Second Edition

URBAN LIFE

Readings in Urban Anthropology

Edited by George Gmelch and Walter P. Zenner

URBAN LIFE

Readings in Urban Anthropology

Second Edition

Edited by
George Gmelch
Union College

Walter P. Zenner
State University of New York, Albany

WITHDRAWN

WAVELAND

PRESS, INC.

Prospect Heights, Illinois

For information about this book, write or call:

Waveland Press, Inc.
P.O. Box 400
Prospect Heights, Illinois 60070
(312) 634-0081

Cover photograph: Radda in Chiante, Italy by Sharon Gmelch.

ISBN 0-88133-332-8

Printed in the United States of America

7 6 5 4 3 2 1

To our mentors,
Charles J. Erasmus and Conrad M. Arensberg

CONTENTS

Contents

PREFACE

The first edition of *Urban Life* was published in 1980. Five years later we began collecting ideas on possible improvements in the book, and, in 1987, those ideas were incorporated into this second edition published by Waveland Press. In this edition, we have added eleven new essays, ten of them written expressly for *Urban Life*. Several authors of the original essays who had been back to the field since the first edition have written epilogues which provide updates on changes that have occurred in their field settings. Also, we have added a new section to the book entitled "Community Formation and Urban Neighborhoods," as well as expanded the section on urbanism to include new articles on the origin and nature of early cities, the effects of city living on human health, and urban danger. We have also updated and reworked most of the introductory essays.

These changes reflect the many conversations we have had with our students and with urban anthropologists regarding the first edition of *Urban Life*. We also distributed a questionnaire to instructors who had assigned *Urban Life* in their classes to learn what was beneficial in the first edition and what needed to be changed. We believe that the new edition will continue to gain and to hold student interest.

In our selection of readings, we have chosen work giving broad coverage of the topics central to urban anthropology. We have also provided a wide geographic range of research and analysis. Too, we have sought a balance between classic studies of enduring interest and important recent work, including seventeen articles published here for the first time. Always, with the student in mind, we have looked for clear writing which captures the interest of the reader.

Urban Life is organized into six parts, each corresponding to a major focus of the field and each introduced by an editorial essay. These essays offer an overview of the general topic addressed by the readings and provide background and context for the selections. Each article is prefaced by a brief note highlighting its particular significance.

The selections in Part One discuss the effects of urbanism on the social life, personality and health of city dwellers. Part Two looks at the manner in which anthropologists have adjusted their outlook and their research methods in response to the study of urban life. In Part Three the cityward migration of rural peoples and their adaptations to city life are examined. Part Four focuses on family and kin, personal relations and gender roles in urban society. Part Five treats ethnicity and class in the city. Finally, Part Six deals with community formation and urban neighborhoods.

The parts of this collection are interwoven and informed by several underlying themes made explicit in the editorial essays. One theme is that of cross-cultural comparison, the testing of generalizations based on one culture with the experiences of other groups and contexts. A second theme is the importance of small intimate groups for most city people; such groups serve as a focus of urban life and help members to maintain a meaningful pattern of expressive and emotional relations. Most important is the familiar anthropological theme of *adaptation*, the strategies that people, both as individuals and as members of groups, use to cope with the demands of life in the city. Our chief concern here is with the unique demands posed by urban social environments and the ways in which human cultures have dealt with them. Implicit in this orientation is a comparison of the urban with the rural—in particular, how customs and institutions which evolved in small-scale societies have been transformed in urban settings. While the focus is often on the urban adaptation of individuals and groups, the city is also seen as part of the broader national and international system.

Our publishers, Bob Woodbury for the first edition and Neil Rowe for the second edition, gave us wise counsel at every stage. Arnold Foster, Sharon Gmelch, Robert V. Kemper, Mark LaGory, Kathleen Logan, Owen Lynch, Barbara Martin, Michael Whiteford, Miriam Lee Kaprow, Maurice Richter, Dave Simms and several anonymous reviewers made valuable suggestions which guided our selection of articles. Ron Farrell, Richard Nelson and the late Paul Meadows gave advice on editorial matters. Rita Michalec, Joann Somich and Betty Kruger typed the essays. Finally, we are indebted to our colleagues who have written original essays for this volume and who have generously agreed to our request that royalties earned by this book be given to the Society for Urban Anthropology.

George Gmelch
Walter P. Zenner

Albany, New York
January 1988

Part One
Urbanism

WIRTH'S MODEL

Once upon a time there was a mouse who lived in the country. It played out in the fields and lived off the simple products of the land in a poor hole. One day this mouse was visited by its cousin from the city. The city mouse complained about the hard work which the country mouse put in to get its simple food and poor accommodations. When he left, he suggested that his country cousin come with him to the city. And he did. The city mouse lived in an apartment. There was much excitement and variety in the city and many kinds of free food. When the shadow of the cat appeared, however, the mice shivered with fear in a small corner. The country mouse then fled from the city and was happy to return to the country.

This fear expresses the common-sense view of the differences between country life and city ways. Country life is tranquil but dull, while city life has variety and excitement and fear. Country people are plain and moral. They know and care about each other. Indeed they know so much about each other's doings that there is little or no privacy. Whereas material concerns, loneliness, and privacy are the hallmarks of city life, in the country "life is with people," to quote the title of a book presenting such a folk society (Zborowski and Herzog 1952).

This stereotype of the differences between the village (country) and the city was the starting point for social scientific research on rural-urban differences. It found its way into Louis Wirth's model of "Urbanism as a Way of Life." The interest of sociologists in the city, which led to Wirth's formulation, had its

1

roots in the rapid growth of industrial cities in Europe and North America. Chicago, where Louis Wirth lived, was an excellent example of this explosion in that Chicago started as a village in the early nineteenth century and within a century had become a metropolis of over three million. While clearly emphasizing modern industrial urbanism, Wirth wrote as if he were describing a *universal* model. The model stresses size, population density, and heterogeneity as characteristics of the city. Wirth relates these features of the city to the breakdown of primary groups, such as the family and the community, and the resultant individualism and *anomie* (normlessness, alienation, anarchy). Bureaucracy – an impersonal type of social structure – arises, and people have a sense of individual impotence.

Wirth's theory has prompted a great deal of research by anthropologists and sociologists. For example, Robert Redfield (1947), a colleague of Wirth's at the University of Chicago, after comparing four communities in the Yucatan area of Mexico that ranged from a city (Merida) to a small indian village, developed the concept of "folk society" as an opposite of Wirth's urbanism. Where urban society is impersonal, heterogenous, and secular, folk society was posited to be personal, homogenous, and sacred. Village life was seen to be satisfying, peaceful, well integrated, and comparatively free of strife. This idealization of the rural strengthened the perception of the urban as being negative, as having harmful effects for its inhabitants.

Miner applied the Chicago urban paradigm to the small African city of Timbuctoo (pop. 6000) that he studied, with mixed success. He found that while it worked for the macro level characteristics of the city it did not hold true at the neighborhood and family level which were more integrated and personal than Wirth would have predicted. Similarly, Bascom (1955) studied the Yoruba of Western Nigeria, who lived in dense concentrations comparable to cities elsewhere. Yet they did not exhibit the kind of alienation from primary groups or collective behavior which was hypothesized by Wirth as characteristic of urban places and of people in such circumstances. In fact, Yoruba cities are less sharply distinguished from their countrysides than our Western stereotypes of cities envision (Bascom 1955; Wheatley 1970).

Sally Engle Merry (*Urban Danger*) in a recent study of a multi-ethnic neighborhood in an American city also finds that Wirth's vision of the effects of urbanism are not wrong but partial. The anonymity, disorder and exploitation that Wirth described are characteristic of the city, but they are found mainly at the *boundaries* between different groups of people (e.g., the Chinese, blacks, Hispanics and whites in the neighborhood Merry studied). The lives of urbanites within each of these localized ethnic groups is personal and intimate with enduring social ties, but the coexistence of very separate ethnic groups in the same neighborhood who neither know nor try to communicate with one another breaks down social order.

Other social scientists have criticized Wirth's model of urbanism for having a Western bias. Arensberg believes that a closer examination of the "green cities" of India, pre-Columbian America and West Africa would lead to a very different conceptualization of what is urban. A sociologist, Gideon Sjoberg (*The Preindustrial City*) who spent ten years trying to distill the essential characteristics of the preindustrial cities of Europe and parts of the third world today, concluded that Wirth's model only applied to Western industrial cities. The preindustrial city, according to Sjoberg, is based on a technology which relies on the power of humans and animals, rather than on machines. While the majority of people in the whole society are cultivators, the society is ruled by an elite living in cities. Strong kin and other particularistic ties unite the ruling elite. *Who* you are, not *what* you are, is the guiding principle. Such a city is obviously quite different from the one seen in Wirth's model.

Many anthropologists, however, have been as critical of Sjoberg's theory of preindustrial urbanism as of Wirth's. While recognizing that there is something distinct about cities—all cities, as opposed to peasantries or hunting bands—they prefer a different strategy than that of trying to delineate a single model or even a few types. These anthropologists recognize that there are certain characteristics which are generally considered "urban" when they appear together, such as a large number of people, a high degree of economic specialization for people, buildings, permanent zones designated for specific functions (e.g., government, trade, and religion), and literacy. Yet there may be societies which have centers that can be seen as being urban which lack one trait or another. The Yoruba and the Dahomeans had cities, for instance, without having a system of writing (Bascom 1955; Wheatley 1970; Arensberg 1968).

The different ways in which cities began and the functions which cities played varied. These functions affected the nature of the relationship which cities had to the countryside. In some areas, cities started as ceremonial centers and were natural outgrowths of simpler folk societies, while elsewhere cities were imposed on an unwilling peasantry by foreign traders and conquerors (Redfield and Singer 1954). The realization that there are many different kinds of cities has made it difficult for comparative scholars to agree on a single classification.

INDUSTRIAL URBANISM

There have been elaborations of the Wirth model, seeing it as an explanation of modern urbanism. After all, most social scientific research, even that done by anthropologists, has been conducted in modern industrial and colonial cities. Anderson (1962) has interpreted Wirth's formulation as one which shows how modern society as a whole—not only urban settlements—differs from its predecessors. Modern industrial society in this view has the following characteristics:

1. a high degree of specialization in labor and mass production of goods and services;
2. almost total commitment to mechanical power, both in work and nonwork situations;
3. increasing detachment of the individual from traditional controls, greater transiency in contacts and loyalties, and increasing dependence on secondary institutions (such as corporate and government bureaucracies);

4. high mobility—in daily movements, changes of jobs and residences, as well as changes in social status;
5. continuous change in the man-made elements of the urban environment, including structural renewal and technological innovation;
6. the almost complete subordination of the individual and the group to mechanical time and increasing control by clock time over appointments and coordination of movement;
7. considerable anonymity which is related to transiency (nos. 3 and 4);
8. expectancy and devotion to continuous change;
9. increasing commitment to records and conformity to their use in verification of actions, contacts, pledges, and presences.

Rather than stressing such features as heterogeneity and density per se, Anderson emphasized the impact of the new technology—as exemplified by the use of mechanical power, the clock, and the computer—on modern society. While the full impact of such devices is felt most fully in urban areas, modern agriculturalists are as tied into it as urbanites. For instance, corn and pig farmers in Iowa rely on fertilizers and tractors, some of which are air-conditioned and contain tape decks. The farmers use machines produced far away and are acutely aware of the international market for grain and meat, which affects the farmers' yearly fortunes.

Anderson's definition of modern industrial urbanism is a fine complement to the delineation of preindustrial society which was made by Sjoberg. Sjoberg and others have emphasized the importance of a complex society based on animal and human power. Anderson's formulation sees the importance in technological elements like transportation, clock time and record keeping in accounting for the relative impersonality of modern society, including the transiency of relations, easy mobility, and the expectancy of change. But like Wirth, he does not devote much thought to how such devices may lead to countervailing tendencies as well. For instance, the letter, the telegram, and the telephone call make it possible for individuals to maintain meaningful intimate relationships over long distances without face-to-face contact. To quote a Bell system ad, "Its the next best thing to being there" (Aronson 1971).

THE URBAN ENVIRONMENT

The themes of heterogeneity and density have been elaborated by other scholars. Milgram's article ("The Urban Experience") is a good example of this genre. Laboratory psychologists use mice and rats to experiment on the behavioral effects of crowding on rats in cages. They have suggested that the behavior of rats in these situations is analogous to humans in small rooms and apartments. The psychologists have also conducted research which places human subjects in actual situations of crowding. These studies, particularly those of American and British college students, tend to confirm that crowding produces detrimental effects. These effects include aggressive acts and lack of concern for others (Mercer 1975).

Laboratories do not provide natural settings. The short-term encounters characteristic of such experiments do not permit the rearrangement of living patterns which humans may adopt in crowded conditions. Different cultures maintain different expectations of physical contact among individuals, including the normal space between individuals while having a conversation, touching each other, and feeling the breath or smelling the odors of the others. Many sociologists and anthropologists remain unconvinced that crowding, noise, and the increase of stimulation present in the urban environment produce the detrimental effects attributed to them (Fischer 1976:154-164). On the other hand, some research on the relationship of overcrowding to health tends to confirm the theory that crowding does affect humans adversely, at least in Western settings (Gove, Hughes, and Galle 1979).

Obviously more research on this problem needs to be done. While anthropologists in the past have made few contributions to crowding theory, the observational and cross-cultural approaches of cultural anthropology can add a valuable dimension to this research. Actual observation of how individuals react to crowding in natural settings can be enhanced through the use of videotapes and other new devices. Anthropologists can also be expected to carry out such research in cities outside North America.

SMALL GROUPS IN THE LARGE CITY

The major contribution which urban anthropologists, in conjunction with community sociologists, have made to the theory of modern urbanism has been in the criticism of one aspect of Wirth's theory. The thesis that the modern metropolitan environment leads to a breakdown of primary social relationships, to powerlessness, and to lawlessness has come under attack. The initial view of Wirth and his predecessors and followers stressed the loss of community in the modern urban setting, while the first wave of critics discovered the existence of intense intimate relations and community solidarity in urban slums, in middle-class suburbs, and in the elites of modern society. The heterogeneity and population density of the city was seen as less important than it did to Wirth, while the economic position of individuals, their cultural characteristics, and their familiar status seemed more important in determining their membership in primary groups. The work of anthropologists like Lewis ("The Culture of Poverty"), Liebow (1967), and Stack ("The Kindred of Viola Jackson") and sociologists utilizing ethnographic approaches like Whyte (1955), Gans (1962), and Young and Willmott (1957), were among those showing the persistence of "communities" in the city.

Gans (1962), for instance, described an Italian-American neighborhood in Boston as an "urban village." Social life, according to this view, takes place at the level of small groups, such as the family, the church, and the block; one is not merely "lost in the crowd" on most occasions. Proponents of this view stressed the need of a modern social system with a high degree of occupational specialization for social solidarity, sociability, and mutual assistance both in work and leisure situations, but they were not concerned with the effects of population density on urban groups.

Of late, a synthesis between the Wirthian view and its critics has begun to emerge. While acknowledging the crucial roles which the family, the neighborhood, and the ethnic and occupational communities continue to play in contemporary urban society, these social scientists attribute importance to the concentration of large numbers of different kinds of people in cities, to the new forms of communication, and to the high degree of mobility of people today. A large number of people sharing a common ethnic identity or another interest in a city make it possible for them to form a group which develops the traits of a "Subculture" (Fisher 1976). The new forms of communication and greater mobility make it possible for individuals to maintain a sense of community with people who are far away while these same individuals can be indifferent to their next-door neighbors.

In traditional villages, there was often an overlap between neighbors, kin, and friends. Urbanites today may have many different kinds of alliances, cliques, and other kinds of links to their fellows. While spatial propinquity is still important, many significant relationships are with those who are not in the next house or on the next block, but many miles away. Many urbanites do have people on whom they can rely for assistance in an emergency, but they may lack a sense of community because of this multiplicity of relationships. The fact that an individual in Boston has relatives in Chicago, neighbors who are friends across the street, and another set of friends from work in the suburbs — most of whom rarely meet — does not provide one with the feeling of a closely knit society.

While anthropologists once went out to study communities—which were visualized as containing a single village hall and church—today urban social scientists view the social network as the key. A network is a set of links between individuals. Each individual in a particular place has a different series of links with others, many of whom live in other places and cities. With some persons they have strong ties, while with other people the links are casual and weak. The network perspective provides a new view of modern society (Wellman 1979; Lauman 1973; Stack "The Kindred of Viola Jackson").

In this volume, we have chosen to concentrate our attention on the way in which groups have persisted and been transformed in modern urban settings. The study of this phenomenon has been the *forte* of urban anthropologists. As indicated in this section, anthropologists have made important contributions to the general theory of urbanism together with their colleagues in other social sciences. They have provided a cross-cultural perspective to such a general consideration. Some anthropologists like Gulick (1967), Price (1972), Waldron ("Within the Wall and Beyond"), and Fox (1972) have tried to study cities as a whole. In recent years, Marxist anthropologists have adopted the perspective of Marxian economics in relating the groups, networks, and cities which they study to the larger socioeconomic system in which these are embedded. The example of how rural-urban migration in a Third World country is affected by decisions made in the commodities markets of Europe and America is an example of this interdependency. It requires looking at cities as part of a world system (see Rhoades "European Cyclical Migration"; Bossen "Wives and Servants"; Buechler "The Networks of Doña Rosa"; Rollwagon "The World System"; and Zenner "The Syrian-Jewish Web of Relations").

All these contributions by anthropologists to urban studies are welcome and indeed exciting. Still, the main task of urban anthropology is to describe and analyze the lives of the people who live in cities and their satellites. The macroscopic perspectives of holists and Marxists are needed to sharpen our analyses, but it has been our singular function to provide the "worm's-eye view."

Walter P. Zenner

George Gmelch

ON THE ORIGIN AND NATURE OF CITIES

Bruce E. Byland

Bruce Byland views cities as places where complex societies offer a diversity of specialized services and where large numbers of people live and function together as parts of a complex social organization. The rise of such localities is seen in this essay as a product of environmental stresses which are largely ecological in nature and processes of adaptation to those stresses which are largely cultural. Byland takes a middle ground between environmental determinism and free human will. He looks at the rise of the Mexican city of Teotihuacan as an illustration of this process of urban development.

INTRODUCTION

This brief paper will attempt first to establish a theoretical and practical notion of what a city is, then to examine how such a thing could have come into being and, finally to illustrate both the city itself and the process of its origin in the case of the largest and best known early pre-Columbian city in the New World, the Classic period city of Teotihuacan, located in the Basin of Mexico.

The questions of how cities began and how or why they are different from other patterns of human settlement are indeed intriguing ones. Social and natural scientists of all stripes are interested in the patterns of behavior which are manifest in cities today. No one field can hope to provide a comprehensive explanation of how cities came into being or how their functions have come to be as they are, but the discipline in the position to provide the most direct information about these questions is archaeology. Only archaeology can directly examine the remains of the earliest cities. Only archaeology has the long diachronic view which can relate the changes in human behavior observed in the material and historic records to processes of development. Further, since archaeology is part of anthropology, it has the unique advantage of being able to shamelessly borrow concepts and ideas from any other field as appropriate.

The study of early cities is frought with difficulty. Archaeologists interested in such questions have a number of logistical and technical problems to overcome before significant theoretical questions can be addressed. The sheer scale of the subject matter presents staggering problems. Even early cities are large things. When one

SOURCE: Article written expressly for *Urban Life*.

reckons the cost of mounting a comprehensive study of even a single early urban center the costs are daunting, to say the least. Rene Millon's mapping project of the city of Teotihuacan in the Basin of Mexico required almost ten years to simply draw a detailed map of that single early city. Analysis of the data upon which the map is based continues today, more than 15 years later. Teotihuacan at its height, between about 100 and 500 A.D., covered roughly 20 square kilometers and had a mean population estimate of about 125,000 people. To be sure, it was one of the largest of all early cities anywhere in the world, but similar scale problems can be expected in the investigation of any of the hundreds of early cities worldwide.

One must also not forget that early cities did not exist for the convenience of modern archaeologists. They didn't appear instantaneously, flourish for a brief time and then suffer rapid abandonment with unequivocal causes at every step of the way. The characteristics of a place which would make it a desirable location for settlement are likely to be geological and ecological. Such traits are generally stable. Human utilization of the advantageous qualities of a location, like good water, soil, slope, or available food, will surely vary through time so a palimpsest of consecutive occupations could develop which would rapidly obscure the earliest levels of occupation. The city of Teotihuacan was occupied, for example, for over 1500 years. The earliest levels of the occupation at the site are difficult to examine because of the overburden of later occupation. Furthermore, during 1500 years, construction projects undertaken by the inhabitants of the city frequently borrowed building material from one part of the site for the erection of structures in another. The resultant pattern of mixing makes the problem of interpretation all the harder.

In many cases, especially in the Old World, later layers of a city build up continually over earlier levels of occupation to create a "tell" or a huge mound which may be tens of meters tall. The problems attendant to devising a reasonable excavation strategy to identify and explore the earliest levels of a large, deep site like this are practically insurmountable. How could one hope to design an excavation which would adequately sample the earliest occupation of such a site, knowing that before the excavation is conducted the placement of the early city beneath the mound cannot be known? With infinite time and money perhaps the whole site could be excavated. In the real world it is difficult to secure infinite resources so the archaeologist must accept limitations on research imposed by the practical constraints of research.

WHAT IS A CITY?

In order to effectively discuss the origin and nature of cities we must begin with a bit of a definition of terms. No "cookbook" definition of "city" is going to be sufficient to include every settlement which we might wish to think of as a city. The effort to establish a simple all inclusive definition is a futile one. What is required is a set of guidelines or considerations which can, in any particular context, lead us to an informed discussion. We needn't pigeonhole sites into categories such as cities or towns or villages so long as we clearly understand how these terms are being used.

How then is the idea of urbanism, the meaning of 'city,' to be understood and differentiated from 'town' or 'village.' The rise of cities was the culmination of a process of growth and development of social forms which involved many aspects of life. In order to distinguish cities from forms of settlement which arose at earlier points in human history we must establish a few criteria, not as hard and fast rules for identifying cities but rather as guidelines for recognition. Cities must be different in some recognizable way from other settlement forms.

Perhaps the most important criteria which we can define concern the diversity of both cities and the cultural environment within which they are found. Clearly cities are more complicated places in which to live than villages or towns but they exist in relation to such smaller and simpler residential patterns. The complexity of urban society is found both within the city and in the relationship between the city and its hinterlands. The complex character of urban life has many consequences which can be archaeologically visible.

The people who inhabit a city, by virtue of their membership in a complex political organization, will have a wide variety of specialized roles. One of the most fundamental tasks to be done by the inhabitants of any community is the production of food. Farmers in an urban society produce agricultural surpluses which make possible the support of other people who do not grow their own food. Between administrative specialists like leaders and bureaucrats, religious specialists or priests, craft specialists, merchants, and soldiers, there are many jobs to do which do not involve the production of food. In other words many of the residents of cities are not agriculturalists even though their very existence depends upon the surpluses farming provides. Put another way, the complexity of the city is supported by farmers but provided by others.

The emergence of full-time specialization in nonagricultural tasks is a key aspect of the rise of the complexity of cities. In simple egalitarian societies most people have food production as their primary economic role. Of course some people will occasionally trade with neighboring groups and some will mediate reciprocal feasts or celebrations but few other activities have a direct bearing on the economic standing of the group. In somewhat more complex societies one is likely to find that some members of the group have other specialized roles in addition to producing food. These might include jobs such as adjudicators of disputes, shamans or priests, weavers, woodworkers, or potters. These specializations can be part-time tasks which can be fit into the food production schedule as time allows. As these tasks become more and more important in maintaining a stable social organization they are more than a little likely to require more time. Ultimately, full-time specialization will emerge in which some practitioners of these or other specializations are completely freed of the responsibility of growing their own food.

As this group grows, new burdens are imposed on societies which maintain ever larger numbers of non-food producers. Some system of redistribution of food must exist so that the full-time specialists may have enough to eat. This is not so simple a task as it sounds. A means of gathering the food from the producers must exist, which implies some form of taxation or tribute. The taxes must be stored and parceled out to the specialists which means an administrative structure involving still more specialists. The relative value of the labor or products of the labor of non-agricultural specialists in terms of food produced by the farming part of the community must be established. The fair measure of the value of a person's time and skill in any task is still a point of contention even today. There is no reason to suppose that it was any easier during the time that the organization of cities was just being established and people were first wrestling with the problems of equitable valuation of work. The emergence of a group of people who could control these decisions, who could provide the administration necessary to hold the fabric of society together in the face of these stresses, seems to be prerequisite for complex societies and cities.

The question then becomes explicit, to what extent are cities necessarily associated with stratification and states? Are large agglomerations of people who are not subject to the dominion of rulers properly called cities? I think most archaeologists equate cities with a certain level of social organization which is fundamentally hierarchical. If so then the state as a political form is a prerequisite for the existence of a true city. Cities can exist only as part of civilizations or, perhaps a bit more precisely, only within very complex societies or states.

The recognition that cities are part of complex societies forces another level of understanding upon us. Cities do not exist in a vacuum but rather within a complex settlement system. The arrangement of smaller communities around central cities is such that the goods and services produced in the urban centers can be efficiently distributed to those other communities. Similarly, the movement of the products of smaller communities to the cities is facilitated. Cities are distinguished because they are the most complex places within the system. The variety of products and services available in the city centers is greater than that which is available in other, smaller communities. If only a few people offer certain goods or services which are unusual and desirable then they are likely to be found in only a few locations. It can be argued that the most efficient distribution of such services in a landscape is from central places where a variety of special activities can be clustered together. In this way the transport costs of collecting them can be minimized. The elite people who reside in cities provide services to the residents of the city and to the people who live in surrounding communities. The people from the countryside feed the specialists in the city in return for their administrative support and the specialized goods produced there. If, for example, a resident of a small village needs to acquire four rare items and talk to two administrators it is certainly more efficient for that person to go to one central place where those things are aggregated than to have to travel to six different localities to complete all six transactions. Cities grow as simple solutions to the problem of governing large areas and delivering services to the inhabitants of the hinterlands, and incidentally of extracting goods and labor from those same people.

To create a list of criteria which we can use as guidelines to identify cities as they first develop we need to identify characteristics which are fundamentally associated with the complexity of the cities and of the emerging states in which they are found. Early cities have an economic structure which includes both full- and part-time specialists. As a direct result of this they have a political organization which is rigid and hierarchical. Similarly they support a wide variety of specialized services for residents. These services also extend to smaller communities in the surrounding area which depend on the city for central organization. Finally cities tend to be large population centers. Though large aggregations of people are not always cities and settlements which we might want to call cities are sometimes relatively small, we can generally say that a city will have a population of 5,000 or more people and that some of them will not be agriculturalists. This characterization of cities focuses on the political and economic organization of early urban centers. As such it is representative of approaches which appeal to archaeologists who use material remains to measure such things.

This approach explicitly avoids other variables like the existence of elaborate art styles, a sophisticated writing system, a developed literary tradition, the development of knowledge in formal sciences or the existence of a system of codified law. These sorts of things are often not very visible across the thousands of years required to study the emergence of cities and furthermore, they are as likely to be consequences of cities and states as they are to precede them. The classes of cultural variables we are relying on to identify cities are fundamentally economic and political, and focus on the social relations which operate in an environmental context.

The city then is the place in which the activities which distinguish a complex society from a simple one go on. It is the bearer of the very nature of the nation, the place which both defines and is defined by the society in which it is found.

THE ORIGIN OF CITIES

In order for us to understand how urban centers first came into being we must establish a context for their development. It will be helpful to this process to also create a conceptual framework which draws attention to those aspects of urban centers which are crucial in explaining how and why they exist.

To understand the origin of cities we need to think, for a bit, about both the social and environmental characteristics which allow for the origin and development of this settlement form. In any location where cities later are found there is a historical shift from mobile to sedentary settlement patterns which is related to the availability of a secure, reliable, and predictable source of food. Though this may begin based upon an extraordinarily productive wild food resource it must ultimately be based upon the security and the expandability of agricultural production. In order for the subsistance system to produce adequate quantities of food to support the needs of a growing class of people who do not produce their own, agriculture is an absolute requirement. In no case have cities come into being without the support of agricultural regimes which can produce large quantities of food in limited areas.

The expansion of a relatively simple village into a city as defined above is a complex process though, which requires a consideration of more than just subsistance energetics. Many of the things used here to identify early cities also rely on the relations of people to each other. That is above and beyond the relations of the people to the productive parts of their environment.

Just as the economic underpinning of the city is its agricultural base, the cultural and social essence of the city is its complexity. An understanding of the development of cities will incorporate an understanding of the rise of ranking and stratification in the political organization of states. The "rise of ranking and stratification" refers to the entire process of increasing complexity in social, political, and economic organization which has occurred in those instances where the state has emerged. Clearly there is a relationship between the use of agricultural production to support elites, the emergence of full-time non-agricultural specialists, increasing social order, the establishment of hierarchical organizations of control, and the rise of cities.

The origin of social and political stratification in states which is the basis of urbanism and city life has been the subject of study for decades. Kent Flannery has suggested that an explanation of the rise of complex societies must be based on an understanding of the processes of cultural change, the mechanisms by which change occurs, and the stresses which motivate the change and select the mechanisms actually employed (Flannery 1972). This tripartite systems explanation is certainly the objective of most modern inquiries into the rise of complex societies. Few satisfying answers have been found, however, because of the difficulty of articulating the three parts of the explanation. I would argue that the changes observed in human behavior are best understood as being generated by one of two processes of human social interaction. These are the complementary processes of cooperation and competition between people. The stresses which drive these processes into action are socio-environmental in nature. A careful examination of many of the specific explanations of culture change which have been proposed in the past will show that most of them rely on ecological relations of their motive force. The root causes of change are seen as growing out of the biological character of human populations.

Robert Carneiro's suggestion that competition grew out of stresses imposed by a limited, or circumscribed, environment in the face of population growth is such a case. In this case social change is seen as a result of the efforts of various groups to insure their access to the limited resources of the region in which they live. When populations rise, Carneiro suggests, competition increases thus imposing a hierarchy of communities. The successful competitors will rank higher than the losers and will develop central administrative roles.

Marx's suggestion that as non-agricultural specialization began, competition arose because of emerging differences in access to the wealth generated by labor is another case in point. As the modern Marxist anthropologists see it the sequence of causes and effects begins with the increasing wealth which can be produced given a productive agricultural technology. Surplus production means that some members of society can become craft specialists at least part time. Craftspeople could exchange their products for the agricultural products of their neighbors and thus begin to amass wealth. This represents the beginning of socioeconomic class differentiation. The rich and the poor, craft producers and agriculturalists, have very different interests in the operation of an economic system. Both groups want their products to have high value relative to that of the other so that their status will be elevated. Hence comes class conflict and the eventual formation of the state as a mechanism to maintain the position of the ruling class.

Wittfogel's view that the rise of an administrative elite grew out of organizational stresses imposed by the technological advances made by people is a similar case. In this explanation of the origin of the state, the rise of an administrative structure is seen as a consequence of the development of a technological solution to the problem of maintaining high agricultural productivity. Wittfogel used the case of progressively larger scale irrigation systems as an institution which required cooperation among large groups of people. He argued that for such a system to succeed much planning had to go on and a coordination of effort had to be organized. Thus a central institution of control would develop gradually to insure that the public utility, in this case the irrigation works, would continue to function for the common good. The development of a managerial elite would result in the rise of the state.

I would venture to say that most of the linear, uni-causal sorts of explanations like these which have been proposed over the years grow from some sort of ecological stress as a motive force for change. In each of these cases the rise of the state as a political institution is defined by the development of a controlling elite, either powerful communities or a powerful class or powerful managers, in response to an ecological stress. The rise of the city as a place where the many services controlled by these elites are available is, in a circular way, a direct result of the existence of such a variety of services. We can stipulate that the development of elites and elite governance is defined by a certain limitation of access to positions of power within societies. The limitation of the number of positions of power means that the central services performed by people in such positions will necessarily be restricted in space. Cities function as central places where these services, and others, are congregated so that communication up and down the hierarchy is maximized at minimum cost. Hence the expected human response to ecological stress is cultural.

THE RISE OF TEOTIHUACAN

Knowing that no single case can be an adequate illustration of so complex a process as the origin of cities, we can choose a case to demonstrate the process in a general way. Perhaps the best studied early city in the world is Teotihuacan, located in the Basin of Mexico. Rene Millon's map of the site is unparalleled in detail and comprehensiveness (Millon 1973). The collections of artifacts made by the Teotihuacan Mapping Project under Millon's direction provide an extraordinary, fine grained view of the internal structure of the city. This has been coupled with the extensive surveys of Teotihuacan's hinterland conducted by William Sanders and his colleagues in The Basin of Mexico Survey Project (Sanders, Parsons, and Santley 1979).

The rise of Teotihuacan must be placed in the context of the development of economic and political systems in the whole of the Basin of Mexico. The earliest sedentary communities in the basin are found at about 1500 B.C. and are isolated in the southernmost part of the valley. This is a time when agricultural products probably accounted for more than half of the diet. This southern region is the portion of the Basin of Mexico which has the most rainfall and the richest soil. That the first settled farmers in the valley chose to live there is no mystery. During this period there is little evidence that anyone had any special elite status. Communities were all either small or tiny.

In the succeeding periods the drier, more northerly parts of the basin were gradually settled including the first settlement at the future site of Teotihuacan. Some of the communities in the richer, southern area came to be significantly larger than their neighbors. One of these, the site of Cuicuilco (in the southwest basin) may have had a population of 5,000-10,000 people by 650 B.C. This site and about five others all demonstrate an emerging hierarchical organization in the appearance of monumental civic-ceremonial architecture. Furthermore, a clear organizational hierarchy is evident in the settlement system with at least three levels of site sizes observable. During this time the site of Teotihuacan was first settled as a small, undistinguished farming community. Cuicuilco may well have been a city by our criteria even at this early date.

By about 300 B.C. the situation had changed drastically, Teotihuacan had grown to be, with Cuicuilco, one of two major centers of population and control in the basin. Somehow the previously marginal area that Teotihuacan occupied had been transformed into one of the most densely populated places in the entire basin. These two communities each had populations estimated at greater than 20,000, perhaps as many as 40,000 people. By this time there is no denying that these sites were cities. Each of them certainly had both the size and the internal complexity with numerous administrative, religious, and craft specialists to qualify unequivocally as urban areas. These two sites are so much larger and more complex than any other site in the basin that it is certain that they represented a new level of control in the Basin of Mexico.

By about 100 B.C. or so Teotihuacan had become the single dominant site in the entire basin. Cuicuilco had been largely devastated by the eruption of a major volcano and the consequent lava flow. In the aftermath of this natural disaster the rulers of Teotihuacan adopted the strategy of transforming their city into a huge metropolis with roughly 125,000 residents. This meant that over 80% of the population of the basin resided at this site. If there was any doubt about the status of the site as a city earlier, by this time there cannot be. In fact, at this time Teotihuacan was one of the largest cities in the world.

There is ample evidence of economic specialization in the city of Teotihuacan at this time. It has been suggested that at 100 B.C. about 6% of the population were nonfood producing specialists. By 300 A.D. that percentage had gone up to at least 30% or about 40,000 people who had to be supported by the community in one way or another. Obsidian workers represented perhaps 15,000 of this number and many of them were producing blades for export rather than for local consumption. Other specialists included makers of high status products to be consumed only by members of the local elite, makers of mundane products such as pottery and textiles for common consumption both locally and abroad, and building craftspeople such as plasterers, stonecutters, and muralists. In addition, there certainly were administrators, bureaucrats, priests, and other service personnel who produced no physical product.

The emergence of Cuicuilco as a city in the fertile southern part of the basin is clearly an extension of the pattern of preference accorded that area since the original settlement of the basin. Located in the most fertile and best watered part of the region, population growth, the development of wealth, and the emergence of governmental structures to administer the system could rely on the rainfall agriculture and the chinampa cultivation of the shallow freshwater lakes of the area. Similar advantages were not present in the Teotihuacan Valley. This area was fertile but had much less rainfall. It did have large steady springs but these were of little use until canal systems were developed which could harness the water for human use. Though there is as yet no direct evidence of this, it is overwhelmingly likely that large scale irrigation began at Teotihuacan by about 300 B.C., coincident with the rapid growth of the city.

It is not my place to speculate as to the exact operation of the cause and effect sequence in all of this. It is enough to observe that Teotihuacan became a massive and complex city when the capacity to technologically transform a marginal environment into a productive one was developed. The stresses involved are ecological, the processes cultural, and the mechanisms bewilderingly complex and largely unstudied.

The growth of Teotihuacan is an example, one might even say a typical example, of the process of development which has led to the ever increasing urbanization of the world. By looking closely at this case we can see the relationship between a settlement form and a social and political structure. The city is a manifestation of the state. The study of the origin and nature of cities can help us to better understand their position in our own world.

CITIES AND HUMAN HEALTH

Lawrence M. Schell

> What is the relationship of urbanism to human health? How does
> living in cities affect our biological adaptation? In this essay, Lawrence
> Schell examines how urban environments influence human biology.
> He critically looks at the stereotype of the city as a dreadfully
> artificial and unhealthy place and disentangles the characteristics of
> the urban environment that are linked to health and disease.

In this exploration of the relationship of urbanism to health, the stereotype of
the city as an artificial and unhealthy place will be undermined by identifying
specific characteristics of urban environments that pertain to health and disease.
In addition, the influence of urbanism on human biology and the significant
challenge to human biological adaptation which it poses will be discussed. While
it is customary to think of human biological adaptation and evolution as processes
which were replaced by culture as the means of human adaptation, it is precisely
the environment most conditioned by culture, the urban environment, that poses
the greatest challenge *biologically* and to which Homo sapiens must now adapt.

THE PROBLEM OF URBANISM

The characteristics of hominids evolved over five or more million years and
became established in the hominid line at least 50,000 years before today's cities.
Virtually all human evolution, from the first hominids to the appearance of *Homo
sapiens sapiens,* occurred in response to the demands of a physical and social
environment which modern humans in urban environments never experience.
Indeed, the genus Homo, for more than 99% of the time that it has existed on
earth, has congregated in numerically small, technologically simple bands of
migratory hunters and gatherers. The extreme difference between the
environment of our early biological adaptation and the environment of today's
populations has consequences for modern people in urban surroundings.

SOURCE: Article written expressly for *Urban Life.*

HUMAN SETTLEMENTS AND HEALTH IN THE PAST

The Transition to Settled Village Life

One way to gauge the effect of urbanism on health is to examine human societies before the appearance of permanent settlement. In presettled societies, human beings lived in small, loosely organized bands or tribes. The populations of hunter-gatherers were small, usually not more than fifty individuals, and there was little contact with other bands. People had a migratory subsistence pattern based on hunting and gathering which involved much physical activity and a highly varied diet which was low in animal protein, animal fats and sodium. Resources (food, shelter, tools) were distributed without sharp inequalities within the society. The only domesticated animal was the dog.

With the advent of village life, the earliest form of urbanization, most of this changed. Agriculture replaced hunting and gathering and made possible settled village life. Population size increased slightly, the variety of the diet decreased, and the domestication of animals (e.g., sheep, goat, cattle) resulted in increased contact between people and animals. All these changes had a profound impact on human health, slowly at first and then more powerfully as each trend became more pronounced.[1]

When agriculture replaces hunting and gathering as the primary source of nutrients, a narrower range of nutrients is consumed. This focus on a few domesticated foods makes possible nutritional diseases, especially vitamin or mineral deficiencies. In hunting and gathering societies, these are rare because of the wide variety of food sources utilized. In addition, agriculture involves risk. If only a few crops provide all the foods, there is a greater risk of famine and of dietary deficiency. Seasonal fluctuations in supply occur, and crops may be lost to drought, insects, or plant diseases at any time. Malnutrition due to protein or calorie deficiency is more characteristic of poor agricultural societies than of today's isolated hunting and gathering ones. Early agriculturally based villages and small cities may have been characterized by occasional malnutrition or by vitamin and mineral deficiencies.

Increases in population size can also have a profound impact on health. Many diseases require a minimum population size year after year. These diseases, often called acute community infections, either kill those they infect or, if the host recovers, leave the host permanently immunized against the disease. Measles is an example of an acute community infection, but the flu is not. A natural bout of measles (not the vaccine) leaves permanent, lifelong immunity among the survivors, but people get influenza year after year, there being no permanent immunity to every influenza type. Diseases that leave surviving hosts with permanent immunity need new hosts or the disease-causing organism (pathogen) will perish and no new cases of the disease will occur. If all the adults in a community are the survivors from previous years of infection, the only new hosts are immigrants and newborns. In small populations, like bands, there are not enough of either to sustain an acute community infection. In larger societies with high birth rates, new hosts are produced faster than the rate of natural immunity building, and the disease persists. Measles represents a prime example of an acute community infection, and the population size necessary for maintaining this disease is well over 500,000. This urban size was not attained in any one city until rather recently (consider Table 1). Because of their small population size, infectious diseases may not have been prevalent in early agricultural villages. Skeletal remains from these villages do not show much infectious disease; however, our samples of skeletal remains are too scanty at present to rule out the possibility of an increase in infectious disease before the advent of large urban centers 1000 years ago, at which time acute community infections were prevalent in European cities.

A major change that occurred with sedentariness and agriculturally based subsistence was increased contact with animals. Humans had increased contact with two kinds of animals: the domesticated animals such as cats, dogs, horses, and sheep, and, secondly, the pests such as rats, raccoons, mice, and insects that share human domiciles. Human settlements provided stable environments to which these pests adapted and which were thus instrumental in their evolution. Both types of animals increase the variety of pathogens with which humans come into contact, as well as increase the frequency of their appearance.

The problems posed by more frequent contact with disease-harboring animals are made worse by rudimentary sanitary engineering. While there are reports of drained latrines, piped drinking water, and water cleansed lavatories from

Table 1

The World's Largest Cities
(*from* Chandler and Fox 1974)

Era	Number of Cities with Population over:		Largest City	
	50,000	100,000	Name	Population
1360 BC	3	0 or 1	Thebes, Egypt	100,000
1200	4	0 or 1	Memphis, Egypt	?
430	25	12	Babylon, Mid. East	250,000
200	35	14	Patna, India	
100 AD	45	16	Rome, Europe	650,000
361	25	14	Constantinople, Rome	350,000
622	46	10	Constantinople, Bzy.	500,000
800	58	16	Changan, China	800,000
900	60	15	Bagdad, Persia	900,000
1000	61	19	Cordova, Spain	450,000
1200	69	25	Hangchow, China	255,000
1400	74	24	Nanking, China	473,000
1600	75 +	37	Peking, China	706,000
1800	179	66	Peking, China	1,100,000

archeological excavations of ancient cities in India, Greece and Egypt, these facilities were available only to the elite. For the masses, hygiene and sanitation was probably ineffective, and infectious material of animal or human origin sometimes contaminated food and drink. Because many parasites are transmitted from feces to the mouth via food or drink, settled villagers with rudimentary sanitary facilities can develop a heavy burden of parasitic disease. In contrast, the migratory hunters and gatherers had less contact with animals, moved too often for pests to adapt to people's domiciles, and left their own waste behind with each move to a new camp. Only parasites with exceptional powers of survival outside a host can survive the drying and heat or cold to remain infectious long enough for migratory hunters and gatherers to reinfect themselves.[2]

Health problems stemming from ineffective sanitation were probably new during early urbanization, and they may have become endemic (always present at a constant level) in the populations as urbanization increased. Lewis Mumford (1961) distinguishes two stages in the history of the city pertaining to health: an early stage of small houses, usually of one or two stories and separated by kitchen gardens with some domesticated animals, with farms nearby, and a second stage characterized by greater population, multistoried dwellings so close together that there is no room for kitchen gardens, and fields at a greater distance from the city. In the first stage, the production of waste was balanced by its use as fertilizer in adjacent kitchen gardens and nearby fields. In the second stage, however, the production of waste was much greater, and there were no uses for waste within the city—cesspits contaminated local wells, and, by each multistoried dwelling, there accumulated a dung pile waiting for removal to the countryside. Unsanitary cesspits and dung piles provided an opportunity for contamination of water and food that was far greater than in earlier, small cities or villages, and certainly greater than the hunting and gathering existence of human societies that had preceded the development of village settlements.

The Preindustrial City: Plagues and Pestilences

Given the characteristics of early city life just described, it is no surprise that, for many centuries, human populations experienced substantial mortality and morbidity due to infectious diseases. Actually, in many countries today, infectious diseases still are responsible for much morbidity and mortality, especially in children. The features of urban life so important to the spread of infectious disease are common in many cities: poor hygiene and sanitation, crowding, large population size, malnutrition or suboptimal nutrition, and contact with infected individuals (pests, domesticated animals and humans).

Although Europe was not alone in its experience of infectious disease, the chronicles of its history provides a rich and detailed story of human experience with infectious disease. From the rise of large towns to the development of cities with a half million or more inhabitants, epidemic after epidemic of infectious disease is recorded in great detail as an essential part of the history of Europe.

Leprosy provides but one example. While some historians of medicine claim that leprosy was present during biblical times, this conclusion assumes that ancient investigators could distinguish the disease from other skin disorders. Indisputable evidence is lacking, but the disease is well known from the time just following the fall of Rome. It was widely disseminated in the eleventh and twelfth centuries, probably by the Crusades, and pandemics (the spread of disease over large land areas) are known from the thirteenth, fourteenth and fifteenth centuries. The reason for its subsequent decrease is something of a mystery. Today, the disease still afflicts thousands, though not in Europe. A curious feature of leprosy is that its transmission requires prolonged contact, and its incubation takes years. It is plausible that hygienic conditions in medieval Europe were so poor that infected parents transmitted the disease to their children before the parents showed any symptoms.

In contrast to leprosy, the Plague is easily transmitted. The Bubonic Plague, as it is sometimes known, can take several forms, all of which are caused by a bacterium, *Pastuerella pestis*. The Plague is a city disease, because, in cities, the transmission of *P. pestis* is greatly facilitated. *P. pestis* infects the fleas that infest rats. It is believed that wild animals first harbored the disease, and they transmitted it, through their fleas, to the rats which shared habitations with humans. There, infected fleas could spread the disease to humans either directly or after living on domesticated animals. The flea can also survive on pigs, cats, calves, chickens and geese. Except for the rich, common people shared their living quarters with domesticated animals, slept on straw as a family, stored grain in the home, and generally provided few barriers to rats. Once the disease was started in humans, it could spread from person to person by an aerosol route. In a cough, droplets of saliva carrying *P. pestis* from the lungs would have been inhaled by anyone living in close quarters. In a crowded city, the disease would be able to spread quickly. Since the disease is often fatal and survival does not provide immunity for very long, if at all, the disease could kill millions. In Europe in the sixth, the fourteenth and, again, in the seventeenth centuries, it did. By some accounts, half of the European population perished in each of the first two epidemics. The epidemics, some of which lasted for decades, were accompanied by a variety of social changes including urban outmigrations, debauchery, religious piety, and the development of a number of now quaint remedies and preventive measures. One of these was a scented water that was meant to prevent infection and was named after its town of origin, Cologne (Eau de Cologne).

A variety of other infectious diseases related to sanitation, contact with animals and crowding in cities became epidemic at one time or during several periods. When several epidemics raged at once, the world must have seemed hideous indeed. One can imagine a resident of sixteenth century Europe gauging the disposition of infectious disease epidemics across the continent in somewhat the same way that an average citizen of the United States watches the television news of severe weather conditions across North America. A district physician of Regensburg, Lammert comments in the year 1602 (from Zinsser 1935, p. 272):

There was severe winter, a cold April, a hailstorm in the summer. The wine was scarce and of poor quality. In this year, there was plague in the Palantine, through Saxony and Prussia. In Danzig 12,000 people died in one week. There was a smallpox epidemic in Bohemia; another in Silisia. In southern Germany, there raged the terrible

Bauch krankheit [probably dysentery or typhoid]. There was a famine in Russia accompanied by pestilences of plague and typhus, and in Moscow alone [probably a gross exaggeration] 127,000 people are said to have died of pestilence.

Transition to the Twentieth Century

Many of the factors that contributed to the high rates of morbidity and mortality in preindustrial cities are no longer characteristic of cities in developed countries. Historians of health point to the beginning of the twentieth century as a turning point in health for the United States, especially for cities. At this time, piped water, sanitary removal of wastes, eradication of vermin and pests, food industry regulation, and reduction of overcrowded dwellings became prevalent. These improvements are generally credited with the decline in deaths from infectious disease which occurred in the late nineteenth and early twentieth centuries (Omran 1977; Perry 1975). However, public health reforms cannot be held completely responsible. Tuberculosis deaths began their decline before most reforms were initiated, and the twentieth century has been characterized by several major infectious disease epidemics: poliomyletis in the 1940s and 1950s, influenza in 1918, and Acquired Immune Deficiency Syndrome in the 1980s. Despite the threat of future epidemics, infectious diseases do not cause most deaths now. They have been replaced by deaths due to heart disease and cancer. The reason for the ascendance of these new common causes of death may be found in changes in the urban environment.

CITIES IN DEVELOPED NATIONS

There are still many cities that struggle with the problems of sanitation, hygiene, crowding, nutrition, and the control of infectious disease; still other cities have solved these problems and now face others that affect human health, such as pollution and psychosocial stress. There are other problems which stem from population size and the economic hardships of the underclass, as well as their related effects on health, but these subjects are too large and complex to be considered here.

Cities in developed nations can be classified by their health problems. Those cities characterized by problems with psychosocial stress and from pollution caused by current industrial activities or from past industrialization (e.g., toxic waste dumps) can be called *post-industrial* cities. Health-related environmental factors distinguish these cities from industrializing ones in which problems with industrial pollution are just beginning to surface, and in which problems with sanitation, nutrition and crowding likewise prevail.

In considering health and cities, there are two ways to proceed: by direct comparison of rural and urban rates of diseases, deaths and of other measures of well-being, such as child growth and longevity, or by identifying the factors or characteristics of cities that should affect human health. Both approaches offer insight into the complex relationship between urbanism and health.

URBAN ENVIRONMENTAL FEATURES RELATED TO HEALTH

Stress

Although noise may be considered as urban pollutant, biologically it is usually classed as a stressor. Other common stressors are crowding, light and psychological stress. Considering noise as a stressor rather than as a pollutant has to do with the definition of stress. Although, in nonscientific literature, *stress* refers to the stimulus that provokes the body, in biology, *stress* refers to the body's *response* rather than to the stimulus and *stressor* is reserved for reference to the *stimulus* for that response (Selye 1956). Stimuli that do not provoke the body to react in certain, well-defined ways are not, strictly speaking, stressors (Selye 1956). By this definition, noise is a stressor because it provokes a particular constellation of features.

Figure 1 shows the major features that define the stress response. After experiencing a physical stressor, a perceived stressor or an imagined one, reactions occur along two, interconnected pathways: the neurological and the endocrine. The overall reaction used to be called the fight or flight response, but this label may be an overinterpretation—the response may have many functions. Nevertheless, the immediate reaction does enable a fast energetic reaction (Bieliauskas 1982). The heart beat increases, pumping more blood, with the oxygen and nutrients that it carries, into the body. The circulatory system moves more blood to the skeletal muscle, heart and brain, while decreasing the flow to the stomach and intestines (digestion slows or ceases for a while). Sources of energy for muscular work (such as that performed by the heart and skeletal muscle) are released into the bloodstream. The brain itself is more alert. Chemicals that stimulate the nervous system (adrenalin and noradrenalin) and hormones that promote tissue repair and reduce inflammation are secreted by the adrenal gland.

These chemicals can be measured in an individual after stressful experiences and in different populations characterized by different urban features. In one comparison, nonurban Pacific Islanders had lower levels of adrenalin than more urbanized populations in Africa, the United Kingdom and the United States (Jenner et al. 1987). These results are preliminary and need to be replicated in more communities along the urban-rural continuum before it can be proven that people living in urban environments are characterized by more biological stress than people in less urbanized environments. Although proof is elusive, a study of the residents of a small town near Oxford University in England suggests some of the sources of biological stress (Reynolds 1981). Among men, higher levels of adrenalin were related to particular types of answers to a lifestyle/occupation questionnaire. Among the many results reported was the observation that men who were physically tired at the end of the workday had lower levels while men who were mentally tired had higher levels. In general, the amount of adrenalin measured increased along with the amount of personal responsibility and unpredictability in the job. This relationship was apparent only on workdays; on restdays, it was absent. The frequency of time pressures and challenges was an important factor, and people who had to juggle numerous deadlines had high

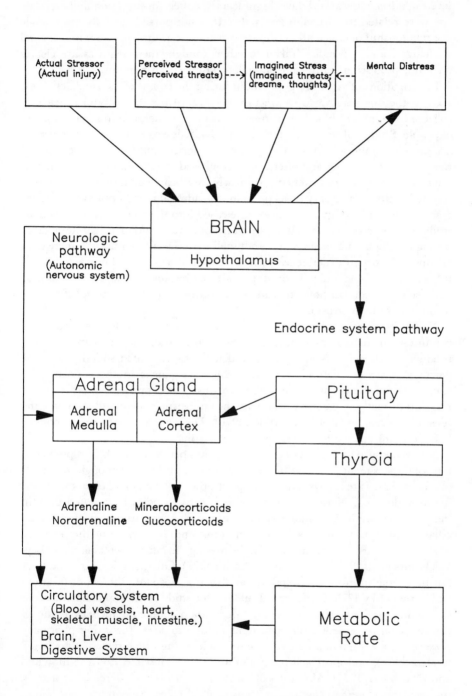

Figure 1. Pathways of the Stress Response

levels of adrenalin on workdays. Significantly, coffee consumption and cigarette use were related to adrenalin levels also. It is not possible to fully disentangle the relationship of coffee and cigarette consumption, time pressure and mental challenges, and adrenalin. Taken together, though, these features are clearly stressful, producing significant physiological effects in humans.

Investigations of an entire population during the course of its usual activities, such as the one near Oxford, are rare because of the difficulty of repeatedly collecting samples of blood or urine to measure adrenalin from large numbers of people. Studies of smaller numbers of individuals exposed to specific stressors are more common and still reveal pertinent information. One study examined race car drivers during and after a race (reviewed in Carruthers 1976). As you might expect, heart rate went up to nearly 200 beats per minute (a common resting heartbeat is seventy beats per minute), adrenalin and noradrenalin levels rose steeply, and energy reserves were released into the bloodstream. A similar study was done of people driving in rush hour traffic. After a half-hour drive during rush hour, adrenalin and noradrenalin levels were significantly increased. Distinctively urban experiences such as driving during rush hour are difficult to pick apart scientifically. Is driving a stressor because of the activity itself or because of the competition, the rude road companions, or the noise? Each one of these may be a stressor.

Noise, itself, is a physiological stressor and is usually louder and more continuous in urban environments where transportatioin and manufacturing produce much noise. Noise is usually defined as unwanted sound; thus, one person's music, or celebration, or desired home repair is another's noise. As a component of the urban scene, noise can raise blood pressure, increase heart rate, alter breathing patterns, stimulate the endocrine system and stimulate the release of adrenalin (Welch and Welch 1970). These are all short-term responses, but there are other effects that are longer lasting.

Noise exposure has been associated with a number of chronic health problems. One of these is mental illness (Tarnopolsky and Clark 1984). Although the causes of mental illness are always difficult to specify, the contribution of emotional stress is rarely doubted. Noise is such a stress, and two studies have noted that, in the areas they studied, mental hospitals had more patients from the communities adjacent to nearby airports than from communities away from the airports, suggesting that the noise contributed to increasing the rate of mental illness (Abey-Wickrama et al. 1969; Meecham and Smith 1977). Other studies, however, have not been able to link noise exposure and mental hospital admissions (Gattoni and Tarnopolsky 1973; Frerichs et al. 1980). One study of the population adjacent to the international airport serving Amsterdam found an increased rate of consumption of remedies for conditions related to stress (counting pharmacy prescriptions written in an area is one way of learning which maladies are being treated there), and more self-reports of anxiety (Knipschile 1977a; Knipschild and Oudshoorn 1977). Also, rates of cardiovascular diseases were higher among the residents closest to the airport (Knipschile 1977b). Researchers also found that the birthweights were smaller among the children born to mothers who had lived nearest to the airport (Knipschild et al. 1981). Reduced birthweights were also observed by scientists working independently who studied communities near airports in Japan (Ando and Hattori 1973, 1977) and in the United States (Schell 1981, 1984). One study of births around the Los Angeles airport reported that the number of congenital malformations was higher among the most noise exposed areas (Jones and Tauscher 1978). This last finding needs to be replicated (Frerichs et al. 1980) by other human biologists working independently at other locations before we can classify noise as a human teratogen (causer of malformations).

All of these effects are believed to occur because of the body's stress reaction to noise; however, in addition to these effects, noise also has a direct effect on hearing. Loud noise can make the ear temporarily less sensitive to sound. Too much noise exposure over a short period of time without break can lead to permanent loss of hearing. In both cases, the ear usually first becomes less sensitive to higher frequencies (Kryter 1970). Considering both the auditory and nonauditory effects, it is important to realize that the ear need not be damaged in order to have more profound physiological effects. Sounds may affect our physiology at a level too low to affect the ear itself. In summary, noise is both a physiological and auditory stressor that affects numerous aspects of human biology, from the auditory to the cardiovascular to the reproductive systems, and it may affect mental health as well.

Pollutants

A large variety of materials in urban environments act as pollutants. Lead, PCBs (polychlorinated biphenyls), mercury, carbon monoxide, and even naturally occurring substances such as methane, are pollutants. A pollutant may be defined as an unwanted substance, in much the same way that a weed, however beautiful or useful, is defined as an unwanted plant. Pollutants cannot be defined by their origin, composition or distribution in the environment. In fact, many urban pollutants are common in rural areas. Some are a consequence of manufacturing or of farm use and, since rural areas have frequently been used as dumping grounds for industrial waste, many others are also present. For example, waste disposal sites in rural areas of eastern New York state may contain substantial amounts of PCBs. Likewise, biologically significant chemicals are likely to turn up in pesticides used on farms; thus, rural areas and the people living there may be carrying a higher chemical burden than urban dwellers. Dairy farmers in upstate Michigan were exposed to PBBs (polybromated biphenyls) that were accidentally added to cattlefeed and subsequently entered the food chain. While some of the worst cases of widespread mercury poisoning are in fishing communities, the source of the mercury which poisoned so many people in the Japanese cities of Minamata and Niigata was an industrial process. Cities are not free of responsibility, but rural areas are not as ecologically separate from urban ones as we might wish.

Despite the conceptual problems with dividing pollution into urban and rural types, some pollutants do appear to be more characteristic of urban environments, particularly air and lead pollution. A problem with any classification of urban pollution is that air pollution contains many elements, including lead, carbon monoxide, ozone, sulfur, and nitrogen. Furthermore, any element can come in a variety of forms, such as an air pollutant or as a water pollutant.

Let us first examine the major components of urban air pollution: carbon monoxide and nitrogen and sulfur compounds, all of which result from combustion. Sulfur is produced from the combustion of fossil fuels, such as oil and coal, which contain high levels of sulfur. When burned to generate heat or electricity, for example, oxides of sulfur are produced (SO_2, SO_3, and SO_4), with varying health effects (Waldbott 1978), and the ability to combine with other elements to form new toxic materials. Mild exposure to oxides of sulfur is corrosive to the upper respiratory tract and severe exposure to concentrated sulfur oxides can cause constriction of small passageways in the lungs, coughing, constriction of larger bronchial passages, and even pulmonary edema or the release of fluid from the circulation into the lung (Waldbott 1978).

Nitrogen is also produced as a result of the combustion of a variety of materials, most commonly automobile emissions. Combustion produces nitric oxide which, when rapidly cooled, becomes nitrogen dioxide. Nitrogen dioxide is four times more toxic than nitric oxide (Waldbott 1978). When formed as nitrous acid or nitric acid, it is corrosive to lung tissue, but, unlike the oxides of sulfur, it is less soluble and is not absorbed into the lining of the upper respiratory tract. Instead, it damages the terminal branches of the lung, the alveoli. Small doses in humans lead to temporary airway resistance (closing down of the small passages). Larger doses over an extended period may cause emphysema, a pathological condition of the lung in which the alveoli coalesce, reducing the available surface area for oxygen exchange and, ultimately, reducing the amount of oxygen getting into the tissues. There are other direct effects and important secondary effects, such as strain on the pulmonary side of the heart, that impair living and shorten life. Carbon monoxide (CO) is another important component of air pollution. Carbon monoxide binds to hemoglobin, the oxygen-bearing protein present in red blood cells. If too much hemoglobin binds with carbon monoxide instead of with oxygen, cells will malfunction and die. The brain is extremely sensitive to oxygen deprivation.

Air contains oxygen (about 21%), nitrogen (about 78%), argon (just under 1%) and CO_2 (about 0.03%). In good, clean air, oxides of sulfur amount to perhaps 0.0001%, while CO and oxides of nitrogen are even rarer. Air in urban environments contains measurable amounts of oxides of sulfur and nitrogen; levels can reach 0.5 parts per million parts of air. Nevertheless, gauging the effects in humans is difficult, and special situations of higher exposure are examined closely to study the effects of environmental pollutants.

Occupational exposures to polluted air provides important information. A classic example is the study of workers in automobile tunnels. In one study of employees of the Triborough Bridge and Tunnel Authority in New York City, the average CO level over thirty days was sixty-three parts per million (Ayres et al. 1973). Forty-seven of the nonsmoking workers had 3% of their red blood cells' hemoglobin bound with CO instead of oxygen (a significant percentage), and there was a high percentage of workers with symptoms suggesting bronchitis. In another study, which examined lung function in children in a number of United States cities found a relationship between forced expiratory volume, a useful measure of lung function, and pollutant levels (Shy et al. 1973).

Air pollution may even affect reproduction. One study of birthweight, a common measure of newborn health, found that the average weight of babies born in parts of Los Angeles with heavy air pollution was less than that of the babies born in the areas with cleaner air. This was true even after taking into consideration some socio-economic factors and mothers' cigarette smoking (Williams et al. 1977). The effect of air pollution may also be seen in mortality rates. Increased mortality rates in Los Angeles have been tied at specific times to increased carbon monoxide levels there (Hexter and Goldsmith 1971), and increased mortality in the New York metropolitan region have been related to increased levels of SO_2 (Buechley et al. 1973). Thus, it has been established that air pollution, a characteristic of cities where combustion of fossil fuels is common, is associated with significant effects on human physiology, reproduction and survival.

Lead is also a component of air pollution. Although it constitutes less than the contribution made by carbon monoxide and sulfur or nitrogen oxides, it is important. Lead produces significant biological effects in people and is plentiful in dust around and in homes. Unlike the air pollutants discussed earlier, lead dust gets absorbed primarily through ingestion rather than through respiration (Barltrop 1982). In terms of exposure to children, dust gets onto toys and hands both of which get into the mouth. Also, children generally pass less lead through the gastrointestinal system than adults, and they absorb more into the bloodstream where it then reaches the brain and the blood-forming portions of the bone (Annest 1982). The source of lead in city dust is the emissions from vehicles that burn leaded gasoline (now much less common) and from the rubble and paint scrappings from houses that had been painted with lead-based paint. Other, lesser sources include materials such as solder, while major occupational sources that affect groups of workers include, for example, fabricators of lead storage batteries for automobiles. The latter sources, however, affect fewer people or are not unique to cities.

The effect of lead varies with the type of exposure, from a poisoning (a large dose over a short period of time) to a chronic low-level lead exposure. Chronic exposure is more prevalent in cities (poisoning has been more common in occupational exposures), and is associated with several biological effects, including the impairment of the process by which new red blood cells are built, and neuropsychologic deficits (Lin-Fu 1979; Needleman 1983). The most troublesome of the latter are subtle effects on cognition and attentiveness, which together may impair the ability of children to learn in school. The number of children with lead in their blood at levels that might produce some of these effects is high in urban areas in comparison to rural locations (Annest 1982).

Place of residence within the city and race are substantial risk factors for elevated blood lead among urban children. According to a report from the U.S. Center for Health Statistics (Annest 1982), nearly one in five black children living in the central portion of large cities in the United States has an elevated blood lead level. Inner-city white children living in older cities frequently have elevated blood lead levels, but not as frequently as black children in the same environment.

To make matters worse, children who are on diets poor in minerals, especially calcium and phosphorous, generally absorb more lead than children on mineral-rich diets. In animal studies, a high-fat, low-mineral diet was associated with blood lead levels fifty times higher than in animals on the better diet (Barltrop 1982). Between the diet and the higher levels of lead in the dust in urban areas, cities may be breeding children who are experiencing biological effects of lead exposure which may be hindering their education and job preparation. This, in turn, may make it harder for them to find well-paying jobs and may result in their residence in poor areas of cities where their children, in turn, will be exposed to lead. Hence, lead pollution may be influencing the social and cultural characteristics of our cities.

COMPARISON OF DISEASE RATES BETWEEN URBAN AND RURAL AREAS

Heart Disease

According to the American Heart Association and the National Center for Health Statistics, heart disease (diseases of heart and blood vessels) was responsible for 975,550 deaths in the United States in 1979, establishing it as the leading cause of death. In comparison, cancer killed less than half as many people in the United States. The number of deaths due to heart disease, specifically ischemic heart disease (obstruction of the blood supply), is usually higher in urban than in rural areas, but the size of the difference varies. The reason for this variation should help us to understand the disease itself.

In one study, Kleinman (1981) found that deaths due to ischemic heart disease occurred more often in urban than in suburban counties in the United States, although the difference was slight among the age groups at highest risk (65-74 years of age). Marmot (1980) reviewed urban-rural differences in heart disease around the world. In developed countries such as the United States and Britain, the difference is small, with the rate of death among males due to ischemic heart disease in the urban centers being 13% more than the rate in rural areas. In Yugoslavia, where urban-rural differences in the environment are more pronounced than in England and Wales, the urban rate is approximately 200% of the rural rate. In traditional, rural societies, such as the Samburu of east Africa, rates of death from heart disease are very low to nonexistent. In summation, the rate of deaths due to heart disease differs greatly between rural and urban areas when there are marked environmental or lifestyle differences between them, but, in developed countries where specific risk factors for heart disease (cigarette smoking, for example) are more evenly distributed between urban and rural areas, the differences in disease rates are very slight or nonexistent. Urban residence *per se* is not clearly the cause of heart disease in cities. On the contrary, lifestyle differences among people are likely to be more important causes.

Cancer

Cancer has long been associated with the urban environment. In 1775, the British surgeon, Percivall Pott, noted that chimney sweeps in London had a high rate of cancer of the scrotum. Sweeps climbed into chimneys to clean them, and the soot that lodged into the dermal crevices is now known to contain carcinogens (cancer-causing elements). Today, the urban environment is still associated with cancer. Studies of the distribution of cancer in developed countries show a higher rate of cancer in urban areas (urban areas are often defined differently in different studies, thus hindering a broad generalization). Table 2 shows the difference in cancer rates between thirteen urban and 957 rural counties in the United States (Goldsmith 1980). The differences are substantial and consistent: urban rates are always higher than rural ones. The reason for the difference is interesting and may aid scientists in understanding the disease itself. The cause may not be urban living *per se,* but rather, in the case of the chimney sweeps, there are occupations in urban areas that employ carcinogens. Usually, employees who use such chemicals are at greater risk for cancer. Insofar as these jobs, and their chemicals, are more common in urban areas, these areas have higher incidence rates of cancer. In short, some of the excess cancer in cities may be due to the occupations of the residents.

The problem of determining the true causes of the differences between urban and rural cancer rates has been intensively examined by Goldsmith (1980). Because air pollution contains carcinogens and is more common in cities where lung cancer is also prevalent, we are tempted to attribute increased lung cancer to the air pollution characteristic of cities. However, Goldsmith points out that the greatest difference between urban and rural rates of lung cancer is between rural counties and the small urban counties with populations of 10,000 to 50,000.

Table 2

Urban-Rural County Ratios of Cancer Mortality Rates
(adjusted for age), U.S. White populations,
1950-1969[1] (*from* Goldsmith 1980)

Male		Female	
Site	Urban-Rural	Site	Urban-Rural
Esophagus	3.08	Esophagus	2.12
Larynx	2.96	Rectum	2.11
Mouth & Throat	2.88	Larynx	1.92
Rectum	2.71	Nasopharynx	1.66
Nasopharynx	2.17	Lung	1.64
Bladder	2.10	Breast	1.61
Colon	1.97	Bladder	1.58
Lung	1.89	Other Endocrine Glands	1.52
All Malignant Neoplasms	1.56	All Malignant Neoplasms	1.36

[1]957 counties are 100% rural and 13 counties are 100% urban.

The rate in large urban centers with populations greater than 500,000 lies between the two. This does not support the theory that the pollution of cities increases the rate of lung cancer, since larger, more polluted cities do not seem to have the highest rate of lung cancer. Also, life-long residents of cities do not necessarily have the highest rate of lung cancer when compared to other city residents. If exposure to pollution is related to lung cancer, then the life-long residents who have had the most exposure should have the highest rate, but, in fact, migrants to the city have the highest rate (Goldsmith 1980).

To discover the true causes of urban-rural differences in cancer, we should look beyond air pollution to the behaviors of urban and rural people. Cigarette smoking may be related to the urban-rural difference and to the higher rate among migrants, and stress might also play a role. In studies of the distribution of any disease, it is difficult to extract the role of one factor, in this case urban living, from the interconnected network of many other factors such as stress, smoking, and diet. Cigarette smoking is a very difficult factor to control in urban-rural comparisons because it is believed to strongly influence the risk of lung cancer, yet, at the same time, it is difficult to measure an individual's exposure to it. Interestingly, in a study of nonsmoking doctors in Britain, no rural-urban difference was found in the rate of lung cancer (Doll 1978).

Mental Health

Considerable controversy exists over the relationship between urbanism and mental health. Results from different studies do not always agree. Again, some of the reasons for this discrepancy are similar to those impeding generalizations about urbanization and other diseases (e.g., heart disease and lung cancer): definitions of urban vary from study to study; definitions of the disease also vary. One generalization does emerge though, namely that extremely isolated communities have higher rates of certain types of mental impairments or psychiatric disorders than do more settled and diversified communities (Webb 1984). Beyond the impact of isolation, few generalizations are not contradicted by one study or another. One review of many studies concluded that there is a consistently higher rate of psychiatric disorder in urban areas (Dohrenwend and Dohrenwend 1974). On the other hand, in individual studies, rural and suburban areas are sometimes found to have a higher rate than cities (Wagenfeld 1982; Engelsmann et al. 1972). Webb (1984) persuasively argues that whatever differences do exist among rural areas, small and large towns, and cities, they are not large differences. Results from his study of scores of psychiatric symptoms derived from interviews of persons in rural and urban areas show that the differences between rural and urban areas are small and not consistent (Webb 1978). It is important to remember that the variety of results from studies is due partly to the variety of approaches taken to study a difficult problem, and from the simple fact that the studies have been conducted at different times and in different places. Indeed, a variety of results among well-conducted studies can be beneficial, since it may suggest specific factors within the rural and urban environments that contribute to psychiatric disorders whether in urban or rural places.

Child Growth

Measuring child growth, unlike mental health, is more straightforward and nonsubjective. If the children are measured accurately, the assessment of the pattern of physical growth of a community's children can provide important information about the health of the children and indirectly about the suitability or healthfulness of the habitat for children and adults (Schell 1986). Child growth depends on a large variety of physiological pathways, and untoward environmental factors can influence many of these and impede physical growth. Provided that the communities under comparison are similar genetically and that nutrition is adequate, comparison of child growth patterns becomes a comparison of the habitability of the respective environments.

Comparisons of the heights of urban and rural children in the United States show no differences (Hamill et al. 1972). In Canada, the difference in height is small, although, when present, it favors rural children (Thibault et al. 1985). In other parts of the world, urban children are generally taller (Eveleth and Tanner 1976). There is variation in the amount of the urban advantage, depending on the age of the children being compared and whether the comparison is between girls or between boys. Even at the same age and within one sex, the urban-rural difference varies. Rural Finnish eight-year-old boys are about one inch shorter than their age- and sex-matched peers from the capital, Helsinki. In Greece, the difference is nearly two inches. The urban-rural difference is larger at adolescence, as adolescence is a time of very rapid growth. Since urban children reach adolescence earlier (Eveleth and Tanner 1976), the increase in size contributes to the urban-rural difference. Figure 2 shows that, for girls, there is an earlier age at menarche (first menses) among urban girls. After adolescence, when the slower growers have caught up, some small urban-rural differences remain among adults.

There may be a pattern to urban-rural differences in child growth. The differences are small in developed countries such as Canada, the United States and Australia, and are larger in Finland, Poland and Greece (Eveleth and Tanner 1976). In the 1960s, when studies of urban-rural growth differences in Finland, Poland and Greece were conducted, they may have had more marked differences between rural and urban areas in economy and in health services for pregnant women and children than when studies of Canada, Australia and the United States were conducted. There are probably factors other than economy and health services, but the urban environment itself does necessarily promote or retard growth. Studies of urban slum children show the depressing effect of poverty, regardless of the degree of urbanization.

Generally, as rural environments around the world become better, and urban-rural differences lessen, we expect to see the difference in child growth lessen also. However, in well-off, industrialized countries, pollution, crowding and stress may cause urban environments to deteriorate, and then the physical growth of children may become poorer in urban areas in comparison to rural ones. This possibility is presented by the few studies that have isolated specific factors that, for now, are more common in urban environments, such as noise (Ando and Hattori 1973, 1977; Schell 1981, 1984; Knipschild et al. 1981), air pollution

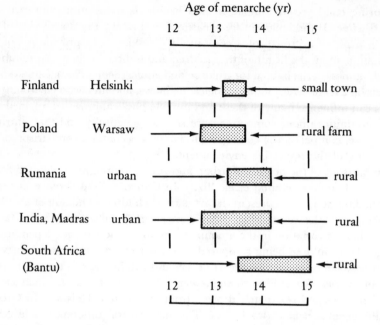

Figure 2. Median Ages of Menarche in Urban and Rural Areas
(from Bielicki 1986; and Eveleth and Tanner 1976). Reproduced with
permission from both Plenum Press and Cambridge University Press.

(Williams 1982), and toxic waste (Paigen et al. 1987). These studies suggest that
future urban areas may be less healthy; currently, however, the difference between
urban and rural children appears to depend on many social factors rather than
on the physical features of the two environments.

CONCLUSION

Cities have a reputation for unhealthfulness that is based on their history and
a failure to understand their present characteristics. Although past comparisons
of rural and urban health indicators have often revealed differences favoring rural
areas, we now know that the advantage depends on the characteristics of the
specific urban and rural environments that are compared. Some features of the
environment are more important than others to human health, and, when urban
and rural environments are similar in these respects, health differences are
minimal. Current research focuses on those specific features of urban and rural
environments that pertain to health and avoid gross generalization.

NOTES

1. Other essays have focused on changes over time in the relationship between settlement pattern and health (Armelagos and Dewey 1970; Black 1975; Cockburn 1972; Polgar 1964). The reader is encouraged to consult these valuable sources.
2. Resource centers that may be shared with infected people or wild animals, waterholes for example, could have provided a source of parasitic infection for migratory hunters and gatherers, though the opportunities for infection and reinfection are far smaller than those open to villagers with domesticated animals and ineffective sanitation.

URBANISM AS A WAY OF LIFE

Louis Wirth

In this famous essay Louis Wirth speculates on how cities influence the social organization, attitudes, and personality of their inhabitants. Wirth begins his analysis by defining the city sociologically as a type of community which is large, dense, and comprised of socially heterogeneous individuals. He then deduces the essential properties of urban existence — anonymity, transitory and impersonal relationships, secularization of thought and so on. In short, Wirth is less concerned with the ecological and demographic aspects of urbanism than with its social and individual properties. Elsewhere in this section, Milgram ("The Experience of Living in Cities") and Merry ("Urban Danger") test and expand upon Wirth's model.

THE CITY AND CONTEMPORARY CIVILIZATION

Just as the beginning of Western civilization is marked by the permanent settlement of formerly nomadic peoples in the Mediterranean basin, so the beginning of what is distinctively modern in our civilization is best signalized by the growth of great cities. Nowhere has mankind been farther removed from organic nature than under the conditions of life characteristic of great cities. The contemporary world no longer presents a picture of small isolated groups of human beings scattered over a vast territory, as Sumner described primitive society.[1] The distinctive feature of the mode of living of man in the modern age is his concentration into gigantic aggregations around which cluster lesser centers and from which radiate the ideas and practices that we call civilization.

The degree to which the contemporary world may be said to be "urban" is not fully or accurately measured by the proportion of the total population living in cities. The influences which cities exert upon the social life of man are greater than the ratio of the urban population would indicate, for the city is not only in ever larger degrees the dwelling-place and the workshop of modern man, but it is the initiating and controlling center of economic, political, and cultural life that has drawn the most remote parts of the world into its orbit and woven diverse areas, peoples, and activities into a cosmos.

The growth of cities and the urbanization of the world is one of the most im-

SOURCE: *American Journal of Sociology*, XLIV (1938): 1–24. © 1938 by University of Chicago. Reprinted by permission of the University of Chicago Press.

pressive facts of modern times. Although it is impossible to state precisely what proportion of the estimated total world-pдpulation of approximately 1,800,000,000 is urban, 69.2 per cent of the total population of those countries that do distinguish between urban and rural areas is urban.[2] Considering the fact, moreover, that the world's population is very unevenly distributed and that the growth of cities is not very far advanced in some of the countries that have only recently been touched by industrialism, this average understates the extent to which urban concentration has proceeded in those countries where the impact of the industrial revolution has been more forceful and of less recent date. This shift from a rural to a predominantly urban society, which has taken place within the span of a single generation in such industrialized areas as the United States and Japan, has been accompanied by profound changes in virtually every phase of social life. It is these changes and their ramifications that invite the attention of the sociologist to the study of the differences between the rural and the urban mode of living. The pursuit of this interest is an indispensable prerequisite for the comprehension and possible mastery of some of the most crucial contemporary problems of social life since it is likely to furnish one of the most revealing perspectives for the understanding of the ongoing changes in human nature and the social order.[3]

Since the city is the product of growth rather than of instantaneous creation, it is to be expected that the influences which it exerts upon the modes of life should not be able to wipe out completely the previously dominant modes of human association. To a greater or lesser degree, therefore, our social life bears the imprint of an earlier folk society, the characteristic modes of settlement of which were the farm, the manor, and the village. This historic influence is reinforced by the circumstance that the population of the city itself is in large measure recruited from the countryside, where a mode of life reminiscent of this earlier form of existence persists. Hence we should not expect to find abrupt and discontinuous variation between urban and rural types of personality. The city and the country may be regarded as two poles in reference to one or the other of which all human settlements tend to arrange themselves. In viewing urban-industrial and rural-folk society as ideal types of communities, we may obtain a perspective for the analysis of the basic models of human association as they appear in contemporary civilization.

A SOCIOLOGICAL DEFINITION OF THE CITY

Despite the preponderant significance of the city in our civilization, however, our knowledge of the nature of urbanism and the process of urbanization is meager. Many attempts have indeed been made to isolate the distinguishing characteristics of urban life. Geographers, historians, economists, and political scientists have incorporated the points of view of their respective disciplines into diverse definitions of the city. While in no sense intended to supersede these, the formulation of a sociological approach to the city may incidentally serve to call attention to the interrelations between them by emphasizing the peculiar characteristics of the city as a particular form of human association. A sociologically significant definition of the city seeks to select those elements of urbanism which mark it as a distinctive mode of human group life.

The characterization of a community as urban on the basis of size alone is obviously arbitrary. It is difficult to defend the present census definition which designates a community of 2,500 and above as urban and all others as rural. The situation would be the same if the criterion were 4,000, 8,000, 10,000, 25,000, or 100,000 population, for although in the latter case we might feel that we were more nearly dealing with an urban aggregate than would be the case in communities of lesser size, no definition of urbanism can hope to be completely satisfying as long as numbers are regarded as the sole criterion. Moreover, it is not difficult to demonstrate that communities of less than the arbitrarily set number of inhabitants lying within the range of influence of metropolitan centers have greater claim to recognition as urban communities than do larger ones leading a more isolated existence in a predominantly rural area. Finally, it should be recognized that census definitions are unduly influenced by the fact that the city, statistically speaking, is always an administrative concept in that the corporate limits play a decisive role in delineating the urban area. Nowhere is this more clearly apparent than in the concentrations of population on the peripheries of great metropolitan centers which cross arbitrary administrative boundaries of city, county, state, and nation.

As long as we identify urbanism with the physical entity of the city, viewing it merely as rigidly delimited in space, and proceed as if urban attributes abruptly ceased to be manifested beyond an arbitrary boundary line, we are not likely to arrive at any adequate conception of urbanism as a mode of life. The technological developments in transportation and communication which virtually mark a new epoch in human history have accentuated the role of cities as dominant elements in our civilization and have enormously extended the urban mode of living beyond the confines of the city itself. The dominance of the city, especially of the great city, may be regarded as a consequence of the concentration in cities of industrial and commercial, financial and administrative facilities and activities, transportation and communication lines, and cultural and recreational equipment such as the press, radio stations, theaters, libraries, museums, concert halls, operas, hospitals, higher educational institutions, research and publishing centers, professional organizations, and religious and welfare institutions. Were it not for the attraction and suggestions that the city exerts through these instrumentalities upon the rural population, the differences between the rural and the urban modes of life would be even greater than they are. Urbanization no longer denotes merely the process by which persons are attracted to a place called the city and incorporated into its system of life. It refers also to that cumulative accentuation of the characteristics distinctive of the mode of life which is associated with the growth of cities, and finally to the changes in the direction of modes of life recognized as urban which are apparent among people, wherever they may be, who have come under the spell of the influences which the city exerts by virtue of the power of its institutions and personalities operating through the means of communication and transportation.

The shortcomings which attach to number of inhabitants as a criterion of urbanism apply for the most part to density of population as well. Whether we accept the density of 10,000 persons per square mile as Mark Jefferson[4] proposed, or 1,000, which Willcox[5] preferred to regard as the criterion of urban settlements, it is clear that unless density is correlated with significant social characteristics it can furnish only an arbitrary basis for differentiating urban from rural communities. Since our census enumerates the night rather than the day population of an area, the locale of the most intensive urban life—the city center—generally has low population density, and the industrial and commercial areas of the city, which contain the most characteristic economic activities underlying urban society, would scarcely anywhere be truly urban if density were literally interpreted as a mark of urbanism. Nevertheless, the fact that the urban community is distinguished by a large aggregation and relatively dense concentration of population can scarcely be left out of account in a definition of the city. But these criteria must be seen as relative to the general cultural context in which cities arise and exist and are sociologically relevant only in so far as they operate as conditioning factors in social life.

The same criticisms apply to such criteria as the occupation of the inhabitants, the existence of certain physical facilities, institutions, and forms of political organization. The question is not whether cities in our civilization or in others do exhibit these distinctive traits, but how potent they are in molding the character of social life into its specifically urban form. Nor in formulating a fertile definition can we afford to overlook the great variations between cities. By means of a typology of cities based upon size, location, age, and function, such as we have undertaken to establish in our recent report to the National Resources Committee,[6] we have found it feasible to array and classify urban communities ranging from struggling small towns to thriving world-metropolitan centers; from isolated trading-centers in the midst of agricultural regions to thriving world-ports and commercial and industrial conurbations. Such differences as these appear crucial because the social characteristics and influences of these different "cities" vary widely.

A serviceable definition of urbanism should not only denote the essential characteristics which all cities—at least those in our culture—have in common, but should lend itself to the discovery of their variations. An industrial city will differ significantly in social respects from a commercial, mining, fishing, resort, university, and capital city. A one-industry city will present different sets of social characteristics from a multi-industry city, as will an industrially balanced from an imbalanced city, a suburb from a satellite, a residential suburb from an industrial suburb, a city within a metropolitan region from one lying outside, an old city from a new one, a southern city from a New England, a middle-western from a Pacific Coast city, a growing from a stable and from a dying city.

A sociological definition must obviously be inclusive enough to comprise whatever essential characteristics these different types of cities have in common as social entities, but it obviously cannot be so detailed as to take account of all the variations implicit in the manifold classes sketched above. Presumably some of the characteristics of cities are more significant in conditioning the nature of urban life than others, and we may expect the outstanding features of the urban-social scene to vary in accordance with size, density, and differences in the functional type of cities. Moreover, we may infer that rural life will bear the imprint of urbanism in the measure that through contact and communication it comes under the influence of cities. It may contribute to the clarity of the statements that follow to repeat that while the locus of urbanism as a mode of life is, of course, to be found characteristically in places which fulfil the requirements we shall set up as a definition of the city, urbanism is not confined to such localities but is manifest in varying degrees wherever the influences of the city reach.

While urbanism, or that complex of traits which makes up the characteristic mode of life in cities, and urbanization, which denotes the development and extensions of these factors, are thus not exclusively found in settlements which are cities in the physical and demographic sense, they do, nevertheless, find their most pronounced expression in such areas, especially in metropolitan cities. In formulating a definition of the city it is necessary to exercise caution in order to avoid identifying urbanism as a way of life with any specific locally or historically conditioned cultural influences which, while they may significantly affect the specific character of the community, are not the essential determinants of its character as a city.

It is particularly important to call attention to the danger of confusing urbanism with industrialism and modern capitalism. The rise of cities in the modern world is undoubtedly not independent of the emergence of modern power-driven machine technology, mass production, and capitalistic enterprise. But different as the cities of earlier epochs may have been by virtue of their development in a preindustrial and precapitalistic order from the great cities of today, they were, nevertheless, cities.

For sociological purposes a city may be defined as a relatively large, dense, and permanent settlement of socially heterogeneous individuals. On the basis of the postulates which this minimal definition suggests, a theory of urbanism may be formulated in the light of existing knowledge concerning social groups.

A THEORY OF URBANISM

In the rich literature on the city we look in vain for a theory of urbanism presenting in a systematic fashion the available knowledge concerning the city as a social entity. We do indeed have excellent formulations of theories on such special problems as the growth of the city viewed as a historical trend and as a recurrent process,[7] and we have a wealth of literature presenting insights of sociological relevance and empirical studies offering detailed information on a variety of particular aspects of urban life. But despite the multiplication of research and textbooks on the city, we do not as yet have a comprehensive body of compendent hypotheses which may be derived from a set of postulates implicitly contained in a sociological definition of the city, and from our general sociological knowledge which may be substantiated through empirical research.

The closest approximations to a systematic theory of urbanism that we have are to be found in a penetrating essay, "Die Stadt," by Max Weber,[8] and a memorable paper by Robert E. Park on "The City: Suggestions for the Investigation of Human Behavior in the Urban Environment."[9] But even these excellent contributions are far from constituting an ordered and coherent framework of theory upon which research might profitably proceed.

In the pages that follow we shall seek to set forth a limited number of identifying characteristics of the city. Given these characteristics we shall then indicate what consequences or further characteristics follow from them in the light of general sociological theory and empirical research. We hope in this manner to arrive at the essential propositions comprising a theory of urbanism. Some of these propositions can be supported by a considerable body of already available research materials; others may be accepted as hypotheses for which a certain amount of presumptive evidence exists, but for which more ample and exact verification would be required. At least such a procedure will, it is hoped, show what in the way of systematic knowledge of the city we now have and what are the crucial and fruitful hypotheses for future research.

The central problem of the sociologist of the city is to discover the forms of social action and organization that typically emerge in relatively permanent, compact settlements of large numbers of heterogeneous individuals. We must also infer that urbanism will assume its most characteristic and extreme form in the measure in which the conditions with which it is congruent are present. Thus the larger, the more densely populated, and the more heterogeneous a community, the more accentuated the characteristics associated with urbanism will be. It should be recognized, however, that in the social world institutions and practices may be accepted and continued for reasons other than those that originally brought them into existence, and that accordingly the urban mode of life may be perpetuated under conditions quite foreign to those necessary for its origin.

Some justification may be in order for the choice of the principal terms comprising our definition of the city. The attempt has been made to make it as inclusive and at the same time as denotative as possible without loading it with unnecessary assumptions. To say that large numbers are necessary to constitute a city means, of course, large numbers in relation to a restricted area or high density of settlement. There are, nevertheless, good reasons for treating large numbers and density as separate factors, since each may be connected with significantly different social consequences. Similarly the need for adding heterogeneity to numbers of population as a necessary and distinct criterion of urbanism might be questioned, since we should expect the range of differences to increase with numbers. In defense, it may be said that the city shows a kind and degree of heterogeneity of population which cannot be wholly accounted for by the law of large numbers or adequately represented by means of a normal distribution curve. Since the population of the city does not reproduce itself, it must recruit its migrants from other cities, the countryside, and—in this country until recently—from other countries. The city has thus historically been the melting-pot of races, peoples, and cultures, and a most favorable breeding-ground of new biological and cultural hybrids. It has not only tolerated but rewarded individual differences. It has brought together people from the ends of the earth *because* they are different and thus useful to one another, rather than because they are homogeneous and like-minded.[10]

There are a number of sociological propositions concerning the relationship between (a) numbers of population, (b) density of settlement, (c) heterogeneity of inhabitants and group life, which can be formulated on the basis of observation and research.

Size of the Population Aggregate

Ever since Aristotle's *Politics,*[11] it has been recognized that increasing the number of inhabitants in a settlement beyond a certain limit will affect the relationships between them and the character of the city. Large numbers involve, as has been pointed out, a greater range of individual variation. Furthermore, the greater the number of individuals participating in a process of interaction, the greater is the *potential* differentiation between them. The personal traits, the occupations, the cultural life, and the ideas of the members of an urban community may, therefore, be expected to range between more widely separated poles than those of rural inhabitants.

That such variations should give rise to the spatial segregation of individuals according to color, ethnic heritage, economic and social status, tastes and preferences, may readily be inferred. The bonds of kinship, of neighborliness, and the sentiments arising out of living together for generations under a common folk tradition are likely to be absent or, at best, relatively weak in an aggregate the members of which have such diverse origins and backgrounds. Under such circumstances competition and formal control mechanisms furnish the substitutes for the bonds of solidarity that are relied upon to hold a folk society together.

Increase in the number of inhabitants of a community beyond a few hundred is bound to limit the possibility of each member of the community knowing all the others personally. Max Weber, in recognizing the social significance of this fact, pointed out that from a sociological point of view large numbers of inhabitants and density of settlement mean that the personal mutual acquaintanceship between the inhabitants which ordinarily inheres in a neighborhood is lacking.[12] The increase in numbers thus involves a changed character of the social relationships. As Simmel points out:

> [If] the unceasing external contact of numbers of persons in the city should be met by the same number of inner reactions as in the small town, in which one knows almost every person he meets and to each of whom he has a positive relationship, one would be completely atomized internally and would fall into an unthinkable mental condition.[13]

The multiplication of persons in a state of interaction under conditions which make their contact as full personalities impossible produces that segmentalization of human relationships which has sometimes been seized upon by students of the mental life of the cities as an explanation for the "schizoid" character of urban personality. This is not to say that the urban inhabitants have fewer acquaintances than rural inhabitants, for the reverse may actually be true; it means rather that in relation to the number of people whom they see and with whom they rub elbows in the course of daily life, they know a smaller proportion, and of these they have less intensive knowledge.

Characteristically, urbanites meet one another in highly segmental roles. They are, to be sure, dependent upon more people for the satisfactions of their life-needs than are rural people and thus are associated with a greater number of organized groups, but they are less dependent upon particular persons, and their dependence upon others is confined to a highly fractionalized aspect of the other's round of activity. This is essentially what is meant by saying that the city is characterized by secondary rather than primary contacts. The contacts of the city may indeed be face to face, but they are nevertheless impersonal, superficial, transitory, and segmental. The reserve, the indifference, and the blasé outlook which urbanites manifest in their relationships may thus be regarded as devices for immunizing themselves against the personal claims and expectations of others.

The superficiality, the anonymity, and the transitory character of urban-social relations make intelligible, also, the sophistication and the rationality generally ascribed to city-dwellers. Our acquaintances tend to stand in a relationship of utility to us in the sense that the role which each one plays in our life is overwhelmingly regarded as a means for the achievement of our own ends. Whereas, therefore, the individual gains, on the one hand, a certain degree of emancipation or freedom from the personal and emotional controls of intimate groups, he loses, on the other hand, the spontaneous self-expression, the morale, and the sense of participation that comes with living in an integrated society. This constitutes essentially the state of *anomie* or the social void to which Durkheim alludes in attempting to account for the various forms of social disorganization in technological society.

The segmental character and utilitarian accent of interpersonal relations in the city find their institutional expression in the proliferation of specialized tasks which we see in their most developed form in the professions. The operations of the pecuniary nexus lead to predatory relationships, which tend to obstruct the efficient functioning of the social order unless checked by professional codes and occupational etiquette. The premium put upon utility and efficiency suggests the adaptability of the corporate device for the organization of enterprises in which individuals can engage only in groups. The advantage that the corporation has over the individual entrepreneur and the partnership in the urban-industrial world derives not only from the possibility it affords of centralizing the resources of thousands of individuals or from the legal privilege of limited liability and perpetual succession, but from the fact that the corporation has no soul.

The specialization of individuals, particularly in their occupations, can proceed only, as Adam Smith pointed out, upon the basis of an enlarged market, which in turn accentuates the division of labor. This enlarged market is only in part supplied by the city's hinterland; in large measure it is found among the large numbers that the city itself contains. The dominance of the city over the surrounding hinterland becomes explicable in terms of the division of labor which urban life occasions and promotes. The extreme degree of interdependence and the unstable equilibrium of urban life are closely associated with the division of labor and the specialization of occupations. This interdependence and instability is increased by the tendency of each city to specialize in those functions in which it has the greatest advantage.

In a community composed of a larger number of individuals than can know one another intimately and can be assembled in one spot, it becomes necessary to communicate through indirect mediums and to articulate individual interests by a process of delegation. Typically in the city, interests are made effective through representation. The individual counts for little, but the voice of the representative is heard with a deference roughly proportional to the numbers for whom he speaks.

While this characterization of urbanism, in so far as it derives from large numbers, does not by any means exhaust the sociological inferences that might be drawn from our knowledge of the relationship of the size of a group to the characteristic behavior of the members, for the sake of brevity the assertions made may serve to exemplify the sort of propositions that might be developed.

Density

As in the case of numbers, so in the case of concentration in limited space, certain consequences of relevance in sociological analysis of the city emerge. Of these only a few can be indicated.

As Darwin pointed out for flora and fauna and as Durkheim[14] noted in the case of human societies, an increase in numbers when area is held constant (i.e., an increase in density) tends to produce differentiation and specialization, since only in this way can the area support increased numbers. Density thus reinforces the effect of numbers in diversifying men and their activities and in increasing the complexity of the social structure.

On the subjective side, as Simmel has suggested, the close physical contact of numerous individuals necessarily produces a shift in the mediums through which we orient ourselves to the urban milieu, especially to our fellow-men. Typically, our physical contacts are close but our social contacts are distant. The urban world puts a premium on visual recognition. We see the uniform which denotes the role of the functionaries and are oblivious to the personal eccentricities that are hidden behind the uniform. We tend to acquire and develop a sensitivity to a world of artefacts and become progressively farther removed from the world of nature.

We are exposed to glaring contrasts between splendor and squalor, between riches and poverty, intelligence and ignorance, order and chaos. The competition for space is great, so that each area generally tends to be put to the use which yields the greatest economic return. Place of work tends to become dissociated from place of residence, for the proximity of industrial and commercial establishments makes an area both economically and socially undesirable for residential purposes.

Density, land values, rentals, accessibility, healthfulness, prestige, aesthetic consideration, absence of nuisances such as noise, smoke, and dirt determine the desirability of various areas of the city as places of settlement for different sections of the population. Place and nature of work, income, racial and ethnic characteristics, social status, custom, habit, taste, preference, and prejudice are among the significant factors in accordance with which the urban population is selected and distributed into more or less distinct settlements. Diverse population elements inhabiting a compact settlement thus tend to become segregated from one another in the degree in which their requirements and modes of life are incompatible with one another and in the measure in which they are antagonistic to one another. Similarly, persons of homogeneous status and needs unwittingly drift into, consciously select, or are forced by circumstances into, the same area. The different parts of the city thus acquire specialized functions. The city consequently tends to resemble a mosaic of social worlds in which the transition from one to the other is abrupt. The juxtaposition of divergent personalities and modes of life tends to produce a relativistic perspective and a sense of toleration of differences which may be regarded as prerequisites for rationality and which lead toward the secularization of life.[15]

The close living together and working together of individuals who have no sentimental and emotional ties foster a spirit of competition, aggrandizement, and mutual exploitation. To counteract irresponsibility and potential disorder, formal controls tend to be resorted to. Without rigid adherence to predictable routines a large compact society would scarcely be able to maintain itself. The clock and the traffic signal are symbolic of the basis of our social order in the urban world. Frequent close physical contact, coupled with great social distance, accentuates the reserve of unattached individuals toward one another and, unless compensated for by other opportunities for response, gives rise to loneliness. The necessary frequent movement of great numbers of individuals in a congested habitat gives occasion to friction and irritation. Nervous tensions which derive from such personal frustrations are accentuated by the rapid tempo and the complicated technology under which life in dense areas must be lived.

Heterogeneity

The social interaction among such a variety of personality types in the urban milieu tends to break down the rigidity of caste lines and to complicate the class structure, and thus induces a more ramified and differentiated framework of social stratification than is found in more integrated societies. The heightened mobility of the individual, which brings him within the range of stimulation by a great number of diverse individuals and subjects him to fluctuating status in the differentiated social groups that compose the social structure of the city, tends toward the acceptance of instability and insecurity in the world at large as a norm. This fact helps to account, too, for the sophistication and cosmopolitanism of the urbanite. No single group has the undivided allegiance of the individual. The groups with which he is affiliated do not lend themselves readily to a simple hierarchical arrangement. By virtue of his different interests arising out of different aspects of social life, the individual acquires membership in widely divergent groups, each of which functions only with reference to a single segment of his personality. Nor do these groups easily permit of a concentric arrangement so that the narrower ones fall within the circumference of the more inclusive ones, as is more likely to be the case in the rural community or in primitive societies. Rather the groups with which the person typically is affiliated are tangential to each other or intersect in highly variable fashion.

Partly as a result of the physical footlooseness of the population and partly as a result of their social mobility, the turnover in group membership generally is rapid. Place of residence, place and character of employment, income and interests fluctuate, and the task of holding organizations together and maintaining and promoting intimate and lasting acquaintanceship between the members is difficult. This applies strikingly to the local areas within the city into which persons become segregated more by virtue of differences in race, language, income, and social status, than through choice or positive attraction to people like themselves. Overwhelmingly the city-dweller is not a home-owner, and since a transitory habitat does not generate binding traditions and sentiments, only rarely is he truly a neighbor. There is little opportunity for the individual to obtain a conception of the city as a whole or to survey his place in the total scheme. Consequently he finds it difficult to determine what is to his own "best interests" and to decide between the issues and leaders presented to him by the agencies of mass suggestion. Individuals who are thus detached from the organized bodies which integrate society comprise the fluid masses that make collective behavior in the urban community so unpredictable and hence so problematical.

Although the city, through the recruitment of variant types to perform its diverse tasks and the accentuation of their uniqueness through competition and the premium upon eccentricity, novelty, efficient performance, and inventiveness, produces a highly differentiated population, it also exercises a leveling influence. Wherever large numbers of differently constituted individuals congregate, the process of depersonalization also enters. This leveling tendency inheres in part in the economic basis of the city. The development of large cities, at least in the modern age, was largely dependent upon the concentrative force of steam. The rise of the factory made possible mass production for an impersonal market. The fullest exploitation of the possibilities of the division of labor and mass production, however, is possible only with standardization of processes and products. A money economy goes hand in hand with such a system of production. Progressively as cities have developed upon a background of this system of production, the pecuniary nexus which implies the purchasability of services and things has displaced personal relations as the basis of association. Individuality under these circumstances must be replaced by categories. When large numbers have to make common use of facilities and institutions, an arrangement must be made to adjust the facilities and institutions to the needs of the average person rather than to those of particular individuals. The services of the public utilities, of the recreational, educational, and cultural institutions must be adjusted to mass requirements. Similarly, the cultural institutions, such as the schools, the movies, the radio, and the newspapers, by virtue of their mass clientele, must necessarily operate as leveling influences. The political process as it appears in urban life could not be understood without taking account of the mass appeals made through modern propaganda techniques. If the individual would participate at all in the social, political, and economic life of the city, he must subordinate some of his individuality to the demands of the larger community and in that measure immerse himself in mass movements.

THE RELATION BETWEEN A THEORY OF URBANISM AND SOCIOLOGICAL RESEARCH

By means of a body of theory such as that illustratively sketched above, the complicated and many-sided phenomena of urbanism may be analyzed in terms of a limited number of basic categories. The sociological approach to the city thus acquires an essential unity and coherence enabling the empirical investigator not merely to focus more distinctly upon the problems and processes that properly fall in his province but also to treat his subject matter in a more integrated and systematic fashion. A few typical findings of empirical research in the field of urbanism, with special reference to the United States, may be indicated to substantiate the theoretical propositions set forth in the preceding pages, and some of the crucial problems for further study may be outlined.

On the basis of the three variables, number, density of settlement, and degree of heterogeneity, of the urban population, it appears possible to explain the characteristics of urban life and to account for the differences between cities of various sizes and types.

Urbanism as a characteristic mode of life may be approached empirically from three interrelated perspectives: (1) as a physical structure comprising a population base, a technology, and an ecological order; (2) as a system of social organization involving a characteristic social structure, a series of social institutions, and a typical pattern of social relationships; and (3) as a set of attitudes and ideas, and a constellation of personalities engaging in typical forms of collective behavior and subject to characteristic mechanisms of social control.

Urbanism in Ecological Perspective

Since in the case of physical structure and ecological processes we are able to operate with fairly objective indices, it becomes possible to arrive at quite precise and generally quantitative results. The dominance of the city over its hinterland becomes explicable through the functional characteristics of the city which derive in large measure from the effect of numbers and density. Many of the technical facilities and the skills and organizations to which urban life gives rise can grow and prosper only in cities where the demand is sufficiently great. The nature and scope of the services rendered by these organizations and institutions and the advantage which they enjoy over the less developed facilities of smaller towns enhance the dominance of the city and the dependence of ever wider regions upon the central metropolis.

The urban-population composition shows the operation of selective and differentiating factors. Cities contain a larger proportion of persons in the prime of life than rural areas which contain more old and very young people. In this, as in so many other respects, the larger the city the more this specific characteristic of urbanism is apparent. With the exception of the largest cities, which have attracted the bulk of the foreign-born males, and a few other special types of cities, women predominate numerically over men. The heterogeneity of the urban population is further indicated along racial and ethnic lines. The foreign born and their children constitute nearly two-thirds of all the inhabitants of cities of one million and over. Their proportion in the urban population declines as the size of the city decreases, until in the rural areas they comprise only about one-sixth of the total population. The larger cities similarly have attracted more Negroes and other racial groups than have the smaller communities. Considering that age, sex, race, and ethnic origin are associated with other factors such as occupation and interest, it becomes clear that one major characteristic of the urban-dweller is his dissimilarity from his fellows. Never before have such large masses of people of diverse traits as we find in our cities been thrown together into such close physical contact as in the great cities of America. Cities generally, and American cities in particular, comprise a motley of peoples and cultures, of highly differentiated modes of life between which there often is only the faintest communication, the greatest indifference and the broadest tolerance, occasionally bitter strife, but always the sharpest contrast.

The failure of the urban population to reproduce itself appears to be a biological consequence of a combination of factors in the complex of urban life, and the decline in the birth-rate generally may be regarded as one of the most significant signs of the urbanization of the Western world. While the proportion of deaths in cities is slightly greater than in the country, the outstanding difference between the failure of present-day cities to maintain their population and that of cities of the past is that in former times it was due to the exceedingly high death-rates in cities, whereas today, since cities have become more livable from a health standpoint, it is due to low birth-rates. These biological characteristics of the urban population are significant sociologically, not merely because they reflect the urban mode of existence but also because they condition the growth and future dominance of cities and their basic social organization. Since cities are the consumers rather than the producers of men, the value of human life and the social estimation of the personality will not be unaffected by the balance between births and deaths. The pattern of land use, of land values, rentals, and ownership, the nature and functioning of the physical structures, of housing, of transportation and communication facilities, of public utilities—

these and many other phases of the physical mechanism of the city are not isolated phenomena unrelated to the city as a social entity, but are affected by and affect the urban mode of life.

Urbanism as a Form of Social Organization

The distinctive features of the urban mode of life have often been described sociologically as consisting of the substitution of secondary for primary contacts, the weakening of bonds of kinship, and the declining social significance of the family, the disappearance of the neighborhood, and the undermining of the traditional basis of social solidarity. All these phenomena can be substantially verified through objective indices. Thus, for instance, the low and declining urban-reproduction rates suggest that the city is not conducive to the traditional type of family life, including the rearing of children and the maintenance of the home as the locus of a whole round of vital activities. The transfer of industrial, educational, and recreational activities to specialized institutions outside the home has deprived the family of some of its most characteristic historical functions. In cities mothers are more likely to be employed, lodgers are more frequently part of the household, marriage tends to be postponed, and the proportion of single and unattached people is greater. Families are smaller and more frequently without children than in the country. The family as a unit of social life is emancipated from the larger kinship group characteristic of the country, and the individual members pursue their own diverging interests in their vocational, educational, religious, recreational, and political life.

Such functions as the maintenance of health, the methods of alleviating the hardships associated with personal and social insecurity, the provisions for education, recreation, and cultural advancement have given rise to highly specialized institutions on a community-wide, statewide, or even national basis. The same factors which have brought about greater personal insecurity also underlie the wider contrasts between individuals to be found in the urban world. While the city has broken down the rigid caste lines of preindustrial society, it has sharpened and differentiated income and status groups. Generally, a larger proportion of the adult-urban population is gainfully employed than is the case with the adult-rural population. The white-collar class, comprising those employed in trade, in clerical, and in professional work, are proportionately more numerous in large cities and in metropolitan centers and in smaller towns than in the country.

On the whole, the city discourages an economic life in which the individual in time of crisis has a basis of subsistence to fall back upon, and it discourages self-employment. While incomes of city people are on the average higher than those of country people, the cost of living seems to be higher in the larger cities. Home ownership involves greater burdens and is rarer. Rents are higher and absorb a larger proportion of the income. Although the urban-dweller has the benefit of many communal services, he spends a large proportion of his income for such items as recreation and advancement and a smaller proportion for food. What the communal services do not furnish the urbanite must purchase, and there is virtually no human need which has remained unexploited by commercialism. Catering to thrills and furnishing means of escape from drudgery, monotony, and routine thus become one of the major functions of urban recreation, which at its best furnishes means for creative self-expression and spontaneous group association, but which more typically in the urban world results in passive spectatorism on the one hand, or sensational record-smashing feats on the other.

Being reduced to a state of virtual impotence as an individual, the urbanite is bound to exert himself by joining with others of similar interest into organized groups to obtain his ends. This results in the enormous multiplication of voluntary organizations directed toward as great a variety of objectives as there are human needs and interests. While on the one hand the traditional ties of human association are weakened, urban existence involves a much greater degree of interdependence between man and man and a more complicated, fragile, and volatile form of mutual interrelations over many phases of which the individual as such can exert scarcely any control. Frequently there is only the most tenuous relationship between the economic position or other basic factors that determine the individual's existence in the urban world and the voluntary groups with which he is affiliated. While in a primitive and in a rural society it is generally possible to predict on the basis of a few known factors who will belong to what and who will associate with whom in almost every relationship of life, in the city we can only project the general pattern of group formation and affiliation, and this pattern will display many incongruities and contradictions.

Urban Personality and Collective Behavior

It is largely through the activities of the voluntary groups, be their objectives economic, political, educational, religious, recreational, or cultural, that the urbanite expresses and develops his personality, acquires status, and is able to carry on the round of activities that constitute his life-career. It may easily be inferred, however, that the organizational framework which these highly differentiated functions call into being does not of itself insure the consistency and integrity of the personalities whose interests it enlists. Personal disorganization, mental breakdown, suicide, delinquency, crime, corruption, and disorder might be expected under these circumstances to be more prevalent in the urban than in the rural community. This has been confirmed in so far as comparable indices are available; but the mechanisms underlying these phenomena require further analysis.

Since for most group purposes it is impossible in the city to appeal individually to the large number of discrete and differentiated individuals, and since it is only through the organizations to which men belong that their interests and resources can be enlisted for a collective cause, it may be inferred that social control in the city should typically proceed through formally organized groups. It follows, too, that the masses of men in the city are subject to manipulation by symbols and stereotypes managed by individuals working from afar or operating invisibly behind the scenes through their control of the instruments of communication. Self-government either in the economic, the political, or the cultural realm is under these circumstances reduced to a mere figure of speech or, at best, is subject to the unstable equilibrium of pressure groups. In view of the ineffectiveness of actual kinship ties we create fictional kinship groups. In the face of the disappearance of the territorial unit as a basis of social solidarity we create interest units. Meanwhile the city as a community resolves itself into a series of tenuous segmental relationships superimposed upon a territorial base with a definite center but without a definite periphery and upon a division of labor which far transcends the immediate locality and is world-wide in scope. The larger the number of persons in a state of interaction with one another the lower is the level of communication and the greater is the tendency for communication to proceed on an elementary level, i.e., on the basis of those things which are assumed to be common or to be of interest to all.

It is obviously, therefore, to the emerging trends in the communication system and to the production and distribution technology that has come into existence with modern civilization that we must look for the symptoms which will indicate the probable future development of urbanism as a mode of social life. The direction of the ongoing changes in urbanism will for good or ill transform not only the city but the world. Some of the more basic of these factors and processes and the possibilities of their direction and control invite further detailed study.

It is only in so far as the sociologist has a clear conception of the city as a social entity and a workable theory of urbanism that he can hope to develop a unified body of reliable knowledge, which what passes as "urban sociology" is certainly not at the present time. By taking his point of departure from a theory of urbanism such as that sketched in the foregoing pages to be elaborated, tested, and revised in the light of further analysis and empirical research, it is to be hoped that the criteria of relevance and validity of factual data can be determined. The miscellaneous assortment of disconnected information which has hitherto found its way into sociological treatises on the city may thus be sifted and incorporated into a coherent body of knowledge. Incidentally, only by means of some such theory will the sociologist escape the futile practice of voicing in the name of sociological science a variety of often unsupportable judgments concerning such problems as poverty, housing, city-planning, sanitation, municipal administration, policing, marketing, transportation, and other technical issues. While the sociologist cannot solve any of these practical problems—at least not by himself—he may, if he discovers his proper function, have an important contribution to make to their comprehension and solution. The prospects for doing this are brightest through a general, theoretical, rather than through an *ad hoc* approach.

NOTES

1. William Graham Sumner, *Folkways* (Boston, 1906), p. 12.
2. S. V. Pearson, *The Growth and Distribution of Population* (New York, 1935), p. 211.

3. Whereas rural life in the United States has for a long time been a subject of considerable interest on the part of governmental bureaus, the most notable case of a comprehensive report being that submitted by the Country Life Commission to President Theodore Roosevelt in 1909, it is worthy of note that no equally comprehensive official inquiry into urban life was undertaken until the establishment of a Research Committee on Urbanism of the National Resources Committee. (Cf. *Our Cities: Their Role in the National Economy* [Washington: Government Printing Office, 1937].)

4. "The Anthropogeography of Some Great Cities," *Bull. American Geographical Society,* XLI (1909), 537–66.

5. Walter F. Willcox, "A Definition of 'City' in Terms of Density," in E. W. Burgess, *The Urban Community* (Chicago, 1926), p. 119.

6. *Op. cit.,* p. 8.

7. See Robert E. Park, Ernest W. Burgess, *et al., The City* (Chicago, 1925), esp. chaps. ii and iii; Werner Sombart, "Städtische Siedlung, Stadt," *Handwörterbuch der Soziologie,* ed. Alfred Vierkandt (Stuttgart, 1931); see also bibliography.

8. *Wirtschaft und Gesellschaft* (Tübingen, 1925), Part II, chap. viii, pp. 514–601.

9. Park, Burgess, *et al., op. cit.,* chap. i.

10. The justification for including the term "permanent" in the definition may appear necessary. Our failure to give an extensive justification for this qualifying mark of the urban rests on the obvious fact that unless human settlements take a fairly permanent root in a locality the characteristics of urban life cannot arise, and conversely the living together of large numbers of heterogeneous individuals under dense conditions is not possible without the development of a more or less technological structure.

11. See esp. vii. 4. 4–14. Translated by B. Jowett . . .

12. *Op. cit.,* p. 514.

13. Georg Simmel, "Die Grossstädte und das Geistesleben," *Die Grossstadt,* ed. Theodor Petermann (Dresden, 1903), pp. 187–206.

14. E. Durkheim, *De la division du travail social* (Paris, 1932), p. 248.

15. The extent to which the segregation of the population into distinct ecological and cultural areas and the resulting social attitude of tolerance, rationality, and secular mentality are functions of density as distinguished from heterogeneity is difficult to determine. Most likely we are dealing here with phenomena which are consequences of the simultaneous operation of both factors.

THE URBAN EXPERIENCE:
A PSYCHOLOGICAL ANALYSIS

Stanley Milgram

Some social scientists have tested Wirth's theory of ways in which large concentrations of people can affect the individual. These scientists have refined the concepts of density and heterogeneity so that specific operations could be performed in these experiments which would prove or disprove Wirth's theory. In this article Milgram reviews the results of such experiments. Milgram presents the concept of "psychic overload" to explain why crowding has certain effects on people, such as their politeness to strangers. Milgram's stress is on crowding in public places. See Oscar Lewis's "The Culture of Poverty" for a consideration of the effects of crowding in the home.

"When I first came to New York it seemed like a nightmare. As soon as I got off the train at Grand Central I was caught up in pushing, shoving crowds on 42nd Street. Sometimes people bumped into me without apology; what really frightened me was to see two people literally engaged in combat for possession of a cab. Why were they so rushed? Even drunks on the street were bypassed without a glance. People didn't seem to care about each other at all."

This statement represents a common reaction to a great city, but it does not tell the whole story. Obviously cities have great appeal because of their variety, eventfulness, possibility of choice, and the stimulation of an intense atmosphere that many individuals find a desirable background to their lives. Where face-to-face contacts are important, the city offers unparalleled possibilities. It has been calculated by the Regional Plan Association[1] that in Nassau County, a suburb of New York City, an individual can meet 11,000 others within a 10-minute radius of his office by foot or car. In Newark, a moderate-sized city, he can meet more than 20,000 persons within this radius. But in midtown Manhattan he can meet fully 220,000. So there is an order-of-magnitude increment in the communication possibilities offered by a great city. That is one of the bases of its appeal and, indeed, of its functional necessity. The city provides options that no other social arrangement permits. But there is a negative side also, as we shall see.

SOURCE: "The Experience of Living in Cities: A Psychological Analysis," Stanley Milgram, *Science,* Vol. 167 (March 13, 1970), pp. 1461–68. Copyright 1970 by the American Association for the Advancement of Science. Reprinted by permission of the author and *Science*.

Granted that cities are indispensable in complex society, we may still ask what contribution psychology can make to understand the experience of living in them. What theories are relevant? How can we extend our knowledge of the psychological aspects of life in cities through empirical inquiry? If empirical inquiry is possible, along what lines should it proceed? In short, where do we start in constructing urban theory and in laying out lines of research?

Observation is the indispensable starting point. Any observer in the streets of midtown Manhattan will see (1) large numbers of people, (2) a high population density, and (3) heterogeneity of population. These three factors need to be at the root of any sociopsychological theory of city life, for they condition all aspects of our experience in the metropolis. Louis Wirth,[2] if not the first to point to these factors, is nonetheless the sociologist who relied most heavily on them in his analysis of the city. Yet, for a psychologist, there is something unsatisfactory about Wirth's theoretical variables. Numbers, density, and heterogeneity are demographic facts but they are not yet psychological facts. They are external to the individual. Psychology needs an idea that links the individual's *experience* to the demographic circumstances of urban life.

One link is provided by the concept of overload. This term, drawn from systems analysis, refers to a system's inability to process inputs from the environment because there are too many inputs for the system to cope with, or because successive inputs come so fast that input A cannot be processed when input B is presented. When overload is present, adaptations occur. The system must set priorities and make choices. A may be processed first while B is kept in abeyance, or one input may be sacrificed altogether. City life, as we experience it, constitutes a continuous set of encounters with overload, and of resultant adaptations. Overload characteristically deforms daily life on several levels, impinging on role performance, the evolution of social norms, cognitive functioning, and the use of facilities.

The concept has been implicit in several theories of urban experience. In 1903 George Simmel[3] pointed out that, since urban dwellers come into contact with vast numbers of people each day, they conserve psychic energy by becoming acquainted with a far smaller proportion of people than their rural counterparts do, and by maintaining more superficial relationships even with these acquaintances. Wirth[4] points specifically to "the superficiality, the anonymity, and the transitory character of urban social relations."

One adaptive response to overload, therefore, is the allocation of less time to each input. A second adaptive mechanism is disregard of low-priority inputs. Principles of selectivity are formulated such that investment of time and energy are reserved for carefully defined inputs (the urbanite disregards the drunk sick on the street as he purposefully navigates through the crowd). Third, boundaries are redrawn in certain social transactions so that the overloaded system can shift the burden to the other party in the exchange; thus, harried New York bus drivers once made change for customers, but now this responsibility has been shifted to the client, who must have the exact fare ready. Fourth, reception is blocked off prior to entrance into a system; city dwellers increasingly use unlisted telephone numbers to prevent individuals from calling them, and a small but growing number resort to keeping the telephone off the hook to prevent incoming calls. More subtly, a city dweller blocks inputs by assuming an unfriendly countenance, which discourages others from initiating contact. Additionally, social screening devices are interposed between the individual and environmental inputs (in a town of 5000 anyone can drop in to chat with the mayor, but in the metropolis organizational screening devices deflect inputs to other destinations). Fifth, the intensity of inputs is diminished by filtering devices, so that only weak and relatively superficial forms of involvement with others are allowed. Sixth, specialized institutions are created to absorb inputs that would otherwise swamp the individual (welfare departments handle the financial needs of a million individuals in New York City, who would otherwise create an army of mendicants continuously importuning the pedestrian). The interposition of institutions between the individual and the social world, a characteristic of all modern society, and most notably of the large metropolis, has its negative side. It deprives the individual of a sense of direct contact and spontaneous integration in the life around him. It simultaneously protects and estranges the individual from his social environment.

Many of these adaptive mechanisms apply not only to individuals but to institutional systems as well, as Meier[5] has so brilliantly shown in connection with the library and the stock exchange.

In sum, the observed behavior of the urbanite in a wide range of situations appears to be determined largely by a variety of adaptations to overload. I now deal with several specific consequences of responses to overload, which make for differences in the tone of city and town.

SOCIAL RESPONSIBILITY

The principal point of interest for a social psychology of the city is that moral and social involvement with individuals is necessarily restricted. This is a direct and necessary function of excess of input over capacity to process. Such restriction of involvement runs a broad spectrum from refusal to become involved in the needs of another person, even when the person desperately needs assistance, through refusal to do favors, to the simple withdrawal of courtesies (such as offering a lady a seat, or saying "sorry" when a pedestrian collision occurs). In any transaction more and more details need to be dropped as the total number of units to be processed increases and assaults an instrument of limited processing capacity.

The ultimate adaptation to an over-loaded social environment is to totally disregard the needs, interests, and demands of those whom one does not define as relevant to the satisfaction of personal needs, and to develop highly efficient perceptual means of determining whether an individual falls into the category of friend or stranger. The disparity in the treatment of friends and strangers ought to be greater in cities than in towns; the time allotment and willingness to become involved with those who have no personal claim on one's time is likely to be less in cities than in towns.

Bystander Intervention in Crises

The most striking deficiencies in social responsibility in cities [occur] in crisis situations, such as the Genovese murder in Queens. In 1964, Catherine Genovese, coming home from a night job in the early hours of an April morning, was stabbed repeatedly, over an extended period of time. Thirty-eight residents of a respectable New York City neighborhood admit to having witnessed at least a part of the attack, but none went to her aid or called the police until after she was dead. Milgram and Hollander, writing in *The Nation*,[6] analyzed the event in these terms:

> Urban friendships and associations are not primarily formed on the basis of physical proximity. A person with numerous close friends in different parts of the city may not know the occupant of an adjacent apartment. This does not mean that a city dweller has fewer friends than does a villager, or knows fewer persons who will come to his aid; however, it does mean that his allies are not constantly at hand. Miss Genovese required immediate aid from those physically present. There is no evidence that the city had deprived Miss Genovese of human associations, but the friends who might have rushed to her side were miles from the scene of her tragedy.
>
> Further, it is known that her cries for help were not directed to a specific person; they were general. But only individuals can act, and as the cries were not specifically directed, no particular person felt a special responsibility. The crime and the failure of community response seem absurd to us. At the time, it may well have seemed equally absurd to the Kew Gardens residents that not one of the neighbors would have called the police. A collective paralysis may have developed from the belief of each of the witnesses that someone else must surely have taken that obvious step.

Gaertner and Bickman[7] of The City University of New York have extended the bystander studies to an examination of help across ethnic lines. Blacks and whites, with clearly identifiable accents, called strangers (through what the caller represented as an error in telephone dialing), gave them a plausible story of being stranded on an outlying highway without more dimes, and asked the stranger to call a garage. The experimenters found that the white callers had a significantly better chance of obtaining assistance than the black callers. This suggests that ethnic allegiance may well be another means of coping with overload: the city dweller can reduce excessive demands and screen out urban heterogeneity by responding along ethnic lines; overload is made more manageable by limiting the "span of sympathy."

In any quantitative characterization of the social texture of city life, a necessary first step is the application of such experimental methods as these to field situations in large cities and small towns. Theorists argue that the indifference shown in the Genovese case would not be found in a small town, but in the absence of solid experimental evidence the question remains an open one.

More than just callousness prevents bystanders from participating in altercations between people. A rule of urban life is respect for other people's emotional and social privacy, perhaps because physical privacy is so hard to achieve. And in situations for which the standards are heterogeneous, it is much harder to know whether taking an active role is unwarranted meddling or an appropriate response to a critical situation. If a husband and wife are quarreling in public, at what point should a bystander step in? On the one hand, the heterogeneity of the city produces substantially greater tolerance about behavior, dress, and codes of ethics than is generally found in the small town, but this diversity also encourages people to withhold aid for fear of antagonizing the participants or crossing an inappropriate and difficult-to-define line.

Moreover, the frequency of demands present in the city gives rise to norms of noninvolvement. There are practical limitations to the Samaritan impulse in a major city. If a citizen attended to every needy person, if he were sensitive to and acted on every altruistic impulse that was evoked in the city, he could scarcely keep his own affairs in order.

Willingness to Trust and Assist Strangers

We now move away from crisis situations to less urgent examples of social responsibility. For it is not only in situations of dramatic need but in the ordinary, everyday willingness to lend a hand that the city dweller is said to be deficient relative to his small-town cousin. The comparative method must be used in any empirical examination of this question. A commonplace social situation is staged in an urban setting and in a small town—a situation to which a subject can respond by either extending help or withholding it. The responses in town and city are compared.

One factor in the purported unwillingness of urbanites to be helpful to strangers may well be their heightened sense of physical (and emotional) vulnerability—a feeling that is supported by urban crime statistics. A key test for distinguishing between city and town behavior, therefore, is determining how city dwellers compare with town dwellers in offering aid that increases their personal vulnerability and requires some trust of strangers. Altman, Levine, Nadien, and Villena[8] of The City University of New York devised a study to compare the behaviors of city and town dwellers in this respect. The criterion used in this study was the willingness of householders to allow strangers to enter their home to use the telephone. The student investigators individually rang doorbells, explained that they had misplaced the address of a friend nearby, and asked to use the phone. The investigators (two males and two females) made 100 requests for entry into homes in the city and 60 requests in the small towns. The results for middle-income housing developments in Manhattan were compared with data for several small towns (Stony Point, Spring Valley, Ramapo, Nyack, New City, and West Clarkstown) in Rockland County, outside of New York City. As Table 1 shows, in all cases there was a sharp increase in the proportion of entries achieved by an experimenter when he moved from the city to a small town. In the most extreme case the experimenter was five times as likely to gain admission to homes in a small town as to homes in Manhattan. Although the female experimenters had notably greater success both in cities and in towns than the male experimenters had, each of the four students did at least twice as well in towns as in cities. This suggests that the city-town distinction overrides even the predictably greater fear of male strangers than of female ones.

Table 1. Percentage of Entries Achieved by Investigators for City and Town Dwellings

| | ENTRIES ACHIEVED (%) | |
Experimenter	City*	Small town†
Male		
No. 1	16	40
No. 2	12	60
Female		
No. 3	40	87
No. 4	40	100

* Number of requests for entry, 100.
† Number of requests for entry, 60.

The lower level of helpfulness by city dwellers seems due in part to recognition of the dangers of living in Manhattan, rather than to mere indifference or coldness. It is significant that 75 percent of all the city respondents received and answered messages by shouting through closed doors and by peering out through peepholes; in the towns, by contrast, about 75 percent of the respondents opened the door.

Supporting the experimenters' quantitative results was their general observation that the town dwellers were noticeably more friendly and less suspicious than the city dwellers. In seeking to explain the reasons for the greater sense of psychological vulnerability city dwellers feel, above and beyond the differences in crime statistics, Villena points out that, if a crime is committed in a village, a resident of a neighboring village may not perceive the crime as personally relevant though the geographic distance may be small, whereas a criminal act committed anywhere in the city, though miles from the city-dweller's home, is still verbally located within the city; thus, Villena says, "the inhabitant of the city possesses a larger vulnerable space."

Civilities
Even at the most superficial level of involvement—the exercise of everyday civilities—urbanites are reputedly deficient. People bump into each other and often do not apologize. They knock over another person's packages and, as often as not, proceed on their way with a grumpy exclamation instead of an of-

fer of assistance. Such behavior, which many visitors to great cities find distasteful, is less common, we are told, in smaller communities, where traditional courtesies are more likely to be observed.

In some instances it is not simply that, in the city, traditional courtesies are violated; rather, the cities develop new norms of noninvolvement. These are so well defined and so deeply a part of city life that *they* constitute the norms people are reluctant to violate. Men are actually embarrassed to give up a seat on the subway to an old woman; they mumble "I was getting off anyway," instead of making the gesture in a straightforward and gracious way. These norms develop because everyone realizes that, in situations of high population density, people cannot implicate themselves in each other's affairs, for to do so would create conditions of continual distraction which would frustrate purposeful action.

In discussing the effects of overload I do not imply that at every instant the city dweller is bombarded with an unmanageable number of inputs, and that his responses are determined by the excess of input at any given instant. Rather, adaptation occurs in the form of gradual evolution of norms of behavior. Norms are evolved in response to frequent discrete experiences of overload; they persist and become generalized modes of responding.

Overload on Cognitive Capacities: Anonymity

That we respond differently toward those whom we know and those who are strangers to us is a truism. An eager patron aggressively cuts in front of someone in a long movie line to save time only to confront a friend; he then behaves sheepishly. A man is involved in an automobile accident caused by another driver, emerges from his car shouting in rage, then moderates his behavior on discovering a friend driving the other car. The city dweller, when walking through the midtown streets, is in a state of continual anonymity vis-à-vis the other pedestrians.

Anonymity is part of a continuous spectrum ranging from total anonymity to full acquaintance, and it may well be that measurement of the precise degrees of anonymity in cities and towns would help to explain important distinctions between the quality of life in each. Conditions of full acquaintance, for example, offer security and familiarity, but they may also be stifling, because the individual is caught in a web of established relationships. Conditions of complete anonymity, by contrast, provide freedom from routinized social ties, but they may also create feelings of alienation and detachment.

Empirically one could investigate the proportion of activities in which the city dweller or the town dweller is known by others at given times in his daily life, and the proportion of activities in the course of which he interacts with individuals who know him. At his job, for instance, the city dweller may be known to as many people as his rural counterpart. However, when he is not fulfilling his occupational role—say, when merely traveling about the city—the urbanite is doubtless more anonymous than his rural counterpart.

Another direction for empirical study is investigation of the beneficial effects of anonymity. The impersonality of city life breeds its own tolerance for the private lives of the inhabitants. Individuality and even eccentricity, we may assume, can flourish more readily in the metropolis than in the small town. Stigmatized persons may find it easier to lead comfortable lives in the city, free of the constant scrutiny of neighbors. To what degree can this assumed difference between city and town be shown empirically? Judith Waters,[9] at The City University of New York, hypothesized that avowed homosexuals would be more likely to be accepted as tenants in a large city than in small towns, and she dispatched letters from homosexuals and from normal individuals to real estate agents in cities and towns across the country. The results of her study were inconclusive. But the general idea of examining the protective benefits of city life to the stigmatized ought to be pursued.

Role Behavior in Cities and Towns

Another product of urban overload is the adjustment in roles made by urbanites in daily interactions. As Wirth has said: "Urbanites meet one another in highly segmental roles. . . . They are less dependent upon particular persons, and their dependence upon others is confined to a highly fractionalized aspect of the other's round of activity."[10] This tendency is particularly noticeable in transactions between customers and individuals offering professional or sales services. The owner of a country store has time to become well acquainted with his dozen-or-so daily customers, but the girl at the checkout counter of a busy A & P, serving hundreds of customers a day, barely has time to toss the green stamps into one customer's shopping bag before the next customer confronts her with his pile of groceries.

Meier, in his stimulating analysis of the city,[11] discusses several adaptations a system may make when confronted by inputs that exceed its capacity to process them. Meier argues that, according to the principle of competition for scarce resources, the scope and time of the transaction shrink as customer volume and daily turnover rise. This, in fact, is what is meant by the "brusque" quality of city life. New standards have developed in cities concerning what levels of services are appropriate in business transactions. . . .

McKenna and Morgenthau,[12] in a seminar at The City University of New York, devised a study (1) to compare the willingness of city dwellers and small-town dwellers to do favors for strangers that entailed expenditure of a small amount of time and slight inconvenience but no personal vulnerability, and (2) to determine whether the more compartmentalized, transitory relationships of the city would make urban salesgirls less likely than small-town salesgirls to carry out, for strangers, tasks not related to their customary roles.

To test for differences between city dwellers and small-town dwellers, a simple experiment was devised in which persons from both settings were asked (by telephone) to perform increasingly onerous favors for anonymous strangers.

Within the cities (Chicago, New York, and Philadelphia), half the calls were to housewives and the other half to salesgirls in women's apparel shops; the division was the same for the 37 small towns of the study, which were in the same states as the cities. Each experimenter represented herself as a long-distance caller who had, through error, been connected with the respondent by the operator. The experimenter began by asking for simple information about the weather for purposes of travel. Next the experimenter excused herself on some pretext (asking the respondent to "please hold on"), put the phone down for almost a full minute, and then picked it up again and asked the respondent to provide the phone number of a hotel or motel in her vicinity at which the experimenter might stay during a forthcoming visit. Scores were assigned the subjects on the basis of how helpful they had been. McKenna summarizes her results in this manner:

> People in the city, whether they are engaged in a specific job or not, are less helpful and informative than people in small towns; . . . People at home, regardless of where they live, are less helpful and informative than people working in shops.

However, the absolute level of cooperativeness for urban subjects was found to be quite high, and does not accord with the stereotype of the urbanite as aloof, self-centered, and unwilling to help strangers. The quantitative differences obtained by McKenna and Morgenthau are less great than one might have expected. This again points up the need for extensive empirical research in rural-urban differences, research that goes far beyond that provided in the few illustrative pilot studies presented here. At this point we have very limited objective evidence on differences in the quality of social encounters in city and small town.

But the research needs to be guided by unifying theoretical concepts. As I have tried to demonstrate, the concept of overload helps to explain a wide variety of contrasts between city behavior and town behavior: (1) the differences in role enactment (the tendency of urban dwellers to deal with one another in highly segmented, functional terms, and of urban sales personnel to devote limited time and attention to their customers); (2) the evolution of urban norms quite different from traditional town values (such as the acceptance of noninvolvement, impersonality, and aloofness in urban life); (3) the adaptation of the urban dweller's cognitive processes (his inability to identify most of the people he sees daily, his screening of sensory stimuli, his development of blasé attitudes toward deviant or bizarre behavior, and his selectivity in responding to human demands); and (4) the competition for scarce facilities in the city (the subway rush; the fight for taxis; traffic jams; standing in line to await services). I suggest that contrasts between city and rural behavior probably reflect the responses of similar people to very different situations, rather than intrinsic differences in the personalities of rural and city dwellers. The city is a situation to which individuals respond adaptively.

NOTES

1. *New York Times* (June 15, 1969).
2. L. Wirth, *American Journal of Sociology*, Vol. 44, No. 1 (1938). Wirth's ideas have come under heavy criticism by contemporary city planners, who point out that

the city is broken down into neighborhoods, which fulfill many of the functions of small towns. See, for example, H. J. Gans, *People and Plans: Essays on Urban Problems and Solutions* (New York: Basic Books, 1968); J. Jacobs, *The Death and Life of Great American Cities* (New York: Random House, 1961); G. D. Suttles, *The Social Order of the Slum* (Chicago: The University of Chicago Press, 1968).

3. G. Simmel, *The Sociology of Georg Simmel,* K. H. Wolff, ed. (New York: Macmillan, 1950). [English translation of G. Simmel, "Die Grossstädte und das Geistesleben," *Die Grossstadt* (Dresden: Jansch, 1903).]

4. L. Wirth, *American Journal of Sociology.*

5. R. L. Meier, *A Communications Theory of Urban Growth* (Cambridge, Mass.: M.I.T. Press, 1962).

6. S. Milgram and P. Hollander, *Nation,* Vol. 25, No. 602 (1964).

7. S. Gaertner and L. Bickman (Graduate Center, The City University of New York), unpublished research.

8. D. Altman, N. Levine, M. Nadien, J. Villena (Graduate Center, The City University of New York), unpublished research.

9. J. Waters (Graduate Center, The City University of New York), unpublished research.

10. L. Wirth, *American Journal of Sociology.*

11. R. L. Meier, *A Communications Theory of Urban Growth.*

12. (Graduate Center, The City University of New York), unpublished research.

URBAN DANGER: LIFE IN A NEIGHBORHOOD OF STRANGERS

Sally Engle Merry

In a landmark study, Wirth argued that the urban way of life is characterized by relations between strangers. Despite considerable research which shows that urbanites' social lives include intimate and enduring social ties, relations between strangers continue to define an essential and problematic quality of urban social life. Sally Engle Merry's ethnographic study of a multiethnic housing project in a high-crime neighborhood shows how the boundaries between social groups contribute to the sense that the city is dangerous. The existence of social boundaries makes the project a fertile place for crime, while the residents' awareness of danger comes from their belief that they live in a world of dangerous and unpredictable strangers. These strangers are people in other social networks, known across the social boundaries which divide the intimate worlds of the project.

In "Urbanism as a Way of Life," Wirth describes cities as places of anonymity and disorder, as settlements in which people treat each other with indifference, competition and exploitation. A city is a place of strangers. The web of gossip, social pressure and concern about the opinions of others was unable to hold in check the criminal, the prostitute and the social deviant or to prevent the personal breakdown of the increasingly isolated individual. Wirth's famous article, written in 1938, distills the ideas of two decades of urban research done by sociologists and anthropologists at the University of Chicago during the early twentieth century. He argues that the ecological conditions of size, density, permanency, and heterogeneity create a social world of impersonal, superficial, transitory relationships in which individuals are detached from close ties to social groups, such as communities and families, and are freed from the constraints of social control. Intimate ties of family and neighborhood become less important, while more impersonal and instrumental relationships come to predominate. Cities are characterized by anomie: by a sense of normlessness, both in the sense of the individual's lack of attachment to a moral code and of a collective loss of moral consensus.

In the fifty years since Wirth's article was published, numerous studies of the social life of cities have challenged his theory. Many researchers have described neighborhoods, workplaces, religious communities, and other urban settings in which

Source: Article written expressly for *Urban Life*.

people know one another and treat each other in terms of intimacy and interdependence (e.g., Whyte 1943; Young and Willmott 1957; Gans 1962; Hannerz 1969; Lewis 1972; Stack 1974; Hannerz 1980). In these places, the close community life which Wirth saw as characteristic of villages flourished. Other critics argued that Wirth was really describing the impact of industrialization, not urbanism. Preindustrial cities lacked the anonymity and disorder of large industrial cities (Sjoberg 1960; Krapf-Askari 1969; Fox 1977). Still others claimed that, despite the apparent disorder of the city, particularly its lack of cohesive neighborhood communities, new forms of community have emerged in modern industrial cities based on social networks, voluntary association and other more ephemeral, yet important, *quasi-group* which stretch across neighborhoods and regions (Mitchell 1969; Boissevain 1974).

Despite these serious and legitimate criticisms of Wirth's vision of the city, however, sociologists and anthropologists still return to his article because they have a lingering sense that he has special insight into the issue, that there are some features of the city life he describes which do resonate with the experience of living in the modern industrial city. Such cities do have many strangers, and strangers are particularly taxing and troubling for urbanites. They lie behind the problems of urban crime, the fear of crime and even the fear of immigrants and newcomers, of people who are culturally strange and different.

Although Wirth's theory of urbanism does not describe the totality of urban social life, it does apply to particular aspects of city life. It describes the boundaries between separate social worlds. Neither Wirth nor Park, an early and influential sociologist at the University of Chicago, thought that the city lacked close-knit urban villages, but saw the city as a collection of these small communities. Park described the city as "a mosaic of little worlds which touch but do not interpenetrate" (1952:47). It is at these boundaries that the characteristic features of urban social life, as Wirth described them, appear. Such social boundaries within a single housing project – Dover Square – and how they generate both crime and a sense of danger will be explored.

LIFE IN A HIGH-CRIME NEIGHBORHOOD

Inspired by Wirth's vision of urban social life, the author decided to conduct a cultural study of urban danger. The items to be researched included how people who live in high-crime urban areas think about danger, how they deal with it on a daily basis, and also how anonymity fosters crime. After perusing crime statistics and neighborhood descriptions, a subsidized housing project located deep in a neighborhood with one of the highest crime rates in a major northeastern city was selected. Since the intent was also to investigate the impact of several ethnic groups living side-by-side, a neighborhood which had a broad mixture of residents was chosen. After locating an ideal small development housing 300 white, black, Chinese, and Hispanic families, the author moved into an apartment three blocks from the project and spent a year and a half carrying out anthropological field research. The residents were questioned regarding how they thought about danger and about how they handled the high rate of crime surrounding them. Project residents who committed crimes against their neighbors were also interviewed concerning their views of crime and danger.

In the mid-1970s, when the study was conducted, the neighborhood was slowly changing from a depressed area populated by homeless alcoholics and characterized by deteriorating housing projects to a trendy neighborhood attractive to wealthy professionals. More daring members of this group bought the old buildings, some of which had a tarnished elegance about them, and renovated them into attractive townhouses. In the ten years since the completion of the study, this process of gentrification in the surrounding neighborhood has continued, but the project has remained much the same. The ethnographic present will be employed to describe the project.

The residents of the Dover Square project are 55% Chinese, 14% black, 9% white, and 9% Hispanic, by population, although the number of families is more evenly distributed. The Chinese residents, most of whom speak little or no English, are largely recent immigrants from Hong Kong, although their children are typically fluent in English. They plan to stay in the United States. Many of the blacks arrived in the city in the 1950s during the massive black migration from the South and have lived in less attractive parts of the city for ten years or more. A substantial number of the whites are connected to an established Syrian-Lebanese community nearby dating from the early 1900s. Some of this community was razed to build the project. The Hispanics are recent arrivals from Puerto Rico and many do not speak fluent English. Many plan to return to their homeland and consider their stay in the city temporary.

The project is federally subsidized, designed to house both low- and moderate-income families. It opened in the mid-1960s and, ten years later, had a remarkably stable population for a housing project: well over half the families had lived in the development since it opened, and the rate of turnover was under 5% per year. Yet, despite this stability, the neighborhood has not become a community. It is not a cohesive, integrated social system, but rather a series of distinct, unconnected social networks occupying the same geographical space. Each ethnic group is scattered throughout the development, yet residents maintain virtually all of their close social relationships with neighbors of the same ethnicity. Consequently, neighbors who belong to different ethnic groups often remain strangers, despite years of sharing the same stairwells, porches and walkways.

A social network is a way of conceptualizing those parts of social life which do not form bounded, enduring social groups (see Barnes 1954; Bott 1957; Epstein 1961; Mitchel 1969; Boissevain 1974). Each person is the center of a group of friends and kinsmen, the central point from which radiates a series of links to other people. This constellation forms a egocentric social network. Members of this network also know others, some of whom the first person does not. These are second-order links, friends of friends. By extension, each second-order link also has social contacts, so that one can imagine a network of social relationships extending outward from any individual to first, second, and further orders of contact. Since these networks of relationship are also potential communication channels, mapping their structure and boundaries provides important clues to the flow of gossip and information through a social system (Merry 1984). Boundaries in social networks tend to be gaps in the flow of information.

In Dover Square, intimate networks, links to close friends and relatives, are almost always restricted to a single ethnic group. An extended network of acquaintances cross-cuts ethnic lines at a few points, but also tends to remain within a single ethnic group. A few individuals have social networks consisting almost entirely of a different ethnic group, such as the white youths who regularly hang out with a gang of young black men and women. Since each ethnic group is scattered throughout the area, the social organization of the project consists of a series of discrete, overarching social networks. One can imagine this social composition as several layers of fishnet strung over the same space with a few threads running between the layers.

The social boundaries between ethnic groups persist because each group is encapsulated within a network of social relationships and a set of institutions which stretches to nearby black, white, Chinese, and Hispanic communities. The majority of families in the project regularly visit kinsmen, friends, religious groups, and social organizations in their nearby ethnic communities. Chinatown lies on one side of the project, an established Syrian-Lebanese community on another, the black community is close by on another side and a substantial Hispanic settlement is in the middle of the slowly gentrifying neighborhood nearby. Jobs, friends, marriage partners, churches, social services, and recreational opportunities are all primarily available within these communities. Consequently, relations with members of the same ethnic group carry an expectation of continuity that is not characteristic of relations with neighbors in Dover Square. Neighbors are only temporary associates, here today but gone whenever they move away, while people in the same ethnic group are connected by enduring ties. The denser mesh of personal ties and group affiliations within ethnic groups means that Dover Square residents are far more accountable to their fellow ethnics than they are to their neighbors of different ethnicity.

Because of the boundaries between ethnic groups, neighbors are often anonymous. This anonymity provides opportunities for crime, since criminals can rob their neighbors with little fear of apprehension. Many project residents observed that, in general, criminals prefer not to work close to home where they can too easily be identified by their neighbors, but here, where neighbors are often strangers, a resident can rob or burglarize people close to home without fear of identification. This means that a project resident can commit crimes on his home territory, which is relatively safe, predictable and familiar, while appearing to victims as a stranger from a distant area. The same people can be robbed whose daily habits and material possessions are easily visible.

At the same time, the widespread fear and distrust of neighbors undermines community efforts at controlling crime. As one of the leaders of the youth group active in committing crimes in the area put it:

> The people who are being affected by crime don't understand that they are the cause of crime. I think a lot of people around here don't want other people's houses to be safe. People are beginning to be cold-hearted, not caring enough, because, if people cared enough about other people, they would care about theirs. In order to protect your house, you have to protect your neighbor's.

Social control is undermined by this structure of social networks since the implementation of sanctions, of punishments for rule-breaking, is unlikely across the social boundaries. For sanctions to be effective in discouraging rule-breaking, they must be both powerful and certain of implementation. A sanction which is severe will have little deterrent effect if the offender feels that there is little chance that she will feel its weight. When the offender is anonymous to his victim, it is obviously difficult to catch him or to impose any penalty on him. If the person who observes a crime knows who the perpetrator is or even where he lives or who his friends are, she might be able to impose some kind of pressure on him. When the perpetrator is a stranger, however, even observing the crime act leaves the observer powerless. The strategies Dover Square residents develop to cope with living in a hazardous environment reveal the critical role played by this knowledge of who the dangerous people are, both in protecting the individual from victimization and in reducing the sense of danger.

CONCEPTIONS OF DANGER

As the author became further acquainted with the residents who lived in the project, it was discovered that they differed greatly in their perceptions of and approaches to the dangers in their environment. One young Chinese woman, for example, never returned home alone on foot after dark. When she arrived by car, she honked the horn to alert her parents and then dashed the twenty feet to her door. A white man cautiously packed his suitcases into his car under cover of darkness before leaving for a trip to escape being noticed by potential burglars. A middle-aged black woman sneaked surreptitiously from her home at 6:00 A.M. to do her laundry before the neighborhood youths gathered in the laundromat to visit and smoke. She was anxious not to leave her home vacant, even for a few minutes, lest the burglars she constantly feared notice that her house was unguarded.

Yet, in the same neighborhood, a young black woman moved freely, visiting neighbors late at night with no thought of danger. Young men would rendezvous in dark secluded hallways even though they were aware that they risked being mugged. A Chinese man, reputed to possess marvelous skill in the martial arts, was studiously avoided by youths seeking safe and profitable robbery victims. He walked through the project without fear. Lastly, an adult black man declared that his neighborhood was very safe because he knows everyone, and everyone knows him.

All of these people face the same hazards, yet their attitudes, fears, and modes of coping vary enormously. Why do they respond so differently to the same risks? Urbanites, in general, continually make decisions about which situations and persons they consider dangerous, but these judgments are rarely based on detailed statistics about where and when crimes occur. Nor are such peoples' attitudes proportional to the statistical risks of victimization, either in this project or nationwide. A survey of the victimization experiences of two-thirds of the 300 households suggested that the rates of victimization of black and Chinese households are roughly the same: about half of each had experienced a robbery, burglary or assault since moving into the development ten years earlier. Yet, when asked how dangerous they found their environment, the Chinese residents reported much higher levels of fear: 30% of those interviewed said the project was dangerous in contrast to only 13% of the black respondents, and 18% said it was not at all dangerous, while 65% of the blacks interviewed felt this way. National statistics show a similar discrepancy between fear and the chance of victimization: although fear focuses on the random, unpredictable attack of the stranger, the risk of assault and murder by friends is far greater.

Clearly, danger cannot be equated with the statistical probability of being the victim of a crime. Instead, it is the individual's interpretation of the surrounding environment. The process of forming attitudes about which kinds of people, places, and times of day and night are safe or dangerous, and the cues which identify them, is one facet of the elaborate process by which an individual comes to know her world. Information from the mass media, from friends and neighbors, and from the urbanite's own experience is constructed into a mental map of the city which guides behavior and creates a sense of safety in the midst of danger. What the individual considers harmful is itself a cultural product. For some, danger is the risk of losing property; for others, it is name calling and personal humiliation; and for others, the degradation of abusive police and social service workers.

The term *risk* is used to refer to the likelihood of experiencing a crime or some other harm. It is thus a concept which refers to the external world and to the hazards it contains. Danger is a cultural construct which describes the way an individual conceptualizes the hazards and risks in his or her world and assesses what they mean to him or her. Fear refers to the inner emotional state an individual experiences as he or she contemplates the danger he or she believes to exist. Thus, both danger and fear are subjective in a way in which risk is not. On the other hand, they are not inevitably connected. Some may see a situation as dangerous but not regard it with fear, while others may see the same situation as dangerous and feel fearsome about it. Ideas about danger are a component of culture: they are learned, shared within groups and influence the way the world is interpreted and understood. Fear is more individualized, depending on each person's experience with harm, sense of competence and control, sense of vulnerability in general and other psychological characteristics.

Other cultures similarly define danger in terms of more general belief systems about their world. For example, a group of Indians living in remote forest settlements in Canada, the Salteaux, do not fear wolves or bears but consider snakes, toads, and frogs dangerous (Hallowell 1938). Although these are among the most harmless of the inhabitants of the forest, they are believed to be emanations of powerful supernatural forces, capable of acting as emissaries for sorcerers, of exuding malevolent magic, and of serving as omens of ill fortune. Monster toads and frogs roam the forest. On the other hand, the Azande farmers of East Africa consider dangerous the man who is quarrelsome, spiteful and dirty, as well as the person who defecates in others' gardens and eats house rats, since he is believed to possess witchcraft, the power to inflict misfortune, wasting disease and death on others (Evans-Pritchard 1937).

Notions of danger in American cities, as in other cultural settings, draw on more general social understandings of who and what is dangerous, the kinds of persons who are believed to be violent and immoral and the characteristics of people who are believed likely to commit crimes. In both simple and complex societies, those who suffer misfortune do not always know exactly where the final responsibility lies. In small-scale societies, the witch or supernatural forces are blamed; whereas in American cities, the faceless criminal receives the blame. Yet, in both, it is the outsider, the stranger, who is held responsible. Such persons are not full members of the observer's social and cultural world, but are people whose behavior appears strange and irrational.

The attitudes of the project residents I talked to vividly illustrate these images of danger. Danger has a variety of meanings for project residents. It means encounters with muggers on deserted streets, invasion by culturally alien neighbors, or the nuisance of disheveled drunks asleep on the sidewalk. Essentially, danger is fear of the stranger, the person who is potentially harmful and whose behavior seems unpredictable and beyond control. Those residents who are the most convinced that their environment is dangerous tend not to be those most victimized, but rather those who lack any social connection to street youths. Such people see themselves awash in a sea of dangerous strangers.

To Chinese residents, the blacks, all of whom seem to look alike and are thought to be robbers whose favorite victims are Chinese, appear most dangerous. Whites seem dangerous because they are members of a dominant group which has long excluded the Chinese from full membership in its social institutions and has treated them with disdain and indifference. Yet, to blacks, who recognize that only a small proportion of the project youths are actually involved in crime (only 10% of the black families have children who commit crimes), the project appears as a safe place in which they know almost everyone and can anticipate which few youths might be inclined to rob them. As one young black woman said to a young Chinese woman, also a resident of the project:

> To you, all the blacks are dangerous because you can't tell them apart, but to me they are George, Johnny, and Jamesy, and I know who to look out for and who will not bother me.

Black adults who endeavor to guide their children into a life of steady jobs and stable family ties find the project youths who pursue a glamorous life of hustling, easy money, and the *fast lane* dangerous in that they threaten to tempt their children away from their values. Some whites find the blacks dangerous, but those who know the black families and have watched their children grow up know which youths are active in crime and hustling, which are not and take comfort in the belief that, because they know them, they will not bother them.

Places which seem dangerous are not those where crimes occur most often, but those which are unfamiliar or are favorite hangouts of tough-looking youths. Nor are places thought to be safe free from crime. A playground in the center of the project, a favorite hangout for a group of youths blamed for local crime, was generally seen as very dangerous, although few crimes actually took place there. On the other hand, the area seen most often as safe was the street in front of each person's house. Yet this was also one of the most common places for robberies. Most people said that their side of the project was safe, but they feared to venture to the other, more dangerous side. Those who lived in the center of the project avoided the edges and those who lived on the periphery regarded the center of the project as a dangerous place to be carefully avoided. The victimization survey revealed no differences in the rate of robberies on any one side of the project. Thus, notions of safe and dangerous places do not simply reflect crime rates, but take into account ideas about territory, ethnic hostilities and conflicts, the presence of hostile strangers, familiarity, the availability of allies and the design of spaces.

Not all crimes are dangerous, nor are all dangerous events crimes. Some crimes which are technically serious are not so perceived by their victims, while others which are not considered serious by the police loom large as dangerous experiences. For example, crimes of violence or threatened violence committed by strangers seem dangerous even if little or no property is taken, such as unsuccessful robbery attempts or attempted burglaries. These incidents are reported when residents are asked if they have been the victims of crimes, but rarely elicit a phone call to the police. On the other hand, assaults by people who know each other are not perceived as crimes, even though they are technically defined as crimes by the police. Those who were assaulted in vicious, interpersonal battles never mentioned these incidents when queried about their experiences with victimization. Assaults by strangers on the other hand, are regarded as crimes and engender fear, not knife fights between rivals for a woman's affection or punches between neighbors over barking dogs or damaging gossip.

Residents of this high-crime environment respond to the dangers which surround them by constructing mental maps of the kinds of people and locations which are dangerous and safe. These maps are subjective representations imposed on the physical realities of space and time, constructions of reality that reflect the individual's past experience and knowledge. They guide movements through the project and channel behavior toward strangers. Yet not all mental maps are equally accurate or helpful. The process of constructing these maps involves drawing distinctions and making generalizations. Maps of areas that are well known are more finely differentiated, while maps of unfamiliar areas are blank or vague. Those with greater knowledge of the potentially hazardous people around them and of the particular uses of the surrounding spaces develop more accurate and differentiated mental maps. Such people also find their environment far less dangerous.

Chinese residents, for example, were generally unable to tell the black residents apart, lumping them all into a criminal and predatory population, despite the fact that 90% of the families had no connection to crime. They also failed to make fine distinctions between the relative danger of different parts of the development. On the other hand, the blacks were far more sophisticated in drawing distinctions between black residents and were equipped with highly differentiated locational maps of the project. Yet, they lumped all Chinese together into the category of rich restaurant owners, despite the fact that the vast majority were poor cooks and waiters in Chinese restaurants. The use of these unsophisticated mental maps thus exacerbates residents' feelings that they are surrounded by a faceless mass of dangerous strangers.

How do these people cope with their dangerous environment? Some residents adopt a defensive strategy, turning their homes into fortresses barricaded with expensive locks and elaborate window bars, stockpiling guns, learning to live with large guard dogs in small apartments and calling the police to report every incident. They are always cautious, staying at home at night and avoiding social contact with anyone but close friends and relatives. These are the people whose lives are most constricted by the fear of crime: the elderly, residents who speak only Chinese and social isolates. Their mode of defense is escape and retreat, but, if the fragile shell of safety around their homes is violated by a crowbar mark on the door or an attempted purse snatch on the porch, the loss of a sense of security is devastating.

Others adopt offensive strategies, developing reputations as dangerous, tough people who are willing to fight back if abused, either by violence, by calling the police or by going to court. These people are still vulnerable to victimization by outsiders who do not know their reputations or by insiders who are angry at them, but they do not feel the same sense of helplessness in the face of anonymous dangers. Unlike the defensive residents, who are vulnerable every time they leave their homes, those who adopt offensive strategies carry their protective armor around with them. Thus, the residents of this project range from those who cower in fear in a barred haven of safety to those who traverse the city at any time of day or night with a sense of confidence and ease springing from their mastery of the urban environment and their extensive knowledge of its locations, its residents, and its cultural patterns.

A THEORY OF DANGER

This analysis suggests a more general theory: that the sense of danger is rooted in feelings of uncertainty, helplessness and vulnerability triggered by encounters with strangers who belong to unfamiliar, hostile and potentially harmful groups. A stranger is not perceived as a unique individual having a personal history, reputation and location in social space. Instead, visible cues such as age, sex, dress, demeanor, ethnicity, location and mode of speaking are used to place a stranger in a social category associated with certain expected behaviors. Mitchell terms this a categorical relationship, one which arises in situations in which interactions are superficial and perfunctory (1966:52). Such categories codify and order social interaction in otherwise uncertain, unstructured urban situations. These categories are constructed through experience and shared cultural conceptions, but the process of construction is rarely conscious or deliberate; rather, it proceeds through the creation of implicit categories which feel like instinctive descriptions of the world.

Categorical identities inevitably ignore individual variation and are likely to lump very different individuals together. Because finely honed categories develop through familiarity and contact, socially distant and unfamiliar strangers will be assigned to grosser and less refined categories than those who inhabit more familiar social worlds. The less contact an individual has with members of other groups, the less accurately will she categorize these groups. Entire ethnic or age groups can be lumped into the dangerous, immoral or threatening camp. The dangerous group generally differs in ethnic background, but suspicions may also arise due to differences in class and lifestyle.

Predictions of behavior based on categorical identities are far less certain than predictions based on knowledge of the particular habits and propensities of a specific person. The stranger's behavior is likely to appear unexpected and unprovoked, leaving the observer with the feeling that there is little she can do to avoid attack. Psychological research suggests that fear comes from the experience of helplessness in the face of harm, the sense that there is no place or time of safety nor any course of action which will guarantee safety (Seligman 1975).

In Dover Square, the coexistence of separate social worlds divided by sharp social boundaries creates conditions under which residents are likely to experience their environment as dangerous. Those who make contacts across the boundaries, who come to know those in other social networks, see the project as much less dangerous than those who do not, who consequently function with far less differentiated and accurate categorical identities and who lack the sense of certainty and control provided by knowing who the potentially harmful people are. Knowing their identities does not protect one from harm, but it does diminish the sense of living in a world of unpredictable and uncontrollable strangers.

Wirth argued that individuals who are detached from organizations and groups pose the greatest threat to social order because they are not controlled by any social group or moral code (1938:76). However, it is not those who are detached, but those who appear detached, who are responsible for crime, disorder, and fear. These individuals are least susceptible to social control. Although they are firmly anchored in existing social groups, their social moorings are unknown to the observer, who sees them as *detached* persons. Criminals in Dover Square actively fostered their appearance of anonymity, of detachment, in order to escape punishment from their victims. Thus, it is the separation between social worlds, as much as the detachment of individuals, that produces anomie and social disorder.

URBAN SOCIAL THEORY AND SOCIAL BOUNDARIES

This description of life in a multiethnic neighborhood suggests that Wirth's vision of urbanism as a way of life was not wrong, but only a partial view. Primary and intimate relationships exist within urban villages and social networks, but the problematic interactions are those that lurk in the gaps between these worlds. Wirth and the Chicago sociologists hinted at the problem of the relationship between the pieces of the urban social mosaic, but it was generally ignored. These pieces may be geographically based communities or nonlocalized social networks (Jacobson 1971). Several nonlocalized networks can occupy the same space, as they do in Dover Square. Whatever their configuration, the question of how these networks articulate with one another is a critical problem for urban anthropology. It is here that the breakdown of social control is the greatest and the freedom to be different the greatest challenge. Anthropologists tend to focus on enduring ties, yet it is these fleeting relationships and social boundaries between enduring groups which are most problematic for urban social life.

THE PREINDUSTRIAL CITY

Gideon Sjoberg

In this pioneering study of the preindustrial city, Sjoberg seeks to understand the characteristics of cities before they are transformed through industrialization. Preindustrial cities throughout the world, he claims, show certain similarities. For one, their technology is based on the use of human and animal power, rather than on machines; and their relationship to the countryside differs from that of industrial cities. The preindustrial city also differs from the industrial city in its lifeways. For these people, city living does not mean participation in a society marked by impersonalization. At the same time there is a sharp division between the ruling elite and the rest of the population. For a portrait of a contemporary preindustrial city, read Waldron's article "Within the Wall and Beyond."

In the past few decades social scientists have been conducting field studies in a number of relatively non-Westernized cities. Their recently acquired knowledge of North Africa and various parts of Asia, combined with what was already learned, clearly indicates that these cities are not like typical cities of the United States and other highly industrialized areas but are much more like those of medieval Europe. Such communities are termed herein "preindustrial," for they have arisen without stimulus from that form of production which we associate with the European industrial revolution.

Recently Foster, in a most informative article, took cognizance of the preindustrial city.[1] His primary emphasis was upon the peasantry (which he calls "folk"); but he recognized this to be part of a broader social structure which includes the preindustrial city. He noted certain similarities between the peasantry and the city's lower class. Likewise the present author sought to analyze the total society of which the peasantry and the preindustrial city are integral parts.[2] For want of a better term this was called "feudal." Like Redfield's folk (or "primitive") society, the feudal order is highly stable and sacred; in contrast, however, it has a complex social organization. It is characterized by highly developed state and educational and/or religious institutions and by a rigid class structure.

SOURCE: *American Journal of Sociology,* LX (1955): 438–445. © 1955 by University of Chicago. Reprinted by permission of the University of Chicago Press.

Thus far no one has analyzed the preindustrial city per se, especially as it differs from the industrial-urban community, although Weber, Tönnies, and a few others perceived differences between the two. Yet such a survey is needed for the understanding of urban development in so-called underdeveloped countries and, for that matter, in parts of Europe. Such is the goal of this paper. The typological analysis should also serve as a guide to future research.

ECOLOGICAL ORGANIZATION

Preindustrial cities depend for their existence upon food and raw materials obtained from without; for this reason they are marketing centers. And they serve as centers for handicraft manufacturing. In addition, they fulfil important political, religious, and educational functions. Some cities have become specialized; for example, Benares in India and Karbala in Iraq are best known as religious communities, and Peiping in China as a locus for political and educational activities.

The proportion of urbanites relative to the peasant population is small, in some societies about 10 per cent, even though a few preindustrial cities have attained populations of 100,000 or more. Growth has been by slow accretion. These characteristics are due to the nonindustrial nature of the total social order. The amount of surplus food available to support an urban population has been limited by the unmechanized agriculture, transportation facilities utilizing primarily human or animal power, and inefficient methods of food preservation and storage.

The internal arrangement of the preindustrial city, in the nature of the case, is closely related to the city's economic and social structure.[3] Most streets are mere passageways for people and for animals used in transport. Buildings are low and crowded together. The congested conditions, combined with limited scientific knowledge, have fostered serious sanitation problems.

More significant is the rigid social segregation which typically has led to the formation of "quarters" or "wards." In some cities (e.g., Fez, Morocco, and Aleppo, Syria) these were sealed off from each other by walls, whose gates were locked at night. The quarters reflect the sharp local social divisions. Thus ethnic groups live in special sections. And the occupational groupings, some being at the same time ethnic in character, typically reside apart from one another. Often a special street or sector of the city is occupied almost exclusively by members of a particular trade; cities in such divergent cultures as medieval Europe and modern Afghanistan contain streets with names like "street of the goldsmiths." Lower-class and especially "outcaste" groups live on the city's periphery, at a distance from the primary centers of activity. Social segregation, the limited transportation facilities, the modicum of residential mobility, and the cramped living quarters have encouraged the development of well-defined neighborhoods which are almost primary groups.

Despite rigid segregation the evidence suggests no real specialization of land use such as is functionally necessary in industrial-urban communities. In medieval Europe and in other areas city dwellings often serve as workshops, and religious structures are used as schools or marketing centers.[4]

Finally, the "business district" does not hold the position of dominance that it enjoys in the industrial-urban community. Thus, in the Middle East the principal mosque, or in medieval Europe the cathedral, is usually the focal point of community life. The center of Peiping is the Forbidden City.

ECONOMIC ORGANIZATION

The economy of the preindustrial city diverges sharply from that of the modern industrial center. The prime difference is the absence in the former of industrialism which may be defined as that system of production in which *inanimate* sources of power are used to multiply human effort. Preindustrial cities depend for the production of goods and services upon *animate* (human or animal) sources of energy—applied either directly or indirectly through such mechanical devices as hammers, pulleys, and wheels. The industrial-urban community, on the other hand, employs inanimate generators of power such as electricity and steam which greatly enhance the productive capacity of urbanites. This basically new form of energy production, one which requires for its development and survival a special kind of institutional complex, effects striking changes in the ecological, economic, and social organization of cities in which it has become dominant.

Other facets of the economy of the preindustrial city are associated with its particular system of production. There is little fragmentation or specialization of work. The handicraftsman participates in nearly every phase of the manufacture of an article, often carrying out the work in his own home or in a small shop near by and, within the limits of certain guild and community regulations, maintaining direct control over conditions of work and methods of production.

In industrial cities, on the other hand, the complex division of labor requires a specialized managerial group, often extra-community in character, whose primary function is to direct and control others. And for the supervision and coordination of the activities of workers, a "factory system" has been developed, something typically lacking in preindustrial cities. (Occasionally centralized production is found in preindustrial cities—e.g., where the state organized slaves for large-scale construction projects.) Most commercial activities, also, are conducted in preindustrial cities by individuals without a highly formalized organization; for example, the craftsman has frequently been responsible for the marketing of his own products. With a few exceptions, the preindustrial community cannot support a large group of middlemen.

The various occupations are organized into what have been termed "guilds."[5] These strive to encompass all, except the elite, who are gainfully employed in some economic activity. Guilds have existed for merchants and handicraft workers (e.g., goldsmiths and weavers) as well as for servants, entertainers, and even beggars and thieves. Typically the guilds operate only within the local community, and there are no large-scale economic organizations such as those in industrial cities which link their members to their fellows in other communities.

Guild membership and apprenticeship are prerequisites to the practice of almost any occupation, a circumstance obviously leading to monopolization. To a degree these organizations regulate the work of their members and the price of their products and services. And the guilds recruit workers into specific occupations, typically selecting them according to such particularistic criteria as kinship rather than universalistic standards.

The guilds are integrated with still other elements of the city's social structure. They perform certain religious functions; for example, in medieval European, Chinese, and Middle Eastern cities each guild had its "patron saint" and held periodic festivals in his honor. And, by assisting members in time of trouble, the guilds serve as social security agencies.

The economic structure of the preindustrial city functions with little rationality, judged by industrial-urban standards. This is shown in the general nonstandardization of manufacturing methods as well as in the products and is even more evident in marketing. In preindustrial cities throughout the world a fixed price is rare; buyer and seller settle their bargain by haggling. (Of course, there are limits above which customers will not buy and below which merchants will not sell.) Often business is conducted in a leisurely manner, money not being the only desired end.

Furthermore, the sorting of goods according to size, weight, and quality is not common. Typical is the adulteration and spoilage of produce. And weights and measures are not standardized: variations exist not only between one city and the next but also within communities, for often different guilds employ their own systems. Within a single city there may be different kinds of currency, which, with the poorly developed accounting and credit systems, signalize a modicum of rationality in the whole of economic action in preindustrial cities.[6]

SOCIAL ORGANIZATION

The economic system of the preindustrial city, based as it has been upon animate sources of power, articulates with a characteristic class structure and family, religious, educational, and governmental systems.

Of the class structure, the most striking component is a literate elite controlling and depending for its existence upon the mass of the populace, even in the traditional cities of India with their caste system. The elite is composed of individuals holding positions in the governmental, religious, and/or educational institutions of the larger society, although at times groups such as large absentee landlords have belonged to it. At the opposite pole are the masses, comprising such groups as handicraft workers whose goods and services are produced primarily for the elite's benefit.[7] Between the elite and the lower class is a rather sharp schism, but in both groups there are gradations in rank. The members of the elite belong to the "correct" families and enjoy power, property, and certain highly valued personal attributes. Their position, moreover, is legitimized by sacred writings.

Social mobility in this city is minimal; the only real threat to the elite comes from the outside—not from the city's lower classes. And a middle class—so typical of industrial-urban communities, where it can be considered the "dominant" class—is not known in the preindustrial city. The system of production in the larger society provides goods, including food, and services in sufficient amounts to support only a small group of leisured individuals; under these conditions an urban middle class, a semileisured group, cannot arise. Nor are a middle class and extensive social mobility essential to the maintenance of the economic system.

Significant is the role of the marginal or "outcaste" groups (e.g., the Eta of Japan), which are not an integral part of the dominant social system. Typically they rank lower than the urban lower class, performing tasks considered especially degrading, such as burying the dead. Slaves, beggars, and the like are outcastes in most preindustrial cities. Even such groups as professional entertainers and itinerant merchants are often viewed as outcastes, for their rovings expose them to "foreign" ideas from which the dominant social group seeks to isolate itself. Actually many outcaste groups, including some of those mentioned above, are ethnic groups, a fact which further intensifies their isolation. (A few, like the Jews in the predominantly Muslim cities of North Africa, have their own small literate religious elite which, however, enjoys no significant political power in the city as a whole.)

An assumption of many urban sociologists is that a small, unstable kinship group, notably the conjugal unit, is a necessary correlate of city life. But this premise does not hold for preindustrial cities.[8] At times sociologists and anthropologists, when generalizing about various traditional societies, have imputed to peasants typically urban kinship patterns. Actually, in these societies the ideal forms of kinship and family life are most closely approximated by members of the urban literate elite, who are best able to fulfil the exacting requirements of the sacred writings. Kinship and the ability to perpetuate one's lineage are accorded marked prestige in preindustrial cities. Children, especially sons, are highly valued, and polygamy or concubinage or adoption help to assure the attainment of large families. The pre-eminence of kinship is apparent even in those preindustrial cities where divorce is permitted. Thus, among the urban Muslims or urban Chinese divorce is not an index of disorganization; here, conjugal ties are loose and distinctly subordinate to the bonds of kinship, and each member of a dissolved conjugal unit typically is absorbed by his kin group. Marriage, a prerequisite to adult status in the preindustrial city, is entered upon at an early age and is arranged between families rather than romantically, by individuals.

The kinship and familial organization displays some rigid patterns of sex and age differentiation whose universality in preindustrial cities has generally been overlooked. A woman, especially of the upper class, ideally performs few significant functions outside the home. She is clearly subordinate to males, especially her father or husband. Recent evidence indicates that this is true even for such a city as Lhasa, Tibet, where women supposedly have had high status.[9] The isolation of women from public life has in some cases been extreme. In nineteenth-century Seoul, Korea, "respectable" women appeared on the streets only during certain hours of the night when men were supposed to stay at home.[10] Those women in preindustrial cities who evade some of the stricter requirements are members of certain marginal groups (e.g., entertainers) or of the lower class. The role of the urban lower-class woman typically resembles that of the peasant rather than the urban upper-class woman. Industrialization, by creating demands and opportunities for their employment outside the home, is causing significant changes in the status of women as well as in the whole of the kinship system in urban areas.

A formalized system of age grading is an effective mechanism of social control in preindustrial cities. Among siblings the eldest son is privileged. And children and youth are subordinate to parents and other adults. This, combined with early marriage, inhibits the development of a "youth culture." On the other hand, older persons hold considerable power and prestige, a fact contributing to the slow pace of change.

As noted above, kinship is functionally integrated with social class. It also reinforces and is reinforced by the economic organization: the occupations, through the guilds, select their members primarily on the basis of kinship, and much of the work is carried on in the home or immediate vicinity. Such conditions are not functional to the requirements of a highly industrialized society.

The kinship system in the preindustrial city also articulates with a special kind of religious system, whose formal organization reaches fullest development among members of the literate elite.[11] The city is the seat of the key religious functionaries whose actions set standards for the rest of society. The urban lower class, like the peasantry, does not possess the education or the means to maintain all the exacting norms prescribed by the sacred writings. Yet the religious system influences the city's entire social structure. (Typically, within the preindustrial city one religion is dominant; however, certain minority groups adhere to their own beliefs.) Unlike the situation in industrial cities, religious activity is not separate from other social action but permeates family, economic, governmental, and other activities. Daily life is pervaded with religious significance. Especially important are periodic public festivals and ceremonies like Ramadan in Muslim cities. Even distinctly ethnic outcaste groups can through their own religious festivals maintain solidarity.

Magic, too, is interwoven with economic, familial, and other social activities. Divination is commonly employed for determining the "correct" action on critical occasions; for example, in traditional Japanese and Chinese cities, the selection of marriage partners. And nonscientific procedures are widely employed to treat illness among all elements of the population of the preindustrial city.

Formal education typically is restricted to the male elite, its purpose being to train individuals for positions in the governmental, educational, or religious hierarchies. The economy of preindustrial cities does not require mass literacy, nor, in fact, does the system of production provide the leisure so necessary for the acquisition of formal education. Considerable time is needed merely to learn the written language, which often is quite different from that spoken. The teacher occupies a position of honor, primarily because of the prestige of all learning and especially of knowledge of the sacred literature, and learning is traditional and characteristically based upon sacred writings.[12] Students are expected to memorize rather than evaluate and initiate, even in institutions of higher learning.

Since preindustrial cities have no agencies of mass communication, they are relatively isolated from one another. Moreover, the masses within a city are isolated from the elite. The former must rely upon verbal communication, which is formalized in special groups such as storytellers or their counterparts. Through verse and song these transmit upper-class tradition to nonliterate individuals.

The formal government of the preindustrial city is the province of the elite and is closely integrated with the educational and religious systems. It performs two principal functions: exacting tribute from the city's masses to support the activities of the elite and maintaining law and order through a "police force" (at times a branch of the army) and a court system. The police force exists primarily for the control of "outsiders," and the courts support custom and the rule of the sacred literature, a code of enacted legislation typically being absent.

In actual practice little reliance is placed upon formal machinery for regulating social life.[13] Much more significant are the informal controls exerted by the kinship, guild, and religious systems, and here, of course, personal standing is decisive. Status distinctions are visibly correlated with personal attributes, chiefly speech, dress, and personal mannerisms which proclaim ethnic group, occupation, age, sex, and social class. In nineteenth-century Seoul, not only did the upper-class mode of dress differ considerably from that of the masses, but speech varied according to social class, the verb forms and pronouns depending upon whether the speaker ranked higher or lower or was the equal of the person being addressed.[14] Obviously, then, escape from one's role is difficult, even in the street crowds. The individual is ever conscious of his specific rights and duties. All these things conserve the social order in the preindustrial city despite its heterogeneity.

CONCLUSIONS

Throughout this paper there is the assumption that certain structural elements are universal for all urban centers. This study's hypothesis is that their form in the preindustrial city is fundamentally distinct from that in the industrial-urban community. A considerable body of data not only from medieval Europe, which is somewhat atypical,[15] but from a variety of cultures supports this point of view. Emphasis has been upon the static features of preindustrial city life. But even those preindustrial cities which have undergone considerable change approach the ideal type. For one thing, social change is of such a nature that it is not usually perceived by the general populace.

Most cities of the preindustrial type have been located in Europe or Asia. Even though Athens and Rome and the large commercial centers of Europe prior to the industrial revolution displayed certain unique features, they fit the preindustrial type quite well.[16] And many traditional Latin-American cities are quite like it, although deviations exist, for, excluding pre-Columbian cities, these were affected to some degree by the industrial revolution soon after their establishment.

It is postulated that industrialization is a key variable accounting for the distinctions between preindustrial and industrial cities. The type of social structure required to develop and maintain a form of production utilizing inanimate sources of power is quite unlike that in the preindustrial city.[17] At the very least, extensive industrialization requires a rational, centralized, extra-community economic organization in which recruitment is based more upon universalism than on particularism, a class system which stresses achievement rather than ascription, a small and flexible kinship system, a system of mass education which emphasizes universalistic rather than particularistic criteria, and mass communication. Modification in any one of these elements affects the others and induces changes in other systems such as those of religion and social control as well. Industrialization, moreover, not only requires a special kind of social structure within the urban community but provides the means necessary for its establishment.

Anthropologists will in the future devote increased attention to the study of cities throughout the world. They must therefore recognize that the particular kind of social structure found in cities in the United States is not typical of all societies. Miner's recent study of Timbuctoo,[18] which contains much excellent data, points to the need for recognition of the preindustrial city. His emphasis upon the folk-urban continuum diverted him from an equally significant problem: How does Timbuctoo differ from modern industrial cities in its ecological, economic, and social structure? Society there seems even more sacred and organized than Miner admits.[19] For example, he used divorce as an index of disorganization, but in Muslim society divorce within certain rules is justified by the sacred literature. The studies of Hsu and Fried would have considerably more significance had the authors perceived the generality of their findings. And, once the general structure of the preindustrial city is understood, the specific cultural deviations become more meaningful.

Beals notes the importance of the city as a center of acculturation.[20] But an understanding of this process is impossible without some knowledge of the preindustrial city's social structure. Although industrialization is clearly advancing throughout most of the world, the social structure of preindustrial civilizations is conservative, often resisting the introduction of numerous industrial forms. Certainly many cities of Europe (e.g., in France or Spain) are not so fully industrialized as some presume; a number of preindustrial patterns remain. The persistence of preindustrial elements is also evident in cities of

North Africa and many parts of Asia; for example, in India and Japan,[21] even though great social change is currently taking place. And the Latin-American city of Merida, which Redfield studied, had many preindustrial traits.[22] A conscious awareness of the ecological, economic, and social structure of the preindustrial city should do much to further the development of comparative urban community studies.

NOTES

1. George M. Foster, "What Is Folk Culture?" *AmericanAnthropologist,* LV (1953), 159–73.
2. Gideon Sjoberg, "Folk and 'Feudal' Societies," *American Journal of Sociology,* LVIII (1952), 231–39.
3. Sociologists have devoted almost no attention to the ecology of preindustrial centers. However, works of other social scientists do provide some valuable preliminary data. See, e.g., Marcel Clerget, *Le Caire: Étude de géographie urbaine et d'histoire économique* (2 vols.; Cairo: E. & R. Schindler, 1934); Robert E. Dickinson, *The West European City* (London: Routledge & Kegan Paul, 1951); Roger Le Tourneau, *Fès: Avant le protectorat* (Casablanca: Sociétu !arocaine de Librairie et d'Édition, 1949); Edward W. Lane, *Cairo Fifty Years Ago* (London: John Murray, 1896); J. Sauvaget, *Alep* (Paris: Librairie Orientaliste Paul Geuthner, 1941); J. Weulersse, "Antioche: Essai de géographie urbaine," *Bulletin d'études orientales,* IV (1934), 27–79; Jean Kennedy, *Here Is India* (New York: Charles Scribner's Sons, 1945); and relevant articles in American geographical journals.
4. Dickinson, *op. cit.,* p. 27; O. H. K. Spate, *India and Pakistan* (London: Methuen & Co., 1954), p. 183.
5. For a discussion of guilds and other facets of the preindustrial city's economy see, e.g., J. S. Burgess, *The Guilds of Peking* (New York: Columbia University Press, 1928); Edward T. Williams, *China, Yesterday and Today* (5th ed.; New York: Thomas Y. Crowell Co., 1932); T'ai-ch'u Liao, "The Apprentices in Chengtu during and after the War," *Yenching Journal of Social Studies,* IV (1948), 90–106; H. A. R. Gibb and Harold Bowen, *Islamic Society and the West* (London: Oxford University Press, 1950), Vol. I, Part I, chap. vi; Le Tourneau, *op. cit.;* Clerget, *op. cit.;* James W. Thompson and Edgar N. Johnson, *An Introduction to Medieval Europe* (New York: W. W. Norton Co., 1937), chap. xx; Sylvia L. Thrupp, "Medieval Gilds Reconsidered," *Journal of Economic History,* II (1942), 164–73.
6. For an extreme example of unstandardized currency cf. Robert Coltman, Jr., *The Chinese* (Philadelphia: F. A. Davis, 1891), p. 52. In some traditional societies (e.g., China) the state has sought to standardize economic action in the city by setting up standard systems of currency and/or weights and measures; these efforts, however, generally proved ineffective. Inconsistent policies in taxation, too, hinder the development of a "rational" economy.
7. The status of the true merchant in the preindustrial city, ideally, has been low; in medieval Europe and China many merchants were considered "outcastes." However, in some preindustrial cities a few wealthy merchants have acquired considerable power even though their role has not been highly valued. Even then most of their prestige has come through participation in religious, governmental, or educational activities, which have been highly valued (see, e.g., Ping-ti Ho, "The Salt Merchants of Yang-Chou: A Study of Commercial Capitalism in Eighteenth-Century China," *Harvard Journal of Asiatic Studies,* XVII [1954], 130–68).

8. For materials on the kinship system and age and sex differentiation see, e.g., Le Tourneau, *op. cit.;* Edward W. Lane, *The Manners and Customs of the Modern Egyptians* (3d ed.; New York: E. P. Dutton Co., 1923); C. Snouck Hurgronje, *Mekka in the Latter Part of the Nineteenth Century,* trans. J. H. Monahan (London: Luzac, 1931); Horace Miner, *The Primitive City of Timbuctoo* (Princeton: Princeton University Press, 1953); Alice M. Bacon, *Japanese Girls and Women* (rev. ed.; Boston: Houghton Mifflin Co., 1902); J. S. Burgess, "Community Organization in China," *Far Eastern Survey,* XIV (1945), 371–73; Morton H. Fried, *Fabric of Chinese Society* (New York: Frederick A. Praeger, 1953); Francis L. K. Hsu, *Under the Ancestors' Shadow* (New York: Columbia University Press, 1948); Cornelius Osgood, *The Koreans and Their Culture* (New York: Ronald Press, 1951), chap. viii; Jukichi Inouye, *Home Life in Tokyo* (2d ed.; Tokyo: Tokyo Printing Co., 1911).

9. Tsung-Lien Shen and Shen-Chi Liu, *Tibet and the Tibetans* (Stanford: Stanford University Press, 1953), pp. 143–44.

10. Osgood, *op. cit.,* p. 146.

11. For information on various aspects of religious behavior see, e.g., Le Tourneau, *op. cit.;* Miner, *op. cit.;* Lane, *Manners and Customs;* Hurgronje, *op. cit.;* André Chouraqui, *Les Juifs d'Afrique du Nord* (Paris: Presses Universitaires de France, 1952); Justus Doolittle, *Social Life of the Chinese* (London: Sampson Low, 1868); John K. Shryock, *The Temples of Anking and Their Cults* (Paris: Privately printed, 1931); Derk Bodde (ed.), *Annual Customs and Festivals in Peking* (Peiping: Henri Vetch, 1936); Edwin Benson, *Life in a Medieval City* (New York: Macmillan Co., 1920); Hsu, *op. cit.*

12. Le Tourneau, *op. cit.,* Part VI; Lane, *Manners and Customs,* chap. ii; Charles Bell, *The People of Tibet* (Oxford: Clarendon Press, 1928), chap. xix; O. Olufsen, *The Emir of Bokhara and His Country* (London: William Heinemann, 1911), chap. ix; Doolittle, *op. cit.*

13. Carleton Coon, *Caravan: The Story of the Middle East* (New York: Henry Holt & Co., 1951), p. 259; George W. Gilmore, *Korea from Its Capital* (Philadelphia: Presbyterian Board of Publication, 1892), pp. 51–52.

14. Osgood, *op. cit.,* chap. viii; Gilmore, *op. cit.,* chap. iv.

15. Henri Pirenne, in *Medieval Cities* (Princeton: Princeton University Press, 1925), and others have noted that European cities grew up in opposition to and were separate from the greater society. But this thesis has been overstated for medieval Europe. Most preindustrial cities are integral parts of broader social structures.

16. Some of these cities made extensive use of water power, which possibly fostered deviations from the type.

17. For a discussion of the institutional prerequisites of industrialization see, e.g., Bert F. Hoselitz, "Social Structure and Economic Growth," *Economia internazionale,* VI (1953), 52–77, and Marion J. Levy, "Some Sources of the Vulnerability of the Structures of Relatively Non-industrialized Societies to Those of Highly Industrialized Societies," in Bert F. Hoselitz (ed.), *The Progress of Underdeveloped Areas* (Chicago: University of Chicago Press, 1952), pp. 114 ff.

18. *Op. cit.*

19. This point seems to have been perceived also by Asael T. Hansen in his review of Horace Miner's *The Primitive City of Timbuctoo, American Journal of Sociology,* LIX (1954), 501–2.

20. Ralph L. Beals, "Urbanism, Urbanization and Acculturation," *American Anthropologist,* LIII (1951), 1–10.

21. See, e.g., D. R. Gadgil, *Poona: A Socio-economic Survey* (Poona: Gokhale Institute of Politics and Economics, 1952), Part II; N. V. Sovani, *Social Survey of Kolhapur City* (Poona: Gokhale Institute of Politics and Economics, 1951), Vol. II; Noel P.

Gist, "Caste Differentials in South India," *American Sociological Review,* XIX (1954), 126–37; John Campbell Pelzel, "Social Stratification in Japanese Urban Economic Life" (unpublished Ph.D. dissertation, Harvard University, Department of Social Relations, 1950).

22. Robert Redfield, *The Folk Culture of Yucatan* (Chicago: University of Chicago Press, 1941).

Part Two
Urban Fieldwork: Anthropologists in Cities

Although rural communities are rarely as simple as they are often characterized, they are markedly more homogeneous than cities. The anthropologist studying a tribal group or peasant village can assume that there is a high degree of uniformity in the lifestyles and values of his population, although status and wealth differences exist even here. Such an assumption cannot be made by the urban fieldworker. One of the defining characteristics of cities is complexity and heterogeneity. The typical city contains a wide spectrum of subcultures based upon class, ethnicity, occupation, religion, and so forth. In response to the problems of understanding such a diverse population, most urban anthropologists have restricted the scope of their inquiries to small, clearly segmented groups within the complex urban mosaic. And there have been few attempts to understand cities as wholes in the tradition of the community study method.

UNITS OF ANALYSIS

The range of social units in which urban anthropologists have worked has been outlined by Eames and Goode (1977): (1) units based on common residence such as a neighborhood or a cluster of blocks in a city; (2) groups based on common culture of origin such as ethnic or minority groups; (3) groups based on a common belief system—religious or political—such as Hare Krishna or radical political communes; (4) groups based on common work, notably occupational groups; and (5) units based upon primary relationships such as households, kinship units, and social networks. Most urban research to date has been on the first type—residential units which have definable boundaries and in which the population is somewhat homogeneous. Such spatially bounded units in which most of the inhabitants are of the same ethnic or at least class background, where there is a high degree of face-to-face interaction and a sense of community, are similar enough to the traditional units of the tribal or peasant village to enable the anthropologist to use conventional ethnographic techniques of field research. But even within small bounded groups there may be numerous cross cutting components which the urban fieldworker must take into account. In a study of prostitutes, Jennifer James (1972) found her research complicated by the diverse backgrounds and attitudes of her subjects. Instead of a homogeneous occupation, she encountered major differences between the prostitutes who were full-time professionals and the drug addicts who worked only when the need arose. Moreover, the attitudes of the women were influenced by their different ethnic backgrounds: blacks tended to see prostitution as a legitimate occupation while whites saw it as deviant and illegitimate.

THE PEOPLE ANTHROPOLOGISTS STUDY

Imagine all the varied neighborhood, community, ethnic, and other social groupings which exist, placed on a vertical continuum according to socioeconomic status, with the very rich at the top and the very poor at the bottom. Now, for every urban anthropological study, imagine placing a black dot corresponding to the socioeconomic status of the group along the continuum. The result would be a dense mass of ink at the lower end and a mere spattering of dots at the middle and top. It is no exaggeration to say that for every anthropological study done in upper- and middle-strata neighborhoods there have been ten studies conducted in slums, ghettos, and squatter settlements. This concentration on the poor is due to several factors. First, anthropology's traditional techniques of collecting data, most importantly participant-observation, were designed for working with fairly homogeneous groups localized in one area. The condensed neighborhoods of the urban poor offer a field situation. more suitable to the anthropologist's methods than do the more spread-out, dormitory suburbs of the middle class. Second, poor people are more accessible. Perhaps harboring fewer image pretensions, perhaps gratified that someone cares, and perhaps less aware of their legal rights, the poor are not as resistant to being studied as those in the strata above them. In most societies, the middle and upper classes are less willing to tolerate the intrusions of anthropologists and their endless questions. Third, anthropologists have always been concerned primarily with people and societies that are marginal in terms of national political power and wealth. Tribal and peasant peoples, long the staple of anthropological fieldwork, are clearly outside the mainstream. It has been anthropologists' adopted role to study (and be the spokesmen for) the marginal peoples of the world. Other social sciences have focused primarily on the mainstream, and particularly on Western societies and their elites. And fourth, to some degree anthropologists may be attracted to the poor because they are "exotic." A middle-class Irishman is not really very different from myself, but the gypsy-like Irish Tinkers whom I studied certainly are. Apart from the added interest of working among people who possess a culture different from one's own, the more divergent the cultural patterns of the group being studied, the more clearly they stand out to the observer.

THE NATURE OF URBAN FIELDWORK

The hallmark of anthropological fieldwork has been the intensive participation of the anthropologist in the life of the community. This is usually accomplished when the anthropologist takes up residence in a village. Unlike sociologists or political scientists who often commute to the people they study, anthropologists try to live among their subjects, participating in and observing activities as fellow residents. Among urban groups, however, residence is often not possible. A severe shortage of housing or dispersed residential pattern of the group under study may necessitate living outside the community. Michael Whiteford ("Doing It") recounts how he was unable to find accommodation in the poor urban barrio in which he was conducting research and instead had to live in a nearby middle-class neighborhood. In a study of cityward migrants to Belgrade, Yugoslavia, Andrei Simic (1974) found private housing so scarce that he spent the first two months of his fieldwork looking for a suitable place to live. Because he was white, Elliott Liebow found it impractical to reside in the black Washington, D.C., ghetto he studied. Whatever the reason, nonresident fieldworkers often have more difficulty gaining the confidence of the people they intend to study. In addition, important activities often take place at times when commuting anthropologists are not present.

Whether anthropologists live in the community or commute, gaining access to informants is often more difficult in the city than in the village. With less outdoor space available than in rural areas, urbanites tend to spend more time inside and therefore are less observable and not as easily approached. Also important are the nature of urban work and the constraints of time. Most urbanites are employees: they work for someone else and receive an hourly wage. Unlike rural anthropologists who may accompany their informants on a hunt or visit them in their fields, urban anthropologists generally cannot interview their informants in their workplace without interfering. Hence, in urban societies key informants are unavailable for much of each day.

Anthropologists studying a nonlocalized group spread across an entire city, such as the Tzintzuntzeños studied by Robert Kemper (see part two), may lose much time just traveling to and from informants' homes. And without telephone and advance notice of their visit, anthropologists may arrive after a long journey through traffic to find their informant not at home. In one year of fieldwork, Kemper traveled 9,000 miles by car to visit migrants living in more than forty neighborhoods. In a rather extreme case, James Watson (1974) estimated that in his study of Chinese restaurant workers in London he spent four hours of travel time for every one hour of interviewing. Clearly, the urban anthropologist, not unlike the peasant migrant adapting to city life, must develop new strategies for working in urban settings.

Counterbalancing some of the difficulties of urban field research are certain benefits absent in peasant and tribal societies. Often available to urban anthropologists is an enormous amount of statistical data collected in government censuses and surveys. Sharon Gmelch ("The Fieldwork Experience") also points out the psychological boost such sources of information can give fieldworkers during emotional lows or slack periods in their research. In tribal and many peasant societies the fieldworker collects the necessary information on the demography and household structure of the community through the time-consuming administration of a household census. In most urban societies this data can be obtained by a trip to the government statistics office. Because urbanites tend to be better educated and are more likely to be literate than their rural counterparts, they are often able to help in the research process. For example, they sometimes fill in questionnaires and keep detailed records of their own activities or expenses.

A psychological benefit of urban fieldwork is the ease with which the anthropologist can escape the stresses and insecurities of the field situation. In traditional rural fieldwork, especially in remote tribal societies, anthropologists are isolated, completely cut off from their own society. When feeling lonely or alienated they must fall back on their own resources. They may retreat into the imaginary world of novels, but there is no physical escape. In the city anthropologists can leave the small world of their informants by simply hopping a bus for "downtown." In the city center, whether it be Bogota or Katmandu, anthropologists may, if they need to, speak their own language, read *Time* or the *Washington Post,* watch an American film, and buy a hamburger. And as Foster and Kemper note in their paper, anthropologists may also make contact with local scholars, who can offer sound advice and assurances that field problems—real or imagined—are not as serious or unresolvable as they often appear.

The need for new approaches to the study of urban groups is evident. Two such approaches, at opposing levels of analysis, are suggested in articles by James Spradley and Jack Rollwagen. Spradley ("Adaptive Strategies of Urban Nomads") adopts an ethnoscientific approach in his study of an urban subculture, analyzing the cognitive domains into which tramps categorize their experiences. In his article he focuses on the emic category of making a flop (finding a place to sleep). Jack Rollwagen ("New Directions in Urban Anthropology"), on the other hand, pleads for a macro-level analysis, arguing that anthropologists have been ignoring the "world cultural system" of which all people today are a part. The real problem for urban anthropologists, according to Rollwagen, is not a methodological one, but a basic conceptual and theoretical one—the need to place the subjects of anthropological inquiry in their societal and global context and trace out the linkages between the small groups and the larger political-economic system.

George Gmelch

ANTHROPOLOGICAL FIELDWORK IN CITIES

George M. Foster and Robert Van Kemper

This article traces the development of the fieldwork tradition in anthropology, placing the relatively new field of urban anthropology in its historical context. The authors discuss how the fieldwork tradition begun in rural areas, first among tribesmen and then peasants, has shaped the interests of anthropologists working in urban areas. They conclude with a discussion of some of the problems and advantages encountered in urban research, including which aspects of anthropology's conventional field methods remain useful. The need for survey and questionnaire data, as well as a reevaluation of anthropologists' traditional role as neutral observers rather than advocates for the people they study, is noted.

Anthropologists are latecomers to urban research. More than fifty years ago sociologists began systematic research in American cities, especially through the efforts of the "Chicago" school, and since that time most sociological research has dealt with urban phenomena. In contrast, the earliest anthropological research on city life took place scarcely a generation ago, and widespread interest in urbanization has developed only in the past decade. Whereas urban sociology is a mature discipline, urban anthropology is still in its infancy.[1] We have yet to define the parameters of the field, identify the topics to be studied, settle upon the most appropriate research strategies, and come to grips with new problems of ethics and relevance.

This recent interest in cities is the third—and probably the final—major revolution in anthropology's definition of its subject matter. When anthropology emerged as a formal science at the end of the nineteenth century it was concerned exclusively with "primitive" (i.e., nonliterate) peoples. Then, about 1940, interest began to shift to peasant societies, the rural dimension of traditional cultures. Now, as we turn to cities, we are again on the threshold of a major change. During these transformations the research goals, the definitions of problems, and the kinds of hypotheses that intrigued anthropologists have varied greatly. One principle, however, has remained constant: the anthropologist's dedication to fieldwork as his primary data-gathering strategy.

SOURCE: Revised from George M. Foster and Robert V. Kemper, eds., *Anthropologists in Cities* (Boston: Little, Brown, 1974), pp. 1–17, "Introduction: A Perspective on Anthropological Fieldwork in Cities." Copyright © 1979 by G. M. Foster and R. V. Kemper. Reprinted by permission of the authors.

Whether interested in tribal peoples, peasant villagers, or city-dwellers, anthropologists believe that the richest, most complete information on how people live comes from direct, personal participation in gathering this information.

IN THE BEGINNING

Anthropologists have not always insisted that fieldwork is their basic data-gathering technique. With rare exceptions nineteenth-century anthropologists relied upon the descriptions of native life published by missionaries, colonial administrators, and travelers for the data on which they based their theories and hypotheses. Only when anthropology became a legitimate academic discipline at the turn of the century, with formal Ph.D. graduate programs, was field research accepted as essential to professional preparation and practice. In America, Franz Boas was the teacher most influential in standardizing this new approach to data gathering.

In some ways research methods have changed very little since those early days. Most anthropologists still draw the greater part of their data from first-hand contact with relatively small numbers of people. In other ways, though, the changes have been great. New research goals have been formulated, and field trips have grown longer. When Boas, Clark Wissler, A. L. Kroeber, Robert Lowie, and others of their generation began their research, anthropology was assumed to be an historical discipline rather than a social science. Faced with a bewildering array of languages, cultures, and physical types, anthropologists saw as their task the discovery of the origins and migrations of the world's people, especially "primitive" societies lacking written histories. In the United States, most indigenous cultures had already changed greatly as a consequence of white contact. Because even greater changes seemed inevitable, a related goal of field research here was to draw upon the memories of the oldest surviving Indians to reconstruct as completely as possible the "untouched" precontact situation.

Since most data gathering consisted of sitting with elderly Indians (who were usually paid for their help) and writing down what they remembered of earlier years, anthropologists needed little field equipment. As late as 1937, when Foster was preparing for his first research among the Yuki Indians of California, the only advice he received from his professor, A. L. Kroeber, was to "buy a pencil and a stenographer's notebook." In the United States prior to World War II, field trips were usually short, often limited to a summer's vacation. Even the largest departments of anthropology had only three or four staff members, and long leaves were difficult to arrange. Moreover, the research goals of ethnographers led them to see little advantage in spending twelve or more continuous months in the field; instead, they worked over several summers, beginning again each year where they had stopped the summer before. In the first quarter of this century, most American Indian tribes were disrupted and acculturated. This fact, plus the "memory culture" orientation of fieldworkers, combined to convince anthropologists that no single group needed or justified more than a few months' study. Because native peoples appeared to be dying out, anthropologists felt it their scientific responsibility to survey all groups, rather than to study intensively a few and neglect the rest.

Even in these relatively short, early field trips the distinctive methodological characteristic of anthropology was apparent. From the beginning anthropologists formed close personal ties with the people they studièd, and almost all anthropologists of that period have written affectionately about their key informants, some of whom became lifelong friends. Anthropologists quickly realized that the best and most accurate data come from persons who like and trust them. Hence, "establishing rapport" came to be an anthropologist's first assignment upon arriving in the field: to search out the most knowledgeable individuals, present oneself to them in a plausible and empathetic role, and make friends. Without fully realizing it, these early anthropologists were inventing the "depth" interview—the ability to talk with, to probe, to "pump" an informant, day after day, in order to extract from him maximum information about his people and their history. Today, in cities as in rural areas, most anthropologists retain this basic philosophy: good rapport with good friends, trust and confidence, and abundant conversation over long periods of time.

Fieldwork in the United States during the first third of the century was strongly conditioned by restrictions of time, distance, and money. Research in the West involved train trips of from three to six days in each direction, often followed by stage coach, river boat, or horseback rides to the final destination. Sources of financial support were limited, and long and costly trips of the type now routinely undertaken would have been difficult indeed. When, in the late 1920's and 1930's, American anthropologists began to embark on research in more distant areas, it was not unusual to spend six weeks in merely reaching the field site. Now that the most distant parts of the earth are rarely more than twenty-four hours away, young anthropologists often forget how huge the world was only a little over a generation ago.

As long as the emphasis of American anthropology was on the disappearing tribe, field research methods, including "scientific" equipment, changed very little. The first bulky portable typewriters, the Kodak camera, and primitive cylinder recording machines were occasionally carted to the reservation, but the pencil (or fountain pen) and the stenographer's notebook continued to be the only indispensable items of equipment.

THE BRITISH REVOLUTION

In England, meanwhile, a revolution in the concept of field research was occurring: long-term analysis of a viable community, emphasizing form and function in their synchronic rather than their diachronic dimensions. Tribal origins, it was assumed, were lost in dim antiquity; they could never be known. What *could* be known was the structure of the contemporary group, its form and content, and the way this system functioned. Anthropology was thus converted into a social science. Although he was not the first anthropologist to live for a long period with a single people, the Polish-born, British-naturalized Bronislaw Malinowski justly receives credit for introducing this new approach to fieldwork. Beginning in the early 1920's at the London School of Economics, he taught his students what he had discovered a few years earlier on the Trobriand Islands: live with the people, learn their language, observe their activities, question, speculate, theorize.

Malinowski and his students were favored in their revolutionary endeavors by conditions in the British Empire. Most of the Commonwealth's "native" peoples belonged to viable societies which functioned with much of their pre-contact vigor; they certainly were not disappearing. There was little need to press for "salvage" ethnography, to record while there was still time. Consequently, young anthropologists with enough financial support could afford to spend as much time as needed with a single group, untroubled by the nagging thought that they should turn their attention to disappearing groups elsewhere. Wherever they worked, field researchers were not foreigners; they were simply in parts of the Commonwealth where the societies were more exotic than at home. The British colonial service encouraged anthropological research, and the Union Jack flying at the District Officer's headquarters symbolized the special privileges that anthropologists could expect from government and native peoples alike. Under Malinowski's tutelage, and favored by the colonial setting—especially in Africa—a new generation of British social anthropologists produced superb monographs on a wide variety of topics which even today are required reading in most doctoral programs.

In the United States, research sophistication lagged behind that of England for a number of years; we lacked a Malinowski, and we were still committed to recording the ways of disappearing societies. The first American anthropologist to adopt the new approach, ten years after Malinowski's pioneering efforts, was Margaret Mead, who in 1925 set out for nine months' research in American Samoa. She was soon followed by Robert Redfield, who spent eight months in Tepoztlán, Mexico, during 1926–1927, and by Hortense Powdermaker, who went to Lesu, in New Ireland, for ten months during 1929–1930. (Although American-born, Powdermaker was a student of Malinowski, so she is perhaps best thought of as carrying on a British tradition in the United States rather than beginning an American style of fieldwork.)

In spite of the demonstrable advantages of long-term fieldwork, quickly brought to the attention of American anthropologists in *Coming of Age in Samoa* (Mead 1928), *Tepoztlán* (Redfield 1930), and *Life in Lesu* (Powdermaker 1933), extended field trips did not become commonplace until after World War II. Although a growing number of American anthropologists made long trips to India and Africa shortly before the war, most doctoral candidates (and their professors as well) continued the old tradition of short trips.

After the war, however, American researchers rapidly adopted the British research pattern, for several reasons. First, we had just about run out of Indians. The fairly exhaustive product of fifty years of North American research, coupled with the accelerating rate of acculturation of native North Americans, meant that these tribes looked much less attractive as research subjects than they had a generation earlier. Second, transportation to distant parts of the world had vastly improved; even in 300-mph piston planes, most places were no more than forty-eight hours from the United States. Research support, too, was becoming more abundant than in earlier years, and for the first time anthropologists could seriously contemplate prolonged research in foreign countries.

THE DISCOVERY OF PEASANTS

In growing numbers American anthropologists now traveled to Latin America, Europe, Africa, and Asia. Some—particularly in Africa—studied tribal peoples, but a majority chose to work in small rural communities in modern or developing nations, for it was soon discovered that these peasant villages made ideal research sites. During the 1950's and 1960's, half or more of American anthropological fieldwork was carried out in such communities.

With the study of peasants came greatly improved data-gathering techniques. Now fully aware of the importance of observing as much as possible, of being present when significant events occurred, anthropologists tried to be as close as we could to the people we studied. Under ideal circumstances we were able to live with village families, to sleep and work in a spare room, and to share meals with them. When this was not feasible, we rented a house near the center of the village, usually hiring local women to cook, clean, wash clothes, babysit—and simultaneously to serve as informants to explain the meaning of what we saw. Now we had opportunities to attend weddings, funerals, baptisms, and other family and community rites on a scale that had never before been possible. For the first time that familiar, but much abused, phrase "participant observation" really came alive. We did not simply ask informants how people behaved; we saw with our own eyes what happened, so that our notes took on a richness, a depth, a detail rarely if ever achieved by earlier researchers.

Because we were observing real people acting out real roles, we needed to know more about them as individuals than in the earlier days of salvage ethnography: where they lived, who their relatives were, their occupations, their incomes and socioeconomic statuses, and the like. To gather this data we adopted the census as a basic technique to provide a factual and statistical framework for our observations and interviews. We also buckled down and learned the local language. Prior to this time relatively few American anthropologists had mastered the language of the people they studied, preferring to use bilingual informants or interpreters. Now we realized that language competence was essential to good fieldwork, and intensive language training became a basic part of every well-planned field trip.

In the post-World War II era more elaborate recording and coding techniques to control and retrieve ever greater quantities of data came into common use. For many anthropologists, the 5″ × 8″ card or sheet, filed according to the Human Relations Area File code, replaced the stenographer's notebook (Murdock, *et al.* 1961). Technological advances likewise vastly facilitated field-work: portable typewriters became truly lightweight, miniature cameras replaced the old Kodaks, and flash equipment was perfected. Transistors made possible small tape recorders, which greatly simplified recording linguistic texts, folklore, and other data such as dreams and projective tests (e.g., the Rorschach and Thematic Apperception Tests), where textual accuracy is essential. Antibiotics reduced the apprehension of serious illness in the field, and with radios and telephones, anthropologists were usually less isolated even in remote countries than their professional ancestors had been among Indian tribes in Canada and the western United States. For those who had known the conceptual limitations and technological handicaps of earlier field research, the fifties and sixties were a great time to be a practicing anthropologist.

URBAN ANTHROPOLOGY

After about a generation of intensive fieldwork in peasant communities, anthropologists realized that significant changes were occurring in the research situation. For one thing, we felt that we had defined rather completely the parameters of peasant societies and had constructed models to explain much of their cross-cultural variation. So, as with the Indians a generation earlier, we appeared to be approaching a point of diminishing returns. At the same time, many of our peasant friends were ceasing to be peasants. Influenced by radio and television, work experiences in foreign countries, and the modernity that follows new roads, many of them gave up their folk costumes and their fiestas; they adopted tractors, fertilizers, and insecticides in farming; and they sent their children to secondary schools and universities. Others simply packed up and moved to cities, where they found work in factories or service fields and after a few years became townsmen themselves.

To a large extent the transformation of traditional peasant societies and the mass exodus to the city explain the new interest of anthropologists in urban research. Beyond this, many of us are genuinely concerned with the social, ethnic, and economic problems so clearly seen in cities; we believe that anthropology, along with the other social sciences, can help to ameliorate these problems. Together these events and convictions have created a new field, *Urban Anthropology*.

From the beginning, the urban research of anthropologists has differed significantly from that of other social scientists and historians. While they have been concerned primarily with the technologically developed countries of Europe and North America, we have been especially interested in the growing cities of Latin America, Africa, and Asia. Our theoretical orientation, too, is different. Because the first people we knew well in these countries were peasants and tribesmen, who today are moving to the cities in increasing numbers, we have been curious about what happens to them in urban environments. As a result, anthropological urban studies have dealt largely with *urbanization,* the process by which rural emigrants settle in and adjust to urban life, rather than with the way of life in cities, which is commonly referred to as *urbanism* (cf. Wirth 1938). In addition, because we have been interested primarily in how people adjust to urban life, we have paid much less attention than have other social scientists to broader issues involving the operation of the urban *system* (i.e., the network of cities within a nation, the ways in which these cities are interrelated, and how the lives of urbanites and rural residents are influenced by large-scale demographic, political, economic, and sociological processes). And finally, although anthropologists have occasionally utilized the results of comparative statistical studies, which have become so important in political science, economics, and sociology, we have continued to offer theories about urbanization on the basis of first-hand field research.

The anthropological urban studies that have appeared since World War II, and especially during the past ten.years, make it possible for us to trace common patterns in the urbanization process and to discern fruitful directions for future work. But with few exceptions (e.g., Whyte 1943; Liebow 1967; Leeds 1968) these reports tell us little or nothing about the urban fieldwork experience. For the anthropologist, how does this research compare with that undertaken in peasant villages and tribal groups? What research techniques are equally valuable in both settings? What new methodologies must be developed (or borrowed from other disciplines) to investigate urbanites? Is the anthropologist working in a city a new breed of scientist, an "urban anthropologist," or does he differ from his rural-based colleagues only by his choice of field site? That is, is the urban anthropologist simply the mirror image of the rural sociologist?

In the second part of this [essay] we . . . discuss how the rural fieldwork tradition consciously and unconsciously shapes the anthropologist's definition of urban problems, what features of conventional methodology are useful in the city, what urban research topics arise that require new approaches, and how urban research may force a reevaluation of the profession's present dilemma regarding "relevance" and ethics.

URBANITES AS RURAL PEOPLE

Accustomed as we are to working in small, "bounded" rural communities, anthropologists are often disconcerted by the amorphous and heterogeneous populations of large cities. How are the boundaries of the urban sample to be determined, and how should the fieldworker proceed with his study? As Anthony Leeds has pointed out (1968:31), we often try to solve this problem by concentrating on slums, squatter settlements, or ethnic minorities, on the assumption that they are analogous to the small rural villages we know, and that they can be investigated in similar fashion. . . . This tendency to see urban peoples in the light of our rural experiences may have serious consequences, as Peter Gutkind has pointed out for Africa:

> The methodological traditions brought to this [urban] field of research are mostly those acquired by social anthropologists working in rural areas. It is this background which for long fostered the view that we were studying tribesmen in town and not townsmen in town (1967:136).

As a consequence, he continues, "Far less attention has been paid to those Africans who have been resident in urban areas for a considerable length of time . . . than to migrants and those less committed to urban life" (1967:143–144). . . . We believe that [Gutkind] is correct in noting that anthropologists have been shortsighted in ignoring long-settled urbanites.

In urban research the anthropologist faces one insurmountable problem: defining a population in the holistic context taken for granted in rural fieldwork. He may investigate a group of migrants from a single village, migrants from many regions, or a group composed of migrants and urban natives. The group may be dispersed throughout the metropolitan zone, clustered in a few neighborhoods, or restricted to a single spatial unit as small as an apartment house (as in Oscar Lewis's well-known studies of *vecindades* in Mexico City). Alternatively, the population may be defined in social terms, as members of a religious sect, a voluntary association, a professional or occupational category. Selecting and delineating the urban population segment to be investigated is *the* critical first step in urban anthropological research.

Once this decision is made, another issue emerges: should the anthropologist concentrate on the internal structure of the group or on the relations of its members to the rest of the urban population? Most anthropologists, following the community study approach, have chosen the former. But, as Leeds argues, this "has led to a thorough failure to justify the units of study used and the failure to show mutual effects between the asserted 'units' of study and the city in which they are immersed" (1968:31–32). . . .

GETTING SETTLED

Although the fieldworker faces different problems in defining the group to be studied in rural and urban settings, the difficulties of settling in—of finding a place to live, experiencing culture shock, establishing a plausible role, and finding informants—remain much the same. As we have seen, in village fieldwork the anthropologist usually lives with a family or maintains quarters in the middle of town; in either case he resides among the people he is studying and constantly observes their daily life. In cities, arrangements of this kind are more difficult; families studied by anthropologists almost always live in crowded quarters with barely enough room for themselves, much less for a researcher and his or her family. Rented rooms, too, are usually less attractive in urban slums than in peasant villages. Moreover, unless the anthropologist decides to study a compact population—a suburban neighborhood, an inner-city slum, or a peripheral squatter settlement—he almost literally cannot live "with" his informants. As a result, when an anthropologist studies a general social institution or a group of people spread throughout the city, he nearly always finds an apartment or house in a convenient area, then commutes to visit informants.

This arrangement has advantages and disadvantages. On the one hand, the anthropologist gains privacy, a comfort often denied him in tribal or village areas where he is a constant object of curiosity. When tired and irritated, and on those days when he hopes never to see another informant, he can retire to his comfortable lodgings to rest and recuperate. On the other hand, many anthropologists who have lived like this feel both guilty and cheated. Conditioned by his colleagues to expect a close emotional identification with the people he studies, even the most conscientious researcher may come to ask himself whether he is doing a good job and whether he is in fact a true anthropologist, if he must carry out fieldwork in circumstances where he is isolated much of the time from the target population. . . .

MEETING INFORMANTS

When he begins research in a village, the anthropologist sometimes has letters to a few people, who in turn can introduce him to others. More often, though, for the first few days he simply wanders the streets, talks to as many people as he can, leans over fences to chat and make friends, gives candy and balloons to children, cigarettes to men, and in other encounters tries to explain why he is in the village and what he hopes to accomplish. In this informal way, he develops friendships. Often the anthropologist "scouts" several communities, then chooses the one where he feels most accepted. All of the people he meets in these early contacts are potential informants.

In contrast, only a few of the people the urban anthropologist meets in the course of a day are potential informants. Although casual encounters . . . may offer insights into city life, the researcher must work at building a network of informants. As intermediaries he may use members of the group itself (e.g., a migrant whom he already knows), local officials, or other social scientists who are known to the people the anthropologist has selected for study. . . .

Just as rapport-building techniques vary from one fieldworker to another, finding a suitable role depends as much on circumstances as on planning. . . . For doctoral candidates, the role of students preparing themselves for teaching careers and required by their professors to learn about another way of life is usually satisfactory. For older anthropologists, the reverse role of professor seems to work best, at least outside of the United States. Sometimes it is as difficult to avoid a negative role as to establish a positive one; most anthropologists have at one time or another been accused of being a CIA agent, a Protestant missionary (if working in a Catholic community), a social worker, a tax collector, or even a misguided tourist.

OFFICIAL AND PROFESSIONAL TIES

Whether an anthropologist undertakes research in a foreign country or in the United States, it is considered proper—and usually it is essential—to notify the appropriate governmental and anthropological authorities of the research plan and to obtain their permission *before* beginning work. These formalities sometimes seem a nuisance, but for the urban anthropologist they often provide an introduction to potential associates in his fieldwork. Precisely because cities are centers for universities and government agencies, urban fieldworkers need not be isolated from professional and official assistance.

Relationships with government officials are extremely important to all anthropologists, for an unsympathetic person in a position of power can make research impossible, while a helpful official can open otherwise closed doors. Ties with local anthropologists can be especially rewarding. As experts in residence, they can point out possible problems in the research design, suggest alternate groups for investigation, and introduce the newcomer to potential informants. Of course, local social scientists may not always be helpful, but taking them into one's confidence at the outset may prevent subsequent misunderstandings and usually makes for good relationships in the future. This is especially important if the anthropologist plans to return later to continue the research project or wishes to carry out related fieldwork in other cities in the same country.

The urban anthropologist is more fortunate than his rural counterpart in that he can easily repay professional and social obligations to his local colleagues by attending their professional meetings, joining their societies, teaching part-time in their institutions, and (if he maintains a separate residence during fieldwork) bringing them into his home. In addition, he may be able to include local scholars and students in the research project, an important advantage in equalizing anthropological skills and training throughout the world. Urban fieldwork also offers young anthropologists an opportunity to meet the community of scholars they will know and cooperate with throughout their careers. . . .

RURAL RESEARCH MODELS IN THE CITY

We have already seen that anthropologists tend to view urban populations from a rural perspective, to look upon them as transplanted villagers. Not surprisingly, then, research design and problem definitions are often based on rural models, on the assumption that what works well in the country will also work well in the city. . . . This "jack-of-all-trades" approach stands in sharp contrast to most other social science models for urban research, where team members are chosen to provide interdisciplinary and interethnic perspectives. Although rich data and valuable theoretical insights have emerged from these anthropological studies, the size and complexity of urban environments clearly place limits on what can be accomplished by a lone fieldworker, even when aided by a trained spouse. Paid assistants are a partial solution to this problem, especially in taking a census and conducting social surveys, but they are no substitute for a genuine team approach, whose advantages have been summarized by John Price:

> The team represents a wide variety of academic skills and personalities that together produce a wider variety of ethnography than an individual does over a long period of time. Through formal and informal discussions, the team is able to create a productive information exchange. It also accelerates the generation and testing of hypotheses much more rapidly than individuals working alone (1972:27).

Although the lone researcher will continue to make important contributions to urban studies, we believe that anthropologists working in cities will increasingly do so as members of social science teams.

In still another way, [urban anthropologists] reflect a decidedly rural bias: [often many] of their best data [come] from the personal relationships rural fieldworkers have long cherished. Although they do not provide a full picture of city life, friendship and the depth interview, with contact over a long period of time between anthropologist and respondent, should continue to be a major research technique in the city. When combined with the statistical survey approaches favored in the other social sciences, it may well prove to be the single most important contribution anthropologists can make to urban studies.

But despite the benefits of [such] deep and continuing relationships, [there is clearly a] need for census and questionnaire data beyond the limits common in rural research. Chance contacts alone are insufficient to provide the balance that marks first-class research. The conclusion we draw is that anthropologists contemplating urban fieldwork will need to devote much more attention than they have in the past to sociological research techniques such as survey research and the design and pretesting of interview schedules. Familiarity with computers, too, . . . will be essential if anthropologists are to make the best use of census and questionnaire materials.

Whether the urban anthropologist carries out fieldwork alone or as a team member, he must strike a balance between "total immersion" and dependence on the more formal techniques of the other social sciences. Andrew Whiteford has described the dilemma we face:

> Such approaches as sampling techniques, the use of census data, and statistical analysis of masses of data would appear to be absolutely necessary for understanding [urban phenomena], but their use also tends to impersonalize the research and deprive the worker of his most satisfying experience, the personal identification with the people being studied (1960:2).

. . . Anthropologists become easily disenchanted when close friendships with informants are replaced by limited, impersonal contacts with "subjects" or "respondents." But, however we might wish it were not so, we must recognize that in cities we can neither observe our informants with the same ease as in villages, nor expect as many contact hours with factory workers as with craftsmen who labor at home. Thus, unless we are content to limit ourselves to the "street corner" variety of urban research (e.g., Whyte 1943; Liebow 1967), we must learn to combine the most valuable features of traditional research models with the quantitative methods common in the other social sciences.

ETHICS AND RELEVANCE

Urban research introduces many new ethical problems to anthropology. . . . We are not dealing with nameless faces in the crowd when describing and commenting on important people in cities. Their roles are distinctive enough to make them easily identifiable no matter how we try to disguise them in our reports. And when . . . the attitudes and life styles of the urban elite strike the anthropologist as unattractive, and when our analyses are constantly unflattering, what are we to do? Like tribesmen or peasants, these upper-class urbanites have great power over us, to the point of making our research impossible.

Even the least visible city-dwellers we study often are literate. They are more interested than villagers in the end product of our research, and they are anxious to see what we say about them. Increasingly anthropological publications are translated into the languages of the people studied, and they can read about themselves. As anthropologists, we must become more concerned about their privacy, and about the harm that careless revelations might cause them.

Although [most anthropologists have] carried into their urban research the traditional anthropological stance of objectivity—the desire to find out about what life was like in the community in question, without major concern for resolving social problems—it seems inevitable that future urban research will be more concerned with "relevance," that it will be more "applied" than earlier work. Already we see signs of this. During her two years of fieldwork in the Ciudad Guayana project in Venezuela, Lisa Peattie found herself becoming an advocate of the poor people she studied and lived among, defending them against the "system" represented by the project coordinators and their elite clientele. Her description of the role of "The Social Anthropologist in Planning" (1967) and her "Reflections on Advocacy Planning" (1968a) make thought-provoking reading for urban anthropologists concerned with the relevancy of their work. In the same way, the Valentines have argued convincingly that the urban fieldworker owes a debt to the people he studies, the people who make his job possible. This debt can best be repaid, they believe, when the anthropologist becomes attentive to community needs and attempts to help his informants to cope with the urban system (Valentine and Valentine 1970).

This combined emphasis on ethics and applied urban anthropology has led to a reevaluation of the anthropologist's "prime directive"—his commitment not to interfere with "native" life unless it is absolutely necessary. This in turn has raised an even more fundamental question: Is the best fieldwork performed by "outsiders" or "insiders"? For instance, can Anglo anthropologists understand the life styles of urban blacks, Chicanos, or native Americans—or, for that matter, any group outside the white middle class—without falling prey to unconscious prejudices? Anthropologists have assumed that on many points insiders are less perceptive observers than outsiders, just as a fish is unaware of the water it lives in until the tank is drained. As the literate, predominantly urban, ethnic minorities in the United States strive to establish their identities, and similar forces are at work in developing nations, this fundamental bias of anthropological research is being put to the test. And more often than not, it is the urban anthropologist rather than his rural colleague who must withstand these pressures.

The net result of these transformations is still unclear, but it seems unlikely that future anthropologists will be allowed to carry out their research without some regard to contemporary social problems or to the needs and feelings of their informants. Just as the peasant migrant to the metropolis faces a new world, so anthropologists moving from the "bush" to the city must adapt their ideas regarding fieldwork to fit a new environment.

The future of anthropology, we believe, lies largely in urban research. Yet the [available] evidence indicates that urban fieldwork is more difficult than rural, and that it is often emotionally less satisfying, because of the problems of maintaining close affective ties with informants. At the same time urban research presents anthropology with challenges and opportunities that cannot be ignored if the profession is to increase its contributions to social science theory and to the resolution of society's problems.

And if, as Morris Freilich suggests, "the critical tool in anthropological research is the researcher himself" (1970:33), then the ingenuity anthropologists have shown in working in tribal and peasant communities will serve in equal measure to master the problems of urban fieldwork. Just as in rural areas, urban anthropologists will find adequate housing, establish good rapport, define a suitable social role, overcome culture shock, deal successfully with government officials and anthropological colleagues, and ultimately combine the best in traditional research methods with the new techniques required for sound urban research.

NOTE

1. A journal, *Urban Anthropology,* and its companion, *Urban Anthropology Newsletter,* the first anthropological publications devoted to urban research, began only in 1972.

ADAPTIVE STRATEGIES OF URBAN NOMADS: THE ETHNOSCIENCE OF TRAMP CULTURE

James Spradley

In this article James Spradley applies an ethnoscientific approach to the study of one urban subculture—tramps. According to Spradley, each ethnic and social group within the city develops different strategies for adapting to urban life. These exist as cognitive or mental maps which categorize their worlds of experience into meaningful units. In order to discover the areas of experience meaningful to tramps, Spradley first conducted several months of participant observation. From this he discovered the major importance of "making a flop" (finding a place to sleep). Formal interviews were then conducted which probed for the tramps' own classifications of this cultural domain. The ethnoscientific approach is one way for anthropologists to overcome some of the problems inherent in urban research.

Urban anthropology includes a variety of approaches. Nearly every subfield of anthropology can bring its methods, techniques, and theories to bear upon human life in the urban setting. At the same time, there are certain unique contributions which anthropologists may be able to make by virtue of their cross-cultural and non-Western orientation. In fact, it is argued here that we may be in danger of selling our birthright for orientations developed by others who have been studying the city for decades. Research in non-Western societies has helped us lay aside our cultural blinders, a prerequisite for discovering the behavioral environment or socially constructed reality of those we study. This is not an easy task in any society, but for the urban anthropologist there are additional problems. Urban groups do not live in the "city" but in their own socially constructed definition of the city. This paper[1] begins with a discussion of five interrelated problems faced by the researcher: (1) cultural pluralism, (2) ethnocentrism, (3) subcultural interpreters, (4) similar cultural forms, and (5) relevant social units. An ethnographic approach to an urban subculture will then be presented as an effective strategy for urban research. Five major steps in the research will be discussed along with data from the subculture under

SOURCE: Reproduced by permission of the Society for Applied Anthropology from *The Anthropology of Urban Environments,* Monograph Number 11, 1972.

consideration. Finally, I shall raise a number of issues which need further exploration by urban anthropologists.

URBAN RESEARCH PROBLEMS

Cultural Pluralism

When the ethnographer studies his own urban society, attempting to discover the meaning of objects and events according to the conceptual systems of city dwellers, he is confronted with a complex multicultural situation. In addition to the thousands of different roles in the city, resulting from specialization, there are many distinct life styles in a myriad of subcultural groups. Considerable strain is placed upon the holistic bias of the anthropologist in conceptualizing the city as a cultural phenomenon. Concepts such as "rural-urban," "primitive-civilized," and "ecological zone" have been used to understand cities as a whole, but they often obscure the cultural pluralism of the urban situation. If we are to understand the city as a functioning whole, we must begin by looking at the different units of that whole. Only then will we be in a position to fruitfully develop conceptual models of the city as a unit to be compared with other cities as well as peasant villages and nomadic tribes. After the various parts of an urban culture have been described and compared, even wider comparisons will be more valid; in fact, we may find that the minority group described here has more in common with nomadic tribes than it does with other urban subcultures. It is of utmost importance, then, for anthropologists to recognize, identify, and describe the various subcultures within the city, for, as Wallace (1962:351) has pointed out, "All of the comparative and theoretical work of cultural anthropology depends upon thorough and precise ethnographic description."

Ethnocentrism

The belief that one's traditions, values, and ways of life are better than those which exist in other societies is probably universal. Anthropologists have long championed the need to recognize the validity and dignity of diverse cultural traditions while not abandoning a commitment to one's own heritage. The contemporary urban scene throughout the world is heavily influenced by Western culture and the researcher has learned values and definitions about urban life which will profoundly influence the questions he asks and the research he undertakes. The use of hallucinogenic drugs by students in American cities is evaluated differently from their use by an isolated Indian tribe living in the Amazon basin. The drinking behavior of men in the Skid Road district of the city is similar to that of the Camba Indians, but Westerners define and evaluate them quite differently.[2] It may not be easy for one studying a remote tribe in New Guinea to overcome his feelings that their way of life is inferior to his own, but that difficulty is even greater when one studies the culture of those who live in his own society but have a very different style of life. Much of the research on the urban population considered here has been criticized for such an ethnocentric bias. Wallace (1965:159) discusses this problem:

> When the sociologist arrives on skid row with precoded, pretested survey questionnaire in hand, every one of his questions implicitly assumes the person is a failure and asks why. Even though this question remains unstated, both questioner and questioned perceive its fundamental reality.

It is naive for the researcher to believe that he can study urban subcultures without being influenced by his own culture. While "value free" research is impossible, the problems in approaching this ideal are much greater in the study of urban subcultures for which the researcher's own socialization has provided him with traditional definitions.

Subcultural Interpreters

Isolated tribesmen or villagers have little knowledge of the anthropologist's culture and informants have no basis for responding to questions based upon that culture. The field worker does not expect them to translate their way of life into the categories and terms which have significance in his way of life. Instead, he immerses himself in the field situation, learns the native language, discerns not only the answers to questions but also which questions to ask, and finally describes the culture in a way which his colleagues and students will understand. The ethnographer's job is one of translating and interpreting the culture he studies into terms which can be understood by the outsider. Urban anthropologists are faced with a different situation. Literacy, communication, and interaction among members of different subcultures have provided informants with a knowledge of the researcher's culture. This is especially true among the groups which are deprived of status and power within the city, for their very survival requires that they know the life styles of members of superordinant status groups. They are keenly aware of attitudes, values, and individual differences among the power holders. As a result the anthropologist who studies an urban population encounters many informants with the ability to translate their way of life into his language and culture. Informants act as subcultural interpreters; their translation competence may lead the anthropologist to describe another subculture in terms of his own without realizing he is doing so. Questions are formulated in the researcher's dialect of English and based on the categories of his culture. When they are put to an informant, they are quickly translated and thus "understood." Then the informant responds to questions he has imperfectly understood with answers phrased in the idiom of the researcher's culture. The ethnographer may thus guide his informants to conceptualize their culture from the perspective of the outsider. Such interpreters may provide a wealth of data which can be analyzed, but the investigator has been effectively prevented from discovering the meaning and definition of experience from the insider's point of view.

Similar Cultural Forms

Urban communities contain distinct subcultural groups which share many similar cultural forms and appear to live in the same environment. They live in the same geographic area and climatic zone, often sharing transportation systems, law enforcement agencies, educational institutions, and many other facets of city life. It would be easy to conclude that different groups actually have the same culture and that a description of these aspects of urban life for one group would be an accurate description for all groups. This appearance of sharing similar forms may even be empirically verified if culture is treated as a statistical description of behavior. But if culture involves the forms people have in mind, the fact that people share the "same" urban environment and institutions may obscure important culture differences. . . . Men who live on Skid Road participate in many of the major institutions of the city. They visit missions, work in jail, go to the theater, walk the streets, get into bathtubs, visit cemeteries, and go to junkyards. Other city dwellers also engage in these activities but define them differently. The underlying attributes, values and meanings which each group assigns to urban life must be discovered if we are to do justice to the pluralistic nature of the city. . . .

Relevant Social Units

All behavioral science is faced with the task of specifying the units and classes of behavior to be described and explained. This has always been a thorny problem for anthropologists and may be seen in such controversies as what is meant by a "tribe." The task has been easier in studying nonurban societies by the coincidence of geographical and social unit boundaries, less mobility, limited communication among social units, and greater linguistic variation. If the city is not a homogeneous sociocultural unit, how are we to identify the unit we are studying and establish its boundaries? Some scholars have studied "Skid Road" using geographical criteria to identify the subculture reported on here. Some even determine the boundaries of this area by asking professionals who attempt to help those who live on Skid Road. Are such professionals to be considered as part of this social unit? Is every individual in such a locale to be treated as part of that subculture? If the city is multicultural in nature then the identification of units which make up this pluralistic phenomenon is of utmost importance. The criteria for treating minority groups, black ghettos, urban Indians, and other units as relevant for research must be explicitly stated in order to make replication and comparison possible. All too often urban research has been carried out with an implicit mixture of biological, social, geographical, historical and cultural criteria which leads to confusing results. Even more crucial is the arbitrariness involved in the selection of criteria for identification of a subculture. . . .

Different approaches or models have been used in the many studies made of the urban population to be considered here. A brief consideration of these models may highlight some of the research problems discussed above for this particular group. The social units which appear to be similar have been referred to variously as "Skid Road alcoholics," "homeless men," "vagrants," "hoboes," "tramps," or "indigent public intoxicants." The *folk model* is the stereotype of this population held by the majority of urban society. They are seen as people who fail abysmally, are dependent on society, lack self-control, drink too much, are unpredictable, and often end up in jail for criminal behavior. In a word, they are bums. The *medical model* defines this social unit in terms of its primary illness—alcoholism. The concept of being an alcoholic is hardly better defined among medical professionals than the idea of being a bum among others in society. Skid Road alcoholics in particular are sometimes considered to be like "burned-out, backward schizophrenic" (Solomon 1966:165) patients who are almost without culturally organized behavior. The *legal model* defines these people as criminals guilty of many minor crimes, but especially public drunkenness. The criminal court in the city studied had a special file for keeping track of this population and they were officially designated as common drunkards. The *sociological model* defines this unit in terms of a variety of criteria including homelessness, age, sex, race, income, drinking behavior, and geographic location. Each of these four models tends to predefine the social unit in terms which are considered relevant to the outsider, using criteria determined by folk, medical, legal, or sociological standards. The folk model in particular has heavily influenced the criteria used by the others. The focus upon drinking behavior and homelessness, for instance, reflects the American cultural values of sobriety, self-control, and the home. All of these approaches are, in different ways and to different degrees, outsiders' models. The *ethnographic model* to be presented here avoids the predefinition of what is to be considered relevant and aims at discovering the insider's view of his social world. While all of these models are useful for certain purposes, it is argued here that, because of their training and experience, anthropologists can make a unique contribution by discovering the insider's model for any particular urban subculture.

AN ETHNOSCIENTIFIC APPROACH TO THE STUDY OF URBAN AREAS

The methods of ethnoscience hold promise of partially overcoming some of the problems of urban research. I consider the task of ethnography to be the discovery of the characteristic ways in which members of a society categorize, code, and define their experience. Ethnographic descriptions based on techniques of ethnoscience have been largely limited to a few selected domains in non-Western societies, such as kinship, color categories, and plant taxonomies.[3] The application of these techniques to an urban subculture is based on the premise that "the units by which the data of observation are segmented, ordered, and interrelated be delimited and defined according to contrasts inherent in the data themselves and not according to a priori notions of pertinent descriptive categories" (Frake 1962a:54).

The various ethnic and social groups within the city have developed different strategies of adaptation. Each subculture provides such strategies in the form of cognitive maps which are learned through socialization. These cognitive maps categorize the world of experience into equivalence classes which eliminate the necessity of responding to every unique event in the environment. This is one of the most important ways that culture enables human beings to survive. . . . If we are to discover different strategies of adaptation among urban groups we must discover the different category systems they use to reduce the complexity of their environment and organize their behavior. Category systems enable the individual to identify those aspects of the environment which are significant for adaptation, provide direction for instrumental activity, and permit the anticipation of future events (Bruner et al. 1956:11–14). Thus, an important avenue to understanding both the strategies of adaptation and the environment to which urban groups are adjusting is in the study of category systems through ethnoscientific techniques. . . .

How shall we approach this goal? The present study was begun by means of participant observation at an alcoholism treatment center on Skid Road and in a municipal criminal court. The first few months were spent in observation and recording casual conversations among informants in order to discover relevant questions. This was followed by more formal ethnographic interviews using a number of different discovery and testing procedures. . . .

THE SUBCULTURE OF URBAN NOMADS

Tramps and Their Domains

[As we have discussed,] the category of men considered in this paper could be characterized in many different ways depending upon the criteria selected. They live part of their lives on Skid Road (geographic criteria); join small groups for drinking (behavioral criteria); violate city ordinances which prohibit public drunkenness, begging, urinating in public, and drinking in public (legal criteria); and are characterized by low income and homelessness (sociological criteria). . . . My first task, however, was to discover how these men identified themselves and to formulate appropriate questions. . . . It was found that informants identified their subcultural membership with the lexeme *tramp*. There were at least eight major categories of tramps recognized by informants: *working stiffs, mission stiffs, bindle stiffs, airedales, rubber tramps, home guard tramps, box car tramps,* and *dings*. This category system constitutes one of the major social identity domains in this subculture. The significance of these findings is that the identity of this subculture has most often been based on *external* criteria. External definitions of the primary social identity of any group profoundly influence the kinds of questions asked and data gathered by the researcher. It may be important for some purposes to identify this population as "homeless men" or "chronic alcoholics," but it does not necessarily reflect the insider's conception of his own social identity. It may even preclude discoveries of great cultural significance.

A semantic analysis of this domain revealed that the underlying criteria in statements elicited from informants were mobility-related. The different kinds of tramps were differentiated in terms of their degree of mobility, mode of travel, type of home base, and economic survival strategies. For example, *home guard tramps* travel very little while the other kinds of tramps travel extensively. *Box car tramps* customarily travel by freight train in large continental circuits which cover most of the United States. *Rubber tramps* travel in their own cars, while *working stiffs* may ride freight trains or use commercial vehicles. The criterion of homelessness was not significant to these men in defining their social identity but rather the type of home base they had. The *airedale* and *bindle stiff* both carry their "homes" with them in the form of a pack and bedroll. *Rubber tramps* live in their cars, *mission stiffs* at the mission, and *dings* who are professional beggars have no home base. While many tramps drink and drunkenness is institutionalized in their world, drinking behavior was not a defining criterion for their social identity. Once it was established that informants conceived their primary social identity to be anchored to a mobile, nomadic life style, the importance of other facts which might have appeared trivial came to light.

Tramps are arrested often and taken to jail where they move through a series of inmate identities. Initially they are *drunks,* whether their crime has been public drunkenness, begging, shoplifting, or urinating in public. After a period of waiting in a drunk tank they are taken to a criminal court for arraignment where over 90 percent of them plead guilty and are sentenced for their crimes. Most courts follow a sentencing procedure which is graduated so that on each successive conviction, especially for public drunkenness, a man's sentence is increased. Sentences for this crime may begin with two to five days in jail and increase to as much as one year in jail where a man will work as a *trusty,* remain confined to a time tank as a *lockup,* and finally become a *kickout* just prior to his release. The judges often believe that this approach curbs the drinking behavior in the constant repeater. The validity of this belief need not concern us here, but graduated sentences act as a strong reinforcement for a nomadic way of life and the individual's identity as a tramp. After several arrests in one city he is motivated to move on to another in order to escape the longer sentences. Even a suspended sentence often induces a man to increased mobility since, if he stays in town and is arrested too soon, it will mean serving time on the earlier suspended sentence in addition to the current charge. . . . Even sleeping behavior is influenced by the nomadic quality of their lives, as we shall see later in this paper. While observations, interview data, and life histories all support the contention that the dominant life style of these men is nomadic, most important is the fact that these reflect their cognitive world. These men are *tramps,* members of a subculture which is present in most large American cities, the subculture of *urban nomads.*

The problems and vicissitudes of urban nomads are different from those encountered by members of other urban groups. As socialization occurs in this subculture a variety of strategies are learned for satisfying biological needs, achieving subcultural goals, and adjusting to the environment. In each of the major scenes in the world of the tramp there are specialized modes of action for solving common problems. These scenes include *buckets* (jails), *farms* (treatment centers), *jungles* (encampments), *skids* (Skid Roads), and *freights* (railroad cars). Tramps learn to solve certain problems in the bucket, for example, as they acquire the categories and rules of this subculture. In jail there are the common problems of restricted freedom, restricted communication, and lack of resources such as food, cigarettes, and clothing. The specialized modes of action for alleviating these perceived deprivations are referred to as *hustling.* Hustling is a cover term for a larger number of specific actions which tramps group into the following equivalence classes: *conning, peddling, kissing ass, making a run, taking a rake-off, playing cards, bumming, running a game, making a pay-off, beating, making a phone call.*[4] These adaptive struggles used in jail are very important to this group of men who often find themselves in a new jail with no other way to meet their needs. Many have actually spent years in jail on short sentences. One tramp had been sentenced to a total of fourteen years in one city alone on convictions for public drunkenness. As one informant stated, "You aren't a tramp if you don't make the bucket." While "hustling in the bucket" is important, tramps have a large number of adaptive strategies which may be employed in almost any scene. In the remainder of this paper we shall consider those related to satisfying their need for sleep in the wider urban environment.

Making a Flop

The ethnographic description which follows has resulted from a variety of research methods and techniques. Previous studies in ethnoscience and cognitive psychology have been especially valuable in this regard.[5] Some aspects of this research are difficult to make explicit, such as the values of the researcher, intuitive insights, and the complex relationship between researcher and informant. While these factors can never be eliminated, a major goal in ethnography is to increase the degree to which all operations may be explicitly stated. This will provide the possibility for replication, an important criterion for evaluating the adequacy of ethnographic descriptions (Conklin 1962). It is for this reason that the following description includes a statement of the procedures used in gathering and analyzing the data presented. While interviewing, recording, observing, and analyzing often occurred simultaneously, the data will be presented here in terms of several research steps. These data represent a partial description of the cognitive map for some members of the population studied. The extent to which other members of the population share this map is an empirical problem. It is assumed that systematic differences will occur depending on social identity, length of socialization into this subculture, geographical area of major socialization experiences, and other characteristics of each informant. Some of these have been examined and all are important areas for further research.[6] It is beyond the scope and purpose of this paper to deal with many of these theoretical and methodological problems in detail.

1. *Hypothesizing the area as culturally significant.* The researcher's cultural background precluded the prediction that sleeping and places to sleep would be culturally revealing or significant. The popular image of the "bum" or "derelict" in American culture portrays these men as sleeping in cheap hotels or passing out in an alcoholic stupor. Although very little review of previous studies on this population was done prior to beginning the study, subsequent research has shown that, with a few exceptions, sleeping has not been considered very important in the published works. Participant observation, carried out among the population at the alcoholism treatment center, revealed the importance of "making a flop." Conversations among tramps at informal gatherings, meals, card playing groups, and "bull sessions" were recorded. As these men related their experiences to one another there were many references to "making a flop." Friends were identified as someone you would "make a flop with." Comments about making a flop were often linked to other important behavior such as being arrested, drinking, and traveling. Informants made such statements as "The most important thing is something to eat and a place to flop." A study (Wallace 1965:29) of Skid Road in a midwestern city emphasized the importance of this aspect of behavior:

> A place to sleep is, in some ways, more important to the men who live on skid row than food to eat or something to drink. This is so for two reasons. First, a man sleeping in the open is an easy victim for the weather, as well as for assailants be they jack rollers or police. Secondly, the law uniformly requires that "everyone must have a bedroom" if he is not to be charged with vagrancy. . . .

This author then discusses the different places where these men sleep, giving the following list: single room hotels, cubicle hotels, mission hotels, dormitories, transportation depots, buses, subways, movie houses, flop houses, box cars, hobo jungles. Thus, in discovering which questions to ask and by examining other studies, it was hypothesized that making a flop was a significant aspect of this subculture.

2. *Recording a corpus of relevant statements.* At this stage, conversations were recorded and statements gathered which all related to the general focus of sleeping. Earlier field notes on other subjects were combed for verbatim statements made by informants about this domain. The tramps' membership at some time in the dominant American society enables them to translate their concepts into those of the researcher. Because of this, very few questions were asked at this stage of the research. One approach that helped overcome their bias in interpreting similar cultural forms was to ask a group of informants to discuss their "experiences of making a flop." In such situations the individuals

often talked among themselves rather than to the researcher. The following examples are drawn from these tape recorded sessions: . . .

A lot of guys make them halls over at the Puget Sound. Either they sleep in the hallway or they sleep in the bathtub over at the Puget Sound (laughter). I've gone up to sleep in the bathroom. You know where they got those trash cans, up on the fourth floor. No one ever looks up there. That Jap says, "I got 300 rooms," he says, "and twelve hundred tramps come out every morning" (laughter). . . .

You know where they got this little private club, down at the end of the block, towards Alaska Way from the Bread of Life, that little dock back there? (Others: yeh) There's garbage cans back there, but they're paper cans, not garbage. They're clean. And many a night, you know, in the summer time, I'd go in there, turn the barrels over, and put a pasteboard box there, and turn that barrel and stick my feet in it, and maybe I'd stick my head and shoulders in this damn pasteboard box, well I was out of sight. I'd lay there with half my body in a garbage can and the upper half in a paste-board box. Until someone kicks that can or tries to load it and you'd better get out! (laughter) (Another informant: I never corked out like that!) Well, that way no one knows. . . .

I usually hit a car lot. I'd either get in the back row, or go right up by the office. They're gonna look for you in the dark. But you pick out the best lighted place and they ain't looking for you in the light, but you get in a dark place and they come looking for you with a flashlight, right by the office, crawl in a car, 'cause they ain't looking for you in the light.

Statements made by one member of this subculture to another member and those which could be placed within a larger verbal context were most valuable. At the same time, written statements, statements made to the researcher, and fragmentary statements were extremely useful. The following examples indicate the variety and range of such data:
"I got my flop for the night."
"Where you gonna bed down for the night?"
"I flopped out in the weeds."
"In a stairway you got to sleep with one eye open or someone will bang you on the head or start taking your shoes off."
"I'm not bothered if I flop in a broom closet."
"I paid for my banner."
"In a flophouse you can cop a heel, double up, hit the deck."
"The Sally is a one night flop."
"I robbed a whole clothesline to make a bed." . . .
"Got me ten or twelve newspapers back in the Frye Hotel . . . had a bed that thick." . . .

3. *Examining the corpus of statements for possible domains, question frames, and substitution frames.* For this study, a domain was considered to be a category system which was labeled with a cover term or a set of terms which all occurred in some restricted environment. There are a number of domains or category systems within the general focus of making a flop which could be

analyzed. These include, but are not limited to, the following: (1) kinds of "flops"; (2) ways to "make a flop"; (3) ways to "make your own flop"; (4) kinds of "people who bother you when you flop"; (5) ways to "make a bed"; and (6) kinds of "beds." Some of these domains are sets of terms referring to objects; others refer to modes of action. This does not exhaust the possible domains and subdomains within this area, nor does it consider "covert categories" (Berlin et al. 1968:290–299) which tramps utilize but which do not have cover terms. While several of these domains will be discussed, the focus of this study is primarily on kinds of "flops." Question frames were derived primarily from the cover terms for the various domains. Such questions as the following were developed:

"What kinds of flops are there?"

"What are the different ways to make your own flop?"

"What kinds of persons can bother you when you sleep?"

Substitution frames were discovered by inspecting the statements related to making a flop for those with terms that appeared to be replaceable by other terms. The following examples show several frames which were utilized:

"(*The sally*) is a one night flop."

"I'm not bothered if I flop in (*a broom closet*)."

"I flopped in a bathtub in (*a flophouse*)."   ˏ

4. *Eliciting the categories of the domain.* The most important question frame for eliciting the categories of the domain labeled "flop" was, "What kinds of flops are there?" This resulted in a large number of terms which are ordered on the principle of inclusion and form a folk taxonomy (Table 1). Some of the terms were discovered through examination of previously recorded texts and others overheard in informal conversations. While the taxonomy appears to be clear cut, the persistent application of the above question frame with different informants did not yield unambiguous results. The final taxonomy given in Table 1 is a result of informant responses, intuitive insights, and some ordering of categories during analysis to satisfy the aesthetic values of the researcher! . . .

First, there were a number of terms which were excluded from the taxonomy because they were extremely rare or very little information could be gathered on them for further analysis. One informant indicated [for example] that one kind of flop was a *mortar box*. He recalled "My wife and I were hitchhiking to Chattanooga and we slept in an old filling station that was closed, in an old mortar box. We picked up some grass they had just cut along the highway and used it for a bed." Further investigation may reveal that there is a category of flops called *boxes* which would include *mortar box* and *trash box*, but the latter was the only box included here as a kind of flop. . . .

Second, there were a variety of places "in buildings" which informants identified that were not included, and the taxonomic status of those which were included is problematical. In most urban environments there are many public buildings which are accessible to tramps. Within these buildings there are public places which make good sleeping quarters because they are heated.

Table 1. Taxonomic Definition of Flops

1. Paid flop
   A. Motel
   B. Hotel
   C. Apartment
   D. Flea bag
      1. Dormitory
      2. Wire cage
      3. Flophouse

2. Empty building
   A. Motel
   B. Hotel
   C. House
   D. Apartment
   E. Abandoned
   F. Under construction
   G. Being torn down

3. Weed patch
   A. Pasture
   B. Cemetery
   C. Viaduct
   D. Bridge
   E. Riverbank
   F. Field
   G. Orchard
   H. Between buildings
   I. Park
   J. Sidewalk
   K. Jungle
      1. Town
      2. Railroad
   L. Railroad track
   M. Alley
   N. Dump

4. Railroad flop
   A. Switchman's shanty
   B. Conductor's quarters
   C. Coal car
   D. Box car
   E. Flat car
   F. Reefer
   G. Piggyback
   H. Station
   I. Gondola
   J. Passenger car
   K. Sand house
   L. Crummy

5. Mission flop

6. Car flop
   A. Truck
   B. Used car lot
   C. Junk yard
   D. Transit bus
   E. Harvest bus
   F. Car on street
   G. Own car

7. Places in a paid flop
   A. Lobby
   B. Toilet floor
   C. Hallway
   D. Bathtub
   E. Closet
      1. Broom
      2. Clothes

8. Window well

9. Under building

10. All night laundromat

11. All night bar

12. All night restaurant

13. All night show

14. Paddy wagon

15. Cotton wagon

16. Hay barn

17. Furnace room

18. Newspaper building

19. Barroom

20. Night club

21. Bus depot

22. Brick yard

23. Scale house

24. Harvest shack

25. Bucket

26. Tool house

27. Stairwell

28. Park bench

29. Penny arcade

30. Church

31. Trash box

32. Doorway

33. Apple bin

34. Haystack

35. Loading dock

These include depots, hotels, business buildings, police stations, etc. Many men reported that one kind of flop was a *toilet floor*. Further inquiry revealed that there were many different places where *toilet floors* could be found. For instance, informants reported: . . . "I have no trouble walking in a second floor, second rate hotel upstairs and curling up and going to sleep in the men's room. If it's very late at night I know there's a very poor possibility of anyone wanting to take a bath, so I just sleep in the bathtub." These places are not considered kinds of "paid flops," yet very often they are in hotels or flop-houses. . . .

Third, the discovery of some middle level terms in the taxonomy presented certain difficulties. Informants responded freely with the most generic term, *flop*. They also responded freely with specific instances of places where they had flopped, such as "I slept in a crummy," or "We slept in a big truck that was loaded with cotton from seats of old cars." Initially the taxonomy appeared to be primarily made up of a generic and specific level. In order to discover the middle levels, the question frame, "What kind of a flop is that?" was used with the specific terms elicited. Through this process it was possible to discover that a *crummy* (a caboose on a train) was a railroad flop, and the big truck noted above was a *junk yard truck* which is a kind of *junk yard car flop*. . . .

Fourth, there was a tendency to assume taxonomic relationships by confus-ing the form and function, as well as different functions, of an object. It will be noted by examining the taxonomy given in Table 1 that the terms categorize objects, not according to their physical form, but according to the function they serve for tramps and not other members of urban society. While this phenomenon has long been recognized by anthropologists, urban anthro-pologists face greater problems because they often share similar forms with those they study, but the functions are defined differently. One cannot assume similarity of taxonomic relationships but must test all such relationships em-pirically. For instance, at first it appeared that *paddy wagon* and *cotton wagon* might be included in the term *wagon flop*, but informants denied this relation-ship. There are several terms which include the phrase "all night," such as *all night laundromat*. When asked to sort these into similar categories, or asked if they were to be considered similar kinds of flops, informants refused to include them in any more generic term than flop. The discovery of taxonomic rela-tionships for similar terms which exist in two or more urban subcultures is one way of demonstrating that such terms are or are not homonyms. Many terms in the domain of flops would be classed only as *vehicles* by this researcher. In-formants classified some objects which were vehicles separately and some ob-jects which were not vehicles, such as *sand house*, together with vehicles.

Fifth, it was necessary to check those terms constantly which might be hom-onyms or synonyms. The problem of intercultural homonyms has already been noted in the preceding paragraph. I shared the term *cemetery* with my in-formants, yet it was included in the terms *weed patch* and *flop* for them but not for me. This type of intercultural homonym contrasts with intracultural homonyms such as informants' dual use of the term *hotel*. One refers to a kind of *paid flop* and the other a kind of *empty building flop*. There were many synonyms used by informants such as *fleabag flophouse*. Some men referred to all kinds of cheap Skid Road hotels as *fleabags*; others used the term *flophouses*. There was some confusion over this since in the city studied there were no *dormi-tory flops* or *wire cage flops*, so informants could use the cover term *flophouse* without specifying the level of contrast, i.e., what terms it contrasted with, since there were only specific flophouses in that city.[7] Some other synonyms encountered were the following: *crummy-caboose, mission-sally,* and *jail-bucket-can.* When a choice was to be made between terms which informants reported "meant the same thing," preference was given to terms used by those who had been members of this subculture for a longer period of time and also reflected the predominant usage of the geographical location of the research. Dialectal variation among tramps was encountered frequently, especially among those who had been socialized into this subculture in the southern part of the United States.

It should be noted that the lower level terms in the taxonomy do not refer to specific objects, but classes of objects judged as equivalent. For some of these terms it was possible to elicit more specific named objects which were members of the class. For instance, *park* is a kind of *weed patch flop,* but there were many different parks where informants had slept. Some different kinds of parks were elicited which are not included here, such as *hobo park.* The discovery of more specific terms was carried out in some cases with the question frame, "What are the different kinds of_____?" or "Can you tell me the names for the different_____where tramps flop?" Some category terms such as *box car* refer to a large number of different objects, but these are not named. Instead, informants would distinguish between members of a set by such statements as "I slept in a box car outside of Omaha on a rip track where I was bothered by the railroad bulls." While *empty buildings, weed patches,* and *railroad flops* are not generally named at a very specific level, other subdomains such as *flophouse* and *mission* have many specific named members reflecting the importance of these subdomains for this population.

We may now ask what this taxonomy says about the subculture of urban nomads. How culturally revealing is it to elicit the categories which this group uses to order their environment in relationship to sleeping behavior? While this category system is not exhaustive it contains nearly one hundred *categories* of sleeping places. Furthermore this taxonomy has five levels and could have been extended to at least six by including more specific terms. Several tentative conclusions may be drawn from these facts. First, the importance of nondrinking behavior such as sleeping appears to have been underestimated by most researchers in this field. Even the study quoted earlier which stressed the importance of finding a place to sleep lists only eleven categories of places to sleep. While the initial participant observations led to the impression that "making a flop" was important and would be culturally revealing, we now have a basis for comparison with other domains, both intraculturally and interculturally. While I would not contend that a simple count of the number of terms or the levels of a taxonomy are conclusive evidence of importance, they cannot be easily dismissed. Preliminary work with other domains in this subculture have not revealed any other category system which organizes so much of the environment or in such a detailed fashion. There are many different kinds of *bars, bulls, time,* and *ways of making it,* but none of these are as elaborate as the different kinds of *flops.* The domain which comes closest to being as elaborate is the kind of *people in the bucket,* or social roles in jail. Further research is necessary to make a more complete intracultural comparison.

Only superficial intercultural comparisons are possible at this time, since, to my knowledge, similar domains in other cultures have not been studied by this means. Sleeping places do not appear to be culturally revealing in the rest of American culture. In fact, the eleven categories of sleeping places noted above from other research are probably more than most Americans use. It is interesting to compare the usage of the two terms *flop* and *sleep*. *Flopping* is used by tramps to refer to the activity which other Americans refer to as *sleeping,* although most tramps will also use *sleeping*. When we consider the use of these two terms in their noun form, an interesting difference appears. The noun *flop* refers to a place in the environment where the activity takes place, while the noun *sleep* refers to the bodily state of rest or to the occasion of sleeping. Thus the verbs may be considered translations of each other but this is not so for the nouns. Tramps, in their language, stress the place where sleeping occurs, while other Americans do not. . . .

It seems apparent that tramps communicate information regarding places to sleep in a wider variety of sociocultural settings than do members of the larger American society. One is not surprised that sleeping behavior has been largely overlooked by those who have studied this group. The social scientist in his own culture has learned that there are relatively few places to sleep, that places to sleep do not enter into a wide variety of sociocultural settings, and probably holds the implicit assumption that places to sleep are not culturally relevant. While the major basis for designating these men as urban nomads was their own definition of social identity, this taxonomy strongly supports such a designation. Although a nomadic way of life does not necessarily require a large number of categories for places to sleep, we are not surprised to find this is so for these men. We might well be surprised to discover a group which is sedentary and also had such an elaborate category system for places to sleep.

A taxonomic definition is culturally revealing but it does not take us far enough in understanding this group of men. It tells us that tramps have many places to sleep but it does not tell us very much about what they consider significant about each place for sleeping purposes. It does not tell us much about how they choose one place to sleep instead of another. There are a very large, if not infinite, number of criteria which could be used to define such objects as *cemeteries, box cars, bridges,* and *bathtubs.* All of these items have at least one feature of meaning in common for the population under consideration: they are all *flops,* places to sleep. If we are to understand what meaning these places hold for tramps, we must discover the underlying semantic principles by means of which tramps differentiate one kind of flop from another. This leads us to the next step in the research.

5. *Discovering the semantic principles of the domain.* The procedures used to discover the underlying semantic principles of a domain have been referred to as componential analysis (Goodenough 1956). A set of objects or events which are identified as equivalent and labeled with a category term are not necessarily identical. All of the objects referred to by the terms in Table 2 are classed as equivalent. They all share at least one feature of meaning but there

Table 2. Dimensions of Contrast for Flop Domain (Highest level of contrast)

1.0 Monetary resources	6.0 Civilian interference
1.1 Not required	6.1 Waitress
1.2 Required to pay for the flop	6.2 Night watchman
1.3 Required to pay for something else	6.3 Bartender
	6.4 Manager
	6.5 Owner
2.0 Atmospheric conditions (weather)	6.6 Farmer
2.1 Almost no protection	6.7 Engineer
2.2 Out of the rain/snow	6.8 Tramps
2.3 Out of the wind	6.9 Anybody
2.4 Out of the wind, possibly out of the cold	6.10 Minister or priest
2.5 Out of the wind and rain/snow	6.11 Truck driver
2.6 Out of the wind and rain/snow, possibly out of the cold	6.12 Probably no civilian
2.7 Out of the wind, rain/snow, and cold	7.0 Police interference
	7.1 Police check and may also be called
3.0 Body position	7.2 Police check
3.1 May lie down	7.3 Police must be called
3.2 Must sit up	7.4 Police do not interfere
3.3 Should sit up but may lie down	8.0 Security
4.0 Intoxication	8.1 Public/Concealed/Protected
4.1 Must be sober	8.2 Public/Concealed/Unprotected
4.2 Must be drunk	8.3 Public/Unconcealed/Protected
4.3 Any state of intoxication	8.4 Public/Unconcealed/Unprotected
5.0 Drinking restrictions	8.5 Nonpublic/Concealed/Protected
5.1 Low risk drinking	8.6 Nonpublic/Concealed/Unprotected
5.2 High risk drinking	8.7 Nonpublic/Unconcealed/Unprotected
5.3 Purchase drinks	

are many differences among them. Each term *contrasts* with the other terms and those at the same level of contrast make up a *contrast set*. The dimensions of meaning which are important in differentiating among members of a contrast set are the *dimensions of contrast*. Each dimension of contrast has two or more values. The differences in meaning among members of a contrast set are indicated in terms of the values on each dimension of meaning. By specifying how each term included in the *flop* domain contrasts with every other term, we would be stating, in part, the underlying semantic principles which organize the domain. If the dimensions of contrast reflect the cognitive world of our informants, we would also be stating, in part, the significant criteria which they use in selecting one place to sleep over another. This study was aimed at a description which approximated the psychological reality of informants. . . .

It is assumed here that any componential analysis of a category system will fall somewhere between an exact replica of the cognitions of informants and one which is completely divorced from how they perceive the world. . . .

Several techniques were used to elicit the dimensions of contrast employed by tramps and to avoid imposing dimensions relevant only to the investigator. The underlying goal of all these techniques was to elicit from informants those differences in meaning which they felt existed among members of the set. Probably the most useful approach was the triadic sorting task (Kelly 1955; Romney and D'Andrade 1964). Informants were presented with three terms for different categories of *flops* and asked to indicate which two were most alike and/or which one was different. *After* a selection was made they were queried regarding the basis of their choice. Substitution frames were formulated from these responses or from other textual material. For example, an informant would be presented with the frame "If you flop in the *(main jungle)* you may be bothered by other *(tramps)*" and asked to indicate what other terms would appropriately go together in the two spaces. This approach is very similar to the "grid method" discussed by Bannister and Mair (1968) in a recent work based on Kelly's personal construct theory of personality. Another approach was to ask informants to sort the terms into two or more groups in any way they desired. Then they would be asked to indicate why they had grouped the terms in a particular way. These techniques led to the discovery of the dimensions of contrast for this domain. Some of those used for defining the terms at the highest level of contrast are listed in Table 2 and a componential definition of these terms is provided in Table 3. . . .

A componential definition does not tell us everything there is to know about a domain. The definition in Table 3 does provide us with the information which some tramps use to identify objects they consider places to sleep with the appropriate label. It also enables us to see how most terms are distinguished from one another. Sleeping *under a building* is both similar to and different from sleeping in a *window well,* and this componential definition shows us how these places are alike and different from the tramp's perspective. They are similar kinds of flops because they require no money, permit lying down, allow any state of intoxication, involve low risk of arrest for drinking, are relatively free from civilian interference, and are checked occasionally by the police. They differ in that when a man sleeps *under a building* he has more protection from rain and snow as well as concealment from other people. At this level of contrast there are two sets of terms with identical values for each dimension of contrast and thus it is not possible to discriminate among them by means of elicited criteria. A *barroom, all night bar,* and *night club* have the same values, a fact which suggests that there may be a covert category which includes these three sleeping places. *Apple bin* and *cotton wagon* are not distinguished; they are both rather concealed places in the vicinity of farms or orchards. Further

Table 3. **Componential Definition of Flops *(Highest level of contrast)***

FLOPS	1.0	2.0	3.0	4.0	5.0	6.0	7.0	8.0
					DIMENSIONS OF CONTRAST*			
Paid Flop	1.2	2.7	3.1	4.3	X	X	7.4	X
Empty Building	1.1	2.6	3.1	4.1	5.1	6.2,6.8	7.1	8.6
Weed Patch	1.1	X	3.1	X	5.1	X	X	X
Railroad Flop	1.1	X	X	X	X	X	X	X
Mission Flop	1.1	2.7	3.1	4.1	5.2	6.8	7.4	8.4?
Car Flop	X	X	3.1	X	5.1	X	X	X
Places in Paid Flop	1.1	2.7	X	X	X	X	7.3	X
Window Well	1.1	2.4	3.1	4.3	5.1	6.8	7.2	8.7
Under Building	1.1	2.6	3.1	4.3	5.1	6.8	7.2	8.6
All Night Laundromat	1.1	2.7	3.3	4.3	5.2	6.5	7.2	8.4
All Night Bar	1.3	2.7	3.2	4.3	5.3	6.1,3,4	7.1	8.4
All Night Restaurant	1.3	2.7	3.2	4.3	5.2	6.1	7.1	8.4
All Night Show	1.3	2.7	3.3	4.3	5.1	6.8	7.4	8.2
Paddy Wagon	1.1	2.5	3.1	4.2	5.2	6.12	7.2	8.7
Cotton Wagon	1.1	2.5	3.1	4.3	5.1	6.12	7.4	8.6
Hay Barn	1.1	2.6	3.1	4.3	5.1	6.6	7.4	8.6
Furnace Room	1.1	2.7	3.1	4.3	5.1	6.2,7	7.3	8.6
Newspaper Building	1.1	2.7	3.1	4.3	5.2	6.4	7.3	8.6
Barroom	1.3	2.7	3.2	4.3	5.3	6.1,3,4	7.1	8.4
Night Club	1.3	2.7	3.2	4.3	5.3	6.1,3,4	7.1	8.4
Bus Depot	1.1	2.7	3.2	4.3	5.2	6.9	7.1	8.4
Brick Yard	1.1	2.7	3.1	4.3	5.1	6.4	7.3	8.6
Scale House	1.1	2.6	3.1	4.3	5.1	6.8	7.3?	8.6
Harvest Shack	1.1	2.7	3.1	4.3	5.1	6.8	7.4	8.1
Bucket	1.1	2.7	3.1	4.3	5.2	6.8	7.4	8.4
Tool House	1.1	2.5	3.1	4.3	5.1	6.12	7.3	8.6
Stairwell	1.1	2.4	3.1	4.2	5.1	6.5,8	7.1	8.7
Park Bench	1.1	2.1	3.1	4.3	5.2	6.8	7.2	8.7
Penny Arcade	1.1	2.7	3.2	4.3	5.2	6.12	7.2	8.4
Church	1.1	2.6	3.1	4.3	5.2	6.2,10	7.1	8.6
Trash Box	1.1	2.5	3.1	4.3	5.1	6.12	7.2	8.6
Doorway	1.1	2.1	3.1	4.2	5.1	6.8,9	7.1	8.7
Apple Bin	1.1	2.5	3.1	4.3	5.1	6.12	7.4	8.6
Haystack	1.1	2.7?	3.1	4.3	5.1	6.12	7.4	8.6
Loading Dock	1.1	2.1	3.1	4.2	5.1	6.2,8,11	7.1	8.7

* See Table 2 for the meaning of each numerical symbol. A question mark (?) indicates lack of information while an X indicates variability among the terms at the next lowest level. In column 1.0, *car flop* has an X because some kinds require money and others do not.

research would probably yield more criteria which would distinguish among these terms. . . .

Does this analysis provide insight into broader aspects of the culture of tramps or is it merely an exercise in analyzing trivial "ethnoscientific trait lists" (Berreman 1966b:351)? Although a more complete discussion of this domain and its relationship to other important features of the culture of urban nomads is presented elsewhere (Spradley 1970), we may note several important themes which have emerged from this analysis. Tramps define sleeping places in terms of some of the most important concerns in their lives: they experience poverty (1.0); as nomads they must be aware of changing weather conditions (2.0); drinking groups and drunkenness are institutionalized (4.0, 5.0); they experience the rejection and harassment from the dominant society which is common to many minority groups (6.0); many do life sentences on the install-ment plan as a result of their encounters with the police (7.0); and they survive, in part, by reducing their visibility and thus increasing their security (8.0). The ethnographic approach not only led to the discovery that "making a flop" was one of the most important features of life for tramps, but through an analysis of this domain many other significant aspects of their culture were revealed.

CONCLUSION

This paper presented a study of the adaptive strategies of urban nomads by means of an ethnoscientific analysis of one domain in their culture. This ap-proach, based on a recognition of the multicultural nature of urban life, allowed informants to identify the relevant social units and the criteria for membership in these categories. The methods used were designed to reduce the influence of that form of ethnocentrism which not only prejudges the value of tramp culture but also predefines the categories and meanings of that culture. Native terminological systems were studied in ways which avoided the tendency of informants to act as subcultural interpreters, translating their way of life into terms which are acceptable to members of the dominant culture. It was shown that while tramps share such objects as cars, missions, jails, brick yards, cemeteries, and bathtubs with other urban dwellers, the meaning of such ob-jects varies greatly from one subculture to another. Those who live in cities may share the same locality but they are actually cultural worlds apart. One important part of *urban* anthropology must be the careful ethnographic description of these cultural worlds.

Ethnography is only a beginning and this study raises many questions for further research. How do those living by different subcultures within the city interact in predictable ways, i.e., how do urban societies manage to "organize diversity" (Wallace 1961)? Can the methods of ethnoscience enable us to map the equivalence structures of the interaction between tramps and the police, bartenders, or social workers? Would it be possible to correlate certain features of tramp culture, as viewed from the inside, with the categories of behavior which are the focus of the medical and sociological approaches? How is mo-bility related to alcoholism, homelessness, and criminal behavior? What are the inherent limitations of the ethnographic approach outlined here in studying urban cultures? Ethnoscience and similar approaches to ethnography cannot begin to answer all the questions which must be asked to increase our understanding of urban man. They can, however, make us sensitive to the culture-bound nature of human existence, whether as social scientists we are investigating other cultures or as tramps we are looking for a place to flop.

NOTES

1. This paper is a revised and expanded version of "Ethnoscientific Study of a Tramp Subculture," a paper presented to the 67th annual meeting of the American Anthropological Association, November 21–24, 1968, Seattle, Washington. Some of the materials used to illustrate the methods of research are drawn from Spradley (1970), where they receive much fuller treatment along with many other domains in the culture of urban nomads.
2. Skid Road is used here in preference to "skid row," which appears in much of the literature. Skid Road is a term which originated in Seattle to describe the road down which logs were skidded to the sawmill and where bars, flophouses, and gambling houses were prevalent. There is an extensive literature on Skid Road and the men described in this paper. Those who are interested may consult Wallace (1965).
3. Since there are many studies which have not been published it is difficult to estimate the degree to which ethnoscience techniques have actually been used in the study of urban groups. There are a number of reports on American kinship terms: Ward Goodenough (1965); A. K. Romney and R. G. D'Andrade (1964); one on American law terms, Mary Black and Duane Metzger (1965); and one on German beer terms, Per Hage (1968)—all pertaining to urban problems.
4. A more detailed analysis of *hustling* may be found in two other publications on tramp culture: Spradley (1968) and (1970).
5. The work of George Kelly (1955) provides one of the closest links between psychology and ethnoscience. Anthropologists whose work has been especially helpful include: Harold C. Conklin (1962, 1964); Charles O. Frake (1961; 1962a; 1962b); Ward Goodenough (1956); Paul Kay (1966); Duane Metzger and Gerald E. Williams (1963; 1966); and Black and Metzger (1965).
6. Some differences among informants regarding different kinds of tramps have been investigated. A sample of about sixty-five men were asked to respond to a questionnaire based on the criteria used by informants to define the domain of "tramps." Relationships between a self-image adjective checklist, social identity as a kind of tramp, and knowledge of this particular taxonomy are being analyzed.
7. See Frake's discussion of the use of the same linguistic form at different levels of contrast for further discussion of this kind of problem (Frake 1961).

DOING IT: URBAN RESEARCH IN POPAYÁN, COLUMBIA

Michael Whiteford

In this article Michael Whiteford offers a personal glimpse of his
experiences in the Colombian city of Popayán. The unit of analysis is a
working-class neighborhood, Barrio Tulcán, on the edge of the city. Due
to limited housing within the barrio, Whiteford is forced to live outside the
community, commuting each day to work. But by using one family's home
as a base, he manages to approximate participant observation. He also
uses a range of other research techniques. Whiteford concludes with some
remarks on the role and value of anthropology's traditional, personalistic
fieldwork methods in urban settings.

After months of planning and ten days of traveling through Mexico and
Central America, my wife, Patty, and I deplaned in Bogotá in May, 1970. At
last we had arrived in Colombia, where I would conduct thirteen months' fieldwork.[1] Two days later we arose with great excitement: on this day we would fly
to Popayán, a town I had lived in twice as a child but had not seen for eight
years. The day began ominously; we had no Colombian pesos, and discovered
that no one would cash our traveler's checks since it was a holiday. At last, the
hotel manager agreed to cash enough checks—at far less than the official rate of
exchange—to cover our bill and taxi fare to the airport.

Still smarting from this gouging, we climbed into a taxi and implored the
driver to rush us to the airport, since we were now late for our plane. No problem, we thought, as Colombian cabbies drive like Grand Prix racers. But this
one pampered his machine, driving at a leisurely pace, and despite my complaints, insisted on giving us a scenic tour of Bogotá. Perhaps he knew something we did not, for on arriving at the airport we were informed that our flight
and the following one to Cali had been canceled. The airline agent was con-
fident, though, that everyone could be accommodated on the afternoon flight.

For the next four hours we sat amid our suitcases and boxes watching other
passengers leave for Mexico City, Los Angeles, and Madrid. Finally word
came that our flight was scheduled to leave. En masse we turned and raced
down the corridor, all of us hoping for a seat. Patty and I were among the
lucky ones.

SOURCE: Article written expressly for *Urban Life*.

We debarked in Cali and staggered into a wave of heat and humidity. Anxious to finish our trip, we spent only enough time there to find another taxi for the two-hour trip to Popayán. Like a thoroughbred racer our driver sped by the huge fields of sugar cane and pastures of regal Brahman cattle.

When at last the lights of Popayán appeared, Patty and I gave simultaneous sighs of relief. We had made it. The streets, wet after a recent rain, gave back reflections of Popayán's colonial architecture. People walked alone, returning home from movies and restaurants or just taking an evening stroll. It was good to be back.

A FAMILIAR FIELD

I first came to Popayán at the age of six, when my father, also an anthropologist, brought his family on a fieldwork expedition. In many ways this was an excellent prelude to becoming a fieldworker myself; I learned Spanish at an early age and experienced a different culture without really being conscious of it. We returned to the field several times while I was growing up, and as an undergraduate I took part in ethnological field sessions in Latin America.

Initially I had thought about working in Mexico. I had done my most recent fieldwork there, and I knew other research was under way which paralleled what I would be doing. Nevertheless, I had very pleasant memories of Colombia, and the idea of returning to Popayán to study migration intrigued me. Furthermore, I was aware that much of the current literature on Latin American urbanization dealt with peasants who arrive in large, industrialized, often capital cities. Comparable data on provincial towns were less abundant. Although these towns have little or no industry and relatively small populations (from ten or twenty thousand to two hundred thousand), they still receive many migrants, who see the towns either as stages in longer journeys or as a final destination.

Although Popayán has not grown as fast as Bogotá, Cali, or Medellín, between 1951 and 1964 the population showed a 46 percent increase—from 31,866 to 58,500 (DNP 1969:21), and in 1970 the city had an estimated population of 77,000 (DNP 1969:57). As a result of this population growth, new barrios were springing up on Popayán's outskirts. This expansion had been fairly orderly, and the edges of the city lacked the jumbled appearance of many other Latin American cities. Although some of these new neighborhoods were being built for Popayán's upper and middle classes, who were gradually moving out from the city's center, most were built to accommodate the influx of working-class migrants.

GETTING ORGANIZED

Unlike most anthropologists entering the field site, Patty and I had a place to stay when we arrived in Popayán. Old family friends graciously housed and fed us for two weeks while we looked for a house of our own. My father was also in Popayán doing fieldwork and was able to offer me on-the-spot advice during my first weeks in the field.

After weighing various research alternatives, I eventually decided to concentrate my efforts on a single migrant population, Barrio Tulcán,[2] a low-income neighborhood of 1,780 inhabitants, built without government assistance.

TULCÁN

Barrio Tulcán is in the southwest corner of Popayán, half an hour's walk from the city's central plaza. Geographically it stands apart from the city; a distance of no less than one kilometer separates the houses of the barrio from those of its nearest neighbor, Barrio Alfonso López. The barrio is hidden by a tall, thick barrier of willows, bamboos, eucalyptus, and cypress. Its entrance is a well-traveled road which skirts the perimeter of the municipal stockyards. Tulcán is situated at the juncture of two small streams, above which rise grassy hills speckled with grazing cattle.

To the casual observer, Tulcán appears more rural than urban. Chickens, ducks, sleeping dogs, and an occasional pig or horse vie for space in its narrow dirt streets with bicyclists, men pushing two-wheeled carts, and women balancing heavy shopping baskets on their heads. From time to time, even cattle are driven through the barrio. Large plots of sweet manioc, corn, coffee, and bananas, as well as a variety of other garden vegetables, add to the countryside ambience, while the hodgepodge of architectural styles further sets the barrio apart from the colonial Popayán. Even the bright yellow and green façades of the houses distinguish the barrio from the more subdued hues in the town.

LIVING ARRANGEMENTS

Even after I made the choice to work in Tulcán, we continued to live in town. Rental houses in the barrio were few, and we were only a short distance—ten or fifteen minutes by foot or about three minutes on my motorcycle—from Tulcán. At first I was distressed not to live among Tulcaneses twenty-four hours a day, but in the long run I came to feel that the advantages of living in town adequately compensated for the disadvantages. Living where we did gave me a valuable opportunity to meet middle-class Payaneses, and in talking with them I gained another perspective on what the Tulcaneses told me. In the end, this important if unforeseen contribution to my fieldwork allowed me to see Barrio Tulcán more objectively in the context of the entire city. Life in Tulcán shut down at night. Because most of the houses lacked electricity, families usually went to bed shortly after sundown. Even if I had lived in the barrio, most of my involvement in its activities would have been during the daylight hours.

Every day I parked my motorcycle in back of a house owned by the Arias family, and began the morning by talking to various members of the family before I set off to work. Whenever necessary, I could return there to rest or jot down notes. I visited with the Arias family at least three times a day and had complete freedom of access to the house and yard. Several times they remarked that I must be one of them because their dogs would never let others come and go as freely. In this way I did experience some of the advantages of living with a family in Tulcán.

FIELDWORK BEGINS

Once I had made the decision to work in Tulcán, I was faced with the problem of getting people to talk to me. Would they be cooperative? Would they like me? Many such questions passed through my mind and, having no answers, I tried without success to block them out. Although I knew I had to stop *planning* the fieldwork and actually begin *doing* it, I kept procrastinating. One more trip to some office for a report on a new barrio that might be better than the one I had chosen, one more search for a map of Tulcán—these were what I occupied myself with. Finally, one day I decided I would begin work the next morning. And to my amazement, I did.

A government office in Popayán had given me a list of leaders of the barrio's governing body. Armed with the names of three of its officers, I made my entrée. The first few people I approached had never heard of any of the names—my initial clue to mobility in the barrio—but they seemed friendly. Nobody snarled; people discussed at length who the leaders might be and then accompanied me until we found someone who told me that my list was a year old, and that the barrio now had a new group of leaders. This led to an informal discussion of how the barrio was organized and managed, and gave me a chance to explain briefly to a polite and curious audience of three my plans for studying the barrio. They nodded in seeming comprehension.

I learned later that my idea to study Barrio Tulcán was not entirely novel. Before my arrival various groups—among them researchers from the *Instituto de Crédito Territorial* ([ICT] the Colombian government's agency for housing and urban development) and engineering and medical undergraduates from the local university—had undertaken short investigations of this, the city's poorest barrio. With the exception of some medical students, who came weekly for one semester to visit specific families, the studies had lasted only a few weeks, and I now believe that the people I talked to on my first day in Tulcán thought my study would be just as brief. After several weeks, residents were amazed that my interest was still keen, and this hastened their confidence and trust in me. They were pleased and flattered that I was interested in doing an in-depth study of them and was truly concerned with *their* views on life.

It was two and a half months before I knew enough people in Tulcán to feel comfortable. This initial phase was the most difficult and discouraging part of my fieldwork. I tried to meet new people every day, but at times it was tempting to believe that I had done enough for the day. Coming upon some unsuspecting person in a store or outside a house, I would walk up to him or her and make small talk, generally asking questions about the barrio which almost inevitably led to conversation. In this way I initially contacted a number of people, noting who they were, where they lived, and whether I wanted to interview them later.

During those first few months I felt that my interviewing was inadequate to my needs. I questioned my ability to collect meaningful data, and I was aware that time was not standing still, and that my apprenticeship counted in the total time we had in Colombia. After working in Tulcán for about a month, I woke up one morning having dreamed I had gone back to Berkeley with only enough data to write a one-page dissertation. Gradually my fear of not getting enough data subsided, although it never went away entirely.

I always explained my role to barrio residents candidly, saying I was a graduate student gathering materials for my doctorate in anthropology. Although this did not mean much to them, the concept of a thesis was not entirely foreign since the local university students who had worked in the barrio were preparing to write senior theses for their graduation.

RESEARCH TECHNIQUES

While my field techniques ranged from simple observation to a detailed questionnaire on migration, most of my information came from interviews. I used two kinds of interviews, lasting from thirty minutes to two and a half hours: in open-ended interviews, I tried to pursue a single line of questioning on a specific topic, but with considerable flexibility in the discussion; whereas the more rigorous and tightly organized interviews followed a written and numbered schedule.

Both casual and participant observation were important in acquiring data. In the former I would gather data just by watching, a technique helpful in learning about how children play, how people greet each other and interact, and countless other things. I participated to some degree in activities I would later describe—fiestas, baptisms, political discussions, and *cantina* (bar) culture. Some of my best insights on life in Tulcán came as a result of observation.

To record data, I always carried a small notebook in my back pocket. Tulcaneses knew what my notebook was for, and sometimes I asked whether or not I could write down interesting facts or the words of a saying or limerick. In some cases I asked to take notes, perhaps to record something I might not otherwise remember exactly. Some interviews, such as those involving life histories, involved considerable detail of a nonsensitive nature, and these too lent themselves to on-the-spot note taking. But sometimes I did not want to interrupt the speaker, and other times I did not take notes on sensitive topics such as politics, interpersonal relations with neighbors, and witchcraft. In these instances I stored the information in my head and left as quickly as possible, hoping to remember most of what I had heard when I wrote it up at home.

I recorded my thoughts in a permanent and organized way at least twice a day. Of all the aspects of fieldwork, this is perhaps the most tedious and boring, yet I learned early that recording notes is not something that can be postponed; otherwise bits and pieces will be forgotten. I organized my data according to the format of Murdock's *Outline of Cultural Materials* and typed my notes in triplicate on 5″ × 8″ paper, noting at the top the informant's name, the date, and the place. The original copy was a key-sort punch card which I kept with me in the field for reference, and every six weeks I mailed the others back to the States for safekeeping.

Three and a half months after I began work in the barrio, I hired three residents to help me conduct a house-by-house census. My chief assistant, president of the barrio Junta, was well known, respected, and extremely hard-working. At his suggestion, I hired two teenaged girls, one the Junta's secretary and the other the queen of Tulcán's soccer team. Choosing the Junta president was fortunate; he was very conscientious about his work, and people freely gave him the information we asked for. The girls, though, were not effective census takers. Taking a census is meticulous work because interviewees must understand all of the questions, and the work can become boring. In addition, when household heads were not at home we had to make several trips in order to complete the census for the family. Unfortunately, my assistants lacked the necessary patience; either they skipped houses where no one was home, claiming later that the dwelling was vacant, or they tried to get the information from small children. Moreover, a friend pointed out what I suspected and feared: some residents were reluctant to reveal personal information to teenagers. After two days, I dismissed the girls and recensused the area myself.

My camera was useful both in getting to know people and in recording events. After residents discovered my willingness to take pictures, I received many requests, and I soon became the unofficial barrio photographer. Taking pictures helped me to meet many people I would have otherwise missed, and returning later with a print provided a basis for further contact.

My cassette tape recorder also served a dual purpose. Music was a primary source of entertainment among barrio residents, and I sometimes recorded singing. Many people played guitars or *tiples* (an eight-string, guitar-shaped instrument), and frequently men practiced together in informal groups. Recording singing was always a marathon event; the participants practiced every song before it was taped, then heard it replayed once when they finished and again when we were through with the session. Toward the end of our stay, I also used the cassette to record responses to Thematic Apperception Tests. Tulcaneses were not reticent about talking into the machine. On the contrary, they thoroughly enjoyed it and usually insisted that I replay everything in front of family and friends.

Finally, I collected what little printed material existed concerning Tulcán. The director of the Instituto de Crédito Territorial gave me a copy of the demographic study his office had conducted in October, 1969, and I found reports on the barrio in local and national newspapers, usually regarding government grants for improving Popayán's poor barrios.

Time was an important methodological intangible. Only long-term residence permits the fieldworker's picture of a community to develop accurately. For example, for many months Hernán Granada told me that he had come to Popayán to get a job—a common reason for migrating. But late in my stay, he told me a long story about how, when he was young, he had gotten into a machete fight with a drinking companion whose family forced him to flee his village. Incidents like this one convinced me that fieldwork cannot be rushed.

LEISURE TIME

One of the advantages of urban research is that the anthropologist can retreat from the field situation more easily than if he were in a peasant village. Although Popayán is a small, provincial city, it offered us periodic concerts, bullfights, soccer matches, and movies. We also had non-Tulcanese friends we visited on a regular basis. We read a great deal, too, and I cannot overemphasize the importance of having good books in the field. Our short-wave radio was an excellent source of entertainment and information; we enjoyed getting international and North American news, and we felt reassured to hear Eric Sevareid put it all in perspective.

FRIENDSHIPS

Certainly one of the most rewarding aspects of fieldwork is making friends. A number of people in Tulcán I never regarded as informants, but more as friends. On the other hand, some very good informants were not particularly good friends. Several Tulcaneses were protective of our friendship and were quite concerned about which of their neighbors we visited or interviewed. One family was quite upset when its members learned that I was getting information from another family they thought undesirable and "without culture." After he had seen me talking with María Molina, Jaime Arias informed me that she was no good, behaved in a scandalous manner, and probably was not telling me the truth. After coming to visit us, Carmen Martínez asked us not to mention her visit to one of her neighbors, some of our good friends, "because they would get mad at me for visiting you."

There were several reasons for this protectiveness. Occasionally we made small loans, all of which were reciprocated in one way or another. Some of our acquaintances did not want to strain our friendship by tapping our resources too often, nor did they want their neighbors to make such demands. Furthermore, our friendship was a source of prestige, since they ascribed to us high social and economic status. But in the end, friends grudgingly recognized that I had to establish contact with a large number of people throughout the barrio.

LEAVING THE BARRIO

When the time came to leave the field, saying goodbye to our friends in Tulcán was awkward. When we arrived late at one party given in our honor, we found our host and most of the celebrants semicomatose, an unusual occurrence in a barrio where drunkenness was rare. In some houses, people would stand looking at the floor, shuffling their feet in uncomfortable silence before saying simple goodbyes. With others we would sit drinking coffee or beer and visit just as though we would be back in a week or two. Our last stop was at the house of the Junta president, where we not only said goodbye but also offered our gratitude. I tried to speak eloquently about how grateful I was for the barrio inhabitants' cooperation in my study. I realized that they had done a great deal for me and felt guilty that I had not done more for them. We wanted to do something for the entire barrio but did not know just how, so we left many of our household goods with the parish priests and asked that they be distributed to the residents of Tulcán.

No matter how thorough I tried to be, I frequently worried that I would get back to Berkeley only to find large holes in my data. I envied friends working in Mexico, for they could always return to their field sites, while distance and cost precluded my returning to Colombia. Although I was unsure how much data I needed on a given topic before I could turn my attention elsewhere, I decided to consider my information sufficient when responses from several informants became repetitive. This problem was partially alleviated when, with five months remaining in the field, I wrote a forty-page paper on my work. Having to sort through my field notes and marshal my data into meaningful sections allowed me to see more clearly the areas on which I would have to concentrate during my remaining months in the field.

The following day, as we were driving to Cali, I thought about our year in Colombia. Thirteen months earlier we had arrived in Popayán, with ambivalent feelings: I was eager to begin fieldwork but was worried that I might not succeed. Now as we raced across the flatlands of the Cauca Valley, I had mixed feelings once again. Psychologically we were ready to leave—during the previous few weeks everything was done with departure in mind—yet nearly two hours before we left I found I missed Popayán already. I wondered how many of our friends we would see again and when we might return. As I reviewed the year's events—good and bad—I was amazed at how quickly the time had passed. It had been an unforgettable experience, and now it was over.

THOUGHTS ON NEIGHBORHOOD STUDIES

Since so many of our discipline's efforts have been directed at life in the countryside, it is natural that anthropological fieldwork conducted in the cities raises comparisons with that done in rural areas. This is particularly the case for anthropologists working in urban neighborhoods where the issues are germane and at times bewildering. Perhaps this is because in both village and neighborhood settings the investigator usually has a socially, geographically, and perhaps even a politically bounded unit of analysis. Yet there are some interesting similarities, as well as important differences, between them.

Because in both cases the investigator is dealing with relatively small populations, the traditional data-gathering tools used in village studies are convenient and generally adequate for looking at urban neighborhoods. But in working in the city we must be ready to adapt and expand our techniques. As George Gmelch notes in the introduction to this section, neighborhoods as units of analysis might be, and often are, more heterogeneous than most peasant villages. For example, although the majority of the adult population of the two neighborhoods I studied in Popayán were migrants from southern Colombia and certainly shared a number of very similar traits, they also were very different from each other in a variety of important ways. In most cases to talk about the Tulcaneses required gathering more individual data than would have been needed on any particular peasant community with its assumed homogeneity. Out of necessity, the urban anthropologist becomes more quantitatively oriented than students of peasant society often are.

We must be careful not to think of either of these settings as truly isolated units. In the past students of both neighborhoods and villages have been correctly chastised for treating these settings as discrete entities and often for failing to integrate villages into their regional contexts and neighborhoods into their urban ones, and in this way not considering the whole picture. Perhaps the urban anthropologist is more cognizant than his/her rural-oriented colleagues of linkages with the larger whole, in this case the city. We should ask: what does the study of a neighborhood tell us about life in general in a particular city? Unfortunately, one small area often tells us very little.

Finally, something should be said about the nature of the data-gathering and theory-generating process. One of the things which attracts people to ethnology is the personal work which the anthropologist has with the target population. In both village and urban neighborhood studies we interact intensively with a relatively small group of individuals, on a daily basis, over a prolonged period of time. We get to know them, and they us; we participate in the rites of passage of their children, and celebrate other important occasions with them. The nature of this relationship is not one of working with faceless individuals represented by IBM numbers on a fortran sheet, but of dealing with people who live and breathe, and have faces which smile and grimace. They are "real" people. Lamentably, as the units of analysis become larger than what the anthropologist can handle on a one-to-one basis, there is a tendency to lose some of this identity. Thus, while no neighborhood study can tell the reader everything he or she wants to know about any particular city, the reader will be provided with a view of it through the eyes of a certain, but real, segment of its population. These perspectives do convey particularistic experiences and interpretations from a personal point of view, something which should not be lost by anthropologists.

RETURNING TO POPAYÁN

By the fall of 1973, I had finished my graduate training, taken a job, and was in my second year of teaching. When I completed my initial fieldwork in Tulcán, several important changes were scheduled to take place during the next few years: after abandoning their original idea of simply bulldozing the barrio and completely rebuilding it, the municipal government designed a series of improvements. I wanted to return to see if these plans had come to fruition and what effects they might have had on the barrio.

In June, 1974, Patty, out one-year-old son Scott and I left for Colombia. At first glance, Popayán seemed little-changed: more residences for the upper, as well as for the working, classes had arisen on the outskirts of town, as had a shopping mall, which occupied an entire city block. In spite of occasional letters, the flow of correspondence had not been very regular, and, although we repeatedly promised to return, most of our barrio friends were very surprised to see us. It was a happy reunion indeed.

WORK BEGINS

Since the primary objective of our return was to study change in the barrio, I wasted no time in beginning the research process. Among other obvious changes, I found the barrio now had regular bus service and, as a result, the bridge leading into the area had been replaced, and a new one permitted traffic to exit in a different location. Many of the old and dilapidated bamboo electrical poles had been replaced with sturdy concrete poles. Some new houses had been built by private individuals, but the ICT's scheme for a block-by-block renovation to improve existing houses and to build eighty new dwellings never transpired. Although the master plan had been approved in Bogota, engineers in Popayán stated that the problems of getting access to all of the land titles kept the project from ever getting off the ground. The barrio sewer was still in the planning stage, and, while blueprints existed, funds were never appropriated.

I began interviewing residents about their attitudes toward the barrio and their feelings regarding what had (and had not) taken place. This went quite quickly, and it was during this time that I began to conduct a comparative investigation of another low-income neighborhood. Unlike Tulcán, Barrio Alberto Lleras was built by ICT. It, too, was a migrant neighborhood with close to two-thirds of the household heads born outside of Popayán. Prospective residents were required by ICT to apply to live in Alberto Lleras. As part of the application process, one had to supply the previous year's income tax receipt, furnish statements on employment, get police clearance, present records of military service and provide a health certificate. The process of qualifying for housing alone provided some interesting and important contrasts with Tulcán.

It was at this time that an old friend, who was teaching a statistics course for anthropology students at the state university, asked me if I would give a couple of guest lectures on urban anthropology. I agreed and was surprised and pleased when, several days later, he approached me and said that the class wanted to know if I needed any research assistants. I jumped at the chance, and a team was prepared.

Because of my familiarity with the research setting, I was able to devise a culturally appropriate, semi-openended, structured interview schedule which would allow us to collect quantitative data for comparative purposes from the two barrios. This was supplemented by participant observation and long, intensive interviews along the same lines as the schedule. We divided the two neighborhoods into segments of approximately equal spatial representation, and then began interviewing household heads. I was able to use interviews from about 35 percent of Barrio Tulcán's household heads, and we collected information from slightly more than 20 percent of the heads of households in Alberto Lleras.

It was an excellent training experience for the students, and it provided me with some data that, because of time constraints, I never would have collected on my own. Like anthropologists working in cultures other than their own, some of these students had to overcome stereotypes, not only ones which they had about the people they were interviewing, but also ones which these working-class people possessed about them as university students (a group which many in Tulcán and in Alberto Lleras felt was pampered and spoiled). A couple of students clearly were uncomfortable working in low-income neighborhoods, and two quit before the end of the first day. After talking with them, it was apparent that, as upper- or middle-class university students, it was difficult for them to relate to the people they were interviewing. Further, some of the migrants were tired of being surveyed again by university students whose attitudes in the past had tended to be patronizing and condescending. Yet, importantly, most of the students managed very well, with most enjoying the work and showing genuine understanding, empathy and compassion.

NEW ROLES WITH OLD FRIENDS

Not only had Barrio Tulcán changed, but I, too, had gone through a metamorphosis. When we left Popayán in 1971, my friends in the barrio bid goodbye to someone who had been in their midst for a year, poking around, asking questions, at times being somewhat of a nuisance, but always curious and ever-present. I was a university student and some had been puzzled that I seemed to need so much schooling. For example, it was immediately apparent that some of my barrio friends, with only a year or two of formal education, were undeniably more adept at math than I.

Three years later, I returned as a university professor. My status in the barrio increased with my age and profession. When I told friends in Tulcán that I was writing a book about them, they truly seemed pleased. I had been with them long enough, they reasoned, to be able to present an accurate picture. They wondered if having a book about them would improve their situation, and I was somewhat saddened at having to confess that it probably would not, but that it might make a difference to some.

When we returned to Popayán in the summer of 1974, some of the acquaintances of my youth, who had not been there in 1970-71, had returned to Popayán, and, although they were now only in their late 20s and early 30s, they definitely held positions of power and influence in the community. It was through my interactions with these community leaders, or people who would soon assume such ranks, that I obtained a sense of how Popayán operated, what directions the community would soon be taking, and how its leadership envisioned the role of low-income neighborhoods like Tulcán and Alberto Lleras in the grand scheme.

THE EARTHQUAKE OF 1983

About five minutes before my class was to begin, I was looking over some notes when a student rushed into my office and blurted out "Did you hear about the earthquake in Popayán?" I looked up in amazement. No, I responded, what had she heard? She explained that, while driving to campus, she had been listening to a report of an earthquake striking southern Colombia and that the commentator had mentioned Popayán. Any student who has even taken a course from me has heard about Popayán, so it was not surprising that the name rung a bell with her. That evening, we watched the news with uneasy anticipation. There was a thirty-second clip on the destruction of Popayán, which showed the cathedral and a graphic display of several other scenes depicting the impact of the calamity.

At approximately 8:15, Thursday morning, March 31, 1983, Popayán's residents were awakened by the shaking of buildings accompanied by a thunderous, roaring sound, like that of a jet airplane, coming from the ground beneath them. The oscillations and the initial loud noises were followed by sounds which were described as *diabolical* moans and groans. Although the whole process lasted only eighteen seconds, when it was through one of the most beautiful cities in the New World had been severely damaged, at least 200 people had been killed, and more than 30,000 inhabitants were left homeless. The earthquake struck as Popayán was celebrating Easter week, the most important time in the lives of many of Popayán's residents. Not only is it a period of celebration of a series of events in the life of the Church, but it is also an occasion for families to gather together. In recent years, tourists from various parts of Colombia, as well as from other countries, have crowded into the city to visit its churches and to watch the nightly activities. Although the evening processions generally are solemn affairs, the hotels are jammed, the shops are full, and a carnival atmosphere pervades the air. The city is never more beautiful than during this time of year. Traditionally, Easter is the time when the exteriors of houses get new coats of paint. Midafternoon rains wash Popayán's streets clean and the blooming hibiscus, jacaranda and bougainvillea give the city an additional sprinkling of pinks, reds, yellows and purples. Easter week of 1983, unfortunately, ended on a tragic note.

When the tremor struck, Samuel Samboni, a baker in Barrio Tulcán, was still in bed. Usually at this time, Samuel would be at work delivering bread, but that day was a holiday, and he was enjoying some extra sleep. When the shocks of the quake subsided, Samuel turned on his radio and heard that the center of the city had been destroyed, including the cathedral, whose roof collapsed on worshippers during the 8:00 A.M. mass. Knowing his mother and daughter were there, Samboni raced into town. For several hours, he and other rescuers dug through the rubble. In time, Samboni helped uncover eleven bodies, some smashed beyond recognition. Exhausted, he finally returned home only to encounter his mother waiting for him with news that his daughter had been injured and was in the hospital.

Ignacio Gonzalez and his family lived on the second floor of a relatively new, four-story complex built for members of the city's middle class. At the moment of the quake, Gonzalez was preparing breakfast for himself, the other members of his family having already left for activities elsewhere in the city. When the building started to vibrate, Ignacio hurried to the front door and found that the frame had twisted to the point where the door would not open. Having no time to lose, he kicked out the kitchen window and jumped. By the time he smashed the glass, Gonzalez realized his apartment was now on the ground floor, and he gingerly stepped over the ledge and onto the rubble beneath his feet. Many of Gonzalez' neighbors, who were still sleeping in the ground-floor apartments, were crushed to death in those brief seconds.

Everyone suffered. Families lost loved ones, and, thousands of houses were destroyed, as were places of business – large commercial establishments, small stores, cottage industries and the like. Only one of the city's beautiful baroque churches was left undamaged. Even the dead were disrupted. The walled tombs, in which the city's deceased are encased, were split open by the tremor. Caskets tumbled out, exposing their contents.

Popayán looked as if it had been bombed. For months afterward, the streets were filled with debris, making pedestrian and vehicular traffic tedious and dangerous. The city's parks and the green belt around its periphery became tent cities, as those left homeless crowded into makeshift housing, which lacked adequate, potable water and waste disposal systems. These were the lucky ones. For every family jammed into a tent, at least three were forced to huddle in dwellings made from unmortared bricks, flattened-out oil drums, sheets of plastic, strips of bamboo and cardboard. Farther from the city's center, new squatter settlements spontaneously appeared. Within weeks, the hillsides of Popayán began to have an uncanny and disconcerting resemblance to the slums of larger cities elsewhere in Latin America.

Small communities outside of Popayán similarly experienced the force of the earthquake. The peasant village of Puelenje was turned into a series of small brick mounds. Ruins of the church stood out because the pile of debris was higher than those of residences. Julumito, a small coffee-growing community just outside of Popayán, appeared as though some supernatural force had taken a giant eraser and simply reduced the village to a fine pile of reddish pieces of brick.

However, like flowers in the spring, within days after the earthquake, shops popped up amidst the rubble. In other instances, merchants tacked up notices in empty buildings informing customers where they could be found. More commonly, many store owners lost entire inventories and lacked capital to replenish stocks and open their doors. While there were jobs on both demolition and construction crews, the unemployment situation became serious.

RELIEF FUND

Because of the long relationship between the city of Popayán and my family, when news of the disaster reached us, we immediately moved into action. An emergency relief fund, centered in Ames, collected funds raised by my parents and siblings in their respective cities. Six weeks after the earthquake, I arrived in Popayán to stay with an old childhood friend. After talking with acquaintances about how the funds could most effectively be spent, we decided to dispense most of the monies through the regional office of the Servicio Nacional de Aprendizaje (SENA). SENA is a Colombian government institution designed to train people in occupational skills. The branch in Popayán offers courses in such skills as masonry, pottery making, plumbing, typing and bookkeeping. Immediately after the earthquake, people at SENA moved into some of the most impoverished rural and urban areas and began organizing teams of neighbors to build earthquake-proof housing. Under the direction of a *teacher*, groups of four or five neighbors rebuilt each other's homes. They were taught how to secure the rafters so that the roofs would not collapse during minor quakes. Steel reinforcement rods were employed in the construction as well. SENA was able to acquire building materials at reduced prices and sold them at cost.

BARRIO TULCÁN

The physical damage to Barrio Tulcán itself was minimal — an island of eerie tranquility, left untouched on the edge of such obvious destruction. Like people throughout the city, barrio residents talked of lost loved ones, of the disappearance of jobs, as their places of work often were destroyed, and about the nightmares they had that other quakes would soon follow. In the days after the quake, many Tulcanses worked throughout the city, assisting the relief efforts. After this initial response, they settled back and concentrated on putting their own lives in order. Six weeks after the incident, residents were concerned that the promises made by the government to ease the problems of housing and to assist in the reconstruction of the city would be too slow in coming. Many sarcastically wondered if the monies would ever leave the capital, and, even if it did, how would they benefit? It seemed to some that, once again, they might be bypassed as the assistance went elsewhere. Realistically, they observed, there were many others in more desperate circumstances. Nevertheless, they hoped something positive would come out of this catastrophe for them.

Although there was not time to conduct any type of study, there were other observations about the barrio that indicated it was changing. Aside from some of the new growth, compounded by the nearby squatter settlements, the barrio that I had first studied almost a decade and a half before had aged nicely. Homes made from split bamboo, ill-fitting wooden planks, and brick facing now had evolved into stuccoed and painted abodes. Many of the sons and daughters of families I had previously worked with were now studying in high school or trade school, and some were at the local university — educational levels unobtained by anyone from previous generations in those families. Nemecio Cruz's father told me that his son, then six years old, would go to the university one day. The family had singled out Nemecio as the one who would receive a university degree and decided to make whatever sacrifice necessary to bring this to fruition. Over the next decade, both parents worked to this end. Likewise, after older siblings completed primary school and joined the work force, some of their income was put aside for Nemecio's education. In 1983, he was in his third year at the university and, according to his delighted mother, would graduate in a couple of years.

While I would have preferred to have returned under more pleasant circumstances, it was good to see the people in the barrio again, and I am convinced those strong feelings were reciprocated. For instance, Faustina Arias announced with great emotion to her daughter and husband that, after the earthquake, she knew I would return. We talked of the past, of the current situation, and of what the future held for them. By-in-large, as they had always done, they looked at life with an air of unbridled optimism, tempered by a generous dollop of reality.

NOTES

1. The original fieldwork was supported by the National Institute of Health, and 1974 research was funded by the Wenner-Gren Foundation for Anthropological Research. The author also appreciates the continued support of Iowa State University.
2. The names of the barrio and its inhabitants are pseudonyms.

A FIELDWORK EXPERIENCE: IRISH TRAVELLERS IN DUBLIN

Sharon Bohn Gmelch

In this account of an urban field experience, Sharon Gmelch discusses the personal adaptation required of the anthropologist when studying another culture. Research was carried out among Irish Travellers (Tinkers)—a nomadic, impoverished, gypsy-like population—living in Dublin. From her account we learn that fieldwork in cities need not be less intimate or personal than that conducted in rural areas. We also learn some of the advantages and special requirements of urban field research, and of the dilemma anthropologists face in deciding whether to remain neutral observers or become needed advocates for the people they live among.

I first went to Ireland in the summer of 1970 as a graduate student participating in a field training program in anthropology.[1] The program began with an orientation period in Dublin during which we attended lectures on Irish society and research techniques. We then left the city for small communities in the Irish countryside. This was not surprising given the traditional focus of anthropology on tribesmen and peasants. I went to a fishing village in the West where in true anthropological spirit I remained for the duration of the summer. Only once did I venture by bus into the nearby provincial town—feeling that to do so more often would be reducing the hardship and, therefore, the experience of living in an "isolated" community. In adopting this attitude I was also naively ignoring the crucial role played by urban centers in the lives of people everywhere. My village, though small (pop. 342), was hardly isolated. To a large extent it was a bedroom community for the provincial capital just 7 miles away—many of its residents drove to work there each morning, returning each evening; others commuted longer distances returning only at week's end. A number of its residents had sons and daughters living in cities—in Dublin or "across the water" in London, Birmingham, or New York. Almost every home had television, and everyone read newspapers and listened to radio which brought national and international news as well as urban values into the home.

It was on my way to and from my village at the beginning and end of the

SOURCE: Article written expressly for *Urban Life*.

summer that I first became aware of Tinkers or Travellers[2]—an indigenous, gypsy-like people who lived on the roadside in horse-drawn wagons, tents and trailers and earned their living largely by begging and scavenging for scrap metal. They were a well-known yet little understood group in Ireland—the subject of folklore and fiction rather than serious sociological or anthropological study. I was intrigued. To my eyes, they were exotic. They also matched my interests in poverty and ethnicity. By coincidence my husband, also an anthropologist, was at the same time becoming involved with Travellers. He had arrived in Dublin at the end of the summer and while waiting for my field school to end, collected demographic data for a physical anthropologist who was conducting a genetic study of Travellers.[3]

Before leaving Ireland that summer we acquired a copy of "The Report of the Commission on Itinerancy"—a government report detailing what had become known as the "itinerant problem." It outlined the plight of hundreds of Traveller families living in poverty as well as the problems their nomadic lifestyle created for the settled community, especially in urban areas. Reading the report and the most recent census figures forced the realization that if I pursued my interest in Travellers, I would in fact be doing "urban anthropology." For although many Travellers still lived in rural areas, they were moving into Irish cities at an ever-increasing rate. And for good reason.

The traditional rural-based trades of the Travellers, such as tinsmithing, chimney sweeping and horse dealing, had become obsolete with modernization. Moreover, the city and the advantages it offered exerted considerable pull. Its high population density made begging and scrap metal collecting, the Travellers' newest economic specializations, easier. It was also easier to collect the "dole" (unemployment assistance) and obtain other social welfare benefits. A Dublin-based, volunteer movement—the Itinerant Settlement Movement— had also been organized to help Travellers, particularly to settle. But there were other attractions, too. City life meant street lights to brighten the night, more pubs, cinemas and activity of all kinds. In the space of less than twenty years (1952–1971), the number of Travellers living in the capital city of Dublin had jumped from 158 to 1,435. And the trend was the same in other Irish cities and provincial towns. Thus even the most "isolated" and "traditional" segment of the Irish population had been touched by urbanism and modernization.

The following account emphasizes the field experience more than research techniques, although the latter as they relate to urban areas are treated in a separate section. Anthropological fieldwork, even in cities, is an intensely personal experience. Unlike other social scientists, anthropologists attempt to live among the people they study, conducting research at all times of day for an extended period of time. It is their desire to know a culture from the inside, through the eyes of its members, and to observe actual behavior rather than rely solely on informants' verbal responses that separates anthropologists from other social scientists. It is for this reason that I am focusing on the field experience itself as well as on some of the special problems and advantages of anthropologists conducting urban research.[4]

THE FIELDWORK EXPERIENCE

Preparation and Arrival

While completing my formal graduate study at the University of California, Santa Barbara, I read everything I could on poverty, ethnicity, and itinerant and outcast groups in other countries in order to refine my interests and formulate a research design. I was interested in understanding how Travellers—who, like the settled Irish community, are white, English-speaking, Roman Catholic, and indigenous to Ireland—had for so long maintained a separate ethnic identity. I decided to focus my research on the interaction that takes place between Travellers and settled people as one way of understanding the persistence of their stigmatized identity and the maintenance of social boundaries between the two groups. The population concentration of Dublin made it an ideal place to examine the dynamics of this interaction. My husband, who was also doing his doctoral research among Travellers, planned to investigate their urbanization and adaptation to urban life. With a resolve that these were the two most significant issues to examine, we set off for Ireland.[5]

We arrived on July 19, 1971 and settled temporarily into one of Dublin's many bed-and-breakfast homes. Anxious to begin we made a list of things we needed to do—buy a car, get insurance, rent a flat, obtain a year's visa, and discuss our research with local authorities—and then telephoned a social worker we had met the previous summer. To our surprise and delight we received an invitation to attend a Traveller wedding the next day.

First Impressions

The ceremony took place in Our Good Shepherd Catholic Church in Churchtown, a suburb on the south side of Dublin. I had expectations of a large and gregarious crowd. Instead only thirteen people—counting the bride and groom, my husband, the social worker, and myself—attended. An air of disinterest and perfunctoriness pervaded the gathering. The fifteen-year-old bride appeared shy and woebegone in her wrinkled and ill-fitting wedding dress. The groom wore a dark, rumpled suit and an expression of detached resignation. The bride's father and the handful of women relatives present shifted uncomfortably in the pews, murmuring among themselves. The priest and his assistant arrived and taking the bride and groom by their elbows, jockeyed them into the proper position in front of the altar. Perhaps unnecessarily, I felt acutely embarrassed for them, especially after the priest instructed them in a loud and impatient tone on when and what to say. The customary mass was omitted. About a dozen neighborhood children who had filtered in during the ceremony stood at the back of the church, gaping innocently at the spectacle before them. And then it was over. We all rushed out. The social worker took some quick snapshots to commemorate the event. A squad car pulled up at the curb and called the groom over. A young *gardai* (policeman) leaned out and advised him to "start out right" and be "well-behaved." Johnny was out on bail for the ceremony. Larceny, the social worker informed us, was a growing problem in the city. We left soon after, my head spinning from these glimpses of what was to come.

My first impressions of Travellers were not flattering, nor did they help make interaction easy. The men looked rough and forbidding with their weather-beaten and scarred faces, tattered suits, and dark tobacco-stained fingers. They seldom smiled. The women were less threatening, if only because most were somewhat matronly and many were pregnant. But even they were tough in appearance and wary and evasive in manner. Fieldwork among Travellers, I feared, was not going to be easy.

Beginning Fieldwork

One of the first problems faced by anthropologists when working in the city is delineating the boundaries of the population they intend to study. In my rural research, I had simply lived in a small village. Dublin, on the other hand, was large and heterogeneous. My interest in Travellers defined in ethnic terms the group I was interested in, yet there were close to 1,500 Travellers living in the city. They were spread across Dublin in more than fifty camps. Some were small roadside camps of two or three families; others were large government-sponsored, serviced "sites" of up to forty families. As a single researcher rather than a member of a large research team, I could not regularly visit them all.

After making an initial visit to most of the larger encampments, George and I decided to concentrate on two camps which seemed most appropriate for our purposes. Both had large, relatively stable populations and were within easy commuting distance of the flat we had rented. One, Labre Park, was the first site built for Travellers in Dublin and one of the first of its kind in the country. It accommodated thirty-nine families in one-room, prefabricated dwellings (known as "tigins") with indoor bathrooms and electricity; extra family members spilled over into trailers and wagons parked nearby. The second camp, Holylands, was a temporary and undeveloped campsite located on the edge of a suburban housing estate on the south side of the city. It was little more than a large field ringed by trees with two strips of blacktop on either side to provide hard standing for wagons and trailers. A single water tap and two rarely-used outhouses constituted the amenities for a population of about twenty families.

During this initial phase of fieldwork, we alternated our visits between the camps. Upon arriving in one, we would both get out of the car and walk off in separate directions, approaching individuals or groups of Travellers and attempting to engage them in conversation. A few people had met George the previous summer and had received the photographs he had sent to them, so he was not a complete stranger. But I was. At first most of my contacts were with curious children, teenagers and the elderly. I explained my role—an American university student who would some day be. a teacher—and what I hoped to do—learn what it was like to be a Traveller. I explained about writing a dissertation which they interpreted to mean a book. When they asked how long I was going to stay and I said "a year," they were skeptical. Most of their contacts with outsiders similar to myself had been short-lived—primarily with Irish students doing one-term projects or journalists carrying out brief interviews. After repeated visits, however, the realization that I intended to keep coming became clear. As I became more familiar to people, they in turn became friendlier. Gradually I was developing rapport. No doubt the fact that I was not Irish lessened their suspicions that I might be something other than what I had said. (Nevertheless, I learned that for a period of several months a few people continued to suspect that we were police agents.)

The early weeks were not easy. I can remember the sinking feeling I got when people were cold or walked away from me. When in camp I was always on guard, monitoring my behavior, trying to act appropriately—wanting to be friendly but not too friendly, interested but not too curious. I ate whatever food was offered me, sat casually on the ground and two or three times on urine-soaked mattresses, trying my best to seem indifferent to the odor of unwashed bodies and the filth of the surroundings many lived in. I was repeatedly asked the same questions, often during the course of a single conversation, partially because Travellers—especially the women and teenage girls—were genuinely curious about certain things and partially because we had so few common experiences on which to base a conversation. But I also came to view this questioning as a test of my truthfulness and consistency. "Are you married? How long have you been married? How old are you? How old were you when you got married? Is he your husband? Do you have any children? Don't you like children? Are you from America? Do you know Elvis?" Some days I thought I couldn't face driving into camp again. The thought of seeking out people to talk to, of giving the same explanations over and over, and of risking rejection was almost too much to bear.

Although rapport developed with some Travellers, commuting to the camps soon proved unsatisfactory. To begin with, there were logistical problems. Travellers lacked definite work and leisure hours; plans, even for major trips away, were made on the spur of the moment. Some days I would arrive in camp to find virtually everyone gone. Setting up an appointment to talk to a specific individual at a specific time was nearly impossible. Travellers do not live by the clock (few even knew how to tell time). And understandably, my appointments were far more important to me than to them. I also felt that I was missing out on much of the important activity of Traveller life. This fear was reinforced when I would arrive in camp to be told, "You should have been here last night; the guards came up and took Biddy's Jim." Most importantly, I wanted to lose my outsider status and get "backstage," to blend into the background of camp life so that people would act naturally in front of me. Travellers are used to dealing with outsiders in a superficial and manipulative way: the nature of many of their contacts with settled people such as in begging or dealing requires them to be skilled at impression management. I felt it was important for me to view their lives from the inside, in hopes of learning what they really felt and to avoid unconsciously adopting the settled community's stereotypes of them. Moreover, Travellers had never been studied in depth before, and I felt an obligation to collect as wide a range of ethnographic data as possible.[6] Only living in a camp would enable us to do this.

Moving into Camp

After seven weeks of commuting between camps, we selected Holylands as our main research site for a number of reasons. First, the layout of the camp was better for observation. Families were camped along opposite ends of a small central field and consequently the actions of one were readily observable to all. In Labre Park, the tigins were lined up in a single row, each doorway facing the back of the house in front. Secondly, Holylands provided a better cross-section of the Traveller community. Some families had lived in the Dublin area as long as ten years; others were new to the city. Many families were still mobile. Because Holylands was then a temporary site, Travellers were for the most part free to move on and off with their own wagons, trailers and tents. Thus besides the stable core of families who remained the entire year, we were also exposed to new families who stayed for shorter periods of time. Thirdly, and perhaps as important, families at Holylands had been more approachable and hospitable during our visits than those at the other camp. It was at the suggestion of some Holylands residents that we finally bought a wagon and horse and prepared to move in.

The wagon, which was in need of paint and a few repairs, gave us a tangible excuse for coming to camp each day. Moreover, now that it was apparent that we really intended to live and travel like Travellers, the social distance that had naturally existed between us lessened. Our relationship with Travellers improved steadily over the next few days. As we worked on the wagon, people stopped by to give us advice, lend a hand, or simply chat and question us about America, particularly about the west ("What are cowboys like? Are there still Indians?"), the availability of scrap metal, and movie idols ("Do you know Clint Eastwood?"). The transition from regular visitor to camp member was completed the first night we slept in the wagon.

I had spent most of the evening sitting around a wood stove in one of the trailers quietly talking to a family. I had gone to bed fairly early, about ten. An hour or so later I woke to the roar and screech of vans and lorries racing into the site and the sounds of people laughing and talking. This lasted for a half hour and then the camp settled down to sleep once more. Suddenly a loud argument broke out in the trailer next door. Accusations, curses and obscenities were hurled back and forth. I could hear screams, groans and the sound of glass breaking. As I peered out the front window of the wagon, I saw the woman next door stagger from her trailer. A wave of irrational paranoia swept over me and I envisaged being dragged from my wagon and beaten. But gradually things quieted down and the camp fell into a fitful third sleep. The next morning I acted as if nothing had happened. Everyone I saw seemed subdued and sheepish. I was coyly asked by one woman how well I'd slept, but no direct reference to the fight was made. The eight-year-old son of the family involved came closest when he said, "You must have learned a lot last night."

Indeed I had; many of the pretenses and polite public fictions maintained for the "outsider" had been broken.

I soon learned that Thursdays, the day Dublin Travellers received their unemployment payments, were invariably days of heavy drinking and often fighting once the pubs had closed. Most fights started as arguments between husbands and wives, which sometimes escalated into physical beatings. Sometimes they involved other family members, but rarely people outside the family. As the year progressed, I became inured to the sounds of Thursday night violence.

Once living in camp, I fell into a more comfortable fieldwork routine. Much of the Travellers' time was spent out-of-doors, except in bad weather. Hence they were more accessible than house-dwelling villagers in the west of Ireland and most urban dwellers. Each family lit a campfire in the morning and kept it burning until they went to bed at night. A blackened kettle of water was kept boiling, and pots of tea were brewed throughout the day. Informal interviews consisted largely of extended conversations around the campfire and at the pub in the evening. Each morning I made a list of questions and topics I needed to explore and during the course of the day steered conversations to them, learning when (and when not) to ask direct questions as well as what questions to ask and in front of whom. I started with what I regarded as the least intimate and sensitive topics—with aspects of Travelling life that Travellers were proud of. Early weeks were spent learning about the art of Travelling itself, traditional skills such as tinsmithing and peddling, what settled people were like in different parts of the country, and aspects of family history. As time passed, the historical and general were left behind and more contemporary and sensitive issues were discussed—begging, scavenging, welfare, discrimination in the city, drinking behavior, family problems, and trouble with the law. Much of this was discussed spontaneously and at the Travellers' initiation. The anthropologist as a neutral outsider, and someone who has shown great interest in the people he or she is living among, often becomes friend-confessor-psychiatrist. Many people came to our wagon during the course of the year, shut the door, and began talking about their problems.

I rarely took field notes in front of Travellers. I felt it would act as a barrier, reminding them of the differences between us. I also felt it would be insensitive and raise unnecessary suspicions, since they themselves could not read. I tried to be as unobtrusive as possible. Moreover, the proximity of my wagon made note taking immediately after an event or discussion relatively easy. If I had time, I would write down a conversation in detail; at the very least I would jot down important information and reminders to myself to be typed up later as complete field notes.[7] During the last few months of research, I made numerous tape recordings to obtain details of family histories and to record the Travellers' own descriptions and explanations of aspects of their culture. I did not use the tape recorder as often as I would have liked since it always attracted a crowd who wanted to take turns singing into it.

As with other anthropologists, I relied heavily upon the friendship and assistance of several key informants. However, to balance the view of Travellers I was developing by living in one camp, I continued to make periodic visits to other camps in the city and even to areas outside of Dublin.[8] Regular attendance at the weekly meetings of Dublin social workers involved with Travellers also provided an opportunity to cross-check certain impressions and ask questions about Travellers in other parts of the city. For six weeks I acted as a substitute social worker in a commuter town outside of Dublin. This provided me with an opportunity to directly experience some of the problems and misunderstandings that arise between Travellers and settled Irish working in the welfare sphere.

Fieldwork is a process of adjustment. Just as the anthropologist must adjust to the people he or she is studying, so the people must adjust to the presence of an anthropologist. I had numerous "unusual" habits. At first small children gathered around me in the morning to watch me brush my teeth, talking and pointing, "Ah, would you look. Sharon's washing her teeth." More importantly, Travellers had fairly conservative notions about the role of women. They were surprised and curious about why I did not have children (I told them about birth-control pills), that I knew how to drive a car and that I often wore slacks or jeans. My most difficult adjustment was to the lack of privacy. Trailer and wagon walls were thin, and each family's camp was located only a few yards away from the next. Moreover, Travellers are gregarious, the result of large families and crowded living conditions.[9] They freely entered each other's dwellings without warning, sitting down to listen for a while, perhaps without uttering a word themselves, and then abruptly left. As we became an accepted part of camp life, our shelter became a customary stop on the visiting rounds. If someone wanted to talk, he or she simply opened the wagon door and came in. We could have visitors at any hour of the day or night. It was difficult to suggest that people leave without risking offending them. I put a latch on the door which deterred some, but most merely opened the double windows above the door and leaned in to talk or else tugged at the flimsy door until we were forced to open it.

RESEARCH IN THE CITY

Data Collection

One of the advantages of urban research over that conducted in most rural areas is the anthropologist's access to a variety of other information sources—government agencies and personnel, research institutes and their reports, university departments and staff, the census bureau, libraries, and private archives. Depending upon the particular research problem, information from such sources can be as important as that obtained from informants. I spent many hours in the National Library searching out information on the history of Travellers and in the library of *The Irish Times* reading newspaper clippings which documented the growth of the Itinerant Settlement Movement and clashes between Travellers and settled Irish over housing, campsites and trespassing. The latter provided important clues to the stereotypes and attitudes settled people held toward Travellers and their change over the years. The archives of the Department of Folklore at a nearby university contained a variety of information on Travellers, including the results of a questionnaire sent to school teachers across Ireland in the early 1950s. This yielded important data on traditional Traveller culture. Whenever I was depressed or anxious or felt my interaction with Travellers had reached a point of diminishing returns, I went to one of these places and drowned my sorrows in solitary work. This never failed to cheer me up, providing me with a wealth of information as well as new topics and questions to pursue with Travellers.

When a complete respite from research was needed, the city provided shops, restaurants, plays, movies, museums, art galleries, and the zoo—a range of diversions unavailable to anthropologists working in rural areas. The wide range of contacts with settled Irish we made during the course of the year meant that we were occasionally asked out for dinner or tea. Good food in comfortable surroundings helped place fieldwork in perspective.

An important part of my research involved observing Travellers outside the camp setting as they moved among the settled community. Even had I not been interested in interethnic relations, it would not have been possible to view Travellers as an isolate, especially in their urban context. The population concentration of the city made it the perfect place to examine the dynamics of Traveller-settled Irish interaction. Contact between the two groups was more frequent than in rural areas. On any major shopping street, for example, I would observe the transactions that took place between Travelling women begging for alms and settled passers-by. I could also accompany Travellers scrap collecting and begging and go with them to pubs, shops, cinemas, courts, hospitals, and the like.

To supplement the observations and impressions gained when in the company of Travellers and from informal encounters with settled Irish, I undertook a series of formal interviews. First I outlined the main institutions and spheres of activity within which interaction between Travellers and settled Irish takes place: in the legal system, health and welfare, organized religion, the Itinerant Settlement Movement, and economic exchanges. Interviews were then arranged with authorities and personnel from each of these spheres—justices, social workers, local police, nuns, priests, settlement committee members, doctors, nurses, and scrap metal merchants. In order to more systematically measure the settled community's attitudes toward Travellers, however, a methodology requiring more than participant observation and interviewing was needed. Eight months into the research, using the insights gained from participant observation, I designed a questionnaire which elicited information on the frequency and contexts within which settled Irish meet Travellers. Administered to 300 Irish men and women in Dublin and three rural areas, the questionnaire also explored settled Irish attitudes toward the Travellers.

Few cultural groups today are truly isolated; all are part of larger politico-economic systems. This becomes especially apparent when one is conducting research in urban areas. Dublin Travellers are dependent not only on the settled Irish community for support (in the form of social welfare benefits, charity, and trade) but also have social networks which extend to England. Many families Travel there for part of each year; others move to English cities to find conventional employment. Recognizing this I left for a three-week trip to England in January 1972, after being in the field for five months. By going to England I would see for myself where many Irish Travellers migrated and the conditions they lived under. My primary destination was Birmingham. There I visited relatives of families from Holylands who were living in the slums and interviewed social workers, probation officers, and the like to gain some understanding of the situation of Irish Travellers in English cities. This trip was especially important to me since moving to England and "passing" as working-class Irish is one of the major ways Irish Travellers are able to escape their stigmatized identity.

Neutral Observer or Advocate?

Urban research raises new dilemmas for the anthropologist. As George Foster and Robert Kemper point out in their essay ("Anthropological Fieldwork in Cities"), the groups studied by anthropologists in urban areas are often faced with major social problems. This was true of Travellers who not only lived in poverty and suffered discrimination at the hands of the settled community but also had to cope with a rapidly changing environment. The Itinerant Settlement Movement was actively seeking to settle them on official sites and in houses. At the time of our research the movement stressed integration with the settled community as the ultimate solution to the "itinerant problem." It was difficult not to become a spokesperson or advocate for Travellers' rights.

Travellers were then, and still are, an emotive subject in Ireland. The people working to help them wanted answers and reassurance that they were doing the right thing. Since I attended settlement committee meetings, I was often asked my opinion. I refrained as much as possible from giving advice to settlement workers during the course of my research. For one, I saw my role as that of a dispassionate observer. I also wished to avoid making ill-informed statements while I was still learning. What help I gave Travellers was generally on a smaller, more direct level such as reading medicine labels, filling out medical card and housing applications, interpreting legal notices which arrived in the mail, writing and reading personal letters to the families who received them, obtaining telephone numbers, and when necessary acting as a chauffeur.

Yet the pressures to give advice continually fought with my desire to remain neutral and simply carry out my fieldwork. By the end of the research, I had decided that I was sufficiently knowledgeable to make a few common-sense suggestions to settlement workers. I also felt I owed it to Travellers. To be truly dispassionate when working with people, particularly a stigmatized poverty group like Irish Travellers, is in some ways inhuman. Moreover, anthropologists are in a far better position than most outsiders to speak for the people they have lived among. At the urging of a prominent settlement worker we wrote an open letter to settlement committees, assessing their work from the Traveller point of view. Later we wrote a critique of the settlement movement for an Irish journal.[10] Our recommendations were modest and included urging the provision of serviced campsites for Travellers who wished to continue Travelling rather than focusing all efforts on permanent settlement. We strongly recommended that Travellers be involved actively in settlement work, particularly that they be given a voice in planning. In our letter to settlement workers we advised against being patronizing in their dealings with Travellers and against making promises that could not be kept. These suggestions were endorsed by some, resented or ignored by others. It is difficult to assess their impact. Since the time of our research, Travellers have become more involved in the settlement movement, but their numbers are extremely small and their involvement minimal. The official goal of the movement has also been moderated. The stress is now placed on settlement as an "alternative" to life on the road rather than the path to integration, and no campsites have been constructed for Travellers who wish to remain nomadic.

CONCLUSIONS

Urban fieldwork, like urban life itself, is varied and complex. Most anthropologists employ a wider range of research techniques in the city than are typically used in rural areas. In my own work, participant observation and interviewing were supplemented by a social survey and extensive archival research. Far more data sources are available in the city than in rural areas. Thus fieldwork in urban areas often requires considerable imagination in order to take advantage of the wealth of data collected by other people—government agents, journalists, and other social scientists—which are pertinent to the anthropologist's own interests. When one is conducting research in the city it is necessary to place the group under study in its larger politico-economic context. This is true of rural research as well, but is especially important in the city, where groups are less autonomous. This often requires research outside the bounded unit the anthropologist has chosen to study. I lived in a camp, yet I also worked outside it observing interactions between Travellers and settled Irish, interviewing various officials, and administering a questionnaire. I also spent time outside the country. In rural research the anthropologist, while aware of the influences of the larger system, is less likely to be drawn outside his community for actual research.

Yet urban research need not be any less intimate or personal than village fieldwork. The principal goal of anthropology, whether conducted in rural or urban areas, remains that of gaining an understanding of human society. It is based on the belief that only intense, day-to-day involvement with people over an extended period of time can provide real understanding. Thus while urban anthropologists may, and indeed should, make use of historical, demographic, and survey techniques, they should not do so at the expense of the insights gained from traditional methods such as participant observation. Even in cities anthropological fieldwork should remain an intensely personal experience, for only through in-depth interaction in small groups and intimate familiarity with the field setting can we truly understand other cultures.

NOTES

1. The field school was sponsored and organized by the Department of Anthropology, University of Pittsburgh and funded by the National Science Foundation.
2. "Traveller" and "Travelling People" are the terms most frequently used by the people themselves. "Tinker" is the term traditionally used by members of the settled community and the name by which most foreigners know the group. Within Ireland, however, it has derogatory connotations. "Itinerant" is the government designation and the term used by the news media.
3. See Crawford, M. H., and George Gmelch (1974).
4. Few of the results of my research with Dublin Travellers are presented here. The interested reader can consult other accounts if he or she wishes (see S. Gmelch 1974, 1975, and Gmelch and Gmelch 1974, 1976, 1978).
5. Financial support for my research was provided by a NDEA fellowship and by the Institute of Social and Economic Research of the Memorial University of Newfoundland.
6. The only study of Travellers then completed was a master's thesis in sociology. See McCarthy, Patricia Walsh (1971).
7. Even after moving into Holylands, we retained a room where we kept our typewriter, books, field notes, and the like, which we did not have space for in the wagon. It was also a place to take much needed baths, since Holylands had no bathing or toilet facilities.
8. Travellers living in campsites or houses in Athlone, Ballinasloe, Bray, Carlow, Clones, Dundalk, Ennis, Enniscorty, Galway City, Kilkenny, Loughrea, Monaghan, Roscrea, and Tuam were visited during the course of the year.
9. Traveller families were large; most households contained six or seven children. The fertility rate of 10.4 children per prolific woman over age forty is one of the highest recorded. This high fertility rate can be explained in part by the long reproductive careers of the women who marry young and continue reproducing until they are forty or forty-five years of age. At Holylands, three women had each given birth more than twenty times although not all infants survived childhood.
10. See Gmelch, Sharon Bohn, and Gmelch, George (1974).

NEW DIRECTIONS IN
URBAN ANTHROPOLOGY

Jack Rollwagen

Jack Rollwagen argues that anthropologists have for too long adopted an
"isolationist" perspective, naively looking for societies untouched by the
outside world and treating socieites that are integrated with the outside
world as isolated. They need instead to recognize the interdependency of the
world's cultures by adopting a truly "holistic" as well as an evolutionary
approach. But first they need to redefine some basic concepts. The special
problems of anthropologists working in cities, in Rollwagen's view, are not
really methodological, but theoretical and conceptual. Anthropologists must
search for the "most significant context" within which to relate their
particularistic cultural studies to the whole of the world's political-economic
system.

INTRODUCTION

The creation of a significant urban anthropology depends upon a reassessment
of some of the basic premises derived from cultural anthropology upon which
contemporary urban anthropology has been built. Perhaps the most fundamental of these is the premise that encourages the search for the quintessential
nature of a cultural system by its conceptual isolation from the other cultural
systems with which it is intertwined. The goal of traditional ethnography has
been to recreate the essence of a culture system at such a time in its evolution
before that essence was destroyed by acculturation to the larger outside world.
The major paradox of anthropological research during the past century of
anthropology's existence as an academic discipline is that anthropologists have
devoted so much of their energies to the search for societies which have not
been totally obliterated or totally transformed by the rapid expansion of the
world system, yet they have devoted only minimal attention to the nature of
that world system itself and to the processes of its evolution. As a result, the
entire frame of reference within which cultural anthropological research is
conducted has been skewed in the direction of conceptualizing cultural systems
in vacuo. Vocabulary, methodology, theory, frame of reference, and ultimately

SOURCE: Article written expressly for *Urban Life*.

the very perspectives which call them into being reflect this isolationist perspective.

That such a fundamental skewing could have arisen within a discipline that prides itself upon a broad overview of the evolution of human beings wherever they may be found and throughout time demonstrates the degree to which cultural anthropologists have departed from the foundations upon which general anthropology as a discipline evolved. Cultural anthropology has become too centrally a search for the quintessence of conceptually isolated cultural systems. Ethnography has become too centrally the description of such conceptually isolated systems. Ethnology has become too centrally the comparison of such conceptually isolated systems. If cultural anthropology is to move beyond this restrictive framework, a perspective that provides alternative vocabulary, methodology, theory, frames of reference, and perspectives must be developed. An evolutionary perspective on cultural anthropology provides the means through which the problems inherent in a conceptually isolationist cultural anthropology can be overcome. The use of an evolutionary perspective is particularly important in urban anthropology and the anthropology of complex societies since an evolutionary perspective provides the temporal and causal framework necessary for the study of urban cultural systems that are intricately interrelated to the world political economy.

The basis of an evolutionary perspective is in the concept of process. All cultural systems are in the process of continual adaptive interaction with their total environment. The overwhelming majority of cultural systems in the contemporary world are adaptively interacting with each other within one large, totally unified, and hierarchical system of cultural systems which may be termed "the world system" (see Rollwagen 1980). The evolution of this world system provides the context for the continuing evolution of the various cultural systems within it since each individual cultural system is an adaptive interaction with the whole. The evolution of contemporary cities, world urbanization, can most productively be examined within the evolution of this world system.[1]

The concept of a world system of cultural systems in adaptive interaction with one another provides the impetus for the exploration of causality at the systemic level. This world system perspective is absent from much of the research conducted in cultural anthropology. The varieties of colonialism and the heritage it bestowed upon the various cultural systems that it encapsulated or created become a major context for urbanization throughout the world during the past 500 years, both for the colonies and for the colonial powers. Research on contemporary rural-urban migration becomes more meaningful when migrations are perceived to be local evidences of the adaptive interaction of cultural systems to major political-economic processes in the evolution of the world system.

The massive rural-urban migrations in the United States that characterized the early years of the twentieth century, for example, are but one repercussion of the functioning of the world system. The lives of blacks and Chicanos in the cities of the United States are directly affected by the unemployment that results when American manufacturers contract with manufacturers in other areas of the world such as Korea, Poland, and Mexico for the production of goods more inexpensively produced there than in the United States. The economic support of such dense populations as are found in Hong Kong is dependent upon a world system that supplies those populations with work.

The world system approach provides a unified explanation of the worldwide forces and processes that shaped and are shaping our contemporary world. The industrial revolution and colonialism, for example, can be integrated into the world system approach as two inextricably interrelated aspects of the securing of raw materials and markets and the regulation of competition. Development and underdevelopment and their perpetuation are the results of the unequal distribution of access to power by the world's cultural systems. The current division of the world into two major military power blocks is a geopolitical attempt to preserve (or upset) a particular economic status quo of the hierarchy of the world cultural system. Changes in the functioning of the world system due to political-economic factors and/or innovations bring about redistributions in the functions performed by the various components of the system. Cities (populations of individual human beings involved in an enormous number of cultural systems that may be local or that may extend through transnational levels) provide and perform aspects of the functions necessary to keep the integrating and overarching world system functioning.[2]

The choice of a perspective or a frame of reference that emphasizes the search for the quintessence of culture in conceptually isolated cultural systems permits the avoidance of the very questions of political economy that have transformed the study of human beings in other social science disciplines and which could have provided extremely valuable frames of reference for anthropological research. The result of this divergence in choice between anthropology and the other social sciences is that anthropologists are in a less advantageous position than their fellow social scientists in terms of overall perspectives. Anthropologists, however, have the advantage of an approach that emphasizes intensive ethnographic fieldwork focusing upon a much greater range of cultural systems than other social scientists. Another advantage is that this research incorporates more sophisticated theoretical perspectives on emic and etic methodologies than do other disciplines (see Rollwagen 1980). The strengths that emic analyses have given to the study of those small-scale systems that anthropologists most frequently select for study must not blind us to the fact that both emic and etic analyses may be employed in the analysis of the world system that provides the context for those small-scale systems.

The theories used by anthropologists too often have emphasized the culture of the individual social system as if the culture of the individual system by itself accounted for the nature of that cultural system and the situation of the individuals within it. What is needed in cultural anthropology in general and in urban anthropology in particular is a reconsideration of the conceptual framework within which anthropological research is viewed. The isolationist perspective and its search for the quintessence of cultural systems must be set aside in favor of a perspective that recognizes the interdependency of the world's cultural systems and deals with this interdependency in the conduct of anthropological research. Pursuing this new direction in research will provide two immediate benefits: first, anthropological research will be more coordinate with research in the other social sciences without losing the valuable insights that its own tradition provides; second, the efficiency, power, and scope of the explanations presented will increase since those factors that are beyond the scope of the research in an isolationist perspective but which are conditional to the nature of that system are included as central determinants of the nature of the particular social system chosen for anthropological attention in an evolutionary world system approach.[3]

The world system approach and its value as a framework for urban anthropological research may be more apparent through the discussion of one topic with numerous correlates in urban anthropological research. The massive redistribution of economic resources that is the function of the world economy redistributes resources unevenly (see Hay 1977:85–86). Many of the cultural systems receive little in return for the participation of their members. André Gunder Frank's phrase "the development of underdevelopment" (Frank 1969) suggests that there is a skewing of the world system to the continuing benefit of some cultural systems and to the relative detriment of others. Similarly, the concepts of colonialism, neocolonialism, and internal colonialism indicate mechanisms that vary with the nature of the individual cultural systems involved but which are central to the nature of the world system and its functioning. Despite the plethora of studies by anthropologists of cultural systems that benefit least from the functioning of the world system (the studies of the poor, the peripheral, and the powerless), the majority of these studies are descriptive accounts of the functioning of the particular system chosen as object without a corresponding probing of the larger system, the functioning of which conditions the existence of that individual system.[4] Thus, there are descriptive accounts of once self-sufficient "primitives" whose increasingly rapid incorporation into the world system since 1500 A.D. has destroyed the very fabric of their cultures; there are descriptive accounts of peasants who are the suppliers of raw materials to the world economy and consumers of its manufactured products; there are descriptive accounts of the urban poor who eke out a living in a relationship marginal to the control of the means of production in their society but who remain essential to its functioning. The significance of much of this research is destroyed because the isolationist tradition in cultural anthropology places more emphasis on the search for ethnographic case studies than upon a search for cause or process in the larger system which produced the results that are depicted in those descriptive accounts.

Accepting the idea of a world system as a system of causality that affects all of the other cultural systems of the world does *not* imply that the "products" of the operation of a world cultural system must be identical. It is obvious that they are not. Mexican cities, Cuban cities, and Puerto Rican cities (to select examples from one geographical area of the world) are not ethnographically identical or even very similar because their participation in the world system is quite different. It is logical to expect, because the nature of the participation of individual cities in the functioning of the world system is different, that the nature of the cultural systems that comprise those cities and the cultural systems that link them to other systems in the hierarchy will be as varied as the functions that they fulfill.

A RECONCEPTUALIZATION OF TERMS

What is needed is a new direction in urban anthropological research. The skewing toward an isolationist perspective in cultural anthropological research must be compensated for by a return to the holistic perspectives embodied in general anthropology and by a reintegration of anthropology into the mainstream of social science. A major step toward the reestablishment of a nonisolationist perspective in urban anthropology is a reconsideration of the implications of the very terms that are the building blocks of the perspectives with which anthropologists view their subject matter. The isolationist perspective has produced a set of definitions that support an isolationist viewpoint. If anthropologists are to begin to deal with cities, nations, and the world system, the terms that embody the perspectives with which they approach their study must facilitate their objectives and not militate against them. An evolutionary perspective suggests definitions that have repercussions in the methodology, the theory, and the frames of reference used in research. A consideration of some of the most important of these definitions will indicate what some of the implications of the evolutionary perspective are for urban anthropology.

The most important term for urban anthropologists and for anthropologists in general is the term "culture." Operationally, the term "culture" in cultural anthropology has become too closely tied with the unit of "society." Thus, societies have a culture but units smaller than societies, units within societies, are said to have a "subculture" of that society. The implication, of course, is that the proper relationship between culture and society is one of exact equivalency. Units smaller than a society have something less than culture and there can be nothing larger than a society because there can be nothing larger than culture. A reconsideration of what *culture* is and how it is generated indicates the restrictiveness of this kind of definition and how it is in accord with the isolationist perspective. The implication of studies too numerous to mention is that humans are constantly interpreting their world, creating a mental world within which they exist. Although each individual being does this, groups of human beings in association support one another in the elaboration of interpretations and in the application of value judgments to support such interpretations. This elaboration of interpretations occurs in all human groups, regardless of the number of individuals involved and regardless of the function of the group. Every individual belongs to numerous groups, each of which has a set of evolving interpretations of its world. Each set influences the interpretations of the members of its group as well as the interpretations of members of other groups with which it comes into contact. Couples who live together elaborate a set of interpretations of their world; members of voluntary associations elaborate a set of interpretations that guide the members of that association; members of all levels of government elaborate a set of interpretations with which to deal with the problems they face; the list is endless in number and variety. The world in this view is filled with culture-generating groups of human beings whose membership is endlessly overlapping. "Culture" is thus not the sole property of a level of human beings called "society" but rather a *process* of creation and interpretation that occurs whenever two or more human beings interact for any extended period of time.

Accepting the perspective that culture is a process of cognitive elaboration and interpretation that human beings engage in continuously as individuals in all of their associations facilitates the comprehension of an infinite set of culture-elaborating units different from societies in form and function. The participation of individuals in the elaboration of interpretations and their agreement to participate in the application of these elaborations in some mutually understood manner are the bases of the formation of a culture-evolving system. These systems may be smaller than societies (that is, included within societies), but they can also cross cut the boundaries of those conceptual systems that we term "societies." Indeed, some are conceptually above the level of society. Some examples of cultural systems that operate beyond the boundaries of individual societies, over a much larger territory than any individual society, and, in a sense, above the level of individual societies are the United Nations, the Red Cross, the Roman Catholic Church, the World Bank, and General Motors. Each of these cultural systems is an organization with tremendous impact upon millions of people throughout the world.

The addition to this list of the world system, a political-economic cultural system elaborated and accepted by human beings throughout the world over the past 500 years, is simply a logical extension of the culture-elaborating process discussed above. This system does not have at its base a corporation or a charter as in the case of the examples given above, but its operation, although diffuse, is no less formal. The world system is a cultural system of elaborations and interpretations that structures the nature of the major economic transactions of the world and thereby influences the nature of the other functionally related cultural systems. The perception of such a system as the largest unitary cultural system yet devised in human evolution, a cultural system that operates within, above, and often in spite of individual nations, societies, and governments (but most frequently with the compliance of the national elite), does not generally constitute a basic premise for the conduct of research in urban anthropology. My position in this paper is that urban anthropologists must accept the existence of such a cultural system, the operation of which provides the primary context for all of those other cultural systems selected for research.

This approach has several advantages over the position taken by the isolationists and their use of the concept of culture. It renders meaningless the opposition between "macrostructure" and "culture" suggested by Hannerz (1969:179–180) and others. Macrostructure *is* cultural and therefore cannot be opposed to it. "Culture" is a term that refers to the varied cognitive systems in the constant process of elaboration by human beings as members of an infinite set of groups with overlapping membership, cognitive systems that structure and influence the total range of behavior of the participants in those cognitive systems.

Political systems (for example, governments) are one kind of cultural elaboration, one kind of cultural form. Economic systems (for example, mercantilism or capitalism), no matter how large, are also cultural elaborations. The contemporary world system, a political-economic cultural system elaborated by millions of individuals over the past 500 years throughout the world and integrating nations into its fabric along with other cultural units down to the smallest cultural system, is the most complex cultural system yet devised by human beings. It is the system which structures the lives of nearly all human beings in all of the contemporary societies and in all areas of the world. It is logical to assume that the functioning of the world system influences the nature of even the smallest cultural system in cities, for example, since the cities and the nations in which these cities exist are intricately interconnected with that world system. The recent example of the changes in the supply and price of oil on the world market and its effects on all of the world's cultural systems is only the best-known example of a set of political-economic relationships structured by the world system that effects the lives of individuals in every cultural system of the world.

This reconceptualization of the concept of culture to accord with the existence of a political economy that is worldwide in scope with ramifications into every other cultural system necessitates a redefinition of the concept of "holism." In a world that is united into one cultural whole by a world system of political economy, that which becomes the cultural whole is the totality of the participating cultural units involved, regardless of their form or function. The growing interest by social scientists in the history of the evolution of the world political-economic system provides anthropologists with an expanding and absolutely essential framework within which to conduct their ethnographic and ethnological research. The incorporation of the general political-economic frameworks provided by the other social sciences into anthropological research will result in mutual benefits. Anthropologists will benefit from the integration of anthropological research into the mainstream of the research in the other social sciences, which have devoted a considerable amount of their research effort to an exploration of the world system. In return, anthropologists can provide to the other social sciences through the emic and etic research which they have evolved the descriptive and analytic case studies of cultural systems that are so necessary if the complexity and diversity of the functioning of the world system is to be understood in its endless variety of manifestations.

With the increasing growth in interrelationships that integrate individual cultural systems throughout the world into one world cultural system, the cause-and-effect relationships that exist will become increasingly apparent. Only an approach that is holistic in the world system sense can expect to explain why cultural systems at all levels are as they are.[5] The use of the holistic approach as a concept in studying the cultural systems of cities in the world system is essential in explaining the functioning of those cultural systems in any significant sense. This position is in direct contrast to that of Hannerz, who suggests that "The holistic culture concept has a long and venerable tradition in anthropology, of course, but as a tool of dynamic analysis it is of very limited utility" (1969:179–180). The process of world urbanization during the past 500 years can in no way be separated from the evolution of the world system. Every cultural system in the contemporary world is directly conditioned by the nature and functioning of the world system. To regard the holistic approach (in which the "whole" is the world system) as having limited utility is not only isolationist but productive of sterile analysis.

The exhortation to study a chosen cultural system holistically in urban anthropology carries with it the same restriction of relativity that is inherent in any anthropological study. One simply cannot study "everything." But that is not what is implied in a "holistic" approach, just as it is not implied in ethnography that one describes "everything" about a cultural system. A holistic approach simply suggests that any aspect of a cultural system that is chosen for study be examined in terms of that which forms its pertinent or significant context in the larger system of which it is a part. Since the context of any one aspect of a cultural system is composed of sets of cultural systems integrated in various ways into one whole, the problem is to discover those factors that are *most* pertinent to the explanation of the *central features* of the cultural system being studied. The central features of a cultural system will vary according to the cultural system chosen for study, of course. A relativistic definition of a holistic approach to cultural systems would attempt to sort out "the most significant context" for the interpretation of the particular cultural system chosen for study from that which is less significant. Any critical analysis of the process of social science would necessarily conclude that choice and perspective are fundamental aspects of social science. The concept of the world system in studying the holistic context of cities and their cultural systems provides a framework for anthropological research that avoids the limitations inherent in an isolationist approach.

The term "context" has become increasingly more evident in urban anthropological studies. Although urban anthropologists find the concept an important one and are quite willing to use it in their research, the tradition of "absolute relativism" still persists in anthropology. In the framework of "absolute relativism," each society/culture must be considered as if it existed in a universe unto itself. That "absolute relativism" is a product of the isolationist tradition in cultural anthropology is quite apparent. The thread of the argument in this paper, however, is that the isolation of societies/cultures in the world, if it was ever a significant actuality, has long since been replaced by an amalgam of cultural systems unified by a common political-economic cultural framework. The context that is the ultimate context for the functioning of all cultural systems in the contemporary world is thus the world system. Ethnographic and ethnological research which does not indicate the relationship between the operation of particular cultural systems and the world system cannot expect to indicate the nature of process since it cannot approach the question of cause.

The approach suggested in this paper also permits the resolution of what seems to be a recurrent question in urban anthropology: how can anthropology approach the study of such large-scale systems as cities? This question, among others, is expressed by Basham (1978:6):

> In moving to larger-scale societies, anthropologists have been forced to reconsider the benefits and limitations of the traditional methodology. In the past, ethnographic work has depended upon the development of close rapport with a relatively few informants from whom anthropologists have attempted to construct descriptions of entire cultures. Such an approach can work quite well in communities of a few hundred or even a few thousand people. But what happens to anthropological methods in cities of tens of thousands or even millions of people?

It is apparent that this problem is not a methodological one but a theoretical and conceptual one. In conducting research on cities, anthropologists must utilize both emic and etic approaches on a number of kinds and levels of cultural systems. If one uses an emic approach, research may be conducted on the nature of any number of cultural systems that are incorporated into the hierarchy of cultural systems that, taken with the other cultural systems that link it to the systems beyond it, make up the city. The nature of these individual cultural systems as well as the nature of the city taken as a whole may be examined through the perspectives of the participants in these individual cultural systems. By contrast, urban anthropologists bring etic approaches to the study of individual cultural systems within a city and to the study of a city as a whole through their knowledge of and use of theory and data from the social sciences. Thus, their knowledge of how the political economy of a city that they have chosen to study operates gives them a distinct advantage in providing the context for the functioning of the social systems within it; their knowledge of the functioning of the world system gives them an advantage in comparing the functioning of the city chosen for study with some other city or cities. These comparative approaches must become a much greater part of urban anthropological research. In short, the emic and etic approaches in combination with one another allow both the investigation of diversity and the contextualization that are necessary to study any kind of cultural system selected for study, from those that are very small to those that are very large. In terms of population, cities are very large. But the fact that they are composed of numerous kinds of cultural systems arranged into a hierarchy of power allows the exploration of individual cultural systems through emic approaches to research on the nature of that cultural system itself, through exploring emically the nature of the view that participants hold of other cultural systems in a city (or of a city taken as a whole), and through etic approaches to all of a city's cultural systems. This approach permits a complete range of explorations, from the study of Goffmanesque kinds of impression management of cultural systems by their participants (Goffman 1959) to the use of census data. In fact, an evolutionary approach utilizing the concept of an infinite number of evolving cultural systems united into one world system is integrative of much of what have been regarded as "different" approaches to research.

SUMMARY

The suggestions incorporated in this paper do not imply that all cultural systems should be regarded in research as identical products of one massively unitary system, as Lynch (1979:2) seems to fear. Indeed, to the contrary, the implication of the world system perspective is that the diversity of the parts of which the system is composed allow the system to function as a whole (see Wallerstein 1976:230). The world system, after all, is a cultural system like other cultural systems; that is, a set of ideas and behaviors accepted by and interpreted by a collectivity of individuals. The collectivity in this case is the total human population of the world that participates in the world system in all of its manifestations. These individuals participate in an infinite set of continuously generated cultural systems that are integrated into the world system. Some individuals and some cultural systems are in effective control of resources that are significant in the power relationships that structure the world system hierarchically. Others are relatively less powerful. Some are in effective control only of their physical and mental energies within a framework that assigns such resources little value. The distribution of power within the world system is uneven, both among societies and among other cultural systems and the individuals who participate in them. Power often becomes redistributed among the cultural systems of the world, as the recent world petroleum crisis has demonstrated. The diversity of the bases of power within the world system and the diversity of the physical locations of this power, as well as the constant factor of change, provide ample opportunity for anthropological research. Anthropologists must incorporate the existence of unity as well as the existence of diversity into their frameworks for research and analysis.[6] They must reintegrate their discipline and the other social sciences in the exploration of an evolving world system and begin the emic and etic research that will build an ethnography and ethnology of the world system.

NOTES

1. There is, in a sense, a question whether there should be an "urban" anthropology. This question is really at least three questions rolled into one: first, whether there is any value to anthropology in choosing to study cities; second, whether there can be a study of cities and their cultural systems apart from the study of the larger systems in which they exist (that is, whether anthropologists should proceed to the anthropology of complex societies and not elect to study cities as a specific subject matter); third, whether anthropology as a discipline has anything to contribute to the study of cities in comparison to (a) the other social science disciplines, which are already heavily involved in the study of cities, or (b) some to-be-evolved entity entitled "urban studies" (see, for example, Leeds 1972:4–5).

   The position taken in this paper is as follows: first, cities and their cultural systems are appropriate subjects of research and necessary ones if anthropologists are to fulfill anthropology's commitment to study human beings wherever they may be found in order to understand the nature of human beings and their cultural systems. Second, cities and their cultural systems cannot be understood apart from the cultural matrix in which they are embedded. Therefore any "urban" anthropology is a result of a conscious choice to select particular kinds of cultural systems which were not extensively studied by anthropologists earlier and to examine them within the context of the world's hierarchy of cultural systems (herein called "the world system") which conditions their natures. Third, anthropology's emic and etic approaches to the study of cultural systems (see specifically Harris's definitions of emic and etic [1968:571, 575]) provide the perspective and data that are essential for the explication of how cultural systems function, a perspective that complements those provided by other social sciences.

2. As some examples of anthropologists who are conceptualizing research within what I would call an evolutionary world system framework, I would cite Epstein (1972), Gugler and Flanagan (1978), Jorgensen (1971), Rhoades (1978), and Wolfe (1979).

3. Any discussion of the literature from the other social sciences that would be pertinent to the creation of a world system approach for urban anthropology would be a major undertaking, a task much beyond the scope of this article. The social science literature pertinent to the development of a world system perspective is increasing rapidly and is transforming the nature of much of the research in the social sciences. Although a great deal of this literature is Marxian, neo-Marxian, or is considered to be such by those who do not find themselves in sympathy with it, one does not have to be totally committed to Marxism as a "true believer" in order to recognize the value of the framework provided by Marx and his proponents. As S. M. Miller (quoted in Walton 1979:8) points out:

> By "political economy" I do not mean to center only on what are considered to be Marxian analyses, but rather to focus attention on the broader political and economic setting and implications of the issues with which we deal. Obviously, the various Marxian approaches have much to offer but one need not be a Marxist nor a radical to be able to think about broad influences on the development and course of what gets defined or undefined, treated or untreated, as social problems. What is important is that we avoid narrow frames of reference and that we do not neglect broader issues of how political and economic forces affect daily life.

4. The cultural systems which are the subject of anthropological research have often been peripheral to power in what I am calling "the world system." The instances in which such cultural systems demand power are not rare at the local levels of the hierarchy of power, but the instances in which the poor and disenfranchised gain any significant power in the world system are exceedingly rare. When they do occur at any significant level in the world system they are termed "revolutions." It is apparent, however, that all such revolutions have failed if the intent of their participants can be construed to create a cultural system without a hierarchy of power or one which was not subject to the hierarchy of power that is the world system.

5. The acceptance of an infinite set of cultural systems overlapping in social space and continually changing through time because of the participation of the individuals who compose them in the constant process of cultural elaboration appears to be difficult for anthropologists. One of the basic "premises" in cultural anthropology has been to search for an idealized "steady state" in cultural systems. The search for a quintessential "time before things changed" in anthropological research is a search for a mythical past when it concerns the majority of cultural systems in the world during the past 500 years. As André Gunder Frank notes:

> A mounting body of evidence suggests, and I am confident that future historical research will confirm, that the expansion of the capitalist system over the past centuries effectively and entirely penetrated even the apparently most isolated sectors of the underdeveloped world. Therefore the economic, political, social, and cultural institutions and relations we now observe there are the products of the historical development of the capitalist system no less than are the seemingly more modern or capitalist features of the national metropoles of these underdeveloped countries (1969:5).

The isolationist position in anthropology which calls for the conceptual isolation of whatever cultural unit is chosen for study, whether it be primitive band or urban ethnic group, has its parallel in other social sciences. Goering, for example, contrasts two paradigms for sociological research on cities:

> The Chicago School has assumed that cities and constituent communities are clearly defined spatial entities, whose autonomy is often assumed. This assumption involves a curious hypostatization of the city. As Clark says: "Practically no social unit in industrial societies is entirely autonomous, but for analytical purposes, various units may be conceived as distinct systems" (Clark 1968:85). The city is conceptually and empirically bounded by the (increasingly) arbitrary boundaries of the political city. Given the assumption of relative autonomy, the Chicago School urbanists then pursue the laws of urbanism and urbanization by which "the city" is presumed to operate and develop.

> The Marxian argument begins with the assumption that cities have long ago lost most of their putative independence and have become mere dependent creatures of regional and national political and economic forces. The economic linkages within the corporate economy—capitalism—are central for understanding the loss of autonomy and vulnerability of cities and urban regions (1978:79).

Thus, it is not only anthropologists who have adopted a strategy of research that excludes those factors which are essential to the explanation of the nature of the cultural systems chosen for study. Any research method which avoids confronting the question of cause in the description or analysis of a cultural system will be less valuable than one that does. Anthropologists must accept the functioning of the world system as directly related to the functioning of any cultural system that they may choose for study. Urban anthropologists, regardless of the level of the cultural system which they choose for investigation, must also conceptualize their research within the framework of the functioning of the world system in order to explain the functioning of that cultural system at any significant level.

6. The acceptance of diversity and its study has always been the strength and joy of anthropology. The ability to accept a unity that recognizes diversity has always been its weakness. The major stumbling block to the acceptance of a unity incorporating diversity has always been that unity seemed to require an approach that implied the homogenization of the constituent parts. In this regard, the concept of "culture" when applied to complex societies such as the United States, for example, too often seems to require a degree of similarity in the participants that does not accord with the research findings. The skepticism with which many anthropologists will regard the world system concept will probably be based to a great extent upon the fear that it will tend to treat all cultural systems as if they must be alike or moving toward a homogeneity. Anthropologists will fear that they must give up the joy of diversity in order to come to some understanding of the whole. This is *not* a requirement for the acceptance of an evolutionary model *per se* but rather only what some people have implied in their own particular interpretations of evolutionary models. The very basis of the world system model is in the unity of the world political economy which is predicated upon the integrated functioning of a necessary diversity of the constituent cultural systems of the world. It is the treatment of this diversity and how individual cultural systems are integrated into the whole that is the subject matter and approach that will be the most productive of insight in urban anthropology in the coming years.

Part Three
Migration and the Adaptation of Migrants to City Life

By 1985 more than thirty percent of the world's population were living in cities of more than 100,000 inhabitants. The growth of urban centers has been due in large measure to the cityward migration of rural peoples. Since World War II the increase in urban migration has been phenomenal. Mexico City is one of the most striking examples. From 1960 to 1985, the population of the metropolitan area grew from less than 5 million to nearly 15 million, with cityward migrants making up over forty percent of the increase. The flow continues today at a rate of about 15,000 new migrants each month – an average of 500 new persons each day. All new arrivals need food and water, shelter, employment, and schooling for their children.

Anthropology has given much attention to migration, as have some of the other social sciences, notably sociology, demography, and economics. Indeed, more urban anthropologists have conducted research on rural-urban migration than on any other single topic (Gmelch and Zenner 1978). There are several specialized journals devoted solely to migration studies, such as *International Migration Review* and *International Migration,* though they cross the lines of several disciplines. There are also a half-dozen anthologies on the topic and a similar number of bibliographies which list more than 2,500 individual titles dealing with migration. In fact there is so much literature that "many social scientists believe that migration has achieved status as an independent field *sui generis*" (Kemper 1979:10).

Most anthropological studies of migration have been of rural peasants or tribesmen moving to industrialized cities, usually within their own society but also internationally. There the peasants obtain unskilled or semiskilled work and frequently live among their own kind—coethnics and often covillagers. While peasant migrants of this type comprise the vast bulk of rural-to-urban movements, there are also other groups in the migration stream. These groups include merchants, students, small town elites moving to larger cities, and even some upper-class landowners. These middle- and upper-strata migrants, whose migration behavior and adaptation in the city tend to be individual-oriented, have not been the concern of many anthropologists. Some reasons for this neglect will be discussed in the introductions to parts five and six.

EARLY STUDIES

Early studies of migration focused on mass movements, particularly the trans-atlantic movement of people from Europe to the New World in the late nineteenth and early twentieth centuries (Jackson 1969; Kasdan 1970). In analyzing the causes of migration, the larger economic and social forces were stressed. Comparatively little attention was given to the characteristics and motives of individual migrants or to selectivity—why in the same circumstances some individuals choose to leave while others remain at home.

Once the migrants were in the city, researchers focused on problems of adjustment rather than the successful ways in which most migrants adapted. In large part this focus was the result of prevailing views about the differences between rural and urban society. The pioneering writings of Louis Wirth and Robert Redfield, for example, described urban society as disorganized, secular, and individualistic. This led observers to expect that cityward migration by rural peoples would be disruptive and would cause social disorganization, culture conflict, and even anomie and alienation. Oscar Lewis's (1952) landmark study "Urbanization Without Breakdown" was the first study to question this view. Among his Tepoztecan migrants, urbanization did not result in weakened kinship bonds, social disorganization, change in religious beliefs, or alienation. Lewis's findings were corroborated by Janet Abu-Lughod's study of Egyptian migrants in Cairo ("Migrant Adjustment to City Life"). The Egyptian migrants had to make some adjustments to nonagricultural wage labor and to reduced space caused by the high population density of the city, but otherwise no major shift in behavior occurred. They readily adapted to the city with little disruption of their traditional ways.

A NEW APPROACH

Since the 1950s more attention has been given to the individual migrant: to decision-making processes and the strategies migrants develop to cope with city life. Today's migrant is less likely to be viewed as a pawn automatically responding to large structural forces than as a volitional individual who understands his situation and alternatives open to him and who rationally chooses among them (Kasdan 1970). Take the example of a poor Italian (or Spanish,

Yugoslav, Turkish, Greek) peasant whose lands are not large enough or fertile enough to make a satisfactory living. He does not blindly migrate to a new land; rather he has a number of alternatives to consider: (1) he may choose to continue working his land as best he can; (2) he may be able to remain at home while commuting to a nearby town to work; (3) he may move to a large city, leaving his wife and family at home but returning on weekends; (4) he may move his entire family to the city and give up his village home; or (5) he may leave the country altogether and go to a city in one of the northern, industrialized nations such as Germany or Switzerland to work, either going alone or taking his wife and family with him. Not all of these alternatives, of course, are open to every rural villager, but there are nearly always a number of possibilities to be considered. Hence migration must be viewed as a process in which individuals consciously change their own situations in search of a more rewarding life.

The decision to migrate is usually based on a complex and careful consideration of many variables. It is reached when the anticipated advantages of life in the city outweigh the strength of social bonds at home and the individual's attachment to the predictable and familiar. The attractions of the city must overcome the fears and insecurities associated with moving to an unfamiliar and alien environment in which the migrant must start a new life (Simic 1973). Only in extreme cases of hardship such as famine, genocide, or war (as in the saturation bombing of the Vietnamese countryside) is migration motivated by a single factor.

THE PUSH-PULL FRAMEWORK

In describing the underlying factors that enter into the decision to migrate, anthropologists often speak in terms of "push" and "pull." Push factors are the conditions or attributes of the rural homeland which induce individuals to leave. Common among them are soil erosion, low crop yields, land shortage, disputes, and political factionalism. Pull factors are the attractions of the city which draw or pull individuals to it. These include jobs, educational opportunities, conveniences, the excitement and lure of "city lights," and hopes of success. Since few migrants have prior experience living in cities, pull factors often tend to be stereotypes of city life and what it has to offer. Not surprisingly then, expectations are sometimes inaccurate or unrealistic. Although the push-pull framework has been criticized as being simplistic, it is nevertheless a useful framework for categorizing the range of factors encouraging migration.

ADAPTIVE STRATEGIES

Once in the city the migrant must find a place to live, get a job, and develop a network of friends to satisfy his emotional and social needs. Of great concern to urban anthropologists are the strategies migrants adopt to do these things. These strategies may be *individualistic,* in that the migrant may depend primarily upon his own resources and initiative, or they may be *group-oriented*, with the migrant relying upon others—usually kinsmen or fellow villagers—for assistance (Graves and Graves 1974). A migrant seeking housing, for example, may find accommodation on his own or may rely upon kinsmen to assist him. Often migrants who do the latter reside with their kinsmen for several months until suitable accommodation can be obtained. Similarly, in establishing friendships the migrant may seek contacts with other members of the wider urban society or he may choose relationships solely from among his own kind—kinsmen, fellow villagers, or coethnics.

Perhaps the best example of group-oriented strategy is the voluntary association. This is the subject of Kenneth Little's essay. Comprised of members of the same ethnic group or even individuals from the same home village, voluntary associations assume many of the functions that were performed by kinship groups in the migrants' home villages. As Little demonstrates, the voluntary association—much like guilds in preindustrial cities—gives the migrant a sense of belonging; it also provides financial aid in times of need, and organizes dances and other recreational activities. Village-of-origin mutual aid societies are found among the Egyptian migrants in Cairo studied by Abu-Lughod. In short, such associations provide a strong support group which eases the migrant into the urban world.

Similarly, squatter settlements are a group response to the shortage of low-cost housing in cities in much of the developing world, particularly Latin America. Through careful organization, migrants as well as longer-term urbanites have successfully invaded government-owned lands and constructed their own rent-free settlements (Mangin 1967, Safa 1974). In time the squatters are often able to secure title to their homesites as well as cajole the government into providing electricity and piped water. In some cities squatter settlements are so numerous that their populations comprise a major segment of the total urban population. The genesis of squatter settlements in the Brazilian capital, Brazilia, is examined by David Epstein in part five.

Most migrants develop and utilize both individual and group-oriented strategies. However, individualistic strategies tend to be more typical among migrants in Western society and particularly among better educated, middle-class migrants who have a better understanding of how the urban system operates. Strategies in which the migrant relies upon kinsmen and fellow ethnics for help in getting established in the city are most common among tribal and peasant migrants in the cities of developing countries. Examples, however, can also be found in the United States, such as migrants from the hollows of Appalachia who rely heavily upon their kinsmen already residing in midwestern industrial cities to help them find jobs and get a foothold in the city (Brown and Schwarzweller 1971).

MIGRATION INTENTIONS

Not all migrants who arrive in the city remain permanently. Some return home; others move on to other cities or emigrate to a new country. Many persons moving to the city go as *temporary* migrants who do not intend to stay. They migrate only with the intention of accomplishing a specific objective, usually saving a sum of money. In some societies the dominant migration pattern is a circular one in which individuals move back and forth periodically between their rural homes and urban centers. This pattern, known as "circular migration," is essentially a movement between two economic systems, with the villager leaving the rural area where resources are limited for the city where he will obtain a wage-earning job. While the migrant may spend much time in the city and develop a network of social ties there, his primary identification remains with his home village. Once enough money has been earned to satisfy his consumption needs at home, he returns home and remains there either permanently or until economic need propels him once again to the city in search of work.

There are also migrants who intend or at least hope to make the city their permanent home but are forced to return, often because of family circumstances, such as the need to look after ill or elderly parents, or because of a failure to find work. Still others may return because they cannot adapt. This is more often the case in international migration where persons are moving not only from a rural to an urban setting but to an unknown setting in a new society with language, customs, and people which are strange to them. Unless they have kinsmen or belong to a voluntary association or some other support group, the psychic pain of being separated from close friends and the familiarity and security of the home environment may be too much to bear.

The return movement of Spanish migrants from German industrial cities to their rural homelands in southern Spain is the subject of Robert Rhoades's essay. He identifies several types of migration streams, each one generating its own unique return pattern. While the essays by Kemper, Simić, Gmelch, and Abu-Lughod are mainly concerned with the impact of the city on the migrants, Rhoades explores the impact of return migrants on their home communities, with special attention to the role they might play in the development of their homelands.

AN ALTERNATIVE APPROACH: MACRO-LEVEL ANALYSIS

Before concluding this introduction, it is important to call attention to the work of a few scholars who are attempting macro-level analyses of migration. Their approach, sometimes termed the "historical-structural" (as opposed to the micro-level "culturalist" approach adopted in this book), focuses on the *contexts* of population movements. Migration is seen as the dependent variable in a larger process involving an economic imbalance between the highly urban-industrialized societies and regions of the world and rural, largely agrarian societies and regions. This perspective is found in varying forms, including the "dependency theory" and the "internal colonialism" and "center-periphery" models (Kemper 1979:10).

The problem for future migration scholars will be how best to integrate the micro-level analyses, such as those of the anthropologists represented in this reader, with the macro-level analyses of some anthropologists, political economists, and others. As Robert Kemper states, the issue is "how can we cross the 'frontier' between the *culturalist* and *historical-structuralist* territories without, on the one hand, sacrificing the fine-grained ethnographic fieldwork among individuals and small groups or, on the other, ignoring the important national/international forces which influence the migration process. . . ." (1979:10).

George Gmelch

MIGRANT ADJUSTMENT TO CITY LIFE: THE EGYPTIAN CASE

Janet Abu-Lughod

In this excellent case study Janet Abu-Lughod examines the adjustment of
Egyptian villagers to life in Cairo. The author questions the notion that
rural migrants must radically change their behavior and personality to
adjust to city life. The migrants do change in response to the demands of
the new, nonagricultural work, to smaller houses with less outdoor space,
and so forth. But the urban milieu does not require for these migrants a
major shift in identification and behavior from the rural or folk pattern to
the urban pattern—from one end of the folk-urban continuum to the
other. This phenomenon is explained by the fact that Cairo is very rural
in character despite its size. Abu-Lughod's study also raises questions
about the validity of Wirth's theory of urbanism for cities of the
developing world, in which a large percentage of the urban populations
are comprised of rural migrants. These cities do not exhibit many of the
classic urban traits.

One of the most dramatic phenomena of recent decades has been the urbanization of large segments of the world's peasant folk, particularly in rapidly industrializing countries. In few places has this urban growth been as vigorous as
in Egypt—at first spasmodically in the 1940's stimulated by a war economy,
then more gradually in the 1950's in response to the indigenous demands of a
developing economy[1]—until, at present, one out of every three Egyptians lives
in an urban place having 20,000 or more persons.

Migration from rural areas has been chiefly responsible for Egypt's soaring
rate of urbanization, even though natural increase, still as high in cities as in
rural areas, accounts for half the annual rate of urban growth. This migration
has favored the very largest cities of the country, bypassing those of moderate
and small size. Therefore there has been a tendency for cities to conform to the
principle of allometric growth, with high growth rates correlated positively
with rank as to size.[2] Indeed, for the last three decades, cities of highest rank
size have sustained average rates of growth which are more than twice the rate
of natural increase, while smaller towns, of between 20,000 to 30,000, have
failed to keep pace with rates of natural increase, i.e., have actually experienced
net losses of population.

SOURCE: "Migrant Adjustment to City Life: The Egyptian Case" in *The American
Journal of Sociology*, XLVII (1961):22–32. © 1961 by the University of Chicago. Reprinted by permission of The University of Chicago Press.

Migration, then, has had its prime impact on the largest cities, and the towering giant of Cairo, with a present population of close to three and one-half million, has been the most important recipient of the newly urbanizing population. This paper, therefore, concentrates on the adjustment of Egyptian villagers to life in Cairo, inquiring into its nature and exploring the elements which mediate any dramatic transition between rural and urban life.

THE RURAL AND THE URBAN IN CAIRO

Sociologists studying the adjustment of rural migrants to city life have been trapped in a dilemma of their own making. Even after the replacement of the rural-urban dichotomy by the more reasonable continuum, the sequence and dynamics of adjustment have still been deduced as though the dichotomy were valid; the unconscious assumptions have led many students to an oversimplified image of a one-way adjustment of rural man to a "stable" urban culture, despite lip service paid to feedback and mutual assimilation.

This adjustment is assumed to be disorganizing in the extreme. Physically, it is envisioned as drastically altering the dwelling, changing the accouterments within the home as well as the neighborhood surrounding it, transforming the appearance and dress of the migrant himself. Economically, the migrant is seen as adjusting to changed occupations and rhythms of work, to a new division of labor within the family, and to different relationships between work associates. Socially, it is hypothesized that the migrant weans himself from the intimacy of the village to the harsh superficial relationships inherent in urban life, adapts himself from the homogeneous peer group to the diversified reference groups of the city, and suffers a reduction in proximity-centered social life and neighboring. Culturally, he is assumed to undergo a revolution in motivation, values, and ideology. In short, according to the rural-urban dichotomy, a hypothetical villager is to be dropped, unarmed, into the heart of urban Cairo to assimilate or perish. He is to be granted no cushions to soften his fall.

It is our contention here that the dichotomy is as invalid in Egypt and in many other newly awakening nations as it is in the Western nations, but for a somewhat different reason. In these cases the dichotomy has not yet sharpened due to the continual ruralization of the cities.[3]

Only one fact need be cited to support this allegation: More than one-third of the permanent residents of Cairo have been born outside the city, that is, one out of every three Cairenes is a migrant of one sort or another, and the overwhelming majority are from the rural hinterlands within Egypt.[4] To speak about one-way assimilation to a stable urban culture when so large a minority comes equipped with needs and customs of rural origin is folly. Numbers alone should alert us to the probability that migrants are shaping the culture of the city as much as they are adjusting to it.

These rural migrants are drawn from two extreme types which face basically different problems of adjustment. One type, qualitatively the cream but numerically the less significant, consists of bright youths who migrate in search of education or wider opportunities. These have both the drive and the facility for rapid assimilation into the culture of the city. This paper ignores their real but different problems. The second type, referred to here as the "non-selective" migrants, are drawn primarily from the have-nots of the village. Numerically dominant, they are as much driven from the village by dearth of land and opportunity as they are attracted to the city.[5] With a lower capacity for assimilation, they tend to build for themselves within the city a replica of the culture they left behind. They are the subject of this article.

A second circumstance which has kept Cairo more rural than would be expected is the continual incorporation into the built-up metropolitan region of pre-existing villages. While some of these villages go back into history, such as Mataria, the pharaonic town of On (Greek, Heliopolis), some are of fairly recent origin. It would take a keen observer indeed to distinguish between a village within Cairo and one located miles beyond its fringes. In fact, the city of Cairo contains within its boundaries an extensive rural-urban fringe which stands juxtaposed against modern villas on the west, intervenes on the alluvial flats between urban Misr Qadima and suburban Maadi on the south, dips deep into the very heart of the city from the north, and, in somewhat different fashion, encircles Medieval Cairo on its eastern border. There are vast quarters within the mosaic of Cairo where, physically and socially, the way of life and the characteristics of residents resemble rural Egypt.

While full proof of this contention lies outside the scope of this paper,[6] a few figures may illustrate this point. High literacy is associated in Egypt with urbanism. In the largest urban centers, literacy rates in 1947 ranged between 40 and 45 per cent, while smaller towns and villages had literacy rates of under 25 per cent. Yet, in one out of eight census tracts in Cairo, the literacy rate was less than 25 per cent. As might be expected, the rural-urban fringe had the lowest literacy rates (5 and 7 per cent), but, surprisingly enough, even some of the more inlying zones contained populations no more literate than the rural. Similar comparisons made for other urban variables, such as refined fertility rates, religious and ethnic homogeneity, and condition and type of building, reveal the same inescapable fact that within the city of Cairo there exist numerous subareas whose physical and social characteristics closely approximate the villages of the countryside.

WHERE MIGRANTS SETTLE IN CAIRO

It is therefore possible for migrants to live in any of the large sections of the city which retain basic similarities to the village. To what extent do they actually select such areas as their ports of entry into the city's structure? Since our hypothesis is that one of the major cushions in the assimilation of rural migrants is the nature of the subcommunity to which they gravitate, our concern will be with the areas of first settlement of "non-selective" migrants.

Direct evidence of where migrants settle in the city is not available in the Cairo census.[7] In our attempt to approximate their ecological distribution, however, we are aided by several circumstances: First, small sample studies made in Egypt and other industrializing countries indicate that a fairly typical pattern of initial settlement is followed by many rural immigrants.[8] The typical migrant, here as elsewhere, is a young man whose first contact in the city is often with a friend or relative from his original village, with whom he may even spend the first few nights. Later, more permanent lodgings are found, usually within the same neighborhood. This process, in the aggregate, results in a concentration of migrants from particular villages within small subsections of the city, far beyond what would be expected by chance. Second, migration to Cairo has tended to occur in major spurts, the most important of recent times occurring in the early 1940's. Therefore, not only did the typical migrant gravitate to a small area of the city already containing persons from his home village, but he was not the only newcomer at the time of his arrival.

These two factors, operating together, resulted in the formation of small conclaves of ex-villagers sharing a common past in the village and a similar and often simultaneous history of adaptation to the city. A parallel between this and the ethnic ghettos of large American cities at the turn of the century readily suggests itself. While the congregations of villagers from Kafr Bagour and Garawan are smaller than were the Little Sicilys and although villagers are segregated (and segregate themselves) from the main stream of urban life by less powerful barriers than language and Old World customs, they also have developed the protective pattern of physical proximity and certain social institutions which help mitigate the difficulties of transition.

The formal associations founded for and developed by migrants are important, directly, in the dynamics of rural to urban adaptation, but are even more important indirectly, since their location and distribution in the city offer the *only* evidence as to where migrants settle in Cairo. Before analyzing the locational pattern of these institutions, however, some explanation of their nature is essential.

The *Directory of Social Agencies in Cairo*[9] lists more than 110 village benevolent associations. The Garawan Benevolent Society is typical. Garawan, a village of 8,000, is located in the heart of the Egyptian Delta some forty miles northwest of Cairo. Population pressure resulted first in the formation of several daughter villages, but eventually many of the men had to seek work in Cairo. (The village has a heavy excess of females.) The Garawan Benevolent Society was founded in 1944 to "extend aid to members" and to "provide burial facilities." Self-supporting, it sustains its activities through the dues contributed by "320 Egyptian Muslim adult males from Garawan," according to the directory's entry. Using a most conservative estimate of size of family (two dependents per adult male), one estimates that approximately 1,000 persons are to some extent involved in the core community of ex-Garawan residents.

One must make two basic assumptions if the locations of these societies are to be used as indirect evidence of migrant settlements. First, it must be assumed that migrants from specific villages are not distributed randomly throughout the city but that the processes described above result in aggregate settlements of persons from the same village.[10] Second, it must be assumed that the office of the migrant association is located in or near the subarea of the city which contains the maximum concentration of members. While this would not be true in every case, one might reasonably expect some relationship between office and clientele.

Even if these assumptions were absolutely beyond question (which they are not), an analysis of the locations of the associations would be irrelevant if they were scattered capriciously throughout the entire city. This, however, is fortunately not the case. When the addresses listed in the directory are located on a spot map, a definite, although not simple, pattern emerges which indicates in rough fashion the areas where rural migrants seem to be concentrated. Most associations fall within the elliptical belt around but never within the central business district. The arc contracts both east and west to a bare quarter of a mile from central business district and expands north and south to more than a mile from city center, thus conforming to the general contours of the city.

Northern Settlement. One-third of the migrant associations cluster in the segment of the city which radiates northward from the central business district, circumscribed south and east by major rail lines, and bounded by the Nile to the west and an agricultural zone to the north. This section contains two subareas of densest concentration: the first in the vicinity of the Khazindar bus station; the other in Al Sharabiya, northeast of the main train terminal.

The Khazindar bus station has served since the 'twenties as the terminus of bus lines connecting Lower Egyptian provinces (the Delta) with Cairo. Within a radius of one-fourth of a mile of this station are eight village associations, all representing Delta villages; within half a mile are sixteen associations, ten actually concentrated in a four-by-six-block area just northeast of the station. This area has a strange mixture of urban and rural features. Behind the main street on which the station stands, narrow unpaved streets and alleys harbor prematurely aged, badly deteriorated, urban housing interspersed with the rural type of structure. The two- and three-story buildings contrast markedly with the six- to eight-story structures which dominate the main street. A cluster of blackgarbed women squat to gossip; old men sit in doorways; a sheep bleats; children swarm in packs. When this area received its major influx of migrants, it was an outpost of urban settlement. As recently as 1940 there were farms just to the north. By now, however, the city has swept beyond it.

The second concentration of migrant associations is located in the tiny quarter of Al Sharabiya, where seven associations almost all from Delta villages are located within four blocks. Occupationally, many residents are bound to the rail yards that virtually surround it. Despite its geographically central location, this section presents a distinctly rural aspect and retains a close functional tie to the rural fringe, since farms bound it where rail lines do

not. Lower buildings, some of mud brick, predominate. Commercial establishments are those of the large village or small town. Al Sharabiya and Khazindar
areas contain most of the migrant associations of the city's northern quadrant.

Most of the associations in this quadrant represent Lower Egyptian villages.
Hence many migrants have presumably settled close not only to their point of
origin but, even more specifically, to their point of entry into the city, i.e., the
bus terminal. Moreover, the migrants settling in this part of the city selected
areas which were, at the time of settlement at least, on the outer edge of the
built-up city.

Southern Settlement. Another third or more of the migrant associations are
clustered directly south of the central business district, quite distant from the
southern rural-urban fringe. The densest concentration is found in the transitional business district—a curved interstitial belt buffering the Western-style
commercial zone north and west of it from the native market and residential
quarters to its south and east. Twenty-five associations are located in this zone,
while the remainder are scattered farther south toward Old Cairo.

Most striking is the fact that the majority of these associations represent
villages of Upper Egypt. Thus the principle of least effort seems to determine
migrant distribution. Villagers coming from north of the city favor the northern
quadrant of the city, while those coming from the south prefer location in the
southern quadrant. But, whereas the former have their associations in family
residential zones near the city's fringe, the latter have theirs in a marginal commercial district characterized by a heavy excess of unmarried males.[11] Further
examination reveals that the latter are primarily in rented offices, whereas the
former are frequently in the home of the association's president.

What accounts for the remarkable difference? One hypothesis can be offered
here. Migrants from Delta villages follow a different pattern of migration and
hence make a different type of adjustment to the city than do migrants from
Upper Egyptian villages. First, migrants from the Delta move primarily in
family groups, while those from the south either remain single or leave their
wives and children in their home villages. In Cairo in 1947, of the 400,000 migrants from Lower Egypt, half were males and half females, but 200,000 out of
the 250,000 migrants from Upper Egypt were males. Thus the sex ratio of
Delta migrants was remarkably well balanced, while there were four men for
every woman among Upper Egyptian migrants in Cairo.

Second, significant occupational differences between the two migrant groups
affect both adjustment patterns and spatial distribution. Upper Egyptian
migrants go primarily into domestic and other personal services or work in
unskilled labor gangs, while the occupations followed by Lower Egyptian
migrants are both more varied and less likely to include housing as a part of
wages.[12]

In the light of this the major differences between the location of migrant
associations representing Upper and Lower Egyptian villages become more
comprehensible. The associations of Upper Egyptians are located in an area

which serves as a leisure-time focal point as well as a residential area catering to single men. This is both cause and effect of the character of Upper Egyptian migrants. The associations play a more active role in their lives, in part because their members are denied access to the alternative social unit, the family.

Central Zone, East and West of the Central Business District. The remaining associations are divided between Boulaq, which forms the western quadrant of the ellipse, and Bab al-Shariya and Waily, the eastern portion of the belt. Ten associations are located within the former zone, while twenty have addresses in the latter. Just as the ecological position of these areas is midway between the northern concentration of Delta village associations and the southern concentration of Upper Egyptian associations, so, sociologically, they lie midway, containing associations from both regions of the country in roughly equal proportions. They share still other similarities. Both are close to the central business district; both rank low in socioeconomic status (below both shubra and the transitional business zone); both are primarily family areas; and both contain the densest slums of the city: densities of up to 900,000 persons per square mile are recorded for small subsections of Boulaq, and the over-all density of the community area of Bab al-Shariya is the highest in the city. Of the two, Boulaq is the older and hence the one retaining more rural qualities in its buildings and streets, but even Bab al-Shariya, despite its uniformly high apartment buildings looming above narrow access alleys, contains a population more rural than urban in its ways.

These, then, are the areas to which migrants have gravitated within the city. That they are relatively scarce in the highest rental zones of the city is attributable to their low socioeconomic status. Migrants are relatively absent, also, from the rural-urban fringe proper which would, as we have seen, provide them with the most familiar and protective environment. The lack of rental housing in these areas (privately owned farms with villages for laborers only), the dearth of public transportation, and their desire to live close to their new jobs are undoubtedly important reasons for their rejection of these areas. A second area surprisingly overlooked in the search for "near-the-fringe" living is Medieval Cairo, that rectangular belt of oldest structures toward the eastern edge of the city. The complete absence of new housing in these districts, coupled with a low turnover rate (the population works at traditional crafts and trades where production, selling, and living quarters are often in the same structure), have probably prevented mass invasions by new migrants.

HYPOTHESES CONCERNING MIGRANT ADJUSTMENT

Earlier, the hypotheses of migrant adjustment were broken down into four classes: physical, economic, social, and ideological. In light of the locational material presented above, plus observations of both rural and city life in Egypt,[13] these will be defined here in an attempt to describe the peculiarities of migrant adjustment in Egypt.

Physical. We have already suggested that many migrants gravitate to areas lying close to the rural-urban fringe, while others settle in areas which have at least a cultural resemblance to semirural areas. In these sections, interior streets and alleyways are seldom used for wheeled traffic, leaving undisturbed the rural functions of the street as pathway, meeting place, playground, and tethering area for animals.

Greater adjustments are required with respect to both the dwelling and the physical neighborhood. Housing occupied by the majority of migrants is more urban than rural in style. This results in functional overcrowding more severe than in the villages. The village home minimizes the number of inclosed rooms in order to maximize private open space (a ground-level interior courtyard or a protected roof courtyard in a more commodious two-story home). This cherished space is eliminated in the multifamily flats of the city. While many of the tasks assigned to the courtyard are no longer performed in the city (drying dung cakes, storing crops, tethering animals), other social uses such as cooking, eating, and just sitting are driven indoors or to the streets in the city.

Not only is the home more compressed due to the loss of outdoor "overspill" space, but the neighborhood is also more concentrated. While residential densities in Egyptian villages are surprisingly high, they nowhere approach the densities of Cairo's poorer districts. Many families using a common stairwell and public utilities means, paradoxically, more intensive contact with neighbors than in the village; and adjusting to the inadvertent intimacy may be extremely difficult for people new to the city, particularly for women.

Within the home itself are other changes, of which the loss of the overroom is perhaps the most important. In the rural home one full room is devoted to the massive flat-topped oven in which bread is baked daily and which, during the winter months, heats the adjacent areas and provides a snug bed for a blanketless family. That its loss is viewed with distress by at least some migrants is evidenced by the fact that some seek the top floor of an urban dwelling to construct a village oven and advise newcomers from their village to do the same.[14]

Other changes in the home are viewed more favorably, since they conform to the aspirations of villagers. Among the objects high in status found in the most prosperous rural homes are small kerosene burners instead of dung-cake fires for cooking, wardrobes and china closets to store a growing stock of consumption items, and the high four-poster bed with its black wrought-iron frame embellished with gilt, which remains, in the city as in the village, the *most* important sign of status. These are items with which migrants tend to crowd their urban homes, as soon as they can afford them.

The dress of migrants changes little in the city. Only the selective migrants change completely from the *galabiya* (long loose robe) to pants and shirts; for non-selective migrants the change is rarely required to conform to the urban pattern, and it is occupation rather than status per se or place of birth which dictates appropriate attire. It is perhaps because of this that the change is more frequently attempted by Delta than by Upper Egyptian migrants.

Change in dress presents more difficult problems for the women. The universal dress of village women is a high-necked, long-sleeved printed gown which is then covered by a black one of similar cut. A kerchief and then a black mantilla completely cover the hair. While many village women retain this attire in the city (as do many old city residents), some of the younger of them first discard the black garment and later may adopt a modified urban version of the printed gown with cutout neckline and daring three-quarter-length sleeves.

The foregoing remarks apply best to Delta families making a relatively permanent adjustment to the city. They do not apply with equal force to Upper Egyptian migrants working as domestic servants or in other occupations where housing is provided or to those who remain unmarried or leave their families in the village. Paradoxically, this group, exposed most intensively to a completely new physical environment, is least assimilated to Cairo. A lifetime spent in sections of the city which contrast sharply with the village environment affects a superficial sophistication unmatched by the manual laborer from the Delta living in a quasi-rural district. It seems, however, that the very lack of gradual transition and of the mediating influences of family and neighborhood has the reverse effect of prolonging the period when one is a stranger. This type of migrant often completely rejects urban life, confining his periodic social contacts to co-villagers often in his own profession and his "real" life to infrequent sojourns to his village family.

Economic. In their villages of origin, migrants were engaged almost exclusively in agriculture. Men worked long and hard during the three sowing and harvesting periods in the Delta and the two crop-change periods in Upper Egypt, these periods of intense activity being followed by slower seasons of maintenance and community sociability. The basic rhythm of rural life thus dictated large finite jobs alternating with lighter routine work. The length of the work day varied with the stage of the cycle.

Women's work was more evenly distributed, with child care, the preparation of food and bread, the making of dung cakes, and the tending of livestock performed daily. Work in the fields was done during the early morning hours, except during the busy seasons, when it absorbed a greater portion of the day. Labor was communal within the extended family home and, when outdoors, was usually performed in company.

Laundry is a case in point. In the village, washing is done in the canal or now, increasingly, at the communal water taps. It is never a solitary activity. Contrast this with how laundry is done in Al Sharabiya, a migrant area described above.[15] Water is also secured from communal taps, but a man guards the tap, effectively discouraging women from washing at the site. Women carry their water home to wash in solitude within their dwellings. Other functions are similarly driven indoors or eliminated altogether. Thus the ex-village woman experiences a reduction in her work load (except where outside employment is taken), but, at the same time, she experiences an even greater reduction in the social life which formerly attended her labors.

The experience of migrant men, on the other hand, is often the reverse. The work of a city manual laborer is probably more taxing, certainly more evenly distributed over time, and usually *less* solitary than rural work. Exceptions must be made for migrants working as itinerant peddlers, shoe-shiners, tea-makers, etc., and, of course, for those working as domestic servants. These occupations are both more independently regulated and somewhat more isolating from contacts of a primary nature.

To what extent do migrants working at steady jobs in the company of others come into contact with associates from different backgrounds? Social heterogeneity is one of the distinguishing characteristics of urbanism, but for this to create the mental counterpart—cultural relativity—heterogeneous persons must come into intimate contact with each other. While in large-scale factories the mixing of diverse people undoubtedly occurs, the overwhelming majority of commercial and industrial firms in Cairo employ only a few persons, often within the same family. Furthermore, migrants often depend upon their compatriots to guide them to their first jobs. Sometimes, migrants seek out well-known "successes" from their village to give them employment. Thus migrants cluster together not only residentially but also on the job as well. In the smaller firms of Cairo, then, a far greater homogeneity of the work force exists than would have been expected by chance. Far from isolating the migrant from his fellow villagers, his job may actually consolidate his village ties.

Social. The hypotheses presented by Louis Wirth in his logical statement[16] of the differences between the rural and urban ways of life have been misused, as if they were facts, and many of the concepts almost self-evident to sociologists studying American cities have proved less valid when applied to the growing body of data about non-Western and preindustrial cities. While isolated refutations have appeared,[17] as yet there has been no major reformulation of the theory.

Wirth hypothesized that the ecological determinants of a city (large numbers of heterogeneous people in dense, permanent settlement) would have certain social consequences, notably anonymity, dependence upon impersonal relations and sanctions, sophistication, and tolerance of change. To what extent do the social relationships in Cairo conform to these predicated types, and, further, how much does the rural migrant really have to adjust his personality to become a functioning member of urban society?

While these questions are too ambitious to be answered here, two propositions are suggested. First, the culture of Cairo fails to be characterized chiefly by anonymity, secondary contacts, and the other attributes of urban life. Second, migrants to Cairo are active creators of a variety of social institutions whose major function is to protect migrants from the shock of anomie.

Middle Eastern culture places a high value on personal relationships, even at a sacrifice of privacy and internal development. This, combined with a system of relationships based on the extended kinship group, serves to increase the number of primary ties far beyond what Western sociologists, reasoning from their own experience, dare to assume possible.[18] This network of personal associations enmeshes not hundreds but thousands of individuals.

Were Cairo merely an amorphous mass of individuals, this network, large as it is, might account for but a small fraction of the individual's contacts. However, Cairo is not one community but, rather, many separate social communities. Functional sections of each community may be geographically separated—residence in one section, business in another, recreation in still another. A member of one community may pass daily through the physical site of communities other than his own, neither "seeing" them nor admitting their relevance to his own life. But, within his own community, there is little if any anonymity.

It is within this context of "urbanism" that the Egyptian migrant is called upon to adjust. His adjustment is further facilitated by the formal and informal institutions he develops within his small community, one of which has already been mentioned—the village benevolent society. Through it many migrants receive moral support from their compatriots as well as insurance against the insecurities of urban life, that is, isolation in poverty, sickness, and death.[19] It is unlikely, however, that more than 100,000 migrants are involved in these associations, while it will be recalled that their number exceeded 600,000 in 1947. Thus, even if these associations are important to the persons they serve, they fall short of absorbing most migrants.

Other formal institutions play a relatively minor role in providing social groups for migrant identification. Labor unions (except for craft guilds), civic associations, charitable organizations and political groups are all relatively undeveloped social institutions in Cairo. One must look, then, to the informal social institutions for a fuller understanding of patterns of adjustment. Unfortunately, documentation in this area is totally lacking. While a few may be singled out as playing important roles, no estimate of their magnitude can be offered.

First in importance is undoubtedly the coffee shop in which Middle Eastern males conduct their social and often their business lives. The comparable Western institution is probably the old style of British pub which, with its set of steady patrons and its intimate atmosphere, served as a social focus for the individual's life. Many an Egyptian coffee shop is run by a villager to serve men from that particular village. News of the village is exchanged, mutual assistance for employment is given, and the venture more resembles a closed club than a commercial enterprise.

For the women no such informal association is available. While within the village there are also no purely female informal associations, religious festivals, births, deaths, marriages, circumcisions, etc., are all village-wide events in which women have important roles to play. Within the city, however, these events become more private, and the role of women as full participants is probably reduced. Social life in the city is confined more and more to the immediate neighborhood.

It is this immediate neighborhood, however, which constitutes, after the family, the most important informal social institution for migrants in the city. The cohesiveness of the neighborhood is strengthened by the tendency of persons from the same village to settle together. Similar to the situation elsewhere, it is the women, children, and very old persons who are the most active participants in neighborhood-centered social life.

Motivations and Ideology. The Weltanschauung of the city man is presumed to differ from the peasant's in several significant ways. First, relaxation of the heavy hand of personal social control in the village is assumed to give greater latitude for individual differentiation. Second, cities are assumed to foster a more secular, rational, and mechanistic ordering of activities. Third, cities are gateways to a more sophisticated knowledge of the outside world. Finally, cities have traditionally been the centers of movements of social change, from new religions to new political ideologies and transfers of power.

While these statements are valid premises, data on Cairo are lacking which would permit us to place rural migrants along the continuum from the sacred, conformist, isolated, and relatively static state of the ideal folk society to the extreme of urbanism outlined above. For one thing, the Egyptian village hardly conforms to the ideal prototype of a folk society. Where farmers raise cash crops tied to international markets (cotton and sugar), listen to radios, travel often to market towns, have relatives or friends in the cities, and send their children to schools following a national curriculum, the magic ring of isolation has already been broken. On the other hand, as already demonstrated, it is possible within Cairo to lead a fairly circumscribed existence outside the main stream of urban life. Therefore, while there may be a wide gap between the least-sophisticated villager and the most-sophisticated urbanite, there is certainly no indication that migrants necessarily pass from one pole to the other.

NOTES

1. Expulsion from supersaturated rural environment ranks as an equally important element in this growth.
2. See Charles Stewart, Jr., "Migration as a Function of Population and Distance," *American Sociological Review*, XXV (June 1960), 347–56; George Zipf, *Human Behavior and the Principle of the Least Effort* (Cambridge, Mass.: Addison-Wesley Press, 1949). Application of hypothesis to Egyptian data prepared by present writer.
3. It probably *never* will sharpen to the same extent as it did in the West because simultaneously with this ruralization of the cities is occurring an urbanization of rural areas (extension of roads, education, and social services). These processes were temporarily distinct in Western development.
4. The *1947 Census of the Governorate of Cairo* shows that, of a total population of little more than 2 million, only 1.3 million had been born within the city; 51,000 were born in other governorates (large cities); 59,000 were born outside Egypt. Thus more than 630,000 residents of Cairo came from more or less rural sections of Egypt.

5. See the unpublished findings of two American sociologists, Karen and Gene Petersen, who have made a sample study of 1,250 migrant families from five Delta villages.
6. It is presented in full detail in this writer's *Cairo: One Thousand-One Years of the City* (Princeton, N.J.: Princeton University Press, 1971).
7. A table showing place of birth by census tract of current residence has, unfortunately, never been included in any Cairo census.
8. See H. Saaty and G. Hirahayashi, *Industrialization in Alexandria* (Cairo: Social Research Center, 1959); "Demographic Aspects of Urbanization in the ECAFE Region," in *Urbanization in Asia and the Far East* (Calcutta: Research Center on the Social Implications of Industrialization in Southern Asia, 1957); a variety of papers in UNESCO, *Social Implications of Industrialization and Urbanization in Africa South of the Sahara* (Paris: United Nations, 1956), among others.
9. Prepared by Isis Istiphan and published by the Social Research Center, American University at Cairo, 1956.
10. Obviously, not all ex-residents would be found in the Cairo settlement of maximum concentration, since some, probably the most successful economically, may have already moved to other sections of the city, while others never did follow the typical pattern, for example, the selective migrants or those with intervening experiences, such as army service.
11. The sex ratio here is 129 in the ages most likely to be imbalanced by migration, 15 to 49; in the northern section it is only 104. Forty per cent of males of marriageable age are unmarried here, while only 25 per cent are unmarried in the northern section (computed from 1947 census).
12. The *Directory of Social Agencies* lists the dominant occupations of members of each association. Government and manual workers are listed most frequently for Lower Egyptian associations, while servants, porters, and messengers are the most frequently mentioned occupations for Upper Egyptian associations.
13. The author has spent more than three years in Egypt, one and a half at a UNESCO project in a village area and two years in Cairo studying the structure of that city. Many observations have been further authenticated by anthropologists and social workers with longer and more intimate experience in both areas, to whom the author expresses gratitude.
14. Reported by Hind Abu el Seoud, an anthropologist studying a small Delta village and its ex-residents in Cairo.
15. Account provided by Abdel Monem Shawky, former social worker in the district for fourteen years.
16. Louis Wirth, "Urbanism as a Way of Life," *American Journal of Sociology*, XLIV (July 1938), 1–24, which essentially reformulates the work of earlier German scholars, such as Max Weber, *The City*, ed. and trans. D. Martindale and G. Neuwirth (Glencoe, Ill.: Free Press, 1958); and George Simmel, "The Metropolis and Mental Life," in *The Sociology of Georg Simmel*, tr. Kurt Wolff (Glencoe, Ill.: Free Press, 1950), pp. 409–24.
17. See, e.g., Gideon Sjoberg, "The Preindustrial City," *American Journal of Sociology*, LX (March, 1955), 438–45; Horace Miner, *The Primitive City of Timbuctoo* (Princeton, N.J.: Princeton University Press, 1953).
18. Weber himself rejected impersonal relations as a useful part of the city's definition, noting that "various cultural factors determine the size at which 'impersonality' tends to appear" (*op. cit.*, p. 65). See also Richard Dewey, "The Rural-Urban Continuum," *American Journal of Sociology*, LXVI (July 1960), 60–66.
19. Burial services, offered by almost all associations, parallel the burial-insurance organizations of Negro rural migrants to northern cities.

MIGRATION AND ADAPTATION: TZINTZUNTZEÑOS IN MEXICO CITY

Robert Van Kemper

> Through the writings of George M. Foster, the Mexican village of Tzintzuntzan has become well known to students of peasant societies. Robert Van Kemper, a student of Foster's, followed the migration of Tzintzuntzeños to Mexico City. In this essay, Kemper examines the adaptive strategies of the Tzintzuntzeño migrants in the areas of residential behavior, group organization, employment, and in their psychological adjustment to urban life. Due to the dispersed residential pattern and status distinctions within the migrant community, the Tzintzuntzeños rely more on themselves and their immediate families in coping with city life than do the Egyptian migrants described by Abu Lughod.

During the three decades since Oscar Lewis (1952) carried out his pioneering fieldwork in Mexico City, in which he suggested that migrants from the village of Tepoztlán undergo "urbanization without breakdown," anthropologists have devoted considerable attention to cityward migration in Latin America. The causes and patterns of migration, its effects on communities of origin and destination, and the characteristics of the migrants have been investigated. However, the emphasis of anthropological research has been on the processes and strategies of adaptation among metropolitan migrants. A common approach to studying migration and adaptation involves examination of migrants from a *single* community of origin to a *single* urban destination. Ideally, a fieldworker will generate a detailed longitudinal data base which will permit analysis of continuity and change over an entire generation. This was Lewis's plan for his Tepoztlán-Mexico City research project, and it is my plan for the study of migrants from the community of Tzintzuntzan in Mexico City.

METHODOLOGY OF THE TZINTZUNTZAN MIGRANT PROJECT

From the initial period of fieldwork in 1969–1970, this investigation has been conceived as a logical outgrowth of George M. Foster's (1948, 1967) long-term study of the people of Tzintzuntzan, a *mestizo* peasant village located on the

SOURCE: Article written expressly for *Urban Life*.

shores of Lake Pátzcuaro about 400 kilometers west of Mexico City. When I arrived in Mexico City, I had a list of about twenty migrants' names and just two addresses; when I departed the field sixteen months later, I had gathered information on nearly five hundred persons involved with Tzintzuntzan migrant households in Mexico City. During this first phase of fieldwork, I used the standard array of anthropological data-gathering procedures: participant observation, censuses, household budget surveys, in-depth interviews, questionnaires, projective tests (Thematic Apperception Test), and life histories.

Subsequently, I conducted a mid-decade ethnographic survey of the Tzintzuntzan migrants in the capital. Results of this fieldwork showed that the migrant population had increased 23 percent to reach a total of about 630 persons in just four years. By summer 1974, there were at least 105 identifiable household units located in more than fifty *colonias* (neighborhoods) within the greater metropolitan area of Mexico City. The recent arrivals tend to move directly to peripheral housing areas, thus continuing the center to periphery pattern of mobility found among the earlier migrants.

Since 1974, I have returned to Mexico City and to Tzintzuntzan for several brief periods of fieldwork. Using the ethnographic census conducted in 1970, I have resurveyed the village . . . to ascertain current patterns of migration. These longitudinal data are vital as a basis for carrying out a major decennial restudy planned for 1979–1980. This ten-year follow-up will provide new information on recent migrants, and will permit the testing of hypotheses and ideas generated through the earlier phases of the research project.

BUSCAR LA VIDA: THE DECISION TO EMIGRATE

In the period since World War II, the forces of technology and economic modernization have permanently transformed life in thousands of Mexican villages, and Tzintzuntzan is no exception. Through the effects of health and sanitation campaigns, the once stable population of Tzintzuntzan had by 1970 more than doubled to 2,200 persons. Penetration of the community by highway, rail, radio, and television networks has greatly increased its participation in national affairs. The growing tourist market for the locally produced pottery and crafts and the active involvement of villagers in the *bracero* program of the 1950s and early 1960s (and continuing involvement in illegal labor migration to the United States in the 1970s) have combined to raise the standard of living for nearly all Tzintzuntzan residents. The recent construction of a secondary school in the village (in conjunction with the remodeling of the old primary school) has also stimulated interest in the world beyond the local community.

In this context, migration is becoming a routine matter for the people of Tzintzuntzan. Between 1930 and 1940, when nearly one of every nine Mexicans was moving across state boundaries, only a handful of Tzintzuntzeños ventured outside of the state of Michoacán. In contrast, about 15 percent of all village households had one or more members leave the state between 1960 and

1970. This proportion is in line with the current national average of 14.5 percent for inter-state migration. Although a number of Tzintzuntzan peasants are forced to leave the village to avoid retribution or prosecution for criminal acts, the majority are eager to leave. In their words, they emigrate to *buscar la vida,* to search for life.

Tzintzuntzan migrants in Mexico City offer many reasons for having left the village to pursue the "good life" in the capital. Emiliano Guzmán, a twenty-nine-year-old factory worker, laments the lack of progress in Tzintzuntzan while reciting his opportunities for steady, albeit low-paying, employment in Mexico City. José Zavala, a middle-aged teacher, recalls the tranquility and pleasant pace of village life in contrast to the overcrowded, smoggy, and hectic metropolis—but in the same breath admits that there is no job for him in the village. Raúl Silva dislikes being separated from friends and relatives in the city but at the same time admits that he has no wish to go back to Tzintzuntzan to become a potter like his father. Other migrants make similar comments when asked why they migrated to the capital. Taken as a whole, they weigh the good and bad of village and city, and—like peasants the world over—opt for urban life.

As these examples show, the people of Tzintzuntzan have learned to treat migration as an option to remaining in the village. The decision to migrate is not always simple, nor related directly to visible economic conditions. Tzintzuntzeños select destinations based on their perceptions of available opportunities which they learn about through friends and relatives who already have experiences beyond the local scene. In this regard, we may speak of migration *strategies* by which villagers manipulate (although not always maximize) available contacts to improve their current situations.

Rufino, and many other Tzintzuntzeños like him, can survive their initial encounters with urban life because when they arrive in the capital they can stay *arrimado* ("up close to," i.e., as a guest) with relatives or friends already established in the city. These ties to "senior" migrants have been important in the initial urban experiences of more than 90 percent of Tzintzuntzeños now living in Mexico City. The *arrimado* network—with the promises of assistance in finding housing and work—is certainly responsible for much of the recent growth in the migrant group in Mexico City. Complex social networks now bridge the gap between village and metropolis, transforming what once were individual migration itineraries into a continuing and expanding social process. The set of actors is constantly changing, with each new migrant profiting from the experiences—pleasant and unpleasant—of friends and relatives who preceded him to the capital.

Although the migrants' first residence in Mexico City is usually arranged through friends or relatives, the choice is also constrained by governmental and private sector forces beyond their control. For instance, the prohibition on new residential subdivisions within the Federal District, which was in effect from 1952 to 1970, severely restricted the housing options for new arrivals and for the urban middle class. Rent control policies in the central city zones have had similar effects. As a result, most Tzintzuntzeños now live near the metropolitan periphery, with perhaps half living outside of Mexico City proper.

These limitations on the urban housing stock have encouraged many migrants to reconsider traditional family and household arrangements. Although the conjugal family remains important, enclaves of extended families have appeared in several neighborhoods. Some migrants rent adjacent rooms in a *vecindad* (low-income apartment units) while others purchase lots with kinsmen and share the burden of house building. These urban residential strategies are not mere recreations of the village patterns of living near one's relatives. On the contrary, the migrants have evolved their strategies in an effort to conserve their limited financial and social resources in an overcrowded metropolitan environment.

ORGANIZATIONAL STRATEGIES: WILL THE AGRUPACIÓN SUCCEED?

One way in which many migrant groups maximize their limited resources in urban settings is to establish village-based or regional associations. Until recently, however, the Tzintzuntzan migrants had no such voluntary association and they had little sense of "community" in Mexico City. Absence of such an association meant that social integration among the migrants rested solely on kinship, friendship, or *compadrazgo* (ritual co-parenthood) ties, often established before migration. In addition, the limited social relations among migrants has encouraged an outward search for potentially useful contacts in the city.

Expansion of a migrant's reference group beyond fellow migrants and villagers is a critical phase in the process of urban social adaptation. Urbanization thrusts Tzintzuntzeños into a new social domain: the two great categories of peasant life—"villagers" vs. "outsiders"—are blurred and ultimately obliterated through daily participation in city life. Surviving in the city beyond the initial period of adjustment requires ties with persons beyond the migrant group; the most successful migrants have often drifted away from the other Tzintzuntzeños in the capital as they pursue better jobs, housing, and education for themselves and their families.

In this context, can the *Agrupación* (association) of Tzintzuntzan migrants succeed in creating a sense of community among a growing and increasingly diverse population? Founded in 1975 by a socially minded school principal nearing retirement age, the Agrupación is intended to provide the migrants a common identity by making annual pilgrimages to Tzintzuntzan during the village's patron saint's festival. Beyond this ritual activity, the Agrupación is chartered to provide nominal social assistance to needy migrants and its members pledge to "struggle to maintain a closeness that will permit them to help one another in their physical, spiritual, social, and cultural problems."

Until the establishment of the Agrupación, the Tzintzuntzeños in the capital never united to press for political favors, economic benefits, or social services.

Their geographic and socioeconomic diversity prevented them from organizing. The Agrupación has been helpful in supporting village efforts to construct a secondary school in Tzintzuntzan and it has also made donations for the work of the church in Tzintzuntzan. On the other hand, the efforts of the Agrupación's leader to involve the entire membership in a campaign to "bring to justice" a villager who killed the leader's brother during a recent Tzintzuntzan fiesta is causing considerable controversy among members. In effect, the Agrupación is splitting along traditional kinship and friendship lines rather than providing a mechanism for consolidating the migrants.

More importantly, the Agrupación is primarily a middle-class professional phenomenon. Very few working-class migrants have been recruited into the membership, even though they represent two-thirds of all migrants. Thus, the Agrupación appears to perpetuate—and reinforce—the class barriers among Tzintzuntzan migrants in Mexico City. The differential success of certain migrant families—often linked to their status in Tzintzuntzan prior to emigration—has virtually created two migrant groups within the capital rather than one. Those in the working class turn to fellow workers for help; professionals limit their social interaction to middle- and upper-class colleagues. Extended family ties within the migrant population closely follow class lines and extensions of a migrant's reference group to non-Tzintzuntzeño urbanites do little to create a sense of community among the migrants.

This emphasis on individualistic solutions to social organizational issues does not mean that Tzintzuntzeños are floundering in an impersonal urban world. On the contrary, many belong to unions, neighborhood organizations (e.g., to maintain streets), and parish groups, although few appear to be active in the political arena. When they gather for weddings, baptisms, funerals, and holiday fiestas, the migrants usually entertain a mix of fellow migrants and other urban residents. Under these circumstances, and especially given its middle-class flavor, it remains to be seen whether the Agrupación will succeed as a distinctive organization dedicated to bringing all Tzintzuntzan migrants together, giving their children a sense of belonging to Tzintzuntzan, and creating a spirit of cooperation where individualism has reigned supreme.

PALANCAS: THE STRUGGLE FOR ECONOMIC SUCCESS IN THE CITY

Tzintzuntzeños hold many types of jobs in Mexico City. They are employed as factory workers, school teachers, civil servants, store clerks, musicians, and even as pharmacists, translators, and computer analysts. Many migrant households have more than a single wage earner (the average is 1.75 workers per household), but few individuals attempt to maintain two separate jobs. The unemployment rate among the migrants is quite low (about 7 percent), and rates of upward economic mobility appear to be at least as high as for the rest of the urban population.

Most Tzintzuntzan migrants come to the capital without a job assured; instead, they hope to find work through the assistance of relatives and friends already working there. Thus, in addition to providing temporary lodging, the more experienced migrants often serve as *palancas* ("levers") in finding jobs for new arrivals. The length of time needed to find a "good" job depends on the migrant's personal attributes (especially, his previous work experience and educational background), on the sequence and quality of his experiences outside of Tzintzuntzan, and on his own definition of what constitutes adequate employment. Generally, the migrants find some work immediately upon arrival, but a satisfying job seldom comes quickly. After some initial job instability, most migrants settle into relatively permanent niches. This does not mean that they retain the same job year after year; on the contrary, they continually search for better opportunities, with the final decision to change careers or company affiliations determined by their perception of the best available combination of wages, tenure, and social security benefits.

Few migrants expect to get wealthy in Mexico City, but some hope to make the critical shift from manual to "professional" jobs, and most believe (or hope) that their children will enter the ranks of white-collar workers. The Tzintzuntzeños are well aware that it is difficult to get ahead without adequate educational and job training. For this reason, children are encouraged to stay in school as long as possible and to obtain the best "credentials" possible. Indeed, in recent years, one of the main reasons for the emigration of young people from Tzintzuntzan is to get an advanced education, which will then open doors to professional employment opportunities in Mexico City and in other urban centers.

A shift from traditional to modern concepts of "success" is an integral part of the process of economic adaptation to urban life. When the migrants compare their positions with those of their parents or siblings still in Tzintzuntzan, nearly all conclude that the city offers the better prospects for themselves and for their children. Moreover, very few would consider returning to the village as an alternative to seeking other urban employment if they were to lose their current positions. The most important shift, however, occurs when the migrants come to realize that a dependence on their fellow migrants poses severe limitations on their urban prospects, since their opportunities are unlikely to be superior to those available to their fellows.

Tzintzuntzeños in Mexico City eventually recognize that, while fellow migrants are keys to the initial job, long-term economic success is the result of individual initiative, hard work, and a good network of migrant and non-migrant palancas. As one migrant remarked, "What are my dreams? Well, with hard work a person begins to think about his future, in having his own home, in helping his children and in seeing them achieve a social and economic level that he himself doesn't enjoy." So far, such aspirations have not been crushed by external, uncontrollable forces—such as a national or international economic depression—but should this occur, then frustration, anger, and sadness may replace the migrants' still rising expectations.

IMAGEN DEL MUNDO: PSYCHOLOGICAL ADAPTATION TO URBAN LIFE

Migrating from Tzintzuntzan to Mexico City not only involves people in new residential, organizational, and occupational strategies, it also may require modification of an individual's *imagen del mundo* ("worldview"). The psychological dimensions of urban adaptation must be understood not merely in terms of a rural-urban continuum but also in terms of the relative socioeconomic positions occupied by migrants before and after they leave for the capital. If a migrant holds values inappropriate for city life, these may not be *rural* values, but attitudes acquired in the process of interacting in situations where they have been defined as an inferior.

Tzintzuntzeños near the bottom of the socioeconomic scale in Mexico City face pressures and frustrations which parallel those of the poorest peasants in the village. For both groups, their concern is day-to-day survival, not upward mobility. Of course, since most migrants come from the better educated, more affluent, and more ambitious village families, their economic success in the capital is not surprising. Those migrants with steady urban jobs tend to have an optimistic worldview in which a pragmatic balance is struck between present needs and future hopes. The idea of most working-class Tzintzuntzeños in the capital is to provide a base upon which their children can build even better lives.

The small but growing number of professional-level migrants often face a frustration common to middle sectors of many urban societies. They may earn quite respectable wages, but they can rarely hope to belong to the elite groups whom they emulate. The psychological dangers of excessive "social climbing" haunt long-term as well as recent migrants. For example, the Zavala family was eager to send their daughter to a private academy—preferably, a French-speaking school—because they wanted her to receive a "proper" education (which to them meant an upper-class, foreign-oriented curriculum). Ultimately, however, the financial drain outweighed the benefits, and they enrolled her in the inexpensive public high school near their apartment. Subsequently, she has entered a professional school where she is being trained to work in the growing field of tourism. In this case, the Zavala's reference group was not compatible with their means. Their excessive drive brought with it a greater psychological malaise than if they had been content with their actual middle-class status.

This concern for education as the means to upward social and economic mobility is a key indicator that a "modern" worldview has become dominant among most migrants—as well as among the village families who are now sending their children to the new secondary school in Tzintzuntzan or to boarding schools in other communities. The emphasis on education implies a strong achievement motivation and a healthy future orientation. These values are especially strong among young professionals. For example, Martín Calva works as a well-paid government employee in the computer analysis division of the Treasury Department. He has moved up the job ladder rapidly in the past ten years, so that he now has a nice condominium apartment in which his wife, child, and younger siblings reside. Just as his relatives helped him through the university a decade ago, so he now assists a chain of his own brothers and sisters to get an education and move ahead in the urban system. Martín Calva and other migrants reason that if a primary school certificate was enough to lift an earlier generation of migrants out of the village and into a working-class job in Mexico City, then a secondary or university diploma should guarantee their children a professional position.

Unfortunately, the gap between working class and middle class is too wide for many people to bridge in a single generation. Furthermore, it is likely that the competition for civil service jobs and professional (e.g., doctors, lawyers, engineers) positions in the capital will become increasingly arduous in the 1980s as the metropolitan population passes the 14 million mark. It may be necessary, in order to fulfill their dreams of upward mobility, that young migrants will have to leave Mexico City to take positions in provincial cities and towns. If this occurs, then the migrants' optimism about their future will be rewarded, but not in the anticipated manner. More importantly, the pool of professional-level talent in Mexico City will have been distributed among other communities in need of their services—a prospect much desired by government planners interested in decentralization of Mexico's population and economy.

Already, some migrants born in Tzintzuntzan, raised and educated in Mexico City, and seeking work in other cities can be found among the Tzintzuntzeños. Perhaps higher education can help to overcome the historical concentration of migrants in the capital, where other forces have been unable to influence the massive flood of peasants entering the urban job market. If so, then what psychological adaptations—as well as residential, organizational, and occupational strategies—will occur among these re-transplanted Tzintzuntzan migrants? Only by following these migrants beyond the capital and comparing their experiences to those of migrants who never went to Mexico City can we discover the answers.

CONCLUSION

Most early discussions of migrant adaptation in Latin American cities were framed in terms of the Great Dichotomy, usually labeled "folk-urban" or "rural-urban." A significant corollary of this dichotomous view suggested that cityward migrants from "rural" areas ought to experience major difficulties in adjusting to "urban" culture. Such difficulties were supposed to result in culture conflicts, disorganization of traditional lifestyles, personal anomie and alienation, and breakdown of primary group affiliations. This model of the urbanization process, which Lewis attacked so effectively in his study of Tepoztlán and Mexico City, suffers from a fatal flaw: it is static, and thus fails to account for the continuing changes in the rural communities of origin, in the urban communities of destination, and in the migrants themselves.

In contrast, numerous recent studies demonstrate that contemporary processes of economic and social development in countries such as Mexico are creating an increasingly unified system in which villages and cities each play important roles. Rather than focusing on the separation of city and countryside, social scientists now recognize the interdependencies which connect a metropolis like Mexico City with a village like Tzintzuntzan. The evidence gathered over the past decade shows clearly that, far from being passive pawns moved by impersonal economic and political forces, Tzintzuntzan migrants are active agents in shaping their own destinies and, in turn, the future of Mexico. Moreover, as Tzintzuntzan shifted from the "pioneer" migrations of the 1940s and 1950s to the "mass" migrations of the 1960s and 1970s, so a new phase may dawn in the 1980s.

Whereas the early adventurers who came to Mexico City were usually alone in the metropolis and thus had to rely on their own skills in getting ahead, recent arrivals have learned to use those who preceded them to find urban housing and jobs. The coming decade may generate a conflict between the migrants' willingness to help new arrivals and their desires to help their own children succeed in the increasingly competitive metropolitan setting. If such a shift in orientation does occur, then future social scientists may conclude that the migration processes and strategies common during the 1960s and 1970s were not universal but merely timely adaptations to a specific combination of prevailing social, economic, and political conditions.

BOGDAN'S STORY: THE ADAPTATION OF A RURAL FAMILY TO YUGOSLAVIAN URBAN LIFE

Andrei Simić

In the years following the Second World War, the rapid expansion of the Yugoslav economy and the bureaucracy under a new socialist state brought about the migration of millions of peasants into urban centers. Andrei Simić finds that, in contrast to some peoples in other parts of the world, these migrants quickly became assimilated into city life with minimal signs of social pathology. He concludes that this has been possible because urbanization in Yugoslavia has taken place principally during a period of economic growth and within the context of a relatively stable system of traditional values shared by urbanites and villagers alike. The life history of Bogdan is typical of this phenomenon, and his success in Belgrade is to a large degree typical of the experience of South Slav rural-urban migrants as a whole.

Since the close of the Second World War, the Yugoslavs, like rural peoples all over the world, have opted for urban life with an almost uncritical faith in the promises of industrialization and modernization. However, unlike many of their counterparts in other developing countries, their experience has been largely a positive one. While this was especially true during the three decades of initial urbanization, even today one finds minimal evidence by world standards of the kinds of social and cultural marginality which typify what Lewis (1964) has labeled "the culture of poverty." This phenomenon pervades, despite the fact that the size of most Yugoslav towns and cities has more than doubled and other, serious socio-economic problems exist, such as runaway inflation (currently exceeding 100% a year[1]), chronic unemployment, a cash-poor economy, low productivity and the relative lack of a work ethic, an acute housing shortage, inadequate and inefficient public services, and increasing ethnic and political unrest. The smooth integration of millions of former peasants into the fabric of urban life has largely contradicted the age-old stereotype that urbanism inevitably leads to every sort of social pathology and disorganization (cf. Wirth 1938). Rather, the South Slav experience confirms Lewis's (1952) contention that the process by

SOURCE: Article written expressly for *Urban Life*.

which rural peoples move to cities and adapt to conditions there will differ from one
historical and cultural setting to another.

YUGOSLAV URBANIZATION

Yugoslavia, like the rest of the Balkans, has a very ancient history of urban life. For
instance, Belgrade, the national capital, was the site of a Roman citadel and town
called Singidunum and, dating from at least 100 A.D., has been continuously
occupied up to the present. However, through the mid-twentieth century, Yugoslav
cities remained remote, provincial centers of traditional Middle Eastern,
Mediterranean or Central European types, thus reflecting the diverse influences of
the three great civilizations which met on this southeastern frontier of Europe. For
the most part, Balkan urban populations existed, until recently, as small islands in a
vast sea of peasantry.

At the close of the Second World War, Yugoslavia ranked with Albania, Malta,
and Portugal as one of the four least urbanized countries in Europe, with under 20%
of its people living in centers with populations over 20,000. Not a single paved road
joined its two largest cities, Belgrade and Zagreb, and, even in 1961, only a little over
11% of the population gained its livelihood from industry, with almost 60% still
dependent on peasant agriculture. However, under the influence of an ambitious plan
of industrialization and modernization initiated by Tito's socialist government, there
began a significant shift away from peasant agriculture, which, by 1964, accounted
for only about 20% of the national income. Economic change and the rapid postwar
expansion of the bureaucracy brought about mass migrations from the countryside
into the towns and cities. Clearly, as elsewhere, the motivation to leave ancestral
villages in favor of urban life can be explained as a reaction to perceived unfavorable
rural conditions in contrast to positive expectations regarding the city, what social
scientists have labeled the *push-pull syndrome*. In this respect, Hoyt et al. (1962:485)
estimate that, in the period immediately following the war, the level of migration to
Yugoslav urban centers was 380,000 migrants per year. The Belgrade experience is
typical of this trend. Its population increased from approximately 365,000 in 1948 to
697,000 in 1965, and, by 1982, numbered almost one and a half million (Savezni
Zavod za Statistiku, 1982). This augmentation represents more than a fourfold
increase in less than four decades, almost all of it attributable to the influx from the
countryside.

Belgrade, which is the capital of both Yugoslavia and the Republic of Serbia,
reflects in microcosm the transformations wrought by the past 150 years of Balkan
history. It was only a little over 100 years ago that Ali Rizah Pasha, by order of the
Ottoman Sultan, surrendered Belgrade's Kalemegdan Fortress, thus rendering
insignificant the last symbol of almost 500 years of Turkish domination. At that time,
the Serbian capital was little more than a dusty Moslem market town and garrison.
During the following decades, the city grew to become the modest intellectual and
administrative center of Serbia with 24,000 residents in 1867. The vacuum created
by the retreating Turks was quickly filled by a new native artisan class, the
bourgeoisie, and an elite, drawn to a large degree from the indigenous peasantry.

Another period of modest expansion followed the First World War, when Belgrade became the capital of the newly created Kingdom of the Serbs, Croats and Slovenes (later named Yugoslavia). However, the city remained an essentially quasi-Oriental backwater with a superficially Western European façade. During World War II, many of the modest gains of the interwar period were lost when the city was severely damaged during the German invasion and occupation. With the defeat and expulsion of the Axis powers, due in large part to the efforts of the Yugoslavs themselves, Belgrade became the hub of a new Marxist state and, as Hammel (1969:25) points out, "the final Yugoslav station on the Serbian road to success in migration."[2]

Although Belgrade is the capital of the most multiethnic state in Europe, excluding the Soviet Union, it remains, at the same time, a predominantly Serbian city, Eastern Orthodox by religious tradition (if not practice) and non-Western in its historical and cultural orientation.[3] This ethnic specificity of Belgrade holds particular significance for the integration of peasants into urban life, since rural-urban mobility in Yugoslavia has largely followed internal cultural boundaries. Of equal importance is the fact that, while Yugoslav cities such as Belgrade have been profoundly influenced by rural culture, there has occurred a simultaneous modernization of the countryside (Halpern and Halpern-Kerewsky 1986). Thus, no sharp cleavage has developed between these two major segments of the society. Not only do most Yugoslav families trace direct origins from the peasantry, but, even today, they maintain close ties with village kin regardless of their socio-economic and educational levels. In this respect, an ideology of kinship solidarity associated with an earlier period of Balkan history and typified by large, patrilocally extended households (the *zadruga*) continues to play a salient role, thus easing the stresses associated with rapid urbanization and economic development. This solidarity is expressed in the intense material and ritual reciprocity which links rural and urban kin and which demonstrates the ability of traditional South Slav culture to adapt to new conditions brought about by the transformation of Yugoslav society into a modern, industrial, urban state (Simić 1973; 1983).[4]

Rural-urban migration and urbanization are clearly the result of major economic and social trends rooted in large-scale historical antecedents; nevertheless, these phenomena are fundamentally the result of conscious choices made by individuals from among existing perceived alternatives. For instance, Max Weber (1892), in his classic study of German agrarian society at the close of the nineteenth century, found that, while migration of farm workers from eastern to western Germany could be explained in terms of fluctuations in the world market, in the final analysis, individual motivations played the decisive role. Thus, one way of understanding the dynamics of rural-urban migration and the accommodation to city life in Yugoslavia is to consider such adaptation from the standpoint of the personal histories of those who have experienced this metamorphosis. In this respect, the story of Bogdan and his family is not atypical of the more than two hundred informants I have known over twenty years of periodic field work in both rural and urban Yugoslavia. While the levels of success varied among the peasant migrants, in almost all of the case histories I have collected, the same motivations, values, and strategies appear. Thus, the character and fate of the nation can ultimately be seen to reside in the individual, and one is not intelligible without the understanding of the other.

BOGDAN'S STORY*

The red-tiled roofs of Cerići's almost sixty households dot the green flanks of the valley, stretching for almost two kilometers, like so many Christmas ornaments, along the winding course of the Žabica Creek. Today, a hard-surfaced, but narrow, road spans the twenty kilometers from the regional market town of Gornji Milanovac to the unpaved village plaza around which cluster the Byzantine-style Orthodox church, soccer field, four-year elementary school and community meeting hall (*dom*). Parallel to the road, glistening wires stretched between crudely hewn trunks of young poplars unpredictably deliver power for the electric lights, sewing machines, television sets, stoves, and refrigerators which grace all but a few of the homes. Only a generation ago, Bogdan remembers, life was quite different here in the heart of Serbia, which is little more than an hour's drive south of Belgrade:

> In those days, there was no electricity, and we could barely afford the kerosene lamps which, in any case, we used sparingly. For the most part, we were up with the sun and to bed at dark. I often think of the late fall, when the village paths turned to mud, and how we sloshed through it in our leather moccasins [*opanci*] and scratchy, homespun wool socks. There were times, after the heavy snows, when we could not leave Cerići at all, and, in the best of weather, it took at least half a day to reach Gornji Milanovac by horse-drawn wagon. When we sold our produce at the town marketplace, we would leave in the middle of the night in order to be there by dawn. We were poor by any standard, yet our neighbors were no better off. We didn't feel inferior to anyone, and, after all, we are the descendants of generations of warriors who defended our Serbian traditions against the Turks! Nevertheless, I don't think I could return to the hardships of those times. But, the village is no longer like that, and I will never sever the ties to my birthplace or our kin who still live there.

As in many traditional agrarian societies, until recent times, much of rural Yugoslavia was characterized by widespread poverty. This was due in large part to the relative lack of land resources in respect to the size of the peasant population. In the case of Bogdan, this was a significant motivating factor for leaving the village:

> I lived in Cerići until I was 42 – that was in 1950. I had only three hectares [about seven and a half acres] of unproductive land. Until just before my father's death in 1941, I lived in a *zagruda* [a partrilocally extended household] with my parents, my sister, and my five brothers and their families. There were twenty-two of us, including the children, and, even with fifteen hectares of land, we had a hard time. Just before my father died, he divided the holdings among us sons – my sister, of course, went to live on her husband's land after she got married. In order to support my wife and three children, I had to hire myself out doing any jobs I could find. But the opportunities in the village were limited, and the pay almost nothing. After the war, I worked part time as a clerk in the Cerići agricultural cooperative, but this was barely enough to pay the taxes on our land. Between the five of us, we were somehow able to wrest a living from the soil – even our small children helped. Not that we lived well. We ate what we produced: fresh cheese, milk, beans, bread, onions, peppers, and cabbage for the most part. Meat was a rarity – we couldn't afford to slaughter our animals.

*The names of informants and their places of origin have been changed to protect their anonymity.

Among the most significant stimuli for migration is indirect contact with urban life through the experiences of relatives or neighbors who now live in the city and who return for frequent visits to the village. Through such relationships, it is possible not only to judge the chances of success in migration, and also to be assured of a helping hand during the difficult periods of settlement and accommodation to an unfamiliar environment and way of life:

> After the war, we began hearing more and more about the opportunities in the city from neighbors and relatives who had gone to Gornji Milanovac or even Belgrade. I knew that there must be a better way of life than this. Actually, before the war, I had served a year in Zagreb while in the army, but in those days there were no jobs in town, and the urban poor lived worse than the peasants. In 1949, my wife's cousin, Panto, moved to Belgrade, where he found employment with a construction company, and, when my job with the village cooperative was abolished in 1950, I wrote him and asked him to help me obtain work there. Much to my surprise, he answered right away informing me that there was an opening with his concern as a clerk and that his boss would save the position for me, since he owed Panto a favor. I went immediately and stayed with Panto and his wife. My family remained [in] the village, and I visited them every weekend. Actually this worked out very well, since I could bring food from Cerići back to Belgrade and aid Panto by sharing it with him. I can't say I enjoyed living in Belgrade at first. I just worked and slept for the most part, saving as much money as I could. We ate what Panto and I would bring from the village, and I only spent my earnings for the bus tickets to Cerići. I wasn't like some others who, once they had a few dinars in their pockets, went wild, wasting their money in cafes on drink and Gypsy musicians!

After employment, the most basic problem facing a new migrant in Belgrade is housing. Without space for his family, he cannot really be said to have put down roots in the city. The destruction due to the Second World War and the rapid increase in the urban population have brought about a major housing crisis in all Yugoslav cities, and Belgrade is among the most acutely affected. In spite of the fact that one of the major tenets of the Yugoslav socialist state when it came to power was that the government "owes each family an adequate dwelling unit with minimum standards," this remains largely empty rhetoric (Fisher 1966:144). Theoretically, housing can be obtained by impersonal means via the so-called socialist economic sector, that is, through government agencies or the enterprise where one is employed. In this respect, larger and more successful firms can frequently offer their workers modern housing, or an apartment can be obtained through the municipality, if one does not mind waiting for years. All of this can be expedited, of course, through friends or kin in important positions; however, most migrants must fend for themselves. For an unskilled worker like Bogdan with a minimal education and few significant connections, the process of settling down is likely to be a long one. Thus, for the peasant migrant, there is usually a direct relationship between the length of time in the city and the quality of housing:

> I couldn't continue staying with Panto – he and Milena had only one room they rented from an old lady, and there was barely enough space for the two of them. After about two months, I managed to get a bed in a worker's barracks. There were about twenty of us in an old wooden building on the southern outskirts of the city. It was very cheap, but

life was really worse than in the army or the village. There was only one cold-water tap outside, and the outhouse was always filthy. When it rained, the whole area flooded, and we had to wade through a mire of mud to get to the toilet. The entire place smelled of urine and feces. We workers tried to share our food and prepare meals together, but there was no kitchen, and we had only a small kerosene camp stove. In those days, I went home to Cerići as often as possible. About four months later, I found an old shack made of boards and galvanized iron sheets on an unpaved alley near the barracks. I was able to buy it, but not the land it stood on. It had one small room and a kitchen with a cold-water tap. There was no bathroom, just an outhouse, but, after all, that is what we were used to in the village. I bought a kerosene heater, but it did little to keep out the cold during the winter. In any case, I was able to call for my family and [to] provide a place for them to live. In the meantime, I found a better job through a distant relative as a clerk with the city government (opština). We stayed in the shack for almost three years, while we waited for the housing agency to give us an apartment. We were always short of money, and, if it weren't for the food from the village, we would have never made it. My wife finally found a job in a municipal office making Turkish coffee for the workers and cleaning up, a kind of caretaker, you might say. Finally, we received an apartment through the city in an old part of Belgrade. It was rather primitive, but very spacious with large porcelain stoves heated by coal. Also, for the first time in our lives, we had an indoor toilet, but no hot water. Nevertheless, we had never experienced better! My wife and I slept with the three children in one room just as we had in Cerići. We kept one room for a parlor, and another for guests from the village who were almost always with us. We discovered credit, and gradually began buying the furniture that we now have piece-by-piece. In the beginning, we simply borrowed a truck from a cousin who worked at a motor pool and brought what few things we needed from Cerići. I remember how we slept on homemade straw mattresses. I had no idea how uncomfortable we were! Well, finally they began the renewal of the neighborhood in which we lived, and our building was torn down. By law, when this occurs, a family must be given other housing of at least equal size. Since there was no such space then available, we received two apartments in this modern building where we live today. One was put in my name and the other in that of our son, Mile. We rent Mile's apartment out, even though this is not quite legal. When our daughter, Stana, gets married, it will be her dowry. Actually, we have had a good deal of luck, more than many others!

Bogdan's success in accommodating to Yugoslav urban life can be attributed, to a large degree, to the role of traditional culture and its associated values. In particular, kinship has provided this family with a ready-made set of resources, and, thus, precluded the kinds of alienation and social marginality that have typified rapid urbanization in many other parts of the world. Bogdan's case being not at all atypical, suggests that neither long residence nor even birth in the city necessarily weakens ties to the countryside. Indeed, many native Belgradians are as familiar with their parents', and even grandparents', villages as they are with the capital itself. Moreover, such rural-urban ties are not only of utility during the initial phase of settlement in the city, but may persist over an entire lifetime. For the urbanite, the village constitutes a source of foodstuffs, a place for summer vacations, and, perhaps most importantly, an insurance policy against failure in the city or economic crisis. For the peasant, city kin represent a source of cash for taxes and capital improvements, an initial base for the new migrant, and a place where children may stay while obtaining a higher education. In some cases, the urban household simply constitutes an extension of the village home, and many families continue to behave as if they were still a single unit with two or more residences. In other words, the urbanization of segments of rural-based kinship groups has simply opened up new avenues for continuing the same kinds of reciprocity that have always typified South Slav traditional culture. For example, twenty-four years after migrating to Belgrade, Bogdan was still interacting with both his and his wife's urban and rural kin as intensely as he had the day he left Cerići:

> To tell you the truth, life in Cerići was not entirely bad, and, in some ways, it was much better than in the city. I particularly remember how we would look forward to village weddings, which usually lasted several days, and how we enjoyed going to Gornji Milanovac to the *vašar* [animal fair]. Actually, in reality, I still belong to the village. I never sold my land, but simply g[a]ve it to my brother, Branko, to work. Also, I have let [sic] my nephew live in my house with his wife and three children. That is the house where we were all born, and, even though it is part of my share of the estate, it is really a family home, since that is where our parents lived and died. You must understand what I mean by family. In Cerići, there are seventeen households of Mitrovići, and we are all related through our fathers. In fact, the *mala* [neighborhood] where most of the family houses are clustered is called Mitrovići. My wife is also close to her kin, and we visit her village of Livadice as often as we do Cerići. Family is family, and we remain close to our own no matter where they may be or what they may have accomplished in life. We help each other when we can. No one else will!

In 1974, when questioned about specific recent contacts with kin, Bogdan gave the following account:

> The fifteen-year-old daughter of my *sinovica* [brother's daughter] spent ten days with us in August. Her mother, Miroslava, spent two days here during the same month. Miroslava's husband also visited us for a day in September. Another *sinovica*, Jelena, came with her husband to stay for several days in September. They are from the village of Beli Potok near Belgrade. My brother Nikola came from the town of Ivanjica for a day in October. My wife's unmarried sister from Zemun [a town just across the Sava River from Belgrade] visits us at least once a week. Another sister of my wife from Takovo [a provincial town not far from Cerići] has already visited us four times this year with her husband and five children. They always bring us large amounts of food from their holdings in Livadice — potatoes, garlic, onions, homemade sausages, and *rakija* [fruit brandy]. The young daughter of my brother Milenko from Cerići was with us for a month this summer, and Mira and Rada, the two girls that are here right now, are cousins from the village. Vaso, our *prijatelj* [in-law — the brother of Bogdan's wife's sister's husband], who lives in Belgrade, drops by several times a week. And, of course, my wife's cousin, Panto, and his wife live only a few minutes walk from here, and we see each other quite often. Frankly, we have so many visitors, it is hard to remember them all. Our kin just come whenever they want. We don't expect them to let us know ahead of time. And, we do the same! In June, I went to Gornji Milanovac because I have been feeling badly of late. There is a spa there and taking the water always makes me feel better. I stayed with the daughter of my brother Branko and her husband. He is an instructor in the secondary school there. Of course, I didn't pay them anything, but I took a dress for my niece and a sweater for her fifteen-year-old daughter. I didn't go to Cerići while I was there, but at least a dozen of my relatives came to see me in Gornji Milanovac. Some of my wife's kin also visited me: her *brat od tetke* [mother's sister's son],

her *ujna* [mother's brother's wife], her *brat od strica* [father's brother's son], and my *šurak* [wife's brother] and his wife. Everyone I saw in Gornji Milanovac brought me food from the village to take back to Belgrade — so much I couldn't even carry it all. In late October, I will go to Cerići to visit the family graves on the Days of the Dead [Zadušnice]. This year, my three children spent almost the entire summer in Cerići and Livadice with their uncles. They still love village life, and it is a change from the dirt and confusion of Belgrade.

Bogdan is an example of a conservative peasant migrant whose social universe, even after settling in Belgrade, remained rooted almost entirely in kinship. In fact, his kinship network was so extensive and contained so many diverse social types, that he had no real need for friends apart from family members. Counted among his blood relatives and affines [relatives through marriage] were peasants, industrial and construction workers, skilled craftsmen, bureaucrats and other white-collar workers, a lawyer, an army colonel, an Orthodox priest, a secondary school instructor, an engineer, and a factory director. Among his close relatives were at least a dozen Communist Party members, and an equal number who were deeply religious and hostile to the present Yugoslav regime. In this respect, Bogdan's family is not exceptional by Yugoslav standards, and the vast majority of the more than two hundred families I have studied over the past twenty years exhibit the same diversity. What is even more significant is that such differences in status, educational levels and political orientation do not seem to inhibit kinship relationships to any appreciable degree.

As was the case with most peasant migrants at the time when Bogdan came to Belgrade, he left Cerići hoping to escape from what seemed to be the unrelenting and unchanging drudgery and poverty of peasant life. In exchange, he envisioned a more comfortable and economically secure existence in the city and dreamed of the social mobility that his children might enjoy. For Bogdan, as well as for the vast majority of peasants who settled in Belgrade during the three decades following the Second World War, this desire was largely fulfilled. His son Mile is a graduate of a secondary technical school, and now works as a skilled cabinetmaker for a furniture concern in Belgrade and lives with his widowed mother, wife and two children in the modern apartment his father finally obtained after almost six years in Belgrade. Mile's wife, Zora, was born in a village only seven kilometers from Cerići and supplements the family income as a seamstress working in the private sector. Over the last ten years, they have gradually modernized the family home in Cerići, adding a contemporary kitchen and bathroom. They spend most of their holidays in the village and plan eventually to retire there in a comfort unknown to their parents' generation. Bogdan's daughter Stana finished secondary commercial school and, with the aid of the father of a student friend, found a job as a secretary in a small textile enterprise. She now lives with her husband, a secondary mathematics instructor and native Belgradian, in the apartment her father had promised her as a dowry. Zoran, Bogdan's oldest son, is an epileptic and consequently was unable to finish secondary school or to find permanent employment in the city. He has now returned to Cerići to work in agriculture with his uncles, cashing in the *village insurance policy* that his father had never allowed to lapse.

At the time of his death in 1981, Bogdan must have felt a deep sense of satisfaction from a lifetime of accomplishment. It was largely through his own initiative that he and his family had come to enjoy the best of two worlds. Together with masses of other rural migrants, Bogdan, as an agent of change, participated in a great historical process, the simultaneous peasantization of the cities and the modernization of the countryside (cf. Friedl 1959; Halpern 1965). However, it would be erroneous to suggest that all migrants experience the same level of success as had Bogdan. Many lack his extensive kinship ties, and others come from even poorer and more remote villages than Cerići, villages that are difficult to visit regularly or that can provide little material support. Still others, freed from the bonds of traditional social controls and norms, drift into various forms of maladaptive behavior: alcoholism, poor work habits, family violence and even criminality. The latter, however, does not describe even a significant minority. For instance, there is nothing comparable in Yugoslavia to the so-called American *underclass* or the slum dwellers of Latin America. Moreover, rural migrants in Belgrade do not form a class segment, nor are they, after a few years in the city, readily discernable from the general urban population. Although Belgrade folklore is full of stories about bewildered peasants washing potatoes in the bidet and stalling goats in the living room, the reality is that the cultural gap which separates the new urbanite from the city proletariat is minimal. My case studies and personal observations clearly show that the important cultural contrast does not exist between long-time urbanites and new migrants, but rather can be observed between intellectuals and professionals, on the one hand, and blue-collar workers and peasants on the other. Even this distinction is mitigated by the class-heterogeneous nature of most Yugoslav kinship groups.

CONCLUSION

One measure of successful urbanization is the degree to which rural migrants are able to integrate themselves into all levels of urban society. On the one hand, this depends on the migrant's ability to discard those markers and forms of behavior that readily identify him or her as of recent rural origins, and, on the other, the degree to which barriers exist on the part of the host population to the incorporation of the new settler. In this respect, the generally positive experience in Serbia can be explained in terms of the concurrence of a set of unique historical circumstances. The Turkish conquest in the fourteenth century destroyed the existing indigenous aristocracy, and, in over more than 500 years of Moslem occupation, no native elite of any significance was to emerge until the nineteenth century. However, this small middle and upper class, which was derived largely from the peasantry, was to enjoy only a little more than a century of ascendancy before the socialist revolution following World War II destroyed the existing system of social stratification. Thus, unlike many of the countries of Western Europe and Latin America, in most of Yugoslavia, a centuries-old continuity of asymmetrical class relationships has not prevailed. Until about thirty years ago, Yugoslav urban populations remained very small and were largely derived from peasant migrations of earlier periods. Similarly, contemporary urbanites have recent village roots and have brought with them a repertoire of folk customs which have been superimposed over earlier borrowings of rural culture. Thus, those cultural differences which do exist are not the product of the rural-urban dichotomy, but rather reflect various levels of occupational and educational achievement.

While migrants to Belgrade have encountered a congenial cultural atmosphere, that is, an existing population speaking the same language, sharing the same religious origins, and generally participating in the same kinship-oriented value system, economic factors have also contributed to the relatively trouble-free urbanization of Yugoslav society. The massive movement of rural peoples took place during the first three decades following the war, a time of accelerated economic expansion; therefore, not only was there a balance struck between the creation of new jobs and the rate of migration to cities, but also an expanding occupational pyramid made very rapid vertical mobility possible for many. Consequently, peasant migrants in such cities as Belgrade did not necessarily remain at the bottom of the urban prestige ladder; rather, they were able to enter every level of the productive and bureaucratic hierarchies. This initial phase of the modernization of Yugoslav society represents the simultaneous transformation of an entire people; yet, in many respects, this transformation has been more of an economic and demographic revolution than a cultural one.

It is doubtful that Bogdan's experience will ever be repeated again. He is the product of a particular period in his nation's history. With a deepening economic crisis, it is possible that his son Zoran, who returned to Cerići, represents the wave of the future. Recent reports indicate that land that has lain fallow for decades is again being cultivated. For at least the immediate future, rural-urban migration in Yugoslavia remains a two-way street.

NOTES

1. A report by the Yugoslav News Agency Tanjug, cited in the *Los Angeles Times* (4 July, 1987), states that the rate of inflation increased from 93.3% in 1986 to 100.6% in June of 1987.
2. For a more detailed discussion of Yugoslav urbanization and the history of Belgrade, see Simić (1973:28-71).
3. Yugoslavia is composed of six republics and two autonomous regions roughly corresponding to the settlement of the major ethnic groups. Ethnicity is defined principally on the basis of language and religion. For example, the Serbs, who comprise the largest national category, are of the Eastern Orthodox faith and speak Serbo-Croatian.
4. While traditional concepts governing kinship and other interpersonal relationships have made a positive contribution to the integration of rural migrants into urban life, this same ideology has significantly inhibited the building of efficient large-scale institutions within the economy and bureaucracy. For a detailed discussion of this phenomenon, see Simić (1983).

A WEST INDIAN LIFE IN BRITAIN

George Gmelch

In this essay, George Gmelch examines the migration and adaptation of West Indians to Britain. The oral history of a single migrant, Roy Campbell, is used to give the reader an insider's view of emigration. While the previous essays on Yugoslav and Mexican migration were concerned with rural-to-urban migration within a single culture, this West Indian case concerns international migration and the adaptation of migrants to a new culture. While the Yugoslav and Mexican examples dealt with linear migration in which migrants permanently left their rural homelands, most West Indian migrants only aim to be abroad long enough to satisfy certain economic or educational goals. This article is about return migration, as well as outmigration. The subsequent essay, by Robert Rhoades, examines the impact of returning migrants.

About one of every ten current residents of Barbados has emigrated at one time or another; many others have left and have never returned. High rates of outmigration are common throughout the small, over-populated, and resource-poor islands of the Caribbean. It is so pervasive that, in most villages, nearly every household has a relative or close friend in Britain or North America. Beginning in the 1830s, when slavery was abolished in the British Caribbean, and slaves were free to move, migration has been of such fundamental importance to the islanders' economic adaptation that it has been referred to as "livelihood migration" (Richardson 1983). Success for most West Indians, economic as well as social, depends upon emigration.

Most West Indian outmigration is not *permanent* or *linear*. Most migrants do not intend to settle abroad for good; rather, they see their migration as circular. At the time of their departure, they expect to be away only long enough to achieve a goal – to save enough money to build a respectable house at home, to complete a college education, or to learn a trade. Today, an estimated half million West Indian immigrants live in Britain; three times that number reside in the United States and Canada. Most have arrived since 1955, first going to Britain, and then, after she closed her doors to immgrants in the 1960s, to North America. Most have stayed away from their homeland much longer than they originally intended, yet they cling to the hope that someday, if only at retirement, they will be able to return home. Having an *ideology of return* is important, for it gives the migrants a psychological safety valve, an idea to fall back on when life abroad does not measure up to their expectations.

SOURCE: Article written expressly for *Urban Life*.

WEST INDIAN MIGRATION

In the first fifty years after emancipation (1835 to 1885), the major movement of West Indians was away from the plantations on which they had been enslaved to small holdings and towns on their home islands (Marshall 1982). Some also migrated to other islands within the Caribbean, primarily to British colonies. Much of this inter-island migration was in response to the expansion of sugar cane cultivation in the newer colonies of British Guinea and Trinidad.

After the 1880s, the migrants went farther afield, travelling to Spanish and other non-British territories: to Cuba and the Dominican Republic to work on large sugar estates, to Central America to work on banana plantations, to Bermuda to construct a dry dock, to the United States to work in factories and in fields, and, most notably, to Panama to excavate and build the Canal.

In the following two decades, until World War II, little migration occurred. Likewise, at this time, many earlier migrants returned home. During the Depression, it was generally considered better to scratch out a living on a small parcel of land at home than to be unemployed abroad.

With the outbreak of World War II, a new wave of migration began as workers moved to Britain, the United States and Canada to fill the jobs of citizens who were away in the armed forces. The war, however, was only a prelude to the mass migration to Britain that followed. The war, itself, provided the conditions which promoted such extensive migration, namely the enormous loss of life and the devastation of many British cities which created a high demand for labor. In the 1950s, West Indians migrated in large numbers to *the mother country*. For example, Barbados, in a six-year period from 1955 to 1961, saw nearly 19,000, or eight percent, of its citizens leave.[1]

What prompted Barbadians and other West Indians to leave their homelands? In most of the Caribbean, population growth had outstripped development; on many islands, there were simply too many people for the available resources. On Jamaica, for example, population growth rates of three and four percent per year, which were double those of the nineteenth century, caused the rural population to become so concentrated on small holdings that further increases were not possible without a substantial drop in the standard of living or movement off the land (Lowenthal 1972). It should be noted, however, that no social scientist has yet shown that a causal relationship between economic hardship and the propensity to emigrate existed. Rather, there is wide agreement that postwar migrants were reacting less to internal conditions in the West Indies than to an external stimulus, namely, the demand for labor in Britain (Peach 1968, Rose 1969, Foner 1978).[2] Ceri Peach (1968) examined the migration rates of different islands and compared them to population pressure, income, unemployment, economic growth and other indices for each island and found no correlation showing that these *push* factors were the predominant causes of the movements. Indeed, rates of migration from different Caribbean islands have tended to follow the same pattern regardless of local conditions.

Most West Indians migrated to England alone, not as couples or families. In most households, the male emigrated first, followed by his wife or girlfriend and by some, but seldom all, of their children. Why did men go first? Are they more ambitious, adventurous or independent than West Indian women? Definitely not, according to

Nance Foner (1986) in a study of Jamaican migrants. Rather, in most households, there simply was not enough money for the entire family to emigrate together, and, as men were the principal breadwinners, it was natural that they would go first. If employment and housing conditions abroad were favorable and enough money could be saved for additional fares, women and children followed.

Most West Indian governments made no effort to prevent their citizens from leaving; in fact, emigration was often seen as a safety valve for excess population and high unemployment. Barbados assisted British companies and government agencies to recruit workers. London Transport and the Lyons Hotel and Restaurant Association, for example, set up offices in Bridgetown to interview Barbadians. A Barbadian from a tiny village in the north of the island could make his way to Bridgetown and apply for a job 3,000 miles away as a bus conductor, a ticket taker on the platform at Euston Station, or a dishwasher in a Picadilly restaurant.

Who were the men and women who left the Caribbean to seek jobs in England? What was it like to be a black immigrant in a predominantly white society? How well did they adjust? Did they achieve their goals and were they able to return to the Caribbean? The following pages focus on the experiences of Roy Campbell, one of ten Barbadian migrants whose life histories I recorded in 1985 and 1987. I use Roy's account here because, in many respects, he comes closest to being *typical* of post-war Barbadian migrants in terms of education, jobs, housing and social adjustment.

ROY CAMPBELL: AN IMMIGRANT'S LIFE

Roy grew up in a village in the parish of St. Lucy at the northern tip of Barbados. Like many Barbadian villages, this community is made up of small, brightly colored, wooden houses stretched single file along a narrow main road, with other houses connected by footpaths. Scattered among them is the occasional *wall* or cement-block house owned by a better-off family, often emigrants who have returned from abroad. Bordering the village are the pale green canefields, which cover much of Barbados, and bordering the fields are lines of cabbage palms and casurina trees imported from Australia by the early British planters.

Roy remained in school until age fifteen, earning his *leaving certificate* (equivalent to a high school diploma). He then obtained a job as an apprentice automobile mechanic in a garage in Bridgetown, the capital and Barbados' only city. Four years later, he was still earning apprentice wages of seven dollars per week when British Army recruiters came to Barbados.[3] Roy volunteered, took the physical exam and was accepted, but his father, fearing another war, refused to let his only son go. Instead, he gave Roy money to pay for his passage to England, a new suit of clothes and a suitcase.

> I wanted to go [to England], because I wasn't getting anywhere here in Barbados, and because I wanted to see what England was like after hearing so much in school about the mother country. I was nineteen, and many of my friends had gone over already. I left on the boat the 16th of June, 1962, with my suitcase full of warm underclothing and food: rice, sugar, rum, peppers, pepper sauce, flour, yams, and potatoes. I thought it would be hard to get West Indian food there.

In the early years of West Indian emigration to England, migrants travelled by sea. In 1955, thirteen ships made more than forty sailings, each carrying up to a thousand migrants (Patterson 1963). Over half the ships were Italian, and; in a curious reversal of migration streams, some of the ships carried Mediterranean emigrants to Venezuela on the outward voyage, then picked up West Indians bound for Britain on the return crossing. The fare was expensive and many emigrants sold their possessions and borrowed from relatives to raise the money. Most had never been on a ship before.

> I went on the *Serrienta*, an Italian ship. I was seasick for about three days, but, after I recovered, the days started going too quickly. I wanted to stay on a bit longer – the food was so good, and, at night, you could go down to the cinema. And they had a lounge where you could listen to the news, and they had comics so you could sit down and read if you wanted. And they had a bar where you could have a drink. The ship had an Italian band, but they played samba music so that both the Italians and the West Indians could dance to it. I'll tell you, I didn't want to come off the ship.
>
> After seven days at sea, we stopped at Tenerife in the Canary Islands, then Barcelona, then Naples and then we got off in Genoa. I was seeing places I'd never seen, places I'd never heard of. In Tenerife, I saw policemen walking the streets with guns. I said to myself, "These people are not as free as our people back home." I'd never seen a policeman with a gun. At first, I was terrified. I was afraid if I said anything bad I'd be shot.
>
> In Tenerife and Barcelona, I saw white people begging for the first time. I never knew of such things. Then I saw white people working as refuse collectors, and I thought to myself that I'd never do that job and here are whites doing it. Then I saw white taxi drivers. I said to myself, "Is it going to be like this in England?" My whole attitude began to change. I was going to England thinking of only picking the jobs that I wanted, but seeing white people doing those bad jobs made me think that I might have to do bad jobs too.
>
> From Italy, we took the train across the continent to France and the English Channel, where we got the ferry over to the English side and then the train to Waterloo Station in London. There my sister met me.

More than half the arriving West Indians settled in London; the others gravitated to cities in the Midlands and the north of England, particularly Birmingham, Manchester, Bradford and Nottingham. Where an immigrant settled was determined largely by where his relatives and friends had settled before him. They provided temporary accommodation, helped the new arrival find a job, and assisted in acclimating him to English life – how to ride the bus, where to shop and so forth. As each new immigrant, in turn, assisted others, colonies of transplanted West Indians developed in particular neighborhoods of most major cities. Anthropologist Douglas Midget (1977) found half of the 290 migrant households from the village he had studied on the island of St. Lucia in the same London neighborhood of Paddington.

> The first week, I stayed with my sister, her husband and their boy. Then she got me another room in the same house. I shared it with a Barbadian who worked for London Transport. He did his own cooking and sometimes he'd cook for me, but mostly I'd only sleep there, because I'd go up to my sister's to eat and watch television. When the landlord sold the house, we all had to move. My sister and her husband got a flat with three

rooms, and she rented one of the rooms to me.

It was hard to find a place to stay in England. Rooms were available, but you'd see signs — "No Blacks," "No Coloured," "No Irish." Or you might see "English Only." And when you did get a room, the landlord would put restrictions on you, like telling you all visitors must be out of your place by ten o'clock.

England was rough in the beginning; it wasn't what I expected. The first morning my sister and I walked down to the bus stop, and she didn't say good morning or hello to the people there, and I am thinking, "This is strange." Anywhere in Barbados, you say good morning and hello to people. The next morning, I go to fetch the milk off the stoop, and, when I get there, the lady next door was there to pick up her milk as well. I said, "Good morning." She just looked surprised and didn't answer. When I got upstairs, I told my sister, then she told me that was the custom in England. Nobody says good morning or hello, at least not to black people. I missed all the friendliness that you have in Barbados.

When I first saw all the houses joined together with all their chimneys up in the air and smoke coming out the top, I wondered where the people lived. I thought the houses were factories. I had never heard of people making fires in their houses, and they all looked the same, every building, every street, all the same way. I said to a man, "How do you know which is your house?" He said, "By the numbers." That alone put me off.

When I got to England my thinking was that I'd be away no more than five years. I wanted to save enough money to get a little home in Barbados. At that time, the pound was worth $4.80, and I thought that, if I could save $10,000, I would be able to buy enough building materials to build a home. Building material was pretty cheap then; you'd get a [cement] block for thirty-six cents, a board for about forty cents, and labor was cheap. I wasn't thinking about getting married, settling down, or anything like that. I only wanted to make some quick money, see the country and come back home.

The first winter, I really wanted to go back home. It was so cold, the worst winter they had had in many years, but my father told me before I left Barbados that that was the last money he was going to spend on me and that I was on my own from now on. That stopped me from writing and asking him to send for me. After that winter, I wanted to get back to Barbados as fast as I could, but it took a long time to save any money. And by the time I saved enough for my passage, I was starting to get settled down.

My first job in England was working at a bakery as a porter. It was a Jewish bakery in East London. The pay was 8 pounds, 10 shillings per week. I had to load the van with the cakes, then I'd clean the bread trays, pack the frig with the cakes for the next day, and sometimes I'd sweep up. In Barbados, I wouldn't have done that kind of work, but, as I said, seeing white people doing those jobs, I knew I'd have to do them too. They didn't pay me enough for the work I was doing, but the bakery was walking distance from home, plus they let me have rolls and buns for lunch. I'd bring a piece of ham to work, and I'd eat their rolls. Plus they gave me free milk to put in my tea. So I saved an extra ten shillings a week that I'd have had to spend on lunch if I had worked somewhere else. I guess that's why I didn't leave the bakery, at least not for a long time.

In the bakery, there were a half dozen Barbadians, a couple of Jamaicans, and a half dozen Montserratians. The foreman, assistant foreman, oven man and storekeeper were all Jewish. Only the cakemaker was English. You had more West Indians there than anybody else. That was because we were cheap labor and did all the hard work.

All the West Indians became very friendly. We used to go to each other's house to have a drink and party. There was a lot of mickey taking [poking fun] at each other, especially about the country you came from. Jamaicans would call us "small island" because Jamaica was so much bigger than our islands. Then we'd say that the cricket players from Montserrat can't bowl very fast because, if they take a long run, they'll land in the sea. Or we'd say, they can't even grow pumpkins in Montserrat because the vines have to run and land is so scarce they haven't got anywhere to go. We'd make fun of each other's speech, too. We used to laugh at the way Jamaicans talk, because they talk back to front. Bajans would say the "top of my head" is hurting me, where Jamaicans would say "my head top" is hurting me. I would say "bring me the bottle," but Jamaicans would say "go carry come the bottle." We laughed at them. But they'd just say all small islanders are "fou fou" [foolish].

About this time, in 1963, I met the woman that became my wife. I met her when I went to visit a friend of mine, and she was there. I got talking to her and her girlfriend (she was Barbadian too), and I spent the whole day there. I told Wendy about my work, and she told me about her work at the Lyons Restaurant at the corner of Oxford Street and Tottenham Court Road. She had come to England on a contract with Lyons Hotel and Restaurant; they were recruiting girls in Barbados, and she signed up.

The following day, my friend's girlfriend called me at work to tell me that Wendy wanted to see me again and that she was off from work that day. So I told my boss I had to go home. I caught the bus and went straight there. She made me a cup of tea and something to eat. After that, I'd meet her every night after work and take her home. After two or three months courting I said, "It is not profitable for you paying rent and me paying rent — why not live together?" So we moved in together, and she got pregnant. She lost the first baby, but got pregnant again and, in November, 1966, had the baby.

When she was pregnant, she said, "You know, this is not Barbados. Here, if you have children and you are not married, they look down on you." I said I would try to get a different job to make more money so that we could get married. At the time, there were a lot of colored immigrants working for London Transport, so I decided to give them a try. At the driving test [for bus driver] there were a half dozen of us, five white guys and me. We got in this old Routemaster double-decker bus. We all sat upstairs except for the guy who was being tested on driving. Each guy drove for fifteen to twenty minutes. Well, I drove pretty well, and the guy said, "You drive damn good." When all of us completed the driving, he took us back to the depot. The inspector said to us, "You all let me down; this black boy here drove better than any of you." So then I figured that everything was going to be okay, that I was going to get the job. But he called me to one side. "What I advise you to do," he says, "is take a conductor's job, and maybe later you'll get to drive the bus." Back in the room, I talked to the five white guys, and they told me that they all got through, that they were all going to be bus drivers. When I told them about me, they said, "Blimey, you drive better than us." That really put me off. I didn't bother with the conductor's job then, I just started for home.

On the train on the way back home, I got the *Midday Standard*, and I saw a position for a postman. So I sent in the form. Two days later, I got a reply asking me to come in for a test. Two dozen of us took the test, and after we finished, we all went out in the room and waited. They called out eight of us. I heard them tell the others that they would have to try another time, that they hadn't made it. I really felt good then. I had made it!

They sent me to postman's school to learn the towns and cities in England, Scotland, Ireland and Wales. And I had to learn the London districts, learn the whole of London from North 22, EC 1 to EC 4, WC to WC 2, E 1 to E 18, Northwest 1 to Northwest 11, West 1 to West 14, Southeast 1 to Southeast 27.

At the school we'd test each other:
"Where is Southeast 3?"
"Greenwich."
"Where is Tottenham?"
"North 15."
We had three days to learn all that and nine days to learn all the towns and cities. They gave us a pack of cards to take home at night so that we could study. I would give my girlfriend the cards, and she would test me, even when we were eating:
"Where is Wellingborough?"
"Northhampton."
"Yeah, you know that one. Okay, where is Limerick?"
"Ireland." and so on.

I learned them all with two days to spare. There were three of us colored fellows in a class of eighteen, and we all passed the exam early. Some of the white guys said they couldn't understand how these black people come here and learn these places faster than they who were born here and who lived here all the time. I'd think to myself, "Hey, I am doing great in this white man's country." We wanted to do well, so we really put our minds to it.

I started in the north London post office. There were about eight West Indians and a dozen Africans. At first, they gave us, the black fellows, the dirty jobs, like sorting parcels. Whatever they told us to do, we'd always try to do it to our best so that the governor [supervisor] couldn't come in and say that you, a black person, wasn't doing a good job. My boss used to call me Sam. I asked why he called me Sam and not my real name, Roy. He said that in his school days, they used to call all little black boys Sam, "You know, Sambo. So if I call you Sam," he says, "don't be annoyed."

Another English guy at the post office told me that when he was in school, he thought black boys had tails. He and his friend had followed a black man into a public lavatory to see if it was true. When the black man went into the toilet stall, they got up on the next toilet and looked over the top at him. The black guy pretended he didn't see them peeping on him, but then, when he was done, he rushed for them and banged their two heads together.

West Indians got on better with the whites than with the Africans. The white workers wouldn't show their prejudice. The Africans thought we were inferior to them. They would say that because all West Indians are descended from slaves, and the slavemasters were white people who had sex with our great grandmothers and their mothers. That is why we were much fairer in color than the Africans.

Roy's primary leisure activity in England was playing cricket. After several years in London, playing with other West Indians and in the London Post Office League, Roy was invited to play for an English club.

My friend Winston introduced me to the fellows from Trinity. They were all white except Winston, his brother and me. The first match, I did very badly. I made naught [didn't score any runs]. I felt bad for Winston because he had told them what a good bat I was. But the second match, I did a little better, and the third match I was still better. Eventually I was opening the batting [batting first in the order].[4] Playing on an English team was different from playing in the West Indies. If you did well, say you scored a century [100 runs in one match], you'd have to buy drinks. In the West Indies, they'd buy you the drinks. Playing with the English fellows, you always wanted to do well, but you also knew that if you did well it was going to cost you money.

After my girlfriend, Wendy, had the baby, I said to her that we had to be careful, because we want to go back to Barbados, and, if we have more children, we won't ever be able to afford to go back. So I said, "Let's quit for a while." Then we had a second kid in 1969, and I said "That's it, no more kids." I was eight years in England then, and it was time to start preparing to go home.

After we got married, her mom wrote from Barbados and told us that there was some land being sold, and if we would like a house spot, it would be a good place. We didn't have much money, but we withdrew what we had and sent it home to buy the spot. The price was $3,300.

I came back to Barbados on a visit for the first time in 1968, after being away for six years. You could see great improvement: there were many more cars, the roads were much better and the people were doing better. In the stores, you'd see many of the same things that you'd see in England. In 1973, Wendy and I came back together and had a plan drawn up for a house, and then we went back to England to save more money.

When Roy and Wendy returned to England in 1973 they left their two children behind in Barbados with Wendy's parents. They did so in order to save money and hasten their permanent return to Barbados. Although their children were in good hands, the separation was traumatic for Roy and Wendy. Roy had difficulty even talking about it years afterward. In 1976, they returned to Barbados again, but they still did not have enough money to build the house they wanted. Nevertheless, they contracted a relative to begin construction.

We went to my wife's uncle and asked him if he could start the house and told him to build until our money was gone. He agreed, and he told me to open an account at Plantations Limited, the builders store in Bridgetown. When we left Barbados that time, I said to my wife that the next time we came back, it must be for good. There were the kids to think about, and I really wanted to be back in Barbados to enjoy my own country. Barbados looked so good to me, all the sunshine and the friendliness of the people. In England, you only get three or four months of what they call sunshine, in what they call summer. You always seem to be loaded down with lots of clothes — shoes, socks, t-shirt, shirt, vest, cardigan, coat and what not. The weight on you made you feel old. In Barbados, you can just put on a pair of shorts and walk outside barefoot.

In 1979, six years after leaving their children, Roy and Wendy returned to Barbados for good, having saved enough to finish the construction of their house. Roy, who had slipped and injured his back while working at the post office, was given a medical disability and a pension, which would help support them in Barbados.

We arrived home on the 31st of November, 1979, which was Independence Day. We stayed at my mother-in-law's until our things arrived by boat, and then, just before Christmas, we moved into our own house. Coming home made me a bit nervous. I wondered if I could get a job and what kind of work I would do. My first job was as a security guard. The pay was small, but I didn't have much choice. I had to make some money because the kids were in school. My wife didn't have a job, and the house wasn't finished yet. My post office pension paid some of the bills, but it wasn't enough to support the whole family.

Then I met a friend from England who had come back to Barbados and after a lot of trying he got me a job at the Transport Board. They made me an inspector. Being able to travel all around the island, riding on all the different bus routes, I was able to meet a lot of people. People on the buses or at the bus stops saying, "Good morning, Mr. Campbell," or "Hello, Roy," people knowing your name and wanting to speak to you and you just being back from England — well, that made me feel pretty good. It made me feel glad to be home.

Coming back to Barbados wasn't very hard on me, mostly because I'd come home a few times to visit. I knew what to expect. If I had stayed away for all those years and then come back and tried to settle down, it would have been hard. Plus, I got a job pretty quick, and we were able to move into our home so that we didn't have to pay rent.

Some things, however, do bother me. One thing is that people here are not good at timekeeping. If someone agrees to meet you at eight o'clock, they don't turn up until eight-thirty or maybe even nine, and they don't say they are sorry for being late. If the English say they will get here at eight o'clock, they will be here at eight o'clock. And people here aren't as mannerly. The English always say "please" and "thank you," but you don't hear that said much here.

I wasn't able to adjust myself to the West Indian type of cricket either. I was thirty-five when I came home and the boys here were young and really fast [bowlers], and the pitches were hard. I decided that I had played enough, so I packed it in. I still watch a lot of cricket; when a touring team comes to Barbados, I go out to Kensington Oval to see the match. I meet a lot of the blokes who played for the post office teams in England there. I look around for them and during the intervals, or the lunch and tea breaks, we talk about what we used to do in England and how we used to play over there, and remember the old times.

About a fourth of the Barbadians who emigrated to Britain during the 1950s and 1960s have since returned home. More will return in the future, especially as they near retirement age and get pensions that will help support them in the Caribbean. Why do they return to their less developed homeland where good jobs are scarce, prices are high and services limited? How well do they readjust?

Some migrants are pushed home by unfavorable conditions abroad — unemployment, racial tension and personal problems. The British economy has been recovering slowly from the last recession (1979-82), and what gains have been made have done little for West Indians. The unemployment rate among West Indians in British cities is double that among whites. West Indians have also been disturbed by new signs of racism in Britain, such as the rising popularity of extreme right-wing groups like the National Front. The rhetoric and policies of Margaret Thatcher's conservative administration have also contributed to the growing uneasiness. Some right-wing members of Parliament have proposed that the government encourage West Indians to go home by offering them money, and the British Nationality Act of 1981, which declared that children born in Britain of West Indian parents would no longer qualify for British citizenship, was a slap in the face of West Indians who had given the best years of their lives to Britain.

Some return migration is precipitated by personal crisis: the breakup of a marriage, the death of a spouse, trouble with children, or ill health. One of Roy's neighbors who had been a hotel maid in an English resort town returned after being divorced. "After my husband left, it was just me and the kids in the house, and that's not good for anybody. I was lonely and bored. We needed more relatives around." In Britain, doctors often advise West Indians with serious health problems, especially mental disorders, to re-emigrate. The change of scenery and climate may be good for the patient, but it also helps to reduce the burden on Britain's National Health Service.

While some emigrants go home because they are unhappy with their lives abroad, the vast majority, like Roy, return because of their attachments to Barbados and its people. Many want to be near aging parents and old friends again; others have patriotic reasons.

For most emigrants, however, return migration is best understood as merely the fulfillment of what they had always intended to do, the natural completion of the migration cycle. At the time of their initial emigration, most Barbadians only plan to be away long enough to save money to buy a house and perhaps a car or to acquire a college degree or a trade. Despite such intentions, however, most overseas Barbadians never manage to return for good. Some simply cannot afford the passage or plane ticket back to Barbados. Those who fare poorly overseas are also disinclined to return because they will lose face, since all emigrants are expected to come home with at least enough money to buy a home of their own. Unless they are receiving a pension, most migrants will not return home without good prospects of a job. Because Barbados has scarcely any benefits for the unemployed, they are better off staying abroad. Conversely, the very successful also seldom return. To do so would mean giving up well-salaried positions and a standard of living that cannot be equaled in Barbados. It can also mean costly obligations to share their wealth with less well-off kinsmen at home.

Not all returnees readjust to life in Barbados as easily as Roy Campbell. Many are disappointed with what they find. Barbados is not the same place they left more than a decade before. The number of cars on the roads has doubled, snarling traffic around Bridgetown; crime has increased; the development of tourist hotels has driven up land prices on the coast, putting the hope of buying a house near the sea out of reach; and young Barbadians seem less courteous than a generation ago. In short, the primary source of dissatisfaction among many returnees is the lack of fit between what they had expected to find at home and the modern reality. The most dissatisfied tend to be those who have been away the longest and those who made no or few visits home.

An estimated 15% of returnees are so unhappy that they re-emigrate to Britain or to North America. For others, the dreams and unrealistic fantasies of what the homeland was going to be like fade with the passage of time. They adjust to the comparative inefficiency and petty annoyances of life at home. Gradually, their expectations about what can be accomplished in a day's work are lowered, and the slow pace of island life, rather than being a source of frustration, is seen as a virtue. Many cope with the shortcomings of life at home by getting off the island occasionally. Whether it be a return trip to London or a cheap charter flight to Miami, in the metropole, they can satisfy their appetites for the items they cannot get in Barbados. When abroad, these Barbadians are also reminded of the drawbacks of life there – the impersonality, the unsafe feeling on the streets at night, racial prejudice, and the *rat race* – and, thus, tend to appreciate Barbados and island life all the more.

NOTES

1. During the 1950s, the doors to Britain were wide open to all immigrants from the Commonwealth, though the British government did try to ensure that passports were not given to people with serious criminal records, old people or unaccompanied children (Field and Haikin 1971). Although just about any Commonwealth citizen could enter, the emigrants were, generally speaking, better educated and more skilled than those who stayed behind (Richardson 1983). This changed in 1982 with the passage of the Commonwealth Immigrants Act, which restricted immigration. The Act was the outcome of a campaign that began in the mid-1950s, spearheaded by extreme right-wing political groups and some Conservative members of Parliament and widely publicized by the press, to control immigration – in particular, the immigration of colored people. Support for the Act came largely from those who believed, first, that immigrants were flooding the labor market and, thus, taking jobs away from native Britons, and, second, that too many colored immigrants were creating a *race problem* in Britain (Rose 1969).
2. The sole exception to this pattern was the final year and a half before the imposition of the 1962 Commonwealth Immigration Act when, in the rush to beat the ban, the numbers of arrivals swelled out of proportion to labor demands.
3. All figures are in Barbados dollars. One Barbados dollar equals fifty U.S. cents.
4. Roy was a star batsman for the Trinity team; in 1972, he averaged more than eighty runs per game, and, by the time he left England, he had become the third highest run producer in the history of the Trinity team.

EUROPEAN CYCLICAL MIGRATION AND ECONOMIC DEVELOPMENT: THE CASE OF SOUTHERN SPAIN

Robert Rhoades

A much neglected aspect of migration has been the return flow of migrants from cities back to their rural homelands. Some scholars, who have argued that migration is beneficial to both the host and donor societies, claim that return migration has several important benefits for the migrants' rural homelands. First, workers may bring back valuable work skills and industrial experience that will upgrade the home labor force. Second, the migrants' foreign earnings may be used to establish innovative businesses, cooperatives and farms that will contribute to the revitalization of the rural homeland. Rhoades raises serious doubts about this view in his ethnographic case study of return migrants in a southern Spanish village.

MIGRATION AND DEVELOPMENT: A DEBATE

During Western Europe's twenty-year "economic miracle" (1955–1975), over ten million southern Europeans emigrated to the industrial world north of the Alps and Pyrenees. Lured by promises of higher wages, secure jobs, or simply the hope of escape from poverty, they left the impoverished Mediterranean Basin and sought their fortunes mainly in the labor-deficient regions of Germany, Switzerland, and France. However, these migrations were not terminal, one-shot affairs but governmentally planned, circular movements of labor between Europe's rural fringe and its industrial core. Migrants generally perceived themselves as "target workers" who temporarily went abroad for the purpose of earning enough money to build a new life upon return to their homelands. Correspondingly, labor-recruiting nations and employers looked upon immigration as a temporary, "stop-gap" solution to domestic labor shortages and thus discouraged permanent settlement of alien workers. This dovetailing of individual and national desires has resulted in continuous voluntary and periodic pressured returns of large numbers of migrants since the earliest stages of the post-war migrations.

SOURCE: Article written expressly for *Urban Life*.

The systematic transfer of manpower from Mediterranean regions of high unemployment to labor-starved regions in the North initially seemed a timely answer to many of Europe's economic and political ills. Migration across national frontiers was seen as fostering the cultural mingling of diverse Europeans, a necessary step toward realizing the dream of a "United States of Europe." More importantly, however, southern European countries would receive through remittances the foreign currency needed to overcome balance of payments problems. Also, the return of migrants was optimistically projected as a potential force in the economic uplifting of southern Europe. In fact, officials of northern European governments proclaimed that the exchange of "workers for wages" constituted a special form of "development aid" (Rhoades 1978a). Returning migrants were expected to carry home modern work habits, progressive attitudes, industrial skills, and the necessary capital to rejuvenate their regions' stagnated economies. It was believed that returnees could form a new entrepreneurial class capable of establishing businesses, industries, and modern farms needed for Mediterranean development.

By the early 1970s, however, the development aid interpretation had come under serious question. Critics argued that social and economic "costs" associated with emigration overshadowed actual "benefits." In a reversal of thought, emigration was seen as a "form of development aid given by poor countries to rich countries" (Castles and Kosack 1973:8). Industrialists, they argued, were interested in maintaining high profits through recruitment of a ready-made work force willing to work at lower wages than nationals. Furthermore, during periods of recession and high unemployment, industrial nations could export their unemployment problems by sending foreigners home. Antagonists of the development aid perspective also correctly pointed out that recruiting countries only accepted physically and educationally qualified migrants with at least some urban-industrial experience. However, since foreigners filled lower class, manual jobs no longer desired by northern Europeans, they received no opportunity to learn new skills. At the same time, the absence of a large proportion of their best workers negatively affected southern European agricultural and industrial productivity. Finally, critics argued that it is probably a "myth" that returning migrants invest in a manner conducive to their home communities' development.

Unfortunately, this important debate on migration's role in development has been carried out without information on the actual behavior of returnees and their impact on sending regions. Empirically, virtually nothing is known about how returnees are investing their savings or whether they are applying skills or ideas acquired abroad in an innovative way. However, controversies on this topic can only be resolved through a firsthand study of returnees in their home communities. The purpose of this essay, therefore, is to present the results of an in-depth study of cyclical migration and development in Spain's province of Granada. Although research was confined to one geographical region, the results are relevant to a worldwide debate over the problematic link between migration and development. At the heart of this debate is whether urban regions, via the process of rural-urban migration, exert a positive developmental impact on labor exporting areas.

RETURN MIGRATION: AN ANDALUSIAN DREAM

The movement of migrants back to their places of origin has been described in many terms: return migration, counterstream migration, reverse or homeward migration, and repatriation. Migrants at this stage, now called returnees or repatriates, intend to take up relatively permanent residence in their native lands for the indefinite future. Thus, the return home is not just for a brief holiday or to take care of pressing family business. Social and economic commitments will now again be physically anchored in the home community, not in some distant, alien place (see Gmelch 1980 and Rhoades 1979b for detailed discussions of return migration).

One Mediterranean region which has been strongly affected by return migration has been the Spanish province of Granada. For a quarter of a century, Granada's impoverished villages and towns have sent thousands of native sons and daughters on the northward journey. Most communities have lost one-third of their inhabitants since 1960, mainly young adults who have sought their fortunes in northern industrial Spain and as "guest workers" abroad. Despite this drastic drop in population, however, many villages exhibit an aura of prosperity in the face of general demographic and economic decay. The striking impact of migrant investments in their home communities can be seen everywhere: construction of new homes, renovation of old ones, appearance of new businesses, increase in modern farm machinery and automobiles, and the presence of durable goods. Those who support the "migration as development" thesis point to such outward changes as evidence of their position. Migrants are, it seems, returning and applying their urban-acquired aspirations, values, and earnings to the modernization of their communities.

FATES OF RETURN: FAILURES, SWALLOWS, AND GERMANS

However, closer examination of communities and individual cases reveals that migration is not a monolithic force. There are clearly distinct types of migration streams flowing out of Granada, and each one generates its own return pattern. "Internal" migration to Barcelona, for example, and "external" migration to West Germany have been directed toward industrial employment. However, migrants to Barcelona rarely return permanently to the village while most international migrants intend to return after some years abroad. Most jobs in France and Switzerland have been seasonal and temporary, mainly for a three-month harvest or a six-month construction period. Migrants with these destinations use the village as a home base and return temporarily every year.

Individuals vary widely in their desire or ability to use different migration streams as economic strategies. Although the types overlap, international migrants can be classified as "failures," "swallows," and "Germans."

"Failures" are known in Spanish as *los fracasados*, "those who have failed." These are returnees whose migration experience was short-lived and for whatever reason chose to return home after a few months abroad. Typically, "failures" were unable to adapt to the foreign culture or failed to accept separation from their home community. Frequently, they return home disillusioned with nothing to show from their journey abroad. The "return of failure" has no innovative impact on the village, and *fracasados* rapidly blend in with those who never emigrated (Cerase 1970:220).

José B., an unmarried 28-year-old day laborer who also cultivates his family's small fields, illustrates the case of a *fracasado*. In 1970, his brother-in-law secured him a job in a bolt manufacturing plant near Frankfurt. Although initially elated by the prospects of earning over ten times his village income, José experienced severe "culture shock" within two months of his arrival in Germany. He lived with his brother-in-law in a small, cramped room in company barracks where they also cooked meals on a hot plate. José's contract began in late November, the onset of the German winter. He found the Germans unfriendly, the food not to his taste, the language impossible, and the climate unbearable. By late January, José had had enough and, disillusioned, he walked away from his assembly line post and returned forever to Granada. He arrived home with $575 in savings and a few electronic items purchased in Germany. Still today, he rarely talks of his migration experience.

"Swallows" are known in Spanish as *los golondrinas*, migrants who engage in planned, repeat migration on a seasonal basis. Most international *golondrinas* work in the French grape harvest or in construction in Switzerland. Like their feathered namesakes, "swallows" predictably depart and return by the seasons. Every year during the off-season, they may be active in the local economy. In the Andalusian case, men generally go alone to Switzerland while the French grape harvest frequently attracts complete families. The migratory "swallows" generate greater earnings than *fracasados*. Sometimes they save enough to renovate a house or purchase a parcel of land. However, their migration strategy is subsistence-oriented; that is, their aim is to earn enough to live on until the next work period. "Los golondrinas," villagers will tell you, "eat here in the village what they earn there."

Manuel M. typifies the *golondrina*. In the village he farms two hectares, works at odd jobs, owns a small bar, but every year he applies for a six-month contract to work in Swiss construction. For over a decade, Manuel has travelled to the Spanish emigration branch office in Granada where he applies for a Swiss contract. Generally, he secures work with the same company from Geneva. During his absence, his wife and children take care of the farm and bar. Since this strategy generates income which will be used to support the family throughout the year, it holds limited potential for community development. The impact, therefore, of *los golondrinas* is only slightly more significant than that of *los fracasados.*

"The Germans" or *los alemanes,* as they are locally called, are long-term migrants returning from northern Europe. Village inhabitants consider industrial, intra-European migrants the migration "elite" since they generate the greatest physical impact on villages. Everyone knows the potential for rapid financial gain is enhanced by securing work in Germany or similar industrial positions in France, Holland, or Switzerland. Although males initially emigrate alone, the rest of the immediate family follows after a foothold is gained abroad. Frequently, all family members of age work. After several years abroad, *los alemanes* return with the intention of remaining in the village where they can live "semiretired" on their investments.

Moises V. is an *alemán* who spent 12 years in Germany. He and his wife, who worked abroad 9 years, were able to save more than $40,000. Two of their three children were born there; all speak German better than Spanish. In 1973, Moises and his wife decided to bring their family home. During his annual vacation, he made arrangements to purchase the home of the village physician who had moved to the coast. Moises also acquired four hectares of land and a small tractor. Before leaving Germany, they purchased all furnishings needed for their new home. Throughout their migration experience, Moises and his wife planned and dreamed of their final homecoming. Before going to Germany, Moises was a *campesino* (peasant) who had no land and depended on local landlords for jobs or land to cultivate. Migration, however, was Moises's only chance to change this. As he put it:

> Fifteen years ago, this town was owned by four men. They wouldn't even greet me on the street. They even had a club where I couldn't go. One of them lived here in this house. It's mine now. Everyone knows who Moises V. is. There is no finer house nor furnishings in this village than mine. I owe everything to Germany.

In Moises's community, as in many others, the *alemanes* are largely responsible for the village construction booms, growing bank deposits, presence of modern consumer goods and the general appearance of village prosperity. If there is any hope for development through migration, it must come from this class of returnees. The remainder of this paper, therefore, will focus specifically on village-level activities of returned "Germans."

RETURNEE INVESTMENT

The volume of capital sent home by Andalusian migrants has been staggering. If these funds were properly invested in employment-generating enterprises or in economically sound businesses or farms, fundamental changes could come to Andalusia. Migrant remittances from northern Europe have been so massive in recent years that new banks have opened in many small communities. In 1972 alone, the 179,000 Spanish migrants in West Germany sent or brought home German marks worth almost one billion U. S. dollars (Bundesanstalt für Arbeit 1973). In one village of 1,500 residents, migrants sent home $6 million by 1976. A study of the same village indicated that migrants saved an average of $6,000 each, although a few families saved over $40,000. These earnings are set aside for specific types of investments in a variety of undertakings. The main types of investments are: (1) housing, home furnishings, and durable goods; (2) small-scale businesses (bars, shops, grocery stores); and (3) agriculture.

Symbols of Success: Houses, Furniture, and Durable Goods
A desire to improve housing ranks as a major motivation for emigration, especially among married migrants. This is accomplished by restoring the family home, constructing a new one, or renovating an older, purchased home. Often, migrants begin the construction of their post-emigration residence early in the migration cycle, with the wife or other family members returning to supervise the construction project. It is not unusual for migrants to miscalculate costs and face the need to re-emigrate to earn funds to finish their building project. Half-finished migrant houses with grass and weeds growing around are not uncommon sights in Granada. However, the desire for housing has created temporary local employment for those left behind.

The migration-stimulated housing boom has altered significantly village settlement patterns in many communities. The physical concentration of returnees' homes in villages has been labeled *el centro alemán* (the German Center) by locals. In one village on the plains north of the Sierra Nevada mountains, this shift has been especially dramatic. Prior to migration to Germany, most workers lived in poor housing or caves situated on the village fringe. In 1966, more than one-fifth of the village populace lived in caves; by 1976, however, this percentage had fallen to 8 percent. Since caves symbolize lower status to community members, a central element of return migrant ideology centers on changing residence within the village. Thus, the exodus has been toward the lower barrios along the main village thoroughfare. In this *el centro alemán,* which is a kilometer-long physical concentration of new migrant houses, shops, and bar-restaurants, real estate values have increased over 1000 percent in 10 years.

"German" returnees not only come home wealthy by local standards, they display this wealth through conspicuous consumption of luxury goods acquired abroad. The return lifestyle is distinguished by a characteristic type of home furnishings, goods consumption, and clothing. The German flavor is very strong. Symbols of migration success always include plush furniture, televisions, chandeliers, German tourist wall plaques, ashtrays, and similar paraphernalia. Many migrant households contain wall-long glass cabinets which proudly display German beer steins and glass articles as well as built-in bars stocked with a wide array of liquors. It is no exaggeration to classify many returnees as Germanophiles in terms of consumption. They always bring back their limit of consumer goods on annual trips and upon their final return. Electronic gadgets and appliances are especially desirable.

Villages influenced by heavy return migration from industrial Europe show outward signs of social transformation. Today, former *campesinos* (peasants) or *jornaleros* (day laborers) who emigrated and returned with solid savings live in the most modern houses, frequently next door to former landlords or professionals. However, the old establishment finds it extremely difficult to keep up with the consumption habits of returnees. Moises V., the *alemán* returnee mentioned above, brought his entire household furnishings—including bathtub and doorknobs—to make sure there would be no village residence better decorated than his.

Migrant Businesses

After returnees have satisfied their desires for improved housing and living conditions, they put their energy and remaining savings into some local enterprise. The majority buy a parcel of land to farm, but a number try their hand at a small business. The primary goal in setting up a private enterprise is to live in a semiretired state. Returnees do not plan, initially at least, to take up wage labor in the fields. Instead of "working like Negroes" (*trabajando como negros*), as they claim was the case before, they now live "on their own account" (*por su cuenta*). Returnees with small businesses describe their aspirations in terms of "being independent," "no longer a slave," or "to be one's own boss." As a result, very few actually work in occupations held in Germany since it would mean they would have to become laborers again in Spanish cities. Indeed, many skilled workers (mechanics, carpenters, welders, masons) do not market their skills upon return. Instead, they attempt to live from various investments (Rhoades 1978a:142–143).

Returnees are amazingly predictable in the kinds of businesses they establish: bar-restaurant combinations, grocery stores, shops, and vehicle hire. Investments center primarily on undertakings that are manageable on a family scale. This has caused the number of bars, for example, in one village to rise from three to nine in ten years. Eight of these bars are owned by returnees. The same village, with a declining population and only slightly over 1,500 inhabitants, now contains six grocery stores, one supermarket, and six bread shops. Most of these enterprises were recently added by migrants, and there is evidence that as more return from Germany, the growth of small businesses will continue.

Returnees are not adventurous in investing and are unwilling to gamble savings in risky financial schemes. Even though migrant families frequently return with considerable amounts of capital, opportunity for investment in the village is severely limited. Furthermore, in a few cases, entrenched middle-class entrepreneurs and authorities have conspired to refuse business permits to returnees. The traditional business elite has not departed in the wake of the unexpected competition. They simply sold their shops to returnees and opened more profitable stores, selling modern appliances and furniture to meet returned migrant consumption needs.

Migrant Farming Enterprises: A Questionable Future

The purchase of agricultural land is seen by many migrants as necessary for long-term security and a symbolic ingredient of post-emigration lifestyle. Demand for small cultivable parcels has created strong inflationary pressures in land values. According to local bankers in one village, quality irrigated land now sells for $14,000 to $15,000 per acre while dry land may cost up to $6,000 per acre. Interest in land is due in part to a lack of alternative investment opportunities in the village and returnees' general distrust of risky investment schemes. "Land," the migrants declare, "will always be there, come war, famine, or depression." Land is purchased from landlords who have capitalized on the land-hungry mood of returnees to reap handsome profits. In general, however, returnees are not concerned with modernizing newly acquired parcels as much as continuing with traditional patterns of land use. For a variety of reasons, parcels may not always be intensively cultivated. Often crops or fruit are not worth harvesting due to low prices or lack of cheap labor. Farming alone can no longer support a family and maintain the standard of living migrants have grown accustomed to in northern Europe. Those who attempt to rely strictly on small-scale agricultural investments often must re-emigrate (Rhoades 1979a:65–69).

A number of returnees have invested heavily in modern farm machinery. In one community, for example, the number of tractors rose from 18 to 45 between 1969 and 1976, the years corresponding to heaviest return from Germany. On the plain of Guadix, north of the Sierra Nevada range, several migrants purchased large John Deere tractors for $11,000 each. These large machines are built for deep-plowing or wide-sweeping operations customary on the American Great Plains, not for the shallow-soil cultivation practiced in the area. Since most former migrants do not have sufficient land to justify ownership of a tractor, they attempt to hire out the machine and labor. Unfortunately, demand for tractor time is restricted to planting and harvest seasons. Furthermore, unplanned expenses related to repairs, maintenance, attachments and high fuel costs have sharply diminished their profitability. Tractor owners also admit there are "too many tractors for so little land" and that a saturation point has been reached. Also, the increase in farm machinery is reducing the availability of manual jobs in agriculture. Ironically, return migration investments contribute to the need for more out-migration among the laboring class.

POST-RETURN LIFESTYLES IN SOCIAL CONTEXT

Throughout the long and lonely migrancy period, the typical Spanish migrant yearns to return to his cultural roots. Nostalgia is a prime mover in directing the migrant homeward. If a worker departed for Germany during his twenties or older, the village remains his main social frame of reference while abroad. The desire to emigrate and return a Spanish "Horatio Alger" success is an impelling image. In terms of ideology, the migrant is Spain's modern conquistador whose "cities of gold" are not in the Americas but in the factories along the Ruhr, Rhine, and Saar regions of northern Europe. And his mission, like that of the ancestral conquistador, is to acquire his fortune abroad, and return to bask in the praise of his countrymen. However, only in the context of his village—not among strangers—can he be a proud entrepreneur, landlord, or homeowner. It is not difficult to imagine the emotions of a peasant of humble origins who is now able to return triumphantly to the place which formerly exploited and humiliated him.

Another gauge of the philosophical orientation of returnees is found in the results of the first political elections held since the Spanish Civil War. During the 1977 campaign, emigration was the central political issue for all parties in Granada. Posters and handbills from the left, center, and right proclaimed "stop emigration" as a key slogan. Returnees, however, often were suspected of leaning toward the left in political and labor matters. This image was not helped by a few former migrants who ran for public office on the Communist ticket. After the elections, one of the "folk explanations" why a given village voted Socialist or Communist was that "too many migrants live there" (Rhoades 1979a:69). Especially among the middle and upper classes, a fear was prevalent that emigrants had become "men of ideas" and thus overly critical of the social *status quo*. This was not true, however, of the *alemanes*. Election results demonstrated that communities tied closely to Germany for jobs tended to vote for moderate parties. Successful returnees do not have radical change on their minds but are voices of moderation in Spain's post-Franco political experiment. Bitterness, however, can be found in many parts of Andalusia, especially in the communities characterized by the *golondrina* pattern of seasonal out-migration. Communities lacking a migration outlet or those facing constant uncertainty in the fight for seasonal contracts in France or Switzerland tend to be antagonistic in political matters. The *alemanes*, however, are voices of political and cultural moderation. They are not interested in risking loss of their new status with an uncertain political system.

AN ASSESSMENT

What conclusions germane to the debate over migration and development can be drawn from this ethnographic study of Andalusian returnees? Outwardly, many sending communities verify the thesis that circular migration is conducive to economic development. The improvement in income, material life, housing, and the growth of a small business sector seem to testify to the notion that migration is a positive force which integrates peasant communities into national economies. Since the migrations began, unemployment has actually decreased in some communities, agriculture has been mechanized, and rural credit problems partially overcome. From all appearances, migration has allowed rural populations to "share the fruits of development."

However, serious doubts can be raised as to the permanence of these migration-induced changes. The *centro alemán* can be compared to a "stage prop" which will crumble as soon as the migration drama reaches its final act. As special "worker suburbs" of West German industry located a thousand miles away in Spanish villages, the prosperity of the "German Centers" depends upon the continuing availability of jobs in northern Europe. However, in 1973 Germany abruptly closed its doors to new migrants, and other industrial nations have pursued similar policies. If migrant investments fail, as many have, returnees will not be able to repeat their international migration experience. Most returnees are relatively young men and women in their forties, and it is doubtful if their investments will last the rest of their lives. Even if they "semi-retire" with a restricted standard of living, their children will be forced to seek work outside the region.

Returnees may construct new homes and fill them with modern furnishings, but such investments do not create resources or conditions which will guarantee long-run prosperity. Returnees invest in small-scale, highly competitive businesses located in depressed regions which continue to lose population. Commercial agriculture or agrarian innovations are not a primary concern of former migrants. Most consumer items purchased by migrants are low quality, mass-produced goods which will deteriorate rapidly in value. Given local wages, such goods cannot be easily replaced. Migrant families may enjoy at least short-term social mobility, higher incomes, and improved conveniences, but outside the "glitter" of their homes, the stark village reality continues. Rural communities may have had a new "facelifting" by returnees, but the local infrastructure remains largely unaltered and no new employment opportunities have been created through migrant actions. In other words, the changes brought by migration are only "skin-deep"; they do not represent fundamental structural changes in the economy.

RETURNING TO THE RETURNEES: IMPACT OF MIGRATION AFTER TEN YEARS

Exactly a decade has passed since I lived in Andalusia and conducted migration research. My return to the villages in 1987 was cause of great celebration and endless hours of discussion about my own fortunes and those of my migrant friends since I last saw them. The massive return of migrants was only beginning in 1976 and 1977 when I set forth my hypothesis on migration and change. Today, the former migrants look back nostalgically on those days as *la buena época de emigración* (the great age of emigration). As Spaniards returned home from Northern Europe, they were not replaced by others. The *migration drama* about which I wrote had indeed reached its final act. Now, time was on my side. Ten years are sufficient to determine if the changes brought about by migration were, as I argued, *only skin deep*.

Both returned migrants and government statistics will tell you that the economy of Spain and Andalusia has deteriorated over the past decade. Spain's unemployment rate climbed from 5.2% in 1977 to 16.3% by 1982. Andalusia's unemployment rate shot up threefold, from 7% in 1977 to over 21% in 1982. These increases are due to many factors, including the drying up of the emigration outlet. The Spanish population continued to grow vigorously, while, from 1973 to 1982, an actual decrease in the number of available jobs occurred (Lagares Calvo 1982).

Within the migrant-sending areas, conditions got even worse. Populations of the villages continued to fall another ten to fifteen percent. The Socialist party, which the German returnees initially rebuffed, came to power and won the migrant vote. Unemployment reached crisis proportions, and the governments of Andalusia and Extremadura instituted a rural unemployment compensation system, whereby the government pays up to 180 days of unemployment. In the villages I had studied, this welfare system replaced migration as the main source of income for the rural populace. The *migration as development* thesis obviously had not worked out as European planners had hoped.

Despite negative statistics and the pessimistic views of my migrant friends, however, those villages which had sent migrants to industrial Europe continued to show an outward appearance of prosperity, which puzzled me. In fact, one of my main research villages – Alcudia – continued to enjoy the growth of small businesses and new homes even as the population fell. Here, my *stage prop* had not fallen as predicted, but had, in fact, improved. Since 1977, the number of restaurants in this village of 1300 inhabitants increased from nine to thirteen, the number of supermarkets from one to two. In addition, two new discotheques and four new hairdresser shops opened for business. The *centro aleman* consisted of two to three rows of new, two-story homes, along the main road. The owners, all returned migrants, were now in their 40s and early 50s.

Nearby villages that had sent migrants to the seasonal French harvests or to temporary Swiss construction sites had not fared so well. They continued to see a decrease in population, with no compensation in new construction or small businesses. I was reminded of the *green revolution* debates. Migration had increased inequities between the more prosperous communities (German-linked) and the poorer ones (seasonally French- or Swiss-linked).

I was wrong on another point. There may have been no fundamental economic structural changes in the migrant-sending regions, but I sensed fundamental structural changes in the minds of the Andalusian migrants. Unlike earlier ages of emigration, when their Andalusian ancestors went to the New World and rarely returned permanently, the European migrant did come home to stay. Women and young people, especially, are now aware of alternatives. The village, for most, still remains their base of operation, but they are knowledgeable of the European urban core. For a livelihood, returnees combine diverse strategies, including farming, seasonal migration for tourism, small businesses and unemployment compensation. I admire now, like I did not in 1977, their tenacity and creativity in coping with an economically difficult situation and in managing to somehow come out on top, at least spiritually.

Part Four
Urban Family, Kinship, and Interpersonal Relations

Many theorists from different schools see urbanization leading to the weakening of the family. They feel that urban life tends to sever ties between the nuclear family (parents and unmarried children) and its extended kinfolk (parents of adult children, their siblings, their siblings' children, uncles, aunts, cousins). This weakening is because in the urban context the tasks which the family performs for society are limited to early childhood care, eating, sleeping, and emotional support and expression for nuclear family members. Other functions carried out by the family in a nonurban context are attenuated in the city. They are transferred to other institutions. Credit, for example, is provided by banks rather than by relatives. The workplace is outside of the home, and employment is found through impersonal agencies and advertisements, rather than through the kinship network. Child-care centers and the schools take an increasingly important share of child rearing, while hospitals, public welfare departments, senior citizen centers, and old age homes are more significant than the family and kin in the care of the ill, the needy, and the aged. Sex activity, too, is found outside of marriage and may be quite impersonal. This picture of the family fits in quite well with the Wirthian theory of urbanism as a source of isolation and loneliness (Wirth "Urbanism as a Way of Life"; C.C. Harris 1970).

Much of the criticism of the Wirthian theory comes from studies which have shown that family ties of urbanites are often strong and that connections with extended kin survive in urban settings. Several aspects of this critique will be stressed in this essay and in the articles which follow. The first aspect is that urbanization and industrialization, even in the West, do not necessarily reduce familial ties to those of the nuclear family. The second is that non-Western family types persist in modern cities in the Third World, even though these cities are affected by Westernization and urbanization. The third is that economic function and social status are strong influences on the form of the family and on relationships between nuclear families and their kin. The changing roles of men and women in urban societies are closely tied to changes in the forms and functions of the family.

THE URBAN FAMILY AND INDUSTRIALIZATION

Anthropologists and historians have made a major contribution to theories of urbanism by pointing out that the association of urbanism and attenuated families is by no means simple. They have shown that the rosy picture of people living in extended family households in preindustrial societies is, to a large degree, a wishful idealization. These "history of the family" scholars have shown how important nonfamilial institutions like the wet nurse were for preindustrial urban people. They have also demonstrated how much illegitimacy, prostitution, child abuse and neglect, and dissolution of families existed before modernization. It turns out that the nuclear family household, often truncated, was quite common in premodern Europe (Ranum and Forster 1976; Stone 1977; Laslett 1972).

During and after the Industrial Revolution many changes took place in the Western family, both working-class and of the middle and upper strata. The forms and functions of the family and kinship changed during different stages of industrialization and the rural-urban migration which accompanied it. Young and Willmott (1973:65–100) describe three stages of the transformation of the English family from its preindustrial past to its contemporary form. The stages are: (1) the family as unit of production; (2) disruption of this unit and transition to the family as unit of consumption; and (3) the symmetrical family as unit of consumption. In the first stage, the household is the site of production in both agriculture and handicrafts. All family members engage in productive activities. Among urban craftsmen, the workshop is part of the home. However, the shift from self or familial employment to performance of wage labor for others occurred first in the cities.

The second stage, the transition from the domestic system to the factory system, was still incomplete in the nineteenth century. In some trades, like bootmaking and tailoring, craftsmen still needed to employ their wives. But generally the productive functions of the family were lost, and as factories and other specialized workplaces replaced the family as units of production, schools took over educational tasks. While many women did work in factories, during the child-bearing and rearing years they were often confined to their homes, completely dependent on their husbands for support. The financial resources of the working-class family were especially strained during these years because children needed to be supported and often did not make a contribution to the family income. The battering and abuse of women and children by men, who were themselves oppressed in the factories, desertion of families, and the use of the public house (tavern) for recreation were common features of working class life. Aspects of this second stage in the transformation of the family persist in England and other parts of the Western world to this day. The docker families of Bethnal Green, now part of Tower Hamlets, are a good example of this family type (Young and Willmott 1957).

Family disruption of the type that occurred during the Industrial Revolution continues in Western Europe and North America, particularly among poor migrants, although migration may strengthen other kin ties. Susan Keefe's comparison of Anglo- and Mexican-American families in California follows the line of criticism of those who argue that extended kin ties wither away in modern industrial societies (Keefe, "The Myth of the Declining Family"; Rhoades, "European Cyclical Migration", and G. Gmelch, "West Indian Life"). Sometimes only husbands or wives can go to the city, and some of the children may be left behind. The family may be forced to reside in a furnished one-room apartment; continued contact with their families of origin in the country or in another country is difficult. "On the other hand, the extreme overcrowding of tenants, cooped up in rooms which are too small, and the common facilities for water, washing, and so on bring neighbours into some degree of close contact with the life of the family" (Vieille 1954 in C.C. Harris 1970:99-117). This disruption of family life, however, is usually transitory. Urban poverty can sometimes be met best by receiving and giving aid to both kinsmen and neighbors, as Stack ("The Kindred of Viola Jackson") points out in her article.

The emergence of the symmetrical or companionate family represents the third stage. This family, which first arose in the British and North American middle classes in the last century, is marked by a decrease in births, a rise in the educational level of women, and less segregation of gender roles. For example, more wives are employed and husbands increasingly help with households, although true symmetry is rarely achieved. The use of labor-saving devices in the home permits more time for outside activities, plus it engenders a desire for more income to buy more devices.

Young and Willmott's delineation of stages cannot be applied mechanically to societies, even within the Euro-American industrialized sphere. There is an element of liberal utopianism in the labels "symmetrical" family and "companionate" family, and this type of household may only exist in a segment of the middle class. It certainly was not characteristic of the working class families of East London, studied by Young and Willmott (1957) in the 1950s.

Whether or not development toward a symmetrical family can be at all applied to the Third World is arguable. Middle-class women in Guatemala City, whether they work outside the home or not, bear the full responsibility for child care and housekeeping, unless they hire servants to do these tasks (Bossen "Wives and Servants"). Little (1973) has claimed that African women in towns have achieved a large measure of liberation from the constraints of the traditional culture by their migration to towns. Clignet's studies, however, show that the association of urbanization with the rise of a Western-style family and consequently Western middle-class gender role definitions is problematic (Clignet "Urbanization and Family Structure in the Ivory Coast"; Clignet and Sween

1974). While some conformity to Western ways in a city dominated by European planners and economic institutions is inevitable, still family types based on polygyny and on inheritance and clan membership through one parent only continue to persist. Such institutions continue to have ramifications in modern African cities.

SOCIOECONOMIC STATUS AND EXTENDED KIN

Economic status in both preindustrial and industrial cities has been an important factor in determining the character of family life. The usual picture of modern urban society as one in which the family's functions have been reduced to those of child care and consumption has been challenged by studies which demonstrate the importance of extended kinship ties in economic activity.

Kinship ties in both preindustrial and industrializing societies are most ramified among the political and economic elites. These groups have powerful kin networks; consider, for example, European nobility and royalty. All the royal families of Europe intermarried (Fleming 1973). The emergent ruling classes of modern colonial and industrial societies evidence similar patterns. In Brazil, Argentina, Chile, the United States, and Britain the rise of merchants and landowners to key positions in society often coincided with marriages to members of an older elite. While some of these elites were rural in origin, they often maintained homes in large urban centers where their wealth could be transformed into political office, like the aristocracy before them (e.g., Balmori and Oppenheimer 1979; Lewin 1979). Today these elites tend to be multinational. For instance, Grace Kelly, a Philadelphia heiress and movie star, married the prince of Monaco; her daughter has married a French millionaire. Jacqueline Bouvier was married first to John F. Kennedy and later to Greek shipping tycoon Aristotle Onassis. She also has affinal ties with the Auchincloss family, which is in turn kin to the Roosevelts.

The economic functions of family and kin are weakest among the isolated urban poor such as the urban nomads of Skidrow (e.g., Spradley "Adaptive Strategies of Urban Nomads") and among impoverished recent migrants to the city. But even among these, as Stack and Eames and Goode ("The Culture of Poverty") show, there is a substantial amount of mutual aid provided by kin and friends. The poor may also rely on assistance from unrelated neighbors and friends. The odd complex household of the protagonist in Madame Rosa, an Academy Award winning film, is one example. Madame Rosa was an ex-prostitute who in her old age fostered the illegitimate children of other prostitutes as well as an assortment of other abandoned children. She would fit in well in the furnished rooms of rural French and North African migrants studied by Vieille (1954). This is a world where people must often find friends, for many have no relatives whom they can ask for help.

In modern welfare states, the families of the poor are subject to bureaucratic interference. In the United States, receipt of welfare is contingent on the absence of an employable male in the household, which encourages husbands to desert their wives and children or not marry the women with whom they have children. Nevertheless, as Stack (1974:passim; and "The Kindred of Viola Jackson") shows, the support of the poor by the state is often inadequate and the maintenance of extensive networks of kin and friends is still necessary. Bureaucratic intervention thus changes both the roles of men and women in the family, as well as the structure of the household itself. Governmental action— whether with regard to welfare assistance, protection of children against abuse, or education—affects the poor more than other classes and can transform the family. Whether even well-intentioned intervention by governmental agencies benefits the poor and others is a subject about which there is considerable debate (also see Orent 1977; Handelman and Leyton 1978).

In the middle-status groups, the situation differs. The usual sociological stereotype is that the strong conjugal family with only weak links to extended kin is typical of the middle class. That is where one would expect to find the symmetrical or companionate family which is essentially a unit of consumption, not production. Here again, sociologists and anthropologists have found that middle-class families in countries like Great Britain and the United States often have strong bonds with their extended kin. It is common for grandparents to provide their grandchildren with riding lessons and other expensive amenities which the parents of these children could not pay for on their own (C. A. Bell 1968 in C. C. Harris 1970:209–224). Many Jews of East European origin in New York City are often involved in clubs organized on the basis of kinship, such as cousins (Mitchell 1978). Small businesses are often organized as family firms (Leichter and Mitchell 1967). Thus even urban people in a large metropolis are highly involved with their kith and kin. Not surprisingly, we find that the involvement of family in business has been quite a common pattern, even though it may entangle the business with the emotional tensions of kin ties (see Buechler, "The Networks of Dona Flora," and Zenner, "The Cross National Web of Relations").

While the modern educated middle classes in India and Africa appear to adopt a European style in their lifeways, this emulation of the West is only partial. For instance, in a small Indian town near New Delhi, urbanization/ modernization has had little impact on family life. Marriages even among the Western educated are still arranged, and marrying outside one's caste is still forbidden. Recent rural migrants continue to participate in the joint ownership of rural property which they and their kin share. Ties with distant kin are maintained and the interests of the extended kin group are still considered to outweigh the desires of individual members. Married children who establish new households in the city are expected to care for and take in elderly parents (Vatuk 1972). Clignet's studies also show that traditional patterns are often retained in urban Africa (Clignet "Urbanization and Family Structure in the Ivory Coast"; Clignet and Sween 1974).

Middle-class Japanese also maintain structured ties with kinsmen who live in other households. Even the salaried employees of large corporations who live in Tokyo suburbs frequently live near their parents. It is quite common for children to be assigned to stay with a particular grandparent. The child may bathe his grandparent and the grandparent will play with the child. The relationship may be quite intimate. A child may become grief-stricken if his grandparent dies (Vogel 1967:224–246). Intimate emotional and economic relationships between extended kin are not incompatible with modern urban life, either in the West or in non-Western cultures. In fact, the sociability and mutual aid which urban people find in the family and among extended kin are as effective as what they would find outside the bosom of the kindred. Urban society provides alternatives to kinship ties, but it does not destroy them.

THE RANGE OF INTERPERSONAL TIES WITH KIN AND NONKIN

Despite the stress anthropologists have given to kinship, many individuals have relatively weak ties to their kin. Many only call, write, or visit their parents or mature siblings on rare occasions, like once in seven years. In spite of the emphasis on the perpetuation of closely knit small groups and stable neighborhoods in some studies, connections between many individuals are indeed of a temporary nature. Weak ties with some people did, of course, occur in premodern times. Certainly traders and other itinerants in preindustrial societies had such loose ties with their clientele, but loose ties are more common in this day of the large corporation. In many communities where heads of families are employed by the army or a large corporation, people become accustomed to the fact that some families are here today and gone next year. In some areas of work, like government service, *what* one knows is as important as *who* one knows. The successful worker seeks to impress the stranger with his or her competency rather than prevailing on friends and acquaintances who are obliged to perform favors (Wolfe 1974; Jacobson 1975). Yet emotional friendship ties may become entangled with the presumably "objective," "universalistic" criteria of such rational bureaucracies, as they do in the small family businesses. Such entanglements, especially when they involve hiring and firing, are the stuff that executive suite dramas and novels set in academia are made of.

The strategies that one employs successfully in the corporate bureaucratic world differ from those of a setting where nepotism is the rule, not a violation of the rules. Thus an individual who wishes to succeed may find his chances are better by having several wide-ranging networks of acquaintances (as opposed to friends) who provide that person with information about jobs, grants, and other opportunities for advancement, rather than investing time and emotion in being an active member of an intimate group. The investment in "inbred" group memberships may tie the individual down to a specific job or get one stuck in an unsatisfactory situation (Granovetter 1973). At the same time, those who are mobile and who have few relatives near home may reproduce friendship circles which replace the absence of relatives in the vicinity.

In the late 1950s, in a suburb of a Northeastern American city, an 8-year-old girl reported to her parents who came from New York City that there was one other Jewish girl in her class. The girl's parents were delighted and contacted the other couple. Together the two couples placed an ad in the neighborhood paper, suggesting a meeting of a "Fairville Jewish Club." Other couples in the essentially Gentile suburb responded, and a Jewish club which lasted on and off for nearly fifteen years was founded. The content of the meetings was not particularly Jewish, but the form of a meeting—connected with some kind of eating—resembled that of other Jewish organizations, including the New York City cousin clubs. Friendships formed in that organization have continued long after the dissolution of the club itself (Zenner 1978).

A similar "reproduction" of kin-like groups occurs in child-care cooperatives and car pools which have been studied in Great Britain and North America. Sometimes groups of parents which start to share such functions, otherwise carried out by kin, end up as friendship groups which maintain patterns of cooperation even when some move out of the neighborhood and new people move in (Cohen 1974:27–28; Coombs 1973). Thus while many interpersonal relations in the modern urban society are temporary, patterns of cooperation have emerged to fill gaps left by the absence of extended kin and durable friendships.

So far, gender relations as such have been underplayed in our discussion. Yet it is obvious that whether or not occupations and household tasks are segregated into male and female roles, gender is crucial to our understanding of familial and extra-familial relationships. In all of the articles in this section, as well as other articles in this volume, we can see linkages between reproduction, sexual intercourse, and nurturance in male-female relations. Kathleen Logan's article ("Latin American Urban Movements") in the next section, in fact, sees a clear connection between the traditional roles which women have had as wives and mothers and their participation in political protests throughout Latin America.

Urban settings have also been the scenes for substitutes for certain familial relations. Extra-marital sex for hire is but one example of such specialization. It may supplement sex between husband and wife or it may be the main sexual outlet for many urbanites. The same is true for such nurturing and healing institutions as schools, hospitals, hospices, nursing homes, and convents. While convents in particular may be associated with rural settings, they represent specialization which grow up in complex centers of population. Such settings do involve an intensification of interpersonal ties comparable to the family. Prostitution, on the other hand, can be used as a metaphor for the kind of urbanism described by Wirth, marked by casual contact involving payment for services rendered. In both fictional and ethnographic accounts dealing with prostitution, however, we find the human need for intimacy finding expression. The "lovelorn farangs," discussed by Cohen (below) are good examples of this phenomenon.

Several of the articles in this section demonstrate the persistence and importance of intimate ties between the individual and kin outside of the nuclear family (Keefe, Stack, Clignet). One deals with the interaction between unrelated women in a single household (Bossen "Wives and Servants"). The article by Clignet also shows how members of certain African ethnic groups adapt their originally rural family structures to the urban setting. All of these articles explicitly show how the family in the urban setting is part and parcel of larger social systems, while Cohen's paper shows how even the search for wives has taken on an international character.

The way in which the larger world produces tensions within the family is described well by the different authors.

Walter P. Zenner

THE MYTH OF THE DECLINING FAMILY: EXTENDED FAMILY TIES AMONG URBAN MEXICAN-AMERICANS AND ANGLO-AMERICANS

Susan Emley Keefe

Traditionally, it was assumed that nuclear family systems arise with urbanism due to increased geographic and socio-economic mobility and to the extended family's loss of economic function. Substantial evidence supports the thesis that extended family ties persist among urban Mexican-Americans and Anglo-Americans in southern California. The two ethnic groups differ in reference to the geographic distribution of kin, Chicanos having local kin groups in contrast to the dispersed kin networks of Anglo-Americans, but, for members of both ethnic groups, the extended family endures and contributes in positive ways to ethnic adaptation to urban life.

> It used to be thought that families living in modern cities had little contact with their relatives. This idea was suggested when people compared the apparent individualism of their own family lives with their fondly held, though often misguided, images of the "good old days." During the past two decades, there has been much careful research on kinship ties, and the general findings of these studies are (1) that kinship ties are extremely important in contemporary urban society and (2) that the existence of a vital, all-embracing extended family of the "good old days" was mostly a myth. (Caplow, et al. 1982:195)

The theory that urbanization leads to extended-family breakdown has a long history in the social sciences. As Caplow, et al. (1982) point out, the theory assumes that kinship organization in cities changes from an extended family system to a more isolated, nuclear family system and, furthermore, that urbanization is the cause of this change. The theory has its roots in the nineteenth century with the development of more sophisticated comparative and evolutionary social theories. For example, in his book *Ancient Law*, Henry Maine argued that, as societies become more complex, there is an evolutionary shift from kinship status to contract status:

Source: Article written expressly for *Urban Life*.

The movement of progressive societies has been uniform in one respect. Through all its course it has been distinguished by the gradual dissolution of family dependency and the growth of individual obligation in its place. The Individual is steadily substituted for the Family, as the unit of which civil laws take account (Maine 1861:168).

Other nineteenth-century scholars, including Emile Durkheim, Ferdinand Tonnies, and Max Weber, agreed in general that urbanism is associated with increasing individualism, growing alienation in a mass society, greater geographic and socio-economic mobility, and the loss of a sense of community. More recent neoevolutionists, such as Elman Service (1967), continue the argument that, in comparison to primitive societies where kinship is the most significant organizing principle, urban, state-level societies have other means of organizing public life, and kinship tends to be confined to the private sphere.

Early twentieth-century sociologists and anthropologists adapted these theories to the contemporary process of urbanization and to the associated process of industrialization. Contrasting urban society with rural, preindustrial society, Talcott Parsons (1943), Robert Redfield (1941), Ralph Linton (1949) and, most especially, Louis Wirth (1938), as well as others in the *Chicago School* associated urban life with "the weakening of bonds of kinship" (Wirth) and the "isolation of the nuclear family" (Parsons). In addition to citing the increasing importance of individualism in urban societies as a factor in the decline of the kin group, these theorists emphasized the extended family's loss of significant economic and social functions. In urban, industrial societies, the family is no longer the unit of economic production; moreover, the labor market's demand for work force mobility results in migration and dissolution of local kin groups. With increased socio-economic mobility and an emphasis on individual achieved status, the ascribed status of kinship and the associated resources of inheritance and a family name and reputation become less important. The extended family may survive, but it functions more in affective than in instrumental ways (although it is generally argued that it may remain economically functional among the poor who rely on kin for mutual aid). The extended kin group remains significant in urban societies, it is argued, primarily due to emotional bonds of attachment and to the socializing patterns they produce. Finally, according to this school of thought due to the presumed fragility of affective, noneconomically based bonds, the frequency of visiting such kin is relatively insignificant.

The theory of the declining urban extended family continues to be perpetuated by some more contemporary social scientists (Goode 1963, 1966; Harris 1969; Smelser 1966) and is reported in textbooks read by new generations of social scientists. Moreover, as Caplow, et al. (1982) note, it is a theory held, for the most part, by the general population. Perhaps this is one of the reasons why the theory persists despite the convincing evidence to the contrary amassed by researchers over the last thirty years.

Oscar Lewis (1965) is perhaps best known for proposing that urbanization and industrialization are compatible with extended family bonds when he found "urbani-zation without breakdown" in Mexico City. In fact, cross-cultural studies find the retention of extended family ties in urban areas around the globe: in India (Vatuk 1972), the Philippines (Jacobson 1970), West Africa (Aldous 1962), Brazil (Wagley

1964), Yugoslavia (Hammel and Yarbrough 1973), Canada (Garigue 1956), and England (Young and Willmott 1957), as well as elsewhere. Work with many urban-American ethnic minority groups, including Italian-Americans (Palisi 1966), Jewish-Americans (Winch, Greer, and Blumberg 1967), Puerto Rican-Americans (Garrison 1972), and Japanese- and Chinese-Americans (Light 1972) also indicates the existence of local kinship ties which involve significant levels of visiting and mutual exchange of goods and services. Furthermore, urban-dwelling, mainstream Anglo-Americans are by no means cut off from their extended family ties. As Sussman (1959), Burchinal (1962), Litwak (1960a, 1960b), Adams (1968), and Greer (1956) have demonstrated, Anglo-Americans maintain a *modified extended family*, in which kin ties remain important in affective and instrumental ways despite geographic mobility. Of course, considerable variation in the precise nature of kinship organization exists among these separate cultural groups, but, clearly, urbanism does not necessarily result in the extinction of extended family networks. In Barbados, as Greenfield (1961) points out, a nuclear family system can also arise in nonurban situations, further calling into question any proposed causal relationship between urbanism and nuclear family organization.

This study examines the extended family ties of urban Mexican-Americans[1] and Anglo-Americans in southern California. The findings are based on research conducted in three towns where Chicanos make up a large segment of the population: Santa Barbara, Santa Paula and Oxnard.[2] Data were collected by means of two large-scale surveys of several hundred respondents and a series of in-depth interviews with a small number of informants. In addition to the expected cultural differences between the Mexican-Americans and Anglo-Americans interviewed, significant differences in socio-economic status are evident between the two ethnic groups: most of the Mexican-Americans come from blue-collar households and have not completed high school, while most of the Anglo-Americans live in white-collar households and have completed one or more years of college. Within the Chicano sample itself, there is considerable heterogeneity. Generation accounts for much of the variation by class and culture within the ethnic group, particularly for the contrast between immigrants from Mexico and the more acculturated and assimilated second- or third-generation Mexican-Americans.

Consistent with early social science theory, research on Mexican-Americans has more often than not asserted that the traditional Mexican-American extended family is disappearing with urbanization and acculturation (Alvirez and Bean 1976; Grebler, et al. 1970). Nevertheless, it is also suggested that, in comparison with the Anglo-American nuclear family system, Chicano family ties remain stronger (Gonzalez 1969; Madsen 1964); yet, few studies have actually collected kinship data on both Anglos and Chicanos. Analysis of the data on kin ties from the author's research indicates both ethnic groups retain considerable extended familism; however, there are important ethnic differences in extended family structure and the cultural values associated with familism. In the following section, the extended family systems found in these two urban ethnic groups are described, and representative case studies are presented to illustrate the differences between them.

MEXICAN-AMERICAN AND ANGLO-AMERICAN EXTENDED FAMILIES

Many similarities actually exist between Mexican-American and Anglo-American kinship patterns. Both are founded on the bilateral kindred and affinal extensions. The nuclear family is the basic and most significant familial unit and normally constitutes the household. Relatives in the kindred sometimes interact as a social group and are often relied upon for assistance in times of need. Likewise, members of both ethnic groups remain in frequent contact with relatives who live nearby. Moreover, the distinction between more important, primary kin (parents, siblings and children) and less important, secondary kin applies in both ethnic groups.

Distinctive for Chicanos is the inclusion in the extended family of fictive kin (*compadres*) ritualized through religious, and sometimes secular, ceremonies. Baptismal *compadres* take on special obligations, especially the willingness to assume parenthood of their godchildren, if necessary. As godparents of a child, *compadres* or co-parents have a special link with the real parents of the child and are typically close friends or relatives. Fictive kin often fill the same role as real kin in the Chicano extended family; they are accorded the same attention and affection and render mutual aid when it is needed. The tendency to choose relatives as *compadres* increases with each generation among Mexican-Americans, however, so that the ethnic distinction of having kin who are only fictive is perhaps less significant that has sometimes been portrayed by researchers.

The analysis of family data from the author's research reveals that the distinctiveness between Anglo-Americans and Mexican-Americans emerges more in the comparison of interaction and exchange with real, as opposed to fictive, kin. Moreover, there are significant differences in family organization between immigrant Mexicans and later generations of Chicanos. Finally, consideration of kin *and* nonkin social ties leads to a more comprehensive and realistic comparison of the more kin-isolated lives of Anglos versus the kin-dominated lives of Chicanos.

Turning first to a consideration of kin living in town, Mexican-Americans are much more likely to have relatives in town than are Anglos. Less than half (46%) of the Anglos are related by blood or marriage to other households in town, while 86% of the foreign-born and 94% of the native-born (second and third generation) Mexican-Americans have nearby relatives. Chicanos are also related to larger numbers of households in town than Anglos, although there is a significant difference between native- and foreign-born Mexican-Americans. The second and third generations have an average of seventeen and fifteen related households in town respectively, while the first generation averages only about five related households. The Anglos, in comparison, have an average of only three and a half related households in town.

Anglos and Chicanos are both likely to visit with their relatives in town, but Chicanos visit more kin and more often than the Anglos. Ninety percent or more of the Anglos and three Mexican generations with nearby relatives visit at least one related household weekly. However, Chicanos are more likely to visit households daily; 37% of the first generation, 52% of the second generation, and 54% of the third generation visit at least one household daily compared to 26% of the Anglos.

Numbers of kin visited fall into a similar pattern. Anglos with kin in town visit an average of two households a week while immigrant Mexicans visit an average of three and native-born Mexican-Americans visit an average of four.

Exchange of aid with kin is characteristic of both ethnic groups, but native-born Chicanos far surpass both Anglos and immigrant Mexicans in frequency and variety of exchange. Over 40% of the second and third generations have given all six types of aid inquired about to relatives in town in the last year and have received three to four types of aid. In contrast, 41% or more of the Anglos and immigrant Mexicans have given only two types of aid and received only one type of aid.

In summary, Anglos are unlikely to have a local kin group. If they have relatives in town, they are few in number. However small the local kin group is, Anglos nevertheless visit their kin frequently and exchange goods and services with them. First generation Mexican-Americans have slightly larger local kin networks than Anglos and visit these kin somewhat more frequently; their exchange of aid, on the other hand, is somewhat less frequent than for Anglos. The native-born Chicanos, in contrast, have the largest local extended families. Moreover, they visit with more kin and exchange aid more frequently than either the Anglos or immigrant Mexicans.

Analysis of family organization by kin type rather than residence yields another perspective on ethnic differences. First, considering relations with primary kin (parents, siblings and children), all three generations of Mexican-Americans, as well as the Anglo-Americans, maintain contact with the overwhelming majority of their primary kin. In addition, goods and services are exchanged with the majority of primary kin, although this is more characteristic of the native-born Chicanos. All three Mexican-American generations have more primary kin in town than the Anglos; however, the majority of both the Anglos' and Mexican immigrants' primary kin live outside the local area. This affects the frequency of visiting primary kin. The native-born Chicanos see the majority of their primary kin at least weekly while the Anglos and immigrant Mexicans do not.

While primary kin form the core of the individual's extended family in both ethnic groups, secondary kin tend to dominate numerically as local relatives and in the individual's network of interaction and exchange. Because native-born Chicanos recognize more secondary kin than Anglos or immigrant Mexicans and are more likely to have secondary kin nearby, their local extended families tend to be much larger. Anglos (5%) are least likely to have local secondary kin and have the smallest average number of secondary kin (2.1) in town. The tendency to have locally residing, secondary kin increases from generation to generation among the Mexican-Americans; while immigrant Mexicans have an average of 7.3 secondary relatives in town, the second generation averages 22.7 and the third generation averages 32.7 secondary kin in town. Interaction with secondary kin is much less common than with primary kin among all groups, but it is least common among Anglos who visit with only 12% of their secondary kin regardless of place of residence, compared to the three Mexican-American generations, who see 35% or more of their secondary kin regularly. Exchange of goods and services with secondary kin is infrequent among all groups.

In sum, the native-born Mexican-Americans have far and away the largest, most integrated extended families. The native-born Chicanos count more relatives than the

Anglos or immigrants and interact and exchange aid with more relatives. While the first-generation Mexicans have much smaller kin networks, the networks are relatively well integrated through visiting and mutual aid. Anglos count a good many relatives, but the number included in interaction and exchange is comparatively small. Anglos have an average of only 12 relatives with whom they visit, less than half the number visited by first-generation Mexicans and less than one-third the number seen by the native-born. The Anglos also exchange aid with the smallest number of kin (eight) compared to between thirteen and nineteen for Mexican-Americans depending on generation. Thus, not only are Anglos less likely to have a local kin network than Chicanos, but also their full kin network is smaller and more selective than the Chicanos' kin network. Apparently, kinship as a social system is less important for Anglo-Americans.

Among Mexican-Americans, on the other hand, the kin group grows stronger and more localized with each generation. The first-generation immigrants tend to locate in urban areas where they have secondary kin, but most of their relatives remain in Mexico. Once settled, they generally establish small, but well-integrated, local extended families, primarily through their married children. Second-generation Mexican-Americans thus inherit a fairly large local kin group made up of their parents, siblings, and perhaps more distant kin, which is extended through their own spouse and offspring as well as the spouses and offspring of their siblings. The third generation, which is likely to remain residing locally, has a vast number of nearby kin, although they tend to confine the greater part of their interaction to their primary kin — parents, siblings and children.

This process in which the later, and better-off, generations become more familistic calls into question the idea that Mexican-American extended familism is tied to poverty and the search for resources outside the nuclear family (Alvirez and Bean 1976; Grebler et al. 1970). Research with other groups indicates that the urban poor are likely to have relatives who are equally as poor and have few resources to exchange. Furthermore, social agencies are designed to meet many of the needs of the poor, and, although many needs certainly go unmet, the agencies nevertheless offer tremendous resources of which a number of the poor take advantage (Jacobson 1970; Wagley 1964). Instead of the lower class, therefore, it is the urban middle and upper classes whose members have resources to spare where the tradition of extended familism flourishes.

The primary difference between the extended families of the two ethnic groups, then, involves the nature of their geographical proximity. Chicanos tend to have a *traditional* extended family, defined as a localized kin group consisting of a number of related households whose members interact together frequently and exchange mutual aid (Keefe 1979: 352). Anglo-Americans, on the other hand, tend to have a *modified*, or what I have referred to as a widespread, extended family, in which ties with relatives, especially primary kin, are maintained despite geographic distances separating kin. This difference in extended family structure comes about because of a difference in geographic mobility. Anglos are more mobile than Chicanos, tend to live near few relatives, and consequently visit kin infrequently. Contact may be more frequent by mail or by telephone, however, particularly between primary kin (Keefe and Padilla 1987). Immigration, of course, affects the kin group of foreign-born

Mexican-Americans, but among native-born Chicanos, residential stability is a common trait; 32% of the second generation and 43% of the third generation in the study were born in the city in which they were interviewed (compared to only 4% of the Anglos). This difference in geographic proximity leads to several related differences in extended family structure. While members of both ethnic groups maintain contact with most of their primary kin, Chicanos see their primary kin and exchange goods and services with them more frequently due to their proximity. Secondary kin are less important for both Mexican-Americans and Anglo-Americans, but, due to the fact that Anglos are extremely unlikely to have locally residing secondary kin, interaction and exchange with secondary kin is much less frequent for Anglos. Finally, the relative lack of local kin in general among Anglo-Americans means that most of their social network is made up of non-kin (friends, neighbors, coworkers, etc.) compared to the kin-dominated social networks of Chicanos. While 89% of the Anglos' social contacts in town are non-kin, only about half (52%) of the first generations', 41% of the second generations', and 24% of the third generations' social network is made up of non-kin.

FAMILY CASE STUDIES

In order to fully appreciate the ethnic differences described previously, three case studies are presented in this section representing aspects of immigrant Mexican, native-born Chicano, and Anglo-American family organization. It should be emphasized that each case study represents the life of an individual whose story is unique from every other individual in their ethnic group. Yet, in these case studies we also find a pattern of family organization which, in its broad outline, fits that of the ethnic group at large. It is this pattern which is of primary interest here; the details of the individuals' lives add interest and demonstrate some of the possibilities in variation within the group.

Carmen Munoz: A Mexican Immigrant

Carmen Munoz is a fifty-four-year-old housewife with seven children. She was born in Hermosillo in the state of Sonora, Mexico and has been in the United States for twenty-two years, living mostly in Santa Barbara. Carmen left most of her family in Mexico, and, since she has not travelled back since migrating to the United States, her ties with kin there are negligible. Both of her parents are dead. One of her sisters is living in San Diego and the other is in Tijuana, a Mexican border town. Her brother only recently moved back to Mexico after having lived in southern California. She sees her siblings only rarely now, as she lives in Santa Barbara, but her sister in San Diego helped Carmen when she originally migrated to the United States. Carmen cannot remember many of her other relatives and old friends that are still living in Mexico, having lost contact with them long ago. Her second husband, Miguel, has many relatives in Mexico, including his mother and siblings, and his ties are much stronger to kin in Mexico than are Carmen's. Miguel's mother came to live with them for several years but then moved back to Mexico. Carmen has met few of Miguel's other Mexican relatives and does not feel close to any of them.

Carmen and her first husband chose *padrinos* (godparents) for all of their children when they were living in Mexico, and she sees some of them occasionally on their rare visits to the United States, but, basically, she no longer has contact with those *compadres*. She does, however, have *compadres* in town, her youngest child's baptismal *padrinos*, and she sees them regularly.

Carmen's close social network consists primarily of her children and her children's families. She sees her five married children almost daily and has a high level of exchange of goods and services with them. For example, several times when she became critically ill, her sons or daughters would accompany her and her husband to the emergency room. When one of her daughters was hospitalized, Carmen spent most of her time at the hospital. Presently, another daughter is having financial difficulties and Carmen has taken in all four grandchildren for a while to alleviate some of the burden. Carmen's children often give her rides to the market, to church, and take her on other errands, as she does not drive, and Miguel often works the night shift, sleeping during the day. This type of exchange appears to be limited to her children. Although she knows a few of her neighbors, she does not exchange favors, advice, childcare or money with them. Her exchange with her *compadres* in town is also minimal. There is no one in town who Carmen considers to be a close friend.

Anna Fuentes: A Native-Born Chicana

Twenty-three-year-old Anna Fuentes is a second-generation Chicana, born in Santa Barbara. Anna and her husband, Ruben, were married immediately following her graduation from high school, and, while they are looking forward to it, they do not have children yet. As a native Santa Barbaran, Anna has a large local kinship network and very close relations with her primary kin. Specifically, Anna has her parents, one sister and one brother living in town, while a second brother lives in nearby Oxnard. Ruben has nine siblings, only one of whom does not live in town. Anna estimates that she and Ruben have about forty other relatives in town, and, of these, they see ten at least monthly. Anna usually takes her mother shopping every Saturday, and, on Sunday, she and Ruben have dinner at her parents' house. Every Monday night, Anna and Ruben have dinner at his parents' house. These immediate kin are the only individuals who Anna and Ruben are sure to see socially several times a week. Frequency of contact diminishes rapidly outside of the immediate families, as Anna sees her closest first cousin, on the average, only once a month and her aunts and other cousins perhaps two or three times each year.

Anna tends to be self-reliant and rarely asks for help from others, but, in time of trouble, she says she would rely on her primary kin. On the other hand, she recalls that she has been of service to several relatives in the past year. For example, her mother and sister confide in her about their problems, and several other relatives have also come to Anna for advice about their personal problems. Furthermore, Anna has loaned some money to one of her sisters-in-law, and she has helped her parents with household chores, as well as such tasks as preparing tamales for a party.

Anna feels very close to her family; they are the most important people in her life. She and Ruben have friends, but they are secondary to their relatives. Ruben and Anna have six good friends, all Mexican-Americans. Four of these are *compadres*, as Anna and Ruben are *padrinos* to their children. Anna sees her friends regularly and sometimes has invited them over with her relatives. For example, the one large party she had during the year of interviews was a barbecue with family and friends celebrating her and Ruben's fifth wedding anniversary. Anna does not generally exchange goods or services with friends, preferring when necessary to rely on family.

Amy Cooper: An Anglo-American

Amy Cooper is a thirty-one-year-old mother of two young children. Amy met her husband, Donald, in Santa Barbara, where they have lived for the last eleven years.

Amy has only one relative living in town, Donald's cousin, who they see every month or so and have helped out financially on occasion. She mainly socializes with four female friends whom she has known for ten years or more. Amy not only gets together with each of her friends several times a week, but also talks to them on the telephone frequently. Most of these friends have small children as well, and they often take them to the beach or to the pool together. Amy and her girlfriends talk about shared problems concerning marital difficulties, disciplinary problems with children, worries about sick relatives, and so on. They also help each other out with babysitting, housecleaning, and small loans of money. Amy is also friends with a neighbor at her apartment building, and they often exchange childcare or borrow small items when necessary.

Amy feels very close to her parents, but, because they live elsewhere in California (Fontana), she cannot see them as often as she would like. Still, she manages to visit with them monthly, sometimes at their home and sometimes at hers. During the interviews, Amy's mother came to stay for several days, and they talked at length about the children, Amy's grandmother's illness, her father's drinking problem, and the stress of her mother's job. Amy often takes her problems to her mother for advice, because "she cares about my life and the children." The Coopers seem to have continual financial problems due to Donald's low income in his occupation as a musician and music teacher, and Amy's parents have loaned them money several times beginning when they were first married. Amy's only brother lives in Manhattan Beach, California, and they remain in frequent contact often meeting at her parent's home. Amy worries about his wife, who has had some disturbing psychological problems. Clearly, Amy's primary kin are important to her, and she works to maintain close contact with them. Nevertheless, she has not felt it necessary to move back to the Los Angeles area, content to have her social contact with primary kin remain periodic.

Amy has several other relatives she cares about, mostly on her side of the family, including her grandparents and an aunt. Donald's mother is the only in-law she interacts with much (aside from his cousin in town), since he has no siblings and his father is dead. These relatives also live elsewhere in southern California, limiting social interaction with them, although mutual aid, especially when visiting in each other's homes, is offered.

CULTURAL DEFINITIONS OF CLOSE FAMILY TIES

As the case studies demonstrate, familism in the traditional sense of interacting with a large, local kin group is a pervasive Mexican-American trait irrespective of level of acculturation. Those who immigrate to the United States must leave their relatives in Mexico; thus, their interaction with them obviously declines. They tend to remain emotionally close to their parents and those siblings left behind, however, and any relatives who happen to live in town become important. As the immigrants grow older, time and energy is invested in maintaining a primary kin network like Carmen's, which is based on adult children and their families. Non-kin, including friends, neighbors, and coworkers, on the other hand, never come to figure significantly in their social lives.

For the native-born, the extended kin group becomes large and cohesive. Most significant are the primary kin: parents, siblings, and adult children. Friends and other non-kin are likely to be integrated into the native-borns' social networks but never to the exclusion of relatives. For most native-born, like Anna Fuentes, the kin group is the core of their social life. Familism as a cultural trait is thus nurtured by the first generation only to come into full bloom in later generations due to geographic stability.

As suggested elsewhere (Keefe 1984), Anglo-Americans also maintain a preference for *close* extended family ties; what differs is the ethnic definition of closeness. Mexican-Americans and Anglo-Americans share many interpretations of *closeness*, such as the expression of love and affection between kin, evidence of trust and respect among family members, sharing life experiences as a family, and knowing family members are there if needed. Chicanos differ, however, on one fundamental aspect in defining *closeness*: the need for the consistent presence of family members. Chicanos value the physical presence of family members while Anglos are satisfied with intermittent meetings with kin supplemented by telephone calls and letters. For Mexican-Americans, it is important to see relatives regularly face-to-face, to embrace, to touch, and to simply be with one another, sharing the minor joys and sorrows of daily life. For Anglos, these experiences are integral to nuclear family life but less important with regard to extended family ties. Anglos also feel comfortable having friends function in these roles, while Chicanos reserve them primarily for kin. As Adams (1970) has pointed out, friends and relatives can be interchangeable for Anglo-Americans with regard to social visiting and minor kinds of mutual aid.

Geographic proximity, in other words, is not the basis for the Anglo-American conception of *closeness* in kin ties. In fact, there are many aspects of close family relations that can be unaffected by the physical presence or absence of kin: carrying a family identity as part of a personal identity, talking or worrying about family members and experiencing a psychological feeling of well-being stemming from family members' support. Other aspects can be fulfilled with the intermittent physical presence of kin, including being present during holidays and in times of crisis. Amy Cooper is really somewhat atypical of our sample of Anglo-Americans in that all of her primary kin live in California. Most of the Anglos in the study were born outside of California and have at least some of their primary kin living in other states, which makes them even more inaccessible.

In conclusion, early social theorists, looking at American society in general, were correct in their description of urban life as being less kin-based. This is true insofar as it concerns the face-to-face social communities of the Anglo-American majority, but it is wrong to conclude that this ethnic trait is an urban trait. In many contemporary, urban societies and urban-dwelling ethnic groups, such as Mexican-Americans, extended kinship dominates social life. Moreover, it does not follow that Anglo-Americans lack kin ties because, in fact, Anglos have significant extended-family ties which can be activated immediately and intensely in times of need (Sussman 1965). In rethinking the relationship between urbanism and kinship organization, much remains to be done in describing the extent of cross-cultural variation and potential explanations for that variation. Furthermore, it would appear that focusing on the social lives of individuals, rather than on apparent social communities, would be a better technique to use in future research on the question. In any case, it is clear that the extended family survives in cities and contributes in positive ways to ethnic adaptation to urban life.

NOTES

1. The terms *Chicano* and *Mexican-American* are used interchangeably in this paper to refer to to the entire ethnic group of Mexican descent in the United States. Modified versions of these terms are used to discuss subsegments of the ethnic group (e.g., immigrant Mexicans, native-born Chicanos). The term *Anglo-Americans* is used to refer to white Americans of European descent. Considerable cultural and socio-economic diversity which affects family organization, obviously exists within the Anglo-American ethnic group. My research, however, indicates that Chicano, versus Anglo, ethnicity is the most significant factor affecting extended family organization within the population sampled.
2. The author expresses appreciation to the National Institute of Mental Health which provided funding for this research (Center for Minority Group Mental Health Programs, Grant number MH26099, Principal Investigator: Amado M. Padilla). The first survey randomly sampled residents in three selected census tracts in each of the three cities; the final sample included 666 Chicanos and 340 Anglo-Americans. In the second survey, which produced a sample of 381 Chicanos and 163 Anglo-Americans, respondents who indicated willingness were reinterviewed. For the second set of interviews, a much longer questionnaire was used; in-depth case studies were subsequently done of twenty-four Chicanos and twenty-two Anglos. Cases were selected randomly to cover a stratified range of cultural, socio-economic, and family organization categories. Further description of the research design and findings can be found in Keefe and Padilla (1987).

THE KINDRED OF VIOLA JACKSON: RESIDENCE AND FAMILY ORGANIZATION OF AN URBAN BLACK AMERICAN FAMILY[1]

Carol B. Stack

A common stereotype of the family life of the urban poor is that it is disorganized. Parallel to this image is the portrayal of the black family as one which is centered around a grandmother, her daughters, and her daughters' young children. The prevalence of such a fatherless household has been variously seen as a retention of African culture, as a product of slavery, and as one of the outcomes of urbanization and certain welfare policies. It is often viewed as something which is pathological. Stack, in this article, challenges these portraits. She points out that the idea of "matrifocality" cannot fully describe or explain the variety of strategies by which North American blacks have adapted to the situation of urban poverty. Rather than stressing concepts like household and kin group, she uses dynamic or process concepts like "adaptive strategy" and "alignment." It will be useful to compare her description of the urban black kindred with Oscar Lewis's view of "The Culture of Poverty."

INTRODUCTION

Concepts can become so widely accepted and seem so obvious that they block the way to further understanding. Descriptions of black American domestic life (Frazier 1939; Drake and Cayton 1945; Abrahams 1964; Moynihan 1965; Rainwater 1966a) are almost always couched in terms of the nuclear family and in terms of the fashionable notion of a matrifocal complex. But in many societies the nuclear family is not always a unit of domestic cooperation, and the "universal functions" of family life can be provided by other social units (Spiro 1954; Gough 1959; Levy and Fallers 1959; Reiss 1965). And matrifocal thinking, while it may bring out the importance of women in family life, fails to

Source: Reprinted with permission of The Free Press, a Division of Macmillan, Inc. from *Afro-American Anthology*:Contemporary Perspectives, Norman W. Whitten, Jr. and John F. Szwed, Eds. Copyright © 1970 by The Free Press.

account for the great variety of domestic strategies one can find on the scene in urban black America. The following study suggests that if we shed concepts such as matrifocality we can see that black Americans have evolved a repertoire of domestic units that serve as flexible adaptive strategies for coping with the everyday human demands of ghetto life.

In the fall of 1966 I began to investigate black family organization in midwestern cities. I concentrated upon one domestic family unit—the household of Viola and Leo Jackson—and their network of kinsmen, which proved to number over 100 persons.[2] My immediate aim was to discover when and why each of these people had changed residence, and what kind of domestic unit they joined during the half-century since they had begun moving north from Arkansas.

The data show that during the process of migration and the adjustment of individuals to urban living, clusters of kin align together for various domestic purposes. It soon became clear that matrifocal thinking provided little insight into the organization of domestic units of cooperation, for example, those groups of kin and non-kin which carry out domestic functions but do not always reside together (Bender 1967). In certain situations such as the death or desertion of a parent, the loss of a job, or in the process of migration it was found that an individual almost always changed residence. But matrifocality proved to be a poor predictor of the kind of domestic unit the individual might subsequently enter. Among Mrs. Jackson's kin one can find various assortments of adults and children cooperating in domestic units: children living with relatives other than their parents, and also clusters of kin (often involving the father) who do not reside together but who provide some of the domestic functions for a mother-and-child unit in another location. Not only does matrifocal thinking fail here, but also little or nothing in the current writing on black American family life helps deal with questions such as the following that arise when we examine Mrs. Jackson's kin: Which relatives can a person expect will help him? Which relatives will care for parentless or abandoned children? And who will look after the ill and elderly? I will discuss these questions, and the challenge that Mrs. Jackson's kin and their lifeways put to our powers of explanation. First, however, I will deal briefly with the nature of matrifocal thinking.

THE MATRIFOCAL COMPLEX

Matrifocality has become a popular replacement for the discarded nineteenth-century concept of matriarchy. Some would argue that matrifocality is more sophisticated, but I suggest that it is no more useful than matriarchy for characterizing urban Negro households.

When the rules for reckoning kinship are not explicit, then it is difficult to determine the basis upon which households are formed. As so, as M. G. Smith (1962b:7) has pointed out, by necessity the anthropologist then must rely on data on household composition. It is in this context that the term "matrifo-cality" is most widely used. However, it also has been used to refer to at least three units of information: (1) the composition of a household, (2) the type of kinship bond linking its members, and (3) the relationship between males and females in the household. In fact, matrifocality tells us little about the actual composition of the household, and the relational link upon which the household is formed. Schneider (1961) points out that in the past the terms "matrilocal marriage" and "matriliny" were used interchangeably (see Bachofen 1861) and that the matriarchal complex referred to a household which did not include the husband or father. Both González (1965) and Smith (1962b) use matrifo-cality to refer to the composition of households. These and similar formulations ignore the developmental history of domestic groups (Goody 1958). In addition, they supply no information on the age and circumstances in which individuals join households, the alternatives open to them, the relational links they have with other members, or who the members are. *Matrifocality is not a residence rule, and in particular, it is not a rule for post-marital residence.* Residence, one of the dynamics of social organization, can be understood only if the basis for the active formation of households is known.

A further complication is that notions such as matrifocality, maternal family (C. King 1945), and matriarchy inadvertently are associated with unilineal descent. It was Bachofen's contention (1861) that matriliny (descent through women) and matriarchy (rule by women) were but two aspects of the same in-stitution (Schneider 1961; Lowie 1947). This claim had to be discarded when observers failed to find any generalized authority of women over men in matri-lineal societies. This controversy is well known. What is less widely appreciated is that there is a close parallel between matriarchal and matrifocal thinking, in that both imply descent through women. For example, M. G. Smith (1962b) defines Caribbean matrifocal households as ones which are composed of blood-related women plus all their unmarried children. González (1965:1542) defines consanguineal households in terms of the type of kinship bond linking adult men and women in the households such that no two members are bound together in an affinal relationship. She suggests that consanguineal households may also be matrifocal (1965:1548) and that there is evidence that consanguineal households exist among lower class Negro American groups (Du-Bois 1908; Frazier 1939; C. King 1945). The tentative classification that emerges from studies of black American households as consanguineal or as both consanguineal and matrifocal is confusing. In this confusion the use of the no-tion of matrifocality roughly coincides with Schneider's (1961:3) definition of matrilineal descent units in which he states that the "individual's initial rela-tionship is to his mother and through her to other kinsmen, both male and fe-male, but continuing only through females." *Matrifocality is not necessarily a correlate of matrilineal descent, nor does it imply a structure for linking families in the same community.*

The term "matrifocality" may have value as an indication of the woman's role within the domestic group, but it tells us little about authority, decision-making, and male-female relationships within the household, among extended kin, and in the community. Used in this context to refer to a dominant female role, and as a designate of residence classification, reference to the matrifocal household may lead to confusion between residence and role behavior. Analysis of role relationships and interactional patterns which is limited to their classification as matrifocal is at best uninteresting. The role organization of urban Negro households exists in a dynamic system which can be illustrated by the life histories of individuals in households as they adapt to the urban environment. This adaptation comes out dramatically when one examines Viola Jackson's kin and their many ways of forming a domestic unit.

Frequently, discussions of matrifocality and consanguineal households ignore crucial aspects of family organization. Some of the matrifocal thinkers seem to assume that children derive nothing of sociological importance from their father, that households are equivalent to the nuclear family, and that resident husband-fathers are marginal members of their own homes (M. G. Smith 1957b). A look at Viola Jackson's kindred raises doubts about many of these assumptions.

URBAN FAMILY ORGANIZATION

Clusters of Kin

The past fifty years have witnessed a massive migration of rural, southern blacks to urban centers in the United States. The kindred of Viola Jackson are a part of this movement. Ninety-six of them left the South between 1916 and 1967. Some of them first moved from rural Arkansas to live and work harvesting fruit in areas around Grand Rapids and Benton Harbor, Michigan, and Racine, Wisconsin; eventually they settled in the urban North. Two major patterns emerge from their life histories: (1) relatives tend to cluster in the same areas during similar periods; and (2) the most frequent and consistent alignment and cooperation appears to occur between siblings.

During the process of moving, Viola Jackson's kin maintained communication with relatives in the South. They frequently moved back to the South for short periods, or from Chicago and other midwestern cities to fruit harvesting areas on a seasonal basis. Therefore it is difficult to separate the data in terms of phases such as "migration" and subsequent "urban adaptation." During some seasons bus loads of rural blacks were brought to the North to harvest fruit. Many families worked their way back South only to repeat the process in order to avoid the poverty and unemployment there. This circulatory migration mainly involved the younger families and individuals.

Frequently, migrant workers follow their relatives and large urban neighborhoods reflect the geographical boundaries of the hinterland. Once these facts are established it is important to find out who made the original move, his age at the time of the move, which relatives joined one another to form households, and the context of each move.

Between 1916 and 1967 Mrs. Jackson's kin lived in five states, and groups of 10 to 15 individuals tended to cluster in the same areas during the same time periods. An example of this can be seen in Table 1, which shows where Viola's mother and siblings were living during that time period.

The basis for the active formation of households during migration and urban settlement can only be understood if material developing out of life histories is related to the realities of kinship and non-kinship factors. During this period of migratory wage labor in the young adult's life, the data show that the strongest alignment is of cooperation and mutual aid among siblings of both sexes (after the age of thirteen). Siblings left the South together, or shortly followed one another, for seasonal jobs. They often lived together in the North with their dependents and spouses, or lived near one another, providing mutual aid such as cooking and child care.

Table 1. Residence and Kin Clusters

AREA AND TIME PERIOD	EGO'S MOTHER (MAGNOLIA)	EGO (VIOLA)	B	S	S	S	B
Arkansas 1916–1917	X	X	X				
Arkansas 1928–1944	X	X		X	X	X	X
Blythe, Calif. 1927–1928	X·	X	X				
Grand Rapids, Mich. 1944–1946			X		X		
Benton Harbor, Mich. 1946–1948			X	X	X		X
Racine, Wisc. 1947–1948			X		X		X
Decatur, Ark. 1948–1952	X	X			X		X
Chicago, Ill. 1950–1953				X			
Champaign, Ill. 1952–1954	X	X	X				
Gary, Ind. 1954–1955			X				
Champaign, Ill. 1955–1967	X	X	X		X	X	X
Chicago Heights, Ill. 1959–1967				X			
Chicago, Ill. 1965–1967			X				

Domestic Arrangements

CASE 1

In 1945 *C* left her husband and daughter in the South with his parents and moved to Racine, Wisconsin, to harvest fruit. At the same time *C's* brother's wife died leaving him, *J*, with two young sons. *J* decided to move north and join *C* in Racine. He and his two sons took a bus to Racine where he got a job in a catsup factory. The company furnished trailers which *C* and *J* placed next to each other. *C* cooked for *J* and his two sons and cared for the children. They were cooperating as a single domestic unit. This situation continued for about a year and a half and then they all returned to the South.

CASE 2

By 1946 Viola and Leo had four children and Leo was picking cotton. They were anxious to leave the South in order to find better wages and living conditions. Viola, Leo, and their children joined a bus load of people and moved to join Viola's brother, *L*, in Benton Harbor, Michigan. In Benton Harbor all the adults and the older children worked harvesting fruit. At the same time Leo's twin brother and Viola's brother, *J*, and his two sons moved to Benton Harbor. Leo's twin brother moved into Viola's and Leo's household. *J* and his sons moved into the household of *J's* brother, *L*, and *L's* wife.

CASE 3

In 1948 *C* decided to move north again. This time she took her daughter with her. She moved to Benton Harbor where Viola and her family, their two brothers, *L* and *J*, and Leo's twin brother were all living. *C* and *J* and their children began cooperating as a single domestic unit as they had in Racine.

The pattern described above of cooperation and mutual aid among siblings becomes even more apparent as these individuals move to urban areas. Sibling alignment in the urban context will be discussed in the next section.

SIBLING ALIGNMENT AND KIN COOPERATION IN URBAN AREAS

Understanding residence and family organization for people whose economic situation is constantly changing, and who therefore frequently change households, is not easy. Aside from the common observations of household composition based upon where people sleep, there are many other important patterns to be observed, such as which situations lead to a change in residence, which adults share households, and with which adult relatives are children frequently living.

One pattern, a continuation of a pattern formed during the early stages of migratory labor, is the cooperative alignment of siblings. By the time the majority of Viola Jackson's relatives had established permanent residence and jobs in the North there were numerous examples of siblings forming co-residential and/or domestic units of cooperation. These sibling-based units, apparently motivated by situations such as death, sickness, desertion, abandonment, and unemployment, most often focused around the need for child-care arrangements. Here are two examples:

SISTER/BROTHER

In 1956 Viola and Leo were living in Champaign, Illinois. Viola's brother, *J*, took the train from the South to visit them. After the visit he decided to move to Champaign with his two sons and look for work. *J* rented a house near Viola's and got a construction job. When he brought his sons to Champaign Viola cooked for them and cared for them during the day.

SISTER/SISTER

In 1959 Viola's sister, *E*, was suffering from a nervous breakdown. *E's* husband took their four youngest children to his mother in Arkansas. *E's* sister, *C*, was living in Chicago and she cared for *E's* oldest daughter. After *E's* husband deserted her, *E's* twin sister, *M*, moved into *E's* house. The household was composed of *E*, her oldest daughter who had been in Chicago, *M*, and *M's* two youngest daughters.

These alignments may be largely attributed to adaptation to urban socioeconomic conditions. One such urban pattern is a minimum of emphasis on the inheritance of property. For obvious social and economic reasons, poor and highly mobile urban apartment dwellers do not develop strong ties to a homestead or a particular piece of land, even though they may express strong regional and even neighborhood loyalty or identification. This contrasts with the rural South and Young's and Willmott's (1957) observations that apartments in Bethnal Green were kept in the family. The high frequency of moving from one apartment to another in economically depressed urban areas is related to the degree of overcrowding, the shortage of apartments, urban renewal, and the changing employment situation. Another situation causing these alignments to form is the arrival of a new migrant to the urban area wherein he lives with siblings. With time, if he successfully establishes himself in a job in the urban area he may move out of his sibling's household.

CRISIS SITUATIONS AND THE RESIDENCE OF CHILDREN

It has already been pointed out that migration, unemployment, sickness, and desertion by necessity often lead to a change in residence. Most often these changes are closely related to the need for child-care arrangements. The choices and expectations involved in placing children in a relative's home largely focus around which adult female relatives are available. In selecting the specific relative, the following criteria are considered: the geographical locations of these adult female relatives; their source of financial support, their age, their marital status, the composition of their household, and the ability of the people making the decision to get along with these females. At the same time, due to the flexibility and mobility of urban individuals, decisions frequently center around the relational link the child has with female members of a particular household. This means that the distance and location of a household, for example, are not a great deterrent, and that in fact the economic, distance, and other decisions are made after the kin criteria are met.

Children in the extended kin network of Viola Jackson frequently live with relatives other than their biological parents. The child-female links which most often are the basis of new or expanded households are clearly those links with close adult females such as the child's mother, mother's mother, mother's sister, mother's brother's wife, father's mother, father's sister, father's brother's wife.

Here are some examples.

RELATIONAL LINK	DOMESTIC UNIT
Mother	Viola's brother married his first wife when he was sixteen. When *she* left him, she kept her daughter.
Mother's mother	Viola's sister, *M*, never was able to care for her children. In between husbands, her mother kept her two oldest children, and after *M's* death, her mother kept all three of the children. Her brother offered to keep the oldest girl.
Mother's mother	Viola's daughter (age 20) was living at home and gave birth to a son. The daughter and her son remained in the Jackson household. The daughter expressed the desire to set up a separate household.
Mother's sister	*M* moved to Chicago into her sister's household. The household consisted of the two sisters and four of their children.
Father's mother	Viola's sister, *E*, had four daughters and one son. When *E* was suffering from a nervous breakdown her husband took three daughters and his son to live with his mother in Arkansas. After his wife's death he also took the oldest daughter to his mother's household in Arkansas.
Father's mother	When Viola's younger sister, *C*, left her husband in order to harvest fruit in Wisconsin she left her two daughters with his mother in Arkansas.
Father's sister	When Viola's brother's wife died, he decided to raise his two sons himself. He kept the two boys and never remarried. His residence has consistently been close to one or another of his sisters who have fed and cared for his two sons.

These examples do indeed indicate the important role of the black female. But the difference between matrifocal thinking and thinking about household composition in terms of where children live is that the latter can bring to light the dynamics of household formation, and the criteria, rules, and decisions that the process entails.

The summaries of the social context in which children changed households indicates which adult female relatives are frequently called upon for service. The alignment and cooperation between siblings, such as mother's sister and father's sister, has already been noted. This has been underestimated by workers who select the grandmother household (especially mother's mother) as the only significant domestic unit. It must be noted that the crucial role which paternal as well as maternal grandmothers assume in socialization is a frequent, but definitely not a unique, alternative.

Since social scientists have stressed the existence of female-centered, woman-headed, matrifocal black families, it is of particular interest to look at the formation of grandmother households in Viola's kin. Here is a summary of the households in which Viola's mother, Magnolia, has lived.

MAGNOLIA

AGE	CONTEXT OF DOMESTIC UNIT OR HOUSEHOLD
60	In 1958 Magnolia's second husband died and she was left alone with her daughter's (M) two oldest children. Viola sent her two oldest sons to care for Magnolia and the two children.
62	In 1960 Magnolia moved to Champaign and joined the household of her twin daughters, E and M, bringing M's children with her.
65	After E's death, Magnolia and her daughter moved to Danville, Illinois, with M's two children, who Magnolia raised in the South, and M's two youngest children.
67	After M's death, Magnolia joined her daughter Viola's household for a short time.
67	Soon afterward, Viola and her husband rented a nearby house for Magnolia and the four grandchildren. Magnolia is on welfare, cares for the four children, and constantly receives help from the Jacksons and from her children living in Chicago.

When a grandmother household is characterized as matrifocal we get little insight into the dynamics of its formation. At best, it suggests a mother hen who gathers her chicks about her. After age sixty, Magnolia's residence was determined by her children, who decided to bring her to the urban North to care for her. Her move North was prompted by her children's concern for her health and well-being.

We find that Magnolia has frequently shared households with her children and grandchildren. In fact, she has consistently moved to join her daughter's households to be cared for, or to care for her grandchildren. Instead of simply gathering her flock, each move and new household in which Magnolia lived after age sixty was formed on a different basis.

By the time Magnolia was elderly she was living in the urban North in a grandmother household caring for her grandchildren. This was the result of the illness and subsequent death of one of her daughters. At this time a house was rented and maintained for Magnolia and the four grandchildren by Viola and her husband, Leo. The rented house was one block from Viola's home and the two households functioned primarily as a single domestic unit of cooperation. The cluster of relatives consisted of four generations: Magnolia, the four grand-children, Viola and Leo Jackson, ten of their children, and their grandchild, the son of Viola Jackson's oldest daughter.

This four-generational kin cluster is not a co-residential unit, but a domestic unit of cooperation. The main source of financial support consisted of Leo's seasonal construction work, welfare payments to both Magnolia and Viola's daughter (for her son), and the part-time jobs of some of the teenage children. These individuals used Viola's house as home base where they shared the eve-ning meal, cared for all the small children, and exchanged special skills and services. Frequently, Viola's brother (whose wife had died) ate with the group and participated in the exchange of money, food, care for the sick, and household duties. The exchange of clothes, appliances, and services in crisis situations extended beyond this kin cluster to relatives in Chicago and St. Louis. This group is an example of an urban kinship-based domestic unit which formed to handle the basic family functions.

CONCLUDING REMARKS

The examples from the preceding sections support the suggestion that domestic functions are carried out for urban blacks by clusters of kin who may or may not reside together. Individuals who are members of households and domestic units of cooperation align to provide the basic functions often attributed to nu-clear family units. The flexibility of the blacks' adaptation to the daily social and economic problems of urban living is evidenced in these kinship-based units which form to handle the daily demands of urban life. In particular, new or expanded households and/or domestic units are created to care for children. The basis of these cooperative units is co-generational sibling alignment, the domestic cooperation of close adult females, and the exchange of goods and services between the male and female relatives of these females. To conclude, it is suggested that these households and domestic units provide the assurance that all the children will be cared for.

NOTES

1. The author would like to thank Professors E. Bruner, D. Shimkin, F. K. Lehman, D. Plath, and O. Lewis, and Mr. W. Ringle, for their interest in this work and helpful comments.
2. Names throughout the paper are pseudonyms.

URBANIZATION AND FAMILY STRUCTURE IN THE IVORY COAST

Remi Clignet

Anthropologists have discovered a wide variety of family types and kinship systems throughout the world. Many peoples reckon descent through the father and the male line, while others reckon descent through the mother and the female line. In systems which follow the former pattern (known as patrilineal systems), the individual inherits from his father and male ancestors, while in matrilineal systems inheritance is from mother to daughter, or, in some instances, from mother's brother to sister's son. Unlike our own society, many cultures permit men to take more than one wife. How does urbanization affect peoples whose native cultures prescribe family systems which differ radically from the one most common in the West? Such a question follows from theories of urbanism which propose that relations between the nuclear family and extended kin break down under the impact of modern urbanization. Clignet tries to answer this question by comparing two ethnic groups with distinctive family systems who live in one West African city. One group has a matrilineal system, while the other is patrilineal. They differ in other ways as well. For another example of "controlled comparison," see Keefe ("Myth of the Declining Family").

Urbanization may be viewed as a particular manifestation of social change. As such, it is often defined as a process leading originally distinct social systems to a common destination.[1] As an example, it is supposed to facilitate the universal emergence of a European type of nuclear family.[2] In this perspective, many scholars have been eager to determine the extent to which African patterns of familial behavior lose their traditional specific properties.[3] These researchers have in fact equated the problem of measuring urbanization with the problem of measuring the relative decline and persistence of traditional affiliations. Taking as examples the familial systems of two Ivory Coast peoples, the present paper intends to show some of the limitations of this type of analysis.

The description of the convergencies characterizing manifestations of social change between distinct cultures emphasizes the "empty, mechanical, and reversible" nature of time.[4] Yet there is also a certain amount of variability in the responses of distinct familial systems to urbanization. The social phenomena

SOURCE: *Comparative Studies in Society and History* 8:385–401 (1966). Revised. Copyright © 1966 by Society for Comparative Studies in Society and History. Reprinted by permission of the Cambridge University Press.

which accompany urbanization are determined in part by the unique characteristics of the historical period at which this process takes place. They depend,
also, at least partly, upon the relative exposure to urbanization of the total
social systems under study.

Additionally, the variability of responses to urbanization reflects the original
properties characteristic of the ethnic groups analyzed. The size of the kin
groups prevailing among such peoples and their type of descent will affect the
responses of individuals to the pressures accompanying urbanization. The demands imposed on their members by various types of kin groups are specific,
enforced by varying techniques of social control, and the tension management
system prevailing in each of these groups differs[5]; hence the responses of each
ethnic group to urbanization will be distinctive. All African ethnic groups
respond to urbanization, not only by modifying their familial life styles but also
by selecting new values, norms, and practices that they make fit the preexisting
modes of familial organizations. Moreover they differ in the extent to which they
make use of each of these mechanisms of adjustment to a new situation.[6]

THE SOCIAL ORGANIZATION OF THE ABOURE AND BETE PEOPLES

The first people analyzed here, the Aboures, number about 12,000 and are
concentrated in the southeast part of the country. They are at present divided
into three territorially distinct subgroups. Each subgroup is divided into seven
major clans whose members, even today, occupy a social position which is by
far superior to that occupied by aliens or by the offspring of former slaves. In
effect, the Aboure social and political structure is hierarchical, with authority
concentrated in the hands of chiefly lineages, subject to the consent of the heads
of commoner lineages. In this society clearly defined age groups exert important military, economic, and social influences. Political office and property
are transmitted along matrilineal lines.[7] Originally engaged in fishing and
subsistence farming, the men of this group are increasingly involved in cash
crop agriculture, and the yearly income of the farmers of this area exceeds that
for any other area.

The Bete number 150,000 and occupy a portion of the southwest.[8] They are
a patrilineal people with a typical acephalous political and social structure. At
present, the maximal unit of political and social organization is the village,
which (in contrast to the Aboure) normally is composed of a cluster of minimal
lineages, each of which traces descent to a common agnatic ancestor. Originally
warriors and hunters, Bete men shifted not long ago to subsistence farming,
and a large minority do not yet grow cash crops.

In summary, the two groups can be contrasted as follows: First, the political
organization of the Aboure is more complex than that of the Bete. Stability in
Aboure society is ensured by a hierarchic organization which minimizes conflict
between lineages and affines. Conversely, Bete social stability rests upon a

principle of reciprocity at the horizontal level; the exchange of women and bridewealth between villages circulates wealth. Wives and husbands occupy inferior positions in the village of their respective affines.

Second, the religious life of Aboure people is much more elaborate than that of the Bete, who have no ancestral cult and for whom present conditions of life are more meaningful than memories of an uncertain past.

Third, so far, the economic development of the Aboure area is markedly higher than that of the Bete country, and as a consequence, Aboure are wealthier than their Bete counterparts.

Fourth, although both groups follow virilocal rules of residence, the organization of the descent group is mainly matrilineal among the Aboure and patrilineal among the Bete. In both societies, ties between brothers and sisters are close. With the Aboure, the link is permanent, and the position of a woman in her own lineage is determined by that of her brother. With the Bete, the tie entails reciprocal and successive obligations: the brother wishes the sister to marry as soon as possible in order to effect his own marriage. Thereafter, the sister is able to place very exacting demands on her brothers as a price for her obligation to live outside her natal community.

Lastly, the two groups differ in the extent to which wives are absorbed within their affinal group.[9] The Bete wife, who may enjoy a high status in her own village, must ensure that her offspring acquire a strong position within her husband's descent group. Further, because of her level of participation in the agricultural activities of her households, she is a major determinant of her spouse's wealth. Her expected influence on the functioning of her affinal group probably accounts, at least in part, for the high brideprice which accompanies marriage. Similarly, the variety of functions performed by married women in the household is probably a factor which explains the great incidence of polygyny in this society. By contrast, the ties between Aboure spouses are much looser. Their economic activities and interests tend to be separated. The child's status is meaningful in the wife's descent group but not in that of the husband. This low degree of "social absorption" of Aboure women in their affinal group is associated with a low brideprice; the limited functionality of the role performed by wives is also evidenced by the low rates of polygyny, as well as by the high frequency of divorce.

The ratios of migration of these two groups towards the largest urban center of the Ivory Coast (Abidjan) are quite different and seem to be determined by geographical factors. The Aboure are concentrated in an area close to Abidjan and are more heavily represented in this city than the Bete, whose residence is more remote.

The differential distance separating the rural hinterland of each one of these two peoples from the capital city has affected their respective migratory patterns and modes of adaptation to the urban scene. The disproportion between the numbers of male and female residents in Abidjan is smaller in the case of the Aboure than of the Bete. Further, the various age groups of the first one of these ethnic groups are more evenly represented in the capital city than those of the second one. Contrasts in the distance separating the Aboure and the Bete hinterland from Abidjan imply as well differences in the exposure of these two ethnic groups to French norms, values, and practices. Thus the Aboure were subject to French colonial authority fifty years before the Bete. As a result, 65% of the Aboure men over 14 years old living in Abidjan can read and write French as against only 35% of their Bete counterparts; for adult women, the figures are 16% and 8% respectively.[10] Despite such differences, urbanization presents, nevertheless, similar problems for the two groups. Ties between the nuclear family and the broader kin group become geographically looser. Even in the most rural suburb of Abidjan, Adjame, only one-third of the households comprise subparts of the same extended family. Further, owing to the unpredictability of family income, nuclear families themselves tend to be unstable. More than half of the households where both parents are living together have regular sources of income; of the households which include only one of the parents only one-quarter have regular sources of income.[11]

In summary, although the Aboure and the Bete areas were colonized by Europeans at different times, and, as a consequence, have followed distinctive patterns of migration toward Abidjan, they have faced similar difficulties in the process of urbanization. As an example, the unevenness of the diffusion of schooling between the sexes had a comparable impact upon the two ethnic groups, and women in Abidjan have often lost their opportunities of maintaining financial autonomy.

Given these similarities and these contrasts, we may ask what is the differential impact of traditional organization upon family structure in the urban milieu. To be sure, the structure and the functioning of Aboure and Bete kin groups are changing in the towns, but the question remains to determine the extent to which traditional models affect the direction of these changes. We propose to explore this point with regard to some aspects of the female role. The roles of women reflect the degree of their social absorption in their affinal kin group and vary as between societies to a larger extent than those of men. Because of this initial variability, an analysis of the changes affecting female roles should lead to a better understanding of the convergencies and divergencies underlying the processes of urbanization. The data for this analysis are drawn from interviews conducted by African female fieldworkers with 751 married Aboure and 1074 married Bete women. Survey techniques were particularly appropriate since adequate sampling and control were needed and since a substantial body of more impressionistic ethnographic data was already available.

THE EFFECTS OF URBAN RESIDENCE ON MARRIAGE

Rural communities among the Bete and Aboure, as in other African societies, place a high premium on the early marriage of women and considerably restrict freedom of choice in mate selection. Marriage concerns the family more than the individual, and the status of the family is indeed partly dependent upon the transfer by marriage of the child-bearing abilities and economic contributions of women.[12] The extent to which marriage influences the status of a family is likely to determine the intensity of the pressures that its senior members exert upon its individual female members of marriageable age. The intensity of these pressures can be measured indirectly in various ways. First, it should be noted that the younger women are when they marry, the more likely they are to comply with the wishes of their lineage, with respect to the choice of a mate.

Another index of familial pressures is provided by the ethnic affiliations of the two partners. Since the consistency of parental pressures is likely to be higher when both families belong to the same ethnic group and are culturally alike, the fact that two individuals derived from the same people marry one another implies, on their part, a certain degree of conformity with traditional rules.

In the urban context one would expect that the group's control of the individual would lessen, leading to deferment of marriage, increased frequency of intertribal alliances, and greater freedom of mate selection. The first of these expectations is correct: In Abidjan, only 57% of Aboure women and only one-third of Bete females married immediately after their first menstruation, as contrasted with 82% of rural Aboure and 56% of rural Bete women. Thus, urbanization has similar effects on the age of marriage within both ethnic groups; although the original contrast between these two peoples persists, it diminishes.

Our second hypothesis, concerning the frequency of intertribal marriages, is equally validated. Among the Aboure such alliances characterize only 2% of the rural respondents but one-fourth of their urban counterparts. The variations among the Bete are in the same direction, although of a more limited magnitude; only 1% of the rural Bete women married a mate from a different ethnic group but this percentage rises to 8% in Abidjan. Thus, the rate of interethnic marriages reflects a group's involvement in the processes of modernization.

Although there is a certain decline in the influence exerted by the nuclear family in the choice of a mate when one moves from the villages to the city, the influence of the extended family is more important in Abidjan than in smaller communities. Because urbanization increases the distance between the various generations of the same nuclear family, the uncles or elder siblings often are obliged to play in matrimonial negotiations a role traditionally performed by the father. In this instance, urbanization increases the importance of the extended kin group; this observation is, at least in the short run, hardly tenable with the assumption that urbanization is associated with a decline of traditional affiliations.

There are additional instances in which the family systems of these two cultures are not affected by the urban situation. Irrespective of the nature of the environment, the degree of social absorption of the wife in her affinal group seems to influence the pattern of behavior which is adopted toward her at the time of the marriage, by her husband as well as by her own family. Among the rural Bete families, which are characterized by a high degree of social absorption of wives into their affinal groups, the bridegroom is supposed to offer some presents to the bride, whereas her own family is reluctant to provide her with a dowry. In rural areas, only 36% of Bete wives report that their husband failed to meet such an obligation, whereas 44% of them indicate that their own family did not give them any present. In Abidjan, the corresponding figures are 42% and 53%, respectively.

By contrast, among the rural Aboure, where the loyalties of the wife are consistently more directed toward her own kin group, a reverse pattern is evident. The family of the bride is expected to enable her to fulfill her new domestic duties by providing her with pots and pans, and no less than 91% of rural Aboure families apparently conform to this rule. Conversely, the Aboure bridegroom is not expected to give presents to his spouse and, in fact, 54% of the interviewees indicate that they did not receive any present from their husband. In Abidjan, one-third of the Aboure interviewees reported that their family did not help them at the time of their marriage, and 55% of them indicated that they were not given any present by their husband.

In urban environments, the bride's family and her mate tend to deviate from their expected patterns of behavior, irrespective of their ethnic origin. The extent of this deviation, however, varies with the particular behavior under consideration. Thus, in rural areas the obligation for the Bete bridegroom to offer a wedding present to his future wife is less frequently observed than the obligation for the Aboure family to provide the bride with a dowry. Changes of residence hardly affect the extent to which Bete males fulfill their duties toward their new brides and as a consequence the contrast between the behavior of Bete and Aboure husbands in this respect does not vary significantly between rural areas and Abidjan.

While urbanization may lessen ethnic differentials with respect to certain attitudes and behaviors but may hardly affect the magnitude of such differentials in other instances, it widens ethnic contrasts, for example, with respect to the pattern of relationship between geographic origin and marital choice. No less than 97% of rural Aboure wives married a man from their own village, but this figure drops to 77% among the Aboure women living now in Abidjan. By contrast, although only 26% of Bete partners living in rural areas come from the same village, this characterizes no less than 43% of Bete married individuals now living in Abidjan. In fact, it is possible that the propensity of Bete urban spouses to be married within their natal community reflects strongly the economic orientation which underlies the brideprice in this culture.

However, it is possible also that the degree of involvement of an ethnic group in processes of modernization influences the tendency of urbanized individuals to marry within their own community of origin. When many persons in a given ethnic group have attended school and work in the modern sector, the urbanized members of such a group tend to widen their social networks and acquire new affiliations. By contrast, among peoples whose level of modernization is minimal, urbanization is associated with a "stretching" of preexisting traditional social networks. In this latter case the whole ethnic group tends to maintain a high level of internal cohesiveness and its urbanized members keep close contacts with their village of origin. In the first case, urbanization increases the number of possible inter-ethnic marriages; in the second, it diminishes this number.

In summary, the effects of urbanization on patterns of marriage are highly diverse, in some instances eradicating ethnic differentials, but not always limiting the role of the extended kin group. Though in many respects the trajectories of change are alike for both peoples compared here, they differ markedly in other instances.[13]

THE IMPACT OF URBANIZATION ON THE FUNCTIONING OF THE HOUSEHOLD

We begin by examining similarities in the reallocation of domestic roles in the urban environment. Within the towns men spend more time outside their households owing to the exigencies of employment in the modern sector. In rural areas, conflicts center more markedly on the distribution of authority within the family, but within the towns conflicts largely are caused by the reluctance of husbands to fulfill family obligations. Very simply, in rural areas the husband is greatly concerned with his domestic authority, while in the towns he is more involved with his status in the occupational world. In the latter situation the wife must fill the vacuum generated by the absence of her husband and his disinterest in domestic problems.

However, there is no doubt that urban living vastly increases the role of the husband as sole controller of the family income. Of the rural Aboure wives interviewed, 81% handle their own resources independently from their husband. This figure drops to only 38% in urban districts, where in 55% of the cases the familial budget is centralized in the hands of the husband; the corresponding proportion rises from half among the rural Bete to 62% among the urban families of this group. However, the custom of giving wives fixed allowances still enables them to exert considerable initiative in the spending of money, even where the husband is the nominal controller. Thus, the changes concerning the rules which underlie the allocation of roles between partners are characterized by the fact that women are in a position to take decisions in a greater variety of cases, such as buying clothes for herself.

This increase of authority is associated with a greater psychological and social independence on the part of women. An amusing example of this recently acquired independence was provided by the responses to an adaptation of a traditional Bete game which was included in the questionnaire: "If you were in

Table 1. Who Would You Save? (Percentages)

PERSON SAVED BY THE WIFE	ABOURE		BETE	
	Rural	*Urban*	*Rural*	*Urban*
Husband	84.1 (431)	47.5 (67)	79.5 (518)	54.0 (198)
Mother	13.3 (68)	31.9 (45)	18.0 (116)	40.9 (150)
Nobody	1.8 (9)	13.5 (19)	1.4 (9)	3.8 (14)
No Answer	0.8 (3)	7.1 (10)	1.1 (7)	1.3 (5)
Total	100.0 (511)	100.0 (141)	100.0 (650)	100.0 (367)

a boat with your mother and husband and the boat sank, which one of them would you save if you were the only one able to swim?"[14] Table 1 reveals a sharp contrast between rural wives, who chose to save their husbands because they feared the powerful sanctions which could be brought against them by their in-laws, and urban women, who displayed a greater attachment to their family of origin.

Increasing female autonomy is evident also in changing customs related to the birth of children. Overwhelmingly, rural Aboure women give birth in the house of their mothers and remain there for a considerable period afterwards; only 27% of rural Aboure wives stayed with their husbands for the birth of their children. Conversely, almost one-half of the Bete mothers remained at their husband's home for the birth of their child, and less than one-fifth stayed with their own kin for more than a month after the birth. This contrast reflects in both societies the need for the affirmation of the child's solidarity with his descent group. In the urban context, birth takes place overwhelmingly in maternity centers, but urban women of both groups tend to return to their village of origin, to their own family for increasingly long periods after childbirth. In both cases, they are asserting their increasing autonomy from the husband.

In this instance, the bonds between the woman and her own family far from being severed are reinforced in the urban context. Among the Aboure, this feature merely reflects the fact that the functioning of the matriclan is not affected by the distance between its various components. However, in the case of the Bete, it seems that the most modernized females (whether this modernization is defined in terms of age, residence, or socioeconomic status) deviate from traditional norms and innovate with respect to the fulfillment of their obligations toward their own kin group. To be sure, a trip to their village of origin can be associated with a trip to their affinal group so that their children will be in a position to establish their proper status in the group of their fathers. Nevertheless, it can be suggested that the strengthening of the ties between a woman and her family usually implies an increase in her autonomy from her husband. In this context, .the rates of change of these two peoples differ markedly, that of the Bete being higher than that of the Aboure.

In short, for both groups urbanization implies a restructuring of a wife's relationship to her husband and to her family of origin. Similar conditions in the urban environment produce similar effects in each group; the wife's desire to be autonomous generates tensions with her husband. However, the nature of these tensions varies between the two peoples, in part as a function of the differential character of their respective traditional organizations. It is to this point that we must now turn.

In rural Aboure areas, as we have indicated, wives are not "socially absorbed" into their husband's kin group. This lack of identification makes it easy for them to leave their husbands and thus enables them to exert sanctions. Thus, 54% of rural Aboure wives indicate that their husbands normally give in to them in family quarrels. As we might expect, the reverse is the case with the Bete, where the greater "social absorption" of a woman into the affinal group places her in a weaker position: almost two-thirds of rural Bete women admit that they usually defer to their husband's wishes in family quarrels. In the urban environment, however, the Aboure wife is not so distant from her husband. Her greater financial dependence and her enlarged direct responsibilities for the children are manifested in her greater willingness to concede to her spouse: only 27% of urban women see their husbands as usually yielding in family quarrels. Conversely, the power of Bete women seems to increase in the city and only 52% see themselves as normally giving in under similar circumstances. In this instance, the trajectories of change prevailing in each of the two peoples under study are highly dissimilar.

There are also interesting differences in the causes for family conflicts. In Aboure rural areas sexual infidelity of husbands is the primary source of conflict; in the towns such a concern is less frequent, while a major cause of conflict relates to rights over the responsibilities toward offspring. For example, urban fathers are increasingly reluctant to meet educational costs so long as traditional patterns of matrilineal inheritance persist, while maternal uncles often attempt to shift obligations to the father. In consequence, the mother occupies an uncomfortable position between these two individuals.

By contrast, the nature of quarrels within rural Bete households reflects the marked economic orientation of individuals as well as their greater mutual dependence in this respect; the largest single cause of disputes (35%) reflects the dissent of spouses about the share of profits accruing to familial enterprise. This sort of conflict is exacerbated in urban areas, and disagreement over money is regarded as the main source of tension by 45% of urban wives. It is clear enough here that the urban environment does not change the causes of conflict but merely accentuates traditional sources of tension.

Insofar as urban residence has an impact upon conjugal relations, it is also likely to have consequences for relations between co-wives in polygynous households. Among the rural Aboure matrilineal descent implies a low level of competition and conflict among co-wives, who rarely quarrel and help each other to raise the children. This picture changes in the towns, where interests are more individualized and where a patrilineal orientation is more common. As a result, competition between co-wives increases and only 31% of wives in urban polygynous households cooperate with respect to child-rearing.

Among Bete, of course, a pattern of conflict among co-wives has always been more evident, since the status of a woman is highly dependent on the position of her offspring *vis à vis* her husband's descent group. Formally the hierarchy of wives rests on seniority, but in practice favors are frequently given to younger wives. Few rural Bete women in polygynous families admitted to any form of cooperation with co-wives in child-rearing. In the towns, however, the greater autonomy of Bete co-wives from the head of the household facilitates cooperation, and in 31% of the cases children are cooperatively reared. Here also, changes within the two peoples are dissimilar; urbanization modifies not only the magnitude of ethnic contrasts, but also their direction.

The social representations attached to the child-bearing abilities of the woman partially determine her status within her affinal group and correspondingly influence her relationship with her husband and the co-wives. These representations also influence her child-rearing practices, which are likely to vary with residence, particularly with regard to weaning. In the rural areas, there are initially quite marked differences between the Aboure and the Bete in this respect. Urban living, which entails a decline in polygyny, leads to much earlier weaning.

Urbanization appears also to alter the expectations of mothers concerning the behavior of their children. The hierarchic nature of Aboure traditional society leads rural mothers to be particularly demanding of their offspring in terms of obeying group norms and of paying respect to senior members of the community. In the towns, however, half of Aboure mothers consider academic achievement to be the most significant demand they impose upon their offspring. Clearly, this change reflects the weakening of traditional social constraints and the need for adjustment to a highly competitive occupational structure.

Bete rural society, characterized by much greater individualization of roles and more competition, places considerable emphasis on the acquisition of formal schooling. An interesting reversal seems to occur in the urban setting; there, only 48% of the women rank educational achievement first while 37% consider compliance and respect for elders as most important. This should not be taken to mean that, in absolute terms, Bete urban women attach less importance to educational achievement than do the rural ones; they almost certainly ascribe more importance to it. But we might suggest tentatively that the emphasis upon cohesiveness may be due to the low social status of Bete in the towns, which obliges them to stress group solidarity in the face of strong pressures from other groups that impede their opportunities.

Urbanization also affects the techniques of punishment which mothers use against deviant children. Urban wives, irrespective of their ethnic affiliations, tend to use physical sanctions more often than their rural counterparts. This increased incidence of physical sanctions is probably associated with the increase in domestic and disciplinary responsibilities incumbent upon the housewife in an urban environment. Whatever the deviant behavior of the child, almost two-thirds of the women of either group who live in Abidjan consider themselves the major disciplinarian of the family, and this is contrasted with their rural counterparts.

SUMMARY AND CONCLUSIONS

As mentioned in the introduction, it has been recently asserted that various family systems are moving toward a common pattern. The present investigation shows indeed that in the Ivory Coast urbanization erodes ethnic differentials in some patterns of behavior and generates accordingly some uniform sets of responses. Thus, urban women from different ethnic backgrounds marry at a later age, more often choose a mate outside their ethnic group, enjoy greater initiative in spending money, wean their children earlier, and exert more discipline over them.

To sum up, urbanized African families display many traits similar to those of industrial countries; however, they tend to retain some distinctiveness insofar as they tend to be increasingly matrifocal. The wife has more responsibilities than her rural counterpart and must also undertake new duties. This change results from the various forms of social differentiation associated with the development of a "large scale" society, of which urbanization is but one aspect. Clearly, the expansion of educational and occupational opportunities facilitates the emergence of a social system in which individual status is increasingly based upon individual educational and occupational achievement. Yet, at the same time individuals rely also upon ethnic affiliations, and much evidence indicates that the distribution of the various Ivory Coast ethnic groups within the occupational structure of that country is markedly skewed at the lower and the upper part of the scale. Indeed the various peoples are not evenly represented in the lower and the upper rungs of the occupational hierarchy prevailing in the labor market. As long as opportunities for upward mobility remain limited and most males must accept a low social status, the males' domestic position is likely to be marginal. Under these conditions the new division of duties and responsibilities between spouses does not necessarily exemplify an egalitarian pattern. It results mainly from the more frequent and longer absence of the husband outside the household and from his disinterest in functions which no longer yield meaningful signs of status and authority.

Consequently, the increase in familial functions carried out by the urban wife is accompanied by an increase in her autonomy. Women are eager to manifest their independence from their husband whenever they are given the opportunity to do so. In fact, although urbanization leads to a change in the symbolic expressions of tensions between sexes, these tensions which have prevailed in so many traditional societies seem to perpetuate themselves. However, the domestic autonomy of a woman in the urban environment is not necessarily associated with a rise in her social status nor with her greater participation in the occupational structure. Thus, if it is true that African urbanized women complain that they do not have as wide a range of support and as clearly defined a position as their rural counterparts, it is equally true that for this very reason they tend more than men to maintain their kin affiliations. In Africa, as in other parts of the world, the extent to which kin affiliations determine the allocation of the economic, social and political position of the individual influences not only the frequency but the nature of the ties maintained by the various members of the nuclear family with the extended kin group. The less significant the role of kin affiliations in this regard, the more familial ties will be maintained by women rather than by men; namely the severance of such ties is usually more threatening for the former than for the latter. In effect, the status inconsistencies faced by the urban wife leads her to emphasize traditional ties with her own family of origin. In this context, women are less likely than men to innovate in familial patterns.

However, if, as has been suggested, urbanization makes family systems rather more uniform, the processes of adaptation differ to the extent that traditional models are distinctive. Thus, in our sample, the rates of change of various patterns of behavior vary as between the two ethnic groups; if the Bete women have changed more rapidly than their Aboure counterparts in terms of loyalties toward their own families of origin, the Aboure families have departed more rapidly from their obligations with respect to dowry. Similarly, the trajectories of change of the two ethnic groups differ and this is evidenced at the level of the systems of checks and balances which operate within each type of family. Given the greater autonomy of women in urban areas, this increased autonomy generates tensions whose direction and intensity depend upon the nature of the traditional organization, as in the marked dissimilarity between the objects of the quarrels among urbanized Aboure and Bete spouses and as in the organization of urban polygyny.

The specific nature of African cultures leads their representatives to adjust differentially to the uniform stimuli which accompany urbanization. Not only this, but the various members of the familial group react differentially to modernization just because their position in the traditional structure is unlike. Thus, social changes have heterogeneous effects on both sexes, and this heterogeneity raises some interesting questions. For instance, does the extent to which Ivory Coast urban women reinforce their traditional affiliations constitute a temporary or a permanent phenomenon? Does it reflect only the initial difference of exposure of both sexes to innovating processes or does it reflect a fundamental trait of the woman's social role, especially in African systems?

Another question concerns the extent to which the effects of urbanization along these lines are likely to be differentiated as between various socioeconomic strata. It has been observed that it is the lower class family pattern which usually is the first to change. How does this proposition fit the African context where upper class can be defined either in "western" terms (i.e., in terms of education and of level of participation in the modern sector of the economy) or in traditional terms? In other words, is the most modernized segment of the urban population likely to show characteristics similar to those of the more traditional rural families? Or does this segment adopt patterns of behavior which are even further removed from traditional ones than those which are adopted by the least modernized subsegment of the urban population?[15]

NOTES

1. See A. Feldman and W. Moore, "Industrialization and Industrialism: Consequence and Differentiation," *Transactions of the Fifth World Congress of Sociology*, Vol. II, pp. 151–169.
2. See W. Goode, *World Revolution and Family Patterns* (Free Press of Glencoe, 1963), p. 1.
3. For a critical view, see Ruth Simms, *Urbanization in West Africa: A Review of the Current Literature* (Evanston, Northwestern University Press, 1965), pp. 24–25. See also P. Gutkind, "African Urban Family Life," *Cahiers d'Etudes Africaines*, II, 10, 1962, pp. 149–207.
4. See C. Levi-Strauss, *Structural Anthropology* (New York, Basic Books, 1963), pp. 309 and ff.
5. See A. Feldman and W. Moore, *op. cit.*
6. If, as it is after argued, the pattern of behavior of the African individual is heavily influenced by the traditional society to which he belongs, then it seems possible to suggest that the processes of social change should also be analyzed from the viewpoint of the society under consideration and not only from an external point of view. In this context, the use of the two concepts used by Piaget to describe the centripetal and the centrifugal aspects of the development of meanings in the mind of the child, assimilation and accommodation, seems to be relevant. See J. Piaget, *The Child's Conception of His World* (New York, Harcourt, 1929).

   In methodological terms, I am therefore suggesting that the analysis of the changes incurred by familial systems should be undertaken by taking the very viewpoint of these systems. The first type of change is accommodation oriented insofar as it is centrifugal and leads the system to move further away from its initial position. The second type is assimilation oriented insofar as it is centripetal and reinforces selectively certain traits characteristic of the system.
7. See G. Niangoran Bouah, "Le Village Aboure," *Cahiers d'Etudes Africaines*, I, 2, 1960, pp. 113–127.
8. See D. Paulme, *Une Société de Côte d'Ivoire Hier et Aujourd'hui: les Bétes* (La Haye, Mouton, 1962).
9. Concerning a definition of this concept, see L. A. Fallers, "Some Determinants of Marriage Stability in Busoga: A Reformulation of Gluckman's Hypothesis," *Africa*, XXVII (1957), pp. 106–123.
10. See *Recensement d'Abidjan Résultats définitifs* (Abidjan, Ministère des Affaires Economiques et du Plan, 1958) pp. 69, 79–80.
11. See "Centre International de l'Enfance," *Etude des Conditions de Vie de l'enfant Africain en milieu urbain et de leur influence sur la délinquance juvenile (Travaux et Documents*, XII, Paris, 1959), p. 89, Tableau 40.
12. See J. C. Mitchell, "Social Change and the Stability of African Marriage in Northern Rhodesia," *Social Change in Modern Africa*, A. Southall, ed. (London, Oxford University Press, 1961), pp. 316–328.
13. For the use of this concept see A. Feldman and W. Moore, *op. cit.*
14. Originally, this game concerns men who are asked to choose between rescuing their

sisters, their wives, or their mothers-in-law. See D. Paulme, "Littérature Orale et Comportements Sociaux," *L'homme*, I, 1 (Janvier-Avril, 1961), pp. 37–69.
15. On this question, see R. Clignet, "Environmental Change, Type of Descent and Child-Rearing Practices," in H. Miner, ed., *The City in Modern Africa* (London, Pall Mall Press, 1967).

WIVES AND SERVANTS: WOMEN IN MIDDLE-CLASS HOUSEHOLDS, GUATEMALA CITY

Laurel Bossen

> While most of the articles in part four have touched on the domestic roles of women, few have related their roles within the home to their contribution to the general economy. Bossen tackles this relationship in an article in which she shows how middle-class women in a Latin American city employ poor women in their households. She shows where the roles of the two classes of women overlap and where they are distinct. In this situation there are many underlying tensions. As Bossen points out, the kind of affluence which allows these privileged women to afford domestic servants is related to the poverty of those who become domestics. The women about whom Bossen writes are not extremely wealthy, for most women of the upper class would not work outside the home; yet even the middle class in Guatemala City and many other Third World cities can still afford to hire domestic servants.

INTRODUCTION

The contemporary urban middle-class household of Western society is generally portrayed as a nuclear family that has abandoned many of the traditional tasks associated with rural households. Production is typically removed from the home to large enterprises where there is little need to rely on extended family ties to expand the labor force. The husband becomes the principal money earner working outside the home, while the wife adjusts to a diminished work role in the home combined with continued responsibility for domestic services and childcare. The shrinking of domestic work is encouraged by modern technology which reduces the labor input in a wide range of traditional goods and services that were once produced in the home.

While this model fits the North American experience, there is a noticeable difference in the middle-class household of urban Latin America where the gap

SOURCE: Article written expressly for *Urban Life*.

between rich and poor, urban and rural society is more extreme. In Latin America, high rates of unemployment, the low cost of unskilled domestic labor, and the relative scarcity of labor-saving appliances combine to produce an urban middle-class household which typically includes one or more young female servants as additional residents and participants in household activities. Indeed, the literature indicates that a large part of the surplus female population found in Latin American cities is the result of a general influx of young, single women from poor rural areas who seek work in domestic services (Boserup 1970; Jelin 1977; Chinchilla 1977; Hollandar 1977; Smith 1973).

In the cities, young women who lack specialized job skills are absorbed into middle-class households where they share the labor of middle-class women as housekeepers. Their domestic tasks require that they spend most of their time *with* the family, but they are not *of* the family; they are not kin. Nonetheless, the continuous presence of domestic servants in the home implies an intimate relationship and means that, if they remain for a long time, they may be treated as members of the family in certain limited ways. If they are liked and trusted, they may be treated "like a daughter" and respond with the feeling that their employer is "like a mother." Moreover, they typically play the role of a surrogate mother within the household, caring for the young children when their mother goes out. The fact that many domestic servants are young women with few family ties in the city, or come from urban families that have been splintered by the pressures of poverty means that they may be particularly receptive to such partial incorporation. At the same time, a high degree of distrust and tension can develop between the middle-class woman and the domestic employee. Of course, the young maid-servants occupy an inferior status economically, legally, and socially within the household that employs them. They may be seen as "resident aliens." Within their place of employment and residence, the middle-class household, legitimate kinship claims (and the servant's lack of them) define economic and social rewards.

In this discussion, I compare the position of middle-class wives and their servants—two sets of women who work for, live within, and depend on middle-class households in Guatemala City. By comparing the economic and social roles of these women who live and work side by side, I hope to illustrate how domestic roles articulate with kinship and class relations. First, I show how the work roles of wife and servant are interwoven within urban middle-class households, and then I consider the way the legitimate kinship ties of the wife serve to define her economic and social position, and contribute to the stability of class-stratified urban society.

THE MIDDLE-CLASS COMMUNITY

Villa Rosa is a modern middle-class neighborhood in Guatemala City with slightly more than 4,000 residents.[1] The houses are relatively homogeneous, suburban-style homes, around 15 years old, with electricity, modern plumbing,

6–8 rooms, gardens and driveways. In 1974, these houses were generally worth from \$12,000 to \$18,000. Consistent with the larger Latin American pattern of urbanization (Boserup 1970), the census data for this area show a remarkable surplus of women: 142 females per 100 males! This compares to 111 females per 100 males for Guatemala City as a whole (Guatemala 1974:25). There are two main reasons for the more extreme sexual imbalance found in Villa Rosa. First, while middle-class men's occupations are sometimes based in rural areas or provincial centers, their female kin and children tend to reside in the capital city where they can profit from the greater concentration of cultural, educational, and occupational opportunities. Second, female domestic employees are a significant fraction of the resident population in middle-class neighborhoods. Census and survey samples show that resident female domestic employees comprise just under 11% of the total population in Villa Rosa. Roughly 60% of the households employ them. Indeed, they are considered a normal feature of the middle-class household. These live-in domestic workers are further supplemented by day-workers who commute from neighboring working-class districts and shantytowns, and who are not counted among the resident population.

THE ECONOMIC ROLE OF WIVES AND SERVANTS IN THE FAMILY

In Villa Rosa as in most of Latin America, housework is defined as women's work. Male participation is considered rare and abnormal. Housework is performed both by unpaid family members, and by domestic employees drawn from the rural and urban working classes. In comparing the roles of wives and servants in Villa Rosa, we cannot fail to note the inconsistency of conventional social definitions of work whereby women who work in someone else's home are considered to be economically active, while women who work in their own homes are considered to be fulfilling family obligations, but not "working." In Villa Rosa, approximately half of the wives and daughters of middle-class households earn regular cash incomes.[2] Yet a substantial proportion of the women stay home and dedicate themselves to domestic tasks. Combining the percentage of women who stay home with that of women who are introduced into the home as servants, it is evident that this neighborhood consumes a high level of personal domestic services. Approximately 1 out of every 4 to 5 residents (19–25% of the *total* population) is involved in domestic upkeep.[3]

The presence of domestic servants in more than half of all Villa Rosa households is related to a variety of factors, but does not appear to be closely linked to outside employment by the wife. Households that lack domestic employees are generally characterized by one or more of the following features: the lack of young children, the lack of outside employment by the wife, and the presence of another adult female relative with at least some time available for housework. That is, they seem to have less work per woman (as indicated, say, by a low ratio of men and children to adult women), or a tight household budget. For instance, in a nuclear family lacking young children, housework was shared by a working mother and three daughters attending high school and university. With 4 capable females, they felt it would be unnecessary to hire a maid even though they could afford it. In households that have domestic employees, there may or may not be a high ratio of domestic consumers per woman. The ability to pay seems to be the key factor, whether the services are marginal or central to the well-being of the household.

Housework in Villa Rosa includes a variety of familiar tasks: washing and ironing clothes, buying food and household articles, cooking, washing dishes, general housecleaning, and childcare. As part of their middle-class standard of living, residents of Villa Rosa consume more elaborate meals, fashionable clothing, and home furnishings than most Guatemalans. These consumption patterns entail extra time and effort for the housekeeper. In Villa Rosa, housekeeping is obviously facilitated by some forms of modern labor-saving technology such as stoves and running water for cooking and cleaning, ready-to-wear clothes, and the availability of stores, supermarkets, and processed foods. At the same time, the fast-food industry has not yet transformed daily dining patterns. In many of the households I visited, the husband and children return each day during the two-hour lunchbreak for a home-cooked meal together. In addition to family meal preparation, hand laundry and ironing are time-consuming tasks. Laundromats are scarce, and the few who own washing machines complain that they have broken down and cannot be serviced. Thus, the household of Villa Rosa remains a place of labor-intensive service work, much of it manual.

The economic roles of housewives and servants involve considerable overlap, but have some important differences. To understand their interrelationship, we must consider their social characteristics, the division of labor between them, and the division of rewards for their contribution to the household. Among middle-class women, we find that kinswomen of any age may be involved in housework. They may be unmarried daughters, young wives, or older women and grandmothers. Their educational levels are high, averaging around 9 years for all adult women. In contrast, the domestic servant is typically young (average age of 21), single, and averages only 1.9 years of schooling. As indicated by their youth, most domestic employees do not stay long. In the course of my interviews, I found that a number of households were looking for replacements for employees who had left or been dismissed.

The role of the domestic employee is to perform or assist in the housework for which the middle-class woman is held responsible. In most cases, the middle-class woman supervises or herself performs some of the housework despite the presence of domestic employees. In the few cases where the middle-class woman has very little spare time, she may relegate nearly all of the housework and childcare to one or more domestic employees. There is a division of labor which tends to occur between middle-class women and domestic employees, but it is by no means rigid. The middle-class woman normally wants to maintain control over child-raising, spending, and food preparation. The employees are assigned to the more monotonous and less responsible tasks of washing clothes, ironing, sweeping, mopping, errands, and washing dishes. If the employee is trusted, she is given greater responsibility in shopping, cooking and childcare.

In housekeeping, the economic roles of the middle-class woman and the domestic servant may alternate. If an employee has just quit or been dismissed, or if a family cannot afford one, the middle-class woman will assume the manual tasks of preparing and serving food, and cleaning up after other members of the household. Unlike the occupational roles of middle-class men vis-à-vis lower-class men, the distinction between intellectual and manual labor is not readily applied to women doing housework. This may cause some real discomfort to middle-class women, as in the following case:

> Francesca lives with her husband, two adult sons, a divorced daughter and her young grandson. Although four adults are working outside the home, Francesca finds her access to cash is inadequate. She desperately craves an outside job to increase her personal income, but is unable to find one that is commensurate with middle-class status. Meanwhile, she is expected to provide housekeeping services for the four working adults and grandchild. Her daughter in particular depends on her for childcare and pays Francesca $20 monthly, exactly the average income of domestic employees. Francesca bitterly complains: "They treat me as if I were a servant in the house, only without a salary. At times I despair. Closed-up in the house, it is very depressing. One wants to leave running."

Francesca's comparison with servant status illustrates that the boundary between women of different classes is not clearly expressed in the housework they perform. On the one hand, this could foster certain shared interests between women who, as women, must work in the same milieu regardless of class background. On the other hand, there are obvious tensions, for despite any similarity of actual work roles and economic dependency on the same household funds, the rewards for wives and servants are of a different order, expressing their unequal positions.

The servant is paid a wage—by day, week, or month—whereas the wife receives a "share" of the family estate. More specifically, the average servant in Villa Rosa works for a very low wage, roughly $20 per month, plus room and board. She works without a contract, and is on call for long hours, morning through evening, without formal provisions for holidays, sick leave, pension, or maternity leave. Upon dismissal, she loses not only her wage, but her whole "situation," her temporary home.

In contrast, middle-class wives and kinswomen receive much greater rewards in cash and kind. The wife's rewards are not explicitly settled as to amount or percentage of the husband's income; she depends on the fortunes of her husband's economic ventures and upon his personal discretion in allocating income to her for household maintenance. Interviews with wives in Villa Rosa revealed a wide range of budget variation by which the wife may receive from less than one-fourth to nearly all of her husband's pay, where male earnings averaged $328 per month. Rigorous comparison with the wage of the domestic employee is impossible for the budget of the middle-class woman is clearly not the same as a wage. Much of the money is spent on collective needs for food, clothing, household articles and the children's education. But having the means to feed, clothe, and educate one's children is *part* of a higher standard of living. Unlike the servant, the wife is guaranteed not only her own maintenance, but that of her children. Even if she may not get regular holidays or "time off," she cannot be summarily dismissed from her "job" or from the marital estate, the home. In contrast, the low wages and working conditions of domestic servants are not compatible with raising children of their own. In this context, it is clear that the economic rewards of the middle-class woman are at least several times greater than those received by the domestic employee who shares the same work.

The similarity and proximity of their work, and the disparity of rewards between the wives and servants of the middle class would be expected to produce invidious comparisons and tensions. This occurs on two levels. First, the wives of Villa Rosa appear to share a generalized distrust of domestic employees as representatives of the poor classes. In discussions among middle-class women, the problems of finding "trustworthy" domestic servants, and the inconveniences of dismissing those who were thought to be pilfering, immoral or unreliable workers frequently arise as topics of animated conversation. One housewife who had fired 3 young women within several months was frustrated because she could not find an adequate replacement. With 4 teenaged children for whom she was shopping, cooking, and maintaining stylish clothes, she felt she needed domestic help, but always found it difficult to find young women of "good character." Servants, on the other hand, recount work experiences in which they claim employers withheld pay, skimped on food, falsely accused them of theft, docked their meager wages for the cost of lost or broken items, or fired them without giving notice or full pay.

A second level of tension seems related to the fact that cheap domestic labor, while it lightens the workload, obviously has implications regarding the perceived economic value of the housewife. The middle-class housewife knows that most of her daily work is unskilled, and that there are scores of lower-class women willing to perform the same work for less pay. This tends to devalue the tasks of housekeeping. The cash value of housework is so low that for the same budget money a husband could hire 3 to 4 live-in employees to replace the economic services of the middle-class housewife. Alternately, the middle-class woman who desires to increase her personal spending money from the household budget knows that by dismissing the maid and doing all the housework herself, she only gains about $20 per month. The low market value of housekeeping undoubtedly creates a certain economic uneasiness for the middle-class housekeeper, particularly in a society where the accepted rationale for differential economic rewards is linked to differences in occupational role.

In this situation we would expect the middle-class woman to try to differentiate her domestic contribution from that of her servant.[4] Clearly, little training is involved in washing clothes, ironing, and mopping floors. The middle-class woman does not claim superiority in these areas. Instead, she may attempt to excel in new kinds of housekeeping skills that emphasize and reinforce superior class status for the household. Thus she dabbles in gourmet cooking, fancy needlework and crafts to beautify the home, interior decorating, home tutoring of the children and so forth. By these activities, still outside the market economy, the middle-class woman seeks to demonstrate that her value to the household cannot be matched by the lower-class domestic employee. Overall, such efforts appear to be rather weak and unconvincing in terms of their direct economic worth. It must be remembered that the link between such housework and the productive process of the modern economy is indirect. Capitalist production is removed from the home and even from the neighborhood. In housework, increased output of services does not result in increased cash income. Maintenance and reproduction of the population is still an essential form of work, but in Villa Rosa it is confused with a range of services and consumption that go beyond economic maintenance and extend into the realm of conspicuous consumption of luxuries—activities which are not usually considered "work." Given the inequality of rewards for work of seemingly equal value, we now look more closely at the role of kinship as it relates to social and economic inequality in these middle-class homes.

THE ROLE OF LEGITIMATE KINSHIP

In modern urban society, home and family remain crucial for social reproduction. Broadly defined, social reproduction encompasses three types of activity: (1) the daily feeding and maintenance of the labor force which restores the capacity of employed workers from day to day; (2) the reproduction of the society through caring for children and raising the next generation of productive people; and (3) the reproduction of the class structure. This third aspect involves a means of identifying, training, and channeling children to fulfill different hierarchical positions in society with minimal disruption as they assume their adult roles.

Within the urban middle-class households of Villa Rosa, domestic servants participate in the first and second types of middle-class social reproduction. They perform household maintenance and provide childcare in middle-class homes. But servants are not permitted to engage in the third type. Lacking previous kin ties to the middle class and formal marriage to middle-class men, they are debarred from reproduction of the privileged class. While some may take the view that this type of social reproduction is largely a passive role, others such as Papanek (1979) have suggested that it does involve goal-directed activity which brings real economic rewards. She labels this form of unrecognized work "status production." I would suggest that much of this status production work takes place in the idiom of family and kinship roles in the middle class. Clearly, the most important factor that conditions a middle-class housewife's reward is not her overt work role (which is shared with servants) but her kinship role as defined by her marriage. The kinship role of middle-class women is the basis for the reproduction of the class structure. The marriage contract is the means by which she is able to claim a share of her husband's income. It is not surprising that some 90% of the marital unions in Villa Rosa are legally contracted rather than common-law (the form that predominates among low-income populations).

By virtue of the marriage tie, it might be proposed that the wife provides additional sexual and childbearing services which are outside the province of servants. However, I would maintain that it is neither sex nor reproduction *per se* that distinguishes the wife's contribution. Regarding sex, few would realistically claim that the wife is the only woman to provide sexual services to the middle-class man. Certainly the women of Villa Rosa do not claim this. Other women, including servants, are often enlisted and may even have children by middle-class men. But under these circumstances, the servant, unlike the wife, risks loss of employment and material support for the resulting offspring who are "unrecognized," that is, illegitimate. The resident servant lacks a license to produce middle-class children, and she is generally not permitted to raise lower-class children within a middle-class household. Even though the servant's work role may replicate that of the middle-class wife, it is only the wife who holds the right to bear and raise middle-class children in Villa Rosa and receive greater rewards in the name of (middle-class) motherhood.

The children of servants and ex-servants are not seen in Villa Rosa, for they are raised in the working-class districts and shantytowns of the city, or in the rural villages from which the servants migrated. Thus Julia, a young woman of 21 who had worked for 5 years in the home of Augusta in Villa Rosa, and who had been loved "like a daughter" by her employer during those years, would sadly depart to raise a family in one of the poorer zones of the city, while Margarita, a 24-year-old single mother leaves her 3 children with her own poor mother in the shantytown in order to earn a meager salary of $18 per month in Villa Rosa.

Although servants help to care for middle-class children, it is precisely in the area of motherhood that the middle-class women of Villa Rosa most jealously guard their control. This goes beyond the general rule that domestic servants be childless (See Arizpe 1975, 1977) or able to leave their children with someone else. It includes an active kinship role for the middle-class woman, an emphasis on "mothering" which socializes her children for a privileged position in a class society. It is just this contribution which middle-class women emphasize as uniquely important to them. Many women express concern about the harm that may come to their children if they should decide to work outside the home. A typical expression of their concern is as follows:

Children cannot be left in the charge of servants. They will not learn well. They will acquire the vocabulary of servants. A woman should not work until her children are well formed. The love of a mother is indispensable. . . . Mother's love is special. It offers much security and affection. Others do not care for your child in the same way.

Although there are working middle-class women with children, these women still stress their personal role in instilling cultural values and in supervising the social development of their children.

The problem of establishing children's pedigrees as opposed to illegitimacy is one that affects middle-class men and women differently. Men are free to deny affiliations to children produced with lower-class women provided they do not marry them. The fact that some biological offspring lack fathers to sponsor their entry into the privileged classes need not affect a middle-class man personally provided that he has the economic means to maintain himself independently at the appropriate standard of living. In contrast, women are not able to deny the act of maternity, for it is so obvious. A middle-class woman who produces children without a certificate (legal marriage) of fatherhood from a man with the social status and wealth to maintain her class position risks the loss of membership in that class. Middle-class women must be able socially to "prove" the paternity of their children in order to maintain their class privilege. Social proof generally consists of a marriage contract and the absence of any evidence or insinuation of independent interaction with males other than a woman's kin or husband. She must be above suspicion. Legal, monogamous marriage is the means by which parents of middle- or upper-socioeconomic status establish the right of their children to inherit their class status and privileges. The emphasis on the social aspects of motherhood may be seen as a complementary social function which can be used by women to reinforce their class position. In Villa Rosa, women's economic contribution even if they work outside the home is generally inadequate to support middle-class status. Thus they emphasize their ability to provide legitimate children with the cultural values and social graces which women of other classes generally lack the means to cultivate.

CONCLUSION

In comparing the economic and social roles of the two classes of women that reside in households of Villa Rosa, I have shown that the domestic services they provide are similar. Superficially, they perform the same kinds of tasks in their day-to-day routines, the one substituting for the other in work, if not in reward. The major difference is that the middle-class wife is officially designated to provide regular sexual and socialization services within the household, while the servant may only do so on an informal, illicit, or impermanent basis. Another difference is that the middle-class woman may dispense a significant share of the household operating fund, while the domestic employee is rarely trusted with more than the grocery money, carefully itemized.

Beyond the similarities in the housework they perform, in the final analysis they are not involved in the same kinds of production, or work. The domestic employee produces services that are consumed immediately and are privately valued by the family that employs her. By virtue of the fact that she is nonkin and receives a cash wage for the work, her labor and her reward are defined as social. She is recorded "economically active" in the census, and her earnings are counted in the GNP. In contrast, the middle-class wife is not considered to be "economically active" when she provides domestic services for which she is not "paid." Her reward is privately determined within the family; it does not correspond to any going wage rate in the labor market. However, the middle-class wife does, in a sense, produce a "product" that is ultimately realized in a wider social context. She produces legitimate children who are prepared to assume public roles as the next generation of the middle class. Her domestic role as mother has a recognizable social value for the power structure, since it is the means to reproduce the system of class divisions. It is also her means to maintain her class advantage.

A final question that necessarily arises regarding the roles of the domestic servant and the employer in middle-class households is whether the middle-class woman exploits her employee. Jelin (1976:144), writing of domestic employees in Brazil, has asked, "To what degree, in capitalist societies, does the 'liberation' that upper-strata women attain through getting jobs also entail the exploitation of lower-strata women?" There are several sides to this question. On the one hand, it cannot be denied that domestic employees are exploited. Their rewards are set at a minimal subsistence level, clustering at the bottom of the urban wage scale, and generally considered insufficient to support reproduction. The average wage is so low that it is impossible for most domestic employees to accumulate any savings after meeting their personal clothing and health expenses. Servants frequently complain that they are unable to acquire any assets to safeguard against the day they lose their job. On the other hand, if we assume that modern technology will soon provide alternatives to the employment of domestic labor (laundromats and fast-food services are currently expanding in Guatemala City), then domestic employment may suffer a great drop, much as it has in advanced industrial countries such as the U.S. and Canada relative to the turn of the century (Ryan 1975, Leslie 1974). Vast numbers of rural and urban women will lose their principal alternative to unemployment. If this occurs, the condition of working-class women will probably deteriorate even further, while middle-class women will be free of accusations of exploitng their servants. They will no longer have to cope with anxieties about hiring trustworthy servants to join their households. At that point, the individualistic features of domestic exploitation will fade to reveal a more generalized macro-economic condition wherein still larger sectors of the population are unemployed and lacking any means of livelihood. If such labor substitution by capital-intensive services takes place in the domestic sphere, the urban middle-class household will probably move one step closer to the North American model by giving up the domestic employee, while the displaced servant class—no longer cloistered in middle-class homes—may begin to struggle for social solutions to their problems of unemployment and poverty.

NOTES

1. Villa Rosa, the name of the community, and personal names used are pseudonyms. This discussion is based on research that was conducted in Guatemala City in 1975, supported by a doctoral research fellowship from the Organization of American States.
2. While census figures give 38%, my own survey data show 57% of the women earn some outside cash income.
3. This calculation includes live-in domestics and full-time housewives but not middle-class women who work outside the home part-time or lower-class women who work on a day basis. These would add to the numbers involved in housework in Villa Rosa.
4. If paid employment commensurate with the status and income of middle-class males were available, it could be assumed that the middle-class women would become more active in the market economy. However, such employment opportunities are rare for the women of Villa Rosa (See Bossen 1978).

LOVELORN FARANGS: LETTERS BETWEEN FOREIGN MEN AND THAI GIRLS[1]

Erik Cohen

Loneliness is in the view of many sociologists a characteristic of modern urban life. This comes out in the personal letters produced by Thai girls who a e prostitutes with tourists as clients. The letters exchanged between the girls and their Western clients show the latter's ambivalent feelings of trust and uncertainty about their girl-friends' sincerity. These feelings are complicated by the activities of the "scribes" who write the girls' replies. The analysis shows that while on a macro-social level, the tourists are exploiting the girls sexually, on a personal level, the girls are manipulating and perhaps even dominating their absent boyfriends. This paper illustrates the kind of approach to urban anthropology suggested by Rollwagen ("New Directions in Urban Anthropology").

...Excessive love for the exotic can destroy the white European in the Orient. Many men think they go away from here with their souls intact – but they find in their own countries they've been profoundly changed by their experiences without knowing it. They become outcasts among their own people because everything at home seems insipid in comparison with the East. Then usually they're lured back again by the siren call of what has already ruined them (Grey 1983:254).

BACKGROUND

Dear P.

Long time I miss you so gust[?]. I did return from my hollyday find one note I was tinging [thinking] about you and I did write tiss letter for you because you wore [were a] good girle and I did tinking about [. . .] only one ting you did make cruker [anger?] me wen you faitting you pepule [fighting with your people] for dat I dind [didn't] write you eny more so if you wonded [wanted] I come dea [there] for Xmas and I marry you long if you do not. Be stupid like last time because I dint [didn't] write to you I did put police on you before and day [they] did tole [tell] me you wosed [?]. Go at dat club were [where] I dit pek [pick] you up nea [near]. I do not if I kend ondstand [cannot understand] if you wosed go [were going] whit [with] men or not to dat I did dismist you: afterwis [afterwards] I do not mint [mind] to marry you.

You dont remember at airport I was nearly kray [crying] four you but one ting I wonded [wanted to] told you I bringe you here and you go witdeater [the other] pepule

Source: *Anthropological Quarterly*, (1984):115-127. © Catholic University Press.

remember I'm Italian very bat [bad] thiss words because if I do married you I wonded stopper [stop you]. I do safre [suffer] four you. All so I wonded one photography from you if its possible my dear I do close the letter and say good luk from you love
F.P.
[A letter of an Italian mine-worker in Australia to a Thai bar girl]

Did you enjoy time with your other two men? Please tell me a bit about it; I so much like you to share your experiences with me...

You probably can't imagine the way I am living: spending most of my day *alone*, sitting in my room at my writing table, reading, thinking, writing... while the "real" life passes by outside my window; it's really quite different from your very social, open, sensual and purposeless kind of life-style – which I enjoy, if not without difficulties, while I am with you.

[From a letter of a German academic to a Thai bar girl]

In this article personal letters are analyzed to illustrate the dilemmas involved in the attempt to maintain a personal, intimate relationship over a distance of space and time. Although the data used – the correspondence between Thai bar-girls and their *farang* (white foreigner) boy-friends – are admittedly of a peculiar character, they reflect in an intensified manner the tensions inherent in any attempt to maintain "intimacy-at-a-distance." The foreigners who write letters to Thai girls are almost exclusively Westerners - Europeans, Americans, Australians and New Zealanders. No letters from Japanese tourists came to my attention, and only two or three from Arabs who had received a Western Education.

Thai girls working in tourist-oriented bars and coffee shops typically engage in "open-ended" prostitution (Cohen 1982 and in press).[2] They are prepared to extend single, basically mercenary sexual encounters with *farangs* into more protracted liaisons, which usually involve a complex mixture of sentimental attachment and pecuniary interest on the girls' part (Cohen 1982). Many such liaisons continue for the length of the *farang's* stay in Thailand. Some *farang* men regularly return to Thailand to spend their vacations with their old girl-friends, most of whom continue to engage in prostitution during their boy-friends' absences and may maintain concomitantly several such protracted liaisons, besides having short-time encounters. Some of these liaisons eventually develop a more permanent character, a girl may become a *farang's* mistress, or even his wife, and cease to engage in prostitution, at least as long as she received support from her boy-friend or husband.

For many foreigners, particularly middle-aged married or divorced men, the encounter with open-ended prostitution in Thailand is on the order of a revelation. Many become infatuated with Thai women and strongly attached to girls they initially picked up from a bar or coffee shop for the night. Being tourists, however, their stay in Thailand is ordinarily brief and, they inevitably face a difficult problem: many would like to extend the liaison beyond their departure; but they are also aware that the girls worked in bars or a coffee-shop when they had first met, and will probably return there again to engage in sexual liaisons with other men. The *farangs'* problem becomes one of how to safeguard the relationship, and their girl-friends' attachment or even fidelity, during the long separation between vacations. As a consequence of their attempts to resolve this problem, an astonishingly extensive and lively correspondence develops between the lovelorn *farangs* and their Thai girl-friends.

The *farang's* problem is aggravated by the fact that the liaison itself is usually shrouded in considerable ambiguity (Cohen 1982). Though sexually intensive, the relationship is usually superficial. Language difficulties and cultural differences, particularly when encountered during the brief span of a vacation create an almost insuperable barrier to mutual understanding. The girls, particularly those who have more experience with *farangs*, are highly adept at staging attraction to their customers. They generally understate the mercenary aspect of the relationship and emphasize the emotional one, (Cohen 1982:415-6; on a similar situation in the Philippines, see van der Velden, 1982). Many *farangs* are confused by the girl's conduct: on the one hand, they tend to believe that the girl genuinely likes or loves them; on the other, they are plagued by doubts as to her seriousness, sincerity and faithfulness (Cf. Cohen, 1986). The *farang's* uneasiness grows as the time of his sojourn in Thailand draws to an end and reaches its apex in the period immediately after his departure, and he becomes eager to continue the relationship by correspondence.

The Thai girl, even if she is not genuinely attracted to the *farang*, usually consents to extend their relationship by correspondence. To have a remote *farang* boy-friend is a source of potential financial and emotional support, and offers a possible counter-balance to the uncertainties and fortuitousness of her daily existence (Cohen 1982:422-3). Indeed older girls often purposely nurse a series of such liaisons with different men, and then derive their main support from remittances, rather than from regular work in prostitution.

The life of Thai girls engaged in tourist-oriented prostitution, living mainly in the slums on a *soi* (lane) in Bangkok, was one of the principal topics in my study of *soi* life, conducted during the summers of 1981-1984. The *soi* in which I did research is located near a major tourist entertainment area, and during my study I had ample opportunities to observe and talk to the girls and the *farangs* living on the *soi* or visiting the entertainment area (Cohen 1982, 1984, 1985a, 1986 and in press). I quickly became aware of the correspondence which many of the girls conducted with one or several of their *farang* boy-friends, and was often asked to serve as a "scribe," i.e., to translate letters written in English and other European languages into Thai and to write letters dictated in Thai, in those languages. I have also examined a collection of more than a hundred letters from *farangs* to various Thai girls, left by the girls in the house of an English-speaking Thai. The present paper is based on my own observations and participation in the conduct of the correspondence, a content analysis of the letters which came to my attention and on conversations with Thai girls, their *farang* boy-friends and several "scribes." I followed the work of one scribe for several months, interviewed four others and talked to many *farangs* who occasionally wrote letters for the girls.

THE LETTER AS A COMMUNICATION DEVICE

Private letters are a potential gold-mine for the sociological study of intimate relationships, but one which remains largely unexploited (Cf. Sarabia 1985:169). A major reason for this surprising lack of interest in private correspondence is the scathing methodological criticism to which Thomas and Znaniecki's (1927) monumental work on the Polish peasant in Poland and America, largely based on an analysis of several series of letters, has been submitted (Phillips 1966:128). The use of letters as sociological data has, indeed, several serious drawbacks, of which the lack of representativeness is perhaps the principal one (Phillips 1966:83, 128-9). This problem, however, appears to be particularly serious in studies which seek to derive conclusions regarding public opinion or attitudes from letters (e.g., Brunt 1979; Grey and Brown 1970), but is much less serious when letters are used to gain insight into personal interactions, as in the present study.

The study of letters also poses problems of interpretations. As Simmel acutely noted in his brief but incisive "Excursus on written communication" (Simmel 1908:378-382), there is a conflict in the genre of the letter between its intimate content and its public (written) form; the letter is an "objectivization of the subjective" (Simmel 1908:381), making it questionable whether the letter renders the interpreter real access to the writer's "self" (Ferguson 1981) or merely to a representation of it, intended for the recipient. Personal letters may well be used as a subtle means of manipulation of the partner, who, being personally close but physically remote, lacks the clues, ordinarily supplied by the pragmatic context of a face-to-face conversation, for evaluation of the writer's sincerity and truthfulness. This makes the letter a highly ambigious communication device, and engenders acute problems of interpretation for the recipients, as we shall see in the following sections.

THE MECHANISM OF CORRESPONDENCE – THE ROLE OF THE "SCRIBE"

The correspondence between Thai girls and their *farang* boy-friends is hindered by a serious obstacle which exacerbates the conflict between intimacy and publicity in the genre of the letter – the correspondents do not usually share a written language. The *farangs* do not ordinarily speak Thai. The girls, even if they have acquired some knowledge of spoken English in the course of their work (Cohen and Cooper 1986), are only in exceptional cases able to write or read the language. Moreover, most of the girls are semi-illiterate even in Thai. Most come to Bangkok from poor rural areas in Northern and North-Eastern Thailand (Isan) (Cf. Phongpaichit 1981:18), where the spoken language is either Northern Thai or Thai-Lao and standard Thai is learned only in school. Like the great majority of children in these areas, most of the girls have had no more than four years of elementary education and find it hard to compose and write letters, even in Thai (Cf. Pitayanon 1984:24). Because the correspondence with *farangs* is normally conducted in English, the girls need the help of a third party to compose and read the letters. However, even the intermediacy of English is sometimes insufficient to overcome the problems of communication, because only some of the *farangs* originate in Anglophone countries, while a growing number are German, French, Dutch, Swedish or Italian. These individuals often possess only rudimentary competence in English, often quite insufficient for written communication, as strikingly illustrated by the first letter quoted above.

Owing to the far-flung correspondence of the girls, bilingual individuals able and willing to write letters to the girls' *farang* boyfriends are much in demand. This demand has given rise to a new occupational role – that of the "scribe." Most scribes are Thais, whose knowledge of literary English is limited; some are *farangs*, mostly "drop-out" expatriates living in Thailand (Cohen 1984), who make a living by teaching English in local language schools or from other temporary jobs. A scribe's fee for writing a letter ranges from US $1.50 to US $4.00.

The scribes perform a crucial function in the process of correspondence. They are not simply passive translators, i.e., persons who render the exact meaning of spoken or written words from one language to another (Cf. Schmitt 1982). Rather they are "language brokers" (Cohen and Cooper 1986), whose function resembles that of other linguistic intermediaries between tourists and locals. They not only translate, but also actively interpret, consult, and serve as covert "go-betweens" (Shanklin 1980) in the epistolary communication between the girls and their *farang* boy-friends. Scribes friendly with the girls are not averse to "inventing" a response to a letter received from a *farang* correspondent, while the girl herself is away with another man. They thus actively help to protect the girls' interests, by deceiving their far-off boy-friends and assuaging possible suspicions concerning the girls' activities. In a particular memorable case I witnessed, a girl received a letter from a boy-friend who wrote: "... I know in my heart that I do not love you; and that I will never love you;" he then went on to advise his ex-girl-friend "... to leave Bangkok and the terrible life of bars and sleeping with men behind you," and to "... have some respect for yourself and return to your home..." The girl herself was absent when the letter arrived and her sister took the letter to a scribe. An older girl, a friend of the recipient of the letter, upon hearing the contents, addressed a blistering reply to the girl's ex-boy-friend. She informed him, in the girl's name, that she accepts the break-up of the relationship, does not need his advice and is able "to take care of myself." She now has a new and better boy-friend and will go home once the time is right. The scribe wrote the letter, which was apparently dispatched without the girl in question having even the slightest idea of the whole affair.

Some scribes take an almost professional pride in their adroitness at the composition of letters for the girls and their ability to mislead or deceive the girls' correspondents. When the *farang* boy-friends, mistakingly believe the girls themselves write their letters, compliment the girls for their progress in the English language, the scribe may derive some ironic satisfaction. Some scribes, however, feel uneasy about their part in the deception. One scribe, indeed, adopted a typical stance of role distance (Goffmann 1972:73-134), claiming that he relates to the whole business of letter-writing as a mere joke. However, only in exceptional cases does a scribe dare to disclose to a girl's far-off friend her real doings. There was a rumor around the *soi* of a case in which a *farang* scribe disclosed to a girl's boy-friend the depth of her deception; the girl, who had succeeded in extracting considerable sums of money from that boy-friend, is said to have murdered the scribe in revenge.

His role as a go-between puts the scribe in a position of potential power over the correspondents, which he may try to use to his own advantage. Thus, one Thai corresponded on his own, in a girl's name but without her knowledge, with her *farang* boy-friend, attempting to extricate money from him. The *farang*, however, became suspicious when the scribe asked that the money be transferred to the scribe's own, rather than the girl's, checking account, and refused to send it.

The process of writing a girl's letter to a *farang* is normally initiated by the girl's reception of a letter from him. The letter is brought to the scribe for translation, and after hearing its contents, the scribe is usually asked two specific questions: what, if anything, did he exactly say about sending some money? And when will he arrive? The desire to know the farang's precise date of arrival is not always motivated by longing. Rather, as one journalist acutely observed in an article about letters by girls working in the sea-side resort of Pattaya, "For business sake the girls must make sure that their boyfriends come at different times of the year..." (Sihasut 1983:21).

Having comprehended the salient points in the *farang's* letter, the girl usually sets out to answer it. Her conduct varies between two extremes: in a minority of cases, especially in those in which the girl takes the relationship seriously for emotional or financial reasons, she makes an effort to compose a detailed response. She might even write a draft in Thai and ask the scribe to translate it literally into English; or she may dictate an answer word-for-word and have the final product read out to her for checking and corrections. The composition of such a letter is a fretful affair and may take an hour or more to accomplish. Such conduct is, however, rare. Much more frequently the girl approaches a scribe with only the vaguest instructions as to content of the letter. Thus, one girl who maintains a wide correspondence with several men was observed giving brief instructions to a scribe, adding: "Put on a lot of sugar, he likes sweet." In the extreme case, the girl curtly asks the scribe to "write a letter," declaring that she does not know what to write and hence leaves the content to him. The more experienced scribes develop with time a standard scheme for letters, to whomever they may be addressed, in which the following topics are touched upon; a polite inquiry about the boy-friend's health, some details about the girl, her children or parents, a declaration of love and continued faithfulness, a report on her current (mostly financial) problems, an overt or covert supplication for support, and the expression of the hope for a reunion. Consequently the girls' letters, supposedly a most personal and intimate form of communication, tend in fact to become routinized and very much like one another. But while a girl may keep in touch with several *farangs*, the *farang* typically corresponds with only one girl, and is not in a position to notice the standard character of the letters he receives.

THE FARANG'S LETTERS – THE DILEMMAS OF INTIMACY AND DISTANCE

In the correspondence between the Thai girls and the *farang* men, the letters written by the men are of greater interest than those written by the girls. The *farangs'* letters are much more articulate, specific and varied, even though a number of basic themes or, more correctly, dilemmas, can be encountered in many of them. These will form the subject of the present and the next two sections.

The *farangs'* basic dilemma is created by their desire to maintain an intimate relationship at a distance. Personal intimacy generally implies physical nearness (Cf. Hall 1966:110-2); intimacy and distance are mutually incongruent. This incongruence is the obverse of that contained, in Simmel's view, in the position of the stranger: the stranger is (physically) near but (socially or personally) far (Simmel 1950: 402) The person to whom one writes intimate letters is, on the contrary, personally close but physically far. The writer of letters strives to close the gap by declaring his continuing solicitude, attachment or solidarity (Cf. Thomas and Znaniecki 1927:303). The *farangs'* letters to Thai girls are intended to maintain a love relationship despite separation. Indeed, it appears that for many *farangs* the relationship grows in importance and intensity *after* the separation. During his stay, the *farang* can play "king for a day" (Gottlieb 1982) in the sexual realm. His is a buyer's market with hundreds of girls competing for his attention. Once the *farang* has left, however, their respective circumstances are reversed. His sexual opportunities are typically much more limited as he resumes the routine life in his home environment, or returns to work at a lonely job in a foreign country. Under these circumstances, his Thai girl-friend often becomes a single ray of hope in an otherwise subdued and often depressing existence, and he becomes dependent on her readiness to continue their relationship at a distance. His girl-friend, however, is at liberty to enter new relationships with other men. Jealousy thus joins his feelings of powerlessness over his distant partner. The *farangs'* letters reflect an intense concern with the preservation of some semblance of continued intimacy and mutual attachment, despite the long separation in space and time, and the uncertainty about the girl's activities.

The first reaction to the separation on the *farang's* part, is usually an intense sense of loss and yearning for his beloved. This is expressed in the highly emotional tone of his first letters, as in the one written by a young German with a limited competence in English immediately after his departure:

> Hello V.
> How are you? I hope fine.
> I waiting you. I love you so much and I hope you came [sic!] back to me, very quickly.
> Please write me many letters. My heart is not happy because my heart missing you too much. I hope you missing me too, V., I love you very much, please love me too.
> How are you fly [sic!] please tell me.
> Your home waiting for you [i.e., in D. in Germany].
> All my love only you.
>
>   P.
>
> *I waiting you!*
> *I love you!*
> *I want you!*

Another German gives vent to his feelings in a curious patois of English and German: "[Ich] bin und hab my in you verliebt" ("I am [in love] and have fallen in love with you").

Similarly strong sentiments are expressed in more literary English by other correspondents, e.g., "I die a little bit every day I don't hear from you." Or: "I would volunteer to come back. Even if it was to fight a war, but if that gets me to see you sooner then I go fight." Or, most profusely: "...I feel like coming running down to you... I will! I surely will – there is no doubt about it – I really mean it! I cannot stay any more without you. Oh, my God! He knows how much I miss you... too much...."

Their infatuation with the Thai girls induces the *farangs* to draw a stark contrast between the bleakness and meaninglessness of their life at home or at work, and the time they have spent, or will spend in the future, with their girl-friends in Thailand: e.g., "I have been working 12 to 14 hours every day for the last month, so about all I do is work, eat and sleep." Or, from a letter by a German man:

> Since my holiday is finished I have so much work that in the evening [I am] too tired to do anything. Every day I work 14 to 16 hours. To work is good so I have not too much chance to think about D. [the girl] and me. Alas it is very lonely when I come back to my house.

Other letters express the writer's rejection of life at home: "I am getting sick of work here, K. It's boring with no future." And in a most pessimistic, but resigned note, an Englishman writes to his girlfriend:

> I do not have very much to say except I am glad that you are not here, not because I would not like you to be with me, but because life here is not so good. There is nothing to do here but drink and eat. There are no jobs for anybody, especially me.

Against such background, the girl is made the center of the *farang's* existence. Thailand in general and the girl-friend in particular are exorbitantly glorified in the letters: e.g., a *farang* working in Saudi Arabia writes a letter during a "dreary" night-shift, feeling "glum" and expresses his fervent desire to be "... back there with you in glorious Thailand instead." Another man, an Australian rig worker, writes to his girl-friend: "You have everything I like in a woman, you're very funny, very honest... and, ook! very sexy." As the *farang's* unhappy present leads him to focus on the future reunion with his beloved, the day of return to Thailand, in the words of an Australian, "... will be the happiest day of my life."

These proclamations of love and longing, even if genuine, obviously also contain a meta-message. By expressing his single-minded attachment to the girl, the *farang* signals his faithfulness to her and, by implication, his expectation that she will likewise be faithful to him.

The attempts of *farangs* to breach the distance separating them from their girl-friends are made somewhat easier by "linking objects" (Volkan 1981), particularly pictures of the beloved. Thus, one American working in Saudi Arabia writes that he kisses his girl-friend's picture every day. Many ask for a photo of their girls as does, for example, the Italian mine-worker whose letter was quoted above. Some send pictures of themselves. In the absence of direct contact, letters from the beloved attain an overwhelming importance. Thus, another *farang*, also writing from Saudi Arabia, says, "I am 35 years old, but when I am with you or receive a letter from you I feel like a very young man!" The foreign men repeatedly write of their anxious expectation of their girlfriends' letters, and describe their worry and chafing when none arrive and their happiness when they receive one.

Most of the letters express strong feelings and attest to extraordinary infatuation of some *farangs* with the girls despite their usually brief sojourn in Bangkok. The content of the letters, of course, should not be taken as an indication of the frequency of such infatuation, because it is reasonable to assume that the *farangs* who take the trouble to write letters will be those who get more strongly involved. The *farangs* who take their encounters with Thai women more casually will probably not be motivated to write letters. Some letters, however, express a casual or even cynical attitude to the girls, e.g., "You probably don't even remember me now with all your boyfriends you must have." A cool, self-conscious distance is manifested in the letter of the sophisticated German academic, part of which was quoted above: "Did you enjoy your time with the other two men? Please tell me a bit about it, I so much like you to share your experiences with me." Such letters, however, are exceptional. Most foreign correspondents are seriously involved with the girls, and are therefore gnawed by suspicion even as they tend to trust the girls blindly.

THE FARANGS' LETTERS – THE DILEMMA OF TRUST AND SUSPICION

To maintain an intimate relationship at a distance is difficult under the best of circumstances. It becomes a serious problem under the circumstances surrounding the liaisons of *farangs* and Thai girls. The couple usually spent only a short time together, linguistic and cultural barriers to communication usually preclude closer acquaintance despite sexual intimacy. The circumstances of their first encounter, in the context of tourist-oriented prostitution, also pose a problem for the future maintenance of the relationship, engendering feelings of doubt, anxiety and jealousy in the *farang* after his departure.

The absent *farang* finds himself in a doubly paradoxical situation. While his sojourn in Thailand usually inspired a feeling of sexual and personal dominance over the apparently submissive Thai girl, he now realizes, in his changed situation, his dependence on her, and, while the girl's occupation inspires him to doubt the genuineness of her written expressions of love and faithfulness in the letters, the cognitive dissonance occasioned by the *farang's* psychological and often financial investment in her, induces him to trust her and to explain away his doubts. This ambivalence comes to the fore in a curious mix of promises and threats which often incongruously follow one another in the same or in consecutive letters.

The *farangs* are further confounded by the girl's conduct of their correspondence. In the course of time, many girls, with the help of their scribes, systematically misinform the *farangs* on their activities, assuring the *farangs* of their continued love and faithfulness. Experienced girls and scribes are adept at the right "calibration" of the emotional tone of the letters, and in anticipating the *farangs'* possible doubts and suspicions and allaying them in advance.

Faced by such skillful handling of the girls' correspondence, the *farangs* find themselves at a disadvantage. Because they are unable to check the girls' stories and assurances, and are anyway inclined to believe them, the letters they receive tend to strengthen their trust in the girls. But they often continue to nurse doubts, and become over-sensitive to small clues from which they could infer the truth. This ambivalence clearly emerges from a long intensive correspondence between a middle-aged New Zealander and his girl-friend, whom he in fact eventually married and took to New Zealand. At least for part of the period during which they corresponded the girl had another protracted liaison, unknown to the New Zealander, and possibly also brief encounters with other men. In one of his letters the New Zealander expresses the hope that the girl is:

> ...not angry at me when I joking ask you [during a long-distance telephone conversation] if you have someone with you, but Darling, before you start to speak to me, some guy count some numbers on the line, in German, maybe another telephone operator, right?

The concluding question poignantly expresses the writer's confusion: he trustfully explains away his own suspicion.

The dilemma of trust and suspicion becomes the more acute, the more seriously a *farang* takes the relationship. This is nicely illustrated by a letter in which a *farang*, after formally spelling out his conditions for marriage, warns his girlfriend: "I hope you are serious about this [marriage] and not playing a trick, just to get money out of me. I will trust you till I found out you have lied to me."

The trustful attitude of some *farangs* is sometimes accompanied by a patronizing disbursement of advice and attempts to direct the girls' lives from afar. One of the most pathetic of such letters which came to my attention was written by a German sausage producer to his young mistress of several years. Unfortunately, I was unable to copy the letter verbatim, but its gist was as follows: The man expressed his satisfaction with the news that the girl is studying to be a hair-stylist and that she has only one man in her life, himself. He says that he is a married man, but has no sexual relations with his wife anymore; they sleep in separate rooms. He produces 94 kinds of sausage. He wanted to send her some, but there are difficulties in mailing sausage from Germany to Thailand. Hence he sends her 50 Deutsche Marks (DM) to buy herself some sausage. But she should always buy only small quantities, since in Thailand's hot climate, sausage may go bad very quickly, and bad sausage could cause one's death. He will bring her some sausage when he arrives next time. Following this paternal advice the sausage producer turns to other matters, especially his intention to purchase a house "for us" in Thailand.

Other *farangs* advise their girlfriends on matters such as where to live or what to do with the money they send them. This emerges very clearly from the authoritative tone of a letter of an otherwise sexually insecure *farang*, working in Saudia Arabia:

> Please tell me how the purchase of your farm is doing as it is very important to me...
> I send you plenty of money so you can take care of yourself and prepare for the future.
> How you spend your money will depend on what I decide upon our future, so keep that
> in mind, O.K. I won't say anymore. I will just decide on what I see myself.

The girls, in their letters, succeed in creating the impression of obedience to their boyfriends' wishes. Some *farangs*, however, eventually realize that they have been deceived. If the relationship was a protracted one, and especially if the couple was married, the damage to the *farangs*, both financially and personally, can be considerable. Letters referring to the break-up are bitter: a desperate letter from an American husband to his (apparently estranged) Thai wife, in which he tells her that he was mugged and raped and almost had a nervous breakdown, ends with a postscript in capital letters – "I HAVE GIVEN UP LIQUOR, SO TELL YOUR BOYFRIEND. YOU *ADMITTED* IT. BOY FRIEND. THANKS WIFE."

The financial losses suffered by *farangs* from such relationships can be considerable, as emerges from a letter by a German man, who had been married to a Thai woman, to his new Thai girl-friend. He tells her of his conversation with the Thai ambassador to Germany, in which:

> I told him all, how she have spent all my money and how she was go back to Bangkok and few days later working in the T. Bar and also going with men to their hotel also for money although she was married to me too. All together she has cheat me one more as 50,000 DM.

The German expresses his hope that as a consequence of the ambassador's letters to the Thai police and attorney-general, his ex-wife will end up in jail. However, in case those letters will not have the hoped-for consequence, he threatens that, upon his return to Bangkok, "...I shall to hunt she until the end of this world." His bitter experience, however, did not preclude him from developing a new relationship with the girl to whom he wrote of his unlucky experiences with his ex-wife, a girl who at the time corresponded with at least four different *farangs*.

THE FARANGS' LETTERS – THE DILEMMA OF LOVE AND MONEY

Though there exist considerable differences between the girls in their attitudes toward *farang* boy-friends in terms of degree of attachment, sincerity and importance ascribed to the relationship, most of their letters have a common denominator, money. The request for money does not necessarily indicate that the girl's interest in the *farang* is purely pecuniary. Rather, as I have pointed out elsewhere (Cohen 1982 and in press), a girl expects her boy-friend to show his appreciation by giving her gifts and money. At the peril of some simplification one can say that, in general, the girls prefer money to love, while the *farangs* prefer love to money. The girls generally tend to manipulate relationships to derive whatever benefits they can, by subtle indications of their need for help or by blunt demands. They frequently bring up their own or their family's problems as the immediate reason for their supplication, or merely mention such problems without an explicit request, hoping to provoke their boy-friends' compassion and to induce them to send money.

The *farangs* initially tend to show much understanding for the problems and needs of the girls and readiness to help them. Thus, a German writes to his girl-friend, "From your letter I got to know that you have money troubles, I can understand this very well and it is very good that you informed me about that. Of course I will provide you with some money."

The amounts, frequency and regularity of support extended by the *farangs*, vary considerably. While some men send as little as US $10, others may send as much as US $3,000. Men who work in the Arab countries and whose earnings are high while they suffer from considerable environmental deprivation, tend to send their Thai girl-friends particularly large sums of money. It appears, that the *farangs* tend to be most generous a brief time after their departure; their generosity peters out as time passes, only to be renewed a short time before their return visit. Some, especially those who seriously strive to maintain a permanent relationship with the girls or intend to marry them, support them regularly, in the hope that thereby they will be kept out of prostitution and wait for their boy-friends' return. The bigger sums of money are usually intended for a specific project, such as the acquisition of a rice-field or the construction of a house, and often come in conjunction with a *farang's* plan for marriage. Men who send money regularly are much sought after by the girls, since they are a source of security against the girls' uncertain existence. Some older girls often build up a coterie of three or four permanent boy-friends, all of whom without knowing of one another, support the girls regularly.

Whatever the goodwill and generosity of the *farangs*, as time goes by, some usually feel the strain of their girl-friends' ceaseless supplications and become apologetic, suspicious or even outrightly aggressive in their responses. They sometimes excuse themselves for sending what they consider to be only a small sum. "I am sending you 100 pounds, it is all I can afford." A few, indeed, explain that they cannot send any money, since they had other big expenses, such as buying an air ticket or having new dentures made. Others respond more aggressively to what they consider to be exaggerated demands. Thus, an American working in an Arab country exhorts his girlfriend: "Honey, I am concerned that you ask for money as I just sent you money in December. Eight hundred dollars is a lot of money and you should have plenty of money... I will send you your money 22 Dec... I won't send you money... unless you can show me how you spent the money... This makes me wonder what you do with your money... I want us to have a good future. If this makes you unhappy then maybe you should forget me..."

The most fascinating response to a girl's apparently indirect supplication for money comes from one of the two or three letters written to Thai girls by Arabs from the Gulf states: "...you say in your letter that you cry because you are poor, so why don't you think that there are many people in the world who are more poorer, that who don't have money to have one time to eat;" after this exhortation he continues: "... I don't care if you have money or you are poor because I love you, I only care about that — is that I don't want anybody say that you are Bad Society Girl [i.e., a prostitute]." This is a remarkable *mel entendu*. The man apparently believed the girl was afraid that he would not want her because of her poverty, while he was solely interested in her good name. He apparently did not understand her letter as a supplication, and consequently did not send her any money.

While *farang* men are often prepared to support their girl-friends, so as to maintain the liaison, the very act of sending them money also raises fears of engendering a counter-productive effect. Thus, in a long and intensive love letter, an American working for a major corporation, after expressing his desire for his girl-friend "...to feel safe and secure and protected and happy to be with me," continues: "I do not want you to feel that you care for me because of the money. I will send you money...;" and after learning from a letter from her which just arrived that she was forced to pawn her gold necklace (the first thing the girls usually do when they run out of cash), he sent her US $100, saying: "I would have gladly sent you the money if you had said that you need it."

And another, rather insecure *farang* whom I already quoted above, exhorts his beloved: "Don't love me because I give you things, love me because I am me, O.K.," and then goes on to state that "to me money is not important. It is only important because it keeps you from suffering and helps you get a chance at a good life."

The ambiguous relation between money and love, expressed in these quotations, reflects a broader ambiguity marking most relationships between *farang* men and Thai girls in Bangkok (Cohen 1982 and in press). This ambiguity, however, becomes more pronounced and salient in the correspondence, owing to the intensification of feelings and the uncertainties caused by the distance.

This state of affairs induces some *farangs* to attempt to impose their will upon the girls in a remote-control manner. Some *farangs*, especially those who take their relationships seriously, make their support of the girls conditional upon their future conduct. The desire for control stands out exceptionally strongly in a letter by an American working in Saudi Arabia, who drew up a formal offer of marriage to a girl, which is worth quoting in full:

> (1) We must get legally married (2) I will send to Bangkok 4000 B [US $200] per month for the support of your two children. (3) I will give you a round trip ticket to Saudi Arabia when you are ready to come. (4) After 6 months I will give you another round trip ticket to return to Bangkok to visit your family and children. (5) I will help you get a job here. (6) All the money you make you can keep for yourself. (7) I will give you 1000 B [US $50] per month for spending money while you are here. (8) I will buy you clothes and food while you are here. (9) Anytime you are not happy here you can leave and not come back. Now for all of the above I will ask you the following: (1) Be honest and faithful to me while you are here. (2) Take care of me and my home very well. (3) If I am unhappy with you, you will leave and not give me any trouble in the future.
> Now I don't think that is asking too much.

This proposal is followed by the exhortation about her seriousness, and a warning that if she is dishonest with him "...you will lose a great deal more than me. I have much to offer. If you are good and honest you will win it all."

I am unaware of the girl's response to this attempt to achieve control over her through a formalization of their relationship. But, from my knowledge of the girls' general reactions to proposals about the future made by *farangs*, I guess that she smilingly agreed to enter the contract, without feeling in any way committed to abide by its stipulations.

DISCUSSION: THE FARANGS' LIFE SITUATION AS REFLECTED IN THEIR LETTERS

There exists a voluminous and rapidly growing literature which describes the evils and the exploitation inherent in sex-tourism (e.g., ZEB 1983; Khin Thitsa 1980). My own work on the relations between tourist-oriented prostitutes and foreigners suggests a more discriminating and sophisticated generalization: sex-tourism may indeed engender the sexual exploitation of local women on the macro-social level; but on the micro-level of interpersonal relationships, the state of affairs may often be inverted – the local women actually exploiting the foreigners. The data presented in this paper strongly support this conclusion. They show, in the first instance, the "power of the weak;" the often despondent dependence of apparently powerful, well-to-do and free *farangs* upon the apparently weak and submissive Thai women; this despondency is exploited with consummate skill by the Thai girls, with the help of their "scribes." But, perhaps more importantly, it reflects the dismal personal predicament and sexual distress of the girls' *farang* correspondents, the roots of which have to be sought in their life-situations. The selection of the letters at my disposition is by no means random, and does not permit me to generalize on the characteristics of all the *farangs* coming to Thailand. But it is fairly clear that the *farang* letter writers fall into two principal types: alienated young people, ranging from "drop-outs" to elitist academics; and isolated middle-aged individuals – bachelors, divorcees or men estranged from their wives – many of whom work abroad, particularly in Arab countries. There is little doubt that many of the latter would be considered misfits in their sedate, middle-class societies. But their very isolation enables them to attempt to live out their sexual fantasies in the Orient – an attempt which many of their contemporaries, who lead apparently ordered and satisfying lives, may well desire to make but are precluded from doing so by their personal circumstances. These males are therefore not interesting because they differ from those contemporaries, but rather because they may well express and articulate in their often pathetic letters some general, if covert, aspirations and fantasies of many middle-aged Western men. The fact that many of the hopes and fantasies of the *farang* correspondents eventually end in disappointment, and some in anger and bitterness, does not detract from the significance of their attempt.

To many *farangs* who come to Thailand for the first time, the apparently pliable and submissive young Thai girls appear to provide an opportunity to realize their sexual dreams and fantasies and to prove their manhood. Most of these men stay in Thailand only briefly, and have a few opportunities to penetrate beyond the surface of tourist-oriented prostitution and to realize the game most girls play with their customers. Some are disposed to play the touristic game themselves, and do not delve too deeply, so as not to dispel the fantasy which they are living out (Cf. Cohen 1985b). They enjoy their stay, but then return to routine life. Others, however, take their experience more seriously – and once they return home or to work abroad, their life becomes lastingly transformed; in the drabness of daily life or the loneliness of a remote workplace, the girl with whom they spent a week or a fortnight becomes a sole ray of light, the new center of their life. Mixing fantasy with reality, they write passionate letters, through which they strive to retain the girl they will be separated from for so long. However, since, in the back of their minds they are aware of the unrealistic aspects of their relationships, their enthusiasm mixes with forebodings, their hopes with fears and their trust with doubts. Their letters, with their incongruities, amply express the profound and persisting dilemmas faced by the *farangs*, dilemmas which remain largely unresolved owing to their isolation and to the adroitness with which the girls manipulate them.

CONCLUSION: THE PARADOXES OF INTIMACY-AT-A DISTANCE

The unity of nearness and remoteness involved in every human relation is organized, in the phenomenon of the stranger, in a way which may be most briefly formulated by saying that in the relationship to him, distance means that he, who is close, is far, and strangeness means that he, who is also far, is actually near (Simmel, 1950:402).

The same categories which characterize the relationships of Simmel's stranger, can also be applied to the relationship of intimacy-at-a-distance; only that here the terms are inverted, and so is the incongruity — for Simmel's stranger is physically near but socially far; the remote intimate is physically far but socially near; and both relationships harbor a paradox, which is a source of ambiguity. Thus, the stranger, equally remote from all the locals, may become their *confidante* (Simmel 1950:404), whereas personal intimacies, communicated at a distance through the objectivizing medium of the letter, lose much of the spontaneity and urgency of face-to-face communication.

The paradoxical character of the correspondence is further exacerbated by the role of the scribe. This role most blatantly embodies Simmel's idea that any letter represents an "objectivization of the subjective" (Simmel 1908:381). The scribe is a third person, completely unrelated to the corresponding parties, who translates and writes the most intimate confidences the partners convey to other. And here we encounter the ultimate paradox: partly owing to the routinization of his role, and partly to the distance which his uncomfortable position leads him to adopt, the scribe tends to standardize the letters which he as a "language broker" writes for the girls, often endowing the apparently individual letters in which spontaneous and personal feelings are expressed, with the impersonal character of a circular. His dexterity at composing the letters, however, reinforces the *farangs'* love and trust for their girl-friends and dispels their doubts; it thus ironically helps to perpetuate their attempts at maintaining "intimacy-at-a-distance" and their submissions to the manipulations exercised by their seemingly pliable and accommodating Thai girl-friends.

NOTES

1. This paper is based on data collected in an anthropological study of a *soi* (lane) in Bangkok conducted during the summers of 1981-1984, under a grant from the Harry S. Truman Research Institute for the Advancement of Peace, at the Hebrew University of Jerusalem, the support of which is hereby gratefully acknowledged. Thanks are also due to the National Research Council of Thailand for the kind assistance of its staff during field work and to Yoram Bilu and Elihu Katz for their comments on an earlier draft of this paper.
2. Prostitution is a widespread phenomenon in Thailand, but the number of women engaging in it is notoriously difficult to ascertain. Estimates vary between 500,000 and 1 million. Many women, however, engage in prostitution only on a part-time or seasonal basis, and move in and out of the occupation, so that they can hardly be labelled "prostitutes." The number of women engaging in tourist-oriented prostitution, even if highly visible, represents a small percentage of the total, probably less than 10,000 at any one time. For general information, see e.g., Khin Thitsa 1980, Mingmongkol 1981, Phongpaichit 1981, Truong 1983, Hewison 1985, Ong 1985.

Part Five
Urban Class and Ethnicity

Wirth defines the city as "a relatively large, dense and permanent settlement of socially heterogeneous individuals." The heterogeneity that Wirth refers to includes the different backgrounds of people who live in cities, the many occupational specialties by which people make their livings, and the system of rewards by which some live grandly while others may starve. While the people of the countryside are not completely homogeneous, the degree of heterogeneity in large cities is much higher.

The concepts of "class" and "ethnicity" have been developed by social scientists to understand this heterogeneity. The way in which these terms have been used by social scientists will be examined in this essay. I will then proceed to discuss the role of political and economic conflict in perpetuating urban diversity, the relationship of ethnicity and culture to personal expression, and the development of a common "ethnic" identity by all people in a city. The aim is to clarify the usage of *class* and *ethnicity* and to stress some related themes.

CLASS AND ETHNICITY – TWO OVERLAPPING CONCEPTS

When social scientists construct abstract models of social systems, they generally assume that some division of labor in society is necessary. All human societies have divided certain tasks, at the very least along the lines of age and sex. Only women can bear children and lactate. Young children and old people are generally weaker than ages in between. As societies become more complex, so does the division of labor. The degree to which simple societies, like those of hunters and gatherers, are or were stratified is a matter of controversy, but certainly many horticultural, agrarian, and preindustrial urban social systems were stratified. They gave lesser and greater awards of power and prestige to individuals on the basis of the social position they occupied and the function they presumably fulfilled.

In stratified societies, people are unequal in the goods they own, the control they command over their goods and lives, the material and symbolic rewards which others accord them, and their access to strategic power within the society. In such societies, people are often grouped together with those who have similar power and prestige. We often set up ideal types or construct perfect models of societies. In one type, individuals' status groupings are determined at birth and people within the society cannot change their status during their lifetimes. Often such a society is called a "caste society," although the Indian caste system is much more complicated than such a simple description would suggest. Another type is the "open class society." In an open class society, while individuals are born into a status grouping or class, they may rise or fall in class affiliation. So far, we have talked about social position, power, wealth, and class without mentioning race, religion, national origin, or other components which we think of in relationship to ethnicity.

If people can change their social position, the fact that X once had a higher rank or Y had a humble birth will be remembered. Thus there is a disparity between the status which a person acquired at birth, one's *ascribed* status, and the status he or she has *achieved*. In addition, if we assume migration, religious diversification, racial differences, and the presence of different speech communities in one place, we are dealing with the kind of cultural diversity and multiplicity of self-identities which we have come to call "ethnicity." In a perfect closed "caste" society, ethnicity and class would be identical, but they are not in the complex societies which we encounter everywhere in modern times (Parsons 1951:172; 1975:56–57).

Parsons (1951:172) sees both social classes and ethnic groups as sets or aggregates of families and extended kinship units. He defines social classes by status in a stratified society, while ethnic groups are defined on the basis of descent either from a common ancestor or from "ancestors who all belonged to the same categorized ethnic group." In an open class system, where people may change status, the two would often not be identical. For instance, in India one can find members of a low "Untouchable" caste who are wealthy and powerful and can be considered members of a ruling elite.

Because of this discrepancy between the status into which one was born and the status one has attained, individuals face conflicting claims on their loyalties and groups (whether based on class or ethnicity) and may face internal divisions. Because ethnic loyalties, including those grounded in race and sect, are acquired at birth, they are sometimes called "primordial" by social scientists (Geertz 1973:254–310). Such sentiments are seen as divisive in new nations which seek to unite peoples from a diversity of backgrounds and as irrational by those who see political struggles resting upon the present economic circumstances of different classes.

A. Cohen's essay on ethnicity (1974) stresses its relevance to present circumstances, rather than primordial ties. This comes out in his definition of the condition of "ethnicity." An ethnic group, he writes, can be defined "as a collectivity of people who (a) share some patterns of normative behaviour and (b) form a part of a larger population, interacting with people of other collectivities within the framework of a social system." This definition implies that the ethnic group is a subculture within a larger culture (see Miller, "The Dockworker Subculture," for a definition of subculture). It also contains nothing about descent from common ancestors, whether historical or fictive. An occupational group like construction workers or members of the financial community could be seen as an ethnic group by Cohen, as he shows in his discussion of "the City," London's financial district. Later, however, Cohen does seem to return to an association of ethnicity with primordial ties, for in his last section he speaks of "a new line of cleavage, such as that of social class," cutting across "ethnic lines." Still, by implication, social classes over time become ethnic groups in his eyes. Cohen's emphasis, however, is on the use of a set of common symbols, shared kinship, and religion as useful ways of organizing people on behalf of their common interests.

Miller and Lynch generally share Cohen's view of how ethnic groups utilize a common subculture to further their ends, although each article contains different emphases and nuances. Miller ("The Dockworker Subculture") compares the circumstances among dockworkers which gave rise to a shared subculture. He is not at all concerned with common ancestry. He ignores the fact that dockers in many ports have distinct ethnic identities, such as the Anglo-Americans of Portland, the Italian-Americans of Brooklyn, the Salonicans and Druzes of Haifa, and the Georgians and Moroccans of Ashdod (e.g., Pilcher 1972). Still, the point that the work situation can give rise to sharp class consciousness and to a distinct way of life is well taken. This concern with a subcultural type which cuts across historical and geographic boundaries is like that of Oscar Lewis's "The Culture of Poverty."

Lynch ("A South Indian Caste in a Bombay Slum") in his article is concerned with people who have more than one identity in terms of caste, region and language, and socioeconomic class. He describes how they decide on which aspect of their identity to stress in the new urban situation. Lynch feels that this is an element neglected by Cohen, but it is also an aspect of ethnicity which follows from Cohen's basic view that ethnic groups are interest groups.

Oscar Lewis ("The Culture of Poverty") set out to delineate patterns of behavior shared by a whole class of people, the urban poor. Lewis developed the concept of the "culture of poverty." This was an attempt to develop a model of the behavior of the poor in a variety of cultural settings. No concept in urban anthropology has provoked more controversy and filled more journal pages with criticism and debate than Lewis's culture of poverty. The controversy has overspilled the boundaries of anthropology and has been much discussed by other social scientists and professionals concerned with the poor. While the academic debate is no longer alive, the issues raised by the controversy are important ones. Moreover, the numbers of people living below the poverty line in many industrial and developing nations continues to grow.

In brief, Lewis's culture of poverty is a distinct (and self-perpetuating) way of life that develops among the lowest stratum in capitalistic societies in response to economic deprivation and inequality. Lewis identifies some seventy traits that he considers characteristic of this subculture of American society (actually Lewis claims that only 20 percent of the poor develop a culture of poverty).

According to Lewis, the culture of poverty represents "both an adaptation and a reaction of the poor to their marginal position in a class-stratified, highly individuated, capitalistic society." It represents an effort to "cope with feelings of helplessness and despair that arise from the realization by the poor of the improbability of their achieving success in terms of the prevailing values and goals." Contrary to what Lewis clearly hoped for, his culturalist approach does imply that efforts to provide better economic opportunities and housing for the poor will achieve little in terms of improving their lifeways, which are learned at an early age (Eames 1976).

The views of Lewis have been severely criticized by Charles Valentine (1968), Carol Stack (1975 and "The Kindred of Viola Jackson"), and others who offer a *structuralist* as opposed to a *culturalist* explanation of poverty behavior. They argue that the behavior of the poor is determined by economic conditions established by the larger society, and that those values and behaviors of the poor which are different from those of the dominant classes are the result of their inability to achieve the higher goals defined by society because of their disadvantaged position.

The structuralist interpretation can be seen in several of the essays in this part. Eames and Goode examine the economic adaptations of the poor. The similarities they find in the responses of the poor to low and sporadic income in a wide range of cultural settings support the view that the behavior of the poor is directly "linked to economic social conditions rather than a cognitive or value-based cultural framework."

POLITICAL AND ECONOMIC CONFLICT

Much of the work on class and ethnicity is concerned with political and economic conflict. This is explicit in some of the following articles and implicit in them all.

As Fischer (1972, 1975b) suggests in his subcultural theory, the city intensifies subcultures by bringing more people into them. By bringing peoples bearing different subcultures into one place and by "rewarding" some and "punishing" others, the city sharpens conflict and heightens class and ethnic antagonism. The dockers in large ports are a large enough group to resist the efforts of the employers to prevent them from organizing an effective union. Through their "class consciousness," militancy, and technical conservatism, they seek to retain control over their own lives, despite their employment by powerful outsiders. The class consciousness, which is so well illustrated by the dockers, often develops in the workplace.

Logan ("Latin American Movements") aptly points out that there are many industrial centers and cities in which mobilization for one's interest in the workplace is inhibited. This has been characteristic of Latin America, but the decline of trade union power in the United States and Western Europe in recent years shows that this is not limited to the Third World. Logan suggests that the failure of workplace movements has heightened the importance of residentially based mobilization in which many women participate.

The solidarity of dockworkers in many ports is reinforced by the common ethnic/national origins of the dockers which resulted from a "founder's effect"; that is, early migrants from a certain locality entered a particular occupation and encouraged their compatriots who followed them to the city to do the same. This, in turn, may be the product of a "balkanized" or split-labor market. A split-labor market is one where workers who are classified as belonging to one category (ethnic, racial, religious, or sexual) are channeled into one kind of job. Usually those belonging to one category get more skilled jobs and are paid more, while those who are stigmatized are given jobs paying less. The lower-class domestic servants discussed by Bossen ("Wives and Servants") are a good example of such a segment of a split-labor market. The "pink collar" jobs, such as beautician, typist, or even elementary school teacher and social worker, which typify *female* employment in the United States are another. So are "illegal aliens" in the United States, who often take poorly paid jobs requiring little training. The existence of a group of workers who accept difficult working conditions and less pay than other workers depresses working conditions for all and is often the cause of ethnic antagonism (Bonacich 1972).

Split-labor markets tend to make ethnic and class lines coincide. For instance, in the United States more white males work as skilled workers than do Hispanics or blacks; thus as the interests of the former may differ markedly from those of the latter, they can be seen as reflecting separate class interests. Split-labor markets are only one aspect of economic specialization along ethnic lines. One may also find ethnic specialization in certain trades, such as small businesses opened by minorities like Jews, Lebanese, Chinese, and Greeks (see Zenner).

In some trades and industries, there is actually a cleavage within the ethnic group. In the late nineteenth and early twentieth centuries, many of the factories producing ready-to-wear garments in New York City and elsewhere were owned by Jews. With the mass immigration to the United States from Eastern Europe, penniless Jewish immigrants were employed by these factory owners, often under trying conditions. The Jewish garment workers in New York City organized some militant unions, and the Jewish community was rent by a fierce class struggle (Howe 1976).

While much of our attention is focused on the class and ethnic consciousness of the workers and the disadvantaged, it is important to note that the privileged are often better organized than their less affluent counterparts. Cohen's example of how "the City," the financial district in London, is organized is a case in point. The fact that the most privileged people in any society comprise a relatively small group who may belong to a small set of families, who go to the same schools, and belong to the same clubs makes informal organization of such a class much easier.

Domhoff has suggested that such upper-class solidarity may appear even in a large country like the United States. In one book, he describes some exclusive encampments where rich and powerful men from all over the country come together for a week or so of recreation. Corporation executives and high government officials (including presidents and governors) live and play together. Among their guests are leading entertainers. Such camps are not meetings of a conspiratorial elite, but they do establish a sense of camaraderie (Domhoff 1974). While gatherings like these may not unite the men for political action, it certainly establishes a framework of mutual understanding and accommodation. Cohen's stress on the informal and often invisible organization of ethnic groups and classes is well-illustrated in this instance.

By contrast with the elite, the middle and lower classes are aggregates or categories rather than well-organized interest groups. Those who are well organized have coalesced around such groups as trade unions or certain ethnic organizations. Still, the interests of groups—both urban and rural—who are of lower and middle status in modern societies are usually mediated by other individuals who represent these groups. Sometimes these individuals are elected officials, while at other times they are persons of fairly high status who are linked to the powerful elites. Lynch, in his description of Adi-Dravida participation in political parties, has suggested how members of that caste advance their interests through politicians who belong to particular parties. The study of such mediation through the networks of patrons and clients has been an important aspect of the political anthropology of cities and other complex societies (e.g., Leis and Hicks 1977).

ETHNICITY AND CULTURAL CONTENT

While ethnicity cannot be reduced to political clout or to the group as an economic resource, this is the emphasis we find in this section. The symbols which unite a group are more than weapons in its struggle with others. The symbols have meanings of their own which transcend interethnic and interclass conflict.

Let us use the Mardi Gras and Carnival celebrations as an example. Gonzalez (1970) analyzes the Carnival in a city in the Dominican Republic in terms of how they mirror social and economic differences. But there are more universal meanings expressed in Carnival. The Carnival inaugurates Lent, a period of austerity. The license of Carnival contrasts sharply with the fasting which traditional Christians practice during this six-week period.

In dealing with the choice of symbols and identities, advantages to be gained in a conflict may play a role, but the other factors may have weight as well. For instance, the different identities of the Adi-Dravidas, described by Lynch, will bring different symbols to the forefront. Whether, one of the political parties vying for the Adi-Dravida vote, the DMK, is a "political group with para-ethnic functions" or an "ethnic group with para-political functions" may vary with context; what is clear is that the two are bound into one package. The immigrant may find satisfaction by being with other Tamil-speakers, whether or not this is advantageous, as well as sharing political and economic interests with them. It is similar for Syrian Jews who seek each other's company, both for economic and for ethno-religious reasons.

Just as ethnic and class symbols may have meanings beyond those of economic and political conflict, so aesthetic expression may have political consequences. This point is made very ably by Barbara Kirshenblatt-Gimblett ("Ordinary People/Everyday Life"). While she discusses this primarily with regard to urban celebrations, there is a very complicated field of inquiry in dealing with aesthetic expression and entertainment in a complex urban society.

The question of power is not merely a conflict between elite culture and that of the lower classes. After all, wealthy people control the mass media which generally promulgate tastes for rock music, more than they do for opera or chamber music. In addition, symbols which mark a particular ethnic or religious group publicly may not be what is most significant in terms of the group's own traditions. Thus, Chanukkah is much more visible to American Gentiles, even though it is a relatively minor celebration traditionally, while Jews may find greater significance in observance of the Day of Atonement in the synagogue or Passover at home.

Similarly, the satisfactions and dissatisfactions of ethnic group membership cannot be reduced to the role which they play in competition with others.

CULTURE, STRUCTURE, AND STRATEGY

The articles in Part V, as well as other sections of this book touch on basic issues in anthropology and the social sciences, as well as urban studies. These are questions which relate to issues in our picture of human nature. There are two major thrusts in anthropology as to the role of culture. One is that human beings are basically realistic and rational in aiming to remain alive, healthy and comfortable. The other is that various forces, especially culture in the form of early childhood learning can so shape human behavior that humans will not respond realistically.

The "culturalist" notion of a self-perpetuating culture of poverty implies the latter idea. The structuralists who stress the adaptive nature of the behavior of the poor take the former viewpoint (Eames & Goode, "Culture of Poverty: A Misapplication"). The emphasis on strategy, whether strategies of survival, as in the article "Strategies for Coping with Poverty" (by Eames and Goode), or for mobilization (see Lynch and Logan), also implies realism and rationality. This is also implicit in Buechler's and Zenner's articles about middle-class entrepreneurs.

A related issue in the writing about the "culture of poverty" is the need to define boundaries of such a "subculture," or indeed any subculture in a modern world, in which all institutions and societies on the globe are interconnected. It is not only poverty which is not exclusively an urban problem, but affluence and entrepreneurship. Dona Flora's workshop may be in La Paz, but one may find similar factories outside of urban areas as well. Defining subcultures, whether of poverty or of dockers or of Syrian Jews or of IBM, is thus a difficult task.

The attempts to define culture has been one which has perplexed anthropologists for a long time. As used in the essays here, it includes norms and values which are viewed by the subjects involved as good, as well as practices of the people themselves.

Some stress one, while others emphasize the other side. Miller in discussing the dockers' subculture includes the values of workingclass solidarity and trade unionism. Lewis, on the other hand, seems more interested in the practices of the poor, not in what they give lip service to. Those who stress strategies and the influence of the system on people in cities also seem much more concerned with actual practice, rather than the norms, symbols, and values of the people.

Walter P. Zenner

THE DOCKWORKER SUBCULTURE

Raymond Charles Miller

Cities are divided into zones with distinct functions. In port cities the docks comprise such a zone, and the people who work there have developed their own way of life. Many of the Adi-Dravidas (Lynch "A South Indian Caste in a Bombay Slum") are dockworkers. Despite the differences among such cities as Bombay, Haifa, London, and San Francisco, Miller has discovered a common subculture. Among its features are loyalty to fellow workers, suspicion of management and of outsiders, militant unionism, and a "casual" frame of mind. These elements point to the fact that this subculture is a manifestation of "class consciousness." Miller suggests that the conditions of work in the port are as important to the development of a subculture as are the origins of the dockers. Miller's use of the "subculture" concept follows the way Oscar Lewis ("The Culture of Poverty") has used it.

Following a few introductory comments on the concept 'subculture' and the likelihood of universally similar responses to the industrialization experience, some generalizations are offered here about a dockworker subculture and the conditions that create it. The generalizations are in the form of propositions, not operational hypotheses—certainly not verified generalizations. They are based primarily on written sources, though the author has conducted interviews in San Francisco and Karachi. . . . [1]

The term 'subculture' refers to a culture within a culture, that is, an identifiable human group sharing some of the characteristics of the surrounding dominant culture but separated from it by the special sets of behavior, norms, loyalties, beliefs, etc., manifested and internalized by its members. Milton Gordon argues that subculture is the source of group identification, intimate social relationships, and particularized cultural behavior.[2] A subculture may or may not be geographically confined, though spatial proximity certainly reinforces its separate existence. The members have most of their social interaction, virtually all their primary contacts, with each other. The fewer the communica-

SOURCE: *Comparative Studies in Society and History* 11:302–314 (1969). Copyright © 1969 by Society for Comparative Studies in Society and History. Abridged and reprinted by permission of the Cambridge University Press.

tion channels between members and outsiders, the stronger becomes the internal orientation and the sense of apartness. . . .

An occupational group can . . . manifest its own subculture. In fact, Herbert Gans argues that in the 'early stages of industrialization' occupational grouping is the most productive conception to utilize in studying the society's subcultures and subsocial structures.[3] However, he suggests, as the society becomes highly industrialized, great occupational variations and mobility diminish the utility of this concept as a differentiating factor. Class then becomes more useful. Nevertheless, there are some occupations which, due to their particular attributes, do produce a more entrenched subculture. Seymour Lipset identifies them as possessing an 'occupational community'. He cites several American types: high-status craft groups, such as the printers, and geographically isolated occupations, such as the miners, sailors and longshoremen.[4]

This paper is about the longshoremen or dockworkers, as they are called outside the United States. These are the men who load and unload ocean-going ships. The central proposition of the paper is that certain widely prevalent conditions of dockwork produce a universal dockworker subculture. Today these conditions exist in some places, are just beginning to prevail in other places, and have ceased to exist in others. Some degree of commercialism-industrialism is necessary in order to create them. A high degree of industrialization makes it possible to eliminate them, though, paradoxically, the persistence of the subculture prevents their rapid demise. Only in the highly industrialized countries, especially the centrally planned socialist ones, have they been significantly altered, and even there the legacies of previous conditions remain.

Some limited evidence suggests that longshoremen themselves recognize this universal similarity. Longshoremen from the West Coast of the United States, on overseas visits, perceive their own self-image reflected in their counterparts all over the world, as shown in these comments: 'Longshoremen are the same everywhere you meet them. The French dockers are willing to take job actions to gain their demands when the occasion arises. They are easy to meet and talk to, proud of their occupation and a credit to their communities.'[5] 'As elsewhere, they [longshoremen in Bratislava, Czechoslovakia] have the best pay and working conditions and are proud and cocky.'[6] 'The Polish dockers had the same appearance as other dockers we saw on our trip, and we were given the impression that the independence that dockers enjoy throughout the world was there also.'[7]

A major International Labor Organization (ILO) report also makes generalizations about dockworkers the world over.[8] Another author comments, 'More than in any other industry in a big city, it appears that waterfront jobs belong to particular working class communities'.[9] According to Professors Kerr and Siegel, these waterfront communities have 'their own codes, myths, heroes, and social standards'.[10]

The conditions peculiar to dockland both produce and sustain the subculture. The further local conditions diverge from the following pattern, the less likely is the existence of a subculture which approximates the universal type. There is also a time dimension, due to the effect of cultural lag. Even though present conditions may significantly diverge from the environmental type, legacies of a past environment that did fit the type mean a greater approximation than one might otherwise expect.

The conditions that have been identified as producing the dockworker subculture are:

1. the casual nature of employment;[11]
2. the exceptional arduousness, danger, and variability of work;[12]
3. the lack of an occupationally stratified hierarchy and mobility outlets;[13]
4. lack of regular association with one employer;[14]
5. continuous contact with foreign goods, seamen, and ideas;[15]
6. the necessity of living near the docks;[16] and
7. the belief shared by longshoremen that others in the society consider them a low-status group.[17]

Because of the erratic arrival of ships and cargo, longshoremen have traditionally been hired on a work-available basis. A labor pool usually larger than peak needs competes for the scarce positions. Hiring is done on a daily basis at appointed times and places, a process known as the 'shape-up'. The situation as described for London in 1861 is repeated every work day at numerous ports throughout the world in the 1960s: 'Indeed, it is a sight to sadden the most callous, to see thousands of men struggling for only one day's hire; the scuffle being made the fiercer by the knowledge that hundreds out of the number there assembled must be left to idle the day out in want.'[18] As one would expect, the earnings of the casually employed dockworkers are erratic, low on average, and highly differentiated due to unequal hours of employment.

Various decasualization schemes have been initiated in order to mitigate the uncertainty of employment, but very few ports have complete decasualization. The ports in the Soviet Union are among the few. Such a system means continuous, permanent work for all longshoremen with mandatory attendance.[19] Most Western European ports, despite decasualization schemes going as far back as London's 1891 program, are not so decasualized as ports on the West Coast of the United States. 'All of the various programs of fall-back pay and so forth are simply unemployment benefit schemes. . . .'[20] Casual employment on the docks is very common in underdeveloped economies.

Traditionally, the majority both of the workers and the employers have resisted decasualization—the workers because they feared the loss of the jobs they possessed, and the employers because they feared the costs and responsibilities of regular employment obligations. Both have attempted to make the most of their positions, the workers by stretching the work through time-wasting practices, and the employers by demanding exceptional efforts while evading responsibility for working conditions.[21] Workers in the Port of New York in the recent past have been known to work for forty consecutive hours.

Dock work, except in the most automated operations, requires heavy physical effort—individual loads sometimes exceed 300 pounds. In nonspecialized ports, longshoremen face different types of cargo and new ships almost daily. 'The docker . . . must put his hand to a variety of tasks and is always liable to come up against the unfamiliar, the unexpected, the unpleasant, or even the actively dangerous situation. . . .'[22] The accident rate on the docks is one of the highest in all industrial occupations.

Longshoremen have been called a 'largely homogeneous, undifferentiated mass',[23] because they do the same work, have the same experience and status, and receive the same hourly pay. Thus there is not much occupational stratification and virtually no concomitant promotional ladder. Under the casual system, employers consider all workers on an equal basis, labeling the work 'unskilled'. However, as far back as 1915 Barnes argued that dock work, especially deck (winch, gangway and hooker-on) and hold work (stowing cargo) was a skilled occupation. 'If labor which can be performed satisfactorily only after years of practical training and which carries with it the demand for judgment and the sense of responsibility is not to be called skilled, it is difficult to fix the types of industry to which the term can justly be applied'.[24] In ports outside the United States, where shore cranes are used rather than the ship's gear, the cranesmen form another skilled group. During World War II specially trained Army personnel were sent to replace the striking cranesmen in Bombay; yet their output never exceeded one-fourth of the regular Indian cranesmen's.[25] In fact, dock work is so specialized that the skills acquired are generally not transferable to other occupations. Therefore, longshoremen face limited opportunities for mobility both within and without their occupation.

Longshoremen work in gangs, and the foreman or the boss of the gang is the status position immediately above the 'mass'. His position is an ambiguous one and can be very powerful. Under the casual system, the foreman does the hiring. Thus it pays for the worker to keep on his good side, sometimes through favors or possibly even through a regular kickback. On the other hand, overt friendly contact with the foreman may generate ill feelings among fellow workers.[26] The foreman's favorites in Great Britain are known contemptuously as the 'blue-eyed boys'.[27] Nevertheless, the foreman is frequently a member of the same union as the men in his gang and identifies more with the interests of his gang than with those of his employer. Because of the scattered nature of dock work, the employer must rely on the foreman for supervisory control. Discipline problems are inherent in these arrangements.[28]

Work for the longshoremen comes and goes. Employment demands are irregular and fluctuating. Periods of urgent need are interspersed with indifferent slack. On the job, requirements of speed and agility alternate with delays and inactivity. In other words, the work rhythm possesses both erratic and patterned activity extremes. In ports where employment is casual, the dockworker is forced to accept and accommodate himself to these conditions. If he is to be readily available for uncertain employment at the shape-up several times a day he has to live near the docks. As new ships arrive the employer frequently changes also, so that longshoremen in many ports lack a continuous relationship with any one particular firm (shipping line, stevedoring company, etc.).

Effective decasualization programs diminish the uncertainty and extremes of employment, reduce the need for proximate housing, and in some cases provide a permanent employer-employee relationship. As these programs become more widespread, the outstanding peculiarities of the dockworker subculture as subsequently described are likely to disappear. These developments are occurring in some countries such as the Soviet Union and the United States, but only very recently. Elsewhere, casualness still prevails. Even where decasualization has been effectively implemented, the legacies of previous conditions linger on.

As Bennett Berger reports in his *Working Class Suburb*, the workers may move to the suburbs but they remain working-class in their social relations, attitudes, aspirations and general behavior. Suburbs become 'new homes for old values'.[29] At some ports increased income and greater security of employment have made suburban living possible for longshoremen. Though moving from the waterfront does not mean an overnight transition to middle-class behavior, a watering-down of the subcultural attributes does seem to occur. Longshoremen in the San Francisco area significantly decrease their union activity after moving to the suburbs. Not surprisingly they also frequently refuse to inform their neighbors of their occupation. Lipset suggests that such a pattern appears when income rises faster than the occupation's status.[30]

Succinctly stated, what are some of the characteristics of this dockworker subculture which the above conditions tend to create?

1. extraordinary solidarity and undiffused loyalty to fellow dockworkers;
2. suspicion of management and outsiders;
3. militant unionism;
4. appearance of charismatic leaders from the ranks;
5. liberal political philosophy but conservative view of changes in work practices; and
6. 'casual frame of mind' (free men or irresponsible opportunists).

As Selig Perlman observed forty years ago in his classic work on the labor movement, 'The more distinct the trade identity of a given group and therefore the clearer the boundaries of its particular "job territory", the stronger are normally the bonds which tie the members together in a spontaneous solidarity'.[31] The dock laborer's loyalties belong predominantly to his gang, to his fellow dockworkers and to the waterfront community. These loyalties and related solidarity are highly concentrated and 'exaggerated'. 'As casual labourers in constant fear of underemployment dockers learnt that solidarity was even more vital to them than it was to the ordinary worker; and as a tight community, originally living in a close neighborhood round the docks, they learnt the importance of loyalty and the fear of ostracism.'[32] The longshoremen operate on a 'one in trouble, all in trouble' principle. Many instances have been cited where one man shouting 'all out!' was sufficient to stop work, though none of the workers knew why.[33]

The dockers keep to themselves and have few connections with outside individuals or associations. In some ports (Great Britain and Italy) jobs stay in the family with the son following in his father's footsteps.[34] Intruding outsiders are usually resented or distrusted because the longshoremen see them as either strikebreakers or management spies, or as social workers who hope to reform their 'lazy, shiftless ways'. A deep mistrust of management prevails. 'The belief persists in dockland that employers are ruthless, that they care only for profit and are capable of resorting to all kinds of trickery and subterfuge in order to exact the last ounce of effort from the dockworker.'[35] These beliefs are not based on fantasies, for shippers and stevedores have been notorious for their disregard of workers' rights, welfare and dignity.[36] Many waterfront employers still retain a disdain for the dock laborers, whom they label 'lazy, incapable of thinking, interested only in their wage packets, . . . easily led',[37] and in some cases politically subversive.[38]

The insecurity, shared grievances, apartness, solidarity and location at a critical transportation point all combine to produce an extremely militant form of unionism where government and development conditions are propitious. After village and particularistic ties are sufficiently diminished in the urban environment, the union, unless government control or paternalism prevents this, becomes the major social referent for dockworkers. As industrialization proceeds, dock laborers are in the forefront of union organization and action. The *avant-garde* role of dock labor unions has been noted in countries as disparate as the United States, South Africa and Pakistan.[39] 'The union becomes a kind of working-class party or even government for these employees, rather than just another association among many. Union meetings are more adequately attended and union affairs more vigorously discussed.'[40]

'The strike for this isolated mass is a kind of colonial revolt against far-removed authority, an outlet for accumulated tensions, and a substitute for occupational and social mobility.'[41] There is no doubt that longshoring is among the occupations sharing internationally the highest strike incidences. In an eleven-nation study, it was found that proportionately the most man-days lost due to strikes and lockouts were experienced by the maritime, longshore and mining industries.[42] The militant solidarity of dock labor unions has won high hourly wages for their members and grudging acceptance of time-wasting practices from employers. In fact, in countries as varied as India, Czechoslovakia, Israel, the Philippines, Japan, Puerto Rico, Guatemala and Italy, longshoremen are reportedly the highest paid workers.[43] Unfortunately, in only a small number of ports is high pay matched with regular employment and safe working conditions.

Charismatic leaders may not appear among dockworkers everywhere, but only occupational groups who share some of the same conditions—such as miners—seem to produce proportionately as many from the ranks. Dockworkers seem to respond to powerful personalities in their midst who articulate their grievances. Being one of them is actually a requisite. Harry Bridges, West Coast longshore leader, is a famous North American example of this phenomenon. A current European example is Jack Dash, chairman of the Port Workers' Liaison Committee in London.[44] Conceivably, these leaders are the product of a certain crisis point in industrialization and labor-management relations. In underdeveloped economies such as India, union leaders often come from the intellectual class rather than from the illiterate workers.[45] In completely decasualized ports where the major grievances have been eliminated, it is unlikely that the situation any longer calls for charisma.

Dockworkers are generally liberal or leftist in their political views. Their level of political interest, information and participation is higher than in other groups of workers. 'In general, members of occupations which guarantee a great deal of in-group interaction in many activities and roles, and which involve leadership skills and knowledge about large problems, are more politically aware, vote more, and have a greater commitment to such occupationally linked organizations as trade-unions.'[46] The longshoremen's estrangement from the wider community and from their employers contributes to their readiness to fight the 'big money boys' and all forms of exploitation. Interest in foreign relations is exceptionally high, as might be expected from men whose job is so international in character. The *ILWU Overseas Reports* provide some evidence for these generalizations. One interesting ambivalence noted in them is the holding of concurrent loyalties to nation on the one hand and to fellow workers throughout the world on the other.

Despite the dockworkers' support for significant social change, they are adamant in their opposition to changes in work practices and to technological innovations. Fear of unemployment and wage decreases, and a profound distrust of management, combine to produce these conservative policies. The fear that any change will be for the worse has led casual workers to resist decasualization. Unions have fought all reductions of total work force or of the size of gangs, all new forms of mechanization, and every increase in sling loads; their tactics are stoppages, strikes and go-slow practices. As a result work output has been severely affected in ports as far apart as Calcutta, Havana, Dublin, Sete (France), London and Sydney.[47] The modern port of Los Angeles experienced a 75% decrease in labor productivity from 1928 to 1954 due primarily to a work practice-mechanization struggle between labor and management.[48] The unions, or at least the workers, even refuse to relinquish such practices as 'spelling' or 'welting' wherein a few members of the gang are always resting while the others cover for them.[49] Management is therefore reluctant to introduce labor-saving devices when in fact there is no labor saving, because workers refuse to modify old practices.

In contrast, the ILO report urges unions to take the lead in persuading their members to accept technological innovations, while at the same time making acceptable arrangements for the protection of displaced workers. 'Trade unions thus have a vital and indispensable part to play in the creation and maintenance of conditions in which measures to raise productivity can be taken with the support and cooperation of the labor force as a whole.'[50] There are few dock labor unions in the world who have accepted this function. One notable exception is the International Longshoremen's and Warehousemen's Union (ILWU), with headquarters in San Francisco. In the famous 1960 mechanization and modernization agreement between the ILWU and the Pacific Maritime Association (PMA), the union agreed not to interfere with technical change in exchange for job security, good pay and substantial fringe benefits such as early and well-remunerated retirement.[51]

Finally, casual employment on the docks has either produced or attracted men who already possessed attitudes congruent with casualness. Dockers interpret this 'casual frame of mind' as a positive attribute. They are proud of their independent spirit and freedom from routine. They despise the dull, repetitious demands of most jobs. Consequently, among longshoremen there is likely to be a greater range of independent thought and action than among other labor groups. There is also likely to be a higher proportion of individuals engaged in significant creative endeavors. San Francisco dockers point to their Eric Hoffer as a case in point.

The more widely published interpretation of the 'casual frame of mind' is not so flattering to the dockworker. 'It would indeed be surprising if the casual system of employment in the docks did not induce a more irresponsible attitude than that in industry generally. Casual labour produces a casual attitude. If the employer does not provide work unless he wants to, why should the employee go to work unless he wants to? If a man is used to having work one day and none the next, is there anything very wrong about taking a day off of his own choice, whether for his own pleasure or to air a grievance by a token strike?'[52]

Crichton considers the casual longshoremen 'opportunists'.[53] The ILO report agrees that casualness breeds irresponsibility toward one's job and employer. One of the consequences among dockworkers is poor work discipline. 'This lack of discipline may show itself in a number of ways, including unauthorized rest periods during work, late starts, knocking off early, spelling, go-slow tactics, and, in some ports, pilfering.'[54] Kerr and Siegel explain that the longshoremen 'do not aim to be more considerate of the general community than they think the general community is of them'.[55]

The subcultural characteristics of the dockworker as presented above may be expected to become more prevalent in the non-collective developing countries. As the two key conditions of casual employment and geographical isolation disappear in the more developed countries, regardless of the political-economic system, the previously described idiosyncrasies of the dock laborers as a group can be expected to fade away.

The argument in this paper is akin to the one proposed by Professor Alex Inkeles in his 1960 article, 'Industrial Man'.[56] Inkeles contends 'that the distinctive roles of the industrial system . . . foster typical patterns of perception, opinions, beliefs, and values which are not institutionally prescribed but arise spontaneously as new subcultures in response to the institutional conditions.

. . .'[57] These institutional conditions take their 'form from the occupational structure'. Industrialism is not the same everywhere, and cultural and personal factors have their influence. Nevertheless, the movement toward similarity predominates, and as a consequence the resultant occupational subcultures share some characteristics that cross national and cultural boundaries. . . .

NOTES

1. My thanks to the ILWU for their cooperation and to my colleague, Stanley Bailis, for his helpful comments.
2. Milton Gordon, 'The Subsociety and the Subculture,' in *Assimilation in American Life* (Oxford University Press, New York, 1964), chap. ii, p. 41.
3. Herbert J. Gans, 'The Subculture of the Working Class, Lower Class, and Middle Class', in *The Urban Villagers* (Free Press, New York, 1962), chap. 11, p. 243.
4. Seymour Martin Lipset, *Political Man: The Social Bases of Politics* (Doubleday & Co. Inc., New York, 1960), pp. 408, 432–3.
5. *Third ILWU Overseas Report to the 16th Biennial Convention of the International Longshoremen's and Warehousemen's Union* (Vancouver, British Columbia, 1965), p. 12.
6. *Ibid.*, p. 54.
7. *Official Reports of the ILWU Overseas Delegates to the 14th Biennial Convention of the International Longshoremen's and Warehouseman's Union* (Honolulu, Hawaii, 1961), p. 45.
8. Inland Transport Committee, ILO, *Methods of Improving Organization of Work and Output in Ports* (Geneva, 1956).
9. Richard Sasuly, 'Why They Stick to the ILA', *Monthly Review* (Jan. 1956), p. 370.
10. Clark Kerr and Abraham Siegel, 'The Interindustry Propensity to Strike—an International Comparison', *Industrial Conflict,* Kornhauser, Dublin and Ross, eds. (McGraw-Hill Book Co., New York, 1954), p. 191.
11. Virtually all observers identify this source. In particular, see Charles Barnes, *The Longshoremen* (Russell Sage Foundation, New York, 1915); Boris Stern, *Cargo Handling and Longshore Labor Conditions,* Bureau of Labor Statistics Bulletin No. 550 (U.S. Government Printing Office, Washington, D.C., 1932); Edward Swanstrom, *The Waterfront Labor Problem* (Fordham University Press, New York, 1938); The Department of Social Science, University of Liverpool, *The Dock Worker* (Liverpool University Press, Liverpool, 1956); Inland Transport Committee, ILO, *op. cit.;* and Ministry of Labour, *Final Report of the Committee of Inquiry under the Rt. Hon. Lord Devlin into certain matters concerning the Port Transport Industry,* Command Paper No. 2734 (Her Majesty's Stationery Office, London, 1965).
12. *Ibid.*, and A. J. Crichton, 'Industrial Relations in the Ports', *The Journal of the Institute of Transport* (January 1963), pp. 43–7.
13. Kerr and Siegel, *op. cit.,* p. 192, and Betty Schneider and Abraham Siegel, *Industrial Relations in the Pacific Coast Longshore Industry* (University of California Press, Berkeley, 1956), p. 37.
14. Ministry of Labour, *op. cit.,* pp. 4–11, and Charles Larrowe, *Shape-Up and Hiring Hall* (University of California Press, Berkeley, 1955).
15. Lincoln Fairley, Research Director, ILWU, interview November 1965, and *ILWU Overseas Reports.*

16. Elizabeth Ogg, *Longshoremen and Their Homes* (Greenwich House, New York, 1939), p. 48.
17. Department of Social Science, University of Liverpool, *op. cit.*, p. 50.
18. Henry Mayhew, *London Labor and the London Poor,* Vol. III (London, 1861), p. 313, quoted in Stern, *op. cit.*, p. 71.
19. Harry Bridges and William Glazier, 'Report on Port Operations and Union Structure in Europe, Middle East and U.S.S.R.', ILWU (Seattle, 1959), mimeograph, p. 25.
20. *Ibid.,* p. 13.
21. Ministry of Labour, *op. cit.,* Part I.
22. Crichton, *op. cit.,* p. 45.
23. Kerr and Siegel, *op. cit.,* p. 192.
24. *Op. cit.,* p. 54.
25. Farid Ahmed, Manager, Muhammadi Steamship Company, Karachi, interview, February 26, 1962.
26. Inland Transport Committee, ILO, *op. cit.,* pp. 69-70; Stern, *op. cit.,* p. 73; and Ogg, *op. cit.,* p. 19.
27. Ministry of Labour, *op. cit.,* p. 6.
28. *Ibid.,* pp. 10-11, and Inland Transport Committee, ILO, *op. cit.,* pp. 67-70.
29. Bennett Berger, 'Suburbs, Subcultures and the Urban Future', *Planning for a Nation of Cities,* Sam Bass Warner, Jr., ed. (M.I.T. Press, Cambridge, Mass, 1966), pp. 143-6.
30. Lipset, *op. cit.,* pp. 410-11.
31. *A Theory of the Labor Movement* (New York: Augustus M. Kelley, 1949 edition), p. 275.
32. Ministry of Labour, *op. cit.,* p. 8.
33. *Ibid.,* p. 8.
34. Inland Transport Committee, ILO, *op. cit.,* p. 78.
35. Department of Social Science, University of Liverpool, *op. cit.,* p. 90.
36. Barnes, *op. cit.;* Schneider and Siegel, *op. cit.;* and Ministry of Labour, *op. cit.*
37. Department of Social Science, University of Liverpool, *op. cit.,* p. 91.
38. Harry Bridges, President, ILWU (U.S. West Coast Longshoremen's union), interview, July 1957.
39. Barnes, *op. cit.,* p. 93, and James Sydney Slotkin, *From Field to Factory* (Free Press, Glencoe, Illinois, 1960), p. 118.
40. Kerr and Siegel, *op. cit.,* p. 193.
41. *Ibid.,* p. 193.
42. Kerr and Siegel, *op. cit.,* p. 190. Countries: Australia, Czechoslovakia, Germany, Italy, the Netherlands, New Zealand, Norway, Sweden, Switzerland, United Kingdom and the United States.
43. *ILWU Overseas Reports.*
44. 'Jack Dash: The Rise of a Dockland Leader', *The Illustrated London News,* August 28, 1965, pp. 24-5.
45. *Second ILWU Overseas Report,* p. 36.
46. Lipset, *op. cit.,* p. 200.
47. Inland Transport Committee, ILO, *op. cit.,* pp. 30, 155.
48. Charles Sauerbier, 'Education in Cargo Operations', *Progress in Cargo Handling* (Iliffe & Sons, London, 1955), p. 292.
49. Ministry of Labour, *op. cit.,* pp. 11-17.
50. Inland Transport Committee, ILO, *op. cit.,* p. 35.
51. Otto Hagel and Louis Goldblatt, *Men and Machines: A Story about Longshoring on the West Coast Waterfront* (ILWU-PMA, San Francisco, 1963).
52. Ministry of Labour, *op. cit.,* p. 8.

53. *Op. cit.*, p. 45.
54. Inland Transport Committee, ILO, *op. cit.*, p. 30.
55. *Op. cit.*, p. 193.
56. Alex Inkeles, 'Industrial Man: The Relation of Status to Experience, Perception, and Value', *The American Journal of Sociology* (July 1960), pp. 1–31.
57. *Ibid.*, p. 1.

THE CULTURE OF POVERTY

Oscar Lewis

This selection by Oscar Lewis is probably the most widely cited article
ever written on poverty. Lewis first mentioned the "subculture of poverty"
(later shortened to "culture") in his book *Five Families* (1959), describing
the daily lives of five Mexico City households. The concept appears again
in his *Children of Sanchez* (1961), and later in its fully developed form in
the introduction to *La Vida: A Puerto Rican Family in the Culture of
Poverty* (1966), and in an article in *Scientific American* in 1965.

Through the "culture of poverty" Lewis attempts to show that poverty
is not just a matter of economic deprivation but that it also involves
behavioral and personality traits. Once people adapt to poverty, attitudes
and behaviors that initially developed in response to economic deprivation
are passed on to subsequent generations through socialization. The
implication that poverty is cultural has been severely criticized, as is
discussed in the introduction to part five and in Eames and Goode's essay
("The Culture of Poverty: A Misapplication of Anthropology to
Contemporary Issues").

Although a great deal has been written about poverty and the poor, the concept
of a culture of poverty is relatively new. I first suggested it in 1959 in my book
Five Families: Mexican Case Studies in the Culture of Poverty. The phrase is
a catchy one and has become widely used and misused. Michael Harrington
used it extensively in his book *The Other America,* which played an important
role in sparking the national anti-poverty program in the United States.
However, he used it in a somewhat broader and less technical sense than I had
intended. I shall try to define it more precisely as a conceptual model, with special emphasis upon the distinction between poverty and the culture of poverty.
The absence of intensive anthropological studies of poor families from a wide
variety of national and cultural contexts, and especially from the socialist countries, is a serious handicap in formulating valid cross-cultural regularities. The
model presented here is therefore provisional and subject to modification as
new studies become available.

Throughout recorded history, in literature, in proverbs and in popular say-
ings, we find two opposite evaluations of the nature of the poor. Some
characterize the poor as blessed, virtuous, upright, serene, independent, honest,
kind and happy. Others characterize them as evil, mean, violent, sordid and

criminal. These contradictory and confusing evaluations are also reflected in the in-fighting that is going on in the current war against poverty. Some stress the great potential of the poor for self-help, leadership and community organization, while others point to the sometimes irreversible, destructive effect of poverty upon individual character, and therefore emphasize the need for guidance and control to remain in the hands of the middle class, which presumably has better mental health.

These opposing views reflect a political power struggle between competing groups. However, some of the confusion results from the failure to distinguish between poverty *per se* and the culture of poverty and the tendency to focus upon the individual personality rather than upon the group—that is, the family and the slum community.

As an anthropologist I have tried to understand poverty and its associated traits as a culture or, more accurately, as a subculture with its own structure and rationale, as a way of life which is passed down from generation to generation along family lines. This view directs attention to the fact that the culture of poverty in modern nations is not only a matter of economic deprivation, of disorganization or of the absence of something. It is also something positive and provides some rewards without which the poor could hardly carry on.

Elsewhere I have suggested that the culture of poverty transcends regional, rural-urban and national differences and shows remarkable similarities in family structure, interpersonal relations, time orientation, value systems and spending patterns. These cross-national similarities are examples of independent invention and convergence. They are common adaptations to common problems.

The culture of poverty can come into being in a variety of historical contexts. However, it tends to grow and flourish in societies with the following set of conditions: (1) a cash economy, wage labor and production for profit; (2) a persistently high rate of unemployment and underemployment for unskilled labor; (3) low wages; (4) the failure to provide social, political and economic organization, either on a voluntary basis or by government imposition, for the low-income population; (5) the existence of a bilateral kinship system rather than a unilateral one; and finally, (6) the existence of a set of values in the dominant class which stresses the accumulation of wealth and property, the possibility of upward mobility and thrift, and explains low economic status as the result of personal inadequacy or inferiority.

The way of life which develops among some of the poor under these conditions is the culture of poverty. It can best be studied in urban or rural slums and can be described in terms of some seventy interrelated social, economic and psychological traits. However, the number of traits and the relationships between them may vary from society to society and from family to family. For example, in a highly literate society, illiteracy may be more diagnostic of the culture of poverty than in a society where illiteracy is widespread and where even the well-to-do may be illiterate, as in some Mexican peasant villages before the revolution.

The culture of poverty is both an adaptation and a reaction of the poor to their marginal position in a class-stratified, highly individuated, capitalistic society. It represents an effort to cope with feelings of hopelessness and despair which develop from the realization of the improbability of achieving success in terms of the values and goals of the larger society. Indeed, many of the traits of the culture of poverty can be viewed as attempts at local solutions for problems not met by existing institutions and agencies because the people are not eligible for them, cannot afford them, or are ignorant or suspicious of them. For example, unable to obtain credit from banks, they are thrown upon their own resources and organize informal credit devices without interest.

The culture of poverty, however, is not only an adaptation to a set of objective conditions of the larger society. Once it comes into existence it tends to perpetuate itself from generation to generation because of its effect on the children. By the time slum children are age six or seven they have usually absorbed the basic values and attitudes of their subculture and are not psychologically geared to take full advantage of changing conditions or increased opportunities which may occur in their lifetime.

Most frequently the culture of poverty develops when a stratified social and economic system is breaking down or is being replaced by another, as in the case of the transition from feudalism to capitalism or during periods of rapid technological change. Often it results from imperial conquest in which the native social and economic structure is smashed and the natives are maintained in a servile colonial status, sometimes for many generations. It can also occur in the process of detribalization, such as that now going on in Africa.

The most likely candidates for the culture of poverty are the people who come from the lower strata of a rapidly changing society and are already partially alienated from it. Thus landless rural workers who migrate to the cities can be expected to develop a culture of poverty much more readily than migrants from stable peasant villages with a well-organized traditional culture. In this connection there is a striking contrast between Latin America, where the rural population long ago made the transition from a tribal to a peasant society, and Africa, which is still close to its tribal heritage. The more corporate nature of many of the African tribal societies, in contrast to Latin American rural communities, and the persistence of village ties tend to inhibit or delay the formation of a full-blown culture of poverty in many of the African towns and cities. The special conditions of apartheid in South Africa, where the migrants are segregated into separate "locations" and do not enjoy freedom of movement, create special problems. Here the institutionalization of repression and discrimination tends to develop a greater sense of identity and group consciousness.

The culture of poverty can be studied from various points of view: the relationship between the subculture and the larger society; the nature of the slum community; the nature of the family; and the attitudes, values and character structure of the individual.

1. The lack of effective participation and integration of the poor in the major

institutions of the larger society is one of the crucial characteristics of the culture of poverty. This is a complex matter and results from a variety of factors which may include lack of economic resources, segregation and discrimination, fear, suspicion or apathy, and the development of local solutions for problems. However, "participation" in some of the institutions of the larger society—for example, in the jails, the army and the public relief system—does not *per se* eliminate the traits of the culture of poverty. In the case of a relief system which barely keeps people alive, both the basic poverty and the sense of hopelessness are perpetuated rather than eliminated.

Low wages, chronic unemployment and underemployment lead to low income, lack of property ownership, absence of savings, absence of food reserves in the home, and a chronic shortage of cash. These conditions reduce the possibility of effective participation in the larger economic system. And as a response to these conditions we find in the culture of poverty a high incidence of pawning of personal goods, borrowing from local moneylenders at usurious rates of interest, spontaneous informal credit devices organized by neighbors, the use of second-hand clothing and furniture, and the pattern of frequent buying of small quantities of food many times a day as the need arises.

People with a culture of poverty produce very little wealth and receive very little in return. They have a low level of literacy and education, usually do not belong to labor unions, are not members of political parties, generally do not participate in the national welfare agencies, and make very little use of banks, hospitals, department stores, museums or art galleries. They have a critical attitude toward some of the basic institutions of the dominant classes, hatred of the police, mistrust of government and those in high position, and a cynicism which extends even to the church. This gives the culture of poverty a high potential for protest and for being used in political movements aimed against the existing social order.

People with a culture of poverty are aware of middle-class values, talk about them and even claim some of them as their own, but on the whole they do not live by them. Thus it is important to distinguish between what they say and what they do. For example, many will tell you that marriage by law, by the church, or by both, is the ideal form of marriage, but few will marry. To men who have no steady jobs or other sources of income, who do not own property and have no wealth to pass on to their children, who are present-time oriented and who want to avoid the expense and legal difficulties involved in formal marriage and divorce, free union or consensual marriage makes a lot of sense. Women will often turn down offers of marriage because they feel it ties them down to men who are immature, punishing and generally unreliable. Women feel that consensual union gives them a better break; it gives them some of the freedom and flexibility that men have. By not giving the fathers of their children legal status as husbands, the women have a stronger claim on their children if they decide to leave their men. It also gives women exclusive rights to a house or any other property they may own.

2. When we look at the culture of poverty on the local community level, we find poor housing conditions, crowding, gregariousness, but above all a minimum of organization beyond the level of the nuclear and extended family. Occasionally there are informal, temporary groupings or voluntary associations within slums. The existence of neighborhood gangs which cut across slum settlements represents a considerable advance beyond the zero point of the continuum that I have in mind. Indeed, it is the low level of organization which gives the culture of poverty its marginal and anachronistic quality in our highly complex, specialized, organized society. Most primitive peoples have achieved a higher level of socio-cultural organization than our modern urban slum dwellers.

In spite of the generally low level of organization, there may be a sense of community and *esprit de corps* in urban slums and in slum neighborhoods. This can vary within a single city, or from region to region or country to country. The major factors influencing this variation are the size of the slum, its location and physical characteristics, length of residence, incidence of home and land-ownership (versus squatter rights), rentals, ethnicity, kinship ties, and freedom or lack of freedom of movement. When slums are separated from the surrounding area by enclosing walls or other physical barriers, when rents are low and fixed and stability of residence is great (twenty or thirty years), when the population constitutes a distinct ethnic, racial or language group, is bound by ties of kinship or *compadrazgo*, and when there are some internal voluntary associations, then the sense of local community approaches that of a village community. In many cases this combination of favorable conditions does not exist. However, even where internal organization and *esprit de corps* are at a bare minimum and people move around a great deal, a sense of territoriality develops which sets off the slum neighborhoods from the rest of the city. In Mexico City and San Juan this sense of territoriality results from the unavailability of low-income housing outside the slum areas. In South Africa the sense of territoriality grows out of the segregation enforced by the government, which confines the rural migrants to specific locations.

3. On the family level the major traits of the culture of poverty are the absence of childhood as a specially prolonged and protected stage in the life cycle, early initiation into sex, free unions or consensual marriages, a relatively high incidence of the abandonment of wives and children, a trend toward female- or mother-centered families and consequently a much greater knowledge of maternal relatives, a strong predisposition to authoritarianism, lack of privacy, verbal emphasis upon family solidarity which is only rarely achieved because of sibling rivalry, and competition for limited goods and maternal affection.

4. On the level of the individual the major characteristics are a strong feeling of marginality, of helplessness, of dependence and of inferiority. I found this to be true of slum dwellers in Mexico City and San Juan among families who do not constitute a distinct ethnic or racial group and who do not suffer from racial discrimination. In the United States, of course, the culture of poverty of

the Negroes has the additional disadvantage of racial discrimination, but as I have already suggested, this additional disadvantage contains a great potential for revolutionary protest and organization which seems to be absent in the slums of Mexico City or among the poor whites in the South.

Other traits include a high incidence of maternal deprivation, of orality, of weak ego structure, confusion of sexual identification, a lack of impulse control, a strong present-time orientation with relatively little ability to defer gratification and to plan for the future, a sense of resignation and fatalism, a widespread belief in male superiority, and a high tolerance for psychological pathology of all sorts.

People with a culture of poverty are provincial and locally oriented and have very little sense of history. They know only their own troubles, their own local conditions, their own neighborhood, their own way of life. Usually they do not have the knowledge, the vision or the ideology to see the similarities between their problems and those of their counterparts elsewhere in the world. They are not class-conscious, although they are very sensitive indeed to status distinctions.

When the poor become class-conscious or active members of trade-union organizations, or when they adopt an internationalist outlook on the world, they are no longer part of the culture of poverty, although they may still be desperately poor. Any movement, be it religious, pacifist or revolutionary, which organizes and gives hope to the poor and effectively promotes solidarity and a sense of identification with larger groups destroys the psychological and social core of the culture of poverty. In this connection, I suspect that the civil rights movement among the Negroes in the United States has done more to improve their self-image and self-respect than have their economic advances, although, without doubt, the two are mutually reinforcing.

The distinction between poverty and the culture of poverty is basic to the model described here. There are degrees of poverty and many kinds of poor people. The culture of poverty refers to one way of life shared by poor people in given historical and social contexts. The economic traits which I have listed for the culture of poverty are necessary but not sufficient to define the phenomena I have in mind. There are a number of historical examples of very poor segments of the population which do not have a way of life that I would describe as a subculture of poverty. Here I should like to give four examples:

1. Many of the primitive or preliterate peoples studied by anthropologists suffer from dire poverty which is the result of poor technology and/or poor natural resources, or of both, but they do not have the traits of the subculture of poverty. Indeed, they do not constitute a subculture because their societies are not highly stratified. In spite of their poverty they have a relatively integrated, satisfying and self-sufficient culture. Even the simplest food-gathering and hunting tribes have a considerable amount of organization, bands and band chiefs, tribal councils and local self-government—traits which are not found in the culture of poverty.

2. In India the lower castes (the Chamars, the leather workers, and the

Bhangis, the sweepers) may be desperately poor, both in the villages and in the cities, but most of them are integrated into the larger society and have their own *panchayat* organizations (a formal organization designed to provide caste leadership) which cut across village lines and give them a considerable amount of power. (It may be that in the slums of Calcutta and Bombay an incipient culture of poverty is developing. It would be highly desirable to do family studies there as a crucial test of the culture-of-poverty hypothesis.) In addition to the caste system, which gives individuals a sense of identity and belonging, there is still another factor, the clan system. Wherever there are unilateral kinship systems or clans one would not expect to find the culture of poverty, because a clan system gives people a sense of belonging to a corporate body with a history and a life of its own, thereby providing a sense of continuity, a sense of a past and of a future.

3. The Jews of eastern Europe were very poor, but they did not have many of the traits of the culture of poverty because of their tradition of literacy, the great value placed upon learning, the organization of the community around the rabbi, the proliferation of local voluntary associations, and their religion, which taught that they were the chosen people.

4. My fourth example is speculative and relates to socialism. On the basis of my limited experience in one socialist country—Cuba—and on the basis of my reading, I am inclined to believe that the culture of poverty does not exist in the socialist countries. I first went to Cuba in 1947 as a visiting professor for the State Department. At that time I began a study of a sugar plantation in Melena del Sur and of a slum in Havana. After the Castro Revolution I made my second trip to Cuba as a correspondent for a major magazine, and I revisited the same slum and some of the same families. The physical aspect of the slum had changed very little, except for a beautiful new nursery school. It was clear that the people were still desperately poor, but I found much less of the despair, apathy and hopelessness which are so diagnostic of urban slums in the culture of poverty. [The slum dwellers] expressed great confidence in their leaders and hope for a better life in the future. The slum itself was now highly organized, with block committees, educational committees, party committees. The people had a new sense of power and importance. They were armed and were given a doctrine which glorified the lower class as the hope of humanity. (I was told by one Cuban official that they had practically eliminated delinquency by giving arms to the delinquents!)

It is my impression that the Castro regime—unlike Marx and Engels—did not write off the so-called lumpen proletariat as an inherently reactionary and anti-revolutionary force, but rather saw its revolutionary potential and tried to utilize it. In this connection, Frantz Fanon makes a similar evaluation of the role of the lumpen proletariat based upon his experience in the Algerian struggle for independence. In his recently published book he wrote:

> It is within this mass of humanity, this people of the shanty towns, at the core of the lumpen proletariat, that the rebellion will find its urban spearhead. For the lumpen

proletariat, that horde of starving men, uprooted from their tribe and from their clan, constitutes one of the most spontaneous and most radically revolutionary forces of a colonized people.

My own studies of the urban poor in the slums of San Juan do not support the generalizations of Fanon. I have found very little revolutionary spirit or radical ideology among low-income Puerto Ricans. On the contrary, most of the families I studied were quite conservative politically and about half of them were in favor of the Republican Statehood Party. It seems to me that the revolutionary potential of people with a culture of poverty will vary considerably according to the national context and the particular historical circumstances. In a country like Algeria which was fighting for its independence, the lumpen proletariat was drawn into the struggle and became a vital force. However, in countries like Puerto Rico, in which the movement for independence has very little mass support, and in countries like Mexico which achieved their independence a long time ago and are now in their postrevolutionary period, the lumpen proletariat is not a leading source of rebellion or of revolutionary spirit.

In effect, we find that in primitive societies and in caste societies, the culture of poverty does not develop. In socialist, fascist and in highly developed capitalist societies with a welfare state, the culture of poverty flourishes in, and is generic to, the early free-enterprise stage of capitalism and . . . is also endemic in colonialism.

It is important to distinguish between different profiles in the subculture of poverty depending upon the national context in which these subcultures are found. If we think of the culture of poverty primarily in terms of the factor of integration in the larger society and a sense of identification with the great tradition of that society, or with a new emerging revolutionary tradition, then we will not be surprised that some slum dwellers with a lower per capita income may have moved farther away from the core characteristics of the culture of poverty than others with a higher per capita income. For example, Puerto Rico has a much higher per capita income than Mexico, yet Mexicans have a deeper sense of identity.

I have listed fatalism and a low level of aspiration as one of the key traits for the subculture of poverty. Here too, however, the national context makes a big difference. Certainly the level of aspiration of even the poorest sector of the population in a country like the United States with its traditional ideology of upward mobility and democracy is much higher than in more backward countries like Ecuador and Peru, where both the ideology and the actual possibilities of upward mobility are extremely limited and where authoritarian values still persist in both the urban and rural milieus.

Because of the advanced technology, high level of literacy, the development of mass media and the relatively high aspiration level of all sectors of the population, especially when compared with underdeveloped nations, I believe that although there is still a great deal of poverty in the United States (estimates range from thirty to fifty million people), there is relatively little of what I would call the culture of poverty. My rough guess would be that only about 20 percent of the population below the poverty line (between six and ten million people) in the United States have characteristics which would justify classifying their way of life as that of a culture of poverty. Probably the largest sector within this group would consist of very low-income Negroes, Mexicans, Puerto Ricans, American Indians and Southern poor whites. The relatively small number of people in the United States with a culture of poverty is a positive factor because it is much more difficult to eliminate the culture of poverty than to eliminate poverty *per se*.

Middle-class people, and this would certainly include most social scientists, tend to concentrate on the negative aspects of the culture of poverty. They tend to associate negative valences [with] such traits as present-time orientation and concrete versus abstract orientation. I do not intend to idealize or romanticize the culture of poverty. As someone has said, "It is easier to praise poverty than to live in it"; yet some of the positive aspects which may flow from these traits must not be overlooked. Living in the present may develop a capacity for spontaneity and adventure, for the enjoyment of the sensual, the indulgence of impulse, which is often blunted in the middle-class, future-oriented man. Perhaps it is this reality of the moment which the existentialist writers are so desperately trying to recapture but which the culture of poverty experiences as natural, everyday phenomena. The frequent use of violence certainly provides a ready outlet for hostility so that people in the culture of poverty suffer less from repression than does the middle class.

In the traditional view, anthropologists have said that culture provides human beings with a design for living, with a ready-made set of solutions for human problems so that individuals don't have to begin all over again each generation. That is, the core of culture is its positive adaptive function. I, too, have called attention to some of the adaptive mechanisms in the culture of poverty—for example, the low aspiration level helps to reduce frustration, the legitimization of short-range hedonism makes possible spontaneity and enjoyment. However, on the whole it seems to me that it is a relatively thin culture. There is a great deal of pathos, suffering and emptiness among those who live in the culture of poverty. It does not provide much support or long-range satisfaction and its encouragement of mistrust tends to magnify helplessness and isolation. Indeed, the poverty of culture is one of the crucial aspects of the culture of poverty.

The concept of the culture of poverty provides a high level of generalization which, hopefully, will unify and explain a number of phenomena viewed as distinctive characteristics of racial, national or regional groups. For example, matrifocality, a high incidence of consensual unions and a high percentage of households headed by women, which have been thought to be distinctive of Caribbean family organization or of Negro family life in the U.S.A., turn out to be traits of the culture of poverty and are found among diverse peoples in many parts of the world and among peoples who have had no history of slavery.

The concept of a cross-societal subculture of poverty enables us to see that many of the problems we think of as distinctively our own or distinctively Negro problems (or that of any other special racial or ethnic group) also exist in countries where there are no distinct ethnic minority groups. This suggests that the elimination of physical poverty *per se* may not be enough to eliminate the culture of poverty which is a whole way of life.

What is the future of the culture of poverty? In considering this question, one must distinguish between those countries in which it represents a relatively small segment of the population and those in which it constitutes a very large one. Obviously the solutions will differ in these two situations. In the United States, the major solution proposed by planners and social workers in dealing with multiple-problem families and the so-called hard core of poverty has been to attempt slowly to raise their level of living and to incorporate them into the middle class. Wherever possible, there has been some reliance upon psychiatric treatment.

In the underdeveloped countries, however, where great masses of people live in the culture of poverty, a social-work solution does not seem feasible. Because of the magnitude of the problem, psychiatrists can hardly begin to cope with it. They have all they can do to care for their own growing middle class. In these countries the people with a culture of poverty may seek a more revolutionary solution. By creating basic structural changes in society, by redistributing wealth, by organizing the poor and giving them a sense of belonging, of power and of leadership, revolutions frequently succeed in abolishing some of the basic characteristics of the culture of poverty even when they do not succeed in abolishing poverty itself.

THE CULTURE OF POVERTY: A MISAPPLICATION OF ANTHROPOLOGY TO CONTEMPORARY ISSUES

Edwin Eames and Judith Goode

Edwin Eames and Judith Goode critically assess Lewis's culture-of-poverty concept, offering an insightful analysis of the conceptual, theoretical, and ethical limitations of Lewis's formulation. Beyond this, they comment on anthropological research among the poor. They question whether the study of urban poverty belongs within urban anthropology at all, for poverty is not unique to cities but is generated by modern industrial society.

In almost every volume that has appeared in the rather loosely confederated field of urban anthropology, there is a section devoted to the "Culture of Poverty" concept. Therefore, we would assume that this topic is also included in most urban anthropology courses. The issue of the culture of poverty, the development of the concept, its potential as an explanatory device, and its policy implications, particularly in American society, have all received considerable critical attention in the recent literature.

We feel that a discussion of this concept will serve as a classic illustration of what *not* to do in an emerging urban anthropology. In addition, problems of ethics, methodology, units of analysis, and application of traditional anthropological concepts to complex society can be clarified and illustrated in this discussion.

The development of the culture of poverty concept is intimately linked to the work of Oscar Lewis. . . . The criticisms we make of the culture of poverty concept deal with only one aspect of Lewis's work. His total life's work included many significant contributions, including peasant village studies using innovative data-collecting techniques and further innovations in his studies of slum residents. He was a pioneer in the development of the intensive focus on the family unit in the city, and his development of the method of portraying the "typical day" and the life cycles of individuals did much to accentuate the hu-

SOURCE: Edwin Eames, Judith Granich Goode, *Anthropology of the City: An Introduction to Urban Anthropology,* © 1977 by Prentice-Hall, Inc., pp. 304-319. Adapted by permission of the authors.

320

manistic emphasis of anthropology. His informants were portrayed as real people, and Lewis has received kudos for his incisive biographical portrayals. However, the repercussions of his culture of poverty concept often seem to overshadow the positive contributions of his career.

We can see that Lewis began his career by attacking Redfield's folk society and folk-urban dichotomy; he continued by doing ethnographic studies in Mexico City which initially emphasized strong persistence of organization (family, *compadrazgo*, religion), only later to shift to an almost exclusive concern with the Mexican and Puerto Rican underclasses. These studies culminated in the development of the culture of poverty concept, in which he described the families he studied in terms of their disorganization and pathologies.

Lewis thus became the target of attack in much the same way that Redfield was earlier, when Lewis led the attack. Beginning his career by attacking overgeneralized and weakly documented concepts, Lewis ends his career being attacked for the same reasons. Beginning his work with a direct assault upon the concepts of social disorder and disorganization, he ends his career creating similar models of disorganization for the culture of poverty.

A further peculiarity in the development of Lewis's work is that, in his earlier criticisms of Redfield's folk society concept, he used a variety of scientific and empirically based arguments, which were quite effective. But in the development of his own concept, he made the very same errors of overgeneralization and non-empiricism that he discovered in Redfield's work. . . .

THE CULTURE OF POVERTY CONCEPT

Lewis suggests that the culture of poverty is an integrated set of values, norms, and behaviors characteristic of some of those who live in poverty conditions. It is found in an industrial/capitalist society characterized by a cash economy, production for profit, social mobility, and high rates of underemployment and unemployment. It should be noted that Lewis himself sees the culture of poverty as a response to *industrial capitalism* and *not* to the *urban*. Lewis does not imply that the nature of the city influences the development of the culture of poverty, but many others assume that since his work is done in urban areas, he is implying that poverty and the culture of poverty are *urban* phenomena.

Lewis claims that there are some seventy traits that are diagnostic of those in the culture of poverty. These are subdivided into four subcategories: the nature of integration with the larger society, the nature of the slum community, the nature of the family, and the nature of the individual personality.

Under the category labelled relationship to the larger society, Lewis notes the general lack of participation in the institutions of the larger society (political parties, labor unions, health, education, financial, and cultural institutions). Prisons, courts, and welfare systems, however, are institutions where the poor are overrepresented. He notes that distrust and hostility toward these institutions is also extended toward the church.

Regarding the nature of the community, Lewis notes a lack of organization beyond the family level, but offers little in the way of a description of the community level.

The family is described as a "partial" structure, with high rates of consensual (or informal) unions, desertion, and separation, as well as female-based households. Some of the characteristics of the household units were overcrowding and lack of privacy.

At the individual level, those in the culture of poverty are seen as present-time oriented and fatalistic. They have "weak ego structures" and ambiguity about sex roles, despite an emphasis on masculinity. These latter attributes are allegedly related to maternal deprivation. Certain individual characteristics are related to the nature of the life cycle: an early initiation into sex and a relatively short period of childhood (the period during which the child is protected and dependent).

Lewis includes in his description a number of economic characteristics unrelated to the four-fold classification. These would include high rates of underemployment and unemployment, low wages when employed, frequent purchases of small quantities of goods, lack of savings, borrowing at usurious rates, small-scale informal credit mechanisms, pawning, and the use of secondhand goods.

It should be apparent that lack of organization or evidence of disorganization is found at all four levels in the culture of poverty. Lewis suggests that the culture of poverty, once it comes into existence, tends to be perpetuated through time, *regardless of changes in the circumstances of the people.* He views it as a subculture that is transmitted intergenerationally. He indicates that by the time a child is six or seven, he or she has been irreversibly molded into the culture of poverty. Thus, an individual raised in the culture of poverty is viewed as unable to take advantage of changing circumstances.

THE USE OF ANTHROPOLOGICAL CONCEPTS

There are four continuing themes in anthropology that should be carried over into urban anthropology: ethnography, holism, comparison, and relativism. In the next few pages we will discuss Lewis's culture of poverty in terms of each of these themes and the culture concept.

In Lewis's research in Mexico City, the basic techniques of ethnography were used. He obviously was intimately concerned with his informants, and provided us with detailed descriptions of everyday activities and life histories. The research in San Juan is not as clearly ethnographic. . . . Lewis did not live in the community, nor were his contacts with informants as continuous and long-term as those in Mexico City.

Concerning holism, Lewis's work appears to fit the general model in some ways. His emphasis upon the multiplicity of relationships between the culture of poverty and the larger external system that generates it is quite explicit. However, he frequently confuses the two; that is, he includes as part of the culture of the poor aspects of life that are characteristic of the external system, not responses to it. For example, he talks of unemployment as a trait of the culture, when it is the generator of poverty itself. Unfortunately, Lewis develops a trait list rather than a systemic view of the relationships between aspects of the culture. Therefore, what is finally derived as the culture of poverty is a series of characteristics, not carefully linked to one another or to the nature of the larger society.

While Lewis was comparative, in that he compared Mexico City to San Juan, he did not clearly depict the similarities and differences in the nature of both places, as would be required in a controlled comparison. Moreover, the fact that he did not study any non-Hispanic cultural system, and still generalized to all of the Third World on the one hand and the United States on the other, belies the kind of careful comparison required.

A major difficulty with the use of the culture concept in conjunction with poverty (or with any question relating to complex societies) is that the concept of culture has varied and changed over time. Although accepted as basic, the concept has never been successfully defined in a universally accepted way by anthropologists.

In Lewis's use of the culture concept when dealing with poverty, he emphasized the self-perpetuation of the culture of poverty—the notion that children are doomed to the culture of poverty by age six. The use of early childhood socialization as the explanatory device for the transmission of culture has been characteristic of anthropology since its beginning. . . . More recent studies have focused upon this process as a central research problem in order to determine when early socialization is important and when it is not. Lewis, on the other hand, simply accepts early childhood cultural transmission as the only significant enculturation process, without recognizing the issues involved.

In recent times, one sees two emergent views of culture. In one view, culture is a system of cognitive categories or cognitive maps, which individuals carry around in their heads and transmit through symbolic codes. The *sum* of the overlapping elements of individual cognitive maps is *culture*. The other point of view sees culture as a set of adaptive strategies for survival, usually linked to a particular setting of available resources and external constraints. This is an ecological approach to culture.

Lewis does not recognize these two trends and uses a traditional definition of culture as a "way of life." Thus, the ecological approach—the generation of culture and continued culture change resulting from interaction with the ecosystem—is not found in Lewis's formulation. Lewis views the culture of poverty more as a shared set of cognitive maps. He presents a view of the carbon copy recapitulation of a way of life, generation after generation, without any notion of the interaction of this way of life with changing external systems.

For both the cognitive and ecological approaches, the issue of *change* is fundamental. It is generally recognized that modern society is characterized by rapid rates of change, particularly in the technological and economic spheres. Thus, modern culture concepts must be able to deal with change. In Lewis's definition of the culture of poverty, however, the issue is dealt with by suggesting that those in the culture of poverty are relatively immune to changes in the external system. Thus we have a view of cultural traditions which are self-perpetuating and closed to outside influences.

To some degree, the concept of culture can be useful in the study of urban poor. For one thing, it focuses our attention on shared behavioral patterns, rather than on behavior as individually derived. The culture concept can thus be used productively in showing variability of patterned behavioral responses which differ because of the socioeconomic position of a group in the system to which it is responding. Thus, class subcultures or subcultures of occupational status communities can be fruitfully studied. . . .

The aspect of the culture concept that seems least appropriate in the study of urban poverty groups is that which focuses on intergenerational transmission of basic values and belief systems, which serve as the basis of behavioral responses. We would agree that social learning remains as the major process for the transmission of values and beliefs. However, the learning may be intragenerational in peer groups, rather than intergenerational, leading to persistence for over four hundred years as Lewis suggests. Attributing behavioral responses solely to early parent-child socialization seems unwarranted on the basis of empirical data. We need a modified definition of culture that takes into account different temporal durations and intragenerational modes of social transmission in order to understand modern society. . . .

. . . The transposition of the culture concept to the study of whole complex societies presents many difficulties. Any attempt to describe the total culture of large, industrial nation-states—such as Great Britain or Germany—is bound to fail, since there is no easy way of summing up the totality of the way of life in such large-scale, complex societies. . . .

RELATIVISM AND ETHNOCENTRISM

Lewis's concept lacks the perspective of cultural relativism, a conceptual tool which is one of the *strengths* of anthropology. His ethnocentrism shows in his description of the culture of poverty as a *thin* culture and his equation of the culture of poverty with a "poverty of culture." The latter may indeed be a catchy phrase and a neat linguistic aphorism, but it demonstrates an attitude toward a particular segment of society that is pejorative. This attitude carries over into the discussion of traits, many of which Lewis describes as "lack of _____ " rather than describing what is present. It is obvious that Lewis is working from a framework of middle class notions of what *should* exist.

Lewis suggests that those in the culture of poverty lack organization, but he subsequently notes their ability to develop informal credit groups and mutual aid mechanisms. He obviously views organization from a middle class vantage point, which assumes that only formal structures with specific goals are "organized." We have mentioned [elsewhere] that one strength of urban anthropology is its ability to uncover informal structures and networks that have no labels and titles. It is obvious from Lewis's own data that much informal organization does exist, without the formal characteristics of names, officers, and archives.

This ethnocentric view is particularly apparent in Lewis's description of family patterns and personality types. Disregarding diminishing marital stability throughout the entire class spectrum, Lewis focuses on marital instability for this group alone. In characterizing the female-based household as a partial version of the "normal" family, he is neglecting anthropological literature on domestic cycles and domestic variations that tend to occur under certain conditions. In addition, his description of individuals as having weak ego structures, as being fatalistic and present-time oriented, or as having confused sex identities is obviously based upon class-biased psychological models of what constitutes adequate egos, time orientations, and sex identities.

Also he is comparing the middle class *ideals* of planning for the future and deferred gratification with the actual *behavior* of the poor. This is not the same as comparing middle class *behavior* with poverty *behavior*, since recent middle class consumption patterns indicate a lack of concern for the future. Lewis notes that many of those in the culture of poverty hold middle class ideals about the desirability of a stable nuclear family but do not follow their ideals. This same discrepancy between *ideal* and *real* behavior exists for the middle class as well.[1]

In all fairness to Lewis, his informants are portrayed in their own words as sympathetic human beings. However, the culture of poverty concept denigrated their behavior and their beliefs.

WHAT IS URBAN ABOUT THE CULTURE OF POVERTY?

The emphasis upon poverty groups in urban areas in modern and developing societies is primarily the result of an erroneous association of the term *urban anthropology* with the so-called urban crisis, which leads to an interest in the poor, the marginal, and the disenfranchised. Fox has divided urban anthropology into three categories, the largest of which is "the anthropology of poverty."[2] He includes in this category most of the urban ethnographic literature that does not deal with migration or with the city as a whole. One of the trends in early urban anthropology was a concern with social problems and the search for solutions. However, we would maintain that continued overemphasis of this one area will distort the subfield.

Poverty is not an exclusively urban phenomenon, nor is it generated by the nature of cities. Gulick has noted for American society that poverty, racism, and sexism are fundamental characteristics of the larger social system and not merely aspects of urban localities.[3]

Lewis himself explicitly recognizes that the development of the culture of poverty is a consequence of modern industrial capitalist society—with its labor

market, its materialism, and its profit orientation—rather than the urban setting. He suggests that, as traditional agrarian societies follow a capitalist industrial model, a culture of poverty will emerge. However, his poverty research
has been carried out exclusively in urban areas; his selection of the slum community as the geographic locus in which the culture of poverty will be found
does give the concept an urban appearance.

The culture of poverty issue falls more neatly under the rubric of anthropology of *urban industrial society,* rather than anthropology *in* or *of* the city. If
one were tempted to convert this issue to the anthropology *of* cities, then it
would be essential to study the effects of the urban setting on the poverty population. This would be difficult but could be done. The lack of clearly defined
urban poverty research can only lead to a continuing confusion between urbanism, modernism, and industrialism.

METHODOLOGY

In concept formation, there are two mutually interacting processes involved: in-
duction and deduction. The *inductive process* is one in which a concept or
model is derived from prior empirical research. The *deductive process* is one in
which the theorist starts with a series of assumptions, develops a model in a
logical manner, and then tests the concepts or model by doing empirical research. Most philosophers of science distinguish these two modes, but in reality
they are often joined in a process of formulating and testing.

Lewis's concept was derived from his original fieldwork in Mexico City and
was thus inductively derived. Lewis contends that in his later study of Puerto
Rican slum life, he was testing the validity of the concept in a different cultural
setting. It must be noted that the thrust of Lewis's work was the development
of a cross-cultural, generalizable model of the values and behavior of a poverty
segment of the population. However, it does not appear from the work in San
Juan that the model developed earlier was actually tested in the field situation.
What seems to have happened is that Lewis undertook the study in San Juan
with a preconceived notion of what he would find, and then selected from the
available research material those segments that substantiated his original
formulation. This point is apparent in the *La Vida* volume, where we note a
significant discontinuity between the introduction to the volume, where the concept is outlined, and the rest of the volume, where the data are presented.
Rarely do we find in this volume an interplay between theoretical formulation
and empirically derived data, which could serve to sharpen the theoretical focus
and aid in the interpretation of empirical data.

This disassociation between formulation and data is the basis of Valentine's
critique of Lewis. By selecting from the mass of data presented in the body of
the *La Vida* volume, Valentine is able to demonstrate repeatedly areas in
which the behavior of members of the Rios family completely contradicts the
culture of poverty trait list.[4] These obvious contradictions remain unexplored

and unexplained by Lewis and thus become a basic issue related to the validity of the concept.

In terms of research design, Lewis's initial work in Mexico City was a traditional anthropological study without a problem focus. Lewis felt that he had discovered an unexplored constituency for anthropological fieldwork—the urban slum dweller. He was studying the "way of life" of this group in traditional fashion. In his long-range study of this constituency, he developed the culture of poverty notion as a by-product.

When Lewis shifted his research focus to Puerto Rico, he had more clearly formulated a problem—the testing of the culture of poverty model. In this latter formulation, one could say that the culture of poverty is a dependent variable, or the outcome of a set of society-wide conditions, which are independent variables. However, by not explicitly following this kind of logical procedure, he was trapped into the position of viewing the culture of poverty as a self-perpetuating subcultural system.

In the translation of a conceptual formulation into a research design, an important element is the development of ways to define the variables. When we look at the multiplicity of variables that comprise the culture of poverty, we are given no clues as to how most of them are defined.

Another methodological source of confusion in Lewis's work is the lack of any clear-cut separation of those aspects of the larger social system related to the position of the poor in the social system from those aspects that form the culture (or adaptive response to the position). Thus, when Lewis includes within the *traits* of the culture such items as high rates of unemployment, lack of cash reserves, and other situational constraints, he is adding attributes to the dependent variable that really comprise the independent variables.

Problem of Selecting a Unit of Study

In urban research either a particular unit may be selected to study its characteristics, or a problem may be selected to study within the context of the unit as an ethnographic target population. Lewis's tactic is to take the latter approach. However, the research problem—the description of the culture of poverty—cannot be readily disassociated from the social unit. Lewis assumes that the slum is the geographic or spatial unit within which one can study the culture of poverty. He notes that not all slum residents can be characterized in this way. They cannot even all be characterized as poor. But he never selects a pool of poor defined in material terms as the ethnographic target population. He also notes that not all the characteristics of the culture of poverty can be found in any slum group.

Eventually, he narrows the lens through which one sees the culture of poverty to a single family. Once he turns from the slum community to the family as the unit of analysis, the question of whether the family is an appropriate unit for the study of a culture or subculture is immediately raised. If one were to accept Lewis's notion (which we do not) that there is little organization above the family level, then perhaps one could derive a culture or subculture from family studies. However, it would then be incumbent upon Lewis to describe the similarity in values and behavior *among* the families who share the common tradition of the culture of poverty and indicate the means of social transmission, namely, networks and informal social structures. In Lewis's *La Vida* he relies on only one family, and one which he himself states is atypical. He states that the Rios family is characterized by the most "unbridled id" that he has ever observed. Prostitution is also not typical of other families. Thus we have no indication of the extent to which the Rios family represents a shared pattern that could be called a subculture of poverty.

Going beyond Lewis's work in the culture of poverty, it can be suggested that the study of "the poor" as an urban anthropological research problem brings to the fore many basic issues in the selection of units of study. Selecting an inner-city slum, or an irregular community (squatter settlement), or a minority ethnic group as the unit in which to study the behavior of the poor is a basic error. Even communities and ethnic groups that have a high proportion of poor people within them will still contain large numbers of non-poor or temporarily poor, which make such units inappropriate.

Some examples of the inappropriate use of the ethnic minority group as the unit within which to study poverty can be seen in the work of Valentine and Parker and Kleiner.[5] In both cases, the work was used in relation to the culture of poverty concept. Valentine cites the literature on Black Americans in a discussion of the culture of poverty and he seems to make the assumption that Blacks are equivalent to "the poor." Parker and Kleiner use data collected in a previous project on Blacks and mental illness to discuss whether these Blacks have culture of poverty beliefs. This particular work presents two problems. It assumes that being Black is being poor. It also confuses the relationship between racial minority status and poverty status. If the research in a Black population does indicate feelings of hopelessness and fatalism, are these related to being poor or to being in an oppressed underclass?

The problem of selecting an appropriate social unit is also demonstrated in a number of community studies used to refute Lewis, where it is assumed that the neighborhoods selected are equivalent to "the poor." Mangin uses his experiences with *barriadas* (squatter settlements) in Lima, Leeds his data on *favelas* in Rio, and Safa her data on a shantytown in San Juan to disprove the culture of poverty notion. They do not explicitly point out that their communities were, in fact, not equivalent to *the poor*, but contained people of different occupational levels, career directions, and income.[6]

Poverty must be defined in economic terms, since it is basically an economic condition. The consequence of economic deprivation for behavior is the area that must be studied. However, a population defined merely by income characteristics tends to be a social aggregate of unrelated, non-interacting people. Such an aggregate is not a useful ethnographic unit. A search for a common culture among this aggregate is inappropriate.

Probably the very best unit to use in the ethnographic study of poverty and its consequences would be an occupational status community. In every complex society, there are certain low-paying occupations. Those pursuing such occupations would therefore represent a group who live in conditions of poverty, characterized by instability or intermittency of employment. These jobs are frequently time-consuming and/or require heavy physical effort. They are considered menial, dirty, and unpleasant and are frequently viewed by other members of society as defiling to those who pursue them.

In urban areas, specific occupations that would fall into the poverty level category are: non-mechanized construction labor, dockwork, pedicab drivers, porters (carriers of heavy items), domestics, janitors, scavengers, street vendors, and watchmen. In some of these occupations, the individual is self-employed and has relative autonomy over his time and effort. However, the monetary rewards are minimal, unpredictable, and often lead to depending on creditors for survival. In other cases, the individual works for others, often on a day labor basis, so that he or she has no job security and has little control over the work situation. The common thread in all of these jobs is that returns are small, insecure, and sporadic, so that those who do this kind of work live in conditions of material deprivation and insecurity.

Most of the occupations catalogued above abound in cities in societies that are not fully industrialized. Mechanization frequently leads to the elimination of such work. Another way in which some of these occupations are transformed is through unionization and bureaucratization. For example, construction workers and longshoremen, through union organizations, developed the bargaining power to assure them a secure income above the poverty level. Bureaucratic organization of work has eliminated such jobs as the small-scale watchman, replacing him with private and public security organizations, which are hierarchically organized and guarantee employment security and better pay. In the transformation from a preindustrial to a postindustrial society, many occupations formerly characterized by poverty level income and insecurity are eliminated or transformed.

Despite technology and the organization of work, there are still some analogues to these marginal occupations in the industrialized world. These include menial workers in restaurants and hospitals, janitors, domestics, and vestiges of premechanized construction work and commerce. Even when attempts have been made to unionize or bureaucratize day laborers on some of these jobs, they have not been able to prevent high turnover, mass lay-offs, and the poor working conditions that encourage turnover. Furthermore, some powerful unions seek to exploit the organized low-level worker.

Economists recognize that there is a *secondary* labor market in the United States in which jobs are characterized by short-term employment, low wages, and no fringe benefits. In fact, this labor market recruits from a pool of labor characterized by low income, sporadic employment, and job sequences characterized by horizontal movement rather than vertical career progression. The secondary labor market consists of dead-end jobs.

The phenomenon of poverty in contemporary American society is clearly related to an economic system that, under normal economic conditions, assumes an unemployment rate of approximately six percent. A certain segment of this "normal" population of unemployed consists of those who are long-term unemployed (out of work one year or more). Despite a social welfare system that provides some compensation, the amount of income while unemployed is well below the poverty line.

[Drawing on] this discussion, we would contend that the most appropriate social unit within which the urban anthropologist might study the impact of poverty is one based upon occupation or participation in the secondary labor market, rather than a unit based on space or minority status. Interacting units of people in marginal career cycles or long-term unemployed can be studied.[7] The particular effects to be studied could be selected by the particular researcher, but the independent variable—material deprivation—could be clearly defined and measured. Gutkind is one of the few urban anthropologists to use such a unit. He selected the long-term unemployed as an ethnographic target unit in some of his African urban research. His dependent variables were kinship and network ties.[8]

ETHICS AND POLICY IMPLICATIONS

Anthropologists working with an urban population have a commitment to the group with whom they work. Part of this commitment is to avoid generating data and/or analyses that can be used against informants. They should be aware at all times of the consequences of public use of their data and generalizations.

This criterion pertains as well to the culture of poverty concept. Many of those who have attacked the Lewis formulation have done so on the basis of its implications for the development of programs dealing with poverty. It should be noted that at the time Lewis was writing about the concept, a major thrust of American domestic policy was the eradication of poverty. The various programs that were developed in the 1960s to deal with this problem were subsumed under the notion of the "War on Poverty." For those involved in determining what programs could be established to eliminate poverty conditions, there were two major alternatives: either attack the economic system, which created unemployment and underemployment, *or* attack the values and behavior of the poor, which were assumed to be intergenerationally transmitted and which *by themselves* perpetuated poverty by interfering with upward mobility. Although Lewis did accept the larger social system as generating poverty, his emphasis on the self-perpetuation of the culture of poverty was the point of departure for elaboration by those developing specific anti-poverty programs. Thus, many programs of the War on Poverty were designed to change the behavior and values of the poor. These included compensatory education programs, manpower training programs, and community action programs. Since Lewis himself maintains that the only way of changing the culture of poverty in the United States is through a psychiatric or social work approach, his "scientific credentials" reinforced such government programs.

Another reason for the attractiveness of Lewis's formulation to policy makers was that it explained failures in education, health care, and job training programs. If programs failed, the inappropriate values of their clients could be blamed, instead of the ill-conceived or misapplied nature of the program itself. Finally, the concept was broadly accepted because it bolstered the popular view that had developed since the Industrial Revolution that the poor were responsible for their own condition. Lewis, by providing a "scientific" explanation based on notions of intergenerational transmission and early childhood socialization, was reinforcing already existing beliefs.

Another ethical issue is that of national pride. In his later work in Mexico City and San Juan, Lewis's descriptions of the life of the poor offended many Mexicans and Puerto Ricans. They felt his presentation of life in these countries was unbalanced and pejorative. When one reads some of the anti-Lewis statements, and when one is exposed to Puerto Rican students who have read *La Vida,* this national dismay is quite apparent. Since Lewis's work is so widely read by nonprofessionals, many Puerto Ricans feel it has simply reinforced the negative stereotypes of Puerto Ricans held by the American public. As a result of such strong feelings, Lewis became *persona non grata* in both Mexico and Puerto Rico, making further research in these sites impossible for him.

When he popularly disseminated an untested hypothesis, which was then generalized to the total capitalist-industrial world, Lewis acted contrary to the standards for concern about the uses and possible misuses of anthropological studies.

Once again, we must temper this criticism by looking at Lewis's work in the context of its time. The issue of the social responsibility of the anthropologist was not explicitly raised until the latter part of the 1960s.[9] Lewis's work on the urban poor considerably antedated this. In his day, anthropologists sought "knowledge for its own sake." The belief that one owed one's informants something in return or that one must protect them from the potential misuse of data had not become widespread. It is too easy to castigate with hindsight. And Lewis was by no means the only one responsible for developing notions of cultural deprivation and poverty culture. Many other social scientists also developed similar concepts to explain the non-success of the poor.

The Overemphasis on Poverty

In the larger arena of urban anthropology, the body of literature dealing with poverty segments or underclass segments in the city is the most voluminous. . . . Of great concern is the fundamental social science issue of relating poverty to an understanding of the nature of urban centers and urban processes. We have looked at Lewis's work in some detail and noted that in many ways the fundamental issue of the relationship between the urban and poverty is unexplored.

The poverty literature in urban anthropology has been a dead-end literature. One reason for this is that only the lower segments of society were studied. To understand poverty in urban industrial systems or to study the nature of urban centers, one must also understand the middle and dominant groups in the system, and how they relate to each other. The forces in the larger system must also be examined as to their interaction with all social segments (or ethnographic target populations). . . . No social unit—from the level of the microscopic to the macroscopic—is autonomous or independent. To study poverty by focusing entirely upon the poor is to disregard the larger context and the continuous interactive process. . . .

Unfortunately, the publication of Lewis's work and the controversy generated by the culture of poverty concept directed the attention of a disproportionately large number of urban anthropologists to the study of poverty groups. In many cases, these studies were explicitly designed to test and/or refute Lewis's contentions. Another reason for this concentration on the lower segments was because they seemed easy to define and were relatively accessible. The rich can avoid the anthropologist, while the poor do not have the resources to do this. . . .

Another factor that has led to an overemphasis on lower social segments is the concern with rural-urban migration. In fact, migration literature and poverty literature have become inextricably intertwined in many instances. As an example of this, Mangin, as the editor of a volume specifically concerned with migration, devotes most of his introduction to the culture of poverty concept.[10] Not all migrant groups enter the urban arena at the bottom, but few anthropological studies (especially in America) have focused upon any but the lowest segments. . . .

SUMMARY

We have frequently noted the tendency of urban ethnographers to concentrate upon the poorer segments of the urban population. This bias can be seen in the controversy over the culture of poverty concept.

Oscar Lewis's work has been central to this controversy. A pioneering figure in the development of urban anthropology, he focused toward the end of his career almost exclusively upon the study of poverty. From such studies he developed the notion of a common subculture that characterizes segments of the poor population in many areas of the world.

The poverty subculture concept has many theoretical limitations. Many contemporary anthropologists avoid the use of the culture concept, particularly when dealing with complex societies. Most of the core characteristics of the poverty subculture concept have been questioned by other anthropologists as representing a list of traits, many of which are contradictory, not testable, and negative in tone.

Poverty is obviously not an exclusively urban problem, and a culture of poverty—to the extent to which it might exist—is not a particularly urban problem. The inclusion of the literature dealing with this issue under urban anthropology is an error. It does not fall into the category of anthropology *of* the city, or anthropology *in* the city, but rather the anthropology of complex society. . . .

NOTES

1. For an important discussion of the tendency to confuse ideal behavior with real behavior in comparing class subcultures, see S. M. Miller, F. Reissman and A. Seagull, "Poverty and Self-Indulgence: A Critique of the Non-Deferred Gratification Pattern," in L. Ferman et al. (eds.), *Poverty in America* (Ann Arbor: University of Michigan Press, 1965), pp. 416–32.

2. R. Fox, *Cities in Their Cultural Settings* (Englewood Cliffs, N.J.: Prentice-Hall, 1977).

3. J. Gulick, "The Outlook, Research Strategies and Relevance of Urban Anthropology," in E. Eddy (ed.), *Urban Anthropology* (Athens, Georgia: University of Georgia Press, 1968), pp. 93–98.

4. C. Valentine, *Culture and Poverty: A Critique and Counterproposals* (Chicago: University of Chicago Press, 1968).

5. Valentine, *Culture and Poverty*; and S. Parker and R. Kleiner, "The Culture of Poverty: An Adjustive Dimension," *American Anthropologist*, 72 (1970), 516–28.

6. Mangin, *Peasants in Cities* and "Poverty and Politics in the Latin American City," in L. Bloomberg and H. Schmandt (eds.), *Power, Poverty and Urban Policy*, Urban Affairs Annual Review, vol. 2, 1970; Anthony Leeds, "The Concept of the 'Culture of Poverty': Conceptual, Logical and Empirical Problems with Perspectives from Brazil and Peru," in E. Leacock (ed.), *Culture of Poverty: A Critique* (New York: Simon and Schuster, Inc., 1971), pp. 226–84; and Helen Safa, "The Social Isolation of the Urban Poor: Life in a Puerto Rican Shanty Town," in I. Deutscher and E. Thompson (eds.), *Among the People: Encounters with the Poor* (New York: Basic Books, 1968), pp. 335–51.

7. For a discussion of this issue, see E. Eames and J. Goode, *Urban Poverty in a Crosscultural Context* (New York: Free Press, 1973), Chapter 4; J. Goode, "Poverty and Urban Analysis," *Western Canadian Journal of Anthropology*, 3 (1972), 1–19.

8. P. C. W. Gutkind, "The Energy of Despair: Social Organization of the Unemployed in Two African Cities: Lagos and Nairobi," *Civilisations*, 17 (1967), 186–211.

9. G. Berreman, G. Gjessing and K. Gough, "Social Responsibilities Symposium," *Current Anthropology*, 9 (1968), 391–435; Diane Lewis, "Anthropology and Colonialism," *Current Anthropology*, 14 (1973), 581–602.

10. Mangin (ed.), *Peasants in Cities*.

A SOUTH INDIAN CASTE
IN A BOMBAY SLUM

Owen M. Lynch

Indian society is divided along regional, linguistic, sectarian, and caste lines. A "caste" in India is a group of people who become members of the group at birth through biological descent from other members, who share a common name for the group, and who generally do not marry outside the group. There is a ranking of different castes in terms of power, prestige, and ritual purity. Members of lower castes, especially "untouchables," can pollute members of higher castes through contact. This overly simple explanation of caste in India can help explain one of the several identities borne by the Adi-Dravidas, who are a low-ranking caste from southern India and who have migrated to the metropolis of Bombay in West India. In that city, different political parties compete for their votes. One party calls on them to identify as "untouchables," members of the lowest-ranking caste, on an all-India basis; another party bids them to remember their South Indian roots. The way in which the Adi-Dravidas define themselves politically is thus related both to their position in Bombay as rural migrants from another region and to their caste.

Shantinagar,[1] a pseudonym, has a reputation for being one of the worst—if not the worst—slums in Bombay, India. It is inhabited mainly by squatters from all parts of India. Much of the land is swampy but the squatters are slowly filling it in as their settlements creep across vacant space. Low-lying land is often flooded with black, swampy, garbage-laden water during the monsoon season. Perhaps this location has helped make Shantinagar notoriously famous for the steaming stills producing the bootleg liquor which whets many a thirsty tongue in dry Bombay.

One of the first things which hits the eye, when setting foot in Shantinagar and other places like it in Bombay, is the flags of many political parties waving conspicuously in the wind. Picketed here and there are the red and black of the Dravida Munnetra Kazagham (hereafter the DMK), the blue and white of the Republican Party (hereafter RPI), the orange and green of the Congress Party,

SOURCE: Article written expressly for *Urban Life*.

the red of the Shiv Sena and the green of the Muslim League. What does this mean? Are these flags just for show or are they signs of real political life, activity, involvement, and consciousness?

In this paper a partial answer to these questions will be given by looking at them within the context of one of the communities, the Adi-Dravidas, who live in Shantinagar. The Adi-Dravidas of Shantinagar are highly politicized and easily mobilized for political ends, issues and symbols. They are politically conscious, aware and involved. The first purpose of this paper is, then, to describe political life and its extent among these Adi-Dravidas. The second purpose is to explain their high level of political mobilization in terms of an ongoing process which maintains it.

WHO ARE ADI-DRAVIDAS?

Adi-Dravidas are a Tamil-speaking untouchable caste from Madras state in India. In Madras, or as it is now called Tamilnadu, they are also known as Paraiyan, a name supposedly derived from the Tamil word *parai* for drum and from the association of this caste with drumming at village ceremonies and festivals (Thurston 1909:77). None of the Bombay Adi-Dravidas like the name Paraiyan and only reluctantly admit to it. Adi-Dravida is, however, a more acceptable name, although it is also a name which they show some reluctance to use. Adi means first and Dravida means settler in south India. The Adi-Dravidas claim to be the indigenous people of south India—those who were in India long before the Aryans, Brahmans and Indic-speaking peoples invaded and conquered much of what is north India today. Sub-caste differences among Adi-Dravidas have for all purposes been eliminated, although there are occasional rumors of trouble over this. While there are both Christians and Hindus in the community, inter-faith marriages take place without much difficulty.

Adi-Dravidas began migrating to Bombay about 100 years ago. They came to work in Shantinagar's tanneries which at that time were well outside the city's main settlement. To this day almost all Adi-Dravidas come from the same district of Tinnevelly in the south of Tamilnadu state.

The Adi-Dravida population in Shantinagar continues to increase with new migrants coming all the time. Today's migrants, however, are more sophisticated than the pioneer arrivals. Literacy is high and many, both male and female, read and write. Seventy percent (N 42) of male respondents were literate using a fourth standard or better education as a criterion of literacy. Work in the tanneries has decreased and today Adi-Dravidas work in various occupations throughout Bombay. Eighteen percent (N 11) of respondents worked as dock laborers; fifty-eight percent (N 35) as factory workers; and twenty-three percent (N 14) worked in various jobs such as truck driver, small shop owner, etc. Participation in unions is, moreover, relatively high with sixty-three percent (N 38) of respondents claiming union membership and eighty-seven percent (N 33) of these reporting interest in union activities.

MOBILIZATION

On the whole Adi-Dravida political life in Shantinagar is divided between two parties, the DMK and the RPI. The DMK is a regional party which originated and remains primarily in Madras state or Tamilnadu. At the time of study, the DMK had almost complete control of Madras state government and had won enough seats in parliament for Madame Gandhi and the Congress party to take note and consideration of it.

The DMK was founded in Shantinagar about 1950. Today there are fourteen branches for all of Bombay city. Shantinagar is one of these branches. The Bombay general office and the Shantinagar branch office are one and the same. The meeting house is on a small side street off the main road of Shantinagar and is called, appropriately enough, Dravidian House.

The Shantinagar branch office has ten units of the party in various Adi-Dravida chawls or streets throughout the area. While many of these units have meeting houses, not all are tightly organized and active; some are split by factional quarrels. The Shantinagar branch, however, is tightly organized under four men of the community who have respectable white collar jobs elsewhere in Bombay.

What kind of political life do Adi-Dravidas of the DMK have in Shantinagar? First of all the DMK under its leaders can and does mobilize the entire community. The leaders have organizational skills and experience as well as first-hand contacts with party members throughout the area. These contacts are constantly renewed by visits to the other branches and units, as well as by visits of members to Dravidian House. The ability of the leaders to mobilize the community depends to some extent upon the presence of external threat. Adi-Dravidas are south Indians and in Bombay there is a growing feeling against people from the south. Native Maharashtrians feel that the south Indians are taking away from them much needed jobs. This is one of the reasons for the rise of the Shiv Sena, a local party of Maharashtra state. Indeed, the Shiv Sena was at one time strongly anti-south Indian, though its overt expression of this theme was tempered at the time of study.

In 1968 when the Shiv Sena was particularly active, the DMK was the nucleus around which the Adi-Dravidas gathered for protection. There was one incident in which the police and the Adi-Dravidas of Shantinagar clashed. Knives were drawn and in the end a number of police were hurt and about thirty south Indians put in jail. An association was then formed called the South Indian Association and the DMK leaders were particularly active in it. The Association sponsored a dance program in Bombay's Shanmukhananda Hall. Twenty-three thousand rupees were collected to hire lawyers for the imprisoned south Indians. All were acquitted and the lawyers, all non-south Indians, handsomely rewarded.

In 1967 the DMK was able to organize a number of meetings in which money was raised to support the electoral campaign of the DMK back in Madras state. It is reported that eighteen thousand rupees were raised and that Chief Minister Karunanidhi of Tamilnadu came to Shantinagar and delivered a speech.

The leaders of the DMK have also proven themselves within the community. Before the advent of the DMK there was a caste association of the Adi-Dravidas known as the Adi Dravida Mahajana Sangham (Adi-Dravida Peoples Society). This organization had come under the control of one man whose caste-oriented views did not accord with the broader political views of the DMK leaders and their own quest for leadership status. Through some sort of ma-neuvers, which they admit and which I could never definitely uncover, the DMK leaders were able to sidetrack the Sangham leader and reduce his organiza-tion to one virtually in name only.

More striking than these organizational and defensive activities, however, are the rallies and meetings which the DMK is continually running and sponsoring. These events are attended by large crowds of men and children who come to hear politicians have their say. Whether or not one attends, reports of what was said travel quickly and by the next day are the subject of conversation.

During the 1971 elections to the central parliament, meetings of the various parties in Shantinagar, particularly among the Adi-Dravidas, were at a peak. Adi-Dravidas sponsored some events and attended many others of all parties. Before the elections, election lists were checked and potential voters contacted. On election day itself these lists were assiduously checked to get lazy voters and women to the polls, as well as to resurrect the dead and bilocate the terrestrially displaced. Techniques for voting twice or thrice are well known and relished as a form of political gamesmanship. Children were also paid a few cents to go up and down the roads chanting slogans, carry banners, ride on loud speaker trucks, and distribute campaign literature. Socialization into politics is, then, very much a part of becoming an Adi-Dravida in Bombay.

Behind these activities there is a strong ideological pull from the DMK to which the Adi-Dravidas are drawn. The DMK is a sub-national party representing primarily the interests of the Tamil-speaking peoples of Madras state. For the Adi-Dravidas it is, then, a symbol of, as well as organizational contact with, their "native place," their home districts, their linguistic roots and their Tamil culture. Adi-Dravidas are proud to be Dravidians and take pride in telling of the beauties of Tamil language and culture. This is all very important in Bombay where they are immigrants speaking a foreign tongue and possessing a foreign sub-culture. One informant explained this to me thusly:

> We live in Maharashtra state; therefore, if we don't have the party, people will forget their language and culture. Moreover, it does no good if we become like Maharashtrians and learn Marathi and forget our motherland. Why? Because even then we are treated like south Indians and discriminated against.

Thus, the pride in Tamil nationality and the pleasure derived from Tamil lan-guage and culture are strengthened by the need for protective unity and organi-zation. This need the party can and does satisfy not only by its activities and organization but also by day-to-day events. In the party office and in various other places in Dharavi, one can find reading rooms in which copies of Tamil newspapers and magazines are available. These are read avidly and their news and announcements constantly argued. Political interest and contact are thus kept high.

Among the Adi-Dravidas there is some separation of class, as opposed to caste, issues. When asked the question, "Some say the government does not help the hutment-dwelling people because it is in control of the rich people, others say it does not help the hutment people because it is in control of the upper castes, what is your opinion?" eighteen percent (N 11) replied the government was in control of the upper castes, forty-two percent (N 25) replied the rich people, seventeen percent (N 10) replied both, and twenty-three percent (N 14) replied neither. During the 1971 parliamentary elections no other issue generated more enthusiasm or discussion than Madame Gandhi's promise to eliminate poverty. This issue, as no other, generated a consciousness of kind which temporarily crossed caste, ethnic, and religious boundaries in Shantinagar.

The ideology of the DMK appeals to the Adi-Dravidas through its concern for the poorer classes, its anti-Brahman undertones and its stress on egalitarianism. Adi-Dravidas are both poor and untouchable; the DMK promises to eliminate both poverty and untouchability. Given these anti-upper class and anti-upper caste feelings and their bitter resentment of discrimination, much of the DMK ideology and promises to put rice in every pot and a Brahman in every prison does appeal to the Adi-Dravidas. Yet in my interviews with them there was a definite uncertainty and ambiguity in their feelings about whether or not the DMK *really* was for them and was helping the untouchables in Madras state. Why then do they identify with the party and its goals? There are a number of reasons for this. First, identification with the party in Bombay provides a self in which they can take pride. In Bombay most Adi-Dravidas say, "We are free to go where we will and eat what we want. Nobody here pays any attention to our caste." It would be foolish for them to identify themselves in this city as untouchable and to add the stigma of untouchability to that of being south Indian.

Adi-Dravidas take an evident pleasure in identifying with and being a part of a winning and successful party as the DMK has proved itself to be in Madras. They also take great pride in identifying with Annadhurai, or Anna as he is called, the sainted founder of the party. Anna told them to be proud of their Tamil language and their Dravidian background. Anna, too, traveled overseas to America where he was for some time at Yale University. Now that he is dead, Anna is above question and has become the symbol par excellence around which they can unite. His origins are said to be poor and he was said to be for the poorer classes. Those who depart from what the Adi-Dravidas feel was Anna's message are not true followers of the DMK. Thus, it is not the party which may be at fault, it is only the leaders in it who may be at fault.

The final reason for identification with the DMK lies in the fact that the Adi-Dravidas in Bombay are an immigrant group, speaking a foreign language, and having customs different from those of the native Maharashtrians.

In such a situation ethnicity becomes relevant both structurally and culturally when there is a struggle for scarce resources. The DMK is defined in not only structural but also cultural opposition to the Shiv Sena in Bombay through a clear enunciation and definition of the ethnic symbols of Dravidian culture, language and society. This definition of the situation gives shape to the symbols and organizations selected to protect and enunciate the demands of foreign migrants versus local indigenes. Moreover, the DMK in Madras is a powerful party which even Madame Gandhi must recognize. It is much more useful to link one's survival and one's struggle for existence and respectability in a hostile foreign environment to the DMK star with national influence than to a purely caste-based satellite with little organization or political clout such as the RPI. The sum and substance of the DMK in Shantinagar is that it is not an ethnic group with para-political functions; rather, it is a political group with para-ethnic functions.

While the DMK is the dominant party among the Adi-Dravidas of Shantinagar, there is a significant minority party, the RPI. The RPI was founded in 1956 by the late Dr. B. R. Ambedkar, himself an untouchable, who became the first Minister for Law in independent India. The party is primarily of and for untouchables. In Shantinagar the RPI is not as well organized nor as popular as the DMK. It does have meetings, officers, a small meeting house, and a series of public programs much like those of the DMK. The RPI, unlike the DMK, appeals to those who feel strongly the sting of untouchability. Republicans feel that the DMK has tricked the Adi-Dravidas and is really doing nothing for them.

In addition to their feeling that the DMK is really not doing anything for the untouchables and the Adi-Dravidas, the Republicans also have another reason for belonging to their party and this is a more practical one. In their opinion their party is a national party, not a sub-national one as is the DMK. Moreover, the party has a following in the state of Maharashtra where it is supported by the Mahar caste, Ambedkar's own community. Republican party members have been elected to the Bombay Municipal Corporation. This is a very useful tie for squatters, such as the Adi-Dravidas, in Bombay. With some help from the RPI corporators, it is claimed, the Adi-Dravidas have been able to arrange to have water taps opened in their own chawls, though at their own expense. Getting water taps in a squatter area is a big problem since most of the people are there illegally. Electric connections have also been installed in many chawls through political connections and in 1970 the RPI through its municipal corporator was able to have 10 street light posts installed. During the same year, a latrine for women was opened in one of the swampy fields which was used by the women. Unfortunately no arrangements for water or for sweepers to clean out the place were made so the women still use the fields and the latrine is used as a storehouse for the locally distilled moonshine.

The street lights and the latrine, as well as the electric connections, are a basis for public debate between the RPI and the DMK. Each claims to have done these things and therefore people should join their party.

DISCUSSION AND CONCLUSIONS

The Adi-Dravidas of Shantinagar are politically mobilized; they actively participate in local level politics, are aware of political issues, and have a leadership with organizational skills. Political forms and symbols have also become the major framework upon which the organization of the community is hung. There are important linkages to the arena of higher level structures and issues which are not localized and which integrate them into city, state and national levels of political and social life. The analysis of political mobilization at the micro-level is important, then, because it provides some understanding of the kind and extent of change which is taking place in urban areas of India. It also provides some understanding of what the macro-level changes in political life and socialistic economy mean when they reach down into ongoing social life at the local level.

The major process maintaining this political mobilization is ethnic polarization. This is a process whereby under urban cultural and social constraints rural forms of caste organization are superseded by those of an ethnic form of organization. The phenomenon of ethnicity has largely been overlooked in India because it has been assumed that caste organization subsumes or substitutes for that of ethnicity. Yet there are reasons which negate such an assumption and which on closer inspection make ethnic forms of group organization particularly salient. Ethnicity has been defined as a situation in which

> the members of interest groups who cannot organize themselves formally will thus tend to make use, though largely unconsciously, of whatever cultural mechanisms are available in order to articulate the organization of their grouping. And it is here, in such situations, that political ethnicity comes into being (Cohen: "The Lesson of Ethnicity").

Ethnicity is, then, essentially a political phenomenon, and a form "of interaction between cultural groups operating within common social contexts" (Cohen). In the case of the Adi-Dravidas caste organization has been replaced by that of political party organization at the local level.

This is not surprising when a number of factors are considered. First, in a large city such as Bombay castes, but not the caste system, exist. The caste system of rural India in which there is a hierarchical arrangement of politically, religiously, economically and socially interdependent castes each with its own rights, duties, functions and customs does not exist in large heterogenous cities of India. In such places the principles of social organization are different, more complex, rationalized and bureaucratic; here, castes cannot and do not interact according to the traditional principles of the rural caste system. Rather the principles of caste interaction are primarily political and *competitive*; the valency of the system is political. (Similar arguments have been made by Fox 1967; Bailey 1963; and Leach 1960.) This fact has been quickened by the advent of parliamentary politics and universal suffrage in India.

Second, the Adi-Dravidas themselves are in many ways heterogenous. They come from different counties and villages in Tinnevelly district of Tamilnadu; they are of different religions, Hindu, Protestant and Catholic; they work at different jobs in different parts of Bombay; there exist among them latent sub-caste differences; they are mobile geographically as well as occupationally; and, as individuals in Bombay, they are freer from caste restraints, control and customs than in their native places. Given such heterogeneity there are few traditional leaders and principles of organization to which all give assent and respect. Some form of organization and symbolism other than that of caste panchayats and leaders is necessary to overcome and incorporate this heterogeneity.

At first, it would seem that caste associations might arise in such situations. But this overlooks the definition of the situation in which the Adi-Dravidas of Bombay find themselves and the fact that the Adi-Dravida Mahajana Sangham has been replaced by the DMK. Adi-Dravidas are immigrants and foreigners, as well as culturally distinct in Bombay society. The DMK articulates the symbols, beliefs and myths of Dravidian culture and separateness, and provides the organizational structure within which they can unite as a group in Bombay. The roots of the DMK are in structural *conflict* over access to strategic resources and in cultural *opposition* to other groups, such as the Shiv Sena among Maharashtrians, seeking those resources. In this sense the DMK and the Shiv Sena arise out of similar causes and out of similarly structured definitions of the situation. Caste associations cannot articulate or organize such a definition of the situation in which migrancy and ethnicity are paramount. This definition of the situation in Bombay also helps to explain why there is among Shantinagar's Adi-Dravidas great interest in and support of DMK politics back in Tamilnadu state. This party provides the myths and symbols of ethnic identity and organization in a way that other parties, such as the Congress, cannot and could not because of their all-India orientation and heritage. DMK success and strength in Tamilnadu is indirect support for local ethnicity in Bombay. The stronger the DMK is in Tamilnadu and in New Delhi, the more likely are ethnic demands for defense or help in Bombay to be heard and heeded.

Local-level parties, as ethnic phenomena, are also more salient than caste associations because they are symbolically caste-neutral but structurally allow caste interests to be aggregated and expressed. By the same token they are class-neutral but allow the class-based demands of an urban proletariat to be aggregated and expressed.

The RPI plays on the recessive themes of caste identity and untouchableness in Bombay. There is always the threat that this could become salient and it is not easy for all Adi-Dravidas to suppress it completely. Those who define their situation in these terms are loyal to this party. The RPI is also an organizational complement to the DMK because of its access to the Bombay Municipal Corporation.

The study of ethnicity in India has much to offer in terms of a general theory of ethnicity. First of all, it forces one to look to the definition of the situation which by and large determines the cultural form and symbols a group will select. This is to some extent overlooked by theorists of ethnicity such as Cohen (1974). Second, it shows that ethnicity can be expressed directly through political organization rather than through para-political organization. Finally, it suggests a different and intriguing approach to the dynamics of urban social structure in India. Such an approach pulls aside to some extent the now leaden sociological blinders of caste and casteism and asks us to look at India afresh. It suggests that similar processes, producing similar phenomena, are at work in India as in the USA, Nigeria and elsewhere under the impact of national politics, industrialization and worldwide interdependence of nation states. What is going on in India is a "civil politics of primordial compromise" (Geertz 1973:310) in which the conflicts between new identities and definitions of the situation are brought about by the very process of modernization itself. The problem, then, is not to destroy, but to domesticate them (Geertz 1973:277).

NOTE

1. The research for this paper was conducted for fourteen months during 1970 and 1971. It was generously supported by a grant from the American Council of Learned Societies and was supplemented by a fellowship from the American Institute of Indian Studies. The methods used included participant observation, interviews with leaders, and a questionnaire administered to sixty Adi-Dravidas in Anna chawl of Shantinagar. References to material on squatters in India may be found in Lynch (1979). A full study of ethnicity and identity change among urban untouchables may be found in Lynch (1969).

WOMEN'S POLITICAL ACTIVITY AND EMPOWERMENT IN LATIN AMERICAN URBAN MOVEMENTS

Kathleen Logan

Residentially based mobilizations arising in the new communities of the urban poor have become an important mechanism for social change in Latin American cities. Women, acting to fulfill their traditional roles as mothers, have been on the forefront of these mobilizations. As a consequence of their participation, women have become self-empowered and have begun to change long-established patterns of thinking and behavior. Ironically, by seeking to maintain their traditional roles, women have helped bring societal change to a number of Latin American cities. For other descriptions of Latin American women, see Laurel Bossen's "Wives and Servants" and Hans Buechler's "Dona Flora's Network." Also see Epstein's "Squatter Settlements" for discussion of issues discussed here.

Marxist theory views class conflict as the mechanism of social change in industrial societies. In particular, Marxist theory predicts that the conflict between the bourgeois or property-owning class and the proletariat or laboring class, especially in the workplace, would be the motivating force for social transformation in such societies. This prediction, however, has not held true for the process of social change in contemporary Latin American cities (Portes 1985:31).

Several factors inhibit the workplace from being the locus of mobilizations for social change in Latin American cities.[1] First, the structure of the economy of these cities forestalls effective organization in the workplace. The formal sector of the economy in Latin American cities has not been able to employ the millions of people who need jobs.[2] Consequently, an informal economic sector in which these people do find employment has grown up around, and is interdependent with, the formal sector. Employment in the informal sector is characteristically small-scale, labor-intensive, low-paying and intermittent. It requires no special training or credentials and offers little chance for economic mobility. Many workers in the informal sector

SOURCE: Article written expressly for *Urban Life*.

are self-employed at self-created jobs. Others are employed in very small workshops where little difference exists between owners and employees. Thus, the street vendors, trash pickers, construction workers, domestic servants and open-air market sellers who labor in the informal sector are not able to mobilize in the workplace because their employment is too temporary, too unstable or too small-scale for it to be a nucleus for organization (Portes 1985:31-32). In this way, the structure of the urban economy in Latin American cities simply inhibits the formation of work-based movements such as trade unions.

Second, the political environment in Latin American cities also makes trade union formation quite problematic. In some places, unions are outlawed. In those cities where they have been allowed to form, action by the state has often held their activity in check and thereby circumscribed their ability to bring change. On one hand, outright state repression of trade unions has stifled their potential as agents of change. On the other hand, in those cases where worker organizations have not been impeded overtly, they have been co-opted or controlled by the state so that they are ineffective in bringing real societal change. As a result, trade unions seldom have been the force for social transformation anticipated by Marxist analysis.

Thus, in contemporary Latin American cities, mobilizations ascending from the workplace whereby the laboring class conflicts with the property-owning class, have not been the focal point of social change as once predicted. Instead, another form of mobilization has arisen which succeeds in bringing about social change – the residentially based, popular mobilizations undertaken by the urban poor. Focused upon community needs, these mobilizations have emerged as significant forces in the political environment of Latin American cities (Portes 1985:31-33; Castells 1983:190).

RESIDENTIAL COMMUNITIES AS A BASE

How and why have residential communities become a base for mobilization and a force for change in Latin American cities? Who are the people involved in these mobilizations and what motivates them to act? What are the consequences of these movements?

The rise of residentially based mobilizations in Latin America is rooted in the large population growth of the cities of this region in the second half of the twentieth century. The cities of Latin America have expanded rapidly in population because of the steady influx of rural people migrating to urban areas. In addition, once in the city, these ruralites and their children – the first generation of new urbanites – have a higher birthrate than long-time urban residents, thus multiplying the population growth brought by the initial rural-urban migration (Rusinow 1986:8). The lack of viable, long-range economic opportunities in the city condemn these migrants and their descendants to the lowest levels of the urban economic scale. Thus, Latin American cities not only increase rapidly in population but also grow in the percentage of the population that is low-income.

Given the exponential growth of lower income groups in Latin American cities, how is this expanding population of the urban poor to be housed, employed and educated? It is in the solution to the housing problem for these lower income groups that the locus of residentially based popular mobilizations lies. To understand the rise of urban popular mobilizations, it is important to track the process by which the poor find housing.

Rural migrants commonly live with friends, relatives or *compadres* upon arrival to the city.[3] Later, they rent quarters, as do many of the more established urban poor. Few, however, abandon the idea of owning their own house. Unfortunately, there are major obstacles for them to overcome in obtaining suitable housing. For example, state housing policy and the structure of the housing market almost always foreclose the poor from public housing or that built by private enterprise. Since state housing policy rarely considers low-income residents' housing needs, they seldom find housing in the public sector. In those cases where public housing is available, it contains too few units to meet the housing needs of very many people, or it is accessible only to those who have special connections to the central state, such as some Mexican trade unions which are linked to the federal government (Lomnitz 1977:12-13). Housing provided by private enterprise is geared to middle- and upper-income group markets rather than to the low-income market, and so the urban poor are simply priced out of this kind of housing.

Operating within these limitations, people in lower-income groups (including both recent migrants and the established urban poor) respond to the housing shortage by building their own houses in residential communities that they themselves create. The new communities are formed by invasion, by purchase of land on installment, or by gradual takeover of vacant, unused land, which is usually on the outskirts of the city. Regardless of the kind of community formation undertaken by the residents, however, land ownership is problematic. The threat of eviction looms over the residents, sometimes for years, because their legal title to the land is seldom clear. If the land is state-owned (as in Peru, where much of the land around Lima is owned by the federal government), the residents must persuade the government to give them title. Likewise, if the land in the path of urban expansion is held by *ejidos*, as it is in Mérida, Yucatán, México, then the residents must get state permission to buy the land from the *ejiditarios*.[4] If the land is owned by private entrepreneurs, the residents must either abandon their settlement or convince the property owners to sell the land to them, usually at inflated prices with unfavorable credit terms. Regardless of the original land ownership, getting clear title to the land on which their communities rest is an expensive, difficult process for the urban poor of these new settlements.

Yet, despite the precarious legality of their communities, the residents demonstrate great perseverance, forethought and creativity in building them. The residents make it clear that they intend to establish stable, permanent communities; they carefully plan space for schools, churches and recreational areas. Community-recruited work crews sometimes help build rudimentary streets and sidewalks or other constructions necessary for the community public service infrastructure. Residents also devise ingenious means to hook up their residences to pre-existing electrical and water systems in adjacent communities. In some of the newly formed communities, residents publish newsletters to foster a sense of social community among people who are new neighbors to each other. In some cases, residents are careful to emphasize a public image of their community as stable, law-abiding, patriotic and family-based. By so doing, they try to prevent the state from depicting the formation of the community as a lawless and chaotic process that is harmful to the city, and thereby justifying a government policy to bulldoze the settlement and drive off its residents.

Despite their ingenuity, perseverance and creativity in building their communities, however the urban poor has needs which are beyond their own capacity to fulfill. Consequently, from Buenos Aires to Ciudad Juarez, the residents of the *favelas, barriadas, colonias proletarias, zonas marginalizadas, pueblos jovenes, ciudades perdidas, barrios, poblaciones,* and squatter settlements begin to organize themselves around the necessity of obtaining legal land ownership and basic public services, such as paved streets, electricity, water, sewers and drainage systems, schools, health services and public transportation. Once mobilized to establish their community and to improve its services and facilities, they must remain mobilized, or at least ready to mobilize anew, in case threats of eviction or attempts to exploit the community economically arise. Eviction sometimes threatens the residents when land developers try to drive them off once they have obtained a basic public service infrastructure and, thereby, have increased the value of the community land (Castells 1983:191). In these instances, developers wish to repossess the land they have sold to the residents, so that they can resell it to others at a profit. Attempts to exploit the community economically occur when, for example, bus companies try to raise fares while cutting back service to the community.

The urban poor realize that the deficiency of public services for them is not completely caused by the lack of state funds, because other kinds of public services, like airports, highways and government buildings, do get built (Singer 1982:284). Therefore, the urban poor think it fitting to persuade the state to supply them with the public services they need. To fulfill their community needs, the urban poor can employ a range of strategies employing residentially based mobilizations. They may petition the state for services, establish patron-client ties with powerful politicians and bureaucrats or affiliate with partisan political parties. The involvement of residentially based mobilizations with powerful politicians and bureaucrats or partisan political parties is a double-edged sword, however, for such affiliation comes with the danger that these individuals or parties will take over the movement and use it to further their own ends rather than those of the community. Another danger inherent in this kind of affiliation is that community leaders will be co-opted by the politicians or by the political parties. The urban poor who mobilize in service to their community can also form alliances with other community-based organizations such as women's centers, neighborhood councils and church groups, especially the base communities of the Roman Catholic theology of liberation movement (Portes 1985:33).[5] They can also be confrontational in their choice of strategy by staging strikes, demonstrations, marches, invasions, takeovers and sit-ins. Most commonly, the mobilizations do not pit the urban poor against the dominant classes, but rather against the bureaucrats and technicians that operate the state agencies which are perceived by the urban poor as the institutions most likely to redress their community grievances (Portes 1985:32). Regardless of the strategy they select, however, the efforts the urban poor make on behalf of their individual communities brings a momentum for change that has far-reaching effects in Latin American cities that are only now being analyzed and understood.

THE ROLE OF WOMEN

A notable feature of these residentially based mobilizations is the large number of women who form, lead or participate in them. In fact, it is not unusual for women to make up the majority of participants in some of these movements (Andreas 1985:113, 207; Erlick 1984:66; Logan 1984:78-85; Peckenham and Street 1986:15-16; Singer 1982:296; Thomson 1986:8). Why do so many women participate? Why do they take active roles? How do women participate, and what are the consequences of their participation?

In order to understand women's involvement in residentially based mobilizations, it is important to understand the special significance motherhood has for Latin American women. For many women of this region, motherhood forges their major social role and their major social identity as adults (Harris 1983; Chaney 1979). From childhood, women are reared to expect that motherhood will be their primary occupation in life. Becoming a mother assures a woman a secure and ongoing social status in her community. Being a mother also allows a woman role continuity, for mothers endure as family caretakers despite personal tragedy, social upheaval, economic crisis and political change. As mothers, women nurture the family, provide a stable, secure homelife and absorb the frustrations and disappointments of family members. As mothers, women are responsible for household maintenance and for the care of their spouses and their children. Of these responsibilities, however, women's duties for child care are the most central. For many Latin American women, the primary tasks they set for themselves are to provide for their children and to insure a prosperous, healthy and happy future for them.

It is the compelling responsibility of being a mother that motivates women to mobilize on behalf of their communities. The life-chances of their children cannot be improved without schools, health services and transportation to jobs. Nor can the women's household chores of washing, cooking and cleaning be easily done without an adequate water supply, system of sewers and electricity. Since some or all of these services and institutions are lacking or, if present, are operating inefficiently, in most new communities founded by the urban poor, the circumstances are set for women to mobilize on behalf of their community. Women see community issues as directly related to their duties of child care and household maintenance, and, thus, truly their concern. Since the most obvious community problems fall squarely into what is considered to be a woman's domain in Latin America, women think it appropriate to mobilize around these issues. The irony is that, out of their concern for the responsibilities attendant to their traditional roles as mothers and housewives, an activism on behalf of their communities develops that sometimes brings changes which draw women away from customary patterns of behavior and into new arenas not previously part of the female domain.

In addition to having the motivation to mobilize, many women also have the opportunity to do so, and, under some circumstances, more so than men (Logan 1984:82-83). For example, those women who do not have to work outside of the household can structure their time flexibly to be involved in community activities. For these women, housework and childrearing duties can be rearranged to allow them time to attend meetings or to organize events. In some of these families, children accompany their mothers when the latter participate in community activities or help their mothers with household chores and thus free them to work on community projects (Logan 1984:83). Many other women, however, including the many who are single heads of households, must work their community activism into an already overloaded schedule that includes the double burden of family care and wage-earning responsibilities. It is a tribute to them and to the support networks that they construct that they are able to participate, despite the obstacles they confront.

In contrast, men, because of the structure of their work or because of the time and energy involved in their search for employment, have less time and less control of their working conditions, thus they are restricted in their ability to participate. Also, men's work takes them away from the community and its problems, so they are often less knowledgeable and informed about the community's needs than are women. Finally, men's responsibilities within the family are centered on earning an income and dealing with the world beyond the household. They are less involved with and less responsible for the day-to-day care of household and children. For women, the family and community are their basic political and social reference points. For men, the peer group and the workplace provide the outlet for their social and political energy.

Given the motivation and opportunity to mobilize, many women also have the means. The base from which women mobilize is built upon the solidarity women have among themselves, linked, as they are, to each other by networks of kinship, *compadrazgo*, friendship and neighborhood ties (Butterworth and Chance 1981:156; Logan 1984:76; Lomnitz 1977:131-156; Schmink 1981:45). Since family members often follow each other in rural-urban migration and in settling in new communities, some women have female kinsmen in their neighborhoods. Others have *comadres* living nearby. In addition, women who are neighbors form friendships based on physical proximity, personal compatibility and mutual aid. In these neighborhoods, women help each other by exchanging food, lending each other money and baby-sitting for each other's children. Women in the neighborhoods also socialize by visiting each other, by shopping together, and by mutually celebrating holidays and religious events such as baptisms and saint's days. The links women establish through kinship, *compadrazgo* and neighborhood networks are reinforced by the cultural pattern in Latin America whereby women turn to each other for social support and companionship. Women come to rely on each other to fulfill many of their social needs and come to see themselves as each other's allies. In effect, in many communities, women do not need to create a new structure from which to mobilize, since a structure, based on ties among themselves, already exists from which they can act collectively.

It is important to note that these residentially based movements in which women participate are not feminist movements *per se*. In Latin America, vocal and recognizable feminist movements exist, but they, like similar movements in the United States, arise among the women of the dominant classes and are structured to serve their interests. Feminists of the upper classes are most often concerned with men's exploitation of women and the enhancement of the status of women as individuals. In addition, elite women who espouse feminist goals commonly structure their activism so that it does not threaten dominant class interests. When feminism is straightforwardly a part of a community movement, however, it is cast differently than the feminism propagated by upper-class women.

For the lower-class women of the new, urban communities, feminism is not seen as a gender conflict in which the betterment of individuals as individuals is at stake. To them, feminism is a collective movement to liberate men, women and society from all kinds of oppression (Andreas 1985:200). Such a definition of feminism has helped frame some mobilizations so completely that this interpretation of feminism can be considered the major ideological force behind the movement (Andreas 1985:200). Most residentially based mobilizations center on family and community concerns and thus, focus indirectly on women. Other mobilizations incorporate issues which directly concern women, such as rape or wife-beating. Also, mobilizations, as they improve conditions in the community, can ultimately have the effect of bettering conditions for women even though they do not begin with this goal in mind. Under all of these conditions, however, the feminism of lower-class women is markedly different in its goals and process of bringing change from that of upper-class women.

The residentially based mobilizations in which women participate operate within a complex political, economic, cultural and psychological context. Variables rooted in this context shape the formation, direction and outcome of the mobilizations. Of these variables, the ones stemming from the urban political economy are the most influential and the most widely discussed in the literature about urban mobilizations (Castells 1983; Collier 1976; Cornelius 1973; Gilbert and Ward 1984; Portes 1985).

Since most governments are highly centralized in Latin America, the state controls the resources and services the poor need to build their communities. For this reason, the relationship between the state and the community is the most important variable operating in the political economy that affects the mobilization of lower-income, residential communities. In the 1950s, when residentially based mobilizations first began to be formed, many of the mobilizations did not arise from the communities themselves but rather were imposed on the communities by political actors from outside the communities (Moreira Alves 1984:77). Many politicians helped to found residentially based movements in order to establish patron-client relationships with the urban poor. In such a cliental relationship, politicians could exchange favors for political support. For example, in cases of communities formed by invasion, politicians protected the invasion-formed community from being bulldozed in exchange for the political support of the community residents (Castells 1983:191).

On other occasions, politicians from outside the community started residentially based mobilizations to legitimize the prevailing political system and to encourage compliance with its urban policies (Gilbert and Ward 1984:769). This was especially true when the state wished to gain support for policies unpopular elsewhere in the nation (Castells 1983:191-192). Similarly, politicians sometimes sought to organize residentially based mobilizations to counterbalance other urban mobilizations, such as those undertaken by trade unions (Castells 1983:191-192). In these cases, politicians sought to maintain the *status quo* and viewed the organization of lower-income communities as a means to counter the actions of progressive, change-oriented movements arising in other parts of the urban political landscape.

In all of these cases, the mobilizations organized by political actors outside the community sought to channel the energies of the poor in the direction the former chose and thus kept the poor from mobilizing on their own behalf around the issues the poor themselves selected as important. Although at times, these efforts gave the poor access to much-needed services, the efforts were co-optive and divisive, working against any real social change for the poor. Outside political actors still seek to impose their organization on newly forming, lower-income, urban communities in order to advance the politicians' own interests and causes. Under these circumstances, the relationship between the state and the community is that the former seeks to control the latter directly.

When residentially based mobilizations are truly the product of community-level organization, the relationship between the community and the state becomes one of more subtle control and influence by the state. Nonetheless, the goal of the state or political party is still to attempt to channel the mobilization in the direction that best suits the particular political philosophy of said state or political party. Leftist states and political parties that work with community mobilizations seek to mold them into instruments of revolutionary social change by raising the consciousness of community residents so that they become aware of their socio-economic class position and come to recognize the need for political action against those groups that control power and material resources. Right-wing states and political parties, when interacting with community mobilization efforts, seek to maintain the societal *status quo* by promoting traditional family values among the residents and by encouraging them to become less dependent on the social welfare provided by the state. Centrist states and political parties, in their dealings with community mobilizations, seek to channel any momentum for social change into their own plans to transform society (Gilbert and Ward 1984:769-770). Essentially, then, leftist-oriented political actors (such as Cuba under Castro or Nicaragua under the Sandanistas) want to influence residentially based mobilizations in order to transform society. Rightist ones (nearly any Latin American nation under military rule) want to consolidate traditional values and take charge of the political sphere outside the household. Centrist political actors (such as Mexico under the PRI) want to steer community-based mobilizations into the prevailing political context of gradual reform. Each of these political actors, however, must take care to distinguish between influencing the community and controlling it. Too obvious an attempt to direct the mobilization will ultimately lead to apathy on the part of the community residents (Portes and Walton 1976:108 Gilbert and Ward 1984:770).

How do state-community relations affect women's participation in residentially based mobilizations? At this point in the research, it is difficult to know, since little of the literature analyzing state-community relations discusses the role of women separately. It is important to recognize in any analysis of state-community relations regarding female participation in urban mobilizations, however, that the women involved in these movements always come up squarely against a male-dominated system. Since few politically powerful figures in Latin America are female, activist community women must face the men who control the resources their communities so urgently need. In confronting the powerful male representatives of the state, or even the men of their own communities, the women must also confront *machismo*, a culturally created pattern of male behavior emphasizing male superiority and male dominance.

THE EFFECTS OF MACHISMO

Exactly how does *machismo* affect women's roles in mobilizations? At the state level, male power brokers can simply choose to ignore women's participation in mobilizations and refuse to take their efforts seriously, preferring instead to deal with male community activists, or they can fail to recognize mobilizations as viable movements for social change if they are fueled largely by women. In these cases, female activism is made invisible by the power brokers of the state. Sometimes the opposition to women's mobilization efforts is a combination of *machismo* and ethnic or social class animosity. In such cases, the reaction to women's activism can be unusually cruel and violent. Such an incident occurred in Lima, Peru several years ago when police on horseback rode down migrant Indian women seeking to expand a new community on the outskirts of the city. Many were wounded and some killed in this action by the state (Andreas 1985:92-95).

Machismo also affects women's mobilizations at the community level. Local community men may encourage and rely upon women's support during crisis situations. When the crisis is over, however, women are pushed into the background once again. In this way, women become the surplus labor of community based mobilizations (Erlick 1984:66). Women's participation is also encouraged when it is needed to further men's own interests, but when women put forth their own interests, such as wanting to establish day-care centers or trying to prevent family violence, they are often opposed by men (Andreas 1985:39). As the Ecuadoran activist, Luz Luzuriaga (1980:78) described this pattern, "...most men take women for granted but seldom into account."

Community men may also more openly oppose women when they begin to participate in these residentially based movements (Peckenham and Street 1986:15). Their opposition ranges along a continuum from subtle discouragement to direct confrontation. They may ridicule women's efforts, try to forbid their wives from attending community meetings or oppose women in leadership positions. Men may give women routine, mechanical jobs with no political responsibility (Ardaya Salinas 1986:329). They may also try to limit the women's choice of social associations and their freedom of physical movement, because they think women will waste time gossiping or will have affairs with other men if they get involved with community mobilizations (Arimana 1980:21, 24). Underlying men's opposition is their fear of losing control of women and of losing their superior status *vis-à-vis* women. Sometimes the opposition by men is so great that women simply cease taking part in the mobilizations (Andreas 1985:39). Reporting on women's roles in residentially based mobilizations in Peru, Andreas (1985:205) concludes that no movement has yet completely resolved the issue of cultural attitudes that pit men against women.

Fortunately, *machismo* does not always inhibit women's participation in residentially based mobilizations. At the state level, women do sometimes find male power brokers receptive to their efforts. For example, powerful representatives of the state can establish patron-client relationships with individual female activists. Such a cliental relationship has developed between the state governor and a local female activist in Mérida, Yucatán, México. In this instance, the governor gave land for garden plots to the activist to distribute to community women in exchange for her efforts in mobilizing community support on his and his political party's behalf (Logan, forthcoming).

At the local level, too, there are times when women overcome barriers created by *machismo*. Sometimes, after a movement begins to yield benefits and when the fears of men about women are not realized, then men do come to support women's efforts on the community's behalf (Arimana 1980:22). Also, in some cases, women are able to override *machismo* by convincing men in their community that their activities, because they concern family issues, and thus are part of an appropriate female domain, are fitting for women to do and so the men do not oppose them (Logan 1984:83-84).

Nonetheless, *machismo* remains as a barrier to the greater success of residentially based mobilizations when women are involved. For some, *machismo* is behavior rooted in colorful folklore; for others, it is a philosophically elaborate pattern of male personality (Paz 1961:65-88). For many Latin American women, however, *machismo* is neither. To them, *machismo* is an obstacle preventing them from participating fully in the life of their communities.

PSYCHOLOGICAL EFFECTS OF MOBILIZATION

As has been shown here, there has been substantial discussion in the literature about the effects community-state relations and certain cultural variables have on residentially based mobilizations; however, the variables dealing with the psychological context in which these mobilizations occur, especially regarding women's participation, have been far less fully discussed.

It is interesting in this regard that many women report a change in their thinking and behavior because of their participation in residentially based mobilizations (Andreas 1985; Logan 1984; Thomson 1986; Turner 1980). That is, they feel a sense of self-empowerment, attributed to their participation in mobilizations, that causes them to think of themselves in more positive ways and that enables them to act in new ways they had not previously considered. In this sense, self-empowerment is a process by which individuals begin to develop a sense of their own abilities or capacities to act to bring changes they regard as positive in their lives. It is important to note that this sense of self-empowerment among participants in neighborhood movements occurs even when the movements are not completely successful (Singer 1982:299).

It is perhaps difficult for people from societies where individual development is valued and encouraged to understand the point at which activist women begin their attempt to change deeply embedded patterns of submissiveness and self-effacement. In order to understand the changes in thought and in behavior that women undergo in their journey to self-empowerment, it is important to understand the psychological reality of these women at the start of their odyssey. The lives of many lower-class, urban women are circumscribed by hard work, ill health and weighty family responsibilities. Women endure considerable psychological stress because of the harsh conditions that surround their lives (Ramirez 1980:106-107). Added to the stress of being poor are stresses rooted in the devaluation of women in general and lower-class women in particular. As women, they are seen as less valuable than men. As lower class women, they are assigned the most menial work and given the least priority for health care and education. As such, lower-class, urban women are the targets of both gender and class biases. If the women are defined as part of the indigenous population, they they are also subject to ethnic biases as well. For reasons of gender, class and ethnicity, these women receive daily assaults on their self-esteem. Their denigration ranges from being disregarded and relegated to the sidelines of societal concern to physical abuse, which goes unrecognized by society and unreported by women because women believe nothing is likely to be done about sexual assault and domestic violence (Thomson 1986:32-34).

While women, as housewives and mothers, are expected to absorb the frustrations and disappointments of the family, they have few outlets to express their own concerns. Women are psychological buffers for their families, often sacrificing their own needs and wishes to those of others (Guzman 1983:12). In such a psychological reality, women's own needs as individuals recede before those of family members; yet, despite the central psychological role they have within the family, women are ignored, abused, devalued and taken for granted. All of this takes place within a contex of little choice and few alternatives for women. It is not surprising, then, that many women are shy, passive, timid, silent and fearful of authority, viewing themselves as inferior beings (Andreas 1985; Moreira 1980; Thomson 1986). It is from this humble psychological state that women initiate their participation in mobilizations. For many, activism on behalf of the community brings them empowerment for themselves. Women's activism becomes a quest for human dignity.

The process by which women become self-empowered is not yet known; nonetheless, some aspects of this process can be discussed. Mobilizations in which women play a major part commonly start with women coming together informally in small, local neighborhood groups, sometimes under the auspices of the Roman Catholic Church or of a social welfare program. By coming together in these informal groups, women engage in an activity solely for themselves, apart from their neighborhood and their families — an hour or two of time in the company of other adult women. Out of such groups, a sense of solidarity and of cohesion as community members arises; the sense of isolation and alienation decreases (Logan, forthcoming). This growing sense of community solidarity and group cohesion is especially important for poor women because they much depend on each other for aid and assistance (Singer 1982:283).

At these neighborhood gatherings, women come to realize the common problems they have in living in newly forming communities; i.e., the problems of legalization of land ownership, and of inadequate public services. They also become aware that they share similar family problems, such as poverty, alcoholism, family violence and desertion by spouses. Once women realize their shared problems, they begin to think that they may be able to do something about these problems by acting collectively. Sometimes they form support groups to confront male violence by seeking sanctions through neighborhood councils against the men who physically abuse their families (Guzman 1983:12). Women also organize food cooperatives to make shopping easier and food cheaper or form day-care centers so they can work outside the home and not leave their children unattended (Singer 1982:283). In other communities, women organize boycots of local stores that engage in price gouging. They also wage campaigns to acquire public services by holding marches and sit-ins (Logan 1984:78-81). In still other communities, women learn about health care and establish health clinics (Guzman 1983:12). Finally, in some places, particularly in Nicaragua, women have started night patrols to ensure the safety of community members against the threats of criminals or political opponents (Erlick 1984:66).

In acting to solve community problems collectively, women learn new skills and gain new kinds of knowledge and experience. By acquiring new skills, knowledge and experiences, women increase their self-esteem and enhance their sense of being able to improve at least some aspects of their lives.

Activity in women's community-based groups generates a woman's belief in herself as a person of worth and a belief that she, as an individual, can do something about the problems she faces, two results which are necessary in order for women to be effective agents of change (Arango 1980:94). Self-empowerment results from women's activism in community-based mobilizations because their participation in these movements helps them build solidarity and cohesion among community members. It allows them to see that they share many of the same problems with others and helps them to recognize that they can constructively solve the problems they face. Finally, their participation requires them to learn new skills and thrusts them into new kinds of experiences.

If a growing sense of self-empowerment among female participants is a consequence of their involvement in residentially based mobilizations, what then are the consequences of women's enhanced self-empowerment and continued activism? At its most dramatic, the consequences of self-empowerment and activism by poor, urban women acting from a residential base occur in those places where such movements have been able to become a part of a societal-level mobilization for change. Nicaragua is a case in point. In this nation, residentially based mobilizations, linked with base communities of the popular Roman Catholic Church and involving heavy female participation, have been and still are at the forefront of the Sandanista revolution.[6] Elsewhere, at a municipal level, residentially based mobilizations by the urban poor in which women are significant participants have formed alliances with other kinds of urban mobilizations to bring social change. In Fortaleza, Brazil, such a mobilization helped to elect a female mayor, representing the Brazilian Workers' Party, by allying with the Roman Catholic Church and labor unions. Now this mobilization is active in the campaign to restructure government-community interaction at the municipal level (Peritore 1986:4, 5). In Peru, urban, lower-income women from the *barriadas* of the cities influenced the adoption of legislation that improved the status of women, at least in the legal statutes of the nation. Changes in legislation included banning discrimination against children borne out of wedlock, recognizing trial marriages, granting divorce after one year of separation for both women and men, allowing married women to apply for electoral cards in their own names, and prohibiting definition of parents' responsibilities by gender (Andreas 1985:207).

At another level, the impact of women's growing self-empowerment is more subtle. For example, women's attitudes toward their children's futures have been changed because of their involvement in mobilizations. In some places, women have now chosen to send their daughters to school, as well as their sons (Luzuriaga 1980:80). In other places, women have begun to develop a questioning stance toward institutions, such as the Roman Catholic Church, that importantly influence their lives in ways women may not find wholly beneficial (Andreas 1985:203-4). In still other places, women have chosen to go beyond the bounds of an institutionally sponsored program of community development to take action to bring social changes they see as worthwhile (Logan, forthcoming).

The involvement of women in residentially based mobilizations will continue to be important in Latin America, especially since the number of female-headed households is on the rise all over the region (Harris 1983:5). The circumstances under which these women live and their quest for a more dignified life should guarantee the entrance of many motivated women into the arena of activism. The motivation for these women to act will continue to be rooted in their commitment to motherhood. Women will be led out of the private world of the home into the public battleground of politics by their concern about the issues that affect their families. When political and economic forces impinge on the domestic realm that women consider their own domain, then women do and will act forcefully. Women, acting from their roles as mothers have already been able to wield considerable force in mounting political protests and in changing state policy in some parts of Latin America. In El Salvador, women have organized in protest against the actions of death squads which have kidnapped or killed local political activists (Thomson 1986:107-10). In Argentina, mobilizations by women, especially the "Mothers of the *Plaza del Mayo*," played a critical role in bringing an end to the oppressive military rule of their country (Portes 1985:33, 36). In both these cases, women mobilized because the state sought to silence political opposition by kidnapping, imprisoning, torturing and killing anyone considered a threat to the prevailing political system. By casting their net of oppression so widely, the government of these two nations affected the lives of many. As women saw their husbands, brothers, sisters, daughters, sons and neighbors disappear, they reacted to this threat to their domain by mobilizing against the state.[7] In each case, defense of the women's realm was the precondition of their mobilizations.

The importance of the role of motherhood is so marked that ignorance of its significance in activating women has cost some mobilizations their success. In Santiago, Chile, during the early 1970s, a widespread, residentially based mobilization blunted its efforts for social change in part because the mobilization leaders tried to redefine the role of mothers in a much too militant and nonfamily-oriented way for community women to accept (Castells 1983:206).

What is the future of the residentially based mobilizations in which women participate? In the past, mobilizations to get public services have often ended when the community needs were satisfied or when further campaigns for them seemed fruitless. Less frequently, mobilizations have gone beyond local, particularistic issues; yet, in those instances when the mobilizations have widened to become movements for social change, their influence has been great.

Several important variables will determine the future of these mobilizations. The kind of relationships that develop between the communities and the state and between the communities and powerful institutions such as the Roman Catholic Church will be critical. Mobilizations are certain to continue to produce friction between the state and the communities. Since any state, regardless of its political philosophy, seeks to control political power, emerging community movements are bound to be influenced, directed, co-opted, coerced or suppressed by the state. Yet, in seeking to maintain control, the state must consider that community initiatives, especially in first generation squatter settlements, have done much to improve community services and the quality of life for the urban poor (Rusinow 1986:5). The action of the state to control mobilizations to suit its best interests versus the action of communities to pursue their own interests will lead to continuing conflict. The state reactions to community initiatives will range from accommodation to community demands, in some cases, to certain suppression of the movements in others.

Community relations with the Roman Catholic Church will also shape the future of the mobilizations. If the Roman Catholic Church maintains its stated, preferential option for the poor and seeks to pursue social change actively, then the urban poor who mobilize from a residential base will have a powerful ally. If the Church does not pursue this path, however, it will once again become a mechanism for maintaining the *status quo*, as it has been throughout much of its history in Latin America. At present, the conflict between the Church hierarchy and the popular church in Nicaragua is the best example of this tension within the Roman Catholic Church. Depending upon the choice of the Church, mobilizations by the urban poor will have either an important friend or a significant enemy.

The issue of contradictory cultural values is also a determining factor in the future of mobilizations in which women play a major role. One one hand, Latin American culture encourages women's participation in residentially based mobilizations by defining gender roles so that the most pressing community needs are seen to lie in what are defined as women's areas of concern. Yet, on the other hand, Latin American women are discouraged from participating because of the inhibitions to act placed on them by *machismo*. For women, there is no easy resolution of this tension which is rooted in cultural contradictions, and it will continue to affect their participation as first one and then the other cultural value holds sway.

Women's political activities, arising from their concerns as mothers, as described here, are very different from those Chaney (1979) describes for Latin American women elected or appointed to political office. While Chaney's female politicians also define their roles in public life as extensions of their traditional, familial roles as mothers, Chaney found that this role limits the female politicians, for it isolates them in the less powerful jobs and agencies that deal with what has traditionally been defined as women's areas, such as health, education and social welfare. Such isolation denies the women positions of greater political power and influence, such as in departments of economics and foreign affairs. Chaney also found that, when the female politicians overstep the boundaries imposed by motherhood, they are driven from power. For the community activist women of Argentina, El Salvador, Nicaragua, and elsewhere in Latin America, motherhood seems to allow them more power and latitude to act politically. Seemingly, community-based mobilizations offer women greater political opportunities than do partisan parties.

Since female politicians in Latin American are likely to be from the dominant classes and female community activists from the subordinate ones, perhaps a class variable explains the difference in the political opportunity offered by the motherhood role. It could be that subordinate-class women have more social freedom to maneuver, at least within the context of their local communities, than do dominant-class women within their communal context. It remains to be explained why the role of motherhood, in one case, limits women's political activities and, in the other, expands them.

Finally, the changed consciousness of mobilization participants themselves will influence the future of their movements. The effect of growing self-empowerment is difficult to gauge, since so little research has been done on the psychological effects of participating in mobilizations. It is not yet clear if or how self-empowerment could lead to gender, ethnic or class consciousness. If, however, self-empowered individuals do collectively begin to bring about basic social change, then the *status quo* will be disturbed, and those with an interest in preserving the *status quo* will oppose those who seek change. For women, this is particularly compelling and ironic, since they act in mobilizations out of their concern for fulfilling their traditional roles, yet, by so doing, they are certain to challenge established patterns of culture and politics in contemporary Latin American cities.

NOTES

1. A mobilization is a collective organization to meet familial and communal needs.
2. The formal sector is that part of the economy which contains public agencies and private businesses that employ people in clearly structured jobs. Employment in the formal sector requires education or training credentials, is more permanent and pays higher wages than in the informal sector.
3. The *compadre* is the male coparent (*comadre* is the female coparent) in *compadrazgo* (godparenthood), a form of fictive kinship in which people are linked together by their sponsorship of individuals as they undergo spiritual rites of passage in the Roman Catholic Church. *Compadrazgo* is an important element of social structure throughout Latin America.
4. The *ejido* is community-held land; *ejiditarios* are the communal-land owners.
5. The theology of liberation is a grassroots movement, linked to the Roman Catholic Church in Latin America, which seeks to confront the conditions of poverty and political oppression under which many people live. The philosophy of the theology of liberation movement combines Roman Catholic beliefs about the basic human worth and dignity of each individual with Marxist ideas about structural change, economic dependency and class conflict.
6. The popular church, or grassroots-oriented church created by some Roman Catholic clergy and laypeople, takes an activist stance on social change and follows the tenets of the theology of liberation. In some parts of Latin America, such as Nicaragua, the traditional Roman Catholic Church is at odds with the popular church because the former regards the popular church as a threat to established beliefs and practices.
7. In these settings, women have mobilized as mothers to bring social change. In other circumstances, women have mobilized as mothers to maintain or to recapture the *status quo*. Female supporters of the right-wing A.R.E.N.A. party in El Salvador have mobilized to defend their interests as mothers. Female opponents of the change-oriented Allende government of Chile helped bring down this government by staging a series of street protests in which they emphasized their motherhood. In both of these examples, the women involved were from the dominant classes and, thus, saw social change as a threat to their families and to their way of life. Nonetheless, they share with change-oriented female activists the use of the motherhood role as a political rallying point.

COPING WITH POVERTY: A CROSS-CULTURAL VIEW OF THE BEHAVIOR OF THE POOR

Edwin Eames and Judith Goode

> Whatever the causes of poverty, the poor must develop strategies to cope with low, sporadic income and inadequate resources. In this selection, Eames and Goode examine the adaptive techniques developed by poor people in industrialized societies. The comparative framework they use reveals many similarities in the behavioral responses of the poor despite their different cultural backgrounds. This framework suggests that many behaviors of the poor develop in response to a set of economic and social conditions rather than from a cultural or cognitive origin. (Note the similarity of some of the strategies described here, particularly the role of urban kin groups in providing support, with the group-oriented strategies described among urban migrants in part two.)

Much of the literature dealing with the behavior of the poor in modern capitalist societies attempts to develop a psychological or cognitive understanding of the values of the poor. Individuals, as well as the motives and values underlying their behavior, are frequently used as a basic focus of analysis. To the extent that this emphasis is maintained, the behavior of the poor is often seen as dysfunctional and irrational, and the larger issue of the adaptiveness of common response patterns is obscured. It is these common response patterns that we refer to as coping mechanisms. In the following discussion we will emphasize shared patterns of coping responses found among poor people in industrial societies in as wide and varied cultural settings as possible.

From our perspective, many aspects of the behavior of the poor can be seen as direct responses to the conditions of poverty. Poverty in capitalist-industrial societies is defined by inadequate access to material resources. This means that the poor not only have no accumulated wealth and low cash incomes but their income is sporadic, intermittent and uncertain. Those in poverty are those located in the bottom sectors of the job market, where they not only receive minimal rewards for their work but are in positions where the sources of in-

SOURCE: Adapted from Edwin Eames, Judith Granich Goode, "Coping Responses of the Urban Poor," *Urban Poverty in a Cross-Cultural Context.*

come are frequently cut off. They work in jobs which may often disappear as the needs of the economy change. In addition, their jobs are frequently so menial—lacking the protection of labor laws, unions and social security and lacking in mobility potential—that there is an expected high turnover rate. This is the result of the employer's expectations of turnover, the resultant short-term exploitation of the worker, and the employee's perception of a dead-end situation. Many of these jobs are characterized by heavy labor investment or short-term contracts (day labor). Others involve work in illicit activities or begging, scavenging used goods, or selling minute quantities of goods or services.

Whatever the sources of cash, a variety of similar conservation techniques and strategies have been developed by poor people all over the world to manage this limited and insecure income. One way of conserving resources and adding to them is the development of alternatives to the formal retailing, savings, credit, and insurance institutions in society. These involve informal, small-scale networks to distribute new goods and services, major mechanisms to recycle secondhand goods, or the use of swapping or direct exchanges of goods. Capital is saved by storing it in goods which can be sold or pawned. Insurance is provided by kin and quasi-kin networks and social and economic support systems. The very practices which make survival possible are often viewed by the middle class as indulgent and irrational behaviors perpetuating poverty.

EVERYDAY NEEDS

Food

Basic survival needs include food, shelter and clothing. One of the characteristics of the diets of the poor is that they are composed of basic staples that are high in starch content, such as rice, maize or potatoes (depending on geographic area and cultural traditions). In relation to other foodstuffs available, these items are inexpensive and high in caloric content to meet energy needs. On the other hand, protein sources such as meat and dairy products are very expensive and would not provide adequate caloric intake if the amount of money invested in carbohydrates were invested in them. In such circumstances, it is common to find people who raise a few chickens or hogs to sell for profit so that they can convert the income into carbohydrates. In Oscar Lewis's account of the Sanchez family, Jesus Sanchez occasionally raises hogs, not for consumption but for sale. It is economically rational to do this although dieticians observing these activities might be disconcerted by what appears to be ignorant nutritional behavior (Lewis 1961).

A common characteristic of cash-conserving behavior is the purchase of small quantities of foods at frequent intervals (often on a meal-by-meal basis). In part, this is the result of the lack of storage facilities (refrigerators, freezers, pantry space) available to those with poverty incomes as well as the nature of the cash flow for this population. Frequently one finds tiny stores maintained in households in low-income areas in which it is possible to buy shortening by the tablespoon (Lewis 1965). This enables the vendor to earn cash income and the purchaser to obtain a necessary foodstuff that he or she could not afford in larger quantities in the formal retail market.

The descriptions of squatter settlements are filled with examples of parts of homes being used to store small inventories of foodstuffs for sale. Roberts (1973) found more than 75 percent of the homes in one such settlement in Guatemala City to be engaged in some petty enterprise. Most of them were involved in selling household necessities: food, sewing equipment and fuel. Occasionally residential entrepreneurs will go to the central market daily and then sell small amounts of food and kerosene door to door in their neighborhoods. They are limited to what they can carry and thus sell minuscule quantities—a cup of kerosene, for example.

There are many examples of what Raum (1969) calls the "common mess" in the literature. Often males who are between wives or supporting their families left behind in the countryside practice pooling their money for joint purchases of food and communal preparation. Other variations of this form of economic efficiency are the feeding patterns that occur when members of several households (especially children) are customarily fed by one female in her household. Perhaps they are best described in the work of Carol Stack (1974) who studied domestic cooperation between black poverty families in the United States.

Another variation of this technique can be seen in household food exchanges when several cooks cook more than is necessary for their family and then exchange the surplus. Such cash pooling and bulk purchasing tends to be less expensive, and common preparation conserves fuel, labor and time.

It has frequently been noted that poor people often avoid the cooking of food in their own household units. There is a pattern of purchasing cooked or prepared foods from vendors (street vendors in Asia and Latin America, take-out and fast food restaurants in the United States). Rather than wasting cash resources, this can be seen as a conservative measure since the appliance and fuel costs involved in cooking can often outweigh the cost of buying from vendors, who are in a sense engaged in communal preparation. Another reason for reliance upon food vendors is that the time requirements of the marginal jobs and the supplementary conserving and scavenging activities may make the schedules of different household members so diverse as to preclude their eating together. Thus, working intermittently, at odd hours, and trying to juggle the work schedules of various household members may work against common mealtimes as well as time for the preparation of food. However, in spite of the adaptive nature of street snacking, it is often condemned by outsiders as a symptom of laziness and ignorance.

Housing

A basic strategy related to housing is the development of high density occupation. When several families or individuals share a given residential unit, this can decrease their housing expense. Housing under these conditions may be rented by the group of families or individuals. Often, one family rents an apartment from a landlord but then takes in other families as boarders to augment its income. In Singapore, for example, a family of five cooking, eating, and sleeping in a tiny cubicle manages to augment its cash by renting upper and lower berths in its already constrained living space (Kaye 1966).

Among the poor, renting is almost a necessity due to capital limitations, and the rental housing market for low-income populations consists of units invariably congested and substandard. Such inadequate housing is still highly priced since profit-oriented landlords require as high a return as possible in a high risk market.

The only exception to renting is the widespread occurrence of occupant-built housing or sweat equity rehabilitation throughout the world. In these cases, home ownership is achieved by taking over vacant land or vacant buildings and establishing rights to them through the investment of time and labor. Such irregular settlements of new housing are found everywhere today. In the United States, government policies have recently fostered urban homesteading to recycle and rehabilitate older housing units. These programs are intended to develop a variety of housing for the poor, who can achieve the capital assets of a home through minimal investment of cash but heavy investment of time and labor. Unfortunately, these programs up until now have been used predominantly by the nonpoor.

In much of Latin America, the Middle East and Asia, the spontaneous community of squatters has been very common. Such communities have been studied by a number of anthropologists and some common features have been noted. For squatting to be successful, some degree of organization is necessary in taking over and retaining land which was not formally purchased. As Mangin (1967) noted for Peru, squatters are rarely the most recent immigrants to the city. Contacts and urban experience are necessary for inclusion in the initial squatting attempt. When successful, squatter settlements provide a whole new pattern of housing and housing costs for the poor. Squatters avoid the initial costs of home purchase they would incur in the formal housing market. They also avoid the inevitable monthly payment involved in renting a substandard unit. Instead they intermittently invest cash in building materials and labor in construction. For those with sporadic employment, such labor time is often available.

Municipalities have recognized that such occupant-built housing settlements are cheaper housing solutions than governments can provide. They often develop procedures to legitimize the settlement, create legal land tenure, and provide municipal services to these communities. Community-wide legitimization usually requires a cash outlay in the form of taxes or a labor investment in the communal construction of some public facilities like roads, sewers and water systems. Thus, housing expenses do increase but the self-built house in such an approved settlement becomes a capital asset which can appreciate over time. As an indication of the significance of squatting, 62% of the households in Lima, Peru, 45% in Ankara, Turkey, and over 33% in Karachi, Pakistan, Manila, the Philippines, and Caracas, Venezuela, are located in such settlements (Abrams 1964).

Clothing

As Michael Harrington noted, America's poor are among the best dressed poor in the world. In part this is the result of readily available, cheap and mass-produced clothing. In addition, for clothing probably more than for any other item of consumption, the secondhand market allows the maintenance of the outward manifestation of adequacy. The utilization of secondhand goods conserves cash in two ways. One can buy used goods with minimum outlay and one can later raise cash by selling. In Japan, secondhand clothes hawkers are prominent around urban markets (Caldarola 1968). The wife of Jesus Sanchez was a vendor in the secondhand market in Mexico City (Lewis 1961). In the United States, Goodwill and the Salvation Army are manifestations of this institution.

Used goods can also be acquired directly without the need for cash. Carolina Maria de Jesus, a scavenger in São Paulo, Brazil, notes that she, like most scavengers, acquires shoes and clothing for her family as she rummages through trash and garbage (de Jesus 1962). Secondhand clothing is also distributed by formal charities. In a study of household budgets of the poor in Hong Kong, families often stated that they paid no money for clothes since they received altered clothes from a charity (*Journal of the Hong Kong Institute of Social Research* 1965). A typical source of used clothing is one's patron or employer. According to an eighteenth-century European social commentator, it is an obligation of an employer to a domestic servant to give ". . . from time to time some part of your wardrobe or cast-off clothing" (Taylor 1968:570). Pauw (1963) describes the frequent payments in goods to domestic servants in South Africa, and this is a typical pattern for day workers in the United States.

Another common informal market for clothing and household goods is the marketplace for stolen goods. Such thieves' markets are described as occurring all over the world. Patch mentions that in Lima, Peru, the thieves' market also redistributes the belongings of the recently deceased. Such goods are tainted by their association with death. However, they are bought and sold by the poor (Patch 1967).

EXTRAORDINARY CAPITAL NEEDS

Investment and Savings

Unlike the daily requirements of food, clothing and housing, there are extraordinary expenses which occur at different stages in the life cycle or in crisis events which require large cash outlays. Once again, the shared patterns of the poor can be seen as an adaptive response based upon the need to conserve limited and intermittent cash resources. This point can be seen in the tendency to invest some resources in large appliances and household furnishings which can readily be converted into cash. As Lewis and Leeds point out for poor households in Mexico and Brazil, the purchase of television sets, blenders and other appliances is not simply an extravagant attempt at conspicuous consumption, but is an investment in items which can be pawned in times of emergency (Lewis 1969, Leeds 1971). Obviously, they must be purchased in times of relative affluence. Thus the cycle of relative prosperity and crisis/impoverishment within the condition of poverty is tempered by this modified savings for emergencies. Even bedding (mattresses, pillows, headboards) can be viewed within this framework since it involves pawnable items often purchased at the time of a wedding, when relatives pool resources to help establish a new household.

Because of their economic position, the poor rarely have access to large sums of money. Nevertheless, they have developed techniques to raise large sums for emergencies. These techniques are strikingly similar all over the world. Lotteries, both legal and illegal, are found throughout the world. Since the poor can only afford partial tickets, the winnings are only small windfalls. However, they are often used for the few large purchases made in a lifetime. Marta Sanchez recalls that her father used two minor lottery winnings to buy a radio and a large metal bed (Lewis 1961). Both of these items were potentially pawnable. Thus the purchase of capital goods is a major technique for saving or storing cash windfalls for the future.

Less formally organized institutions for credit also exist. One major type is the informal credit association. One example of such an association is the *ooi* in Hong Kong. The fixed membership in this group pays a small monthly fee. Any member may borrow from the pool in times of crisis (*Journal of the Hong Kong Institute of Social Research* 1965). In Kampala, Uganda, rotating credit associations are found. Again each member contributes monthly, but in this case the monthly fund is lent to each member in rotation, enabling him to make a major purchase (Gutkind 1967). In Mexico City, such groups are called *tandas* and pooled money is distributed by drawing lots (Lewis 1965). Leeds (1971) found that groups of workmates in Brazil developed informal credit pools called *vaquinas* and *caixinhas*. (Literally "little cows" and "little boxes," these words resemble the English "kitty"). Raum (1969) also discovered a varied number of different groupings all designed to "maximize small monthly resources."

Government policies often provide other ways in which a lump sum of capital can be acquired. Peattie (1967) describes the way the residents of one squatter settlement in Venezuela use their severance pay (required by labor laws) as lump sums of capital to be saved or invested. Other examples of similar perceptions and usages of government-provided lump sums are tax rebates and compensation for injury. Such money can be used for major purchases or coping with crises.

Crises

Savings in the forms discussed above are frequently exhausted by crises which take place. Medical emergencies occur particularly during the heavy childbearing years in a family and during old age. Illness has a dual consequence. Medical costs can quickly exhaust savings. In addition, for those employed in the informal sector of the economy, jobs rarely include sick leave or unemployment compensation. In fact, illness is frequently used as an excuse for firing an individual and loss of both current and future income often results.

Another type of crisis frequently faced by this population is conflict with governmental authorities (legal emergencies). Squatters are frequently confronted with the specter of loss of land and housing. They are open to a variety of governmental actions which may threaten the property rights acquired through sweat equity. Adolescent males are often involved in antisocial behavior and harassed and arrested by police authorities. In all of these crises, expenditures for lawyers, bail, and legal documents place a burden upon those already faced with the need to survive on a daily basis.

These as well as a whole variety of other crises force many of the poor to borrow cash from usurers rather than from the banks and legitimate credit institutions that frequently reject them. When money is borrowed from a usurer who demands illegally high interest rates, repayment can become a crisis. Illegal mechanisms of store credit such as those described by Caplovitz (1963) are further examples of usury. Installment buying by the poor can work for and against the buyer. On the one hand, such credit provides the opportunity to obtain the electric appliances which can function as savings. On the other hand, it often commits the buyer to exorbitant payments. With sporadic income, payments are frequently missed with the resulting loss of the item itself or large penalties exacted.

MUTUAL SUPPORT NETWORKS

For many of those in poverty, the source of much cash, goods, services, and social support is a network of extended kin and close friends who behave like kin. Although these kin usually face the same conditions, their collective support becomes an essential element in survival. Crises that affect one household unit at a given point in time may be offset through the help of households linked by kinship or fictive kinship. These units are not likely to have medical or legal emergencies at the same time.

Child care can also be provided by members of an extended kin network to permit mothers to work. This is easiest when kin reside together or in close proximity to one another. In other situations, children are given to other families for months or years to be raised. This frees more members of individual nuclear family units to participate in activities outside the home to generate income.

Mutual aid in emergencies and childcare are but two examples of the aid that can be provided by kin. In addition, much of the feeding, housing and clothing of individuals necessary for survival depends on the strong ties of kinship. Carol Stack has described the household of Viola Jackson, one of her informants, as the central household in a dispersed cooperating kinship network. As economic opportunities in Viola's area expanded, many kin from other areas joined her and became part of the household, contributing to income and sharing in food and shelter. Her brother and his household were located within walking distance. They ate in Viola's house and contributed to its support (Stack 1979). These kinds of cooperative domestic networks are found throughout the world. Peattie describes them in Venezuela, and Lomnitz describes them in Mexico (1974).

A major investment of the poor is in an extended social support system which becomes the ultimate basis of economic and social security. When one is in difficulty, one may withdraw economic or social capital from this kinship bank. On the other hand, when one has periods of relative affluence or windfalls, one must invest in the kinship network. Stack (1970, 1974) has described how important it is to constantly borrow and trade within the network even if one does not need anything. It is necessary to keep the ties strong and the channels of giving and taking open. The network of mutual support which is critical to the survival of the poor is frequently criticized by social analysts. They claim that such commitment to the network prevents an individual or household from moving out of poverty since all "surplus" is redistributed among members of the network. However, it is this basic support mechanism that keeps most of the poor from succumbing to the most deleterious effects of material deprivation. Most attempts to change one's economic position require severing these ties. As a result, such mobility attempts are risky in both the social and economic sense.

DOMINANT CLASS CONCEPTIONS OF THE BEHAVIOR OF THE POOR

A commonly held view of the behavior of the poor is that they lack the ability to defer immediate gratification of basic urges. This view gets translated into three major domains: money, sex, and violence. Several commentators have indicated that such stereotypes have no basis in fact; that the real behavior of the poor is being contrasted to the ideal behavior of the middle class which is perhaps more circumspect about its behavior (Miller, et al. 1965).

The poor are frequently castigated for their inability to save, their consumption of useless status items and costly snack foods, and squandering their limited resources. What we have tried to demonstrate in the previous discussion is that many of the specific behaviors which might appear to be irrational consumption practices are rational indeed within the economic resource setting in which the poor are located.

A widely held view is that poor people are sexually promiscuous, have a pattern of early initiation into sex and are unable to maintain a long-term marital union based upon monogamous mating. There is indeed a high level of consensual (common-law) and extralegal unions among poor people all over the world. This is partly related to the economic expenditures required by church and state in the establishment of marriage. In addition, the legal expenditures of dissolution are often greater than those of marriage. Such avoidance patterns conserve scarce resources. Conditions which become important factors in the instability of both mating and marriage are primarily economic. Although a household unit might try to place all of its members in the job market, conditions of the labor market may make this impossible. The market for women as domestics makes it frequently the case that the woman is more viable in the informal labor market. Frequently, where welfare systems exist, they specifically discourage stable married pairs as eligible, thus encouraging mother-child households.

Within the conjugal family unit, women are usually responsible for the care and well-being of infants and young children. Therefore, adult men who are not significantly contributing to the income of a household are liabilities to the household rather than advantages. For these economic and social reasons, the household unit centers around the mother-child bond. When such families dissolve marriage ties, it is almost always the women who remain responsible for the children. Knowing this, women play an important role in decisions about entering into formal marriage or breaking up marital ties. Very often, women prefer to rely more on their own kin for mutual support than on a spouse who may become a financial liability. This leads to a high frequency of female-headed households consisting of women and their female kin (sisters and mothers) and their children. Marvin Harris (1971:367) points out, "Like all domestic arrangements, the matrifocal family arises under specific and known material conditions and represents an adaptive achievement that is no more or less 'pathological' than any other family form." Such conditions include a general lack of access to strategic resources, with women and men in equal positions in a labor market where single incomes are insufficient to support a family. He points out that while everyone strives for a traditional union, men often prefer temporary unions because they realize their inability to support their families. Women who have the backing of a kinship support unit may also prefer a temporary union to the danger of a permanent male freeloader. Studies in low-income communities in Tokyo, Rio de Janeiro, Guatemala City, Mexico City, Ciudad Guayana (Venezuela), Johannesburg and Witwatersrand (South Africa) all document the high incidence of informal unions in these settings (Southall 1970; de Vos and Wagatsuma 1966; Taira 1968; Peattie 1967; Pearse 1961; Roberts 1970; Whiteford 1964; Phillips 1956; Verster 1967).

Informants' statements seem to indicate that these relationships are seen as allowing for flexibility in situations of financial insecurity. One favela dweller in Rio de Janeiro says about a husband: "I don't have one, I don't want one." She says that married women work terribly hard and their husbands " . . . remain home under the blankets. Some because they can't find jobs, others because they are sick, others because they are drunk" (de Jesus 1962). Marris (1961) encountered a high incidence of broken marriages in Lagos and found people directly linked them to financial situations. Manuel Sanchez articulately states his view of the relationship between one's economic situation and marriage:

> There is also the matter of being poor. If one begins to examine what a marriage comes to, a poor man realizes he doesn't have enough money for a wedding. Then he decides to live this way, without it, see? He just takes the woman, the way I did with Paula. Besides, a poor man has nothing to leave his children, so there is no need to protect them legally. If I had a million pesos, or a house, or a bank account or some material goods, I would have a civil marriage right away to legalize my children as my legitimate heirs. But people in my class have nothing. That is why I say, "As long as I know these are my children, I don't care what the world thinks." . . . And the majority of women here don't expect weddings, even they believe that the sweetheart leads a better life than the wife (Lewis 1961:59).

Thus, ties based on marriage (the conjugal bond) may be weak, but ties to consanguine (blood) kin of the mother are quite strong. This is the very network which is the core of the mutual support mechanism discussed above.

MALE ADOLESCENT ANTISOCIAL BEHAVIOR

In addition to alleged sexual promiscuity, the poor are viewed as prone to violence. In particular, this kind of behavior is associated with male adolescents. This behavior is indeed found in strikingly similar manifestations throughout the world. An obvious "tough" lifestyle is frequently found among poor urban adolescents, related to the nature of their difficulties in entering the labor force in industrial society. These groups share dress, language and recreational patterns involving drinking, physical contests and gambling. Casual illicit activities and challenges to authority are frequent. Such varied groups as the *tsotsi* among young men in South Africa described by Pauw (1963), the *hampones* in Lima, Peru, the gangs (*gallades* and *colleras*) described by Patch (1967), the street gangs in Tokyo described by Caldarola (1968), the gang of Manuel Sanchez in Mexico City (Lewis 1961) and the street corner men described by Hannerz (1970) and Liebow (1967) in the United States are remarkably alike in lifestyle.

These young adult males face a labor market which is worse for them than for their adult counterparts. While marginal occupations such as delivery boy, errand boy and shoeshine boy exist as niches for the young, those between early teens and early twenties are viewed as unreliable. This group has particular difficulty entering even those monotonous dead-end jobs possible for the unskilled. They view these jobs as dull and boring and are viewed with mistrust by their employers. Some of the violence is also associated with a broad range of illicit activities developed to generate income. These would include petty theft, sale of narcotics, pimping and dealing in illegal lotteries.

As one goes through this life cycle stage, there are two paths which usually develop. If a male marries and becomes a family man, he then is viewed as reliable and is pressured to produce income. An example of the shift in one's behavior and friends when this transition is made can be found in the article "From Hell Raiser to Family Man" (Hill 1974), which describes the process in an American Indian group. The other path is to become a professional criminal. Success as a family man is extremely difficult in poverty circumstances, but success as a criminal involves social and physical risks. Often those who fail to become steady, good providers in marriage move in and out of short-term male networks and male boarding house areas throughout their lifetimes. The street corner men in the United States described in *Tally's Corner* (Liebow 1967) and *Soulside* (Hannerz 1970) have their counterparts in cities all over the world.

CONCLUSIONS

A basic characteristic of the behavior of the poor is the similarity of behavioral strategies that have been developed to cope with poverty conditions. An essential element of the poverty situation is low, sporadic income in an industrially based economy. Given such societal conditions, the poor have developed a variety of techniques to survive despite limited resources.

Survival in this lowest and most insecure economic niche is managed through a variety of mechanisms. These include resource conservation, informal savings and credit mechanisms, alternative consumption outlets and most significantly the support of kin-based networks. Movement out of poverty usually involves the risk of cutting oneself off from one's social obligations to, and potential support from, kin.

There are several generally held attitudes about the behavior of the poor. A fundamental view is that poor people are unable or unwilling to defer immediate gratification for future rewards. Three related areas—money, sex, and violence—have been seen as areas of self-indulgence. In all three areas we have linked the behavior of the poor to economic and social conditions rather than a cognitive or value-based cultural framework. Once again, the general cross-cultural similarity in the behavior of poor people in many parts of the world is striking. One can only conclude that poverty in any industrialized cultural setting results in a set of similar behavioral responses which are the basic tools for survival for the urban poor all over the world.

DOÑA FLORA'S NETWORK: WORK RELATIONS IN SMALL INDUSTRIES IN LA PAZ, BOLIVIA[1]

Hans C. Buechler

> In this case study of a small-scale manufacturer in Bolivia, Hans Buechler writes
> of the expression of class in a Third-World city. Buechler explores Doña
> Flora's use of family ties and her relations with her workers in this study of how
> a small firm survives in a highly competitive world market. Such firms are
> extremely important in local and world economies today. The strategies
> employed by workers and managers are well described in this article. This
> analysis points out the weakness of workplace solidarity as described by Logan
> in "Latin American Urban Movements" and the "Cross-National Web of
> Syrian-Jewish Relations" as described by Zenner, both studies which bear
> comparison to the case of Doña Flora.

Our 1956 Willy's Jeep had finally conquered the one-thousand, five-hundred-foot climb up to Doña Flora's woolen garment workshop from the bottom of the two-thousand-foot-deep basin where the city of La Paz is located.[2] Doña Flora's workshop was one of some two hundred small-scale producers my wife, Judith-Maria, and I studied in 1981 and again in 1984. These ranged from artisans, such as tailors, hatmakers, carpenters and shoemakers, with one or two apprentices and/or journeymen to small factories with a workforce of as many as fifty. The factories made a wide variety of products, including plastic containers and sausages.

A young woman, who turned out to be Doña Flora's daughter-in-law, opened a small door in the large sheet-metal gate to the patio, disappeared again — presumably to consult with her mother-in-law — and then led us around an old pickup truck parked in the patio and past a weaver working at a loom stationed in an open shelter. Finally, we entered an expansive room with a large number of sweaters and woven jackets stacked against one wall and several workers sitting at sewing machines.

Doña Flora, a robust woman in her mid-forties (corpulence is considered a sort of status symbol in a society where food is often scarce) gave us a warm reception. Her appearance, the scale of her production and the building housing her business, as well as her own and her daughter's families, established her as an upwardly mobile artisan.

SOURCE: Article written expressly for *Urban Life*.

We learned that she was a second-generation, rural-urban migrant and that the stacks of goods were destined for export and for sale to foreign tourists in La Paz and to Bolivian clients in the city of Cochabamba. Like many other producers of tourist items, Doña Flora is engaged in a wide range of economic activities.

At the time of our first visit, she was involved in a combination of manufacturing, wholesale and retail activities, concerns that entailed manifold commercial ties and labor relations. Since such relationships were among our major interests, one of the first questions we asked was who her workers were. Doña Flora introduced the workers in the room as her children, in-laws and a nephew. However, subsequent observations and information gleaned from interviews with other members of the family cast doubt on the veracity of her claim that she worked only with members of her kin group. Finally, during a later visit, our Bolivian assistant obtained a more probable version from an older woman who was helping Doña Flora to repair defective sweaters. This employee told our assistant that the workers were her own children and that her family was not related to Doña Flora.

Why would Doña Flora have tried to hide the true identity of her workers? The most probable solution to this enigma sheds light on the precarious relationship between owner and worker in Bolivian industries and the cut-throat competition among small-scale producers.

MANUFACTURING IN BOLIVIA

In order to perceive how an answer to this riddle was found, Doña Flora's firm must first be considered in terms of the wider context of the Bolivian economy in general and small-scale production in particular. First, we must understand that, as in many other Third-World countries, manufacturing never played an important role in the Bolivian economy.

Historically, Bolivian entrepreneurs and international corporations were more interested in mining (particularly silver during colonial times and tin since the late nineteenth century) and in commerce than in industrial development. Due to the absence of large internal markets and in the face of competition from already industrialized countries, mining and commerce provided more immediate gains. The manufacturing industries that do exist are themselves heavily dependent on imported capital goods and intermediary manufactures.

Economies that are as dependent as Bolivia is on exporting a narrow range of raw materials are inherently unstable, for they are at the mercy of fluctuations in world demand. In addition, Bolivia, like many other countries in the Third World, has accumulated a very large national debt, a debt which increasingly consists of high-interest loans. As low-interest loans from foreign governments dried up in the early 1970s, new loans had to be assumed at the high prevailing bank rates. Since the early 1980s, Bolivia has not been able to service its debt, so new private bank loans that could be channeled into industry have become unavailable.

Under these conditions, only well-established firms enjoy virtual monopolies in their fields of specializations, state or joint state and private ventures, and small-scale enterprises have a good chance of surviving. Firms in the latter category tend to work with their own rather than with borrowed capital, thus enabling them to contract under adverse economic conditions, only to re-emerge when circumstances permit. Alternatively, they may reduce their profit margin to a bare subsistence minimum.

Some occupations requiring little capital investment, such as tailors and hatmakers, are fiercely competitive. Others are two- or multitiered with low-technology, high-competition production at the bottom and more mechanized production with more sophisticated equipment and generally lower competition at the top. Thus, furniture manufacturing includes both artisans who make crude chairs with equipment rented by the hour and well-equipped factories; sausages are made by family firms in home patios, as well as by foreigners using the latest German and Swiss techniques and technology.

Such adaptations are often complemented by the practice of putting out labor to even smaller firms (or others of similar size), thereby reducing a firm's investment and spreading the economic risks. As a result, small and large firms are often intricately interlinked. Individual shoemakers produce for middlemen who enjoy contracts with specific shoe stores. These, in turn, sell under their own brand names. Seamstresses working with their own machines periodically sew shirts for larger firms that also hire permanent workers. Likewise, women whose main economic activity is trading in street markets also sort coffee by hand for coffee export firms that have mechanized other aspects of their production.

Unlike other areas of the world where tourist crafts are often mass-produced, Bolivian crafts largely continue to be made by individual craftsmen. The production of local crafts for tourists and for export are exemplified by our case. The firm of Doña Flora is, in many ways, typical of small-scale production in general, but also exhibits special characteristics. As in other types of firms, Doña Flora's ties to her workers are highly variable. At the lower end are individuals and families who provide an occasional sweater for sale to middlemen. At the upper end are firms who produce wood carvings or sweaters for mass export in an assembly-line manner: the work process is segmented into small components that are readily mastered by the workers, who become specialized to a greater or lesser degree in specific tasks. Doña Flora's firm lies in the middle- to upper-middle range of this spectrum.

The flexible and uncertain expansion and contraction of such small firms and their variable linkage with each other and with larger firms in general, combined with the special demands for skilled labor in tourist craft firms in particular, provide a likely key to our riddle.

On our first visit, Doña Flora may have suspected that we were foreign buyers in disguise, using our avowed scientific interest as a subterfuge to obtain direct contacts with artisans. Such buyers would have been more hesitant to attempt to lure away close kin, who could be expected to have a long-term interest in the firm. In fact, when she branched out into the manufacture of jackets, the extended family to whom she had put out the sewing was able to make direct contact with her major foreign client, a buyer from London, and began working for him directly. The experience had been particularly galling, since it was the very same client who, in 1973, had encouraged her to diversify from sweaters and ponchos into tailored garments.

Doña Flora's trouble with these workers was symptomatic of a pattern of shifting between work arrangements which entail different degrees of dependence and intensity. The workers she lost sewed in their homes. She would bring the work to them and pick it up when it was ready. In 1978, Doña Flora expanded her workshop and hired workers to work there permanently. By 1984, however, these workers had also set up their own enterprises.

Doña Flora's seamstresses were just one part of an enterprise whose great complexity became more and more apparent to us as we interviewed various other members of her work force. Most notably, our observations of Doña Flora at work further demonstrated the intricate aspects of her business.

Doña Flora generally purchased alpaca wool from altiplano producer-vendors who came to the city to sell it. When she had a large order, however, this source often proved insufficient, forcing her to travel to distant fairs to buy wool directly from the alpaca herders. She then paid elderly women who worked at home in El Alto to spin the wool with wooden spindles. She, herself, also engaged in this activity when she had the time. In addition, Doña Flora purchased machine-spun wool from the would-be state monopoly and, later, when the price they charged became prohibitive, from a factory that produced the yarn clandestinely.

To prepare the warp, Doña Flora combined different natural colors of both hand- and factory-spun yarn. This was a laborious task done with the assistance of anyone who happened to be available: her youngest teenage son, her mother (on her periodic visits from the Titicaca Lake community where she and·her husband had returned after he retired from his job as a porter in the La Paz beer factory), and sometimes an additional worker or two. Her preferred spot for this activity, which requires an area as long as the cloth to be woven, was a plot she owns on the flat El Alto. On the day we accompanied her, her neighbors, two young, recent migrant women from the altiplano, came out to watch and helped her disentangle the yarn in the hopes of learning an aspect of a new trade. With but a few iron pegs and two metal basins, it took four persons six hours to prepare the 200 vara (180 yards) warp without counting the hour spent by the two neighbors unraveling the unruly ball of yarn or the hour travel time to the Alto. That day, Doña Flora took advantage of our presence (and our jeep), to take the warps to a rural community located 15 kilometers away, otherwise she would have had to go by bus or prevail on her younger brother to take her there in his ancient pickup truck.

The community enjoys bus service twice a week from La Paz whence milk vendors come to purchase milk and cheese produced in the community. One of the dairy farm families, to whom Doña Flora was introduced by a former weaver and *compadre* (ritual kinsman) who gave up his trade for a factory job, weaves for her. In addition, Doña Flora also engages the weaver we saw in her patio. A peasant from Lake Titicaca, this man (with whom Doña Flora has established ties of ritual kinship) used to furnish her with cloth when she was selling goods to tourists in a street market.

Doña Flora and her two daughters washed the cloth in a river half an hour away by bus and carded it to give it a smoother appearance, then they handed it over to the four workers we already encountered, who cut it, sewed jackets and made appliqué designs on pillow cases and wall hangings with the shop's two sewing machines.

In addition to goods made from woven woolen cloth, Doña Flora's second major line of craft goods were alpaca sweaters. Her principal source of these sweaters was a kin group in Huarina, while ponchos were knitted for her by women in the

Cochabamba area with wool which she provided. Doña Flora travelled regularly to Cochabamba with machine-knitted alpaca sweaters made in her own shop and other goods made out of artificial fibers that she purchased in La Paz.

On these trips, Doña Flora was accompanied by her younger brother or her cousin's son, Arturo. Her brother was sometimes also sent on business trips as far away as Lima alone. The two-way nature of this productive and commercial venture made the expense and time involved in the 500 kilometer trip well worth her while.

Doña Flora's success with exporting knitted goods from both sources depended in part on her ability to accumulate sufficient quantities (up to several thousand sweaters at a time) and to maintain strict quality control. Her clients were well aware that quality control was one of the major problems in the crafts trade. Some had learned the hard way. One client had amassed 10,000 sweaters through middlemen who purchased whatever they could find in El Alto, but he was forced to throw most of them away when they arrived at their destination because they were poorly made. Doña Flora did not hesitate to reject sweaters that failed to meet her standards. In addition, she, her daughter and the mother of the permanent workers spent a great deal of time mending small imperfections. Finally, when a large shipment had to be prepared, her cousin's son would come after school to help. Often he stayed overnight, repairing ponchos and sweaters and packing them for export. Indeed, during one year when Doña Flora's sons were in the military service, he joined the household altogether.

The sweater business is even more cutthroat than the woven goods business. Shipping agents are frequently approached by producers to direct foreign buyers to their firms, and Doña Flora was not immune to this tactic which she had benefited from on earlier occasions when her son-in-law was still working as a dispatcher. The idea of shipping alpaca woolens to Cochabamba caught on among other La Paz vendors, too, so Doña Flora also faced competition on this front.

Although Doña Flora made most of the crucial decisions regarding her enterprise, she also obtained managerial advice and help from others. Assistance with the paperwork was particularly important, since Doña Flora is illiterate. Her son-in-law, Indalecio, was in charge of the paperwork involved in exporting and shipping. Indalecio, who lived in a separate part of the same compound with his wife, Ricarda, and their children and generally shared meals with Doña Flora, had learned these aspects of the business when he was working for a major dispatching firm. He and Ricarda entered into a partnership with Doña Flora. In addition to Indalecio's managerial assistance, Doña Flora received advice from buyers and hired an outside accountant to go over the accounts with her.

Besides these two major lines of business, Doña Flora, as well as Ricarda, engaged in other, subsidiary ones whose relative importance waxed and waned according to the health of their manufacturing enterprise. Both had market stalls in a biweekly street market where, among other things they sold clothing purchased in El Alto and Laura Ingalls Wilder bonnets. These were of the kind that Bolivians see on television in the dubbed "Little House on the Prairie" series, and were made by Doña Flora's other daughter, who was seventeen in 1981. The two daughters-in-law who lived in La Paz engaged in similar marketing activities. A final source of income was transportation. At one time or another, both Doña Flora and her older daughter owned buses. In 1981, this was true only of Indalecio and Ricarda, who operated it on one of the regular city bus lines. When he had the time, and the bus was in working condition, Indalecio frequently drove the bus himself. At other times, Doña Flora's younger brother took over.

ANALYSIS

The work relationships in Doña Flora's firm are representative of both the range of ties required in the day-to-day operation of an artisan firm and the mutability of the work relationships over time necessary for the survival of both owners and workers.

Work Relationships with Kin

Among kinsmen alone, work relationships in Doña Flora's firm included unpaid collaboration of household members, partnerships with close kin living in semi-dependent households, the companionship and/or collaboration of siblings and more distantly related kin and various other transactions. The latter included the sale of products made by kinsmen and the contracting of a kinsman to transport goods to distant localities in return for the payment of his bus fare and a small variable bonus.

One of the major advantages of kin ties lies in the fact that they can perform many tasks as needed. Individuals are tied to their kinsmen through other kin in a variety of ways, creating a system with considerable feedback. As a result, a firm owner rapidly learns if a kinsman or woman is available to undertake some urgent task or to fill a more permanent position. A kinsman may thus become a part-time or even a full-time collaborator at one time, a companion at another.

On the negative side, an available close kinsman may not be equally suited for all the roles he is called upon to play by a more successful member of his kin-network. Doña Flora's brother was probably a good companion on her trips to Cochabamba, but when it came to collecting a debt in Lima, he was not enterprising or assertive enough to settle the matter, even though it later took the more astute Doña Flora and Indalecio only a day or two to succeed. Similarly, this brother did not make an ideal driver, but he was available and needed the work. Also, his limitations, unlike those of a stranger, were known. As the saying goes *Mejor es el mal conocido que el bien por conocer* (known evil is better than unknown good).

Certain limitations are imposed on a firm that relies heavily on close kin. During an economic downturn, this overreliance on a single major source of income by all members of an extended household may, in fact, be detrimental to their economic well-being. The need for economic diversification was among the reasons why Doña Flora encouraged one of her sons to emigrate to Australia; the bachelor brother ended up as a porter in Washingon, D.C., and the younger son obtained a job in the United States embassy in La Paz. The occasional order for goods from Australia, as well as the possible option of following him there, the generous remittances from Washington and the regular income from the embassy were more important to Doña Flora, at least during the economic crisis of the mid-1980s than the direct involvement of these kinsmen in her firm. Indeed, during such periods of crisis, drawing kin into the firm could backfire; thus, Doña Flora may not have acted in her long-term interest when she insisted that Indalecio join the firm rather than benefiting from his talents in a more indirect or intermittent manner. To be sure, Indalecio could always have spent more of his time driving his bus when export orders dwindled after 1981, but he would not thereby have fulfilled his potential. By 1984, he had divorced his wife and, with his second wife, opened a rival retail store and a shipping firm. Had Idalecio and Ricarda remained in Santa Cruz, the divorce might not have occurred.

Much larger and more capital-intensive enterprises also engage kin extensively. Kin appear as partners in firms inherited from parents; they are hired as managers, technicians or workers; or, having established independent firms engaged in the same speciality, they continue to cooperate in a variety of ways, such as lending one another equipment or raw materials and sending over a worker to help finish a pressing task.

Work Relationships with Nonkin

Arrangements with nonkin are equally variable. At the lowest level of intensity are one-time sales to customers in the market, but producers/middlemen attempt to cultivate and to consolidate ties that could potentially develop into long-term relationships involving repetitive transactions. Doña Flora invited a German buyer, who bought from her regularly, to dinner when he came to discuss a new shipment. She purchased sweaters from the same altiplano producer for many years, thereby assuring a relatively stable source of good quality products, and she established *cacera* (i.e., preferred customer) relationships with knitters and stall owners in Cochabamba. Particularly valuable ties were consummated through bonds of ritual kinship. Both the mother of Doña Flora's in-house workers and the weaver from Huarina, who, upon his entry into a factory, introduced Doña Flora to the family of altiplano weavers to whom she put out work and from whom she bought knitted gloves on occasion, became her *compadres*, as did the anthropologists.

These relationships with nonkin may be intensified over time as confidence builds and/or the need arises. The Latin American who took one of Doña Flora's sons along to Australia was a long-time client. At present, Doña Flora's son carries this man's surname, an indication that he has become fully integrated into the family. Another example of progressive intensification is Doña Flora's relationship with her accountant. By 1984, the latter was assisting her with the establishment of a leather industry that was to be manned by former workers of the very firm for which he was administrator.

Conversely, such long-term ties may also become deactivated or even severed. The latter frequently occurs when one party disappoints the other and sometimes when a worker becomes independent or is no longer needed. In the latter case, however, the relationship may simply become dormant, or it may be downgraded, with only one aspect actively being fostered.

Doña Flora seems to have relied quite heavily on chance encounters to establish her network of work relations with nonkin; yet, in the case of the weaver family near El Alto, she was aided by an outgoing worker. She also re-engaged at least one person with whom she had had a previous work relationship in a new capacity. Chance played an important role in many other small firms investigated; thus, prospective apprentices often went from workshop to workshop in search of openings. Despite the role of chance in building a network of work relations, the initial contact was often less fortuitous. An apprentice could come from a known family in the same neighborhood, or, in the case of first- and second-generation migrants, from the same community of origin. In addition, established workers often recommended their own kinsmen or fellow townsmen.

Spatial Dimensions of Work Relationships

The ties necessary to succeed in craft production of the kind in which Doña Flora engages cut across local, regional and national boundaries. Within the city, she was interactive with her urban kin, clients, shipping agents and sundry officials. Her spinners lived in El Alto where she herself also owned a parcel of land and where she purchased goods from middlemen to sell in La Paz proper. For many reasons, however, her ties had to extend beyond the city. Rural artisans can charge less for their labor because they have additional income, often their principal source, from their land. Migrants, like Doña Flora's weaver, with strong ties to their communities of origin are not forced to switch to another economic activity when business is slack, but can return to their home communities to farm while continuing the relationship with crafts firms on a part-time basis. Cochabambinas, with their special skills and lower wage demands, also constituted an essential component of Doña Flora's network, as did the market vendors in the city of Cochabamba, who opened a new market for alpaca sweaters and goods coming into La Paz from abroad.

The most important ties of all were those with foreign buyers, for only they could open up practically unlimited (albeit very fickle) markets. Participation in international fairs in cities as distant as Caracas and Bogota served the same purpose. Finally, encouraging kinsmen to emigrate to Washington and Australia opened new sources of remittances and potential economic alternatives, sources whose value increases as Bolivia's economy deteriorates.

The spatial expansion of small-scale enterprises, of course, is not a universal phenomenon. Many enterprises operate on a strictly local basis. Nevertheless, although interregional expansion of the kind exhibited by Doña Flora's firm tends to be associated with somewhat larger firms, even small workshops may entail frequent travels that may include remote locations. For example, a lamp maker with several thousand dollars invested in imported chandelier parts also has wooden parts made to order in Santa Cruz, where he also sells lamps on consignment in a store. In a way, such firms act no differently from much larger multinational firms such as a producer of comestible (edible) oil with headquarters in La Paz and factories in Cochabamba and Santa Cruz.

Social Class

Finally, the network of individuals on whom Doña Flora relied to produce and to distribute her goods cut across class boundaries. Although at a social level well beneath her own, herder-market vendors who provided Doña Flora with wool and the elderly women on El Alto who spin for her clearly enjoyed a working relationship of long duration with Doña Flora. They were also many-faceted, for the same women had sold her mantas when she had a stall in a tourist market. In sum, personalistic relationships must be established with all workers regardless of wage levels.

On the next higher social class level, that closer to her own, the differences between Doña Flora and her network contacts diminish. Sewing ponchos entails a higher level of skill than spinning and is commensurately better remunerated. Such skills are also rarer, and it is easier for a dependent worker to become self-employed and, hence, a competitor. Assuring a worker's loyalty to the firm thus becomes at the same time both very important and difficult. Even when a worker leaves a firm, however, the tie may not be broken entirely, for, in small-scale industries, competition and collaboration are not mutually exclusive (Piore and Sabel 1984). Consequently a craft firm that has successfully lured away a customer from a competitor may turn around and subcontract part of the work to the very same rival. This relative openness of artisan production which permits master craftsmen to become proprietors results, with the exception of a few large, highly capitalized state and private craft exporters, in a system with progressive rather than abruptly graded social rankings.

Doña Flora's ties with individuals whom she would consider her social superiors were associated principally with her role as an exporter. She first established ties with foreign buyers when she had a permanent crafts stall in a street market. At that time, she also sold to Bolivian exporters. A Bolivian exporter married to a Californian showed her how the sweaters should look and how to wrap goods for shipping, while his wife taught her the importance of preparing shipments on time. From then on, she dealt with the exporters directly.

The manner in which Doña Flora established ties with exporters is ample proof that she could successfully defend her interests vis-à-vis her social superiors. In this, she is representative of the veteran La Paz *chola* (mestizo) market vendors who instill respect among the lower classes and the elite alike; although, she frequently sought brokers to assist her in her dealings with exporters. While Doña Flora achieved a level of business acumen that enabled her to interact successfully with her social superiors, she nevertheless acknowledged her limitations. We observed that she visited an agent of the Bolivian National Institute for Small-scale Industry and Artisanry (IMBOPIA) alone, but she never travelled to international fairs by herself. In part, this may have been because she felt the need for a male companion, but most likely this was because the transactions at such fairs required literacy, and she could neither read nor write.

Doña Flora's son-in-law, Indalecio, became her principal broker. In 1981, she felt that her daughter Ricarda's marriage to Indalecio was one of the most important links to the middle class that she had been able to establish. Ricarda had met Indalecio when she sent off goods abroad. At first, the couple had moved to Santa Cruz where Indalecio was put in charge of reorganizing the branch office of the shipping firm for which he had worked in La Paz. Doña Flora, however, succeeded in persuading him to return to La Paz and to join her firm. They shared the profits according to the amount of capital each had invested and labor had contributed. Indalecio's education (he was only a year away from obtaining a university degree in economics) and his experience with shipping could not fail to be an asset to the firm. In 1984, after the marriage had broken up, Doña Flora was less positive about Indalecio's contribution. Had he not mixed up two shipments to Spain and England, the firm might have kept the clients it lost as a result. Now, her most important upward link appeared to be that with her accountant who was assisting her in her attempt to switch into the leather industry. She succeeded in creating a multipurpose link, as in the case of the Ecuadorian who took her son to Australia. At first, the accountant could help her with the arithmetic and keep an eye on her interests vis-à-vis her son-in-law, and, now, as an experienced manager of a leather goods firm, he was able to assist her in an entirely new manner.

Personalistic ties that cut across social boundaries are important for elite entrepreneurs, as well as for those who, like Doña Flora, have less advantageous connections. These entrepreneurs often operate in much the same way as those with more humble means, but the elite's high or social status may enable them to gain more ready access to services in return for some future service. For example, a lowly clerk in a government office with whom an elite manufacturer has established a personal relationship may be able to speed some paperwork along the tortuous routes of red tape, or a trusted contact in a lower neighborhood may stand in line for a few loaves of bread when none is available in the upper-class neighborhoods.

Ties that cut across social class boundaries are facilitated by the fact that owners of small enterprises personally engage in many aspects of the productive process. These tasks are not necessarily those for which the owner would have to pay the highest wages. Indeed, the opposite may frequently be the case. A person may also move from one activity into one that is only tangentially related, as was the case with Doña Flora's ex-son-in-law. Much more extreme switching into an entirely unrelated activity may also occur; for example, factory workers have become taxi owners/operators and a bureaucrat with a university degree in economics opened a chandlier and lampshade manufacturing workshop.

Like the social mobility of the workers, the willingness of many owners of small industries to engage in many aspects of the trade may also help to decrease the social distance between owner and worker, although work may still remain quite hierarchically organized. Indeed, perhaps in order to maintain a dominant position, even bosses of small workshops often treat apprentices quite harshly. In addition, men, in particular, may progressively dissociate themselves from productive tasks and become mainly managers. Concomitantly, in the larger, more highly capitalized firms, the social distance between owner and worker is more pronounced than in Doña Flora's firm; however, even in these cases, owner relationships, especially with senior workers, often continue to be couched in personalistic terms.

CONCLUSION

In conclusion, the flexibility required of Bolivian industries to survive uncertain economic conditions affects both their size and the social relations of production. Size is limited not only by a small market, historical dependencies and lack of capital, but also by the need to diversify sufficiently in order to be able to weather a downturn in one of several economic activities. This strategy entails a dispersal of energies and of resources at any given time which may not always maximize economic gain in the short run; however, in the long run, the option of moving from one activity to another or the ability to emphasize a different activity may be crucial for economic survival. For similar reasons, an entrepreneur often engages in a number of different tasks within a given enterprise.

The simultaneous involvement of an entrepreneur in a number of ventures, in turn, requires a far-flung network of personal relationships in order to recruit reliable personnel and to obtain information. Often, it entails a judicious combination of kin and nonkin relationships. Close kin may be employed directly in the firm or used to stabilize the economic situation of the extended family by branching out in terms of occupation and/or geography. More distant kin are frequently hired because they are known and their availability is readily determined. In addition, at least in the long term, an employer has some control over kinsmen because they are less likely to risk a complete break in relations. Finally, nonkinsmen are included in an enterprise in order to extend its access to skills, markets and government bureaucracies. Often, such ties cut across class boundaries. The alternative strategy of manipulating ties with more upwardly mobile kinsmen is often not possible, even when such kin exist. The latter frequently cut off their poorer relatives in order to limit demands placed upon them and in order to hide their own humble origins.

From the vantage point of the worker, the need for high flexibility in an enterprise may entail frequent dislocation, but also opportunities to become independent. Indeed, particularly in the less capital-intensive industries, salaried workers, outworkers or other persons involved in the enterprise may become competitors. To avoid this, some artisans have taken the extreme measures of working alone at all times, but this strategy is successful only in those industries entailing rare skills.

In more general terms, the dynamics of Doña Flora's firm and its relationship to the wider economy argues against the concept of a dual economy (an economy composed of a separate modern sector and a backward, traditional one) that is still prevalent in many discussions of industrialization (Berger & Piore 1980). In these analyses, artisanry and small-scale production are seen as characteristic of an intermediate and transitory stage in a universal evolutionary sequence beginning with small-scale domestic production for household consumption and ending with large-scale factory production for internal and external markets. In industrial anthropology, unlike other subfields of the discipline, change is thus still seen as entailing a sequence of inevitable and irreversible states in a universal progression. Small-scale production in Bolivia is more consonant with the view that industrialization involves flexible accommodation to local, national and international circumstances. The path taken by industrial development also depends upon previous adaptations that continue to shape its course.

The social relationships in small firms are not necessarily less exploitative that those in larger ones, but these firms provide both a wide range of goods and services for local, regional and national consumption that would otherwise not be consistently available and a livelihood for large numbers of people from all social classes. They even permit a degree of upward mobility both within and between economic activities. Rather than constituting a moribund vestige of the past, they represent a dynamic grassroots response within capitalist systems that are subject to extreme fluctuations and/or are consistently marginalized within the world economy.

NOTES

1. Adapted from a book in progress on small-scale enterprises in La Paz, Bolivia. Fieldwork on which this article is based was carried out jointly with Judith-Maria Buechler. It was sponsored by the National Science Foundation and a summer grant from the Syracuse University Senate Research Fund.
2. La Paz is located in a protected cauldron dropping off from a high plateau; however, the newer low-class neighborhoods, including El Alto, spill over only the plateau itself.

THE CROSS-NATIONAL WEB
OF SYRIAN-JEWISH RELATIONS

Walter P. Zenner

Some ethnic groups are international. Familial kin, commercial and charitable ties strengthen ethnic identity in a community which maintains itself in different countries throughout the world. Walter P. Zenner describes such networks in one group. He reminds us that ethnicity is not simply a lower-class phenomenon, but may also be found among middle- and even high-income populations. He also suggests that the process of assimilation is connected to the loosening of such ties.

THE TRADING MINORITY

While urban anthropologists, in general, have concentrated their attention on poor and working-class populations, considerable work has also been done on the social lives of people in the middle and even upper strata of society. Just as poor, rural migrants in cities and working-class people maintain many ties with their kin, with compatriots and with members of their own ethnic groups, so do the more affluent. The nature of such ties varies, depending on the types of economic activities in which members of the group engage, their historical and religious backgrounds and the types of settings in which they are found.

One type of adaptation associated with ethnic groups which occupy a middle status in society has been referred to as the *middleman minority* or the *trading minority*. Trading minorities are ones in which a disproportionate number of members of the ethnic group are engaged in commerce or work for others in their group who are so occupied. Before the rise of the modern, multinational corporation, the only way in which relationships of trust and credit could be enforced across international boundaries and over long distances was through common membership in a family or another community which could enforce discipline on its members. Even today,

Portions of this paper are excerpted from Walter P. Zenner, "International Networks of a Migrant Ethnic Group," which appeared in *Migration and Anthropology*. Seattle: The University of Washington Press for the American Ethnological Society, 1970, pp. 36-48. Published by permission of the American Ethnological Society.

SOURCE: Article written expressly for *Urban Life*.

small firms continue to work over long distances using trusted members of the kin group or co-ethnics as representatives (*see* Buechler, "Doña Flora's Network"; Zenner 1982).

In the case of ethnic groups, there are ties which bind beyond the family. Often, religion, especially in the case of European and Middle Easterners, plays a role in providing a form of social cement between members of the group. These connections may give group members certain advantages, such as other group members giving them loans, easier credit terms or employment. The value of group loyalty is not, however, always an advantage, since the group member must give up much in the way of personal autonomy, and the group itself may be fraught with internal conflict. For instance, a young man employed by his cousins in a small shop may have to work long hours and at lower wages in some instances than if he were working in a corporately owned department store. In addition, the value of ethnicity should not be reduced to its economic worth. Adherence to a common religion, for instance, also connects one's life to the divine and to life beyond one's own span on earth. The intricate web of relations of one trading minority, that of Syrian Sephardic Jews, illustrates the role of ethnic identification in social adaptation.

THE SYRIAN SEPHARDIC DIASPORA

A diaspora is an ethnic group whose members are scattered in different places, either within a country or throughout a region or the world. The Jewish people who had already dispersed during the period of the Roman empire were the group to whom the label was first applied, but the word now pertains to many other peoples as well. Syrian Jewry is, itself, a product of the dispersion of Jews, and it has produced its own diaspora during the past century and a quarter.

Around 1800, the Jewish communities in the large Syrian cities of Aleppo and Damascus were composed of Jews whose ancestors had been in the Middle East since time immemorial and of the descendants of immigrants from Spain, Portugal and Italy. Due to the fact that some of the Jews had a Spanish heritage, these Arabic-speaking communities were considered Sephardic, derived from the Hebrew name for Jews from the Iberian Peninsula. In the nineteenth century, the occupations of Syrian Jews included craftsmen, rural peddlers, government contractors and wholesale merchants.

The migrations of Syrian Jewry occurred as a result of the economic shift in the world economy caused by European domination, and industrialization and the opening of the Suez Canal, as well as of unrest within the Ottoman empire of which Syria was part. In the late nineteenth century, Syrian Jews immigrated to Beirut (Lebanon), Egypt and to Manchester (England). By World War I, they, alongside their neighbors belonging to other religions, were moving in substantial numbers to the New World, to both North and South America. Some, out of religious reasons, moved to the Holy City of Jerusalem at this time, presaging the larger immigration to Palestine/Israel after the First World War. Emigration from Syria continued from this period to the present. After World War I, international boundaries separated Aleppo and Damascas from their hinterlands. The rise of Arab nationalism and its conflict with Zionism made Jewish life in Syria quite difficult. By the 1950s, when

Jews were no longer allowed to leave, the vast majority of Syrian Jews lived outside of Syria. Small numbers thereafter have left either illegally or legally when governments loosened restrictions.

In the cities and countries where they now lived, the immigrants and their descendants often maintained their separate Syrian-Jewish identities in varying degrees. In places where there were high concentrations of Aleppo and Damascus Jews, they formed congregations along former regional lines and strove to contract marriages within their own origin group. In places where the number of Syrians was small, they would meld into the local Jewish community, especially with others from the Mediterranean or Southwest Asia.

This analysis focuses on Syrian Jews in New York, Israel, and Manchester (England), with an emphasis on the international connections which bind the communities together and which stress their common ethnic origin. Those individuals within these communities who are involved in economic, communal and familial activities on an international basis remain strongly identified with the Syrian-Jewish group, while those who lack such activity are more likely to have very loose ties to the group.

The data for this study was collected in New York between 1958 and 1960 and again in 1963; in Jerusalem in 1961 and 1962; and in Manchester in 1987.[1] Some material collected by Zerubavel and Esses (1987) and Sutton (1987) also contributed to the conclusions reached in this study. For the most part, the Syrian Jews studied were born in or descended from individuals who came from the city of Aleppo in northern Syria and were, therefore, often referred to as Aleppians or Halebis. Some were from Damascus, which is in southern syria, and they were called either Damascenes or Shaamis (from the Arabic name for that city, ash-Shaam).

UNCOVERING THE NETWORK

Upon scrutiny, Syrian Jews, whether in the United States, in England or in Israel, exhibit an intertwining network of relationships between the different communities. While engaged in a short study of the Aleppo Jews in New York City in 1958 and 1959, I met a visitor from Mexico, a female cousin, in the first home I visited. One interviewee was married to a woman from Panama, an "import," in the words of one young Syrian. One man was born in Manchester (England), grew up in Brooklyn and lived in Colombia and Panama, before coming to New York. Another grew up in Central America and lived in Israel for a few years. There were also families with business connections in the Far East.

In the institutional sector of the different communities, one also found an international network in operation. Several rabbis and cantors had emigrated over the years from Israel and Syria. They continued to have close ties with other Syrian and Sephardic rabbis in Israel and in the rest of the world. In field work in Israel, I encountered rabbis who had served congregations in Latin America, Europe and the United States before retiring to Jerusalem, as well as younger rabbis from Jerusalem returning home for a visit. There were also contacts between Jews of Syrian origin in Israel and those abroad in the support of institutions for both Syrian and other Middle Eastern Jews in Israel.

This material gives the impression that a substantial segment of Syrian Jewry is extremely mobile, even across international boundaries. There has been no deep-seated inhibition against such mobility, and the connections between different Syrian groups facilitate migration and other contacts.

This point was given new emphasis in Manchester in 1987. In July of that year, I entered a Sephardic synagogue in Manchester. During a pause in the morning prayers, an elderly man told his neighbor that he had heard on the wireless that morning about some political demonstrations in Panama, obviously revealing a personal interest in that area of the world. A few days earlier, I had visited an elderly, but active, textile trader in his office and warehouse. When I asked him about relatives overseas, he took out his address book and gave me addresses of sisters, brothers and their children in various countries in South America, Europe and Asia.

The delineation of waves of migration gives an indication of the general trend (such as out of Syria and to America or Israel), but does not reflect the patterns of back-and-forth migration. Immigrants who did not succeed returned to their former homes, and the children of immigrants emigrated from the second home to another point. These are patterns which ordinary immigration statistics do not reveal. This becomes particularly confusing when one deals with a group like Syrian Jews in which a variety of citizenships and official nationalities are represented. Even in the eighteenth century, Jews born and living in Syria held foreign passports. With the increasing interference of European powers in the Ottoman empire and with greater numbers of migrants, this practice also increased.

KINSHIP AND COMMERCIAL NETWORKS

An important function of kinship among Syrian Jews is that it provides them with links to new economic and/or geographic situations. First, it has been customary for one member of a family to go to a certain country and to set up a store or other business. Then he sends for other kinsmen (brothers, nephews, cousins) to help him in his business. In the past, men who went to work abroad would send money to their families at home. Likewise, marriage may also be involved in economic transactions. Wealth, in some places, is still transferred at the time of a marriage in the form of a dowry. Men, on occasion, will also marry relatively poor relatives from Syria and Israel with practically no dowry.

These patterns can be illustrated by several examples. Ralph Ades was born in Manchester, England, but was brought up in Brooklyn, where his father had a store. Upon completion of his schooling in New York, he joined a brother in business in Barranquilla (Colombia), but moved to Panama City. After serving in the U.S. Army during World War II, he married a cousin from Israel. Now, after living in New York for several years, he has returned to Latin America, where he is working with a brother who has a factory.

Eddie Sitton's family also illustrates the operation of this network. Eddie's wife was born in Panama, but her father was born in Syria and her mother in Mexico. She grew up in Mexico. In an interview, Eddie reported how his own parents came to the United States:

WPZ   Could you tell me a little about your family? Are they Halebi (Aleppine)?

ES   Yes. My grandfather on my father's side sent my oldest uncle to Alexandria
      (Egypt) to escape the (Turkish) army around the time of World War I. The
      Alexandria community supported refugees. Two uncles came to the United
      States. During the war, my grandparents and my aunt died. My father was
      orphaned. The Red Cross contacted his brothers, who sent for him.

WPZ   What did he do in this country?

ES   He was a peddler (I had learned that he had lived in Chicago, where ES still has
      relatives).

WPZ   What did he sell?

ES   Dry goods.

WPZ   What about your mother's side?

ES   My grandfather on my mother's side went to Egypt. Cairo was a big cosmopol-
      itan city compared to Aleppo, which then was a country town. Then he came
      to America.... It was too cold for him. Winters were colder then; they might
      have snow on Rosh Hashanah. So he left for Panama and married. That's where
      my mother was born. My father went to Panama and married. I went to Mexico
      and married....

WPZ   What about cousin marriage; is it common?

ES   There's nothing wrong with it.

WPZ   I know, I just wanted to know if it is common.

ES   Parents will encourage it, especially if the family is rich. *Yihus* (good family line)
      is the main reason. Money is secondary. My parents are second cousins; her (his
      mother's) sister is married to a cousin.

In this interview, Eddie Sitton did not indicate how he met his wife nor her relationship to him, although he indicated that the marriage had not been arranged. In another incident, where a Mexican cousin was visiting a Brooklyn family, I was told that a match between her and a member of that household was under consideration.

The pattern of immigration to a place where one has relatives is very similar to the original relationship between the wealthy merchants of Aleppo and Damascus and the poorer Jewish peddlers who sold the merchandise they acquired on credit to peasants and nomads in rural areas (Zenner 1965).

In Manchester, which is one of the older communities in the modern diaspora, young Syrian Jews, from 1850 to World War I, established another link in the chain from wholesale merchants to retail shopkeepers and peddlers. They acted as shipping agents for the wholesalers in Aleppo and other Middle Eastern Commercial centers, sending cotton goods out from the mills of Lancashire. While the Manchester community was able to achieve a middle-class standing almost from its inception, the situation of most Syrian Jews in the Americas was quite different, with the majority occupied as peddlers. Most of the descendants of these early immigrants are much more prosperous today. In the United States, Syrian Jews for a long time were specialized in the importing of household linens, lace and infant ware. In more recent times, many have been importers of electronic equipment or have opened discount stores (Sutton 1979; Zenner 1982).

Small businessmen in the 1950s and 1960s would still ask relatives living abroad to join them as employees and junior partners. A young Israeli-born Syrian considered an offer from an older brother who was part-owner of a shop in New York. This brother was born in Argentina and had never lived in Israel. When he was mature, he immigrated to the United States and opened a store in midtown Manhattan. In this case, the younger brother, who was imbued with Israeli socialist values, turned down the offer.

The position of Syrian Jews in Israel is somewhat unique. In some ways, Israel has become the impoverished homeland, especially since Syria now has lost most of its Jews and contact with those remaining is restricted. Israel, itself, has not had the type of commercial economy in which Syrian Jews have thrived as in the United States, Latin America and elsewhere. The kind of quick profits which can be obtained in New York's Times Square or in American resort towns cannot be realized in the more controlled Israeli economy. In addition, many of the Syrian Jews in Israel were recruited from among those who were too poor to immigrate to the Americas. With the relative unprofitability of commerce, many have left commerce for unskilled labor, in some cases, and bureaucratic positions in others. Only some of the Syrian families in Israel continue to be involved actively in the commercial-kin network.

Those families which still maintain commercial ties include the families of merchants born in either Syria or Palestine but who made their fortunes abroad. For instance, Moise Kohen was born in Jerusalem. After the war, he immigrated to Colombia and Panama, where he was a shopkeeper for a number of years. After 1948, he retired to Jerusalem for religious reasons. He still has a brother in Colombia with a large family, and he writes to them.

The Israeli-Syrian families with business and communal ties abroad continue to send members out of the country, at least for a number of years. In one family, five siblings born in Israel immigrated to New York within two or three years. One sister had been working in New York. Then two brothers arrived and began to teach Hebrew school. When one of the brothers was about to be married, two more sisters arrived. One of the brothers, in addition to teaching, opened a shop. The family lives in the part of Brooklyn where most of the Syrian Jews live today, and they participate actively in the community.

In addition to the Israelis, other Jews of Syrian origin migrate to and sojourn in different parts of the diaspora, attracted by relatives who are living in that place, whether it is New York, Los Angeles, Mexico or Manchester. Jews of Syrian origin from Egypt, Lebanon and Latin America, for instance, have found their way to the Syrian community in the New York metropolitan area.

Migration between countries is only part of the picture. In the interview cited above, mention was made of movement from Chicago to the New York City area. One finds Syrian Jews following economic opportunities on a worldwide and countrywide basis. Some families move between Bogota, Panama, Cali and Barranquilla or between Hong Kong and New York. Others migrate between New York, Los Angeles and Laredo (Texas). According to one rabbi in a Syrian congregation in New York, many families maintain a shop outside of New York City until their children come of an age when they worry about giving them a Jewish education and about their marrying outside of the Syrian-Jewish and general Jewish folds. During the earlier period, Syrian Jews had extremely strong preferences for marrying other Syrians, but this had declined in both the United States and in Israel.

THE COMMUNAL NETWORK

The network linking the various Syrian-jewish communities is evident in the activities of the merchants, some of whom are communal leaders. The communal network has links with the larger Sephardic-Middle Eastern and generally Jewish arenas of activity, as in the past. The network includes the flow of remittances, which today go primarily from the prosperous and wealthy Syrians in the Americas, Western Europe and East Asia to Israel and other Middle Eastern countries. Israel (in the past, both Syria and Jerusalem) provides rabbis for the scattered Syrian diaspora. In dealing with the flow of remittances and rabbis, the Syrian and'general Sephardic networks overlap and will be discussed.

The remittance network has its roots in the old traditional system of sending contributions for the support of scholars and of the holy places in the land of Israel. Much of this was related to the traditional charities of the Middle Eastern Jew such as support for the poor and needy (including orphans, brides without dowries and widows) in the Syrian cities.

When the Syrian Jews emigrated, this loyalty to tradition was maintained. For instance, a beautiful synagogue, noted for its inlaid wooden Ark, was built in the Nahalat Zion quarter of West Jerusalem with money sent by the Ades family. This family, originally from Aleppo, was resident in Egypt at the beginning of the twentieth century, when the quarter and the synagogue were built. This synagogue was under the jurisdiction of a court of Aleppine rabbis in Jerusalem as late as 1962. An orphanage for Jewish boys in Aleppo was supported by émigrés in the Americas in the 1930s. Some schools in Aleppo and Damascus are funded from abroad as well.

In Jerusalem, a number of Aleppine merchants and rabbinic scholars formed a *Committee of the Aleppine Community* after World War I. All three of the members of this committee were involved in general Sephardic and Jewish affairs, and three went abroad on behalf of both the *particularistic* and *general* communities. The main function of the committee was to support the needy in the Aleppine group in Jerusalem. The heads of this committee were self-appointed, and many of the funds which they used in giving aid were from Aleppines living abroad.

After the establishment of the State of Israel, with its extensive welfare services, many of which are also supported by foreign remittances, the need for private, particularistic philanthropy lessened. In addition, the leadership of the Aleppine group had grown old and was not replaced. Several attempts to reorganize the committee failed. It is likely that one cause of this failure was the fact that younger Israeli residents lacked the contacts with the Aleppines abroad which the older leadership had. In addition, most of the younger men were more involved in general Israeli and Sephardic affairs. By 1962, this organization had largely atrophied, although some remittances were still channeled through it. A Women's Committee, however, was showing signs of activity. This committee, composed of Aleppine women married to businessmen, sold linen seconds at a bazaar. These seconds had been sent to them by a wealthy Syrian wholesaler and philanthropist in New York. Except for this activity, the organization seemed nearly moribund.

The involvement of Syrian Jews in general Sephardic and Jewish activities is important for the flow of remittances. In Jerusalem, and elsewhere in Israel, there are several institutions which were either founded or which receive substantial support from Syrian Jews Abroad. In most cases, the conduct for these funds is a local Syrian Jew.

One institution which receives extensive Syrian-Jewish, as well as other Middle Eastern-Sephardic support, is the Porat Yosef Yeshiva. This rabbinical academy was originally founded in the Old City of Jerusalem on the basis of a bequest from an Iraqi Jew living in India. After the fall of the Old City to the Jordanians in 1948, the new building was erected in West Jerusalem. This new edifice contains many plaques indicating the sources of its endowments, which come from many different non-Ashkenazic groups throughout the world, especially the Americas and Britain. In addition to the Syrians, others who have contributed include Iraqi and Persian Jews.

A more modern vocational school was built in a town near Tel Aviv with money from a North American Aleppine. The man who helped organize the foundation of this school, which is primarily for new immigrants from Africa and Asia, is a well-known politician born in Aleppo. When the North American visited Israel, he ate at the political figure's home in a poor section of Tel Aviv. They also corresponded. While the school was for the larger community of Afro-Asian Jews, the old Aleppine tie linked the two.

This same tie also appeared in other institutions. One young rabbi of Syrian origin was himself uninterested in Aleppo, but since Syrian Jews abroad wanted to give money specifically to needy Syrian boys for the sole purpose of going to a yeshiva, he had to look for such boys. This created a problem, since the Syrians are a small and relatively well-established group among the Afro-Asian Jews. They are somewhat more assimilated into the general Sephardic and Jewish population than more recent immigrants, like the Moroccans. The memory of Syrian origin has significance because of the Syrians abroad.

In addition to Israeli philanthropy, Syrians also contribute to other institutions for Middle Eastern Jews. A leader of the Syrian community in New York was a chief supporter of Ozar HaTorah, an orthodox Jewish school system for those living in Muslim countries and in France. This system was founded by a Polish rabbi who had been working with European refugees in Iran during the Second World War. The manner in which he reached the Syrian philanthropists is unclear, but the Polish rabbi had contacts in Jerusalem, including Aleppine Jews living there.

The importance of the Aleppine rabbis and other religious specialists in this network cannot be overemphasized. Many of the rabbinic families had immigrated to Jerusalem prior to the First World War, but many members of these families traveled to Syria and to the Syrian and other Middle Eastern immigrants in the diaspora. One purpose was to raise money for the sacred institutions in the Holy Land, but also to provide religious services for Sephardic Jews abroad. It was not inconsistent with these purposes to go into business for oneself; hence, some of these rabbis established shops or other commercial enterprises during their sojourns overseas.

Some of these rabbis have lived in the diaspora for most of their careers, while others resided there for only short periods of time. Some who spent most of their lives in countries like Mexico have retired to Jerusalem. In turn, young rabbis from these families go overseas. In rabbinic households, there are frequent visitors from such countries as Peru, Argentina, Great Britain and the United States. Many of these visitors are either the rabbis of these far-flung congregations or else simply members. Sometimes, Syrians in the diaspora will ask well-known, old rabbis in Jerusalem (or elsewhere) for legal opinions or for talismans against some ailment.

In a like manner, one finds Syrian rabbinical students at Porat Yosef Yeshiva and similar institutions from the Americas and elsewhere. These students are guests in rabbinic households and sometimes marry girls from these families. Similarly, one finds such students in yeshivot in New York City, some coming from Syria and others from South America. While this group is not large in number, it adds an additional link to the chain of connections.

The congregations which rabbis of Syrian origin serve are not exclusively Syrian, although most are of Mediterranean or Middle Eastern origin. Neither are those who serve Syrian congregations in the Americas totally Syrian, but, again, those of Afro-Asian origin are most common. Among the Syrian Jews of Brooklyn in the late 1950s, one found a rabbi of Iraqi origin, a school principal from Morocco, an Iraqi-Israeli cantor and a Yemenite-Israeli cantor. There were also several American-Ashkenazic rabbis of European origin and several Syrian-born or Israeli-born Syrian rabbis. The two cantors had both studied certain aspects of the liturgy with Syrian singers in Jerusalem.

In Manchester, the Syrian Jews were always part of a larger group of Mediterranean cotton traders, including Sephardim from Morocco to Iraq. All of the Sephardim participated in the formation of three Sephardic synagogues in the city. While one of these synagogues was seen as more *oriental*, a term designating the Syrian and Iraqi Jews, Aleppians, from the beginning, participated in the foundations of all three synagogues. In the more oriental one, however, the Aleppians were in the leadership position, and they remain so to this day. Still, it can be said that the Aleppians in Manchester have always been much more integrated with other Sephardic Jews than were those in New York City or Mexico City. None of the rabbis in these congregations are of Syrian origin. The small size of the Sephardic enclave there and the lack of firm boundaries between the different origin-groups contributed to the difference between Manchester and New York.

OUTSIDE THE NETWORK

Withdrawal from the network takes various forms. Many Syrian Jews no longer enter traditional commercial occupations. Instead, they become physicians, lawyers or scholars. This reduces their contacts with other members of the community, particularly with those Syrian Jews who live overseas. For others, the change is even more radical. For instance, one woman in Manchester was of Aleppian ancestry and married another English Jew who served in the diplomatic service. Although they did not sever ties with the Jewish community, her husband's career made their social life one which was apart from other Jews, even when they were stationed in places where there were large numbers of Jews.

Ralph Sitt is an example of a Syrian Jew who has lived most of his life outside the Syrian-Jewish network. His father was one of the first Syrian Jews in New York City. Ralph's mother was an Ashkenazi woman from Manchester. He grew up in Harlem, when it was still a Jewish, but not a Syrian-Jewish neighborhood. During the First World War, he joined the U.S. Army and rose to the rank of colonel. While stationed in Panama, he met and married a Gentile woman from Oklahoma who converted to Judaism. After he left the army, he moved to Lima, Peru, where he opened a plastics factory. He maintains membership in the Jewish community, although his autobiography does not indicate his degree of commitment. His son has married a Peruvian Catholic woman, who has not converted to Judaism (Sutton 1987). While maintaining connections with his relatives and with the Lima Jewish community, his relationship appears to be a distant one.

In constrast with these cases are those of Halebis who, in Israel, were uninvolved in Halebi affairs, but who became quite active in the New York Syrian community. Another is that of a Manchester Aleppine woman who married a Syrian-Jewish businessman and who lived most of her adult life among Syrian Jews in the United States.

CONCLUSION

The delineation of international networks among a dispersed ethnic group is something which follows naturally from much of what has been written about migration. Some of the characteristics of the Syrian-Jewish group, of course, may be particular to segments of the Jewish diaspora. The Jewish communities in Syria were themselves products of waves of migration and were always connected to Jewish communities elsewhere; thus, the daughter-communities of Aleppo Jewry are subentities within the Sephardic and Jewish dispersions. As such they reveal much regarding cross-national networks, particularly when considered in terms of general social characteristics.

NOTES

1. The research in New York and Jerusalem was supported by Columbia University and the National Institute of Mental Health. My work in Manchester was financed by a research grant from the Research Foundation of the State University of New York. This support is gratefully acknowledged. I am solely responsible for any errors.

Part Six
Urban Neighborhoods and Community Formation

PLACE AND PLANNING

While it is obvious that cities are places, the way in which such a locale is perceived varies among those who live there. Likewise, the place may be transformed according to the plans of builders and designers; thus, the same location may differ in character according to the manner in which it was developed. Homes may be open to those walking down a street through unhedged lawns and picture windows, or they may be shut off as private spaces surrounded by high walls or hedges and with latticed windows which face an inner court. Towns and cities may center around markets, mosques, cathedrals, bathhouses and other such buildings, or they may center around cafes, taverns, saloons and the like. Streets may form a grid pattern, or they may wind along like a cow path. A city may be centered, as Washington is, with the Capitol Building as a "pivot of the four quarters," the navel of the universe, making secular Washington resemble many sacred cities of the world (Wheatley 1971).

The differences between cities result from a complicated combination of factors. The mental image of what is appropriate combines with the availability of materials, the distribution of power, the ability of planners to convince political leaders to follow their designs, and the creativity of the masses in making the space provided for them their own. These points are well made by the contributors to this section, especially in regard to how even poor and powerless people have influenced the designs of planners and presidents. Epstein shows how Brasilia, a new capital for Brazil, was forced to tolerate squatters in spite of its original design. Kirshenblatt-Gimblett gives us insight into how ordinary New Yorkers utilize the space allotted to them. Deshen shows how immigrants established social control in the new and old cities of Israel. In a discussion of how local voluntary and quasi-voluntary organizations work, Bestor describes how residents in a Tokyo neighborhood maintain their own community and their definition of what that should entail in the face of the municipal government's efforts to impose another definition of community upon them.

THE CITY AS A FOCUS OF IDENTITY

The city, as a physical place, may itself constitute an important source of identity for both present and former inhabitants. Waldron demonstrates this most clearly in relation to the old city of Harar, where the wall constitutes a boundary dividing those within from those without in terms of language and culture. It is an ethnic boundary, much as we might envision the ancient border between the Jebusites of pre-Davidic Jerusalem from their Hebrew and Canaanite neighbors, for, as Waldron illustrates, the inhabitants of this city continue to identify as *ge-usu* even when they migrate to Addis Ababa.

In modern North American cities which are inhabited by descendants or migrants from all over the world, the city may be a weaker focus of identity than in Harar, but it is not insignificant. Civic pride is often associated with loyalty to the local professional sports teams and with the name of the city itself. Bostonians are fierce Red Sox fans, and the New York Yankees have had supporters from a wide variety of ethnic groups. San Franciscans abhor the use of the term *Frisco*, while Chicagoans can detect outsiders by the fact that they do not pronounce the city's name as *shikawgo* but as *shikaago* or even *tchikaago*. Like ethnic loyalty, such civic pride becomes much more marked when residents emigrate or otherwise come into contact with outsiders; thus, a small group of former Chicagoans may continue to root for the Cubs or for the White Sox once living in Los Angeles or New York. The relatively recent phenomenon of civic loyalty in North American cities, as representative of a form of urban social cohesion, deserves additional serious study.

The appearance and location of a city is also of great significance to its residents, as well as to others. While urban neighborhoods may involve the utilization of different cognitive maps so that a Puerto Rican may note the location of *botanicas* on the Lower East Side and ignore the Jewish bookstores, certain features are shared by all such neighborhoods. Among these common features are those provided by the natural environment, although humans can transform these as well. Chicagoans, for instance, consider the lakefront to be of great significance, a view which is given added salience through Chicago's extensive park system which extends along the Lake Michigan shore. By contrast, the Chicago river is less marked in the consciousness of Chicagoans. In Manchester, England, one may cross a bridge over a river and never realize the waterway is there because walls block one's view; hence, the communal focus is consciously placed elsewhere.

NEIGHBORHOODS

In previous sections of this book, we have discussed the effects of migration, wealth, power, prestige and ethnicity on urban centers and the persons who inhabit them. In many ways, these aspects were discussed without reference to location; yet, in fact, they are often localized, even in modern cities. Both commercial areas and residential neighborhoods are still segregated, even if they are not entirely homogeneous.

Locale-specific social networks are generated within urban neighborhoods, isolating them from other neighborhoods. For instance, people maintain some kind of relationship with neighbors in a suburb even when their closest kin or best friends live elsewhere. Children on a block play together, neighbors chat while mowing a lawn or say hello while jogging. Neighbors whose property is adjacent often need to work out arrangements of how to deal with trees that do not recognize property lines.

In a similar manner, shopping malls, the epitome of the city/urban conglomeration created by the automobile, reveal this human tendency to build social networks. Despite the rapid turnover in sales staffs and in individual outlets, one finds social regularities present. The mall rats are the grandchildren of the kids who used to hang around corner drugstores and poolhalls two generations ago. Just as many city dwellers used to go to the neighborhood business district, to Main Street in small towns, or downtown in big cities, so too the present generation visits the malls (Jacobs 1984). The appearance of mall rats on the scene may be just an early sign of the dawning of a new indigenous culture.

Shopping areas, whether traditional markets, downtown areas or contemporary malls, may be segregated on the basis of economic status and ethnic affiliation. They also may be places where individuals of differing heritages may meet. Residential areas have generally been more segregated by class and ethnicity. Both government policies and market forces (sometimes assisted by the actions of buyers and sellers) have played a role in such segregation. The word *ghetto* was first applied to urban quarters in Italy where Jews were compelled to live. These areas had no Christian inhabitants, and they were isolated from the rest of the community each evening by virtue of a gate. Some ghettos in Italy, incidentally, displayed problems which appear in modern times such as overcrowding, the need for building more stories since land was scarce and the neglect of housing because rents were controlled. In this instance, the motivation for segregation was religious, since Catholicism in that period required toleration of Jews, as long as their inferior status was clear (S. Kahn 1903).

In contemporary North America, the underlying patterns which lead to segregation along lines of socio-economic status, ethnicity, age, marital status and even sexual preference are more subtle. Sally Engle Merry, in her essay "Urban Danger," has touched on some aspects of these patterns in regard to renters in a public housing project. Constance Perin shows the connections between the values of social mobility, safety versus danger and/or risk and the way in which land zoning is carried out (1977). Her study employed interviews with real estate developers, bankers and others involved in the production of housing, as well as with those who rent and buy housing to illustrate how the desire to reduce risk to one's investment encourages racial and other forms of segregation, whether this is on the part of homeowners, bankers, or insurance companies. Ms. Perin's work, like all of the studies in the section, further emphasizes the role of location in determining community formation and in defining urban neighborhoods.

Walter P. Zenner

WITHIN THE WALL AND BEYOND: ETHNICITY IN HARAR, ETHIOPIA

Sidney R. Waldron

Harar is the only case of preindustrial "stone" city in this book (cf. Sjoberg "The Preindustrial City)." It has survived as a functioning walled city into the twentieth century, while many other cities of this type like Cairo have become absorbed into modern metropolitan areas. It is also the home of a unique ethnic group with its own language, culture, and identification with the city. The *ge usu'*, as the people of Harar call themselves, are an economic class, too. Sjoberg pointed out that the elite in preindustrial societies were residents of the cities. The *ge usu'* are both a mercantile and a landowning elite who have dominated the peasantry in the surrounding countryside. Waldron thus demonstrates how class and ethnicity overlap. At the end of the article Waldron speculates about the future of the *ge usu'* as they become dispersed in other Ethiopian cities. He suggests that they may form ethnic associations like those found elsewhere in large cities.

Harar, Ethiopia, is a walled preindustrial city whose approximately 20,000 inhabitants[1] speak a unique Semitic language and have an urban culture which is distinct from that of the surrounding peoples. Oral traditions state that the city's wall was built by Emir Nur, who ruled from 1552 to 1566. Since that time, Harar has retained its identity as an ethnic enclave although it has functioned as a vital market area for the surrounding peoples and as an important regional center of Islam. Located about half-way between the Red Sea and Addis Ababa, the capital of Ethiopia, Harar has long served as a trade link between inland Ethiopia and the outside world.

From the vantage point of Mount Hakim, the city of Harar resembles an island of houses in the midst of open country. In many ways, Harar is very much like an island, separated both physically and symbolically from its neighboring ethnic groups. The Harari call themselves *ge usu'*, "people of the city"; call their unique language *ge sinan*,[2] "the language of the city"; and call their way of life *ge 'ada*, "the customs of the city." Outside the city wall, they say, are *derga usu'*, "wild or uncultured people." The religion of the city, Islam, is its major cultural connection to many of the surrounding peoples.

SOURCE: Article written expressly for *Urban Life*.

For an anthropologist, such as myself, one of the most interesting phenomena of the city of Harar is the persistence of its ethnic group, the *ge usu'*, who have maintained their identity despite at least four centuries of frequent and intense contacts with four other ethnic groups. These are the agricultural Oromo, who number some 200,000 in the area of Harar; the pastoral Somali, who are the dominant population in the arid regions; the small group of Argobba villagers; and since the city's conquest and incorporation into Ethiopia in 1887 the highland Christian Amhara.

These outside groups are dealt with for economic, governmental, and many other vital reasons. This discussion will explore the means by which the Harari have maintained their distinct language and culture despite these contacts. Why have they not been absorbed by the surrounding Oromo, who outnumber them ten to one? Why haven't they become Somali, Argobba, or Amhara? Why, in fact, has Harar not become an ethnic melting pot?

SOCIAL SOLIDARITY AND CITIZENSHIP

The first insight into the integrity of the Harari comes from an appreciation of the internal solidarity of the city's society, the high value they place on their way of life, and some of the symbols they use to reinforce cultural self-awareness.

To the outsider, the city of Harar seems congested and maze-like in its complexity. To the *ge usu'*, it is both home and sanctuary. When I first moved into the old city in 1962, I was oppressed by the crowded conditions. Noticing the wide open spaces outside the city, I asked many *ge usu'*, "Why don't you move outside the wall?" The usual answer to this naive question was, "Because everything is inside."

The wall has ceased to be of defensive utility since the mid-nineteenth century. The gates did have an important economic function when Harar was an independent city-state. Each gate functioned as a customs station. Goods were taxed both as they entered and as they left the city (Paulitschke 1888:243). However, neither defense nor taxation explains the continuing importance of the wall. Now it must be viewed as the physical manifestation of the social boundaries which have preserved the Harari ethnic identity and which surround the Harari way of life.

Within the wall, the Harari ethnic group maintains its existence primarily by two means: (1) by defining and emphasizing the social duties of citizenship; and (2) by utilizing symbols of ethnic identity which enhance the consciousness of being Harari.

With few exceptions, the Harari ethnic group is endogamous. A *ge usu'* (Harari) is thus born of Harari parents. A Harari speaks *ge sinan,* the language of the city, as his mother tongue and uses only it within his own society, although he usually knows two or three other languages. Being born in the city and speaking its language would seem to be prerequisites enough for citizenship, but to fully qualify, he must participate in the city's three basic social institutions. These are *ahli,* the family network; *marinyet,* organized friendship; and *afocha,* community organization.

The family network links each person with dozens of other households spread throughout the city (Waldron 1978:15–16). Each has a specific role which is defined for the individual by the kinship system. Unlike many other African societies, corporate kinship groups such as clans are not found in Harar, and unlike many other Muslim peoples, extended patrilineal systems of tracing relationships are not used here. Each person's family network overlaps other individual's networks until the interconnections of families within the city are as numerous and intricate as the crossing of strands in a spider web. Each *ge usu'* is ultimately tied to every other *ge usu',* and closely related to a great many.

If kinship in the city establishes all-encompassing webs of relationships, each with its required form of behavior, friendship provides the *ge usu'* with a small closed group of confidants. Each *ge usu'* belongs to one and only one group of friends, made up of about five or six persons of the same sex. These are formed of playmates from his neighborhood in early youth. Friends are seldom close relatives, and perhaps never are brothers. The explanation for this is that status inequalities are built into all kinship roles, even those between elder and younger siblings. Friends are, above all, equals and thus should not be confused with relatives.

Friendship in Harar is extremely important in adolescence. Young men roam the streets with their friends, and share many of the experiences of maturation in each others' company. Indeed a friendship group sometimes seems to produce a shared responsibility orientation among its members, who are likely to develop a similar way of viewing the world around them.

Friendship groups convene at least once a week in the important institution of the *bercha.* A *bercha* is a calm and deliberative conversational session where friends discuss anything of mutual concern. Much of their conversation centers around the topics of their city, its place names, their legends, and the proper way of telling these in the language of the city. Awareness of the city's culture is thus heightened. Conversation is stimulated by the chewing of the leaves of *ch'at* (*Catha edulis*), called *q̄at* in Arabic. *Ch'at,* chewed in moderation, produces a mild euphoria and mental intensification. The *bercha* epitomizes the nature of friendship in Harar, a tranquil respite from the status considerations involved in the rest of Harari society, and a place where stories are told and advice is sought within the security of lifelong bonds of trust.

The *afocha,* a kind of communal organization, is the focus of social solidarity among the *ge usu',* however. In 1975, there were twenty-four men's *afochas* and fourteen women's *afochas* in Harar. *Afochas* are primarily concerned with weddings and funerals, but their inner workings are much more complex (Koehn and Waldron 1978). *Afochas* are made up of one's neighbors, for the most part, and are likely to include some of one's friends and some of one's relatives. Many friends and relatives will also belong to different *afocha* groups. The overlap of kinship, friendship, and *afocha* membership establishes a very high degree of social solidarity in Harar.

This social solidarity, which could also be called "interconnectedness," affects the ways with which the *ge usu'* behave toward one another. No one within the Harari ethnic group is a stranger, and there are no public acts which remain secrets from one's friends, relatives, or *afocha* mates. Thus a *ge usu'* is very careful how he behaves in public and how he treats other people of the city. Part of this consideration derives from his shared identity with them. But he also knows that if he should quarrel with another *ge usu'*, or otherwise behave against the ethics of the city, he would become the subject of gossip which would eventually reach everyone of concern to him.

Participation in the basic institutions of the city is the essence of Harari citizenship. The total amount of time spent in kinship, friendship and *afocha* functions is extensive. However, the individual who attends to the city's social obligations also knows exactly what is going on inside the walled city. He has accurate and up-to-date information concerning market prices and political conditions, which he obtains in informal conversation at social events. From an overall social perspective, the result of this high degree of participation is an extremely tight-knit ethnic group, effectively closed to those not born in the city, which, in turn, helps explain the persistence of the Harari ethnic group.

SYMBOLS OF IDENTITY

Underlying this tight-knit society is a conscious awareness of what it means to be a *ge usu'*, a member of the city culture. Hundreds of local place names, coupled with their explanatory traditions, make the city a very meaningful place for the *ge usu'*. Although the city is bafflingly complex to the outsider, it is conceptually quite simple for the *ge usu'*. First of all, the city is divided into five quarters. Each of these quarters is further conceptually subdivided into neighborhoods. These neighborhoods are not merely spatial referents. Each has its tales and traditions which enhance the meaning of living in the city.

Usually, neighborhoods are named after *awach*, a category which includes Muslim saints, war heroes and learned men, and which translates directly as "fathers" in the sense of "fathers of the city." Perhaps fifty of the city's neighborhoods are named after *awach*. There are dozens more located throughout the city. (In fact, I recorded one hundred and fifty-six awach shrines in 1975.) Many of these *awach* are shrines of famous Muslim saints which are celebrated in all-night ceremonies by the *ge usu'*, wherein the life of Mohammed and praises to the saint are recited. Harar is thus a kind of holy city; to be a Harari is to live in it, in the constant presence of the *awach*. For the purposes of this discussion, that statement should be reversed: to live in the presence of the *awach* enhances the feeling of being a Harari.

The physical evidence of ethnic awareness is manifold in Harar. Even household architecture plays its role, since every feature of the traditional home has a pattern which is explained in terms of the past of the city. A good example is the explanation of the hard-packed red earth floor of traditional Harari homes. The red color of this specially prepared surface is said to represent the Harari blood spilled at the Battle of Ch'elenqo, where the city lost its independence forever to the forces of the Ethiopian Empire in 1887. Children are thus raised with the distinctiveness between *ge usu'* and other ethnic groups firmly entrenched as part of their surroundings.

Since its conquest, Harar has come into more and more intensive contact with outside groups, especially the Amhara, who comprised the dominant ethnic group of the Ethiopian Empire. The Harari seem to have made adjustments in the ethnic markers used to define themselves vis-à-vis the Amharas, who are Christians, as this contact increased. I can cite only a few examples here.

Richard Burton, who, in 1854, was the first European to vist Harar, reported the Harari to be virtual drunkards, in contradiction to the rules of Islam, which prohibit alcoholic beverages. "High and low," he said, "indulge freely in intoxicating drinks, beer, and mead" (Burton 1966:188). *Gohoy,* a kind of beer, used to be sold in the streets. However, a century later, the Harari do not tolerate the drinking of alcohol: Christians (Amhara) drink; Muslims (*ge usu'*) do not. The *ge usu'* chew *ch'at* extensively; the Amhara eschew it. The *ge usu'* grow the world's most delicious coffee beans, in my opinion, but they seldom drink coffee—it is for Christians. They prefer imported tea, or drinks made from coffee leaves or husks.

One may react to these intensifications of the symbols which define group identity, whether one is Harari or Amhara, with distaste, seeing them as deplorable examples of bigotry and intolerance. Here, however, I am suggesting another perspective, that of a threatened ethnic group, trying against all odds to hold on to its identity, its culture, and its way of life.

BOUNDARY MAINTENANCE AND RESTRICTIONS OF EXCHANGES

Harari in-group solidarity, combined with the symbols of ethnic identity which define the people of the city as separate from all other peoples in the world, provides a strong basis for the maintenance of their ethnic identity. However, probably the most important social mechanisms with which the *ge usu'* have preserved their tiny culture while engaging in daily and important transactions with the surrounding and more numerous ethnic outsiders are those which are used in defining boundaries.

The perspective I have taken in analyzing Harari social boundary maintenance was developed independently of that of the great Norwegian anthropologist, Frederik Barth, but resulted in a remarkably similar conclusion. As Barth says,

Stable interethnic relations presuppose . . . a structuring of interaction: a set of prescriptions governing situations of contact, and allowing for articulation in some sectors or domains of activity, and a set of proscriptions in other sectors, and thus insulating parts of the culture from confrontation and modification (Barth 1969: 16).

The way the people of Harar have held on to their identity is exactly by defining limits for the types of interactions permitted with the members of other ethnic groups. One may trade with an Oromo or an Amhara, but one may not marry a member of the outside group. One may engage in religious celebrations with other Muslims (and the Oromo, Somali, and Argobba are Muslim), but unless the fellow Muslims participate in the three basic social institutions of the city (kinship, friendship, and *afocha*), they are not Harari—they are still outsiders.

In categorizing the types of exchanges which are regulated by the *ge usu'*, I have followed the suggestion of Claude Levi-Strauss (1953:536). He suggests that the crucial exchanges in any society, which my focus restricts to interethnic exchanges, are of three types: (1) exchange of goods and services, or economic exchange; (2) exchange of personnel, (especially marriage, but also including adoption, and assimilation); and (3) exchange of information. One could probably consider biological exchange between groups, or gene flow, but data are lacking.

Sometimes anthropologists speak of social boundaries as if they were single clear-cut lines, as a circle on a map of ethnographic distributions. The approach I have used, however, produces three types of boundaries—each of which is measured as a frequency of interethnic transaction. However, as Barth has made clear, ethnic survival in contact situations is facilitated by forbidding some types of exchanges while permitting others.

The ethnographic details of Harari exchanges with each of the contingent ethnic groups are too complex to be presented here (see Waldron 1974:260–327). However, in the abstract, a pattern of boundary management by the *ge usu'* emerges, which has permitted the survival of their culture. Most important, here, is their restriction of the exchange of personnel across ethnic boundaries. Harari are permitted to marry only other Harari,[3] thus avoiding gradual dilution of their culture. Should a Harari marry a Christian, that person would be shunned and referred to as if he or she were dead.

If endogamy preserves the integrity of the population and its culture, its wealth and energy are derived from profitable economic exchanges with the surrounding groups. Of these, the Oromo have been historically the most important to Harar. Richard Burton described the Harar of one hundred years ago, saying, "Harar is essentially a commercial town: its citizens live . . . by systematically defrauding the Galla Bedouin (Oromo)" (Burton 1966:192). Although much has changed recently in the old system, the *ge usu'* traditionally profited in two ways from the surrounding Oromo peasants. First of all, they owned most of the farmland for miles around the city. This was cultivated by Oromo tenant farmers, who might be expected to yield as much as seventy percent of their crops to the Harari owner. Also, the Harari merchants profitably controlled the city's market, the sole source of regional specialties and imported goods for a vast area of this part of Africa. In a way, then, the Harari exploited the Oromo while forbidding marriage with them, and in this lay the secret of their duration and wealth.

The Harari also controlled the flow of information in and around the city, for they were and are multilingual. Most Harari are fluent in the Oromo language, for instance, although virtually no Oromo can speak the language of the city. The Harari merchants thus could manipulate prices on the spot, using *ge sinan,* the city language, as a kind of secret vehicle for price setting. Many Harari also speak Amharic, Somali, Arabic; many can speak some English. Within the city the knowledge of markets and farms, of political and economic events is pooled within the population of *ge usu'*. It is shared in visits, in meetings of friends, relatives, and *afocha*. In a way, the system of information thus established is like a brokerage of strategic knowledge, and to become a member one must be a *ge usu'*.

BEYOND THE WALL: THE FUTURE OF THE HARARI

The delicate balance of ethnic groups which has been discussed here has been altered irreparably by the events of the twentieth century. As I have indicated, the old farming economy of Harar was based on ethnic stratification: the Harari owned the land, and the much more numerous Oromo paid for the right to work it, often exorbitantly. Such exploitative forms of land tenure were widespread in Ethiopia before the revolution of 1974. Not surprisingly land reforms were one of the first and most necessary changes made by the new government. However, with these reforms, the traditional Harari economy was shattered, and the wealth of the city, which had permitted the *ge usu'* to spend long hours fulfilling social obligations, was gone forever.

In response to this and earlier economic changes, many Harari merchants had moved to the capital of Ethiopia by 1975. In 1977, when I last worked in Ethiopia, this population movement from the old city had become a virtual diaspora: there were more Harari living in Addis Ababa than in their old home city.

I know, from preliminary research in Addis Ababa, that they are adjusting their patterns of friendship and the structure of afocha organizations, and that kinship has taken altered roles. The Harari will not have a wall around them in their new city, nor will they be reminded of their identity by the symbolism of the old city's saints. The literal meaning of the term *ge usu'* will refer less and less to the people who live in their old sanctuary, the city of Harar. However, there will be, for all the foreseeable future, *ge usu'* living in the cities of Ethiopia and contributing their specialities to its culture: they *are* the "people of the city."[4]

NOTES

1. In this paper, I have used the term "Harari" interchangeably with the term of self-reference, *ge usu* ("city person"). This use of Harari is somewhat misleading: (a)

At present the old city, which is discussed here, contains some 20,000 persons. Of these, perhaps two-thirds were *ge usu'* in 1975, and the rest were Amhara and Somali. (b) Outside the old city is a proliferating new urban center at least equal in size to the old city. Ethnically, it is dominantly Amhara, with lesser numbers of Oromo, Gurage and other Ethiopians. The term "Harari," which I have used in a restricted sense, could be used for any resident of the city of Harar, Ethiopia, population 45,000.

2. Until recent years the Harari language, *ge sinan*, was restricted to the city walls. That is to say, one could walk through the Harari speech community in twenty minutes by walking through the city. It is a distinct Ethiopian Semitic language, akin to the national language of Ethiopia, Amharic, but not mutually intelligible with it.

3. Important exceptions to this firm general rule are documented in the complete enthnographic description (Waldron 1974:270). For instance, sometimes a *ge usu'* man might marry an Oromo woman as a second wife. This would be seen as an economic and political stratagem by the *ge usu'*, since, by doing this, he would be gaining a link with her village. He would never, however, bring this wife or any children back to Harar. They would be raised as Oromo.

4. My research in Harar has been generously supported over the years. A Ford Foundation Foreign Area Research Fellowship sponsored the original work, 1962–64. In 1975 and 1977, research was supported by The Social Science Research Council, The State University of New York Research Foundation, and a Summer Stipend from the National Endowment for the Humanities.

ORDINARY PEOPLE/EVERYDAY LIFE: FOLK CULTURE IN NEW YORK CITY

Barbara Kirshenblatt-Gimblett

Studies of urban life often focus on those who hold the most power, whether economically, politically or culturally; and to the extent that these studies examine culture, they are generally concerned with elite culture. Lower-income groups are typically studied in terms of so-called social problems. The analysis of folk culture offers an alternative perspective on the city by asking the question: How do ordinary people, faced with the increasing centralization of resources and power in large cities, find ways to exercise control and autonomy in their everyday lives? Though this study focusses on New York City, the issues are generally relevant to modern social life.

Vernacular culture is rooted in the immediate conditions of social life, homemade, peculiar to a locale and often outside of, if not in opposition to, official or established culture. The street, bar, club, barbershop, vacant lot, rooftop and kitchen are its crucible, rather than the school, museum and symphony hall. Culture in this local sense is a reworking of the materials at hand, from oral traditions and customary practices to the products of the culture industry and elite institutions. Generally absent from the discourse of New York City Culture, vernacular culture is what ordinary people create in their everyday lives. Tacit, often small in scale and informal, vernacular cultural production can reveal how people escape bureaucratic control; create zones of autonomy and choice; resist, oppose or subvert dominant cultural values and practices; and replace and renew what is appropriated from them by the culture industry.

Culture, as an organizing concept in the discipline of anthropology, has been variously defined in the literature (Kroeber and Kluckhohn 1952). Whereas anthropologists have tended to use the term to refer to the total way of life of a particular society, usually non-Western ones that are small in scale, scholars working in complex societies must conceptualize culture in relation to extreme social heterogeneity. Raymond Williams (1982) traces the history of the term, explaining how culture comes to be equated with civilization and the social elite.

Others have used the notion of subculture to capture the diversity of complex societies. In this study, the term *vernacular culture* focuses attention on the

SOURCE: Article written expressly for *Urban Life*.

commonplace aspects of everyday life, in contrast with the elite culture of museums and universities and the *culture industry* that mass-produces our movies, records and fashion.

Key thinkers, such as Theodor Adorno, Max Horkheimer, Jean Baudrillard, Pierre Bourdieu, Henry Lefebvre, Michel de Certeau, Raymond Williams, Stuart Hall and Eric Hobsbawm have disagreed on the nature of vernacular culture and its creative and emancipatory potential. Vernacular culture is variously designated by them and others as folk, popular, residual, emergent, alternative, oppositional, subcultural, genuine, customary or quotidian and is contrasted with official legitimate, dominant, hegemonic, high, or mass culture. The contrasts suggest relationships between vernacular culture and other kinds of cultural formations, relationships that are played out with special clarity in cities.

How then shall we constitute vernacular culture as a subject for study? Typically, the search has led to enclaves and subcultures, to vivid and legible assertions of social autonomy, whether these take the form of identifiable religious sects, such as Hasidim; deviant youth subcultures, such as Punks; artistic subcultures, such as Hip Hop; occupational groups, such as bicycle messengers or distinctive neighborhoods, such as Chinatown or Harlem. Settings and events (clubs, parks, streets, rallies, festivals and parades) have commanded attention as places where, for a time, vernacular culture alternatives can be enacted. Researchers have also searched the interstices in the daily round where alternative and oppositional practices can emerge – in the workplace or at times and places where formal controls are weak. Some have identified vernacular culture with the working class, others with marginal subcultures that can arise in any class and still others with the everyday in *everyone's* life – the quotidian.

There are several recurrent questions which should be addressed in a serious investigation of vernacular culture. With the increasing centralization of both elite and mass cultural production and the massive resources they command, how can local and autonomous vernacular cultures form and survive? Where and among whom are they to be found? What is their makeup and meaning? What are their relationships to other types of cultural formation? How are vernacular values and practices deployed? What are their material consequences? Can we speak of a politics of vernacular culture?

These concerns are important in the conceptualization of urban life less in terms of the haves and have-nots and more as a struggle among diverse sectors and social worlds, where cultural capital, particularly in the form of vernacular culture, may be in greater abundance than economic resources. According to Raymond Williams and others, vernacular culture espouses what the dominant culture neglects, undervalues, opposes, represses or even fails to recognize. In contrast, definition by negation – defining the nature of the have-nots in a society renders certain social sectors invisible as phenomena in their own right by referring to them only in terms of others who have what they lack. Consistent with the discourse of dominant culture is the implication that success is to be measured in terms of upward mobility and economic gain, particularly as achieved through formal educational institutions and the political system. By examining vernacular culture, its processes of formation and deployment, we may be encouraged to question some of these assumptions, to see vernacular culture as commentary, critique, alternative or resistance and to find other standards for measuring its success or failure.

Persistent themes in urban anthropology include territory, politics, social segmentation and work. Should considerations of place be confined to neighborhood, conceptualized primarily in terms of residence? Should the concern with politics be extended to cultural politics? Should ethnic/racial segmentation be viewed not only in occupational terms, but also as highly contingent social constructions? Should the focus on labor be supplemented by attention to domestic life, leisure, religious activity and other aspects of daily reality?

PLACE

"Identity of place is achieved by dramatizing the aspirations, needs, and functional rhythms of personal and group life," according to Yi-fu Tuan (1977:178). Tuan and others have stressed the effort required to transform space into place, to invest a location with meaning. Residence per se is not enough to create a sense of neighborhood: without deep emotional attachments to a location, it is difficult, if not impossible, to mobilize concerted action to protect the interests of those who live there. This is not to underestimate the economic pressures and political forces that shape neighborhoods, but to direct attention to vernacular culture as the medium through which residents make the places in which they live palpable, articulate social relations, give form to values and discover possibilities for action.

Rather than starting with neighborhood as a self-evident unit, we might make the notion problematic. Consider a map of New York City that consists of a series of overlays, each one delineating a particular geography of the city. The boundaries and the territories they define are relevant for certain groups, activities and occasions. They rarely converge, often conflict and shift over time. The various areas include the *bureaucratic territories* (zip codes, area codes, police precincts, electoral districts, school districts, zoning); *areas defined by the delivery of services* (cable television, messenger services, parcel deliveries, taxis, drug traffic); *manufacturing and business areas* (fur, garment, diamond, advertising, electronics, printing, restaurant supply, luxury retail, the territorial organization of vendors and street performers); *local spheres of influence* (parishes, neighborhood associations defined by block, street, square, park or region, gangs, organized crime); *a recreational geography of Culture and entertainment* (Museum Mile, theatre district, landmarks, plaques and historic restorations, concentrations of pornography and prostitution, public spaces, vacant lots and exotic neighborhoods); and *ceremonial centers* (Fifth Avenue, Union Square, Eastern Parkway, Washington Square). Many of these territories cannot be located by means of a map or official marker, but rather are discovered informally through social knowledge, often tacit, and through social action, whether instrumental or expressive, symbolic and ceremonial. Clues may be found in toponomy and orientation, including the official names for areas, name changes initiated by the City Council, new names created by real estate interests and local traditions. For whom is the area near the Port Authority bus terminal Hell's Kitchen rather than Clinton? For whom is the area below Fourteenth Street and east of the Bowery the East Village rather than the Lower East Side? Who refers to Sixth Avenue and who to the Avenue of the Americas? What conception of a territory is at work in the way that directions are given? Is an address on the Bowery to be identified in terms of Lower East Side or Little Italy/Soho cross streets? Individuals who are thoroughly familiar with Prince and Spring Streets may be at a loss if oriented in terms of Rivington and Stanton Streets; yet, all four converge within yards of each other on the Bowery.

Cognitive maps, the ways in which territories are conceptualized by their inhabitants, can offer insights into the complex ways in which space is organized in New York City. Consider the many maps of the Lower East Side that could be drawn by Chinese, Hispanic, Ukrainian, Italian and Jewish inhabitants, children and adolescents as opposed to elderly residents, city planners, real estate developers, the art world, public historians, the tourist industry and New Yorkers whose families once lived in the area. Is the focal point Clinton Street, with its Dominican bridal shops; Essex Street, where Jewish religious articles may be found; East Broadway, now largely a street of Chinese food shops; the art mecca of Alphabetland; the Ukrainian organizations of Second Avenue; the Italian pastry and cheese shops on First Avenue; the vacant lots and abandoned buildings awaiting development; the men's shelters and refuges for the homeless; or the points of historic interest?

Cognitive maps are also enacted in ceremonial ways. The chosen order of march, or route, and the sequence of stops, parades and processions, many of which have a long and well-documented history in the city, dramatize social relations and engage in a spatial articulation of values. As Susan Davis (1986) suggests, "Such public enactments are not only patterned by social forces — they have been part of the vary building and challenging of social relations.... As dramatic representations, parades and public ceremonies are political acts: They have pragmatic objectives, and concrete, often material results."

The Stations of the Cross processions on the Lower East Side and in other parts of the city map sacred history onto the present social reality by establishing a convergence between each stage in Christ's passion and the places in the neighborhood of significance to the parishioners — a housing project, hospital, center of drug traffic, site of an accident or violent death. Placards held aloft at each station may carry statements of protest against abortion, United States involvements in Central America, inadequate facilities for the elderly, the lack of low-income housing, inadequate protection against crime or drug addiction. Groups who participate in such events are also effective in mobilizing community support for improving conditions in their neighborhoods. Processions organized by the Church may make the parish, as a territory, visible for a moment by routing the march along the parish boundaries. Processions organized by saint societies express what Robert Orsi (1985:221) has called "the spirit of defiance in popular spirituality." Home shrines and sidewalk altars, saints' feasts and processions mobilize local communities in alternative, if not oppositional, ways and offer still other notions of territory and neighborhood.

A similar line of argument, with rather different outcomes, could be pursued in regard to other events of this kind. The lion dance processions organized for the Chinese New Year by competing martial arts clubs are viewed by the police, who issue the street activity permit, as one parade. Concerned with the practicalities of rerouting traffic in the small and crowded neighborhood, the police prescribe one route for the dancers to follow. For the dancers, however, Chinatown is a complex area, divided into highly charged provinces of power. What the police, press and visitor consider one parade is, for Chinatown, a series of up to a dozen independent and competitive processions. Each lion dancing team has the right to pass along certain streets, but not others; obligations to go to some spots first, as a sign of deference and respect; and the good sense to avoid crossing paths with a warring team. Elaborate performances lasting almost an hour may occur at prearranged locations and can generate substantial income for the groups, who aim to pick up several thousand dollars in the course of the day. The route, the points at which the dancers stop, the time spent at each place and the elaborateness of the performances constitute a map of social relations and power structures shaping life in the area and beyond.

The annual West Indian carnival procession each Labor Day is not only a celebration, but also an important political event. The sheer number of people who gather, estimated at about one million individuals, is itself evidence of organizational success in turning the numbers out and in coordinating their activity on such a large scale once they are present. Indeed, the West Indian Carnival Association is the largest organization in New York's Caribbean community.

In contrast with the public events staged in the places where people live are those that occur in what have evolved as the city's ceremonial centers. Fifth Avenue has, over the last hundred years, become such a ceremonial center, to the dismay of the Fifth Avenue Association, which sees these events as a nuisance. Dispersed populations, such as the Irish, come together from throughout the metropolitan region and claim one of the most prestigious avenues in the city for four hours in the form of the St. Patrick's Day parade, "the oldest and largest annual civic parade in the United States," according to Jane Kelton (1986).

In contrast with such highly organized, militaristic parades, are events such as the Easter Parade, a tradition for about a century on Fifth Avenue. With no formal auspices or funding, no program, no official route, map or guide, no mailers or paid advertisements, no organizer and no permits, tens of thousands of strangers from throughout the city and beyond gather along Fifth Avenue in their holiday best to see others and to be seen by others. This event, like the activities in Washington Square and other open spaces in the city, is important for the way that it reveals how large numbers of strangers orchestrate an exceedingly complex program of activity on the basis of tacit understanding and customary practice. These events and settings are extraordinary examples of cooperation on a large scale with a minimum of formal control. When exerted, that control is generally repressive, as in the police harassing performers for park permits or noise permits and regulating the solicitation of money (something only religious groups can do).

Events like the Easter Parade, which bring together such a heterogeneous crowd, are also important for the way in which they both crosscut boundaries of class, ethnicity and neighborhood and lay claim to a prestigious public space. These events raise important questions about the nature of public space and the history of legislation in New York to control what can and cannot be done in the city's streets and open areas. Selectively enforced, the law over the last century has gained increasing control over what can occur in public spaces, whether at all or only by permit or license. The hanging of laundry, posting of bills, vending, playing of music and assembly or movement through space are among the activities that can be defined as *quality of life crimes*. Attitudes toward these activities reveal competing notions of the street and differential access to public space, attitudes and notions that are frequently expressed through the rhetoric of crime, public order and respectability.

Perhaps the most vivid, recent example of alternative conceptions of the city being enacted through a delineation of territory other than neighborhood is that of subway graffiti. The basis for association is the subway line. Writers who live near stops on the same line associate with each other, even though their neighborhoods may be widely separated. The drama of control is played out across the entire city on the moving canvas of the trains, as writers vie with each other and with city authorities to achieve the status of *all city*; that is, to have one's tag, or name, well represented on all the major lines. This youth subculture, known as Hip Hop, is worth examining for the conception of the city that it expresses and, from an historical perspective, for the ways in which its expressive modes (graffiti, rapping, breaking, language and dress) have been contested by city authorities, while being coopted by the art world and culture industry.

CULTURAL POLITICS

Emblazoned on a subway car, the epithet "Style Wars" captures not only the spirit of urban graffiti, but also the larger point that style is meaning, that expressive behavior articulates values. Scrawled on a devastated building in Lower Manhattan, the epigraph "Semiotic Guerilla Warfare" acknowledges the conflict of value systems played out in the marks individuals make. The public nature of walls and trains and the outrage of many citizens and city officials are essential as an oppositional context for these marks. As Dick Hebdige (1979) suggests, the *crime* is only a broken code. Both "Style Wars" and "Semiotic Guerilla Warfare" are instances of expressive behavior that derive their meanings from the problematic relations between individual and institution, private and public, property and the law, autonomy and control. These relations inform a vast array of expressive forms in the city, and style provides an important arena for dramatizing these conflicts.

Oppositional styles are frequently appropriated, diffused, and defused, by those they oppose. The movement back and forth is one worth tracing, particularly in the record bin archeology and playing against the groove that are so characteristic of Hip Hop's rap music. At parties held in parks, community centers, schools and clubs, recorded music is the raw material for performances by the DJ, a musician whose instrument is the *wheel of steel* or the turntable. As the record spins, the DJ makes the needle repeat sections, plays two records simultaneously, forces the record to play backwards, adjusts the volume of the two tracks and combines recorded sounds, often taken from obscure records found in the record bins of subway shops, with the electronic beat box or with the live verbal patter of rappers. Like so many other creations in the vernacular, Hip Hop has gained legitimacy and has been reappropriated by the mass media but with unpredictable results.

On the one hand, the legitimate theatre has featured the idiom on its stage, a spate of main release films and videos have gained international visibility for the form, and how-to-do-it books and classes have sprung up to meet the demand for participation by suburban adults and others far-removed from the youth subculture that gave rise to Hip Hop. On the other hand, Maori and Samoan youths as far away as New Zealand, Indian and Caribbean adolescents in England, the children of Turkish migrant workers in Berlin and *bamboo shoot* gangs in Tokyo have identified closely with Hip Hop as seen in films and video, have created their own versions of it and have made it voice their concerns. Such cases call into question what so many critics of the culture industry have characterized as the passive and uncritical consumption of mass culture and the power of the culture industry to displace or to absorb and to domesticate vernacular creations.

Such cases are also an invitation to explore cultural politics. What role do schools, athletic leagues and other institutions, organized and sanctioned by adults, play in homogenizing difference by imposing cultural standards? How do cultural differentiations persist in the face of efforts to eliminate them, whether in the name of respectability, democracy or upward mobility? What are the implications of a middle-class fascination with working-class culture, particularly on the part of disaffected youth? How does style, through the media of music, dance, language, dress and forms of association, articulate the terms in which the conflicts will be played out? With what consequences?

SOCIAL BOUNDARIES

Rather than start with the epithets *ethnic* and *racial* as givens, it would be worthwhile to make the terms problematic, to consider other attributes that contribute to the formation of social categories (age, gender, disability, religion, class), to cast the entire question in terms of the social construction of difference and to view ethnicity in more fluid and socially contingent terms. At one extreme, cases can be cited where objective differences are not a prerequisite for social distinctions, as assimilated Jews who have faced anti-Semitism can attest. At the other extreme, observable distinctions may be inconsequential in the organization of group life. The issue is thus not the degree of cultural difference involved, objectively speaking, but the social significance attributed to any similarity or difference, however small.

Furthermore, identity is not singular and immutable. There are many bases for identifying oneself and being identified by others, and there is a degree of choice. It may not be possible to eliminate an objective difference, but it is possible to render it socially inconsequential. It is therefore important to ask how choices are made and to examine which attributes of the many that could be cited — gender, age, skin color, national origin, residence, occupation, economic status, religion, education, language, political leanings, skills, etc. — are salient in which situations? It is also important to recognize the possibility of multiple identities and multiple cultural repertoires, as well as the ability to select from and to alternate among them. This heterogeneity "brings to consciousness... premises or assumptions hitherto in the main covert or implicit" and is a source of cultural creativity (Keesing 1960). Evident in New York's vernacular music, dance, language, fashion and food, this cultural creativity is worthy of study in its own right.

A promising avenue for research is how culturally specific ways of organizing time shape social identity. Discrepancies between calendars (for example, the variance between the dates of the Greek Orthodox and Roman Catholic Easters) reflect conscientious efforts to differentiate two traditions. As made so clear in the work of Eviatar Zerubavel (1981), each calendar creates its own distinctive rhythms, sequence of moods and dramatic structure not only for those who live by it, but also for others who work and live in the area. Thus, lived calendars are both segregative and integrative, and examples abound of lives lived under more than one calendar.

Calendars are experienced territorially. Either the streets are festivalized by spectacular ceremony or deserted on holidays by those who normally work in the neighborhood:

> New York is not itself on Jewish holy days. Delicatessens are not open. The garment district is silent. All over the city, shops, offices, schools, cleaners, even entire buildings, close down for the day – like so many darkened rooms in a normally well-lighted house.

> Yesterday was Yom Kippur [Day of Atonement], the highest holy day of all, and no-where was it more evident than in the diamond district along West 47th Street between Fifth and Sixth Avenues... (*New York Times*, 9/28/1982).

It would be worth examining how institutions, particularly schools, government offices and the private sector, intercalate civic, Christian, Jewish and other calendars, and to what effect.

When activated in the forms of liturgical recitations and ritual enactments of sacred history, calendars transact the relationship between a very long stretch of history and the short annual cycle of observance. As Lloyd Warner has shown in his analysis of Yankee City calendars manifest a particular view of history in the choice they express of what to celebrate and with what emphasis. The multiplicity of calendars and schedules in New York City is evidence of an extraordinary pluralism and offers an important contrast with the clock, traffic signal and other efforts to synchronize and discipline large numbers of people on a strictly pragmatic basis.

EVERYDAY LIFE

Though a critical factor in any consideration of New York City, work is but one aspect of the lives of New Yorkers. For many, the conditions of work are largely beyond their control. All the more reason to pay close attention to those areas where people have greater autonomy. Herein lies the importance of vernacular culture.

One of the richest areas in which to observe choice and autonomy at a local level is in that of play, the autotelic activity *par excellence*. Streets, buildings and lots intended for purposes remote from pigeon flying and stickball are mobilized in ways that reverse the normal relations between means and ends. In play, as in art, the expressive takes precedence over the instrumental, and the constraints of necessity are suspended for a time in the interests of pure enjoyment: a sewer cap serves as homeplate, fire escape ladders become basketball hoops, fire hydrants delineate boundaries, the stoop becomes a ball court and cars become bases. Small variations in play terminology or practice define regions of the city, while short links in long chains of transmission ensure the integrity and durability of a culture created by and for children who pass on their knowledge of the street to each other and without the intervention of adults. An activity that occurs everywhere, play takes distinctive forms in urban settings, utilizing and transforming features of the environment.

Vertical displacements, such as rooftop gardens and the *tar beach* of urban sunbathers, and aerial extensions such as the flying of pigeons and kites from rooftops, capitalize on the city's extreme verticality. The monumental view from the roof and the unlimited sky often contrast sharply with the street, which in the inner city may be the scene of litter, drugs and devastation. The pigeon game, popular in areas where concentrations of tenements still stand, tests the loyalty of the birds, whose instincts to flock and to home are in conflict when two different flocks mix in the sky. Loyalty and honor, prized values, are dramatized daily in the pigeon game, often in areas where incomes are low, unemployment high and opportunities for suffering personal indignities frequent.

Paradoxically, the very conditions that lead to the impoverishment of urban areas, to the abandoning of buildings and their eventual levelling, also create zones of entrepreneurial opportunity. The lots open up to the unsupervised construction of elaborate gardens and handmade buildings, often without formal sanction. In East Harlem, the South Bronx, the Lower East Side, and parts of Brooklyn, little country cabins mushroom incongruously on vacant lots between tenements and brownstones, some abandoned, others still intact.

These intentionally old-fashioned *casitas*, once common in the Puerto Rican countryside, abound where local men can no longer afford to rent storefronts or basement rooms for their social clubs. One is named *Nostalgia for My Homeland*, others are named for hometowns. The detritus of urban decay is redirected here to materialize pastoral images of another time and place. Though these environments may not significantly change the material conditions of their lives, the enacting of alternatives is both significant in itself and revealing of the larger settings in which these men find themselves.

It is essential that, in our efforts to keep the larger picture in view, we do not lose sight of life as lived in a city such as New York, with all the specificity that gives it its special character. In exploring the interaction of culture, politics and economics, we must take care not to lose sight of processes at work outside of the formal structures and institutions. In our enthusiasm for New York's metropolitan dominance, we must not undervalue the vernacular culture of the city and all that it can reveal to us about the inner life of those that live in New York.

Acknowledgement: This essay was written with the generous support of a Guggenheim Foundation Fellowship, 1986-87. It draws on my earlier study "The Future of Folklore Studies in America: The Urban Frontier," *Folklore Forum* 16, No. 2 (1983): 175-234, and was presented as a position paper to the Committee on New York: The Dual City, sponsored by the Social Science Research Council in October, 1986.

THE GENESIS AND FUNCTION OF SQUATTER SETTLEMENTS IN BRASÍLIA

David Epstein

Squatter settlements are found all over the world. Known variously as *favelas* (Brazil), *barriadas* (Peru), *villas miserias* (Argentina), *colonias proletarias* (Mexico), *bidonvilles* (French-speaking Africa), and *bustees* (India), these settlements have one thing in common: they provide a place to live for poor people, many of them migrants to the city who cannot obtain any other form of housing. The internal characteristics of squatter settlements and their inhabitants have been the subject of much social science research. In this article David Epstein uses an historical-structuralist approach. He focuses on the interconnections between the poor and the dominant strata to explain the function of squatter settlements and why they persist despite government policy to the contrary.

Urban squatting is the fastest-growing, and one of the most widespread forms of settlement in Brazil and in many other countries in the under-developed sector of the capitalist world. Social scientists and public officials have often failed to take into account factors on the international and national levels which account for the existence of squatting in cities such as Brasília, the new "planned" capital of Brazil. The sources of this neglect also underlie many of the widespread misconceptions and mistakes in writing about urban poverty and worldwide underdevelopment in general.

In the case of Brasília, an understanding of the development of the squatter settlement component of the urban settlement pattern requires attention to the class, urban-rural and regional disparities in the economy, and to the requirements for a low-wage labor in the face of low governmental priority for the housing and other needs of workers. Although planners and officials in Brasília inveigh against squatting, it is in fact a product of the same process of development which produced Brasília and in practice is tolerated and regulated by the same institutions that officially condemn it.

A squatter settlement in a city is an area where people build houses in violation of the formal legal rules about property rights, zoning, and type and quality of construction. Squatter settlements (or squatments) may be distin-

SOURCE: Reproduced by permission of the Society for Applied Anthropology from *The Anthropology of Urban Environments,* Monograph No. 11, 1972.

guished from slums in that most squatters (at least initially, and by their own, if not by official definition) own the houses they live in.[1] Large numbers of squatters, though by no means all of them, are members of the urban working class or the urban un- and underemployed, and large numbers of them, though again by no means all, live in housing of low prestige and durability. Slums, on the other hand, are inhabited mostly by renters, and the most common house types are the decayed town house and various types of tenements especially built for rental to the urban poor.

THE DUALIST FALLACY

One approach to squatter settlements is to regard them as fundamentally divorced from the city around them. When squatters are conceived of as in-migrants from rural areas regarded as the "traditional" sector of a dual society, the assumption of urban dualism follows naturally from the dualist image of the national society as a whole. Thus, just as Jacques Lambert (1959) argues that there are "two Brazils," a conclave of social workers in Brasília suggested that there are two Brasílias:

> The phenomenon of marginality which appears in the Latin American countries indi-cates the existence of a *dual urban social structure* and has in the economic factor one of the variables of its appearance.
>
> In addition to this economic variable, which assumes undeniable importance in the configuration of the situation of urban marginality, the concentration of marginalized groups in certain characteristic zones of urban space is observed [emphasis added] (Lambert 1967:2).

While an effort is made to give this term a technical definition, or at least usage, it should be noted that the Brazilian term *marginal* is most often used in crime reporting to refer to individuals from the lower-class, criminal milieu, such as pickpockets, illegal lottery salesmen (*bicheiros*), pimps, and muggers. Use of the term, even in a professional context, must evoke in most middle-class Brazilians associations of the squatting phenomenon with crime, violence, and social pathology in general, in correspondence with their standard prejudices.[2]

Others argue that squatter settlements are in some sense rural, either be-cause of the alleged similarity of architectural forms to those in rural areas or because of the supposed provenience and associated social and cultural charac-teristics of their inhabitants (Bonilla 1962).[3] Bastide suggests that the cultural assimilation of foreigners in Brazilian cities is easier than that of rural migrants who are ". . . bearers of a folk culture, because (a) internal migrations are family migrations . . . (and) (b) the rural family in the city continues to 'so-cialize' its children according to rural models" (Bastide 1964:76).

Building on the concept of subculture, Bastide goes on to suggest that shantytowns are the locales of "microcultures" which are sharply distinct from the urban milieu as a whole.

Other analysts are concerned with the effect on individual personality of the allegedly rapid cultural change taking place in rural-urban migration. Pye, for instance, suggests (and laments) that the maladjustment and insecurity he believes associated with such migration offer a threat to the national and international status quo. This argument relies very heavily on a concept of social duality similar to the arguments of the commentators already cited. States Pye:

> Urbanization is . . . a profoundly disruptive process. In nearly all transitional societies the early emergence of urban centers has produced a *fundamental cleavage* between the worlds of the more modernized cities and the more traditional and village-based people. This *bifurcation of the social structure* is usually matched in the economic realm by the development of *dual economies*. In the psychological sphere the rapid transition from the compact and intimate world of the village to the highly impersonal and anonymous world of the city can leave people with deep personal insecurities.
>
> Thus in a multitude of ways rapid urbanization can cause social, economic, and psychological tensions which, translated into the political realm, become sources of instability and obstacles to rapid nation building [emphasis added] (Pye 1963:84).

Lewis's concept of the *culture of poverty* is more carefully hedged than any of the foregoing discussions, but it also emphasizes the distinctiveness of its bearers from the larger society, rather than the role they play in it. While on the one hand Lewis defines the culture of poverty as a subculture and hence presumably a product of Western capitalism, on the other hand he states:

> It is a culture in the traditional anthropological sense in that it provides human beings with a design for living, with a ready-made set of solutions for human problems, and so serves a significant adaptive function (Lewis 1966:19).

The concept of the culture of poverty focuses attention on the relative lack of organization and the isolation of its bearers. Yet Lewis recognizes that many urban squatters may display a sense of community untypical of the culture of poverty, especially when the settlements are low rent areas of stable residence, physically and ethnically, racially or linguistically distinct from their surroundings (1966:23).

A synthesis of these outlooks would suggest that squatter settlements, contrasting so sharply with the loci of oligarchic traditionalism and the new Latin American consumerism (e.g., the modern superblocks and monumental architecture of Brasília's Pilot Plan), house people who, while they may or may not be bearers of the culture of poverty, are isolated from modern Brazilian national life and are rural, marginal, and maladjusted.[4] Fundamentally, these views suggest the squatters' living conditions and their physical separation from the city derive from their failure to pass from "traditional" rural ways to "modern" urban society, a view evocative of the new unilinealism of the bourgeois liberal development theorists such as W. W. Rostow and Cyril E. Black (Rostow 1960; Black 1966).

The empirical basis for the pathologist-dualist viewpoint lies in the blatant economic and social inequality which pervades every phase of urban life in those cities where squatting exists. The presence of this inequality is made painfully apparent by the frequently close juxtaposition of shabby and foul-smelling squatments with luxury apartments, as in Rio de Janeiro, or with monumental symbolic architecture, as in Brasília.

The policy implications of this view are equally clear—either eliminate these nests of social pathology and potential subversion by means of massive clearance and public housing projects or missionize their residents with community development and other professionally-mediated forms of middle-class morality in order to integrate them into the modern sphere of the society. In fact, the writings of much of this school resemble the older religious missionary forms of colonialist humanitarianism, which translated the poverty and strange customs of the natives into a mandate to provide them as soon as possible with the blessings of clothing and Methodism. Today the Peace Corps tells its applicants that "the most basic contribution a Volunteer can make is to inject some sense of community, some inkling of latent power into a village or slum." This in spite of the fact that squatters have often successfully resisted repeated legal and forcible attempts to remove them and have developed complex networks of voluntary associations of various types!

In fact, both clearance (Safa 1964; Salmen 1969) and community development have been unsuccessful by almost any objective or subjective index. In part this failure is a consequence of the errors of individual programs and their executors, but only in part. It is also a product of the empirical and theoretical inadequacy of the pathologist-dualist position. There is little evidence that squatters are "folk" unable or unwilling to become "urban," or that they have failed to become integrated into the society, and much more evidence that it is the *form* of their integration which has resulted in the spectacular contrast between their lifeways and living conditions and those of their more affluent neighbors. It is not any lack of ties with the dominant sectors of the society that is the problem, but the kinds of ties which exist.

We may apply to dualist analyses of squatting the same criticism which may be made of dualist treatments of the relationship between the Northeast and the Paraiba Valley industrial region in Brazil, Indians and the larger societies of Mexico and Peru, and blacks and whites in the United States. Emphasis on the synchronic, internal characteristics which distinguish a subordinate (satellite, colonized) social group from the group which dominates it (the metropolis) may lead to neglect or even denial of the historic and continuing interconnections between the two groups which gave rise to and sustain the disparity between them. From this first fallacy it is easy to move on to the assumption that the cure for the situation lies in the diffusion of certain characteristics from the dominant sector to the other, or in the full integration of the dependent sector into the dominant. In fact, it is often at least arguable that the solution lies in transforming the nature of the already existing interconnection, or in eliminating the tie completely. To deemphasize the importance of the metropolis-satellite relationship, as the dualists do, is of course to obscure the possibility of such a revolutionary transformation.[5]

In contrast to the cruder imputations of the dualists, many writers emphasize the adaptive or even conservative characteristics of urban squatting. These writers describe a squatting cycle leading from the first tentative efforts to invade private or, more often, public land, to resistance to official challenges to their land tenure and, sometimes, to a high degree of stability as urban neighborhoods (Mangin 1963, 1964, 1965, 1967; Turner 1963). Some writers emphasize that except on the issue of land tenure, squatters tend to be politically centrist or even conservative (Bourricard 1964; Halperin 1963; Peattie, n.d.). Many anthropologists identify with· squatters as with other informants and, in particular, look askance at uncritical schemes to "eradicate" squatting, establish public housing, and "reform" squatters (Safa 1964) and emphasize the relative satisfaction of the migrants with the squatment as opposed to their places of origin, especially when these are rural (Herrick 1966; Pastore 1968).

As a policy prescription, this view seemingly would imply a cautious attitude to mass clearance programs and would tend to suggest that public housing schemes (especially high rise schemes and pay-as-you-go plans) fail to fulfill the needs of many squatters. Rather, where conditions permit, the indicated policy would seem to be one of granting land tenure free or at low cost and promoting improvements in such areas as water supply, electricity, and sewage. Some planners, as in Ciudad Guyana, a new industrial city in Venezuela (Rodwin, n.d.), have even favored regarding squatting as inevitable and setting aside areas where it can be permitted with relatively little disruption of the city plan.

Whatever the virtues of squatting as a strategy of survival or upward mobility, however, squatters continue at or near the bottom of a highly polarized urban social structure—if they are upwardly mobile, their ascent is a fairly shallow one. Even more accurate and less alarmist ethnographic data, if it is focused upon the characteristics of squatters and their settlements to the neglect of their position in the society as a whole and its development, takes the squatters' social position as a given and fails to come to grips with the roots of the problem.

ISOLATE AND SYSTEM

As anthropologists have moved from the study of the most primitive and small-scale of the social units comprising the underdeveloped sector of the global society to rural units in more developed parts of the society to the study of urban society, they have striven manfully to retain two related attitudes. The first is to regard the unit under investigation, whether a tribe, a village, a neighborhood, a family, an individual, or a squatter settlement, as an isolate, a social organism, a largely self-sufficient entity. The second attitude has been characterized by Martin Nicolaus as keeping their "eyes . . . turned downwards, and their palms upwards" (Nicolaus 1968:9–10). In other words, they study the powerless under the auspices of the powerful, and the information they produce is much more readily available to the latter than to the former. This has been true in spite of the fact that many anthropologists have been sympathetic intermediaries between the rulers and the ruled (Gough 1968).

Without reducing anthropological works in general to the level of crude ideology, these two attitudes have tended to minimize the conflict of their holders with the dominant sectors of society. With a few exceptions (e.g., Leeds 1968b), anthropologists have failed to provide much that is helpful to our understanding of elites or of national and international societies, except insofar as the isolates they study may be assumed to be representative.[6] In this sense anthropology has shared what Mills criticized in his *The Sociological Imagination* as the "abstracted empiricist" retreat from the classical tradition of the social sciences.

The increased interest in cities on the part of anthropologists is to a degree a sign that some anthropologists are abandoning the traditional idealization of the exotic and the primitive.[7] Yet they have clung to emphasis upon the study of lower-class and lumpen elements studied as isolates by methods which resemble as closely as possible the methods used in primitive and peasant villages.

The facts of life in cities and the clear lack of demographic, social, and political equilibrium that are apparent on inspection, however, make the simple application of traditional research orientations untenable. Indeed, given a larger-than-local perspective it becomes apparent that the bulk of the ethnographic data we possess consists of "snapshots" (synchronic views) of primitives in the process of being peasantized, peasants in the process of being proletarized, and ruralities in the process of becoming urbanized,[8] whether through migration to cities or through the extension of formerly "urban" technology and institutions to the countryside. Most of the units traditionally studied by anthropologists as if they were microcosms are, in fact, subsegments of subsegments of a global system of social, economic, and cultural relations established in the wake of the worldwide expansion of Western power. Even the nation-states themselves, in many cases, are specialized parts of this global underdevelopment system. The investigator who seeks to explain the forms taken by component units of this system ignores its existence and its specific forms at his peril; the applied social scientist who seeks to effect piecemeal change without considering how his efforts are conditioned by the requirements of the system and its component parts may be bitterly disappointed. The NATO intellectuals and their successors, who seek to explain the global disparities of wealth, power, and prestige as a consequence of the failure of "traditional" societies or "traditional" segments of dual societies to become "modernized," are at best neglectful of the structure and history of the underdevelopment system.

None of the foregoing should be interpreted as a suggestion that specific empirical studies are a waste of time and that all research should be directed toward the characteristics of the global society as a whole. It is rather to assert that such studies must be informed by some notion of what the underdevelopment system is all about and what it implies for the specific nation, region or city, and smaller social unit under examination.

THE CASE OF BRASÍLIA

These rather broad assertions can only be exemplified within the limited scope of the present article or, indeed, even by far more extended discussion about a single city. In the late fifties, Brazil's federal government began to put into practice a century-old plan to build a new national capital in the savanna country (cerrados) of Southern Goiás state in the country's Central Plateau. The construction was guided by a plan written by Lúcio Costa, an eminent Brazilian architect-planner (1957:41–44). Approximately ten years after construction began in earnest, two-thirds of the population of the capital live in areas whose urban ecology and architecture are in direct contradiction to the apartment house superblocks proposed in the original plan. More than 15 percent of the population is housed in technically illegal squatter settlements and over 50 percent in satellite towns whose legality, while unquestioned, was granted in consequence of a last-ditch official effort to limit squatting to some degree. Many of the dwellings in the satellite towns are constructed of the same materials and have the same physical characteristics as those in squatter settlements.

The decision to construct Brasília in the face of the nation's scarce capital resources and the characteristics of the original plan reflected the character of the political and social stratification system of Brazil, in at least the following respects: (1) the monumentalist emphasis on dramatic architecture and broad vistas; (2) the favoring of automotive circulation in spite of the fact that cars remain a luxury for the vast majority of the Brazilian population; (3) the cursory attention paid to the needs and desires of the first residents (the construction workers) and to the lower-class residents in general; (4) the nondevelopmental, static, or skeletal character of the plan, expressed as a final output rather than a process of growth which at all stages would involve human lives; (5) the necessity, given prevailing political practice in Brazil, of finishing the city according to plan within a three-year period (Kubitschek's presidential mandate) if it was not to be later abandoned; (6) the centralized character of the planning and execution processes themselves, with no provision for consultation or participation by any but upper-level technical and political personnel; and finally, (7) the division of the city into hierarchical sectors. The plan is thus false to the nature of social interaction in cities.[9] The general neglect of the social, in any serious sense, as opposed to the esthetic and the symbolic, is one of the hallmarks of the plan and of Brazilian elite culture in general.

SQUATTING AND LABOR SUPPLY

Building Brasília required large numbers of workers, who came from the poorest sections of Brazil, the Northeast (including Bahia), and the Center-West. According to various surveys conducted, from half to two-thirds of the residents of the largest squatter settlement in Brasília, the Social Security Invasion,[10] came from the Northeast of Bahia, and from one- to two-fifths from the Center-West States of Goiás and Minas Gerais.[11] Invariably the migrants themselves cite economic motivations as primary in their decision to move, although some comments in more extensive discussions indicate that many migrants were not unaffected by the more glamorous aspects of the Brasília experiment.

Just as the main strategic resource supplied by Africa in the slavery period was labor, today many underdeveloped regions of economies such as Brazil's have as a principal function the exportation of cheap labor. In Brazil this function is fulfilled by the Northeast and to a lesser extent by some other rural areas, such as in Minas Gerais. The Northeast regularly disgorges migratory streams in accordance with the exigencies of the economy—to the Amazon if the revival of the rubber trade becomes necessary, to the industries of São Paulo, or to Brasília when a new capital is abuilding. Minas Gerais, a secondary source of such migrants, is also a case of the pattern of regional underdevelopment Frank calls "passive involution" (1967). To the extent that the conditions which underlie this exportation of human beings thereby serve the needs of the extant economic and political elites, serious doubts must arise as to the prospects for success of programs administered by these same elites with the declared intention of combating regional underdevelopment.

These considerations also apply to the urban squatter settlements, which serve as reception areas and places of residence for the migrants and some of their descendants and thus owe their existence to the distribution of wealth and power which underlies the migratory process. Rather than viewing such settlements (with alarm or otherwise) as the products of an alleged failure to diffuse urban-industrial values to the rural-oriented lower class or as the pathological consequences of mismanagement or bad planning, we may consider the contribution they make to the provision of an economical solution to the supply of abundant, cheap labor for the urban economy, including not only the industrial sector, but also the largely labor-intensive service sector which is such an important prop to the lifestyle of the upper and middle classes.

The squatments and to a considerable extent the satellite towns serve as reserves, at little cost to the employers, where large numbers of workers may be maintained; proximity to lines of transportation permits easy access to the work sites; high unemployment rates depress wages; domestic, service, and commercial work is available to diminish the effects of (and potential reactions against) this unemployment and ease the burdens of the middle and upper classes; official pressure permits the squatting to be confined to areas of low visibility to the outsider and at a distance from the middle-class zones sufficient to reduce casual contact between the classes; and the location, terrain, and settlement pattern are such as to facilitate military and police measures to repress or contain riot and rebellion should they arise. At the same time, the formal official condemnation of squatting as an evil to be eradicated permits the capital to maintain its symbolic "developmentist" associations in the eyes of the middle class.

On the other hand, from the viewpoint of the in-migrants, the relatively high economic rewards available in Brasília as opposed to the Northeast—especially its rural sector—as well as the generally higher level of public services (education, health, social security) provide the appearance of upward mobility. Squatting, by eliminating the need for payment of rent and property taxes, enhances the squatters' economic position and, in particular, provides a form of security in an unstable labor market characterized by frequent firings, late paychecks (due in part to the dependence of the construction industry on political decisions), and other insecurities. The physical form of the shack permits it to be expanded in accord with the changes in family size and unanticipated receipts of funds. In a society characterized by occupational multiplicity at all levels, the shack may also be used as a business asset: a store, a sewing business, rental of space for a store, or as a source of capital through its sale should the owner decide to move elsewhere.

It is impossible to estimate the numbers of migrants to Brasília who have left, but the rapid growth of the population confirms that a large number, and by all accounts of officials and squatters alike, the vast majority, remain in the new capital. As long as construction continues and the transfer of civil servants from Rio de Janeiro provides a basis for the service sector of the economy, the lower class retains an economic basis. In addition, the availability of public education of better-than-average quality and of medical clinics, such as those of the District Hospital, provides an incentive to remain, even in harder times— and those who have shacks need not concern themselves with paying rent. Women also find in domestic service and in small businesses, especially dressmaking, that they can increase their income and improve their position vis-à-vis their husbands, and in several cases have successfully resisted the migratory urges of their spouses. Most squatters in Brasília, barring disaster or depression, want to stay, and a significant majority want to stay in the squatter settlement. Informants often supposed that the research was connected with the government and wanted to know if they would have any chance of obtaining legal title to their house lots.

Brasília's settlement pattern developed in response to conflicting pressures emanating from the official "planned" construction and from the housing needs of squatters. A tacit bargain was struck at Brasília between the work-hungry migrants and entrepreneurs and politicians. The workers were permitted access to undeveloped public land, readily available in the scantily-populated, relatively flat areas of the new capital and to the waste materials from the construction process, such as the wooden forms used to mold the reinforced concrete employed in most of the monumental and residential apartment buildings.

Another advantage provided by employers is truck transportation from the squatter settlements to the place of work. The marginal cost to the entrepreneurs of providing these advantages was nearly nil, and the advantage to them considerable in terms of permitting the large in-migration to continue and to improve their labor-supply situation. The squatters, on the other hand, possessed a limited bargaining power by virtue of the need for their presence in menial and service roles and of their potential for organized protest and disruption. For active protest to occur required (1) settlements containing large numbers, notably the Social Security Invasion, which in 1967 had over 4,000 shacks, and (2) conditions of threat to the permanence of the settlement or some part of it.

Official and police action has had a regulatory function with respect to squatting rather than (except in occasional declarations of intent) constituting an effort to eliminate or to provide a viable alternative to it for the majority of squatters. Small squatments offering relatively slight prospects of resistance were removed from the centrally planned area housing the urban middle class to the larger and less centrally-located Social Security Invasion. This squatment was the site of two efforts, backed by police force, aimed at removing squatters from privately owned land and from a highly visible position on one of the principal interurban motor routes into the city where their presence would detract from the symbolic and prestige functions of the new capital. While long-term financing for the purchase of publicly sponsored core housing and small agricultural resettlement schemes have been discussed, there is no realistic possibility that official policy toward squatting can do more than to specify its location to some degree and declare the intention to eradicate it.

Brasília's existence up to the present and the economic survival of its poor have in fact been largely dependent upon government expenditures, notably those connected with (1) the construction of the capital, which is continuing under the military dictatorship at a reduced rate, and (2) the salaries of the civil and military employees of the government. Industrial development has been quite restricted, and even agriculture has been limited by natural conditions, the lack of a regional plan, and the commercial manipulations of São Paulo interests concerned with maintaining control of the local markets. The growth of an urban population nearing the half-million mark, more orderly governmental administration by the military, and the completion of the railroad spur to Brasília (officially inaugurated in March 1967, but not in operation until a year later) may change this somewhat pessimistic picture and lead to some industrial employment to substitute for construction work as the city ages and to supplement jobs in the tertiary sector. Yet given the increasingly capital-intensive character of recent Latin American industrialization and the off-center location of Brasília in the Brazilian distribution network, the role of industrial employment is not likely to be great. The probable future decline in expenditures for new building may seriously injure the prospects of the majority of squatters and limit, if not actually reverse, the aggregate effects of migration on population growth in the lower class.

The official policy of the government in regard to squatting, furthermore, tends to discourage—although it does not prevent—the development of small enterprises, other than strictly commercial ones, and of more permanent types of buildings in general. By insistently proclaiming the illegality and eventual demise of the squatter settlements and denying public services such as street lighting, electricity, sewage, and a permanent water system, the government does not prevent the squatter settlement from growing (especially when it moves people into the place in its own trucks!), but it does suppress or deflect some internal entrepreneurial interest and prevent the gradual improvement of many homes beyond the wood-and-tarpaper stage, for which some squatters on occasion have the money and the skills. In the light of the difficult middle-run prospects for employment for squatters in Brasília and the lack of really viable alternate forms of settlement, the governmental policy seems to be somewhat short-sighted.

Thus, what recent in-migrants today see as at least a minimal improvement in their lives may not survive the eventual diminution of the rhythm of construction in the new capital. And in fact, throughout Latin America, current industrialization is largely capital-intensive. It may be that the urban under- and unemployed, when the marginal sense of improvement gained through in-migration and squatting in its initial stages is lost (for instance in the next, urban-born generation), will become a source of political unrest and challenge to the system as a whole (Petras 1969). The development of and prospects for such a challenge, like the genesis of urban poverty and its reflexes in urban ecology, can only be understood on the basis of systemic as well as local variables. Revolutionaries (and counterrevolutionaries) understand this point. Perhaps we can ask at least as much from academic social scientists.

NOTES

1. In Brazil squatter settlements are known as *favelas, invasões, mocambos,* and (when over water, on stilts) *alagados.* Among other terms for them are *callampas* (Chile), *bidonvilles* (French), *barriadas* (Peru), and *gecekondu* (Turkey). In English, they are often referred to as *shantytowns,* but not all squatment structures are shanties and not all urban, shanty agglomerations are squatter settlements.
2. Norman Whitten and James Szwed (1968) use the concept of economic marginality in reference to intermittent or irregular income, a different usage from that dealt with here. Indeed, squatting not involving rent is adapted to marginality in this sense of the term. Use of the term *marginality* for this situation is confusing, however, to the extent that irregular income among sugar workers or urban squatters may be an aspect of their integration into the very heart of the functioning political economy, not of their isolation from it.
3. Anthony and Elizabeth Leeds have effectively demolished this notion in their paper "Brazil and the Myth of Urban Rurality: Urban Experience, Work and Values in 'Squatments' of Rio de Janeiro and Lima," presented in November 1967 at the Conference on Work and Urbanization in Modernizing Societies, St. Thomas, Virgin Islands.

4. William Mangin (1967) suggests without elaboration that urban squatters are less alienated than central-city slum dwellers.
5. This discussion incorporates many of the views of A. G. Frank (1967a, 1967b).
6. See, for instance, one set of proposed criteria of representativity of Conrad Arensberg (1961).
7. This is occurring only to a degree. In part, increased interest in the "urban" reflects the immediate social control and counterrevolutionary concerns of the rulers of American society, efficiently mediated through the academic marketplace, as in the case of the earlier success of "area studies" interests in the social sciences: Russia, China, Africa, Latin America, Southeast Asia. Suddenly we are confronted with poverty and urban studies.
8. A paraphrase of a passage from Scott Cook (1968:259).
9. For a conception of this interaction patterning from a planner's viewpoint, see Christopher Alexander (1966).
10. *Invasão do I. A. P. I.* I.A.P.I. is the acronym for the former Industrial Workers' Social Security Institute, which sponsored the hospital behind which the "invasion," or squatting, began.
11. Discussion of this data is to be found in "Planned and Spontaneous Urban Settlement in Brasília" (D. G. Epstein 1969).

TRADITIONALISM AND IDENTITY IN A TOKYO NEIGHBORHOOD

Theodore C. Bestor

Before 1923, the area now occupied by Miyamoto-chô was a rural hamlet. Now it is part of central Tokyo. In this essay, Theodore Bestor explores what has made this a distinct, not *distinctive*, neighborhood and the activities which breathe life into this identity. He points out that the apparent venerability of the neighborhood itself is the result of instant traditions. Bestor thus gives us a Japanese expression of what Barbara Kirshenblatt-Gimblett discussed in "Ordinary People/Everyday Life."

From the Imperial Palace that marks Tokyo's center to the urban area's outermost fringes, the Tokyo megalopolis stretches in most directions at least 50 kilometers. About 26 million people, roughly 22% of the Japanese population, live within this radius. Yet, despite Tokyo's size and the complexity of the vast institutions of mass society that integrate and sustain it, many Tokyo residents carry out much of their daily lives within tiny, highly localized social arenas, the scale of which seems all out of proportion to the urban complex as a whole.

Older sections of Tokyo often are divided into well-defined neighborhoods.[2] These are not simply bureaucratic devices (such as postal districts or police precincts) that correspond only slightly with the social categories and groupings important in the daily lives of most residents. Nor are such neighborhoods merely emblematic of larger economic, social or ethnic divisions within the city, such as a New Yorker might have in mind when referring to Wall Street, the West Village or Williamsburg. Rather, these neighborhoods are geographically compact, spatially discrete, institutionally well-organized and socially cohesive units with a few hundred to a few thousand residents.[3] Within such neighborhoods, intertwining organizations and institutions provide a wide array of services and sponsor myriad activities for local residents, who are also linked to one another by enduring webs of informal social, economic and political ties that extend throughout the neighborhood.

To the outsider or the casual observer, neighborhood groups and ties are often invisible or transparent. They are easily overlooked for several reasons. In the first case, neighborhood social relations revolve around the undramatic, mundane minutiae of daily life and so are frequently disregarded as unimportant. Second, urban

Source: Article written expressly for *Urban Life*.

community institutions are customarily dismissed as irrelevant anachronisms, remnants of preindustrial urban life out of place and doomed to disappear in the modern industrial megalopolis. Finally, because neighborhood groups and local social ties normally involve close links to municipal agencies, observers routinely assume that neighborhoods do not exist other than as extensions of the government. They, therefore, ignore the pragmatic reality and symbolic significance that local life holds for residents of a neighborhood.

Although the scope and complexity of a neighborhood's social organization may be discerned only locally, local institutions and groups loom large on the social landscape for those residents to whom the services, contacts and activities neighborhoods foster are important. For many residents, neighborhoods are significant spheres of economic activity and usually are organized politically to represent these interests. There are close ties between community groups and local schools, which often serve as focal points for neighborhood activities and social relationships.

Neighborhood organizations make a significant contribution to the quality and safety of urban life. They assist government agencies in delivering services (such as promoting traffic safety, sponsoring sanitation drives or organizing auxiliary fire protection programs). More informally, neighborhood life encourages mutual assistance among residents and, by enforcing local standards of social control, communities prevent crime and discourage potentially disruptive behavior. Neighborhoods provide recreation for residents through organized outings, banquets and events, such as festivals or folk dances, as well as by embellishing even the most laborious tasks with opportunities for camaraderie and mutual relaxation. Ritually, neighborhoods also play important roles, sponsoring festivals and supporting Shintô shrines that house the tutelary deities who protect the parish.

As dynamic, if tightly circumscribed, arenas of social life, urban Japanese neighborhoods maintain themselves organizationally on several levels. First, a wide variety of formally constituted neighborhood organizations and associations exist to accomplish the many political, economic, ritual, educational and recreational ends mentioned above. Chief among these groups are *chôkai*, or neighborhood associations, which are key institutions in the formal structure of many neighborhoods. In addition, neighborhoods are held together by the constellations of individual social networks that link residents to one another. Some one-to-one strands of affiliation, of course, emanate from people's joint participation in local organizations. Other individual ties exist quite apart from any institutional framework, reflecting instead family connections, school ties, shared occupational or economic interests, joint tastes and common hobbies or mutual political leanings. Most residents of a neighborhood can trace ties to many other residents through several alternate paths using one or another of the above sorts of connections. Any individual's networks extend far beyond a given neighborhood's boundaries, but, within these boundaries, residents' networks intertwine and interlock thoroughly, creating an extremely high density of local interpersonal ties.

Neighborhoods are not only internally constituted, but also are defined through their relations with external agencies, chiefly those of the municipal government. In Tokyo, municipal administration is conducted largely by the 23 wards (known as *ku*), each with a population of several hundred thousand. Ward governments routinely rely on community organizations in the day-to-day performance of municipal administration. *Chôkai* play the critical role linking internal dimensions of communities to the municipal government. *Chôkai* are expected to keep the citizenry informed of government programs and policies and to act as a sounding board for government proposals. At the same time, ward governments depend on *chôkai to* supply the labor, the organizational infrastructure and even some of the money required for the delivery of municipal services at the local level. The relationships established between neighborhood associations and municipal governments are close but also potentially exploitative. Neighborhoods can (and sometimes do) resent and resist governmental demands and the presumption that community groups are there to do the government's bidding.

These general features of neighborhood life are common throughout Tokyo, but are more characteristic of older, presumably more traditional areas, particularly those districts that can lay claim (however illusory) to being heir to the traditions of *shitamachi. Shitamachi,* sometimes translated "downtown," refers to the old merchant quarters of preindustrial Edo (as Tokyo was called prior to 1868), in which patterns of premodern urban life – including strong, stable frameworks of neighborhood social life – are presumed to survive. By extension, districts with high proportions of locally self-employed merchants and craftspeople are considered *shitamachi-esque*, whether or not the area possesses any historical link with Edo's *shitamachi.*[4]

In neighborhoods that identify themselves with the *shitamachi* ethos, each dimension of community social structure – the formal institutions, the complexly interlocking personal ties among residents and the external relations between neighborhood and government – are suffused with sentiments of community solidarity and identity. These sentiments nurture the internal social framework of the neighborhood, while at the same time providing a basis for resisting the external encroachments of government agencies. Often this sense of local identity and autonomy is based on traditionalism – the manipulation, invention and recombination of cultural patterns, symbols and motifs to create an aura of stability and legitimacy based on what appears to be historical continuity. In the complexity and fluidity of social life in the Tokyo megalopolis, a neighborhood's ability to sustain itself by claiming (or creating) a link with history and cultural tradition promotes a sense of secure identity, not only for institutions but also for individuals.

MIYAMOTO-CHÔ[5]

One Tokyo neighborhood in which seemingly transparent local institutions and ties that are cloaked with traditionalism sustain a vigorous and thickly textured social life is Miyamoto-chô. The neighborhood is about twenty minutes by commuter train from Tokyo station in what is now a central section of the city. Miyamoto-chô is not particularly old nor is it within the classic *shitamachi* districts; it was part of an outlying agricultural hamlet until 1923 when the Kantô earthquake destroyed old central Tokyo and impelled the outward expansion of the city. By the early 1930s, the region was completely urbanized and distinct, locally organized neighborhoods began to emerge. Miyamoto-chô and six other neighborhoods dating from the late 1920s and early 1930s now occupy the area of the pre-1923 hamlet.

Miyamoto-chô is a rough rectangle measuring about 200 by 400 meters, bounded on the east by railway tracks and on the west by a narrow, heavily travelled road built over an old stream now channeled underground; the northern and southern boundaries are residential and shopping streets that create only barely perceptible divisions between Miyamoto-chô and the neighborhoods on either side.

About 1,920 people in 750 households live in Miyamoto-chô.[6] The neighborhood's population density is close to 30,000 residents per square kilometer, about twice the density for Tokyo as a whole. The neighborhood's density is all the more remarkable because Miyamoto-chô is not a high-rise district. With the exception of three small ferroconcrete apartment buildings (called *manshon* or *mansions*) that rise to four floors, the neighborhood is made up almost entirely of two-story, wooden architecture: homes, tiny apartment buildings, shops and workshops. Miyamoto-chô's tightly packed homes are interspersed with about 100 small shops and 40 tiny workshops or factories. The neighborhood is a middle- and lower-middle-class community, dominated socially, politically and commercially by the self-employed merchants and manufacturers for whom Miyamoto-chô is both home and workplace.

For many residents, Miyamoto-chô is an important sphere of economic activity. The neighborhood is bisected by a bustling street lined with small businesses that cater to the daily needs of residents: stores selling vegetables, fish, rice, *sake*, books, electrical appliances and clothing, as well as service businesses, such as laundries, news agents' stands, plumbing establishments and restaurants. The shopping street's 60 stores and businesses are almost all owned and operated by local residents, generally employing only the labor of family members. Most shopkeepers, craftspeople, factory owners and even professionals (doctors, dentists or accountants) conduct business in tiny shops, workshops or offices attached to their homes, involving family members in all aspects of the household enterprise. Their clientele is primarily local; most local households do the bulk of their shopping for day-to-day needs within a couple of blocks of home.

By the standards of contemporary Tokyo, Miyamoto-chô is an ordinary place similar to hundreds of other neighborhoods that stretch in a wide arc to the north, east and south of central Tokyo. No visible signs of social, economic or cultural distinctiveness set Miyamoto-chô apart from its surroundings. What makes Miyamoto-chô a discrete social unit – distinct, but not distinctive – from nearby neighborhoods are the crosscutting and overlapping institutions and relationships that define Miyamoto-chô as an entity and breathe life into this definition through the activities and interactions they promote. In part, this life is made possible through the accentuation of traditionalism, which, by creating for the neighborhood and its institutions an image of historical venerability, also provides an almost unassailable cultural rationale for their existence and vitality.

FORMAL NEIGHBORHOOD ORGANIZATIONS

Miyamoto-chô contains a wide array of formally organized groups and associations that operate within what these groups collectively define as Miyamoto-chô's boundaries. Some are truly voluntary associations whose menbers and participants join simply out of individual preference, but the most important organizations are at best only quasi-voluntary; although actual participation in the events they sponsor is a matter of personal choice, membership in these is virtually automatic for all Miyamoto-chô's residents. Therefore, all residents are considered by definition members of the neighborhood association (*chôkai*), all adult women automatically belong to the *chôkai's* women's auxiliary (*fujinbu*), the senior citizen's club (*rôjinkai*) nominally includes all residents over the age of 60 and all shopkeepers with businesses along the neighborhood's shopping street belong to the merchants' guild (*shôtenkai*). Although these groups are formally independent, in practice activities, leaderships and memberships so interlock that it is difficult to disentangle one association from another.

Other, more voluntary organizations active in Miyamoto-chô include the neighborhood's festival committee, local schools' PTAs and alumni clubs (*dôsôkai*), politicians' support clubs (*kôenkai*), a volunteer fire brigade (*shôbôdan*) and groups centered on hobbies such as travel, traditional dance, tea ceremony or flower arrangement.

The *chôkai* is unquestionably the neighborhood's most important and visible organization. In some senses, it acts as a semiofficial local government, providing services to residents both at local initiative and at the behest of the municipal authorities. It serves as a conduit for demands, requests and information that flow in both directions. The *chôkai* distributes information on government programs and regulations to residents and assists the government in recordkeeping, census-taking and the conducting of surveys of local conditions. It lobbies the government on residents' behalf; one notable success (achieved by a coalition of adjacent neighborhoods) led the municipal government a decade ago to build a traffic by-pass over a stream that bordered Miyamoto-chô. The *chôkai* helped promote the construction of a new train station on a railway line near Miyamoto-chô. More modest accomplishments include lobbying for the elimination of petty nuisances; for example, pressuring a municipal nursery school to cut down on noise and congestion by prohibiting mothers from delivering their children by bicycle.

Neighborhood groups promote various mutual aid, public health and safety activities. When death occurs, the *chôkai* notifies residents, organizes people to help at the funeral and makes the *chôkai* meeting hall available for the wake. They aid in other emergencies as well; several years ago when a burlap bag factory burned to the ground, a family whose adjoining house was destroyed was put up in the *chôkai* hall for several months while their home was being rebuilt. Local associations have formed a disaster relief team (at government urging) and hold regular earthquake drills. They participate in traffic safety campaigns organized by the police and provide free inspections of children's bicycles. Together, the volunteer fire brigade and the *chôkai* sponsor safety meetings and midwinter patrols and aid the professional fire department in extinguishing blazes. The *chôkai* maintains streetlights on back alleys, and several times each summer, a *chôkai* work crew sprays the entire neighborhood with pesticides. The *chôkai* and its women's auxiliary organize a monthly recycling drive, an important source of the groups' income.

Local organizations also sponsor many recreational activities. Children's outings to parks and playgrounds and trips for adults to hot springs resorts are scheduled throughout the year. Annual events include neighborhood New Year's parties, a springtime cherry-blossom-viewing party, a midsummer *Bon Odori* folk dance festival and the autumn festival for the local Shintô tutelary deity. Even nonrecreational events, such as the fire patrols, the pesticide sprayings, or the earthquake drills, are opportunities for pleasant comaraderie that break daily life's normal routine and which often culminate in banquets or parties for the activities' planners and laborers.

Perhaps no more than a quarter of Miyamoto-chô's households enthusiastically support and participate in the events and activities sponsored by the *chôkai* and other local groups, but the *chôkai* collects monthly dues of 200 yen (100 yen for apartment dwellers from almost all households.[7] Directly or indirectly, the *chôkai's* activities affect the lives of all residents. Through its public service, safety and sanitation campaigns, the *chôkai* improves the living environment of Miyamoto-chô; *chôkai* leaders also argue that by providing these services on a voluntary basis, the organization helps keep government expenditures, and taxes, lower.

The *chôkai* and other formal groups contribute heavily to the maintenance of the fabric of local social life; the relationships established among neighborhood residents through their participation in local groups and activities weave through and mutually reinforce ties established between individual residents in a wide variety of informal, noninstitutional settings. Many of these informal ties would exist even in the absence of local organizations such as the *chôkai*, but the presence of formally constituted groups provides a focus within which informal ties multiply, and local institutions reinforce the neighborhood's density of networks by providing convenient, generally recognized social boundaries. Conversely, informal ties form a base without which many aspects of the formal organizations' activities could not function. Without the informal ties that run throughout Miyamoto-chô, consensual decisionmaking would be impossible, mutual aid and social control would fail, and the *chôkai* and other groups would lack the means to mobilize residents to contribute time, labor and money to neighborhood activities.

THE NEIGHBORHOOD AND THE GOVERNMENT

The *chôkai*, together with other local associations, defines the basic social perimeters of Miyamoto-chô. These groups all share a common definition of the neighborhood and a common set of boundaries based on what local organizations and neighborhood residents regard as Miyamoto-chô's historically legitimate borders. Through the insistence of local groups on maintaining these boundaries and through activities that give life to the neighborhood, the local definition of the community holds its own in the face of municipal government efforts to impose other definitions of community.

Miyamoto-chô's closest contacts with the municipal administration are channeled through a branch office of the ward government. This branch office handles a broad array of official transactions for individual residents, such as the licensing of pets, the acceptance of passport applications, the certification of residence for voting and school registration or the processing of government pension forms. It also acts as a liaison between ten contiguous neighborhoods, including Miyamoto-chô, and the ward government. The ward regards *chôkai* as little more than semi-official agencies of the government itself, and the branch office considers these ten *chôkai* to be under its jurisdiction. *Chôkai* leaders dispute this interpretation of their organization's role and complain (at least among themselves and to an inquiring anthropologist) about the responsibilities they are forced to shoulder by the government in pursuit of the government's, rather than the neighborhoods', goals. Even at the semantic level, there is disagreement over the nature of the relationship; the branch office refers to the ten *chôkai* together as a *burokku* (bloc) under its leadership, while the *chôkai* see themselves as members of a *rengô*, or federation, for which the branch office is merely a source of advice and administrative support.

Beyond coordinating administrative functions, in recent years, the branch office has become the focal point for the ward's increasingly active policy of *machi-zukuri*, or community creation. *Machi-zukuri* policies reflect a bureaucratic attitude that existing patterns and institutions of neighborhood life, as exemplified by *chôkai*, are outmoded and inappropriate in contemporary society. The municipal government therefore feels it must step in and create institutions that will foster a sense of community and citizenship appropriate to a modern, democratic society. Ironically, in its attempts to do so, the municipal government takes the existing neighborhoods and their activities not only as the instruments, but also as the models for creating new senses of community awareness.

The events planned and sponsored by the branch office often duplicate activities of the individual neighborhoods themselves. Frequently, the municipal government's versions involve much of the same traditionalistic trappings and symbolism that characterize *chôkai* activities. Local leaders grumble about being upstaged by the larger, more lavish events the ward government can put on. One example is the extremely elaborate *Kumin Matsuri* (Ward Residents' Festival), modeled on customary *Bon Odori* folk dance festivals held in midsummer throughout Japan. The municipal government first sponsored the *Kumin Matsuri* in 1979, and it included a specially commissioned ward residents' folk song and a folk dance, both of which conform to the conventions of contemporary, commercialized, so-called traditional folk song and dance genres. The ostentatiousness of this first annual festival aroused so much ill will among *chôkai* leaders that, the following year each of the eleven branch offices held separate, scaled-down versions. Despite this, the ward festival continues to be more elaborate than the corresponding efforts of the *chôkai*, and local leaders continue to complain about the cooperation they feel forced to give the branch office in its planning of this event.

If these conflicts seem to be subtle ones, they reflect an undercurrent of tension in the ongoing relationship between *chôkai* and the ward government. The legal disestablishment of *chôkai* in the early postwar period introduced ambiguities into the relationship that can lead to misunderstandings and disagreements on both sides.[8] Local leaders, aware that the municipal government has no direct legal power over *chôkai*, complain of the government's overbearing attitudes and insist that local organizations must be regarded as voluntary bodies organized by and for local residents. Furthermore, the postwar political climate has weakened citizens' subservient attitude toward government officials. Citizens now feel empowered to object to authoritarian directives from the municipal government and complain that officials often seem to forget they are public servants. On top of this, tensions have been spawned by the ward's *machi-zukuri* policies, whose apparent intention has been to supplant *chôkai* both as semiofficial administrative units and as focal points of local residents' activities and identification. These sources of strain in relations between neighborhoods and the government create the potential for dramatic rifts.

An example of such conflict is a dispute over the neighborhood's boundaries and, hence, between external and internal definitions of what the neighborhood is. In 1964, the ward attempted to amalgamate Miyamoto-chô with an adjacent neighborhood. To an outsider, almost nothing differentiates the neighborhoods, yet their residents successfully opposed the merger. True, the municipal government went ahead and redrew the boundaries, and now the two neighborhoods appear on maps as one unit, but today that larger unit is used for almost nothing but numbering houses. The *chôkai* and other local groups do not recognize the larger unit, nor does the ward office; since the ward office depends on the *chôkai* to carry out many of its tasks, it is forced to work within the frameworks, the *chôkai* acknowledge.

The separate political and economic interests of the two neighborhoods would not have been served by a merger. Each neighborhood routinely is able to elect a ward assembly member, so each had political *jiban* (turf) to protect. Merchants' groups in each neighborhood strive to maintain and to increase their share of local trade in the face of competition from other neighborhoods, but when residents explain their opposition to the merger, they present their resistance as an effort to preserve the supposedly distinct traditions and practices in the neighborhoods involved. However minimal such differences may seem to an outside observer, each neighborhood prides itself on its own ways of collecting donations for the annual festival, on the peculiarities of the relationship between its own *chôkai* and merchants' association or on its own methods of selecting neighborhood officers. These minute differences can become the symbolic battlegrounds between neighborhoods (or among groups, each seeking to control the authenticity of tradition within a particular neighborhood). In this instance, neither neighborhood was willing to alter practices they felt best suited their own needs and their own sense of autonomous tradition and identity.

These sentiments, in Miyamoto-chô at least, in part revolved around the neighborhood hall. The issue was not simply a question of sharing ownership of a ramshackle building, but also involved symbolism central to the neighborhood's self-definition.

At the time, Miyamoto-chô was the only neighborhood in the area to have its own hall. During the last year of World War II, as American air raids struck Tokyo more and more frequently, the residents of Miyamoto-chô were ordered to create a firebreak along the adjacent right-of-way of a vital freight line. To create the break, the men and boys of the *chôkai* tore down the homes on either side of the tracks. From the lumber and roof tiles, they salvaged enough to build the neighborhood hall. This hall is now an aging relic, and, compared with newer halls built or acquired by other neighborhoods in the area, it is small and dilapidated, but still the center of local activity and an important symbol of the neighborhood as a community. The prospect of sharing this and other tangible or intangible cultural properties with *outsiders* was an important rallying point for opposing the ward government's plans, and, ultimately, this opposition proved successful.

THE FESTIVAL

A similar expression of community sentiment, indirectly related to neighborhood boundaries and their defense, can be found in the annual autumn festival (*aki matsuri*) for the local Shintô tutelary deity. The two-day *matsuri* is a vivid symbol of the community, and it draws wide participation. It is, of course, a Shintô rite, but for most residents of Miyamoto-chô the *matsuri* is essentially a secular ritual, largely lacking explicit religious significance but replete with social meaning.

Through the *matsuri*, several important, though sometimes contradictory, social themes are expressed. The festival is organized by a festival committee convened each summer by the *chôkai*, but made up of leaders from various local associations, as well as residents who otherwise take no active part in neighborhood affairs. Social stratification and ranking within Miyamoto-chô are expressed and enforced through assignments of positions on the festival committee and by public postings of residents' contributions. Distinctions are underscored between newcomers and longer-term residents. The management of the festival, and even the spatial and temporal distribution of activities during the *matsuri*, reflect rigid sexual and age-graded divisions of labor. Yet, despite the social rankings that play so visible a role, an overt spirit of egalitarianism and community solidarity is presented as the *matsuri's* dominant motif.

The *matsuri* also serves as a compelling marker of the community's boundaries and identity. A central feature of the festival is the *mikoshi*, a portable shrine or palanquin in which the tutelary deity temporarily resides during the two-day festival. The *mikoshi*, carried on a framework of poles by a group of twenty or more young men (and recently women) is taken on what amounts to an inspection tour of Miyamoto-chô; the procession carefully traces the neighborhood's boundaries. When the route of *mikoshi* unavoidably must pass through the territory of an adjacent neighborhood – when roads or alleys linking parts of one neighborhood run through another or when *mikoshi* are brought from other neighborhoods to the shrine in Miyamoto-chô for the priest's blessings – the festival committees from the neighborhoods involved negotiate the route beforehand. When a women's dance troupe, or a *mikoshi* takes a sudden detour through another neighborhood, leaders from the transgressed neighborhood grumble and expect an apology from the offending neighborhood's festival committee.

Although the *matsuri* nominally encourages cooperation and identification with the six other neighborhoods that make up the shrine's parish, the *mikoshi* and their processions provide a venue for interneighborhood competition. In recent years, the neighborhood next door to Miyamoto-chô triumphed with an impressive new *mikoshi*, hand-built by local young men; however, during 1979-81, Miyamoto-chô countered by prominently featuring in its processions the as yet unsurpassed spectacle of a foreign anthropologist and his exotic, red-haired, folk-dancing wife.

Long term, other strategies were required to uphold the neighborhood's standing. In the spring of 1982, younger neighborhood leaders launched a drive to raise funds for a new *mikoshi*; within three months, Miyamoto-chô raised almost $50,000 (U.S.) in cash and pledges from over 400 local households, and, by the time of the 1982 festival, the neighborhood had bought the largest, most elaborate *mikoshi* in the area.

Leaders of the fundraising campaign claim a major objective was to increase participation in the festival and, hence, in neighborhood affairs by making Miyamoto-chô's festival more spectacular and exciting, but they also point out with pride that Miyamoto-chô's new *mikoshi* is more impressive than the adjacent neighborhood's hand-built one and talk with unconcealed pleasure about the failure of another adjoining neighborhood to meet the challenge.

CONCLUSION

Through events such as the festival, and dozens of other, more mundane activities throughout the year, the *chôkai* and other local groups staunchly defend the neighborhood's present-day boundaries and their definitions of the local community. By maintaining Miyamoto-chô's sense of identity and upholding the distinctiveness of each of the local neighborhoods, the festival and similar activities contribute to a sense of resistance to government efforts to reconstitute local social units as part of its *machi-zukuri* policies. Opposition to the government is not the only, nor even the most important outcome of such activities, for, through their participation in events such as the festival, residents maintain the neighborhood as an arena for valued social interactions that bestow prestige, status and recognition on their leaders and participants in ways not duplicated elsewhere in their lives.

In these examples, and in the more general process of socially constructing its identity, institutions and residents of Miyamoto-chô define the neighborhood by referring to particular aspects of its history and its customary practices, selecting certain events or activities with which to press their case. Although many of the events or institutions to which they refer are recent in occurrence or origin, this does not diminish their utility or significance as emblems of neighborhood tradition and distinctiveness. Japanese social institutions have a penchant for *instant tradition* – the ability to cloak new circumstances and institutions with a mantle of traditionalism, imparting depth and resiliency to what might otherwise have shaky foundations.

NOTES

1. This is a substantially revised and abridged version of "Tradition and Japanese Social Organization: Institutional Development in a Tokyo Neighborhood," in *Ethnology* XXIV, No. 2 (April 1985), 121-35.
2. Hereafter, I use *Tokyo* to refer only to the 23 wards (or *ku*) which are the core of the Tokyo Metropolitan Prefecture, itself surrounded by several other highly urbanized prefectures across which the entire egalopolis extends. In 1982, the population of the 23 wards totaled 8.34 million in 592 square kilometers (Tôkyô-to Tôkei Kyôkai 1984).
3. In 1978, Tokyo's 4,067 distinct, nonoverlapping, institutionally organized neighborhoods averaged 801 households on 0.14 square kilometers per neighborhood (Tôkyô Shôbôchô 1978).
4. Seidensticker (1983) traces the cultural history of *shitamachi* through the 1923 earthquake that destroyed most of the old merchant quarters. Other accounts of the social character of *shitamachi* include Dore (1958), R.J. Smith (1960), H.D. Smith (1986) and Bestor (1986).

5. Miyamoto-chô is a pseudonym. I conducted research here from June, 1979 to May, 1981, with brief return visits in 1983, 1984 and 1986. More detailed accounts appear in Bestor (1985; 1986; in press).

6. An additional 180 single men live in two company dormitories in Miyamoto-chô, but neighborhood organizations do not consider these men full-fledged residents, and they rarely are involved in local events.

7. Roughly, one U.S. dollar and 50 U.S. cents respectively during 1979-81.

8. Policy makers during the American Occupation (1945-52) saw neighborhood associations as as potentially undemocratic institutions, tainted by their activities as wartime agents of state control.

SOCIAL ORGANIZATIONS AND POLITICS IN ISRAELI URBAN QUARTERS

Shlomo Deshen

Like other articles in this section, Deshen deals with the relationship between planning and neighborhood life. Deshen sees a positive correlation between careful planning and the social and economic viability of the community. He sees the social variation within Israeli Jewish society as much a product of differences in government programs, as products of the origins of the immigrants themselves.

ISRAELI IDEOLOGY AND TOWN PLANNING

Israel is a new society based on self-conscious ideological movements, Jewish nationalism and socialism. This basic datum, coupled with another constant, the fact of external adversity, causes Israeli society to be introspective and aware of itself. Many of the doings of people are based on decision rather than on ongoing custom. The conscious decision-taking has its most obvious expression in the area of ideology, and among other matters, in the issue of national settlement planning. The prevailing ideologies have always exhibited a marked rural bias. The ideal was to revitalize the Jewish people by returning the land to farming. In line with this, national planning authorities encouraged new rural settlements, while they disdained, or at best ignored, the towns, to which in fact most of the immigrants were drawn by force of material circumstances and personal inclination.

Israeli urban quarters have a built-in problem: they lack the halo of pioneering achievement attributed to rural settlements. For a long time town-dwelling was considered somewhat reprehensible and people tended to be apologetic about it. An important practical social consequence of this situation was that for many decades, and probably even to this day, social organization in Israeli urban quarters was less developed than in the villages. In the latter, particularly in the pioneering cooperative villages (*kibbutzim* and *moshavim*), there developed variegated and intensive networks of people engaged in voluntary activities, ranging from local political and judicial activities to highly sophisticated artistic groups, and on to welfare and public service

SOURCE: Fuller version of this essay appears in the *Jerusalem Quarterly* 22 (1982). Reprinted by permission of the *Jerusalem Quarterly*.

work. Also in the sphere of livelihood Israeli villages exhibit much vitality, and adopt new entrepreneurial ventures in many economic areas besides agriculture (Weintraub, Lissak and Atzmon 1970). In this context, and more so when one bears in mind that the Jewish urban population in Israel was never less than about eighty per cent of the total Jewish population (today it is well over ninety per cent), urban social organization appears much less dynamic than its rural counterpart.

In the 1950s the planners began left-handedly to acknowledge the social facts, and gave some legitimization to non-rural settlements. The new towns were at first designed for about 3,000 (later 10,000) inhabitants only, and even these were legitimized only on a non-urban ideological basis, namely with the slogan of 'Dispersal of the Population' (away from the coastal belt). The new towns were semi-agricultural hybrids: residences were spread over a large area, the idea being that people would work on auxiliary. plots attached to their homes, and thus partly support themselves from the land. The low population density at first gave the towns a marked rural stamp. The towns were supposed to fill economic and cultural functions for their rural hinterlands. But the villages were more viable than the towns and did not require their services; as a result the towns remained largely foreign in their new environments.

At a later stage of development, in the late 1950s and 1960s, urbanism attained a new level of ideological acceptance. The villages developed industrial crops, such as cotton and sugar beet, and these required industrial processing which the new towns were in a position to provide. The towns thus began to fill an actual role in the esteemed agricultural sector. There developed also towns that had an independent economic role, such as towns founded on the mining industry, the processing of phosphates. This gave the towns a novel legitimacy, and freed them from the sensation of inferiority to the rural sector (E. Cohen 1971).

The new legitimacy of the towns in the early 1960s led the planners to change their social policy. Initially little thought had been given to the towns altogether and immigrants were directed to them haphazardly. Consequently the towns were populated by underprivileged people: poor immigrants who lacked skills required by an advanced economy. The early town-dwellers were able to work mainly as unskilled laborers only, in the farming villages. But with the development of advanced and independent economic roles for the new towns the administration made sustained efforts in social planning: particularly it made attempts to attract to the towns skilled workers. These skilled workers also had more education and civic experience than earlier settlers, so that in time the towns gained a stratum of more advanced residents. This element of heterogeneity is an important factor in social organization because it operated to link residents of the new towns to people in the rural hinterland, and gave town-dwelling a respectability that had formerly eluded it.

The attraction to the new towns of Israelis of variegated background, and particularly of old-timers of European background and endowed with advanced technological skills, was not haphazard. It was rooted primarily in the extent to which sustained economic planning efforts were invested in the town. More concretely, in the extent to which the authorities invested to make the town economically viable, by creating sources of income, particularly through the introduction of publicly-supported industry. Administrative decision in these matters, given the limited resources, involved selecting priorities, specific towns and regions. These decisions required weighing national political goals besides the economic factors. Thus, at one time settlement of the semi-arid Northern Negev was considered a prime national goal, while at another time emphasis shifted to the Galilee. At one time towns that provided services to agriculture were promoted, and at another time towns, based on industry, independent of agriculture, were favored. The decisions on priorities were however often idiosyncratic because of combinations of factors over which the authorities had little or no control. Thus world prices of certain minerals or agricultural products might suddenly change and cause specific settlement and industrialization plans to be adapted accordingly. Or a certain country might suddenly change its emigration policy and permit its Jewish minority to leave. The sudden influx of people to Israel requiring housing and livelihood might again drive the authorities to adapt existing plans to the new circumstances. Thus, sub-ethnic heterogeneity and economic viability, important factors in the mode of social organization that evolved in any given urban quarter, were themselves rooted in a combination of both administrative decisions and incidental factors.

Let us now turn to ways in which sub-ethnic heterogeneity and economic viability operated to mould social organization and politics. The first new towns, founded in the early 1950s, were largely populated by Middle Eastern immigrants, particularly from Morocco. The later towns, however, had an element of immigrants from Western countries and of veteran Israelis. Sub-ethnic heterogeneity caused the eruption of ethnic friction, where perviously apathy and despondency had begun to develop. Ethnic friction has played an important role in mobilizing people to civic action. The concentration of Middle Eastern populations in the new towns, and particularly where ethnic friction developed, has facilitated the emergence of local leadership out of these populations. Middle Easterners dominate electorates in many urban quarters and thus provide a power base for the evolving leadership. In the Israeli context this is an important social and political function. Israel was founded by pioneers of European extraction. The latter therefore naturally dominated the administration of the country. The immigrants found it difficult to fill the administrative positions that they found manned by the veterans. The local political level however developed with the new towns, from the grass-roots. Here there developed a new power arena which was open to the new immigrants (Deshen 1970; Aronoff 1973; S. Avineri 1973).

As the new power arena developed and came to be manned by the immigrants, residents of the new towns, local people, gained responsibility over their local affairs. The process of attainment of power by residents *vis-à-vis* the administration that founded the towns can be marked by historical stages. Initially the residents were governed by the absolute rule of the administrators who operated as local representatives of various government bureaucracies (such as the Ministries of Housing, Education, Health, Commerce and Industry). After a few years, however, the administration appointed a local council. This appointed council, while composed of local residents *qua* residents, and not of administrators in their official capacities, was nevertheless close and beholden to the administration. The third stage of local independence was reached when the administration decreed that local elections be held, and thus set the stage for the emergence of grass-roots community leadership (Aronoff 1974).

Most Israeli urbanites are Jewish immigrants of recent decades, some of whom came to live in new planned towns and others in old established quarters that evolved by themselves. Between these two extreme poles of the Israeli urban scene there are various cases of towns and quarters in which there was a limited or certain kind of planning only. Israeli urban quarters thus comprise several distinct types of settings, that can be placed on a continuum, running from a high to a low degree of administrative urban planning.

I operate with the hypothesis that there is a correlation between types of urban planning and types of social organization and politics that emerge in time in the various communities. In the remainder of this essay I will review the state of our knowledge on social organization and local politics in Israeli urban quarters as reported in some of the available ethnographies.

For reasons of space I choose to elaborate mostly with examples of ethnographies that are relatively little-known and obscurely published. In the earlier versions of the paper, mentioned above, I elaborate with many more cases. Starting with an example of "development towns" that have in common a great deal of overall bureaucratic planning, I go on to relatively unplanned quarters toward the other pole of the continuum. The general trend that emerges is that the more detailed and careful planning is, the more viable, economically and socially the town becomes. As a result local grass-roots leadership and political institutions emerge, or, failing such planning, do not emerge.

A DEVELOPMENT TOWN

My first case-study is Ayara (the name, as well as most of those below, is pseudonymous, and I follow the usage of the various researchers), which I myself studied in the mid-1960s (Deshen 1970; 1974).

Ayara was founded in 1955 at a time and in a region where new industrial crops were being introduced, and there developed a functional need for advanced technical services. This encouraged settlement both by immigrants of Westernized background with technological and modern skills as well as by immigrants who lacked these particular skills. The veterans and Westerners raised the quality of demands in areas of public services, schooling and civility generally. Teachers agreed to live in and not commute, and migration and welfare-dependency were low. But altogether overall planning and selection of residents was not nearly as detailed and careful as it was in other such towns where there developed greater local attachment and urban pride. The Ayara people did however exhibit considerable public awareness, they were active in various political parties and sought to make their mark in influencing local affairs. At election time local politicians aroused involvement throughout the population. During the 1960s politics were largely sub-ethnic: political formations, ostensibly ideological but in practice largely sub-ethnic, competed for powerful positions. Politicking very often took place in closed ethnic settings, such as neighborhood and home meetings that were homogeneous, and in synagogues, most of which were in fact ethnic synagogues. But politicking was rarely overtly ethnic, because that was considered improper. People competed under general national political slogans, local politicians were affiliated to general national, non-ethnic parties, and general civic ties crossed sub-ethnic loyalties. Even if the general slogans of the parties were not fully comprehended by the locals and were only paid lip-service, yet their very existence on the local scene was a powerful factor to mute ethnic divisiveness. Thus local social organization was being constantly moulded into general civic directions and away from particularistic ethnic cleavages. Political ethnicity, albeit muted in the way I have indicated, arose to mobilize people into new ways of asserting themselves.

UNPLANNED COMMUNITIES

We now proceed to review urban communities that bore the full brunt of the problems of being haphazardly transplanted. These are the Middle Eastern Jewish immigrants who moved to old-established Jewish cities. Living among essentially similar people, these immigrant communities lacked clear social boundaries, and did not develop social mechanisms to maintain social control and internal cohesion. Such communities constitute a large proportion of Israeli urban quarters, but research on them has been very limited (and this itself is an indicator of deficient public interest and planning). In the paragraphs that follow, we therefore rely on scantier data. Jewish immigrants to Israel hailing from the more remote, least Westernized parts of the Middle East, carried with them the general Israeli national ideal of 'fusion of exiles.'

Also the national system as a whole strove through its educational and other institutions to absorb the motley immigrants, obliterate existing differences and forge them into one nation. But despite the common ideology and the good intentions of the authorities concerned, many problems arose. Due to the lack of.sophistication of those who actually worked with the immigrants, the latter were often subjected to paternalism and to cultural pressure. The immigrants felt that their ways of living in the areas of family life, economic activities, education and general culture, were all depreciated and of little worth. Whereas all Middle Eastern immigrants were under these subjective, and sometimes actual, pressures, in the planned new towns (and even more so in the new villages) these pressures were less acute. Towns such as Ayara were somewhat removed from the centres of Israeli society, the tempo of Israeli society for good and bad therefore affected them less. Also whatever social planning there was in the planned towns, was on the whole beneficial, and encouraged the institutions and indigenous leadership of the immigrant communities. Immigrants who settled in cities such as Jerusalem and Tel-Aviv however, were immediately exposed to the full forces of secularism and urbanism. The assault on traditional culture and life-ways was not cushioned in the cities by administrative thoughtfulness, even of the limited kind that operated in planned towns. Altogether conditions in the cities precluded social and cultural isolation. The upshot of all this was that traditional social structures and internal mechanisms of social control of immigrant society in the cities soon fell to pieces. People became confused in the drastically changed situation. Not only the old religious leadership, but also family authority at the elementary domestic level often became less effective; as a result law-maintenance has become a problem.

A JERUSALEM NEIGHBORHOOD

The Tzur (pseudonym) section in Jerusalem studied by Donna Shai (1970) in the late 1960s is typical of immigrant quarters in the large cities. Populated by immigrants from Kurdistan it has a bad reputation because of juvenile delinquency and a relatively high crime rate in general. The authorities erected modest housing, opened schools, offered the immigrants health facilities, and made jobs available. However, the residents of Tzur constantly rubbed shoulders with the more affluent veteran citizens of European background, in labour and commercial settings, and these contacts undermined the self-respect and confidence of the immigrants. Despite the poor socio-cultural conditions and the weakening of familial control as expressed by cases of delinquency, research has uncovered considerable attachment of youth to their families. The familial ties are ambivalent. On the one hand young people accept the outside evaluation of their quarter as undesirable, and would like to move elsewhere. In actuality people are hindered from doing so because housing elsewhere is much more expensive. But interestingly this is not the only reason; in fact people are attached to their kin and reluctant to part with them. This attachment has positive and negative ramifications. Schooling in Tzur is on the whole poor, and education not valued much, but in the unusual cases when youngsters showed signs of determination and strove to get on with their education, they were subjected to criticism by their peers. The latter were disturbed by the threat to low-level homogeneity. The homogeneity is in fact very pervasive; it reaches into the areas of sub-ethnic background, income and life-style. When occasions for celebration such as weddings arise, festivities are usually lavish, and hundreds of local guests, relatives and friends participate. People will go deep into debt, but not forego large-scale feasting. And, on the contrary, when quarrelling erupts between neighbors, the partisans seek to involve other people in the fight. The partisans will loudly publicize their rival claims, and a crowd will soon gather around them. The aim of the partisans is to sway the sympathy of the crowd to their respective positions. Traditional social controls rooted in the particular sub-ethnic culture of the Tzur people clearly operate, despite the powerful inimical social forces of the city. But in contrast to the situation in the new towns there is little chance in Tzur, because of the dearth of formal organization, for the emergence of a new grass-roots leadership. In the new towns, on the other hand, because of the spatial and social insulation, given minimal economic self-sufficiency, local organizations have more scope for development. Therefore local political leaders have a better chance to emerge in those towns, as the case of Ayara has shown.

TWO TEL-AVIV QUARTERS

We move to the Shabazi quarter in south Tel-Aviv, studied by Gilla Menahem (1972) in the early 1970s. This is one of the oldest parts of the city, founded seventy years ago as a quiet suburb by Jewish Jaffa residents who desired to escape their noisy filthy city, and out of Shabazi and similar adjacent suburbs developed the city of Tel-Aviv. In time the area deteriorated. Prosperous descendants of the founders left long ago, for newer parts of the city further north, and in their stead new immigrants moved in. The area has also attracted numerous small noisy workshops, and some of the deteriorated properties that were not taken up for commercial purposes have attracted shady characters. The quarter has thus lost much of its residential character, and has become altogether a rather unappealing place.

In turning our attention to an urban quarter of this kind we are moving further along the continuum from the planned urban quarter to the unplanned 'natural' urban quarter. The Shabazi quarter is highly heterogeneous. It comprises people who have lived there for many decades, and others who have moved in more recently. Many people have relatives living in the neighborhood, while others are isolated. Particularly lonesome are older people whose offspring have set up their own households in distant, more desirable, parts of the city. Residents hail from a great number of countries of origin, in both Europe and the Middle East, but two categories of immigrants stand out numerically in Shabazi, those from Iraq and from Rumania. Research in Shabazi has focussed on the ways in which the remaining residential families cope with living in their environment. People are concerned that their children should not be influenced negatively from the exposure to the seamy aspects of urban living that are evident in the Shabazi quarter. In line with this we find individual households maintaining networks of relationships among themselves.

The networks of households comprise three to five household units, where people maintain ties of friendship and neighborliness. These are expressed concretely in mutual visiting and gossiping. In the course of this interaction opinions and evaluations are exchanged on the demeanor of people and particularly of the young. The latter are thus encouraged, albeit not at all forcefully, to adhere to the mores of their elders, in matters such as schooling, work, leisure and fashions. The domestic networks are matrifocal, centering exclusively on women who do not work outside their households. These are women of limited education, who lack marketable skills and are tied to their homes by small children. They visit their neighbors while the men are at work and the older children are at school, or their infants sleep. The networks tend to cluster around an older woman, aged over ten years more than the other women. The older woman, being free of the care of small children, maintains an open house, and is available at all times to receive her visiting neighbors and offer friendly hospitality. These 'sociometric stars' are typically old-time residents in the neighborhood, their grown children have moved out, while they remain. In contrast to many other people, including other members of their networks, the leading women hold outspoken positive views of the neighborhood. They propagate the notion that the neighbors 'are just like brothers to each other.' This quasi-kin rationale enables these women to come to terms with their remaining in a deteriorating quarter. Their friendly neighborly activities also enable them to face their very real isolation from people, other than neighbors, such as their relatives. This evaluation of the Shabazi neighbor networks is supported by another striking datum on the leaders. These women tend not to be members of the main ethnic categories of the neighborhood; some of them hail from Poland, others from the Yemen, but none come from Rumania or from Iraq. The leading women are thus isolated also in terms of sub-ethnic variables, and the groups that these women lead are ethnically heterogeneous, being founded only on the factor of spatial proximity. In the face of rather adverse circumstances the Shabazi people have thus developed an indigenous mechanism of social control. By the quasi-kin rationalization of relationships that prevail in the area they seek to maintain local morale, and thereby prevent further deterioration of their neighborhood.

The Hatiqva Quarter studied by Amilia Aviel (1979), also in the early 1970s, has a good deal in common with the Shabazi quarter. But more than that quarter the Hatiqva Quarter has in Israeli parlance become the epitome of a bad area. Located in south Tel-Aviv, it started in the early 1940s as a suburb populated mainly by Yemenite immigrants. In recent decades immigrants from Iraq have become the largest sub-ethnic group, and also people from other Middle Eastern countries have moved there. Hatiqva has high crime rates, but interestingly and in cöntrast to Shabazi, it has retained its residential character. The area is densely populated, families living mainly in small flats in one- and two-storey dwellings that give directly on to narrow streets. Living in Hatiqva, because of the spatial layout, entails high public visibility and minimal privacy. This visibility constitutes the social mechanism that sustains Hatiqva as a residential area. Street life is very lively in the area. Not only is there bustling local commercial activity, but there are many cafés, and altogether people spend a good deal of their time on their doorsteps and in the streets adjacent to their houses. Public territory close to one's home is to a certain extent considered as one's own. This is particularly obvious on weekends and holidays when houses are packed to capacity with people away from their regular occupations. At such times people take to public territory to stroll, chat, relax and while away their time.

Aviel (1979), who studied this Quarter, is the only one of the ethnographers reviewed here who explicitly discusses the subject of social control. The upshot of the data, viewed from that angle, is that the high visibility of people in Hatiqva stymies shady activities. Unknown people are under constant manifold surveillance of housewives staring out of their doorways, of storekeepers from behind their sidewalk stalls, of café patrons at their drinks, and of numerous curious and insistent children. But this mechanism in itself is not sufficient, because many of the residents, particularly adolescents, are known by the neighbors to be lawless people. These lawless adolescents are kept at bay by a series of social mechanisms. Foremost of these is the reputation one gains for physical prowess, and thus the ability to protect oneself by force. Households that have able-bodied men and adolescent sons are thus usually safe, and also other households, if located close to households with vigorous menfolk, enjoy safety. There is a degree of neighborliness and warmth in the Quarter. The ethnographer reports that lonely old folk can also sometimes gain a reputation for power. Thus local hoodlums were apprehensive of an old woman living by herself because of the vehemence of her curses, and she was never molested. Another mechanism of social control was the batting of an eye by people on illicit activities at certain clearly delimited times and places. Thus parents would ignore the taking of drugs, gambling and illicit sexual activities of their offspring in particular locales, but would try, often successfully, to object to such doings elsewhere. As a result of all this Hatiqva Quarter has remained livable to its residents, and its crime rate is kept in check. The criminal potential of the Quarter's population is stymied in its local activities, and tends to be driven to express itself beyond the confines of the Quarter in other parts of the city.

I have presented in this essay materials on several Israeli urban communities. These communities represent a wide spectrum of Israeli quarters, though certainly not all of them. The first case represents communities that have relatively clearly delimited social and spatial boundaries. It has a clearly institutionalized leadership that affects the activities of residents and constitutes an effective mechanism of social control. The institutionalized leadership is linked to the fact that this is a planned community and the relevant planning authorities themselves supply leadership. In the more developed towns of this type, local leadership emerges through infiltration by local people of the general political and administrative systems.

The remaining cases constitute urban quarters typical of modern mass society, in that they lack clear social boundaries, and do not engender an institutionalized leadership of their own. Social control here is vested in the impersonal and abstract mores of society as a whole and in the wielders of general societal power (such as courts of law and police and high-level political figures). Interestingly, however, our review has uncovered various forms of informal and indigenous social control, which lack institutionalized political expression. In Tzur we underlined the role, albeit weak, of extended family cohesion; in Shabazi, the role of matrifocal neighborhood networks; in Hatiqva, the role of street life and public visibility.

This overview of social organization and social control in Israeli urban quarters, based on the pertinent ethnographies, does not give us a definitive formula as to the relationship between types of social policy and types of emerging social organization. For this one would require much more formally-controlled data than I have presented here. The overview does however leave us with one very clear impression: Israeli urban quarters constitute a surprisingly variegated and colorful tapestry, despite the several decades that have passed since the onset of mass immigration. Many observers of the Israeli immigrant scene have felt that processes of acculturation and assimilation among the various immigrant groups have eroded much of the variety of Israeli culture and society. Certainly there is a measure of truth in this. It seems, however, that it is primarily in the kinds of variety that such changes have occurred. While indeed Israeli society seems to have lost some of the colorfulness that was rooted in the variety of traditional cultures, religious and folk practices, a new variety seems to be developing in social areas typical of urbanized and secularized societies. For the social anthropologist, and possibly also for the seeker of the varieties of Jewish social forms, Israel remains an intriguing, often charming, social microcosm.

AFTERWORD: REFLECTIONS OF AN URBAN ANTHROPOLOGIST

Walter P. Zenner

One goal of scholarship and scientific inquiry is an increased understanding of the place of humanity in the universe. Such understanding is always incomplete. In this essay, one of the editors reflects on his ethnographic fieldwork and personal experiences and their contribution to the larger goal.

THOUGHTS ON A DAY IN MA'ARUF

It was a glorious, sunny February day in Ma'aruf, an Arab village in the mountains of Galilee. After the cold, rainy winter months, one sensed the coming of spring. The hills were covered with green and there were white blossoms on the almond trees and red anemones in the fields. I went to my friend's house, as I did whenever I visited this village. He served me coffee in the traditional way, first a cup of bitter coffee—the ritual sign of hospitality—and then a cup of sweet Turkish coffee. We talked about the latest news in the village and the world. For a moment I felt like the nineteenth-century traveler who sensed an "immovable East," barely changed from biblical times.

Then we went out on his terrace, and my gaze wandered to the villagers in the streets. Boys were playing. Men in a truck from the Gaza Strip were selling cheap trinkets and pottery, mostly imports from Hong Kong and Taiwan. Women were going to the bakery to buy bread. Men were returning from work in the city.

Fifty years ago, this village had 500 inhabitants, almost all of them engaged in agriculture. Today there are ten times that number and 80 percent of the men work outside the village, either in factories or in various kinds of government jobs. There is even a small factory in the village itself employing young girls and women to make nylon stockings. Fifty years ago, the villagers grew most of their own food, importing only rice, coffee, and sugar. Today they grow a few cash crops, such as watermelons, tomatoes, and plums, for the market in Haifa, the nearest city, but they also import much food. Fifty years ago, it took several hours to reach the city by foot or donkey. Today taxis and buses go back and forth all day. Most villagers have radios and television sets, and they receive world news from the Israeli radio or from Lebanon, Egypt or Jordan.

They watch the television commentaries of the editor of Egypt's leading paper and listen regularly to the B.B.C.

Fifty years ago, the villagers' life span was short, and the infant mortality rate was high—many babies lived only a few days. Today the women have their babies in hospitals and mortality rates have plummeted. The villagers worry now about the way in which their young people are straying from the traditional ways of life. Many old people receive social security benefits, unknown a generation ago. Fifty years ago, Ma'aruf was a village much as it had been for 500 years—near a city, yet still far away. Today it is but a suburb of Haifa, a sprawling, industrial city, a port of trade with the four corners of the modern world.

As we sat on his terrace, my Ma'aruf friend asked me for advice about his son and daughter. Should his son study art or go to work in a factory? Should his daughter, who had done well in school, go to the university, where she might encounter strange men? I wanted to help him, but what advice could I give? Did I know more about the future than he did? The changes which were engulfing this 500-year-old village in the Galilee mountains were also swirling about my own life.

Unlike my friend in Ma'aruf, whose family had lived in that village in Galilee for half a millennium, I was a wanderer. My family, too, had lived in one place for a long time—a small town in southern Germany. Records showed Zenners living there 170 years ago. Probably the Zenner family had lived in Franconia for centuries, perhaps 1000 years. After World War I, however, my father sought his fortune in the city of Nürnberg. Then, like many other European Jews, my family fled from the Nazi regime. Those who stayed behind were destroyed. Of the many Jewish communities, often centuries old, that existed in Europe and the Middle East in 1800, only a few remain today. The Jewish experience under Hitler was, of course, exceptional. But the breakup or transformation of traditional communities and cultural patterns is a phenomenon that has been accelerating for more than a century.

Since the Industrial Revolution in the early nineteenth century, all sorts of peoples have been on the move—as immigrants to new countries, as peasants seeking jobs in cities, as refugees from famine, persecution and genocide. Arabs, Chinese, Vietnamese, Hindus and South Asians, Muslims, Amerindians, Ibos, Gypsies, Irish, Scots, Welsh, English, French, Italians, Serbs, and many others have joined these streams of humanity leaving their family homes, and often their homelands, for other places. These migrations have reflected changes in technology, in political organization, and in the world economy. As many of these peoples became urban dwellers, some for the first time in their historical experience, the cities themselves were changing in fundamental ways. Now the people of Ma'aruf were joining this movement. Some were working in far-off places, others had become daily commuters, still others were studying abroad. In other Arab villages, people had been uprooted in the past thirty years by wars, land expropriation, and poverty.

ON A VISIT TO LOS ANGELES

A few years after this visit to Ma'aruf, I attended a conference in Los Angeles. When it ended, I stayed another day to see some friends who lived there, whom I had not seen for thirteen years. We had all been living in Chicago then; now my home was in the Northeast and theirs in southern California.

I had known Renee since we were in sixth grade. We had gone to high school and summer camp together. Ernie, her husband, had been my camp counselor. After going away to school, we three had returned to Chicago. Now we were far apart. In Albany, where I live, there are very few people who knew me before I was a college professor and married. Almost no one knew my family before we moved there. One day, when my wife and I were going out and leaving our young daughter with a baby sitter, we realized that if something happened to us, neither the sitter nor our neighbors would know our next of kin. Since then we have made some friends with whom we have become close; yet the feeling is not quite the same with them as with those who have known me since childhood or since college.

For Ernie and Renee, however, it is different. Ernie has two brothers in Los Angeles. There is also a whole colony of ex-Chicago Jews in the city, and one meets old friends from the West Side or the North Side. Even though my friends now live like Californians—enjoying jogging and eating organic foods—they have many links with their past.

In the Los Angeles smog, I suddenly remembered the sunny day in Ma'aruf and realized how close that place is to the clouds of industrial smoke over Haifa Bay. Whether in Los Angeles or Albany with strangers and new acquaintances or in Ma'aruf, surrounded by lifelong friends, enemies, and kin (who often are all rolled into one), we all face the unknown. The great forces of the world in the twentieth century have swept all of us up, and we must find others to help and support us. In this world, we seek the shelter of small groups to give us some protection from life's storms. Now we are all city folk who must find new havens.

REFERENCES

Abelson, P. *Science*, 165(1) (1969).

Abey-Wickrama, I., M.F. a'Brook, F.E.G. Gattoni, and C.F. Herridge. "Mental Hospital Admissions and Aircraft Noise." *Lancet*, ii (1969), 1275-1277.

Ablon, J. "Relocated American Indians in the San Francisco Bay Area: Social Interaction and Indian Identity." *Human Organization*, 23 (1964), 296-304.

_____. "American Indian Relocation: Problems of Dependency and Management in the City." *Phylon*, 26 (1965), 362-371.

_____. "The Samoan Funeral in Urban America." *Ethnology*, 9 (1970), 209-227.

_____. "Retention of Cultural Values and Differential Urban Adaptation in a West Coast City." *Social Forces*, 49(1) (1971).

Abrams, Charles. *Housing in the Modern World*. London: Faber & Faber, 1964.

Abuza, N. "The Paris-London-New York Questionnaires." Harvard University, unpublished.

Adams, Bert N. *Kinship in an Urban Setting*. Chicago: Markham, 1968.

_____. "Isolation, Function and Beyond." *Journal of Marriage and the Family*, 32 (1970), 575-597.

Aldous, Joan. "Urbanization, the Extended Family and Kinship Ties in West Africa." *Social Forces*, 41 (1962), 6-12.

Alexander, Christopher. "A City Is Not a Tree." *Design*, 206 (1966), 46-55.

Altman, D., et al. Graduate Center, The City University of New York, unpublished research.

Alvirez, David, and Frank D. Bean. "The Mexican American Family." In Charles H. Mindel and Robert W. Habenstein (eds.), *Ethnic Families in America: Patterns and Variations*, 1976, pp. 271-292.

Anderson, Nels. "The Urban Way of Life." *International Journal of Comparative Sociology*, 3 (1962), 175-188.

Ando, Y. and H. Hattori. "Effects of Noise on Human Placental Lactogen (HPL) Levels in Maternal Plasma." *British Journal of Obstetrics & Gynecology*, 84 (1977), 115-118.

_____. "Statistical Studies on the Effects of Intense Noise during Human Fetal Life." *Sound & Vibration*, 27 (1973), 101-110.

Andreas, Carol. *When Women Rebel: the Rise of Popular Feminism in Peru*. Westport, CT: Lawrence Hill and Co., 1985.

Annest, J.L., K.R. Mahaffey, D.H. Cox, and J. Roberts. "Blood Lead Levels for Persons 6 Months - 74 Years of Age: United States, 1976-1980." *NCHS Advancedata*, 79 (1982), 1-23.

Arango, Marta. "The Chocó Woman: Agent for Change." In June H. Turner (ed.), *Latin American Women: The Meek Speak Out*. Silver Spring, MD: International Educational Development, Inc., 1980, pp. 85-100.

Ardaya Salinas, Gloria. "The Barzolas and the Housewives Committee." In June Nash, Helen Safa and contributors (eds.), *Women and Change in Latin America*. South Hadley, MA: Bergin and Garvey Publishers, Inc., 1986, pp. 326-343.

Arensberg, Conrad M. "The Community as Object and as Sample." *American Anthropologist*, 63 (1961), 241-264.

_____. "The Urban in Crosscultural Perspective." In Elizabeth Eddy (ed.), *Urban Anthropology: Research Perspectives and Strategies*. Athens, GA: University of Georgia Press, 1968.

Arensberg, Conrad, and Solon T. Kimball. *Culture and Community.* New York: Harcourt, Brace and World, 1965.

Arimana, Carmen. "Squatter Settlement Decision-Making: For Men Only." In June H. Turner (ed.), *Latin American Women: The Meek Speak Out.* Silver Spring, MD: International Educational Development, Inc., 1980, pp. 11-24.

Arizpe, Lourdes. "Indígenas en la Ciudad de México: El Caso de las 'Marías'." Mexico: Sep/ Setentas, 1975.

_____. "Women in the Informal Labor Sector: The Case of Mexico City." In The Wellesley Editorial Committee (ed.), *Women and National Development.* Chicago: University of Chicago Press, 1977, pp. 25-37.

Armelagos, George J. and John R. Dewey. "Evolutionary Response to Human Infectious Disease." *Bioscience,* 20 (1970), 271-275.

Aronoff, M. "Development Towns in Israel." In M. Curtis and M. Chertoff (eds.), *Israel: Social Structure and Change.* New Brunswick, NJ: Transaction Books, 1973, pp. 27-46.

_____. *Frontiertown: The Politics of Community Building in Israel.* Manchester: Manchester University Press, 1974.

Aronson, S. "The Sociology of the Telephone." *International Journal of Comparative Sociology,* 12 (1971), 153-167.

Avineri, S. "Israel: Two Nations." In M. Curtis and M. Chertoff (eds.), *Israel: Social Structure and Change.* New Brunswick, NJ: Transaction Books, 1973, pp. 281-305.

Avriel, A. *Everyday Life in Hatiqva Neighbourhood.* Tel Aviv: Tcherikover, 1979 (in Hebrew).

Ayres, Stephen M., Robert Evans, David Licht, Jane Griesbach, Felicity Reimold, Edward F. Ferrand and Antoinette Criscitiello. "Health Effects of Exposure to High Concentrations of Automotive Emissions." *Archives of Environmental Health,* 27 (1973), 168-178.

Bachofen, J.J. *Das Mutterrecht.* Basel: Benno Schwabe, 1861.

Bacon, Alice M. *Japanese Girls and Women.* Boston: Houghton Mifflin, 1902

Bailey, F.G. "Closed Social Stratification in India." *Archives Européennes de Sociologie,* IV (1963), 107-124.

Balmori, Diana, and Robert Oppenheimer. "Family Clusters: Generational Nucleation in Nineteenth Century Argentina and Chile." *Comparative Studies in Society and History,* 21 (1979), 231-261.

Banfield, Edward C. *The Moral Basis of a Backward Society.* New York: Free Press, 1958.

Bannister, P., and J.M.M. Mair. *Evolution of Personal Constructs.* London: Academic Press, 1968.

Barltrop, Donald. "Nutritional and Maturational Factors Modifying the Absorption of Inorganic Lead from the Gastrointestinal Tract." In V.R. Hunt, M.K. Smith and D. Worth, *Banbury Report No. 11, Environmental Factors in Human Growth and Development.* Cold Spring Harbor Laboratory, 1982, pp. 35-41.

Barnes, Charles. *The Longshoremen.* New York: Russell Sage Foundation, 1915.

Barnes, J.A. "Class and Committees in a Norwegian Island Parish." *Human Relations* 7 (1954), 39-58.

Barth, Frederik. *Ethnic Groups and Boundaries.* New York: Allen & Unwin, 1969.

Barzini, Luigi. *The Italians.* New York: Atheneum, 1965.

Bascom, William. "Urbanization Among the Yoruba." *American Journal of Sociology,* 60 (1955), 446-454.

Basham, Richard. *Urban Anthropology: The Cross-Cultural Study of Complex Societies.* Palo Alto, CA: Mayfield Publishing Company, 1978.

Bastide, R. *Ethnologie des Capitales Latino-Américaines.* D.G. Epstein, trans. *Caravelle,* 3 (1964), 73-89.

Beals, Ralph L. "Urbanism, Urbanization and Acculturation." *American Anthropologist,* 53 (1951), 1-10.

Bell, Charles. *The People of Tibet.* Oxford: Clarendon Press, 1928.

Bell, Colin. "Mobility and the Extended Middle Class Family." In C.C. Harris (ed.), *Readings in Kinship in Urban Society.* Oxford and New York: Pergamon (1968), pp. 209-224.

Bender, D.R. "A Refinement of the Concept of Household: Families, Co-residence, and Domestic Functions." *American Anthropologist*, 69 (1967), 493-504.

Bendix, Reinhard. "Tradition and Modernity Reconsidered." *Comparative Studies in Society and History*, 9 (1967).

Benson, Edwin. *Life in a Mediaeval City*. New York: Macmillan, 1920.

Berger, Bennett. "Suburbs, Subcultures and the Urban Future." In Sam Bass Warner (ed.), *Planning for a Nation of Cities*. Cambridge, MA: MIT Press, 1966.

Berger, S. and M. Piore. *Dualism and Discontinuity in Industrial Societies*. Cambridge: Cambridge University Press, 1980.

Berlin, Brent, Paul Kay, D.E. Breedlove, and P.H. Raven. "Covert Categories and Folk Taxonomies." *American Anthropologist*, 70 (1968), 290-299.

Berreman, Gerald D. "Anemic and Emetic Analyses in Social Anthropology." *American Anthropologist*, 68 (1966), 346-354.

Berreman, Gerald D., G. Gjessing, and K. Gough. "Social Responsibilities Symposium." *Current Anthropology*, 9 (1968), 391-435.

Bestor, Theodore C., "Tradition and Japanese Social Organization: Institutional Development in a Tokyo Neighborhood." *Ethnology*, 24(2) (1985), 121-135.

_____. "*Shitamachi* and the Culture of Urbanism: Subculture, Class, and Community in Tokyo." Unpublished paper presented to the American Anthropological Association, 1986.

_____. *Neighborhood Tokyo*. Stanford: Stanford University Press, in press.

Bieliauskas, Linas A. *Stress and its Relationship to Health and Illness*. Boulder, CO: Westview Press, 1982.

Bielicki, Tadeusz. "Physical Growth as a Measure of the Economic Well-being of Populations: The Twentieth Century." In F. Falkner and J.M. Tanner (eds.), *Human Growth, Vol III*. New York: Plenum Press, 1986, pp. 283-305.

Black, Cyril E. *The Dynamics of Modernization*. New York: Harper & Row, 1966.

Black, Francis L. "Infectious Diseases in Primitive Societies." *Science*, 187 (1975), 515-518.

Black, Mary and Duane Metzger. "Ethnographic Description and the Study of Law." In Laura Nader (ed.), Anthropological Study of Law. *American Anthropologist*, 67(6) (1965), 141-165.

Bodde, D. (ed.), *Annual Customs and Festivals in Peking*. Peiping: Henri Vetch, 1936.

Boissevain, Jeremy. *Friends of Friends: Networks, Manipulators, and Coalitions*. New York: St. Martin's Press, 1974.

Bonacich, Edna. "A Theory of Ethnic Antagonism: The Split-Labor Market." *American Sociological Review*, 37 (972), 547-559.

Bonilla, Frank. "The Favelas of Rio: The Rundown Rural Barrio in the City." *Dissent*, 9 (1962), 383-386.

Boserup, Ester. *Woman's Role in Economic Development*. New York: St. Martin's Press, 1970.

Bossen, Laurel. "Women and Dependent Development." SUNYA: Department of Anthropology, Ph.D. Thesis, 1978.

Bott, Elizabeth. *Family and Social Network: Roles, Norms, and External Relationships in Ordinary Urban Families*. London: Tavistock, 1957.

Bouah, G. Niangoran. "Le Village Aboure." *Cahiers d'Études Africaines I*, 2 (1960), 113-127.

Bourricard, F. "Lima en la Vida Política Peruana." *America Latina* (1964), 89-96.

Braner, J.S., J.J. Goodnow, and G.A. Austin. *A Study of Thinking*. New York: John Wiley and Sons, 1956.

Bridges, Harry (President ILWU). U.S. West Coast Longshoremens Union, interview, July 1957.

Bridges, Harry, and William Glazier. "Report on Port Operations and Union Structure in Europe, Middle East and USSR." (mimeograph) Seattle: ILWU, 1959.

Brown, C. *Black and White Britain: The Third PSI Survey*. London: Heinemann, 1983.

Brunt, L. *Lectori Salutem*, on the analysis of abolition letters in the Netherlands. *Netherlands Journal of Sociology* (1979), 141-153.

Buechley, R.W., W.B. Riggan, V. Hasselblad and J.B. VanBruggen. "So Levels and Perturbations in Mortality." *Archives of Environmental Health*, 27 (1973), 134-137.

Bundesanstalt für Arbeit. *Repräsentativuntersuchung*. Nürnberg: Bundesanstalt für Arbeit, 1973.

Burgess, J.S. "Community Organization in China." *Far Eastern Survey.* 14 (1943), 337-371.
_____. *The Guilds of Peking.* New York, NY: Columbia University Press, 1928.
Burgess, R.W., and D.J. Bogue. *Contributions to Urban Sociology.* Chicago: University of Chicago Press, 1964.
Burton, Richard. *First Footsteps in East Africa.* London: Routledge & Kegan Paul, 1966.
Butterworth, Douglas and John K. Chance. *Latin American Urbanization.* Cambridge: Cambridge University Press, 1981.
Cahn, E.S. (ed.). *Our Brother's Keeper: The Indian in White America.* New York: World, 1969.
Caldarola, Carlo. "The Doya-Gai: A Japanese Version of Skid Row." *Pacific Affairs* 41 (1968), 511-525.
Caplovitz, David. *The Poor Pay More.* New York: The Free Press, 1963.
Caplow, Theodore, Howard M. Bahr, Bruce A. Chadwick, Reuben Hill, and Margaret Holmes Williamson. *Middletown Families: Fifty Years of Change and Continuity.* Minneapolis: University of Minnesota Press, 1982.
Carruthers, Malcom. "Biochemical Responses to the Environment." In G.A. Harrison and J.B. Gibson (eds.), *Man in Urban Environments.* New York: Oxford University Press, 1976, pp. 247-273.
Castells, Manuel. *The City and the Grassroots: A Cross-Cultural Theory of Urban Social Movements.* Berkeley: University of California Press, 1983.
Castles, S., and G. Kosack. *Immigrant Workers and Class Structure in Western Europe.* London: Oxford University Press, 1973.
Centre International de l'Enfance. "Etude des conditions de vie de l'enfant africain en milieu urbain et de leur influence sur la délinquance juvenile." Travaux et Documents XII. Paris, 1959.
Cerase, F. "Nostalgia or Disenchantment: Considerations on Return Migration." In Silvano U. Tomasi and Madeleine H. Engles (eds.), *The Italian Experience in the United States.* New York: Center for Migration Studies, 1970.
Chaney, Elsa M. *Supermadre - Women In Politics in Latin America.* Austin: University of Texas Press, 1979.
Chandler, T. and G. Fox. *3000 Years of Urban Growth.* New York: Academic Press, 1974.
Chinchilla, Norma S. "Industrialization, Monopoly Capitalism, and Women's Work in Guatemala." In The Wellesley Editorial Committee (ed.), *Women and National Development.* Chicago: University of Chicago Press, 1977, pp. 38-56.
Chouraqui, A. *Les Juifs d'Afrique du Nord.* Paris: Presses Universitaires de France, 1953.
Clarke, M. "On the Concept of 'Sub-culture'." *British Journal of Sociology,* 25 (1974), 428-441.
Clerget, Marcel. *Le Caire: Etude de geographie urbaine et d'histoire economique* (2 vols.). Paris: E. & R. Schindler, 1934.
Clignet, R. "Environmental Change, Type of Descent and Child Rearing Practices." Paper presented at the Conference on the Methods and Objectives of African Research in Africa, April 1-3, 1965.
Clignet, R., and J. Sween. "Urbanization, Plural Marriage and Family Size in Two African Cities." *American Ethnologist,* (1974), 221-242.
Cockburn, Aidan. "Infectious Diseases in Ancient Populations." *Current Anthropology,* 12 (1971), 45-62.
Cohen, A. "The Social Organization of Credit in a West African Cattle Market." *Africa,* 35 (1965), 8-20.
_____. "Politics of the Kola Trade." *Africa,* 36 (1966), 18-36.
_____. "The Hausa." In P.C. Lloyd, et al. (eds.), *The City of Ibadan.* Cambridge: Cambridge University Press, 1967, pp. 117-127.
_____. "The Politics of Mysticism in Some Local Communities in Newly Independent African States." In M. Swartz (ed.), *Local-level Politics.* Chicago: Aldine, 1968.
_____. *Custom and Politics in Urban Africa.* London: Routledge and Kegan Paul; Berkeley: University of California Press, 1969a.
_____. "Political Anthropology: the Analysis of the Symbolism of Power Relations." *Man,* 4 (1969b), 217-235.

————. "The Politics of Ritual Secrecy." *Man*, 6 (1971), 427-448.

————. "Introduction: The Lesson of Ethnicity." In Abner Cohen (ed.), *Urban Ethnicity*. A.S.A. Monograph No. 12. London: Tavistock Publications, 1974a, pp. ix-xxiv.

————. *Two-Dimensional Man*. Berkeley and Los Angeles: University of California Press, 1974b.

Cohen, E. "The City in Zionist Ideology." *Jerusalem Quarterly*, 4 (1977), 126-144.

————. "Thai Girls and *Farang* Men: The Edge of Ambiguity. *Annals of Tourism Research*, 9 (1982), 403-428.

————. "The Dropout Expatriates: A Study of Marginal *Farangs* in Bangkok." *Urban Anthropology*, 13(1) (1984), 91-115.

————. "A Soi in Bangkok: The Dynamics of Lateral Urban Expansion." *Journal of the Siam Society*, (1985a).

————. "Tourism as Play." *Religion*, 15 (1985b), 291-304.

————. "Sensuality and Venality in Bangkok: The Dynamics of Cross-cultural Mapping of Prostitution." Invited paper, XI World Congress of Sociology, New Delhi, August 18-22, 1986.

————. "Open-ended Prostitution as a Skillful Game of Luck." To be published in a collection of papers on urban anthropology in Thailand, edited by H. Phillips.

Cohen, E., and R.L. Cooper. "Tourism and language." *Annals of Tourism Research* (1986).

Collier, David. *Squatters and Oligarchs: Authoritarian Rule and Policy Change in Peru*. Baltimore: Johns Hopkins University Press, 1976.

Coltman, R., Jr. *The Chinese*. Philadelphia, F.A. Davis, 1891.

Conklin, Harold C. "Lexicographical Treatment of Folk Taxonomies." *International Journal of American Linguistics*, 28 (1962), 119-141.

————. "Ethnogenealogical Method." In Ward Goodenough (ed.), *Explorations in Cultural Anthropology*. New York: McGraw-Hill, 1964.

Cook, Scott. "The Obsolete Anti-Market Mentality." In Morton Fried (ed.), *Readings in Anthropology*, Vol. II. 2nd ed. New York: Crowell, 1968.

Coombs, Gary. "Networks and Exchange: The Role of Social Relationships in a Small Voluntary Association." *Journal of Anthropological Research*, 20(2) (1973), 96-112.

Coon, Carleton. *Caravan: The Story of the Middle East*. New York: Henry Holt and Co., 1951.

Cornelius, Wayne A. *Political Learning Among the Migrant Poor: the Impact of Residential Context*. Professional Paper in Comparative Politics, Beverly Hills, CA: Sage Publishing Co., 1973.

Costa, Lucia. "Relatorio do Plano Pilato," *Revista Brasileira de Municipais*, Vol. 10 (1957).

Crawford, M.H., and George Gmelch. "The Human Biology of the Irish Tinkers: Demography, Ethnohistory and Genetics." *Social Biology*, 21 (1974), 321-331.

Crichton, A.J. "Industrial Relations in the Ports." *The Journal of the Institute of Transport* (1963), 43-47.

Dash, Jack. "The Rise of the Dockleader." *The Illustrated London News* (August 28, 1965).

Davis, Kingsley. "The Urbanization of the World Population." *World Urbanization, 1950-1970*, Vol. 1: *Basic Data for Cities, Countries and Regions*. Institute of International Studies, University of California, Berkeley, 1969.

Davis, Susan. *Parades and Power: Street Theater in Nineteenth Century Philadelphia*. Philadelphia: University of Pennsylvania Press, 1986.

Deakin, N. *Colour, Citizenship and British Society*. London: Oxford University Press, 1969.

deJesus, Carolina Maria. *Child of the Dark: The Diary of Carolina Maria deJesus*. New York: The New American Library, Inc., 1962.

Departamento Nacional de Planeación (DNP). *La Población en Colombia: Realidad, Perspectivas, y Politica*. Bogotá: Imprenta Nacional, 1969.

Department of Social Sciences, University of Liverpool. *The Dockworker*. Liverpool: Liverpool University Press, 1956.

Deshen, S. *Immigrant Voters in Israel: Parties and Congregations in an Israeli Election Campaign*. Manchester: Manchester University Press, 1970.

_____. "Political Ethnicity and Cultural Ethnicity in Israel during the 1960s." In A. Cohen (ed.), *Urban Ethnicity*, ASA Monograph No. 12. London: Tavistock, 1974, pp. 281-309.

Deutsch, K. "On Social Communication and the Metropolis." *Daedalus*, 90 (1961).

deVos, George, and H. Wagatsuma. "The Ecology of Special Buraku." In George deVos and H. Wagatsuma (eds.), *Japan's Invisible Race*. Berkeley: University of California Press (1966).

Dickinson, Robert E. *The West European City*. London: Routledge & Kegan Paul, 1951.

Dohrenwend, B.P., and B.S. Dohrenwend. "Psychiatric Disorders in Urban Settings. In G. Caplan (ed.), *American Handbook of Psychiatry*, Vol. II, 2nd ed., New York: Basic Books, 1974, pp. 424-447.

Doll, R. "Atmospheric Pollution and Lung Cancer." *Environmental Health Perspectives*, 22 (1978), 23-31.

Domhoff, G. William. *The Bohemian Grove and Other Retreats: A Study in Ruling Class Cohesiveness*. New York: Harper & Row, 1974.

Doolittle, Justus. *Social Life of the Chinese*. London: Sampson Low, 1868.

Dore, R.P. *City Life in Japan*. Berkeley: University of California Press, 1958.

Drake, St. Clair, and Horace R. Clayton. *Black Metropolis, a Study of Negro Life in a Northern City*. New York: Harcourt, Brace, 1945.

Dubois, W.E.B. *The Negro Family*. Atlanta: Atlanta University Press, 1908.

Durkheim, E. *De la division du travail social*. Paris, 1893, 1932. *The Division of Labor in Society*. G. Simpson, ed. New York: Free Press, 1964.

Eames, E., and J. Goode. *Urban Poverty in Cross-Cultural Context*. New York: Free Press, 1973.

Eco, Umberto. "Towards a Semiotic Enquiry into the Television Message." *W.P.C.S.* 3 (1972), University of Birmingham.

Ekwensi, Cyril. *Jagua Nana*. London: Hutchinson, 1961.

Engelsmann, F., H.B.M. Murphy, R. Prince, M. Leduc, and H. Demars. "Variations in Responses to Symptom Check List by Age, Sex, Income, Residence, and Ethnicity." *Social Psychiatry*, 7 (1972), 150-156.

Epstein, A.L. *Politics in an Urban African Community*. Manchester: Manchester University Press.

_____. "The Network and Urban-Social Organization." In J. Clyde Mitchell (ed.), *Social Networks in Urban Situations, Analysis of Personal Relationships in Central African Towns*. Manchester: Manchester University Press, 1969.

Epstein, David G. "The Genesis and Function of Squatter Settlements in Brasília." In Thomas Weaver and Douglas White (ed.), *The Anthropology of Urban Environments*. Society for Applied Anthropology Monographs No. 11. Washington, DC: Society for Applied Anthropology, 1972, pp. 51-58.

Erlick, June Carolyn. "Women of Nicaragua." *Ms.* Nov. (1984), 66-72; 147-150.

Evans-Pritchard, E.E. *Witchcraft, Oracles, and Magic Among the Azande*. Oxford: Clarendon Press, 1937.

_____. *Social Anthropology*. London: Cohen & West, 1951.

Fallers, L.A. "Some Determinants of Marriage Stability in Busoga: A Reformation of Gluckman's Hypothesis." *Africa*, XXVII (1957), 106-123.

Farren, M., and E. Barker. *Watch Out kids*. London: Macmillan, 1972.

Feldman, A., and W. Moore. "Industrialization and Industrialism: Consequence and Differentiation." *Transactions of the Fifth World Congress of Sociology*, Vol. II, pp. 151-169.

Feldman, R.E. *Journal of Personality and Social Psychology*, II (1968).

Fenner, Frank. "The Effect of Changing Social Organisation on the Infectious Diseases of Man." In S.V. Boyden (ed.), *The Impact of Civilisation on the Biology of Man*. Toronto: University of Toronto Press, 1970, pp. 48-68.

Ferguson, F. "Interpreting the Self Through Letters." *Centrum* 1(2) (1981), 107-112.

Ferris, P. *The City*. Harmondsworth: Penguin, 1960.

Fields, F., and P. Haikin. *Black Britons*. Oxford: Clarendon Press, 1971.

Firth, R., J. Hubert, and A. Forge. *Families and Their Relatives*. London: Routledge & Kegan Paul, 1970.

Fischer, C.S. "'Urbanism as a Way of Life': A Review and an Agenda." *Sociological Methods and Research*, 1 (1972), 187-242.

_____. "The Study of Urban Community and Personality." *Annual Review of Sociology*, 1 (1975a), 67-89.

_____. "Toward a Subcultural Theory of Urbanism." *American Journal of Sociology*, 80 (1975b), 1319-1341.

_____. *The Urban Experience*. New York: Harcourt, Brace and Jovanovich, 1976.

Fisher, J.C. *Yugoslavia – A Multinational State*. San Francisco: Chandler, 1966.

Flannery, Kent V. "The Cultural Evolution of Civilizations." *Annual Review of Ecology and Systematics* 3 (1972), 399-426.

Fleming, Patricia. "The Politics of Marriage Among Non-Catholic European Royalty." *Current Anthropology*, 14 (1973), 207-230.

Foner, N. *Jamaica Farewell: Jamaican Migrants in London*. Berkeley: University of California Press, 1978.

Foster, George M. *Empire's Children: The People of Tzintzuntzan*. México, D.F.: Smithsonian Institution, Institute of Social Anthropology, Publication No. 6 (1948).

_____. "What is Folk Culture?" *American Anthropologist*, 55 (1955), 159-173.

_____. *Tzintzuntzan: Mexican Peasants in a Changing World*. Prospect Heights, IL: Waveland Press, Inc.

Fox, Richard. "Resiliency and Change in the Indian Caste System: The Umar of Uttar Pradesh." *Journal of Asian Sudies*, 26 (1967), 575-588.

_____. "Rationale and Reason in Urban Anthropology." *Urban Anthropology* (1972),205-233.

_____. *Urban Anthropology: Cities in Their Cultural Settings*. Englewood Cliffs, NJ: Prentice-Hall, 1977.

Frake, Charles O. "The Diagnosis of Disease Among the Subanam of Mindinao." *American Anthropologist*, 63 (1961), 113-132.

_____. "The Ethnographic Study of Cognitive Systems." In T. Gladwin and W.C. Sturtevant (eds.), *Anthropology and Human Behavior*. Washington, DC: Anthropology Society of Washington, 1962a.

_____. "Cultural Ecology and Ethnography." *American Anthropologist*, 64 (1962b), 53-59.

Frank, André Gunder. *Capitalism and Underdevelopment in Latin America*. New York: Monthly Review Press, 1967a.

_____. "Sociology of Development and Underdevelopment of Sociology." *Catalyst* (1967b), 20-73.

_____. *Latin America: Underdevelopment or Revolution*. New York: Monthly Review Press, 1969.

Frankenberg, Ronald. *Communities in Britain*. London: Penguin, 1966.

Frazier, E.F. "The Impact of Urban Civilization Upon the Negro Family." *American Sociological Review*, II (1937), 609-618.

Frerichs, R.R., B.L. Beeman, A.H. Coulson. "Los Angeles Airport Noise and Mortality – Fault Analysis and Public Policy." *American Journal of Public Health*, 70 (1980), 357-362.

Fried, M.H. *The Fabric of Chinese Society*. New York: Praeger, 1953.

Friedl, Ernestine. "The Role of Kinship in the Transmission of National Culture to Rural Villages in Mainland Greece." *American Anthropologist*, 61 (1959), 30-38.

Gadgil, D.R. *Poona: A Socio-Economic Survey*. Poona: Gokhale Institute of Political and Economic Studies, 1952.

Gaertner, S., and L. Bickman. Graduate Center, The City University of New York, unpublished research.

Gans, Herbert J. "Urbanism and Suburbanism as Ways of Life: A Reevaluation of Definitions." In A.M. Rose (ed.), *Human Behavior and Social Processes*. Boston: Houghton Mifflin, 1962a, pp. 625-648.

_____. *The Urban Villagers: Group and Class in the Life of Italian Americans*. New York: Free Press, 1962.

_____. "The Subculture of the Working Class, Lower Class and Middle Class." In *The Urban Villagers*. New York: Free Press, 1962b.

Garigue, Philip. "French Canadian Kinship and Urban Life." *American Anthropologist*, 58 (1956), 1090-1101.

Garrison, Vivian. "Social Networks, Social Change and Psychiatric Complaints among Migrants in a New York City Slum." Unpublished Ph.D. dissertation, Columbia University.

Gattoni, F., and A. Tarnopolsky. "Aircraft Noise and Psychiatric Morbidity." *Psychological Medicine*, 3 (1973), 516-520.

Geertz, Clifford. *The Interpretation of Cultures*. New York: Basic Books, 1973.

Gibb, H.A.R., and H. Bowen. *Islamic Society & the West*. Volume I, Pt. I. London: Oxford University Press. 1950.

Gilbert, Alan, and Peter Ward. "Community Action by the Urban Poor: Democratic Involvement, Community Self-help or a Means of Social Control?" *World Development*, 12 (1984a) 769-782.

_____. "Community Participation in Upgrading Irregular Settlements: The Community Response." *World Development* 12 (1984b), 913-922.

Gilmore, George W. *Korea from Its Capital*. Philadelphia: Presbyterian Board of Publication, 1892.

Gist, Noel P. "Caste Differentials in South India." *American Sociological Review*, 19 (1954), 126-137.

Gluckman, M. "Anthropological Problems Arising from the African Industrial Revolution." In A. Southall (ed.), *Social Change in Modern Africa*. London: Oxford University Press, 1961.

Gmelch, George. *The Irish Tinkers: The Urbanization of an Itinerant People, Second Edition*. Prospect Heights, IL: Waveland Press, Inc., 1985.

_____. "Return Migration." *Annual Review of Anthropology*, 1980 (forthcoming).

Gmelch, George, and Walter P. Zenner. "Urban Anthropology: A Survey of the Field from a Classroom Perspective." *Urban Anthropology*, 7 (1978), 207-215.

Gmelch, Sharon. *Tinkers and Travellers*. Dublin: The O'Brien Press; Montreal: McGill-Queen's University Press, 1976.

_____. "The Emergence of an Ethnic Group: The Irish Tinkers." *Anthropological Quarterly*, 49 (1976), 225-238.

Gmelch, Sharon, and George Gmelch. "The Itinerant Settlement Movement: Its Policies and Effects on Irish Travellers." *Studies: An Irish Quarterly Review*, 68 (1974), 1-16.

Goering, John M. "Marx and the City: Are There Any New Directions for Urban Theory?" *Comparative Urban Research*, 6 (1978), 76-85.

Goffman, Erving. *The Presentation of Self in Everyday Life*. New York: Doubleday Anchor, 1959.

_____. "Encounters." Harmondsworth: Penguin, 1972.

Goitein, S.D. *A Mediterranean Society*, Vol. III: *The Family*. Berkeley and Los Angeles: University of California Press, 1978.

Goldsmith, John R. "The 'Urban Factor' in Cancer: Smoking, Industrial Exposures, and Air Pollution as Possible Causes." In H.B. Demopoulos and M.A. Mehlman, *Cancer and the Environment*. Chicago: Pathotox Publishers, 1980, pp. 205-217.

Gonzalez, Nancie L. "The Consanguineal Household and Matrifocality." *American Anthropologist*, 67 (1965), 1541-1549.

_____. *The Spanish-Americans of New Mexico: A Heritage of Pride*. Albuquerque: University of New Mexico Press, 1969.

Goode, J. "Poverty and Urban Analysis." *Western Canadian Journal of Anthropology*, 3 (1972), 1-19.

Goode, W. *World Revolution and Family Patterns*. Glencoe, IL: Free Press of Glencoe, 1963.

Goode, William J. "Industrialization and Family Change." In B.F. Hoselitz and W.E. Moore (eds.), *Industrialization and Society*. Paris: UNESCO-Mouton, 1966, pp. 237-255.

Goodenough, Ward H. "Componential Analysis and the Study of Meaning." *Language*, 32 (1956), 195-216.

_____. *Cultural Anthropology and Linguistics*. Washington: Georgetown University Monograph Series on Language and Linguistics, 9 (1957), 173.

_____. "Yankee Kinship Terminology: A Problem in Componential Analysis." *American Anthropologist*, 67 (1965), 259-287.

Goody, Jack (ed.). *The Developmental Cycle in Domestic Groups.* Cambridge Papers in Social Anthropology No. 1. London: Cambridge University Press, 1958.

Gordon, Milton M. "The Subsociety and the Subculture." In *Assimilation in American Life.* New York: Oxford University Press, 1964.

Gottlieb, A. "Americans' vacations." *Annals of Tourism Research* 9(2) (1982), 165-187.

Gough, Kathleen. "The Nayars and the Definition of Marriage." *Journal of the Royal Anthropological Institute of Great Britain and Ireland,* 89 (1959), 23-34.

_____. "Anthropology and Imperialism." *Monthly Review,* 19 (1968), 12-27.

Gove, Walter R., Michael Hughes, and Omar R. Galle. "Overcrowding in the Home." *American Sociological Review,* 44 (1979), 59-80.

Granovetter, Mark. "The Strength of Weak Ties." *American Journal of Sociology,* 78 (1973), 1360-1380.

Graves, Nancy, and Theodore Graves. "Adaptive Strategies in Urban Migration." In Bernard J. Siegel (ed.), *Annual Review of Anthropology.* Palo Alto, CA: Annual Reviews, 1974, pp. 117-151.

Grebler, Leo, Joan W. Moore, and Ralph C. Guzman. *The Mexican-American People: The Nation's Second Largest Minority.* New York: The Free Press, 1970.

Greenfield, Sidney M. "Industrialization and the Family in Sociological Theory." *American Journal of Sociology,* 67 (1961), 312-322.

Greer, Scott. "Urbanism Reconsidered: A Comparative Study of Local Areas in a Metropolis." *American Sociological Review,* 21 (1956), 19-25.

Grey, A. *Saigon.* London: Pan Books, 1983.

Grey, D.L., and T.R. Brown. "Letters to the Editor: Hazy reflections of public opinion." *Journalism Quarterly,* 47 (1970), 450-456, 471.

Guatemala. *Anuario Estadístico.* Dirección General de Estadística, Ministerio de Economía, 1974.

Gugler, Josef, and William G. Flanagan. *Urbanization and Social Change in West Africa.* Cambridge: Cambridge University Press, 1978.

Gulick, John. *Tripoli: A Modern Arab City.* Cambridge, MA: Harvard University Press, 1967.

_____. "The Outlook, Research Strategies and Relevance in Urban Anthropology." In E. Eddy (ed.), *Urban Anthropology.* Athens, GA: University of Georgia Press, 1968.

Gutkind, P. "African Urban Family Life." *Cahiers d'Etudes Africaines II,* 10 (1962), 149-207.

_____. "The Energy of Despair: Social Organizations of the Unemployed in Two African Cities: Lagos & Nairobi." *Civilizations,* 17 (1967), 186-211.

Guzman, Virginia. "Women of the Lima Shanty Towns, Peru." *Latin American Women, Minority Rights Group* 57 (1983), 12.

Hage, Per. "A Structural Analysis of Manchurian Beer Terms and Beer Drinking." Unpublished manuscript.

Hagel, Otto, and Louis Goldblatt. "Men and Machines: A Story About Longshoring on the West Coast Waterfront." San Francisco: ILWU-PMA, 1963.

Hall, E.T. *The Hidden Dimension.* New York: Doubleday, 1966.

Hall, P. *The World Cities.* New York: McGraw-Hill, 1966.

Hallowell, A. Irving. "Fear and Anxiety as Cultural and Individual Variables in a Primitive Society." *Journal of Social Psychology,* 9 (1938), 25-47.

Halperin, E. "The Decline of Communism in Latin America." *Atlantic Monthly* (May 1963), 65-70.

Halpern, Joel M. "The Rural Revolution." *"Transactions of the New York Academy of Sciences,* Series II, Vol. 28 (1965), 73-80.

Halpern, Joel M. and Barbara Kerewsky-Halpern. *A Serbian Village in Historical Perspective.* Prospect Heights, IL: Waveland Press, Inc., 1986.

Hammel, E.A. *The Pink Yo-Yo: Occupational Mobility in Belgrade, ca. 1915-1965.* Berkeley: Institute of International Studies, University of California, 1969.

Hammel, E.A. and Charles Yarbrough. "Social Mobility and the Durability of Family Ties." *Journal of Anthropological Research,* 29 (1973), 145-163.

Hammill, P.V.V., F.E. Johnston, and S. Lemeshow. "Height and Weight of Children: Socio-economic Status." Department of Health, Education and Welfare Publication No. (HSM) 73-1601; Vital Health Statistics Series 11, No. 119. Washington, DC: U.S. Government Printing Office.

Handelman, D., and Shamgar-Handelman, L. "Social Planning Prerequisites for New and Expanded Communities: The Case of Israel." *Contact*, 10 (1978), 86-122.

Hannerz, Ulf. *Exploring the City*. New York: Columbia University Press, 1980.

_____. *Soulside: Inquiries into Ghetto Culture and Community*. New York: Columbia University Press, 1969.

Hansen, A.T. "Review of H. Miner's *Primitive City of Timbuctoo*." *American Journal of Sociology*, 59 (1954), 501-502.

Harrington, Michael. *The Other America: Poverty in the United States*. Baltimore: Penguin.

Harris, C.C. *The Family: An Introduction*. London: Allen and Unwin, 1969.

_____. *Readings in Kinship in Urban Society*. Oxford, New York and Toronto: Pergamon Press, 1970.

Harris, Marvin. *Town and Country in Brazil*. New York: Columbia University Press, 1956.

_____. *The Rise of Anthropological Theory: A History of Theories of Culture*. New York: Thomas Y. Crowell, 1968.

_____. *Man, Nature and Culture*. New York: Thomas Y. Crowell, 1971.

Harris, Olivia. "Latin American Women - an Overview." *Latin American Women Minority Rights Group*, 57 (1983), 4-6

Hay, Richard, Jr. "Patterns of Urbanization and Socio-Economic Development in the Third World: An Overview." In Janet Abu-Lughod and Richard Hay, Jr. (eds.), *Third World Urbanization*. Chicago: Maaroufa Press, 1977, pp. 71-101.

Hebdige, Dick. *Subculture: The Meaning of Style*. London: Methuen, 1979.

Herrick, B.A. *Urban Migration and Economic Development in Chile*. Cambridge, MA: Harvard University Press, 1966.

Hewison, K. "An intimate exploitation." *Inside Asia*, 6 (1985), 33-35.

Hexter, A., and J. Goldsmith. "Carbon Monoxide: Association of Community Air Pollution with Mortality." *Science*, 172 (1971), 265-267.

Hill, T.W. "From Hell Raiser to Family Man." In J. Spradley and D.W. McCurdy (eds.), *Conformity and Conflict*. Boston: Little, Brown, 1974.

Ho, Ping-ti. "The Salt Merchants of Yang-Chou: A Study of Commercial Capitalism in 18th Century China." *Harvard Journal of Asiatic Studies*, 17 (1954), 130-168.

Hobsbawm, E.J. *Primitive Rebels*. New York: Frederick A. Praeger, 1959.

Hollander, Nancy. "Women Workers and the Class Struggle: The Case of Argentina." *Latin American Perspectives*, 4 (1977), 180-193.

Hoselitz, B.F. "Social Structure and Economic Growth," *Economica Internazionale*, 6 (1953), 52-57.

Howe, Irving. *The World of Our Fathers*. New York: Harcourt, Brace, Jovanovich, 1976.

Hoyt, H., G.W. Hoffman, and F.W. Neal. *Yugoslavia and the New Communism*. New York: Twentieth Century Fund, 1962.

Hsu, F.L.K. *Under the Ancestors' Shadow*. New York: Columbia University Press, 1948.

Hurgonje, C. Snouck. *Mekka in the Latter Part of the 19th Century*. London: Luzac, 1931.

ILWU (International Longshoreman's and Warehouseman's Union). *Official Reports of the ILWU Overseas Delegates to the 14th Biennial Convention of the International Longshoreman's and Warehouseman's Union*. Honolulu, 1961.

_____. *Third ILWU Overseas Report to the 16th Biennial Convention of the International Longshoreman's and Warehouseman's Union*. Vancouver, 1965.

Inkeles, Alex. "Industrial Man: The Relation of Status to Experience, Perception and Value." *The American Journal of Sociology*, July, 1960.

Inland Transport Committee, ILO. *Methods of Improving Organization of Work and Output in Ports*. Geneva, 1956.

Inouye, Jukichi. *Home Life in Tokyo*. Tokyo, Tokyo: Tokyo Printing, Co., 1911.

Jacobs, Jerry. *The Mall*. Prospect Heights, IL: Waveland Press, Inc., 1984.

Jacobson, David. "Mobility, Continuity, and Urban Social Organization." *Man*, 6 (1971), 630-645.

Jacobson, D. "Fair Weather Friend: Label and Context in Middle Class Friendships." *Journal of Anthropological Research*, 31 (1975), 225-334.

Jacobson, H.E. "Urbanization and Family Ties: A Problem in the Analysis of Change." *Journal of Asian and African Studies*, 5 (1970), 302-307.

Jelin, Elizabeth. "The Bahiana in the Labor Force in Salvador, Brazil." In June Nash and H. Safa (eds.), *Sex and Class in Latin America*. New York: Praeger, 1976, pp. 129-146.

———. "Migration and Labor Force Participation of Latin American Women: The Domestic Servants in the Cities." In The Wellesley Editorial Committee (ed.), *Women and National Development*. Chicago: University of Chicago Press, 1977, pp. 129-141.

Jenner, D.A., G.A. Harrison, I.A.M. Prior, D.L. Leonetti, W.J. Fujimoto and M. Kabuto. "Inter-population Comparisons of Catecholamine Excretion." *Annals of Human Biology*, 14 (1987), 1-9.

Johnson, Colleen Leary. "Gift Giving and Reciprocity Among Japanese Americans in Honolulu." *American Ethnologist* 1 (1974), 295-308.

Jones, F.N. and J. Tauscher. "Residence Under an Airport Landing Pattern as a Factor in Teratism." *Archives of Environmental Health*, 33 (1978), 10-12.

Jorgensen, Joseph G. "Indians and the Metropolis." In Jack O. Waddell and O. Michael Watson (eds.), *The American Indian in Urban Society*. Boston: Little, Brown, 1971, pp. 67-113.

Kasarda, J.D., and M. Janowitz. "Community Attachment in Mass Society." *American Sociological Review*, 39 (1974), 328-339.

Kasdan, Leonard. "Introduction." In Robert F. Spencer (ed.), *Migration and Anthropology*, 1970, pp. 1-8.

Kay, Paul. "Comment." *Current Anthropology*, 7 (1966), 20-23.

Kaye, Barrington. *Upper Nankin Street Singapore*. Singapore: University of Malaya Press, 1966.

Keefe, Susan Emley. "Urbanization, Acculturation and Extended Family Ties: Mexican-Americans in Cities." *American Ethnologist*, 6 (1979), 349-365.

———. "Real and Ideal Extended Familism Among Mexican Americans and Anglo Americans: On the Meaning of 'Close' Family Ties." *Human Organization*, 43 (1984), 65-70.

Keefe, Susan E. and Amado M. Padilla. *Chicano Ethnicity*. Albuquerque: University of New Mexico Press, 1987.

Keesing, F.M. and M.D. Keesing. *Elite Communication in Samoa: A Study of Leadership*. Stanford, CA: Stanford University Press, 1956.

Keesing, Roger. "Recreative Behavior and Culture Change." In Anthony F.C. Wallace (ed.), *Men and Cultures*. Philadelphia: University of Pennsylvania Press, 1960, pp. 130-131.

Kelley, Augustus M. *A Theory of Labor Movement*. New York, 1949.

Kelly, George. *The Psychology of Personal Constructs*. New York: W.W. Norton, 1955.

Kelton, Jane. "The New York City St. Patrick's Day Parade: Invention of Contention and Consensus." *The Drama Review*, 107 (Fall 1986), 93.

Kemper, Robert V. "Tzintzuntzeños in Mexico City: The Anthropologist Among Peasant Migrants." In George Foster and Robert V. Kemper (eds.), *Anthropologists in Cities*. Boston: Little, Brown, 1974.

———. "Frontiers in Migration: From Culturalism to Historical Structuralism in the Study of Mexico-U.S. Migration." In Fernando Camara and Robert V. Kemper (eds.), *Migration Across Frontiers: Mexico and the United States*. SUNY-Albany: Institute for Mesoamerican Studies, 1979.

Kennedy, Jean. *Here is India*. New York: Scribner's, 1945.

Kerr, Clark, and Abraham Siegel. "The Industrial Propensity to Strike – An International Comparison." In Dublin, Kornhauser, and Ross (eds.), *Industrial Conflicts*. New York: McGraw-Hill, 1954.

Khin Thitsa. *Providence and Prostitution: Image and Reality for Women in Buddhist Thailand*. London: Change, International Reports, 1980.

King, Charles E. "The Negro Maternal Family: A Product of an Economic and a Cultural System." *Social Forces*, 24 (1945), 100-104.

Knipschild, P. "Medical Effects of Aircraft Noise: General Practice Survey." *International Archives of Occupational and Environmental Health*, 40 (1977a), 191-196.

_____. "Medical Effects of Aircraft Noise: Community Cardiovascular Survey." *International Archives of Occupational and Environmental Health*, 40 (1977b), 185-190.

Knipschild, P., H. Meijer, and H. Salle. "Aircraft Noise and Birthweight." International Archives of Occupational and Environmental Health, 48 (1981), 131-136.

Knipschild, P. and N. Oudshoorn. "Medical Effects of Aircraft Noise: Drug Survey." *International Archives of Occupational and Environmental Health*, 40 (1977), 197-200.

Koehn, Peter, and Sidney R. Waldron. "Afocha: A Link Between Community and Administration in Harar, Ethiopia." *Foreign and Comparative Studies/Africa*, XXXI. Syracuse, NY: Syracuse University, 1978.

Kornblum, W. *Blue Collar Community.* Chicago: University of Chicago Press, 1974.

Krapf-Askari, Eva. *Yoruba Towns and Cities: An Enquiry into the Nature of Urban Social Phenomena.* London: Oxford University Press, 1969.

Kressel, G.M. *Individuality against Tribality: The Dynamics of a Beduin Community in a Process of Urbanization.* Tel Aviv: Hakibbutz Hameuchad, 1975 (in Hebrew).

Kroeber, A.L., and Clyde Kluckholn. "Culture: A Critical Review of Concepts and Definitions." Papers of the Peabody Museum of Anthropology, Vol. 47 No. 1 (1952).

Kryter, K. *The Effects of Noise on Man.* New York: Academic Press, 1970.

Lagares, Calvo, M.J. *Déficit público y crisis económica.* Madrid: Instituto de Estudios Económicos, 1982.

Lambert, Jacques. *Os dois Brasís.* Rio de Janeiro: Centro Brasileiro de Pesquisas Educacionais, 1959.

_____. Conclusões, Seminário sobre a Política de Integração de uma População Marginalizada, Brasília.

Lane, Edward W. *The Manners and Customs of the Modern Egyptians*, 3rd ed. New York: E.P. Dutton, 1923.

Larrowe, Charles. *Shape Up and Hiring Hall.* Berkeley: University of California Press, 1955.

Laslett, Peter, et al. *Household and Family in Past Time.* Cambridge: Cambridge University Press, 1972.

Lauman, Edward O. *Bonds of Pluralism: The Form and Substance of Urban Social Networks.* New York: John Wiley, 1973.

Leach, E.R. "Introduction: What Should We Mean by Caste?" In E.R. Leach (ed.), *Aspects of Caste in South India, Ceylon and North-West Pakistan.* Cambridge Papers in Social Anthropology, No. 2. Cambridge: Cambridge University Press, 1960, pp. 1-10.

Leeds, Anthony. "Brazilian Careers and Social Structure: An Evolutionary Model and Case History." *American Anthropologist*, 70 (1968), 1321-1347.

_____. "The Concept of the 'Culture of Poverty': Conceptual, Logical and Empirical Problems with Perspectives from Brazil and Peru." In E. Leacock (ed.), *Culture of Poverty: A Critique.* New York: Simon and Schuster, 1971.

_____. "Urban Anthropology and Urban Studies." *Urban Anthropology Newsletter*, 1 (1972), 4-5.

Leichter, H.J., and W.E. Mitchell. *Kinship and Casework.* New York: Russell Sage Foundation, 1967.

Leslie, Genevieve. "Domestic Service in Canada, 1880-1920." In Janice Acton, et al. (eds.), *Women at Work.* Toronto: Women's Educational Press, 1974, pp. 71-126.

Leis, Philip, and George Hicks. *Ethnic Encounters.* North Sciutate, MA: Duxbury, 1977.

LeTourneau, Roger. *Fès: Avant le protectorat.* Casablanca: Société Marocaine de Librairie et d'Edition, 1949.

Levine, Donald H., Ellwood B. Carter, and Eleanor Miller Gorman. "Simmel's Influence on American Sociology: II." *American Journal of Sociology*, 81 (1976), 1112-1132.

Lévi-Strauss, Claude. "Social Structure." In A.L. Kroeber (ed.), *Anthropology Today.* Chicago: University of Chicago Press, 1953, pp. 524-553.

_____. *Structural Anthropology.* New York: Basic Books, 1963.

Levy, Marion J. "Some Sources of the Vulnerability of the Structure of Relatively Non-Industrialized Societies to Those of Highly Industrialized Societies." In B.F. Hoselitz (ed.), *Progress of Under-Developed Areas.* Chicago: University of Chicago Press, 1952.

Levy, M.J., Jr., and Lloyd A. Fallers. "The Family: Some Comparative Considerations." *American Anthropologist,* 61 (1959), 647-651.

Lewin, Linda. "Some Historical Implications of Kinship Organization for Family-Based Politics in the Brazilian Northeast." *Comparative Studies in Society and History,* 21 (1979), 262-292.

Lewis, Diane. "Anthropology and Colonialism." *Current Anthropology,* 14 (1973), 581-602.

Lewis, O. "Urbanization Without Breakdown." *Scientific Monthly,* 75 (1952), 31-41.

_____. *Five Families: Mexican Studies in the Culture of Poverty.* New York: Basic Books, 1959.

_____. *The Children of Sanchez.* New York: Random House, 1961.

_____. *La Vida: A Puerto Rican Family in the Culture of Poverty.* New York: Random House, 1965.

_____. "The Culture of Poverty." *Scientific American,* 215 (1966), 19-25.

_____. "The Possessions of the Poor." *Scientific American,* 221 (1969), 114-124.

Liae, Tai Chu. "The Apprentice in Chengtu during and after the War." *Yenching Journal of Social Studies,* 4 (1948), 90-106.

Liebenow, J.G. *Liberia: The Evolution of Privilege.* Ithaca, NY, and London: Cornell University Press, 1969.

Liebow, E. *Tally's Corner.* Boston: Little, Brown, 1967.

Light, Ivan. *Ethnic Enterprise in America.* Berkeley: University of California Press, 1972.

Lin-Fu, J.S. "Undue Lead Absorption and Lead Poisoning in Children - An Overview." Department of Health Education and Welfare Publication No. (HSA) 79-5141, (1979), U.S. Government Printing Office.

Linton, Ralph. "The Natural History of the Family." In R.N. Anshen (ed.), *The Family: Its Function and Destiny.* New York: Harper and Brothers, 1949, pp. 18-38.

Lipset, Seymour M. *Political Man: The Social Bases of Politics,* New York: Doubleday, 1960.

Little, Kenneth. "The Role of Voluntary Associations in West African Urbanization." *American Anthropologist,* 59 (1957), 579-596.

_____. "West African Urbanization and Social Process." *Cahiers d'Etudes Africaines I,* 3 (1960), 90-102.

_____. *African Women in Towns.* Cambridge: Cambridge University Press, 1973.

Litwak, Eugene. "Occupational Mobility and Extended Family Cohesion." *American Sociological Review,* 25 (1960a), 9-21.

_____. "Geographic Mobility and Family Cohesion." *American Sociological Review,* 25 (1960b), 385-394.

Logan, Kathleen. *Haciendo Pueblo - The Development of a Guadalajaran Suburb.* Tuscaloosa: University of Alabama Press, 1984.

_____. "Self-Empowerment and Urban Mobilizations in Latin America." Unpublished manuscript.

Lomnitz, Larissa. "The Social and Economic Organization of a Mexican Shantytown." In W. and F. Trueblood (eds.), *Latin American Urban Research,* Vol. 4. 1974.

_____. *Networks and Marginality: Life in a Mexican Shantytown.* New York: Academic Press, 1977.

Lowenthal, D. *West Indian Societies.* New York: Oxford University Press, 1972.

Lupton, T., and S. Wilson. "The Social Background and Connections of Top Decision-Makers." *Manchester University School,* 27 (1959), 30-51.

Luzuriaga, Luz. "Only You Men Have Your Needs Satisfied." In June H. Turner (ed.), *Latin American Women: The Meek Speak Out.* Silver Spring, MD: International Educational Development, Inc., 1980, pp. 73-83.

Lynch, K. *The Image of the City.* Cambridge, MA: MIT Press and Harvard University Press, 1960.

Lynch, Owen M. "Rural Cities in India: Continuities and Discontinuities." In Philip Mason (ed.), *India and Ceylon: Unity and Diversity.* London: Oxford University Press, 1967.

_____. *The Politics of Untouchability: Social Mobility and Social Change in a City of India*. New York: Columbia University Press, 1969.

_____. "Potters, Plotters and Prodders: Marx and Meaning or Meaning vs. Marx." *Urban Anthropology*, 8 (1979), 1-28.

Madsen, William. *The Mexican-Americans of South Texas*. New York: Holt, Rinehart and Winston, 1964.

Maine, Henry. *Ancient Law*. London: John Murray, 1861.

Mangin, William P. "Urbanization Case History in Peru." *Architectural Design* (1963), 365-370.

_____. "Sociological, Cultural and Political Characteristics of Some Rural Indians and Urban Migrants in Peru." Paper presented at Wenner-Gren Symposium on Cross-Cultural Similarities in the Urbanization Process (mimeo), 1964.

_____. "The Role of Social Organization in Improving the Environment." In *Environmental Determinants of Community Well-Being. Pan American Health Organization, 1965*.

_____. "Latin American Squatter Settlements: A Problem and a Solution." *Latin American Research Review*, 2 (1967), 65-98.

_____. "Poverty and Politics in the Latin American City." In L. Bloomington and H. Schmidt (eds.), *Power, Poverty and Urban Policy*. Urban Affairs Annual Review, Vol. 2 (1970).

Maquet, J. *The Premise of Inequality in Ruanda*. London: Oxford University Press, 1961.

Marcuse, H. *One-Dimensional Man*. London: Sphere Books, 1964.

Marmot, M.G. "Affluence, Urbanization and Coronary Heart Disease." In E.J. Clegg and J.P. Garlick (eds.), *Disease and Urbanization*. London: Taylor & Francis, 1980, pp. 127-143.

Marris, Peter. *Family and Social Change in an African City*. London: Routledge & Kegan Paul, 1961.

Marshall, D. "Migration as an Agent of Change in Caribbean Island Ecosystems." *International Social Science Journal* 34(3) (1982), 451-467.

Marx, E. *The Social Context of Violent Behavior: A Social Anthropological Study in an Israeli Immigrant Town*. London: Routledge & Kegan Paul, 1976.

Mayhew, Henry. *London Labor and the London Poor*, Vol. III. London, 1861.

McCarthy, Patricia. "Poverty and Itinerancy." M.A. Thesis, University College, Dublin, 1971.

Mead, Margaret. *Social Organization of Manu'a*. Bulletin 76. Honolulu: Bernice P. Bishop Museum, 1930.

Meecham, W.C., and H.G. Smith. "Effects of Jet Aircraft Noise on Mental Hospital Admissions." *British Journal of Audiology*, II (1977), 81-85.

Meier, R.L. *A Communications Theory of Urban Growth*. Cambridge, MA: MIT Press, 1962.

Menahem, G. "Neighborly Relations in an Urban Slum." M.A. thesis, Tel Aviv University, 1972 (in Hebrew with English summary).

Mercer, Charles. *Living in Cities: Psychology and the Urban Environment*. Harmondsworth: Penguin, 1975.

Merry, Sally Engle. *Urban Danger: Life in a Neighborhood of Strangers*. Philadelphia, PA: Temple University Press, 1981.

_____. "Rethinking Gossip and Scandal." In Donald Black (ed.), *Toward a General Theory of Social Control*, Vol. II. New York: Academic Press, 1984.

Merton, Robert K. "Social Structure and Anomie." In *Social Theory and Social Structure*. New York: Free Press, 1968, pp. 185-214.

Metzger, Duane, and Gerald E. Williams. "A Formal Ethnographic Analysis of Tenejapa Indio Weddings." *American Anthropologist* 65 (1963), 1076-1101.

Midgett, D. "West Indian Migration and Adaptation in St. Lucia and London." Ph.D. dissertation, University of Illinois, 1977.

Milgram, S. "The Experience of Living in the Cities." *Science*, 167 (1970), 1461-1468.

Milgram, S., and P. Hollander. "The Murder They Heard." *Nation*, 198 (1964), 602-604.

Miller, S.M., F. Reisman, and A. Seagull. "Poverty and Self-Indulgence: A Critique of the Non-Deferred Gratification Pattern." In L. Ferman, et al. (eds.), *Poverty in America*. Ann Arbor: University of Michigan Press, 1965.

Miller, W.B. "Two Concepts of Authority." *American Anthropologist* 57 (1955), 271-289.

_____. "Subculture, Social Reform and the Culture of Poverty." *Human Organization*, 30 (1971), 111-125.

Millon, Rene, Bruce Drewitt, and George Cowgill. *Urbanization at Teotihuacan, Mexico, the Teotihuacan Map, Part One.* University of Texas Press, Austin, 1973.

Milton, Gordan. "The Subsociety and the Subculture." In *Assimilation in American Life.* New York: Oxford University Press, 1964.

Mims, Cedric. "Stress in Relation to the Processes of Civilisation." In S.V. Boyden (ed.), *The Impact of Civilisation on the Biology of Man.* Toronto: University of Toronto Press, 1970, pp. 167-181.

Miner, Horace. *The Primitive Cioy of Timbuctoo.* Princeton, NJ: Princeton University Press, 1953.

Mingmongkol, S. "Official Blessing for the 'Brothel of Asia.'" *Southeast Asia Chronicle* 78 (1981), 24-25.

Minis6ere des Affaires Economiques et du Plan. "Recensement d'Abidjan Résultats définitifs." Abidjan, 1958.

Ministry of Labour. *Final Report of the Committee of Inquiry Under the Rt. Hon. Lord Devlin into Certain Matters Concerning the Port Transport Industry.* Command Paper No. 2734. London: Her Majesty's Stationery Office, 1956.

Mitchell, J.C. *The Kalela Dance.* Manchester: Manchester University Press, 1956.

_____. "Social Change and Stability of African Marriage in Northern Rhodesia." In A. Southall (ed.), *Social Change in Modern Africa.* London: Oxford University Press, 1961.

_____. "Theoretical Orientations in African Urban Studies." In Michael Banton (ed.), *The Social Anthropology of Complex Societies,* Association of Social Anthropologists Monograph No. 4. London: Tavistock, 1966.

_____. (ed.). *Social Networks in Urban Situations: Analysis of Personal Relationships in Central African Towns.* Manchester: Manchester University Press, 1969.

Mitchell, William. *Mishpokhe: A Study of New York City Jewish Family Clubs.* The Hague and Paris: Mouton, 1978.

Moreira, Ana. "Our National Inferiority Complex: A Cause for Violence." In June H. Turner (ed.), *Latin American Women: the Meek Speak Out.* Silver Spring, MD: International Educational Development, Inc., 1980, pp. 63-72.

Moreira Alves, Maria Helena. "Grassroots Organizations, Trade Unions, and the Church: A Challenge to the Controlled Abertura in Brazil." *Latin American Perspectives,* 11(1) (1984), 73-102.

Moynihan, Daniel Patrick. *The Negro Family: The Case for National Action.* Washington, DC: Government Printing Office. Prepared for the Office of Policy Planning and Research of the Department of Labor, 1965.

Mumford, Lewis. *The City in History.* New York: Harcourt, Brace and World, 1961.

Murdock, George P. *Social Structure.* Glencoe: The Free Press, 1949. Reprinted New York: Macmillan, 1960.

Needleman, Herbert L. "Lead at Low Dose and the Behavior of Children." *Acta Psychiatrica Scandinavica 67,* Supplement 303 (1983), 26-37.

Niangoran, G. Le village aboure. Cahiers d'Etudes Africaines I, 1 (1960), 113-127.

Nicholaus, Martin. "Radicals in the Professions." *Newsletter of the American Anthropological Association,* November 1968, 9-10.

Ogg, Elizabeth. *Longshoremen and Their Homes.* New York: Greenwich House, 1939.

Ogien, R. "A Slum Area in Tel Aviv." In E. Marx (ed.), *A Composite Portrait of Israel.* London: Academic Press (in press).

Olufsen, O. *The Emir of Bokhara and His Country.* Copenhagen: Gyldendalske, 1911.

Omar, T.P. "Changing Attitudes of Students in West African Society Towards Marriage and Family Relationships. *British Journal of Sociology,* XI, 3 (1960), 197-210.

Omran, A.R. "Epidemiological Transition in the United States: The Health Factor in Population Change." *Population Bulletin,* 32 (1975), 1-42.

Ong, A. "Industrialization and Prostitution in Southeast Asia." *Southeast Asia Chronicle* 96 (1985), 2-6.

Orent, Amnon. *Israel: Three Studies in Urban Anthropology.* Haifa: University of Haifa, 1977.

Orsi, Robert. *The Madonna of 115th Street: Faith and Community in Italian Harlem, 1880-1950.* New Haven: Yale University Press, 1985.

Osgood, Cornelius. *The Koreans and Their Culture.* New York: Ronald Press, 1951.

Paigen, B., L.R. Goldman, M.M. Magnant, J.H. Highland, and A.T. Steegman, Jr. "Growth of Children Living Near the Hazardous Waste Site, Love Canal." *Human Biology* 59 (1987), 489-508.

Palisi, Bartolomeo. "Ethnic Generation and Family Structure." *Journal of Marriage and the Family,* 28 (1966), 49-50.

Papanek, Hanna. "Family Status Production: The 'Work' and 'Non-Work' of Women." *Signs,* 4 (1979), 775-782.

Park, Robert E. *Human Communities.* Glencoe, IL: The Free Press, 1952.

_____. "The City: Suggestions for Investigation of Human Behavior in an Urban Environment." In R.E. Sennet (ed.), *Classic Essays on the Culture of Cities.* New York: Appleton-Century-Crofts, 1969, pp. 91-130 (orig. pub. 1916).

Park, Robert E., and W. Burgess, et al. *The City.* Chicago, 1925.

Parker, S., and R. Kleiner. "The Culture of Poverty: An Adjustment Dimension." *American Anthropologist,* 72 (1970), 516-528.

Parkin, D. *Neighbours and Nationals.* London: Routledge & Kegan Paul, 1969.

Parry, G. *Political Elites.* London: Allen & Unwin, 1969.

Parsons, Talcott. "The Kinship System of the Contemporary United States." *American Anthropologist,* 45 (1943), 22-38.

_____. *The Social System.* Glencoe: The Free Press, 1951.

_____. "Some Theoretical Considerations on the Nature and Trends of Change of Ethnicity." In N. Glazer and D.P. Moynihan (eds.), *Ethnicity: Theory and Experience.* Cambridge, MA: Harvard University Press, 1975, pp. 53-83.

Pastore, J. *Satisfaction Among Migrants to Brasília, Brazil: A Sociological Interpretation.* Dissertation, University of Wisconsin, 1968.

Patch, Richard. "La Parada: Lima's Market." *American Universities Field Staff Report,* West Coast of South America, Vol. 14 (1967).

Patterson, S. *Dark Strangers: A Study of West Indians in London.* London: Tavistock, 1963.

Paulitschke, Phillipe. *Harar: Forschungreise nach den Somal- und Gallaländern Ostafrikas.* Leipzig: F. Brockhaus, 1888.

Paulme, D. "Littérature Orale et Comportments Sociaux." *L'homme I,* 1 (1961), 37-69.

_____. *Une Société de Côte d'Ivoire Hier et Aujourd'hui: les Betes.* The Hague: Mouton, 1962.

Pauw, B.A. *The Second Generation.* Capetown: Oxford University Press, 1963.

Paz, Octavio. *The Labyrinth of Solitude.* New York: Grove Press, 1961.

Peach, C. *West Indian Migration to Britain: A Social Geography.* London: Oxford University Press, 1968.

Pearse, Andrew. "Some Characteristics of Urbanization in the City of Rio de Janeiro." In P. Hauser (ed.), *Urbanization in Latin America.* New York: UNESCO, 1961.

Pearson, S.V. *The Growth and Distribution of Population.* New York, 1935.

Peattie, Lisa. *The View from the Barrio.* Ann Arbor: University of Michigan Press, 1967.

_____. "Social Issues in Housing." Joint Center for Urban Studies. Unpublished manuscript.

Peckenham, Nancy and Annie Street. "This Is How Democracy Works in Our Country." In *Honduran Women: The Marginalized Majority.* New York: Women's International Resource Exchange, 1986, pp. 15-16.

Pelzel, John C. *Social Stratification in Japanese Urban Economic Life.* Ph.D. Dissertation. Harvard University Department of Social Relations, 1950.

Perin, Constance. *Everything in Its Place.* Princeton, NJ: Princeton University Press, 1977.

Peritore, Patrick. "Paulo Freire's Socialism and the Worker's Party of Brazil." *USFI Reports,* No. 8, 1986, South America, pp. 1-86.

Perry, I.M. "The New and Old Diseases." *American Journal of Clinical Pathology,* 63 (1975), 453-474.

Petras, J. "The New Revolutionary Politics in Latin America." *Monthly Review,* 20 (1969), 34-39.

Phillips, B.S. *Social Research: Strategy and Tactics*. New York: Macmillan, 1966.

Phillips, R.E. "The Bantu in the City: A Study of Cultural Adjustment on the Witwatersrand." In *Social Implications of Industrialization and Urbanization in Africa South of the Sahara*. Geneva: UNESCO, 1956.

Phongraichit, P. "Bangkok Masseuses: Holding Up the Family Sky." *Southeast Asian Chronicle, 78 (1981), 15-24.*

Pilcher, William. *The Portland Longshoremen*. New York: Holt, Rinehart and Winston, 1972.

Piore, M. and C. Sabel, *The Second Industrial Divide: Possibilities for Prosperity*. New York: Basic Books, 1984.

Pirenne, Henri. *Medieval Cities*. Princeton, NJ: Princeton University Press, 1925.

Pitayanon, S. "Migration to the Middle East from Thailand Bangkok." Chulalongkorn University, Faculty of Economics, Paper No. 2701.

Pocock, D.F. "Sociologies: Urban and Rural." *Contributions to Indian Sociology*, 4 (1960).

Polanyi, K. *The Great Transformation*. Boston: Beacon, 1944.

————. *Dahomey and the Slave Trade*. American Ethnological Society Monograph, No. 42. Seattle and London: Washington University Press, 1966.

Polgar, Steven. "Evolution and the Ills of Mankind." In S. Tax, *Horizons of Anthropology*. Chicago: Aldine, 1964, pp. 200-211.

Portes, Alejandro. "Latin American Class Structures: Their Composition and Change during the Last Decade." *LARR* 20(3) (1985), 7-39.

Portes, Alejandro and John Walton. *Urban Latin America: The Political Condition from Above and Below*. Austin: University of Texas Press, 1976.

Price, John. "Reno, Nevada: The City as a Unit of Study." *Urban Anthropology*, 1 (1972), 14-28.

Pye, Lucien W. "The Political Implications of Urbanization and the Development Process." In "Social Problems of Development and Urbanization." *Science, Technology and Development*, Vol. 7. Washington, DC: Government Printing Office, 1963.

Radcliffe-Brown, A.R., and D. Ford (eds.). *African Systems of Kinship and Marriage*. London: Oxford University Press, 1950.

Rainwater, Lee, and William L. Yancey (eds.). *The Moynihan Report and the Politics of Controversy*. Cambridge, MA: MIT Press, 1967.

Ramirez, Francisca. "It All Depends on the Teacher." In June H. Turner (ed.), *Latin American Women: The Meek Speak Out*. Silver Spring, MD: International Educational Development, Inc., 1980, pp. 101-110.

Ranum, R., and O. Forster. *Family and Society*. Baltimore: Johns Hopkins University Press, 1976.

Raum, O.F. "Self Help Associations." *African Studies*, 28 (1969), 119-141.

Redfield, Robert. *The Folk Culture of Yucatan*. Chicago: University of Chicago Press, 1941.

Redfield, Robert, and M. Singer. "The Cultural Role of Cities." *Economic Development and Cultural Change*, 3 (1954), 53-77.

Reiss, A.J., Jr. "An Analysis of Urban Phenomenon." In R.M. Fisher (ed.), *The Metropolis in Modern Life*. New York: Doubleday, 1955, pp. 41-51.

Reiss, I.L. "The Universality of the Family: A Conceptual Analysis." *Journal of Marriage and the Family*, 27 (1965), 443-453.

Research Committee on Urbanism of the National Resources Committee. *Our Cities: Their Role in the National Economy*. Washington, DC: Government Printing Office, 1937.

Reynolds, V., D.A. Jenner, C.D. Palmer, and G.A. Harrison. "Catecholamine Excretion Rates in Relation to Lifestyles in the Male Population of Otmoor, Oxfordshire." *Annals of Human Biology*, 8 (1981), 197-209.

Rhoades, Robert E. "Intra-European Return Migration and Rural Development: Lessons from the Spanish Case." *Human Organization*, 37 (1978a), 136-147.

————. "Foreign Labor and German Industrial Capitalism 1871-1978: The Evolution of a Migratory System." *American Ethnologist*, 5 (19.78b), 553-573.

————. "From Caves to Main Street: Return Migration and the Transformation of a Spanish Village." *Papers in Anthropology*, Vol. 20 (1979a), 57-74.

_____. (ed.). "The Anthropology of Return Migration." Special Issue of *Papers in Anthropology*, Vol. 20. Norman, OK: University of Oklahoma, Department of Anthropology, 1979b.

Richardson, B. *Caribbean Migrants: Environment and Human Survival on St. Kitts and Nevis*. Knoxville, TN: University of Tennessee Press, 1983.

Roberts, Bryan. "The Social Organization of Low Income Families." In R.N. Adams (ed.), *Crucifixion of Power*. Austin: University of Texas Press, 1970, pp. 479-515.

_____. *Organizing Strangers*. Austin: University of Texas Press, 1973.

Rodwin, L. *Evolution of a Federalist: William Loughton Smith of Charleston (1758-1812)*. Columbia: University of South Carolina Press, n.d.

Rollwagen, Jack R. "Cities and the World System: Toward an Evolutionary Perspective in the Study of Urban Anthropology." In Thomas Collins (ed.), *Urban Anthropology: Cities in a Hierarchical Context*. Southern Anthropological Society Proceedings No. 14: Athens: University of Georgia Press, 1980.

Romney, A.K., and R.G. D'Andrade. "Cognitive Aspects of English Kin Terms." *American Anthropologist*, 66 (1964), 146-170.

Rose, E.J. *Colour and Citizenship*. London: Oxford University Press, 1969.

Rostow, Walter W. *The Stages of Economic Growth: A Non-Communist Manifesto*. Cambridge: Cambridge University Press, 1960.

Rusinow, Dennison. "Mega-Cities Today and Tomorrow: Is the Cup Half-full or Half-empty?" *USFI Reports*, No. 12 (1986), Europe [DIR 1-86].

Ryan, Mary. *Womanhood in America: From Colonial Times to the Present*. New York: New Viewpoints, 1975.

Safa, Helen Icken. "From Shanty Town to Public Housing: A Comparison of Family Structure in Two Urban Neighborhoods in Puerto Rico." *Caribbean Studies*, 4 (1964).

_____. "The Social Isolation of the Urban Poor: Life in a Puerto Rican Shanty Town." In *Among the People: Encounters with the Poor*. New York: Basic Books, 1968.

_____. *The Urban Poor of Puerto Rico: A Study in Development and Inequality*. New York: Holt, Rinehart and Winston, 1974.

Salmen, L. "A Perspective on Resettlement of Squatters in Brazil." *America Latina*, 12 (1969), 73-95.

Sampson, A. *Anatomy of Britain*. New York and Evanston: Harper & Row; London: Hodder and Stoughton, 1962.

Sanders, William T., Jeffrey R. Parsons, and Robert S. Santley. *The Basin of Mexico: Ecological Processes in the Evolution of a Civilization*. Academic Press, New York, 1979.

Sarabia, B. "Historias de Vida." *Revista española de Investigaciones sociologicas* 29 (1985), 165-186.

Sasuly, Richard. "Why They Stick to the ILA." *Monthly Review* (January 1956), 370.

Sauerbrier, C.L. *Education in Cargo Operations. Progress in Cargo Handling*. London: Hiffe and Sons, 1955.

Sauvaget, Jean. *Alep*. Paris, Librairie Orientale Paul Geuthner, 1941.

Savezni Zavod za Statistiku. *Statistički Bilten 1295* (Statistical Bulletin 1295). Belgrade: Sazezni Zavod za Statistiku, 1982.

Schell, L. "Environmental Noise and Human Prenatal Growth." *American Journal of Physical Anthropology*, 56 (1981), 63-70.

_____. The Effect of Chronic Noise Exposure on Human Prenatal Growth." In J. Borms, R. Hauspie, A. Sand, C. Susanne and M. Hebbelinck (eds.), *Human Growth and Development*. New York: Plenum Press, 1984, pp. 125-129.

_____. "Community Health Assessment through Physical Anthropology: Auxological Epidemiology." *Human Organization*, 45 (1986), 321-327.

Schmink, Marianne. "Women in Brazilian '*Abertura*' Politics." *Signs* 7(1) (1981), 115-134.

Schmitt, C. "Translating and interpreting: Present and Future." *The Incorporated Linguist* 21(3) (1982), 96-102.

Schneider, Betty, and Abraham Siegel. *Industrial Relations in the Pacific Coast Longshore Industry*. Berkeley: University of California Press, 1956.

Schneider, David M., and E.K. Gough (eds.). *Matrilineal Kinship*. Berkeley: University of California Press, 1961.

Schwarzweller, H.K., J. Brown, and S. Mangalam. *Mountain Families in Transition*. University Park: Pennsylvania State University Press, 1971.

Seidensticker, Edward. *Low City, High City: Tokyo from Edo to the Earthquake*. New York: Knopf, 1983.

Seligman, Martin E.P. *Helplessness: On Depression, Development, and Death*. San Francisco: W.H. Freeman and Co., 1975.

Selye, Hans. *The Stress of Life*. New York: McGraw-Hill, 1956.

Service, Elman R. *Primitive Social Organization*. New York: Random House, 1967.

Shai, D. *Neighborhood Relations in an Immigrant Quarter*. Jerusalem: Szold Institute, 1970.

Shanklin, E. "The Irish Go-between." *Anthropological Quarterly* 53(3) (1980), 162-172.

Shen Tsung-Lien, and Shen Chi-Liu. *Tibet and The Tibetans*. Stanford, CA: Stanford University Press, 1953.

Shokeid, M., and S. Deshen. "Distant Relations: Ethnicity and Politics among Arabs and North African Jews in Israel" (typewritten manuscript).

Short, J.F., Jr. "Introduction." In J.F. Short, Jr. (ed.), *The Social Fabric of the Metropolis*. Chicago: University of Chicago Press, 1971.

Shryrock, John K. *The Temples of Anking and their Cults*. Paris (privately printed), 1931.

Shy, C.M., V. Hasselbald, R.M. Burton, C.J. Nelson, and A.A. Cohen. "Air Pollution Effects on Ventilatory Function of U.S. Schoolchildren." *Archives of Environmental Health*, 27 (1973), 124-128.

Sihasut, M. "Love Letters from Pattaya." *Bangkok Post* 17.7 (1983), 21.

Simić, Andrei. *The Peasant Urbanites: A Study of Rural-Urban Mobility in Serbia*. New York: Seminar Press, 1973.

———. "Kinship Reciprocity and Rural-Urban Integration in Serbia." *Urban Anthropology*, 1 (1973), 205-213.

———. "Urbanization and Modernization in Yugoslavia: Adaptive and Maladaptive Aspects of Traditional Culture." In Kenny, Michael and David I. Kertzer (eds.), *Urban Life in Mediterranean Europe: Anthropological Perspective*. Urbana: University of Illinois Press, 1983, pp. 203-224.

Simmel, Georg. "Die Grossstädte und das Geistesleben." In T. Petermann (ed.), *Die Grossstadt*. Dresden: Jansch, 1905. Reprinted in R. Sennet (ed.), *Classic Essays on the Culture of Cities*. New York: Appleton-Century-Crofts, 1969, pp. 47-60.

———. *Soziologie*. Duncker & Humblot, 1908.

———. "The Stranger." In K. Wolff (ed.), *The Sociology of Georg Simmel*. London: Free Press, 1950, pp. 402-408.

Simms, Ruth. *Urbanization in West Africa: A Review of the Current Literature*. Evanston, IL: Northwestern University Press, 1965.

Singer, Paul. "Neighborhood Movements in Sao Paulo." In Helen I. Safa (ed.), *Towards a Political Economy of Urbanization in Third World Countries*. Oxford: Oxford University Press, 1982, pp. 283-303.

Sjoberg, Gideon. "'Folk' and 'Feudal' Societies." *American Journal of Sociology*, LVII (1952), 231-299.

———. *The Preindustrial City, Past and Present*. Glencoe, IL: The Free Press, 1960.

Slotkin, James S. *From Field to Factory*. Glencoe, IL: The Free Press, 1960.

Smelser, Neil J. "The Modernization of Social Relations." In M. Weiner (ed.), *Modernization: The Dynamics of Growth*. New York: Basic Books, 1966, pp. 110-121.

Smith, Henry D., II. "The Edo-Tokyo Transition: In Search of Common Ground." In M. Jansen and G. Rozman (eds.), *Japan in Transition: From Tokugawa to Meiji*. Princeton: Princeton University Press, 1986.

Smith, Robert J. "Pre-Industrial Urbanism in Japan: A Consideration of Multiple Traditions in a Feudal Society." *Economic Development and Cultural Change*. 9(1, part II) (1960), 241-257.

Smith, M.G. "Introduction." In Edith Clarke, *My Mother Who Fathered Me*. London: Allen & Unwin, 1957.

_____. *West Indian Family Structure.* Seattle: University of Washington Press, 1962.

_____. "Domestic Service as a Channel of Upward Mobility for the Lower Class Woman: The Lima Case." In Ann Pescatello (ed.), *Female and Male in Latin America.* Pittsburgh: University of Pittsburgh Press, 1973, pp. 191-208.

Solomon, P. "Psychiatric Treatment of the Alcoholic Patient." In J.H. Mendelson (ed.), *Alcoholism.* Boston: Little, Brown, 1966.

Sombart, Werner. "Städtische Siedlung, Stadt." In Alfred Vierkandt (ed.), *Handworterbuch der Sociologie.* Stuttgart, 1931.

Sorkin, A.L. "Some Aspects of American Indian Migration." *Social Forces,* 48 (1969), 243-250.

Southall, Aidan. "Urban Migration and the Residence of Children in Kampala." In William Mangin (ed.), *Peasants in Cities.* 1970, pp. 150-159.

_____. "The Density of Role Relationships as a Universal Index of Urbanization." In A. Southall (ed.), *Urban Anthropology.* New York: Oxford University Press, 1973.

Sovani, N.V. *Social Survey of Kothapur.* Poone, Gokhale Institute of Political and Economic Studies, 1951.

Spate, O.H.K. *India and Pakistan.* London: Methuen and Company, 1954.

Spiro, Melford E. "Is the Family Universal?" *American Anthropologist,* 56 (1954), 839-846.

Spradley, James G. *You Owe Yourself a Drunk: An Ethnography of Urban Nomads.* Boston: Little, Brown, 1970.

Stack, Carol. "The Kindred of Viola Jackson." In N. Whitten and J. Szwed (eds.), *Afro-American Anthropology: Contemporary Perspectives.* New York: Free Press, 1970.

_____. *All Our Kin.* New York: Harper & Row, 1974.

Stern, Boris. *Cargo Handling and Longshore Conditions.* Bureau of Labor Statistics Bulletin No. 550. Washington, DC: Government Printing Office, 1932.

Stone, L. *The Family, Sex and Marriage in England 1500-1800.* New York: Harper & Row, 1977.

Sumner, William Graham. *Folkways.* Boston, 1906.

Sussman, Marvin B. "The Isolated Nuclear Family, Fact or Fiction?" *Social Problems,* 6 (1959), 333-340.

_____. "Relationships of Adult Children with their Parents in the United States." In Ethel Shanas and G.F. Streib (eds.), *Social Structure and the Family: Generational Relations.* Englewood Cliffs, NJ: Prentice-Hall, 1965, pp. 62-92.

Sutton, Joseph A.D. *Magic Carpet: Aleppo-in-Flatbush.* Brooklyn: Thayer-Jacoby, 1979.

_____. *Aleppo Chronicles.* Brooklyn: Thayer-Jacoby, 1987.

Swanstrom, Edward. *The Waterfront Labor Problem.* New York: Fordham University Press, 1938.

Taira, Koji. "Ragpickers and Community Development: Ant's Villa in Tokyo." *Industrial and Labour Relations Review,* 22 (1968), 11.

Tarnopolsky, A., and C. Clark. "Environmental Noise and Mental Health." In Hugh L. Freeman (ed.), *Mental Health and the Environment.* New York, Churchill Livingstone, 1984, pp. 250-270.

Taylor, Lee. *Occupational Sociology.* New York: Oxford University Press, 1968.

Thiebault, H., L. LaPalme, R. Tanguay, and A. Demirjian. "Anthropometric Differences between Rural and Urban French-Canadian Schoolchildren." *Human Biology,* 57 (1985), 113-129.

Thomas, W.I., and F. Znaniecki. *The Polish Peasant in Europe and America.* New York: A.A. Knopf, 1927.

Thompson, James W., and Edgar N. Johnson. *An Introduction to Medieval Europe.* New York: Norton, 1937.

Thomson, Marilyn. *Women of El Salvador: The Price of Freedom.* Philadelphia: ISHI Press, 1986.

Thrupp, Sylvia L. "Medieval Guilds Reconsidered." *Journal of Economic History,* 2 (1942) 164-173.

Thurston, Edgar. *Castes and Tribes of Southern India.* Vol. VI. Madras: Government Press, 1909.

Tisdale, H. "The Process of Urbanization." *Social Forces*, 20 (1942), 311-316.

Tôkyô Shôbôchô. *Chôkai Jichikai oyobi Bôsai Shimin Soshiki nado Ichiranhyô*. Tokyo: Tôkyô Shôcôchô, 1978.

Tôkyô-to Tôkei Kyôkai. *Dai-34-kai Tôkyô-to Tôkei Nenkan*. Tokyo: Tôkyô-to Tôkei Kyôkai, 1984.

Turner, J. "Dwelling Resources in South America." *Architectural Design* (August 1963), 389-393.

Truong, T.D. "The Dynamics of Sex-Tourism: The Case of Southeast Asia." *Development and Change*, 14 (1983), 533-553.

Tuan, Yi-fu. *Space and Place: The Perspective of Experience*. Minneapolis: University of Minnesota Press, 1977.

Turner, June H. (ed.). *Latin American Women: The Meek Speak Out*. Silver Spring, MD: Inter-Educational Development, Inc., 1980.

U.S. Senate Committee on Labor and Public Welfare, Subcommittee on Indian Education. *The Education of American Indians: Field Investigations and Research Reports.*, Vol. 2. Washington, DC: Government Printing Office, 1969.

Valentine, C. *Culture and Poverty: A Critique and Counterproposals*. Chicago: University of Chicago Press, 1968.

Van Der Velden, L. *Tussen Prostituée en Maitresse: De Hospitality Girls van Ermita Manila*. Amsterdam: Anthropologisch Soziologisch Centrum, Amsterdam University, 1982.

Vatuk, Sylvia. *Kinship and Urbanization*. Berkeley and Los Angeles: University of California Press, 1972.

Verster, J. "Social Survey of Western Township." *African Studies*, 26 (1967), 175-246.

Vieille, A. (Michel). "Relations with Neighbours and Relatives in Working Class Families of the Départment de la Seine." In C.C. Harris, *Readings in Kinship in Urban Sociology*. Oxford and New York: Pergamon, 1970, pp. 99-117.

Vogel, Ezra. *Japan's New Middle Class*. Berkeley and Los Angeles: University of California Press, 1967.

Volkan, V.D. *Linking Objects and Linking Phenomena*. Bloomington: University of Indiana Press, 1981.

Wagenfeld, M.O. "Psychopathology in Rural Areas: Issues and Evidence." In P. Keller and J.D. Murray (eds.), *Handbook of Rural Community Mental Health*. New York: Human Sciences Press, 1982, pp. 30-44.

Wagley, Charles, and Marvin Harris. "A Typology of Latin American Subcultures." *American Anthropologist*, 57 (1955), 428-451.

Waldbott, G.L. *Health Effects of Environmental Pollutants, Second Edition.*, St. Louis: Mosby, 1978.

Waldron, Sidney R. *Social Organization and Social Control in the Muslim Walled City of Harar, Ethiopia*. Unpublished Ph.D. Thesis. Columbia University, Department of Anthropology, New York, 1974.

Wallace, Anthony F.C., and J. Atkins. "The Meaning of Kinship Terms." *American Anthropologist*, 62 (1960), 58-80.

_____. *Culture and Personality*. New York: Random House, 1961.

_____. "Culture and Cognition." *Science*, 135 (1962), 351.

Wallace, S.E. *Skid Row as a Way of Life*. Totowa, NJ: Bedminster Press, 1965.

Wallerstein, Immanuel. *The Modern World-System: Capitalist Agriculture and the Origins of the European World-Economy in the Sixteenth Century*. New York: Academic Press, 1976.

Walton, John. "Urban Political Economy: A New Paradigm." *Comparative Urban Research*, 7 (1979), 5-17

Waters, J. Graduate Center, The City University of New York. Unpublished research.

Watson, James L. "Restaurants and Remittances: Chinese Emigrant Workers in London." In George Foster and Robert Kemper (eds.), *Anthropologists in Cities*. Boston: Little, Brown, 1974.

_____. *Emigration and the Chinese Lineage*. Los Angeles and Berkeley: University of California Press, 1975.

Webb, S.D. "Mental Health in Rural and Urban Environments." *Ekistics,* 266 (1978), 37-42.

———. "Rural-Urban Differences in Mental Health." In Hugh L. Freeman (ed.), *Mental Health and the Environment.* New York, Churchill Livingstone, 1984, pp. 226-249.

Weber, Max. *Die Verhältnisse der Landarbeiter in ostelbischen Deutschland.* Berlin: Drucker and Humbolt, 1892.

Weinberg, Ian. "The Problem of Convergence of Industrial Societies: A Critical Look at the State of Theory." *Comparative Studies of Society and History,* 11 (1969), 1-15.

Weintrub, D., M. Lissak, and Y. Atzmon. *Moshava, Kibbutz and Moshav: Patterns of Jewish Rural Settlement and Development in Palestine.* Ithaca: Cornell University Press, 1970.

Welch, B.L. and A.S. Welch. *Physiological Effects of Noise.* New York: Plenum Press, 1970.

Wellman, Barry. "The Community Question: The Intimate Networks of East Yorkers." *American Journal of Sociology,* 84 (1979), 1201-1231.

Weulersse, J. "Antioche: Essai Geographie Urbane." *Bulletin d'etudes orientales,* 4(1954), 27-79.

Wheatley, Paul. "The Significance of Traditional Yoruba Urbanism." *Comparative Studies in Society and History,* 12 (1970), 393-423.

———. *The Pivot of Four Quarters.* Chicago: Aldine, 1971.

Whiteford, A. *Two Cities in Latin America.* Garden City, NY: Doubleday, 1964.

Whiteford, Michael B. *The Forgotten Ones: Colombian Countrymen in an Urban Setting.* Gainesville: University Presses of Florida, 1976a.

———. "Avoiding Obscuring Generalizations: Differences in Migrants and Their Adaptations to an Urban Environment. In D. Guillet and D. Uzzell (eds.), *New Approaches to the Study of Migration.* Houston: Rice University Press, 1976b.

Whitten, Norman E., and James F. Szwed. "Negroes in the New World: Anthropologists Look at Afro-Americans." *Transaction,* 5 (1968), 49-56.

Whyte, William F. *Street Corner Society.* Chicago: University of Chicago Press, 1955.

Wilcox, Walter F. "A Definition of 'City' in Terms of Density." In E.W. Burgess (ed.), *The Urban Community,* 1926.

Williams, Edward T. *China Yesterday and Today.* Fifth Ed. New York: T.Y. Crowell, 1952.

Williams, Louise, M. Anne Spence, and Susan C. Tideman. "Implications of the Observed Effect of Air Pollution on Birth Weight." *Social Biology,* 24 (1982), 1-9.

Williams, Raymond. "Base and Superstructure in Marxist Theory. In Raymond Williams (ed.), *Problems in Materialism and Culture.* London: Verso, 1982.

Wirth, L. *The Ghetto.* Chicago: University of Chicago Press, 1928 (1956).

———. "Urbanism as a Way of Life." *American Journal of Sociology,* 44 (1938), 3-24.

Wolfe, Alvin W. "Multinational Enterprise and Urbanism." In Thomas Collins (ed.), *Urban Anthropology: Cities in a Hierarchical Context.* Southern Anthropological Society Proceedings No. 14. Athens: University of Georgia Press, 1980.

———, et al. "Social Network Effects on Employment." Prepared for Department of Labor, U.S. Department of Commerce, National Technical Information Service, Springfield, VA (No. PB-231-900), 1974.

Young, Michael, and P. Willmott. *Family and Kinship in East London.* London: Routledge & Kegan Paul, 1957.

———. *The Symmetrical Family.* New York: Pantheon Books, 1973.

Zborowski, M., and E. Herzog. *Life Is with People.* New York: International Universities Press, 1952.

Zenner, Walter P. "Syrian Jewish Identification in Israel." Doctoral Dissertation, Columbia University, Department of Anthropology, Ann Arbor: University Microfilms, 1966.

———. "International Networks of a Migrant Ethnic Group." In Robert F. Spencer (ed.), *Anthropology & Migration.* Seattle: University of Washington Press, 1970, pp. 36-48.

———. "Jewish State Employees in the Albany Area." Albany, NY: State University of New York at Albany, Anthropology Department. Working Paper No. 1, 1978.

———. "Arabic Speaking Immigrants in North America as Middleman Minorities." *Ethnic & Racial Studies* 5 (1982), 457-477.

Zentrum Fur Entwicklungsbezogene Bildung (Zeb). "Tourismus, Prostitution, Entwicklung." Stuttgart: Zentrum fur Entwicklungsbezogene Bildung, 1981.

Zerubavel, Eviatar. *Hidden Rhythms and Calendars in Social Life*. Chicago: University of Chicago Press, 1981.

Zerubavel, Yael and Dianne Esses. "Reconstructions of the Past: Syrian Jewish Woman and Maintenance of Tradition." *Journal of American Folklore*, 100(398) (1987), 528-539.

Zinsser, H. *Rats, Lice, and History*. Boston: Little, Brown and Co., 1935.

Zolberg, A.R. *The One Party Government in the Ivory Coast*. Princeton, NJ: Princeton University Press, 1964.

CONTRIBUTORS' BIOGRAPHIES

Janet L. Abu-Lughod is Professor of Sociology at Northwestern University in Evanston, Illinois and at The New School for Social Research, New York. She holds graduate degrees from the University of Chicago and the University of Massachusetts. Her research interests range from problems of American cities and their design to issues of urbanization in the Third World. She has written books on American housing, about Cairo, Rabat, and Third World cities, has authored numerous monographs and articles on the Arab world, authored a forthcoming text in Urban Sociology and is currently writing a book on the World System in the Thirteenth Century.

Theodore C. Bestor is an Assistant Professor of Anthropology at Columbia University, and is on the faculty of Columbia's East Asian Institute. Previously he was the director of the Social Science Research Council's Japanese and Korean studies programs. He received his Ph.D. from Stanford University in 1983. A book on his research, entitled *Neighborhood Tokyo*, is forthcoming from the Stanford University Press.

Laurel Bossen is an Associate Professor at McGill University. Raised in Chicago, she received her B.A. from Barnard College and her Ph.D. from the State University of New York at Albany, and taught for several years at the University of Pittsburgh. She has conducted extensive research in Guatemala in both Maya and Ladino communities, and is the author of *The Redivision of Labor: Women and Economic Choice in Four Guatemalan Communities* (1984). Her research interests include economic anthropology, development and gender in complex societies, Mesoamerica and China.

Hans C. Buechler is Professor of Anthropology at Syracuse University. He grew up in Bolivia and Switzerland. He received his graduate training at the Sorbonne (Paris) and at Columbia University, where he received his Ph.D. He has taught at the Universite de Montreal. He is author and editor of several books, including *Masked Media: Aymara Fiestas and Social Interaction in the Bolivian Andes* (The Hague, 1980) and *Migrants in Europe* (Westport, CT, 1987) which he edited with Judith-Maria Buechler.

Bruce E. Byland received his Ph.D. degree in anthropology from The Pennsylvania State University in 1980. He has studied the origin and development of states in Mesoamerica, especially in the Mixtec and Zapotec regions of Oaxaca, Mexico. He is now an Assistant Professor of Anthropology at Lehman College and at the Graduate School and University Center of the City University of New York. He is married to Cara Tannenbaum who holds an M.A. in anthropology from the State University of New York at Albany but who is now the proud co-owner and chef of a successful New American restautant called "Quarropas" in White Plains, New York.

REMI CLIGNET is Professor of Family and Community Development at the University of Maryland. Born and raised in France, he moved to the United States in 1963. He has done extensive fieldwork in the Ivory Coast, Cameroun, and Senegal. He has published a number of articles and books on the effects of social change on the familial structures of these countries. He is currently finishing a book on the sociology of the arts.

ERIK COHEN is Professor in the Department of Sociology and Social Anthropology in the Hebrew University, Jerusalem, Israel. He was born in 1932 and he received his Ph.D. at the Hebrew University. His work has been in urban anthropology, urban sociology, the sociology of tourism, the sociology of religion, ethnic relations, and the sociology of the arts. He has done research in Israel, Latin America, and Southeast Asia. He has published numerous articles in sociological and anthropological journals.

SHOLOMO DESHEN is Professor of Anthropology at Tel Aviv University. He studied at the Hebrew University in Jerusalem and received his Ph.D. from the University of Manchester (England). Much of his work was concerned with the integration of North African Jews into Israeli society, as well as the historical reconstruction of Jewish communal life in Middle Eastern countries. He is the author of numerous books and articles in English and Hebrew. His book, *Individuals and the Community: Jewish Society in 18th-19th Century Morocco*, is in press. In the last few years, he has engaged in research on the adaptation of the blind to modern urban society.

EDWIN EAMES is Professor of Anthropology at Baruch College of the City University of New York. He is a native of New York City, where he was born in 1930. After receiving a B.A. from City College in New York, he received his graduate training and Ph.D. at Cornell University. His major fieldwork has been on rural-urban migration in India and the migration of south Asians to British and American cities. His interests center on the processes of urbanization, development, migration, and change.

DAVID EPSTEIN was born in New York in 1943. He received both his B.A. and his Ph.D. from Columbia University. He has been a visiting professor at Queens College and is author of *Brasilia: Plan and Reality*.

GEORGE M. FOSTER became Professor Emeritus at the University of California (Berkeley) in 1979, after teaching for twenty-six years on that campus. Born in 1913, he graduated from Northwestern University in 1935 and took his Ph.D. in anthropology at Berkeley in 1941. His research interests include peasant society,

Latin America, sociocultural change and development, applied anthropology, and medical anthropology. Currently he is continuing a long-term longitudinal study of Tzintzuntzan, Michoacán, Mexico, now in its forty-second year.

GEORGE GMELCH was raised in the San Francisco bay area. He did his undergraduate studies in anthropology at Stanford University and his graduate studies at the University of California in Santa Barbara. Before going to graduate school he played several seasons of professional baseball in the Detroit Tigers organization. He has taught at McGill University, State University of New York at Albany, and Union College, where he is currently an associate professor. He has conducted field research on Irish Travellers, English Gypsies, Alaskan fishermen, and return migrants in Ireland, Newfoundland, and Barbados. He has written and edited four books.

SHARON GMELCH is an Associate Professor of Anthropology at Union College in Schenectady, New York. She received her anthropological training at the University of California, Santa Barbara. She has done extensive field research with Travelling People in Ireland as well as research in Alaska and Quebec. Her chief research interests are interethnic relations, ethnic group formation, culture change, and sex roles. She is the author of *Nan: The Life of an Irish Travelling Woman* and two other books.

JUDITH GOODE is Associate Professor of Anthropology and Director of the Urban Studies Program at Temple University. She was born in New York City in 1939 and spent much of her childhood in Ann Arbor, Michigan, before returning to New York. Her B.A. is from Bernard College, and her Ph.D. is from Cornell University. She has done fieldwork among middle-class professionals in Colombia and with several ethnic groups in Philadelphia. Recently her research interests have centered on the relationship between ethnicity and occupational status, as well as on processes of ethnic group formation and change in dietary systems.

SUSAN EMLEY KEEFE is Professor of Anthropology at Appalachian State University, Boone, North Carolina. Her research on Mexican American families was completed following her graduate work at the University of California, Santa Barbara. Her research interests also include ethnicity, mental health, education, and inequality. She is currently completing research on the concept of ethnicity as applied to Appalachians and the implications for their educational opportunities. She is the author of *Chicano Ethnicity* (with Amado M. Padilla) and editor of *Appalachian Mental Health*.

BARBARA KIRSHENBLATT-GIMBLETT is Professor of Performance Studies, and of Hebrew and Judaic Studies, at New York University. She is a research associate at the YIVO Institute for Jewish Research. Born and raised in Toronto, she studied at the University of Toronto before completing her A.B. and M.A. at the University of California, Berkeley, and her Ph.D. at Indiana University in 1972. Her research on urban vernacular culture was recently supported by a Guggenheim Foundation Fellowship (1986-87), and though focussed on New York City, includes comparative material based on her fieldwork in Japan, India, Kenya, Egypt, Israel, and New Zealand. Her research interests include Ashkenazic Jewry, tourism, and food as a symbolic system. She is the author, with Lucjan Dobroszycki, of *Image Before My Eyes: A Photographic History of Jewish Life in Poland, 1864-1939.*

Oscar Lewis (1914-1971) was born in New York City. He received his B.S. from the City College of New York and his Ph.D. from Columbia University. He did research in Canada among the Blackfoot Indians and in India. He is best-known for his in-depth study of the Mexican village of Tepoztlán and for ·his use of life histories in studying the poor in Mexico, the United States, and Cuba. He was Professor of Anthropology at the University of Illinois from 1948 until his death.

Kathleen Logan is an Associate Professor of Anthropology and Director of the International Studies Program at the University of Alabama at Birmingham. She received her Ph.D. from Bryn Mawr College. She is the author of *Haciendo Pueblo, the Development of a Guadalajaran Suburb*. She has written about medical practices in Mexico and about urban development and the urban poor in Latin America. At present, she is writing a book about the participation of women in urban mobilizations in Latin America, based on her recent fieldwork in Mérida, Yucatán, México. Her current research interests include urban mobilizations, gender roles, and the individual and collective consciousness of grassroots movements.

Owen M. Lynch is Charles F. Noyes Professor of Urban Anthropology at New York University in New York City. A Native New Yorker, he received his B.A. from Fordham University and his Ph.D. from Columbia University. His most important research has been done in India, where he studied untouchables and neo-Buddhists in Agra city and shantytown dwellers in Bombay. He has also directed a study of block associations in New York City. The political manifestations of ethnicity and identity change, as well as modern religious movements, are his main research interests.

Sally Engle Merry is Associate Professor of Anthropology at Wellesley College. She received her Ph.D. in Anthropology from Brandeis University. Author of *Urban Danger: Life in a Neighborhood of Strangers*, she has also published numerous articles on law and community in the United States, mediation, working-class legal ideology, urban design and patterns of conflict, and alternative dispute resolution. She is currently working on a book on the use of courts by working-class Americans which reinterprets the meaning of litigiousness.

Stanley Milgram (1933-1984) was Professor of Psychology at the Graduate Center of the City University of New York. After receiving his Ph.D. from Harvard in 1960, he trained students in urban research and experimental social psychology. Along with Henry From, he produced the award-winning film, *The City and the Self* (distributed by Time-Life Films). He published numerous papers on urban life from a social psychological viewpoint. His book, *The Individual and the Social World* (Addison-Wesley) was published in 1979.

Raymond Miller is Professor of Social Science at San Francisco State University, where he has taught since 1962. He has a B.S. from Denver University, an M.A. from the University of Chicago, and his Ph.D. from Syracuse University. He has done research in Pakistan and Finland. His fields are international development, political economy, and interdisciplinary social science methodology.

ROBERT E. RHOADES was born in rural Oklahoma and early in life experienced migration through the westward "Okie" movements. Like many migrant families of that period, however, he returned to the family farm. Rhoades' academic interests naturally focus on migration and agricultural anthropology. He has studied agriculture (Oklahoma State University), sociology (University of Hawaii) and anthropology (University of Oklahoma), in which he received his Ph.D. in 1976. Rhoades has also worked in Nepal (1962-1964), the Philippines (1976-1978) and is now at the International Potato Center in Lima, Peru.

JACK R. ROLLWAGEN is Professor of Anthropology at the State University of New York College at Brockport and editor of the journal *Urban Anthropology* and *Studies of Cultural Systems and World Economic Development.* He has conducted research in Mexico and the United States. His major research interests include anthropological and political economic studies of the world system (particularly the relationship between world food production and malnutrition) and anthropological filmmaking. He has recently edited a book *Anthropological Filmmaking* and is producing a series of video tapes on Puerto Rican spiritism.

LAWRENCE M. SCHELL is an Associate Professor of Anthropology at the University at Albany, State University of New York. He is also affiliated with the Institute of Behavioral Teratology and the School of Public Health Sciences at the University of Albany. His research interests are the impact of urbanization on health, and the interaction of culture and biology generally. He received his B.A. degree from Oberlin College and his Ph.D. from the University of Pennsylvania.

ANDREI SIMIĆ is Associate Professor of Anthropology at the University of California. He received his B.A. degree in Slavic languages and Ph.D. in anthropology from the University of California at Berkeley. He has carried out extensive field work in Yugoslavia and among Euro-American ethnic groups in the United States. His areas of interest include: urbanization and modernization, ethnicity, social gerontology, and ethnographic film. Dr. Simić's geographic regions of specialization are Eastern Europe and the Mediterranean, Latin America, and the United States. He has currently completed a 60-minute documentary film on Serbians in America.

GIDEON SJOBERG is Professor of Sociology at the University of Texas at Austin. He is author of the *Preindustrial City* and (with Roger Nett) *A Methodology for Social Research.* And he has authored a variety of articles and chapters in books. Currently, he is completing a monograph (with Ted R. Vaughan) on "Ethics, Human Rights, and the Social Science Enterprise," and he continues to write on the nature and impact of bureaucracy in today's world.

JAMES P. SPRADLEY (1933-1982) was DeWitt Wallace Professor of Anthropology at Macalester College, St. Paul, Minnesota. He wrote about tramps, cocktail waitresses, and ethnographic methods. With his brother, Thomas Spradley, he wrote *Deaf Like Me,* the story of Lynn Spradley, who was born deaf.

CAROL B. STACK is Associate Professor of Anthropology and is in the Institute of Public Policy at Duke University in Durham, North Carolina. She is Director of the Center for the Study of the Family and the State, a group of researchers from a variety of disciplines who study the broad spectrum of public and private policies which affect American families. Stack, who received her Ph.D. in anthropology from the University of Illinois at Urbana, is author of *All Our Kin: Strategies for Survival in a Black Community* (1974). Her research interests include social anthropology of complex societies, black families, foster care, welfare, and education.

ROBERT VAN KEMPER is Associate Professor of Anthropology at Southern Methodist University. Born in San Diego, California, in 1945, he received his B.A. degree from the University of California (Riverside) in 1966 and his Ph.D. degree from the University of California (Berkeley) in 1971. His research interests include migration and urbanization, tourism, and Latin America. He is Associate Editor of the journal *Urban Anthropology.*

SIDNEY R. WALDRON is Professor of Anthropology at the State University of New York at Cortland. He worked among the Harari 1962-63, 1975 and 1977, and he is presently completing a monograph on the Harari. In 1981-82 he worked with refugees in Somalia, and in 1985-86 he was a visiting fellow at Oxford University's Refugee Studies Programme. During that period he helped establish a Refugee Studies Center at the University of Juba in the Sudan. He is a member of the advisory board of the American Anthropological Association's Task Force on African Hunger.

MICHAEL B. WHITEFORD is Professor of Anthropology and Professor-in-Charge of the Anthropology Program at Iowa State University. Born in 1945, he received his B.A. degree from Beloit College in 1967 and his Ph.D. degree from the University of California (Berkeley) in 1972. In addition to migration and urbanization, his research interests include medical anthropology, particularly focusing on the social epidemiology of nutritional status. He has done fieldwork in Colombia, Costa Rica, Honduras, and Mexico.

LOUIS WIRTH (1897-1952) was born in Germany. He attended public school in Omaha, Nebraska. He received his B.A., M.A., and Ph.D. from the University of Chicago. Until his death he was Professor of Sociology at the University of Chicago. He was interested in social theory, the social ecology of the human community, and the application of sociology to public policy. In addition to his work on urbanism, he focused attention on the role of thought and ideology in social life and on minority problems. His book *The Ghetto* (1928), which is a study of the Jewish immigrant community in Chicago, is a classic.

WALTER P. ZENNER is Professor of Anthropology at the State University of New York at Albany. He was born in Germany and grew up in Chicago. His B.A. is from Northwestern University and his Ph.D. is from Columbia University. He has done research on Jews and Arabs in Israel, immigrants and state employees in the United States, and Middle Eastern cotton traders in England. He has also done comparative work on middleman minorities. The ramifications of ethnicity in traditional and modern settings is central to his research. His latest work, *Persistence and Flexibility: Anthropological Perspectives of the American Jewish Experience* is in press.